P9-DCR-022

Towards a
European
Civil Code

Towards a European Civil Code

EDITORS
A.S. Hartkamp
M.W. Hesselink
E.H. Hondius
C.E. du Perron
J.B.M. Vranken

AUTHORS
Gerrit Betlem — Th.M. de Boer — Carlos Bollen
J.H. Dalhuisen — U. Drobnig — J.H.M. van Erp
N.E.D. Faber — Gerard-René de Groot
Arthur S. Hartkamp — Ewoud H. Hondius
Geraint G. Howells — S.C.J.J. Kortmann — Ole Lando
G.E. van Maanen — B.S. Markesinis
Peter-Christian Müller-Graff — Madeleine van Rossum
M. Storme — Matthias E. Storme — W.J. Swadling
Denis Tallon — A. Tunc — Hans G. Wehrens
R. Zimmermann

1994
Ars Aequi Libri — Nijmegen
Martinus Nijhoff Publishers — Dordrecht/Boston/London

CIP-GEGEVENS KONINKLIJKE BIBLIOTHEEK, DEN HAAG

Towards

Towards a European civil code / ed. A.S. Hartkamp... [et al.] ; authors Gerrit Betlem ... [et al.]. - Nijmegen : Ars Aequi libri ; Dordrecht : Nijhoff
Met lit. opg., reg.
ISBN 90-6916-162-1
Trefw.: burgerlijk recht ; Europa.

© 1994, Ars Aequi Libri, Nijmegen

All rights reserved. No part of this publication may be reproduced, stored in a retrieval system, or transmitted, in any form or by any means, electronic, mechanical, photocopying, recording or otherwise, without the prior permission of ARS AEQUI LIBRI.

ISBN 90 6916 162 1

Library of Congress Cataloging-in-Publication Data
Towards a European civil code / edited by A.S. Hartkamp ... [et al.].
    p.   cm.
    Includes index.
    ISBN 0-7923-2625-3
    1. Civil law--Europe--Codification.
KJC985.T69 1994
346.4'002632--dc20
[344.0602632]   93-41423

ISBN 0-7923-2625-3

Published by Martinus Nijhoff Publishers, P.O. Box 163, 3300 AD Dordrecht, The Netherlands.
Sold and distributed in the U.S.A. and Canada by Kluwer Academic Publishers, 101 Philip Drive, Norwell, MA 02061, U.S.A.
In all other countries, sold and distributed by Kluwer Academic Publishers Group, P.O. Box 322, 3300 AH Dordrecht, The Netherlands.
All Rights Reserved.

© 1994 Kluwer Academic Publishers

Kluwer Academic Publishers incorporates the publishing programmes of Martinus Nijhoff Publishers.

No part of the material protected by this copyright notice may be reproduced or utilized in any form or by any means, electronic or mechanical, including photocopying, recording, or by any information storage and retrieval system, without written permission from the copyright owner.

Cover-design: Inge Winter

Preface

In 1989 the European Parliament called for the elaboration of a European civil code (*Official Journal of the European Communities* 1989, No. C 158/400). Although the European Commission has not yet shown much enthusiasm for this idea, many legal academics see it as a great challenge.

In September 1991 we decided to ask some distinguished European legal scholars to take up this challenge and write a chapter on the desirability and possible content of a European Civil Code. This book is the result of their enthusiastic efforts.

The book is divided into two distinct parts. The first part examines the general issues which concern the unification of private law in Europe. The second part considers the feasibility of unification of those areas of private law that we considered to be appropriate for a unification on a European level. Because of the numerous references made throughout the book to the UNIDROIT Principles for International Commercial Contracts and to the Principles of European Contract Law, these texts have been reproduced in an annex to this book.

The authors have handed in their articles by January 1 1994. Any developments which have occured after this date could not be taken into account.

The editors would like to express their gratitude to the administrative staff of the Molengraaff Instituut at the University of Utrecht and to Ars Aequi Libri in Nijmegen who prepared the texts for publication.

The editors   's-Gravenhage/Utrecht, April 1994

Contents

PART 2 — *SUBSTANTIVE LAW*

A — *LAW OF CONTRACT*

B — *EXTRA-CONTRACTUAL LIABILITY*

Part 1 — General Issues

CHAPTER 1
Towards a European Civil Code. General Introduction

Ewoud Hondius

1 Introduction

This book is about the development of European civil law. In the past decade, EC directives have led to the introduction of some unified, or at least harmonised, civil law at a European level. A directive on product liability, which goes to the heart of tort law, has been implemented in ten out of the twelve Member States and in some other states as well.[1] A directive on unfair contract terms, which goes to the heart of contract law, is in the course of being implemented. These are but two of the best known objects of EC initiatives in the area of civil law. A list of the relevant directives is reproduced in Chapter 2 by Müller-Graff.

The introduction of these directives has not always been uncontroversial. At the time, the constitutionality of the directive on product liability was doubted by some politicians.[2] The Single European Act and especially the Treaty of Maastricht have put an end to such doubts, but Maastricht has introduced a new theme: is civil law not something to be left to Member States under the principle of subsidiarity?[3] There are other criticisms as well. Not everyone, even when convinced of the constitutionality, is attracted by the quality of EC directives. The draft directive on liability for services has been criticised on this count from every side, academics,[4] producers and consumers[5] alike. These questions raise the issue of whether or not the EC should contemplate the gradual build up of a corpus of civil law. So far, the emphasis has been rather on public law, but several of the prerequisites for a European civil law do already exist. The European Court of Justice has shown itself to be highly competent; it has brought into operation a European administrative law really from scratch, which in turn has influenced the

---

1   See the forthcoming issue 1994/2 of the *European Review of Private Law*.
2   See Geraint Howells, *Comparative Product Liability*, Aldershot 1993, p. 20 ff.
3   See Giscard d'Estaing, A-3-163/90 of 22 June 1990, B of 4 July 1990, footnote 20, B-3-1298-1300/92, B-3-1360-63/92.
4   Erwin Deutsch and Jochen Taupitz (eds.), *Haftung der Dienstleistungsberufe — natürliche Vielfalt und europäische Vereinheitlichung*, Heidelberg 1993; Sigurd Littbarski (ed.), *Entwurf einer Richtlinie über die Haftung bei Dienstleistungen*, Köln 1992.
5   The European Consumer Law Group, a network of academics and lawyers involved in consumer law, for instance was highly critical of the draft.

development of national law.[6] There is a European bar. What is lacking, however, is consensus over the direction which this development should take. Should consensus not be arrived at as to the framework in which future directives in the area of civil law should find a place? Such a framework might eventually be provided by a European Civil Code.

This issue raises several interesting questions. First, there is the question already referred to above: is there a constitutional basis for a European Civil Code in the Treaty of Rome, as amended by the Treaty of Maastricht? Second, is codification of the law, more specifically of the civil or private law, a worthwhile idea? And finally, is this codification feasible on a European level? This book basically aims at answering only the last question: whether or not the various domestic legal systems in Europe are not too far apart to even contemplate unification or harmonisation.

This Chapter will argue that they are indeed too far apart at present. However, in ten or twenty years time this situation may be different. At first sight the difficulty seems to be that the systems are apart not only where the solutions to common problems are concerned but also as to the legal formulation of these problems and the concepts used but this is not always the case as the Common law jurisdictions, England and Wales, and Ireland, are close. This proximity between legal systems also applies to the civil law countries France, Belgium and Luxembourg, and to the Scandinavian systems including Denmark and the European Economic Space States Finland, Norway and Sweden. Even between civil law and common countries,[7] England and Scotland are an example of close co-operation. As these examples show,[8] a common language, or linguistic heritage in the case of the Nordic countries, and a common legal culture often are the basis for such co-operation. It is indeed in this domain that the concept of legal families, set out by Bollen and De Groot in Chapter 7, still plays a role.

A common language — Latin — and a common heritage — Roman law — did of course once exist in Europe. Although the present situation bears little resemblance

---

6   Two examples are the development of the law of legitimate expectations and the reception of the idea of proportionality into English law — see Jürgen Schwarze, *European Administrative Law*, London/Luxembourg 1992, p. 869-870. The reception has met with scepticism from some authors who simply believe proportionality to be non-transplantable as such — see Sophie Boyron, 'Proportionality in English Administrative Law: A Faulty Translation?', (1992) 12 *Oxford Journal of Legal Studies* 237-264.

7   See G. Gandolfi, in: Peter Stein (ed.), *Incontro di studio su il futuro codice europeo dei contratti*, Milano 1993, p. 33.

8   Other examples include both North America — the harmonisation achieved by the Uniform Commercial Code and the Restatements is notorious — and Latin America. As to the latter see Alejandro M. Garro, *Armonización y Unificación del derecho privado en América Latina: esfuerzos, tendencias y realidades*, Roma 1992; the same, 'Unification and Harmonization of Private Law in Latin America', 40 *American Journal of Comparative Law* 587-616 (1992).

to pre-XIXth century Europe, and therefore a 'return' to that period is highly unlikely, yet the present interest in a new European civil law is a fascinating challenge for legal historians. This is set out below in Chapter 5 by Zimmermann. As another German author, Schulze, has observed:

'The present and the past are linked in the concepts of European legal culture and European legal history in two ways: the awakening of interest in research into European legal history is prompted by the experience of the present, namely the present-day efforts towards the development of a body of common European law. The resulting research can in turn influence present-day thinking in that, contrary to another tradition and present-day experience, namely the legal thinking moulded by the nation-state, it contributes from a historical standpoint to a consciousness of a shared European identity. The concept of European legal culture is thus directed at the definition of an identity for the present based on the past whilst research in European legal history is both defined by and directed towards the present'.[9]

Is all this academic speculation, designed at upgrading the profile of the law curriculum? A brief look at what the 'actors of the law' are doing shows us that the interest in the development of a European (civil) law is very real. Legal practitioners all over Europe are forming alliances. Judges are joining their efforts in setting up European courses for their continuing education. The most important event is that future attorneys and judges, the law students of today, are greatly affected by the developments in Europe. Many present day students are participating in various exchange programmes, of which ERASMUS and TEMPUS are the most succesful, and a common legal education is being contemplated in various countries.[10]

Before embarking upon our exercise, I will first have to limit the scope of this book in Section 2.

2 The Subject-matter of this Book

The subject-matter of this book is what continental Europeans call the civil law. This includes contract, tort and restitution, sometimes brought together under the

---

9   Reiner Schulze, 'European Legal History — A New Field of Research in Germany', 13 *Journal of Legal History* 270-295 (1992). See also the author's *Die europäische Rechts- und Verfassungsgeschichte — zu den gemeinsamen Grundlagen europäischer Rechtskultur*, Saarbrücken 1991, p. 19.

10 See for instance F. Ost and M. Van Hoecke, 'Pour une formation juridique européenne', *Journal des Tribunaux* 1990, p. 105-106; H.G. Schermers, 'Jurist voor morgen', *Nederlands Juristenblad* 1991, p. 521-522; R. Verstegen, 'Naar een Europese rechtsopleiding', *Rechtskundig Weekblad* 1990-1991, p. 657-660; G.R. de Groot, 'European Legal Education in the 21st Century', in: Bruno de Witte and Caroline Forder (eds.), *The common law of Europe and the future of legal education/Le droit commun de l'Europe et l'avenir de l'enseignement juridique*, Deventer 1992, p. 7-30. Erasmus is at present being replaced by Socrates.

heading of the 'law of obligations'. Civil law also covers real property, inheritance law and family law. There is little doubt that a future European Civil Code should also encompass what is now dealt with in Europe's Commercial Codes.[11] Did not Europe's impact on private law begin with the company law directives?

Yet, for practical reasons, this book hardly touches upon commercial matters, and family law and inheritance law will not be examined. The latter areas seem to be the least ready for harmonisation efforts, although the harmonising influence of the European Convention on Human Rights should not be underestimated.

Procedural law, however, was considered so important, that Storme Sr. was invited to write a Chapter (6) on this subject.[12] A similar case can be made for including private international law, which is covered in Chapter 4 by De Boer. Private international law and harmonisation of private law have often been considered rivals in achieving legal certainty for crossborder transactions. The rivalry between the Hague Sales Conventions and the Hague Treaty on Private International Law relating to the Sale of Goods is but one example — although these are currently considered to be allied forces.[13] The unification of European private international law, as for instance in the Rome Convention, is an important step because it has already been argued that a European codification of private law strictly for transborder transactions could greatly contribute towards a European Union.[14]

An interesting issue is whether the book should discuss only transnational law or whether it should also include domestic law. An argument for the former approach is made by Wehrens in Chapter 22 on the subject of the *Eurohypothèque* although one drawback of this approach is the disintegration of domestic law through partial harmonisation,[15] which should be a subject for further research.[16]

---

11   See V. Zeno-Zencovich, 'Il diritto europeo dei contratti (verso la distinzione fra 'contratti commerciali' e 'contratti dei consumatori')', in: *Studi in onore di R. Sacco* (in the press).
12   The scope for procedural unification is discussed by Konstantin Kerameus in I.R. Scott (ed.), *International Perspectives on Civil Justice: Essays in Honour of Sir Jack I.H. Jacob QC*, London 1991 and by Manfred Wolf, Abbau prozessualer Schranken im europäischen Binnenmarkt, in: *Wege zu einem europäischen Zivilrecht/Tübinger Symposium zum 80. Geburtstag von Fritz Baur*, Tübingen 1992, p. 35-67.
13   H.U. Jessurun d'Oliveira, 'Towards a 'European' Private International Law', in: Bruno de Witte, Caroline Forder (eds.), *The common law of Europe and the future of legal education*, Deventer 1992, p. 265, 282 sees 'Private International Law from a Community point of view as a halfway house to harmonisation and approximation of the national laws of the Member States.'
14   J.H.A. Lokin, W.J. Zwalve, *Hoofdstukken uit de Europese Codificatiegeschiedenis*, Groningen 1986, p. 363.
15   See Ch.E. Hauschka, 'Grundprobleme der Privatrechtsfortbildung durch die Europäische Wirtschaftsgemeinschaft', *Juristen Zeitung* 1990, p. 290-299.
16   On this issue see also Christian Joerges, Gert Brüggemeier, 'Europäisierung des Vertrags- und Haftungsrechts', in: P.C. Müller-Graff (ed.), *Gemeinsames Privatrecht in der Europäischen Gemeinschaft*, Baden-Baden 1993, p. 233-286.

A comparison of the legal developments in Europe is often facilitated by the common heritage of Roman and canonical law.[17] This common heritage will also be a subject-matter for this book. This common heritage sometimes extends as far as America as the influence of American legal developments occasionally makes an impact on European law.[18] It therefore seems appropriate occasionally at least to mention some of these American developments. The impact of Europe's legal system upon other countries in the world should not be forgotten particularly in those countries with historical links to Europe's old empires. A recent example of a European influence upon legal development is found in Australia's new product liability legislation[19] which is built upon the model provided by the EC Directive.

Community law, as we have just seen, is rapidly gaining ground in the area of civil law, and yet EC law still covers only a fraction of the civil law. It is therefore natural that the law of individual European countries will be discussed. This raises the question of which jurisdictions are to be covered. It will be obvious that these jurisdictions should include not only the Member States of the EC, but also the EFTA Member States which — including Switzerland — have accepted the 'acquis communautaire' to be introduced in their law. An introduction to the various national systems may be found in Chapter 7 by Bollen and De Groot.

Because of a possible future extension of the EC towards East and Central Europe, an extension which has already taken place within the Council of Europe, it will occasionally also be of interest to look eastwards and devote attention to developments in countries such as the Czech Republic, Hungary, Poland and Russia. At the present time of recodification of East European law, civil law is in such turmoil that for practical reasons it is hardly mentioned in this book. In years to come, however, there may be something to learn from East European experiences when work on a future European Civil Code begins in earnest.[20]

3 Constitutionality

Does the European Community have the power to adopt a European Civil Code? This book will not provide an in depth analysis of this interesting question but some attention to this issue is given by Betlem in Chapter 19 on environmental law.

---

17 See H. Coing, *Das Europäische Zivilrecht*, 1985/1989.
18 For instance in the area of product liability: see L. Dommering-van Rongen, *Produktenaansprakelijkheid/ Een nieuwe Europese privaatrechtelijke regeling vergeleken met de produktenaansprakelijkheid in de Verenigde Staten*, doctoral thesis Utrecht, Deventer 1991. For a more general approach see Wolfgang Wiegand, 'The Reception of American Law in Europe', 39 *American Journal of Comparative Law* 229-248 (1991).
19 Trade Practices Amendment Act 1992 — see Jocelyn Kellam, 'Australian Product Liability Reform', *Product Liability International* 1992, 18-21, 25.
20 See A. Harmathy and A. Németh (eds.), *Questions of civil law codification*, Budapest 1990.

Many protagonists of a European Code point to a resolution of the European Parliament. Article 1 of this 'Resolution on action to bring into line the private law of the Member States'[21] reads:

'Requests that a start be made on the necessary preparatory work on drawing up a common European Code of Private Law, the Member States being invited, having deliberated the matter, to state whether they wish to be involved in the planned unification'.

There is no doubt that this is an interesting opinion. For a Dutch lawyer, the fact that the recent recodification of Dutch civil law also began with what seemed an innocuous parliamentary question springs to mind. Yet neither too much should be made of it nor should too much attention be given to the answer of Commissioner Bangemann to a question raised by Mr Filippos Pierros. The question was: 'What practical measures will the Commission take to achieve a minimum degree of harmonization between the Member States on such sensitive matters of substantive and procedural civil law?' On behalf of the Commission, Mr Bangemann answered: 'The Honourable Member is correct in pointing out that discrepancies exist in the Member States as regards substantive and procedural aspects of civil law. While the Community has no direct power in terms of the EEC Treaty to intervene directly in the matters cited by the Honourable Member, Article 220 of the Treaty does permit Member States, where necessary, to enter negotiations with each other to make Conventions with a view to securing benefits for their nationals.'[22]

The Commissioner's answer points to the fact that the European Community has a vast array of instruments available to reach its aims. However, the principle of subsidiarity may thwart an attempt to use these instruments.[23]

4 Codification

Ever since the famous debate between Thibaut and Savigny in early XIXth century Germany, the question has remained on the civil lawyer's agenda: to (re)codify the law or not.

Germany eventually got its codification, after Belgium, France, Luxembourg, Italy, the Netherlands, Portugal and Spain had preceded it. Greece was still to come and then Italy (1942), Portugal (1966), East Germany (1975) and the Netherlands (1992) recodified their civil law. The most recent reform proposals in Germany have only a limited impact, but it should not be overlooked that in the shadow of large scale recodification, updating projects on a far smaller scale have brought

---

21   *Official Journal of the European Communities* 1989, No C 158/400.
22   *Official Journal* C 32/7 of 4 February 1993.
23   Waldemar Hummer, *Zeitschrift für Rechtsvergleichung* 1992, 81-91.

most other codes in line with modern times. One therefore cannot really say that the idea of codification is dead.

However, one may retort: what about the common law countries, or Denmark? Are not the common law countries especially radically opposed to any codification whatsoever? In Chapter 8, Van Erp indeed argues that the adoption of a European *Code* is not possible for England. Yet, one should not forget that as recently as the 1950's, with the establishment of its Law Commissions, the United Kingdom did contemplate the adoption of a codification of at least its law of contract.

Thus, whilst the idea of codification does have some chances of being adopted Euro-wise, this does not necessarily mean that such codification should be European, notwithstanding the fact that regional efforts of harmonisation now seem to have better prospects than global efforts.

Should codification be along the traditional division of the law in private and public law, in substantive and procedural law, that European law be codified? So far, codification along social-economic lines seems to have been a better way. However, with the advent of more harmonised private law, it is important to preserve the rich European tradition in this area and this can best be achieved by keeping traditional divisions intact, even though in most countries these are not as sharp as they may once have been. The one exception is the division of private law in civil and commercial law. As the Italian and the Dutch examples show, this distinction is no longer warranted.

Yet, the practical difficulties of codification, even along traditional lines, seem to be large. With the Italian writer Mengoni one is apt to

'riconoscere che "un codice per l'Europa" non è un'alternativa realistica'.[24]

It is therefore worthwhile to consider alternatives to codification. Such alternatives are set out in Chapter 2 by Müller-Graff. One such alternative may be the elaboration of Principles of European Contract Law, Tort Law, Procedure, etc., as set out in Chapter 3 by Hartkamp.

Once regulation — be it in the form of codification, restatement or otherwise — has been opted for, the question is then related to how to proceed. Some advocate the use of a single text as a point of departure. Several authors, all Italians, have argued that the Italian Civil Code is best equipped to serve as a model for a European Code on Contract Law. For what reason?

'Pour deux raisons fondamentales: tout d'abord pour la position intermédiaire qu'il revêt par rapport non seulement aux deux principaux courants juridique français et allemand (...) mais

---

24 Luigi Mengoni, *L'Europa dei codici o un codice per l'Europa?*, Roma 1993, p. 3.

par rapport aussi au droit anglais; ensuite pour sa modernité intrinsique, une modernité — dirais-je — raisonnablement prononcée, exempte des excès qui ont amené certains pays a faire en toute hâte marche arrière.'[25]

In the practice of the Commission on European Contract Law (the Lando Commission), the text of the new Dutch and Québec Civil Codes are also often consulted. There is a growing literature of those engaged in the various harmonisation commissions as to their experiences,[26] which may well serve to indicate how future codificatory or regulatory work can be organised.

5 Is it Feasible?

'let contract flowers bloom rather than allow the tort elephant to trample them down.'[27]

Having seen that a European Civil Code, although raising serious constitutional issues, is not constitutionally impossible (e.g. by way of Treaty), we now turn to the main question raised in this book. Is a European Civil Code feasible? We shall look at this issue for each of the three main Parts, on Contract, Extra-contractual liability, and Property, separately.

Beginning with the law of contract, Van Erp in Chapter 8 on Formation is sympathetic to harmonisation of the rules on formation, but as yet sees no possibility for this to be reached by way of codification. He discerns a growing divergence between English and continental law, as is demonstrated by the case of Walford v Miles.[28] In this case, the House of Lords considered; 'A duty to negotiate in good faith is as unworkable in practice as it is inherently inconsistent with the position of a negotiating party'. A European Code, which would point to a different direction, would be totally unacceptable to the United Kingdom according to the author. Van Erp sees no problem with the adoption of Principles of Contract Law, since such principles leave more freedom than rules. What the author perhaps overlooks is the criticism with which Walford v Miles has met also in England.

A more positive note is struck by Van Rossum in Chapter 9 and by Lando in Chapter 11. Van Rossum finds a great discrepancy as to error, fraud, duress and undue influence, which in the common law tradition, as opposed to the continental one, are not considered defects of consent. Yet, stimulated by the Dutch Civil

---

25   Giuseppe Gandolfi, Pour un code européen des contrats, *Revue trimestrielle de droit civil* 1992, 707, 726.
26   See the publications listed in the Bibliography on p. 13.
27   H. Kötz, 10 *Tel Aviv University Studies in Law* 195, 212 (1990).
28   [1992] 2 *WLR* 174.

Code's symbiosis of these various approaches, the author does not rule out harmonization. Lando, on the basis of his practical experience, concludes that it is possible to establish a system for non-performance and a terminology accompanying this system. The price to be paid is that it has not been possible to provide general rules on performance and remedies which have any great precision.

In Chapter 10, Storme Jr. starts with the assumption that if there is any aspect of contract law which is resistant to harmonisation, it probably is the validity of contracts. His conclusion is that indeed there are many opposing views, albeit of a mainly technical character.

In Chapter 12, Tallon warns us as to the difficulties in drafting a whole Civil Code, when the preparation of common rules on isolated topics of contract law already provokes so many problems even though this author equally warns us against an excessive pessimism, which breeds resignation or despondency. He rather turns up with some good advice: agree upon the basic concepts and tackle the question of languages. Kortmann and Faber in turn are not convinced that the incorporation of privity of contract and its exceptions into a European Code would succeed (Chapter 13).

We now turn to the area of extra-contractual liability, which includes unjust enrichment and tort. As Swadling concludes in Chapter 14, the English law of restitution has a long way to go before any attempt at codification can be made. Even if English law was sufficiently developed to be susceptible of codification, the author considers it doubtful whether any assimilation of the common law and the civil law in this area could be made.

In his Chapter 15 on the general theory of unlawful acts, Markesinis expresses doubts about a code, but not about the desirability of harmonisation though directives and case-law of the European Court of Justice.

In Chapter 16 on vicarious liability, Van Maanen argues that the rules in the civil and common law tradition correspond on essential points. The author even suggests a legislative text. Yet he considers the chances of success very slim, only in the long run are they better. In Chapter 17, Howells is in the enviable position that product liability has already been harmonised to some extent by the EC Directive of 1985. The lessons to be drawn from the ensuing implementation process are that national legal traditions are difficult to overcome, that formally harmonised laws may yet differ in their application and the limited utility of harmonisation if not all aspects are harmonised.

As for traffic liability, Tunc in Chapter 18 states the case for a traffic accident compensation, which as far as he is concerned, may find a place in a European Civil Code, although the author does see potential adversaries among insurers and practicing attorneys. In Chapter 19 on environmental liability, Betlem shows himself to be an ardent supporter of an Environmental Liability Regulation, which in his view could easily be inserted into a European Civil Code. This author also writes about two aspects which are not taken up by most other authors. First, he sets out the constitutional basis for the Regulation advocated by him. Second, he puts Europe itself in perspective, seeing it not so much as something far larger than what we usually deal with, but rather as part of the world.

Now turning to property law, Drobnig in his Chapter 20 on Transfer of property in corporeal movables sets out the profound differences between the various European countries. For once the English Channel does not seem to be the major divide, but rather an Anglo-French conglomerate versus Germany, Greece and the Netherlands. Yet this author does see a possibility of drafting a European Civil Code, provided this will take into account two basic rules. An important point which the author makes, is that the rules on obligations and property are interdependent to such a degree that an isolated unification of rules of central importance is not advisable.

Dalhuisen in Chapter 21 gives an account of the everlasting struggle of modern business needs for security interests which are compatible with the legal traditions of the various countries of the world. The author does see a possibility for civil law and common law to arrive at a common position through the elaboration of the ownership context. This common position should be arrived at through case-law, which has been the conduit for the development of all modern security rights, and not through legislation.

In Chapter 22, Wehrens strongly argues for the development of a *Eurohypothèque* (mortgage), to be used in case of transfrontier credit transactions as an alternative to domestic mortgage. The author raises two issues which are also discussed in some other chapters. First, does private international law provide a solution for transfrontier credit transactions under mortgage? He answers the question in the negative. A second issue is whether a European regulation should only deal with transfrontier mortgage transactions or should cover all such transactions, even the domestic ones. The major differences between the various mortgage institutions of European countries turn the latter solution into a highly unrealistic and perhaps also undesirable one.

Finally, I have a personal observation to make. On January 1, 1988, the Convention on the International Sale of Goods entered into force. As of 1994, the Convention is in force in a large number of countries, including many EC Member States. If it has been possible to bring about this global harmonisation of a most difficult area, why could it not be achieved for the whole of the civil law?

6 How to Proceed

From the following Chapters the conclusion may be drawn that a European Civil Code may still be a long way ahead, but that it is not to be excluded altogether. It therefore seems appropriate to contemplate the elaboration of a code or restatement, which may at least provide a framework. Such a 'pre-code' may for instance serve to make directives compatible with one another.

Perhaps even more important is the contribution which an exchange of ideas may make towards elaborating a new international framework of concepts and norms of civil law. The necessity of this has been underlined by several authors.[29] It is well stated by Kötz, who suggests 'auch die Grundlagen des Zivilrechts in den Prozess der Rechtsvergleichung einzubeziehen, also einen Bestand allgemeiner Regeln des Vertrags- und Deliktsrechts herauszuarbeiten, der auf einen internationalen Konsens rechnen und dazu beitragen kann, der Rechtsprechung die Anwendung des geltenden Einheitsrechts zu erleichtern, die geschilderten Auslegungsdivergenzen zu vermeiden und den Boden für künftige Vorhaben der Rechtsvereinheitlichung vorzubereiten.'[30]

P. Ulmer has further developed this idea as follows:

'Geeignete Gegenstände dafür bilden Werk-, Dienstleistungs- und Geschäftsbesorgungsverträge, aber auch Darlehens- und Bankgeschäfte, Versicherungs-, Miet- und Leasingverträge, um nur die wichtigsten heute gebräuchlichen Vertragstypen zu nennen. Ziel dieser Arbeiten kann es nicht sein, alsbald Kodifikationsvorschläge zu erstellen. Schon viel ist gewonnen, wenn man auf diesem Wege zur Entwicklung gemeinsamer Grundsätze kommt, die ihrerseits durch Erläuterungen über die jeweilige Rechtslage in den Mitgliedstaaten und über die maßgebenden Erwägungen für die erarbeiteten Vorschläge zu ergänzen sind.'[31]

---

29 In this sense for instance O. Remien, 'Europäische Rechtswissenschaft — Voraussetzung oder Folge europäischer Rechtsangleichung', in: K.J. Hopt (ed.), *Europäische Integration als Herausforderung des Rechts: Mehr Marktrecht — weniger Einzelgesetze, Veröffentlichungen der Hanns Martin Schleyer-Stiftung* 12, vol. 32, Berlin 1990, p. 124, at 131: 'europäische Rechtswissenschaft sollte nicht bloße Folge europäischer Rechtsangleichung sein, sondern ist im Grunde ihre Voraussetzung'.

30 Neue Aufgaben der Rechtsvergleichung, *Juristische Blätter* 1982, p. 355, 361. In his paper on 'Legal education in the future: Towards a European Law School?', in: Bruno de Witte and Caroline Forder (eds.), *The common law of Europe and the future of legal education/Le droit commun de l'Europe et l'avenir de l'enseignement juridique*, Deventer 1992, p. 31, 41, Kötz argues that '[t]he aim of finding a European common core of legal principles (...) is simply to mark out areas of agreement and disagreement, to construct a European legal *lingua franca* that has concepts large enough to embrace legal institutions which are functionally comparable, to develop a truly common European legal literature and the beginnings of a European law school curriculum, and thus to lay the basis for a free and unrestricted flow of ideas among European lawyers that is perhaps more central to the idea of a common law than that of identity on points of substance'.

31 P. Ulmer, 'Vom deutschen zum europäischen Privatrecht?', *Juristen Zeitung* 1992, p. 1, at 7.

All of this requires what Sacco has called the circulation of legal ideas.[32] I warmly support this idea.[33] Domestic law should be given a much wider audience than only the citizens of the state concerned. Smaller nations, especially, should make an effort to 'export' their law. Most Nordic countries already have a tradition of providing government reports with English language summaries. Countries such as Greece, the Netherlands and Portugal would be well advised to take over this tradition. The Netherlands do have a long standing tradition of supplementing doctoral theses with foriegn language summaries. Likewise, some countries publish annual translations or adaptations of major law review articles in English. The *Scandinavian Studies in Law* are perhaps the best known example, but this is not confined to smaller states. Of the larger European countries, Italy has also adopted this system.[34] New law reviews such as the *European Review of Private Law* and the *Zeitschrift für Europäisches Recht* may also help in disseminating legal ideas.

Although for practical purposes, the number of languages used in Europe presents some obvious problems, I do not support the idea that in the future there should be a single European language. Rather the diversity of languages, like that of cultures, seems to give Europe its distinct flavour. On a more abstract level, a case may well be made that the co-existence of several languages may contribute towards a higher quality of legal texts.[35]

7 Conclusion

The impact of European law on the development of private law will become increasingly important in the imminent future. A number of directives already compel Member States to harmonise part of their contract and tort law. Other areas of private law will soon also be the object of efforts towards harmonisation. Not always will the European Community use directives as its sole instrument. Other instruments which have been used by the EC include treaties and regulations. Private self-regulation is another source open to exploitation by those wishing for harmonisation.

---

32 See the *Travaux de l'Association Henri Capitant 1993* (Gênes/Nice), in the press.
33 See for a similar call Anthony Ferner and Richard Hyman, in: *Industrial Relations in the New Europe*, Oxford 1992, p. xvi-xvii: 'Whether "harmonisation" of national industrial relations systems is a realistic possibility must therefore be left to subsequent analysis. However, such policy discussion certainly needs to be informed by an understanding of the similarities and differences between national systems, the evidence of convergence and divergence in recent years, and possible explnations for these trends and characteristics'.
34 See *Italian Studies in Law* (ed. A. Pizzorusso), Dordrecht 1992- ; and *Italian Yearbook of Civil Procedure* (ed. Elio Fazzalari), Milano 1992- .
35 See Olivier Remien, 'Rechtseinheit ohne Einheitsgesetze? – Zum Symposium "Alternativen zur legislatorischen Rechtsvereinheitlichung"', *RabelsZ* 1992, 300, 307.

What is needed at present is a framework in which all these efforts can be placed. Such a framework could be established by a European Civil Code. As yet it is too early to even consider adopting such a Code. As the following Chapters will demonstrate, the concepts and the practical solutions found within Europe are still very much apart and in some areas, such as formation of contract, are diverging rather than converging. However, if a Code is brought about which only aspires to serve as a set of Principles of Civil Law, some practical difficulties seem to diminish. Such a set of Principles may also serve as a source of inspiration to both judges and academics.[36] Judges should play an important role, since it is only through case-law that the major areas of the civil law, such as that of corporeal securities, are formed. Academics are important, since they will have to contribute towards the circulation of ideas with regard to this development.[37] A similar conclusion is reached by Manfred Wolf with regard to the necessity of unification of civil procedure.[38] The new European challenge to lawyers in Europe seems to have been taken up with enthousiasm in a number of countries. This book is one of the fruits of that enthousiasm.

Bibliography

– Ch. Armbrüster, Europäisierung des Schuldrechts? – zur Reform des deutschen Unmöglichkeitsrechts im Vergleich zum Code Civil, *Juristische Arbeitsblätter* 1991, 252-257.
– Christian von Bar (ed.), *Europäisches Gemeinschaftsrecht und Internationales Privatrecht*, Köln etc. 1991.
– J.M. Barendracht, Produktenaansprakelijkheid: Europees Burgerlijk Recht?, *Preadvies Vereniging voor burgerlijk recht*, Lelystad 1987.

---

36 W. van Gerven, 'Court decisions, general principles and legal concepts: ingredients of a common law of Europe, in: Bruno de Witte and Caroline Forder (eds.), *The common law of Europe and the future of legal education/Le droit commun de l'Europe et l'avenir de l'enseignement juridique*, Deventer 1992, p. 339, 348.

37 Such circulation of ideas should in itself, apart from developments at a Community level, make a contribution towards the development of domestic private law. This has always been one of the main functions of comparative law.

38 'Eine Bestandsaufnahme der Prozessordnungen der europäischen Mitgliedstatten lässt erkennen, dass sie auf einer gemeinsamen rechtsstaatlichen Grundlage beruhen, (...). Trotz rechtsstaatlich gemeinsamer Grundlagen bestehen bei der Ausgestaltung im einzelnen manche Unterschiede. Diese Unterschiede, die zum Teil Ausdruck besonderer kultureller Anschauungen, Erfahrungen und sozialer Gepflogenheiten sind, müssen auch in der Europäischen Gemeinschaft nicht volkommen nivelliert werden. (...). Den prozessualen Verschiedenheiten sind in der Europäischen Gemeinscahft aber Grenzen gesetzt, soweit die Handelsbeschränkungen und Wettbewerbsverzerrungen zur Folge haben. (...). Insoweit ist eine Anpassung an die Erfordernisse des Binnenmarkts geboten': Manfred Wolf, 'Abbau prozessualer Schranken im europäischen Binnenmarkt', in: *Wege zu einem europäischen Zivilrecht/Tübinger Symposium zum 80. Geburtstag von Fritz Baur*, Tübingen 1992, p. 35, 67.

- Hugh Beale, Towards a Law of Contract for Europe: the Work of the Commission on European Contract Law, in: Günter Weick (ed.), *National and European Law on the Threshold to the Single Market*, p. 177-196.
- Günther Beitzke, Probleme der Privatrechtsangleichung in der Europäischen Wirtschaftsgemeinschaft, *Zeitschrift für Rechtsvergleichung* 1964, 80-93.
- M.J. Bonell, Unification of Law by Non-Legislative Means: The UNIDROIT Draft Principles for International Commercial Contracts, 40 *American Journal of Comparative Law* 617-633 (1992).
- J.J. Brinkhof, *Europees octrooirecht*, inaugural address Utrecht, Zwolle 1989.
- G. Brüggemeier, Chr. Joerges, Europäisierung des Vertrags- und Haftungsrechts, in: P.C. Müller-Graff (ed.), *Gemeinsames Privatrecht in der Europäischen Gemeinschaft*, Baden-Baden 1993, p. 233-286.
- Richard M. Buxbaum, Klaus J. Hopt, Integration Through Law/Europe and the American Federal Experience vol. 4, *Legal Harmonization and the Business Enterprise*, Berlin etc. 1988.
- Richard M. Buxbaum, Gérard Hertig, Alain Hirsch, Klaus J. Hopt (eds.), *European Business Law/Legal and Economic Analyses on Integration and Harmonization*, Berlin etc. 1991.
- Mauro Cappelletti (ed.), *New Perspectives for a Common Law of Europe*, Leyden etc. 1978.
- Helmut Coing, *Europäisches Privatrecht*, München 1985/1989.
- Helmut Coing, Europäisierung der Rechtswissenschaft, *Neue Juristische Wochenschrift* 1990, 937-941.
- *Corporate Law/The European Dimension*, papers given at the Bar European Group Conference Edinburgh 1991, London 1991.
- Erwin Deutsch, Aspekte für ein europäisches Haftungsrecht — Versuch einer kritischen, dogmatischen Bestandsaufnahme, *Karlsruher Forum* 1992.
- Erwin Deutsch and Jochen Taupitz (eds.), *Haftung der Dienstleistungsberufe — natürliche Vielfalt und europäische Vereinheitlichung*, Heidelberg 1993.
- Ulrich Drobnig, Ein Vertragsrecht für Europa, in: *Festschrift für Ernst Steindorff*, Berlin/New York 1990, p. 1141 ff.
- Ulrich Drobnig, Substantive Validity, 40 *American Journal of Comparative Law* 635-643 (1992).
- J.H.M. van Erp, Europees privaatrecht in ontwikkeling?, in: *Themis en Europa/Een opening van nieuwe grenzen?*, Zwolle 1989, p. 61-70.
- Axel Flessner, Rechtsvereinheitlichung durch Rechtswissenschaft und Juristenausbildung, *RabelsZ* 1992, 243-260.
- Marcel Fontaine, Content and Performance, 40 *American Journal of Comparative Law* 645-655 (1992).
- M.P. Furmston, Breach of Contract, 40 *American Journal of Comparative Law* 671-674 (1992).
- Giuseppe Gandolfi, Pour un code européen des contrats, *Revue trimestrielle de droit civil* 1992, 707-736.
- Alejandro M. Garro, Unification and Harmonization of Private Law in Latin America, 40 *American Journal of Comparative Law* 587-616 (1992).

- Alejandro M. Garro, *Armonización y Unificación del derecho privado en América Latina: esfuerzos, tendencias y realidades*, Roma 1992.
- Jacques Ghestin, L'influence des directives communautaires sur le droit français de la responsabilité, in: *Festschrift Werner Lorenz*, Tübingen 1991.
- Ch.E. Hauschka, Grundprobleme der Privatrechtsfortbildung durch die Europäische Wirtschaftsgemeinschaft, *Juristen Zeitung* 1990, 290-299.
- Georges van Hecke, Intégration économique et unfication du droit privé, in: *De Conflictu Legum (Kollewijn-bundel)*, 1962, p. 198-208.
- Peter Hommelhoff, Zivilrecht under dem Einfluß europäischer Rechtsangleichung, *Archiv für die civilistische Praxis* 1992, 71 ff.
- E.H. Hondius, Naar een Europees burgerlijk recht, *Preadvies Vereniging voor Burgerlijk Recht en Nederlandse Vereniging voor Europees Recht*, Lelystad 1993.
- Erik Jayme, *Ein Internationales Privatrecht für Europa*, Heidelberg 1991.
- Konstantinos D. Kerameus, Procedural Unification: The Need and the Limitations, in: I.R. Scott (ed.), *International Perspectives on Civil Justice, Essays in honour of Sir Jack I.H. Jacob QC*, London 1990, p. 47-66.
- L.A.D. Keus, Europees privaatrecht/Een bonte lappendeken, *Preadvies Vereniging voor Burgerlijk Recht en Nederlandse Vereniging voor Europees Recht*, Lelystad 1993.
- D. Kokkini-Iatridou, *Een inleiding tot het rechtsvergelijkende onderzoek*, Deventer 1988.
- Hein Kötz, Gemeineuropäisches Zivilrecht, in: *Festschrift Zweigert*, 1981, p. 481-500.
- Hein Kötz, Was erwartet die Rechtsvergleichung von der Rechtsgeschichte?, *Juristen Zeitung* 1992, 20-22.
- Hein Kötz, Alternativen zur legislatorischen Rechtsvergleichung, *RabelsZ* 1992, 215-242.
- Hein Kötz and Axel Flessner, *Europäisches Vertragsrecht* (to be published).
- Thijmen Koopmans, The Birth Of European Law At The CrossRoads Of Legal Traditions, 39 *American Journal of Comparative Law* 493-507 (1991).
- Ernst A. Kramer, Europäische Privatrechtsvereinheitlichung, *Juristische Blätter* 1988, 477-489.
- Ole Lando, Principles of European Contract Law, in: *Liber Memorialis François Laurent*, Brussel 1989, p. 555-568.
- Ole Lando, Principles of European Contract Law/An Alternative or a Precursor of European Legislation, *RabelsZ* 1992, 261-273.
- J.H.A. Lokin, W.J. Zwalve, *Hoofdstukken uit de Europese Codificatiegeschiedenis*, Groningen 1986.
- Joseph Lookofsky, The State of the Union... in Contract and Tort, 41 *American Journal of Comparative Law* 89-101 (1993).
- A.G. Lubbers, W. Westbroek (eds.), *Company Law in a European Perspective*, Deventer 1993.
- Marcus Lutter, Die Auslegung angeglichenen Rechts, *Juristen Zeitung* 1992, 593-607.

- Filip De Ly, *Europese Gemeenschap en privaatrecht*, inaugural address Rotterdam, Zwolle 1993.
- H.P. Mansel, Rechtsvergleichung und europäische Rechtseinheit, *Juristen Zeitung* 1991, 529-534.
- Dietrich Maskow, Hardship and Force Majeure, 40 *American Journal of Comparative Law* 657-669 (1992).
- Jacques Massip, L'harmonisation du droit des personnes et de la famille: la contribution de la C.I.E.C., in: *La Commission Internationale de l'Etat Civil*, Strasbourg 1982, p. 15-30.
- Luigi Mengoni, *L'Europa dei codici o un codice per l'Europa?*, Centro di studie e ricerche di diritto comparato e straniero, Roma 1993.
- Anne de Moor, Contract, Justice and Diversity in the Remaking of Europe, *Rechtstheorie* 71-81 (1994).
- P.C. Müller-Graff, *Privatrecht und Europäisches Gemeinschaftsrecht/ Gemeinschaftsprivatrecht*, 2nd ed. Baden-Baden 1991.
- P.C. Müller-Graff, Europäisches Gemeinschaftsrecht und Privatrecht, *Neue Juristische Wochenschrift* 1993, 13-23.
- Peter-Christian Müller-Graff, Gemeinsames Privatrecht in der Europäischen Gemeinscahft: Ebenen und gemeinschaftsprivatrechtliche Grundfragen, in: *Festschrift für Bodo Börner zum 70. Geburtstag*, Köln/Berlin/Bonn/München 1993, p. 303-343.
- Projet de directive sur le rapprochement des lois et règles des Etats-Membres concernant certains aspects de la procédure civile, Rapport final (Storme Commission), Gent 1992.
- Hanns Prütting, Auf dem Weg zu einer Europäischen Zivilprozeßordnung/ Dargestellt am Beispiel des Mahnverfahrens, in: Festschrift Baumgärtel, 1990, p. 457-469.
- Norbert Reich, *Europäisches Verbraucherschutzrecht/Binnenmarkt und Verbraucherinteresse*, Baden-Baden 1993.
- Olivier Remien, Ansätze für ein Europäisches Vertragsrecht, *Zeitschrift für die Vergleichende Rechtswissenschaft* 1988, 105-122.
- Olivier Remien, Möglichkeit und Grenzen eines europäisches Privatrechts, in: *Jahrbuch Junger Zivilrechtswissenschaftler* 1991, p. 11-42.
- Olivier Remien, Illusion und Realität eines europäischen Privatrechts, *Juristen Zeitung* 1992, 277-284.
- Olivier Remien, Rechtseinheit ohne Einheitsgesetze?, *RabelsZ* 1992, 300-316.
- H.D.C. Roscam Abbing, Patiënt en gezondheidszorg in het recht van de Europese Gemeenschap, *Proceedings Vereniging voor Gezondheidsrecht* 1993.
- Arthur Rosett, Unification, Harmonization, Restatement, Codification, and Reform in International Commercial Law, 40 *American Journal of Comparative Law* 683-697 (1992).
- Geoffrey Samuel, Jac Rinkes, *Contractual and non-contractual obligations in English law*, thesis Maastricht, Nijmegen 1992.

- J.G. Sauveplanne, Van verscheidenheid naar eenheid van privaatrecht, *Koninklijke Nederlandse Akademie van Wetenschappen, Mededeling van de Afdeling Letterkunde, Nieuwe Reeks,* 55 no 9, Amsterdam 1992.
- Uwe Schneider, Europäische und internationale Harmonisierung des Bankvertragsrechts/Zugleich ein Beitrag zur Angleichung des Privatrechts in der Europäischen Gemeinschaft, *Neue Juristische Wochenschrift* 1991, 1985-1993.
- Reiner Schulze, *Die europäische Rechts- und Verfassungsgeschichte — zu den gemeinsamen Grundlagen europäischer Rechtskultur,* Saarbrücken 1991.
- Reiner Schulze, European Legal History — A New Field of Research in Germany, 13 *Journal of Legal History* 270-295 (1992).
- Jürgen Schwarze, *European Administrative Law,* London/Luxembourg 1992.
- G.M.F. Snijders, De Europese dimensie van de pacht, inaugural address Nijmegen, Deventer 1993.
- G.J.W. Steenhoff, Naar een Europees privaatrecht?, in: *Recht als norm en als aspiratie,* Nijmegen 1986, p. 85-101.
- Peter Stein (ed.), Incontro di studio su Il futuro Codice Europeo dei Contratti, Pavia 20-21 ottobre 1990, Milano 1993.
- Marcel Storme, Lord Mansfield, Portalis of von Savigny? Overwegingen over de eenmaking van het recht in Europa i.h.b. via de vergelijkende rechtspraak, *Tijdschrift voor Privaatrecht* 1991, 849-887.
- Denis Tallon, Vers un droit européen du contrat?, in: *Mélanges offerts à André Colomer,* Paris 1992, 485-494.
- Denis Tallon, Damages, Exemption Clauses, and Penalties, 40 *American Journal of Comparative Law* 675-682 (1992).
- Jochen Taupitz, *Europäische Privatrechtsvereinheitlichung heute und morgen,* Tübingen 1993.
- Winfried Tillmann, Zur Entwicklung eines europäischen Zivilrechts, in: *Festschrift Oppenhoff zum 80. Geburtstag,* 1985, p. 497-507.
- Winfried Tillmann, *Wirtschaftsrecht,* Berlin/Heidelberg/New York/Tokyo 1986.
- Winfried Tillmann, EG-Kodifikation des wirtschaftsnahen Zivilrechts, *Juristen Zeitung* 1991, 1023.
- B.W.M. Trompenaars, *Pluriforme unificatie en uniforme interpretatie,* doctoral thesis Utrecht, Deventer 1993.
- Peter Ulmer, Vom deutschen zum europäischen Privatrecht?, *Juristen Zeitung* 1992, 1-8.
- F.J.A. van der Velden, Europa 1992 en het eenvormig privaatrecht, in: D. Kokkini-Iatridou and F.W. Grosheide (eds.), *Eenvormig en vergelijkend privaatrecht 1990,* Lelystad 1990, p. 3-28.
- B. Wachter, *Elk volk krijgt het recht dat bij zijn aard past,* farewell lecture Tilburg, Zwolle 1992.
- A.J.O. van Wassenaer van Catwijck, *Naar een Europees verkeersschaderecht,* farewell lecture Vrije Universiteit, Deventer 1993.
- *Wege zu einem europäischen Zivilprozeßrecht/*Tübinger Symposium zum 80. Geburtstag von Fritz Baur, Tübingen 1992.

- Wolfgang Wiegand, The Reception of American Law in Europe, 39 *American Journal of Comparative Law* 229-248 (1991).
- Michael R. Will, Autonome Rechtsangleichung in Europa, in: Fritz Schwind (ed.), *Österreichs Weg in die EG — Beiträge zur europäischen Rechtsentwicklung*, Wien 1991, p. 53-109.
- Bruno de Witte, Caroline Forder (eds.), *The common law of Europe and the future of legal education/Le droit commun de l'Europe et l'avenir de l'enseignement juridique*, Deventer 1992.
- Reinhard Zimmermann, *The Law of Obligations/Roman Foundations of the Civilian Tradition*, Cape Town/Wetton/Johannesburg 1990.
- Reinhard Zimmermann, Das römisch-katholische ius commune als Grundlage europäischer Rechtseinheit, *Juristen Zeitung* 1992, 8-20.
- W.J. Zwalve, De natie en de toekomst van haar codificatie, *Nederlands Tijdschrift voor Burgerlijk Recht* 1992, 92-97.
- K. Zweigert and H. Kötz, *An Introduction to Comparative Law*, second ed. Oxford 1992 (translated by T. Weir).

Private Law Unification by Means other than of Codification

Peter-Christian Müller-Graff

The question of private law unification in Europe by means other than of enacting a European Civil Code focuses attention on the alternatives to a codification[1] of the substantial rules of private law, as far as economic matters are concerned, in the European Community. The value of these alternatives depends upon the definition of the aim of private law unification in the European Community. If the aim is to be the establishment of a coherent set of directly applicable uniform private law rules in all Member States, the question may fairly be raised of whether there is any reasonable alternative to a codification at all. If, however, the aim is to be the establishment of a workable degree of compatibility and conformity of national private law rules for border-crossing activities, or of an advanced degree of common elements in private law inside the European Community, alternatives might be worthy of discussion. This article examines the four most prominent fields of alternative developments towards a higher degree of common private law rules in the Community: European Community Directives (A), voluntary treaties and recommendations (B), 'restatements' (C) and the efforts of UNIDROIT and the Commission on European Contract Law (D). As a matter of fact, the demand for more common private law rules seems to increase as the scope of the freedom to form border-crossing contracts is extended in consequence of the basic freedoms of the EEC-Treaty.[2]

1 Common Private Law by European Community Directives

1.1 The Method

At present the most realistic and preferred way of achieving a higher degree of common private law elements in the Member States of the European Community is the method of fixing 'master rules' for the national legal systems in directives issued by the competent institutions of the EEC. Being legal measures of the Community by their very nature, directives are binding as to the

---

1   For the aim of a codification of private law see *Resolution of the European Parliament*, O.J. 1989, C 158/400.
2   For this effect see Peter-Christian Müller-Graff, *Privatrecht und Europäisches Gemeinschaftsrecht − Gemeinschaftsprivatrecht*, 2nd ed., 1991, p. 17-18.

result to be achieved, upon each Member State to which they are adressed. If the result to be achieved is defined in terms of certain precise private law notions or rules, a substantial choice is excluded for national authorities concerning the implementation. As the Community has been quite active in issuing directives referring to private law,[3] some experience with this method has already been gained.

1.2 The Fields Covered

DIRECTIVES AS SOURCES OF EC. PRIVATE LAW

Several fields of private law have been affected by Community directives to date thereby contributing to the appearance of a certain level of Community private law ('Gemeinschaftsprivatrecht'[4]). This is especially true for contract law where, for example, contracts negotiated away from business premises,[5]

- CONTRACT LAW

consumer credit contracts,[6] package travel contracts[7] and the contractual relationship of self employed commercial agents[8] have been subjected to 'master rules' laid down in directives. Moreover, a proposal has been introduced by the Commission to issue a Council directive on unfair terms in so-called 'consumer contracts'.[9] The law of liability for damages is dealt with in

- TORTS

directives too, especially the rules of liability for defective products,[10] and in cases of violations of the principle of equal treatment of men and women.[11] Proposals for two new Council directives have been put forward by the Commission: one concerning the liability of suppliers of services,[12] the other the civil liability for damages caused by waste.[13] Property law has been part of directives only in the indirect way that conditions of the use of private property are embodied in legal rules in general and in provisions concerning industrial and commercial property in particular. Labour law is the subject of directives to

- LABOR LAW

an increasing degree, for example, in the areas of equal treatment of men and women in labour relations,[14] mass dismissals[15] and the protection of workers in the event of the sale of an undertaking[16] or the insolvency of the

---

3   See Annex.
4   See Peter-Christian Müller-Graff (note 2), p. 27-42; see also Peter-Christian Müller-Graff, *Gemeinsames Privatrecht in der Europäischen Gemeinschaft*, in: Peter-Christian Müller-Graff (Hrsg.) *Gemeinsames Privatrecht in der Europäischen Gemeinschaft*, 1993, p. 7ss.
5   O.J. 1985, *L* 372/1.
6   O.J. 1987, *L* 42/48.
7   O.J. 1990, *L* 158/59.
8   O.J. 1986, *L* 382/17.
9   O.J. 1990, *C* 243/02.
10 O.J. 1985, *L* 210/29.
11 O.J. 1976, *L* 39/40.
12 O.J. 1990, *C* 12/08.
13 O.J. 1989, *C* 251/03.
14 O.J. 1975, *L* 45/19; O.J. 1976, *L* 39/40.
15 O.J. 1975, *L* 48/29.
16 O.J. 1977, *L* 61/26.

employer.[17] New directives have been proposed.[18] Also certain fields of commercial law have been affected by directives such as commercial register publicity,[19] the rules pertaining to annual accounts[20] and the law of commercial agents.[21] Company law particularly has been subjected to 'master rules' laid down in directives on the basis of Article 54 (3)(g) EEC-Treaty.[22] In this context a variety of problems has already been covered including: capital, balance, qualification of auditors, commercial register publicity, one-man-companies, partition of enterprises, mergers of companies, etc.[23] Somewhat surprisingly no equivalent development has taken place in the law against unfair competition. Until now only a directive on misleading advertising[24] has been issued and another on comparative advertising[25] has been proposed despite the projects and hopes for far-reaching approximation in this area in the early times of integration.[26] No urgent need has emerged to lay down 'master rules' for national antitrust law until now,[27] most probably as a result of the existence of a large set of directly applicable uniform Community laws against restrictions, preventions and distortions of competition within the common market[28] (Articles 85 ss EEC-Treaty, EEC-regulations, Articles 65, 66 ECSC-Treaty) and also as a consequence of a gradual autonomous self-approximation of national antitrust law in several states.[29] However, in the field of the protection of industrial and commercial property and copyright some directives have already been issued concerning, in particular, trade mark law,[30] semiconductor protection[31] and the protection of computer software.[32]

---

17 O.J. 1980, *L* 283/23.
18 See RdA 1991, 45.
19 O.J. 1968, *L* 65/8.
20 O.J. 1978, *L* 222/11; O.J. 1983, *L* 193/1; O.J. 1986, *L* 372/1.
21 O.J. 1986, *L* 382/17.
22 See Annex; see as a comprehensive survey and analysis Marcus Lutter, *Europäisches Unternehmensrecht*, 3rd ed., 1991, p. 33ss., 163ss.
23 Id.
24 O.J. 1984, *L* 250/17.
25 O.J. 1991, *C* 180/14.
26 See as a comprehensive comparative analysis Eugen Ulmer (ed.), *Das Recht des unlauteren Wettbewerbs in den Mitgliedstaaten der Europäischen Wirtschaftsgemeinschaft*, 1965.
27 See as suggestions, e.g., Fritz Rittner, in: FIW (ed.), *Integration oder Desintegration der europäischen Wettbewerbsordnung?*, 1983, p. 31ss.; FIW (ed.), *Harmonisierungsbedürfnis zwischen dem Wettbewerbsrecht der EG und der Mitgliedstaaten?*, 1991.
28 As a survey see Peter-Christian Müller-Graff, *Wettbewerbsregeln des gemeinschaftseuropäischen Binnenmarktes*, 1990.
29 See for examples Claus-Dieter Ehlermann, Der Beitrag der Wettbewerbspolitik zum Europäischen Binnenmarkt, *WuW* 1992, 5ss; Peter-Christian Müller-Graff, Die Freistellung vom Kartellverbot, *EuR* 1992, 8.
30 O.J. 1989, *L* 40/1.
31 O.J. 1987, *L* 24/36.
32 O.J. 1991, *L* 122/42.

1.3 Merits and Problems

1   The method of achieving a higher degree of common private law elements in the Member States of the European Community by way of directives undoubtedly has its advantages. First of all it combines the creation of Community-wide conceived 'master rules' on a Community level with the competence and responsability of the Member States to enact the concrete and directly applicable national rules that are deemed to be adequate to the specific legal system (statutory order, case law) and terminology of every State adressed. This method thereby implies the opportunity to add national authority and legitimation to the rules in question and to respect national sovereignty at the same time as far as the form and methods of implementation are concerned. In short, approximation by directives seems to be a way of combining the necessities for uniform Community standards on the one hand and the possibility to tolerate national individualities on the other.

2   However, when looking closer at the requirements as well as into the practice of private law approximation several problems become visible.
    a   Traditionally, private law mainly consists of very precise rules, consequently the method of approximation by directives and national implementation can easily become a dilemma. It tends to either miss the objective of harmonization or to restrict the leeway of national adaptation considerably.
        The latter situation occurs in all cases in which the purpose of private law approximation is to overcome restrictions of trade or distortions of competition in consequence of differences in precise private law rules (e.g., requirements for the validity of consumer credit contracts). Here, even the 'result to be achieved' (e.g., the abolition of certain restrictions or distortions as a result of specific legal differences) requires precise definition. Therefore detailed rules nearly inevitably become part of the result to be achieved in the sense of Article 189 (3) EEC Treaty.[33] In fact, directives for the approximation of private law contain closely knit provisions which can be seen, for example, in the directives concerning product liability or consumer credit contracts. Directives may then partially approach the linguistic structure of regulations in the sense of Article 189 (2) EEC Treaty. Nevertheless, the necessity of national implementation remains and this again implies, among other problems, the risks of delay and of wrongful implementation[34] as well as difficulties of interpretation

---

33   See Peter-Christian Müller-Graff, Europäisches Gemeinschaftsrecht und Privatrecht — Das Privatrecht in der europäischen Integration, 46, *Neue Juristische Wochenschrift* 6 at III 6 (1993).

34   See Peter-Christian Müller-Graff, Common Private Law in the European Community, in: Bruno de Witte/Caroline Forder (eds.), *The common law of Europe and the future of legal education*, 1992, p. 249.

as a result of the need to interpret national provisions in the light of the relevant directive.[35] Moreover, the harmonization by directives requires constant control of the actual implementation in the different Member States by the Commission.

If, however, provisions in private law directives are not formulated in a precise, but in a rather vague way to grant more leeway to the Member States, they are in danger of missing the objective of approximation and of being enacted without the necessary competence to harmonize.

b Another problem in the method of approximation by directives is rooted in the requirement that directives can be based only on certain provisions of the EEC Treaty.[36] As these provisions contain certain prerequisites, it is possible that a particular question may be subjected to a directive, but not some inter-locking questions in the same area.[37] Additionally, legislation by directives implies a certain danger of discharging the directive-issuing institutions of their responsibility to define coherent and applicable rules. Since the directly applicable version of a provision has to be formulated by the respective Member State, the wording of a directive can be wider than is useful for the result to be achieved. A last problem to be mentioned is the rather scattered appearance of the measures taken, both in regard to the areas covered and to the rules created. Coming from an institution that is composed of members of national governments, the directives show a feeling for actualities, but no coherent concept of legislation in private law (except in company law) so far. Thus the experience gained with the directive-method suggests conceiving a more coherent, systematic and possibly codification-orientated approach and prefering the adoption of regulations based on Article 100 A or 235 EEC-Treaty rather than the enactment of directives.

[handwritten margin note: INABILITY OF EC INSTITUTIONS TO ISSUE COHERENT CODIFICATION]

[handwritten margin note: A CASE FOR REGULATION]

2 Common Private Law by Treaties

2.1 The Method

The conclusion of treaties between States containing the obligation to establish certain private law rules in the legal order of the contracting parties can be called the traditional method of achieving a higher degree of common private

---

35 For this need see the cases v. Colson and Kamann (1984) *E.C.R.* 1891; Harz (1984) *E.C.R.* 1921; Kolpinghuis (1987) 3969; Dekker (1990) *E.C.R.* I 3941 at p. 3976.
36 E.g., Articles 54 (3) (g), 100, 100 A EEC-Treaty.
37 For this problem see Peter-Christian Müller-Graff, 'Gemeinsames Privatrecht in der Europäischen Gemeinschaft: Ebenen und gemeinschaftsrechtliche Grundfragen', in: Jürgen F. Baur/Peter-Christian Müller-Graff/Manfred Zuleeg (eds.), *Europarecht — Energierecht — Wirtschaftsrecht, Festschrift für Bodo Börner*, 1992, p. 330.

VARIOUS
ORIGINATING
SOURCES

law elements. Such treaties can have different origins, having been prepared either by intergovernmental commissions or by specialized institutions, the Council of Europe, the OECD, the United Nations or other organisations.[38]

2.2 The Fields Covered

OFTEN
NARROW
IN SCOPE

Common elements of private law based on international agreements of this kind are present in very different fields of private law and they often concern rather particular topics. Among the fields affected in a more comprehensive way rank especially the law of international sales[39] or the law of bills of exchange and cheque law.[40] Particular questions are not only covered, for example, in the areas of securities,[41] liability of inn-keepers,[42] liability for damages caused by nuclear activities[43] and transportation law,[44] but also in family law,[45] the law of inheritance,[46] industrial and commercial property rights and copyright.[47]

2.3 Merits and Problems

MERITS:

OPEN TO
NON MEMBER
STATES

OPEN TO
LATER
ACCESSIONS

1 This traditional method of achieving a higher degree of common private law elements has some advantages. First of all it does not — outside of Article 220 EEC-Treaty — require the identity between participation and membership in the European Community. This method is not therefore restricted to Member States nor is it only applicable if at least all Member States become contracting parties. Moreover the subjects to be harmonized can be chosen more freely than in the context of Community law since the question is not put and does not have to be answered if the Community has a positive competence to act. However, relevant Community law has to be respected to the extent that Member States incur international obligations. A particular advantage of the creation of common private law by treaties can be seen in the opportunity of this method to lead to voluntary acceptance of the involved rules by more States later on. Treaties may also show fields of possible approximation by measures of the Community, since at least some

---

38 For a survey on the status of uniform private law see Gerhard Kegel, *Internationales Privatrecht* 6th ed., 1987, p. 41-74.

39 UN-convention of April 11, 1980; see Peter Schlechtriem, *Einheitliches UN-Kaufrecht*, 1981, p. 118-161.

40 As reference for the agreements see Gerhard Kegel (note 38), p. 43-44.

41 Convention of May 28, 1970 (Council of Europe).

42 Convention of December 17, 1962.

43 OECD-Convention of July 29, 1960.

44 See for references in detail Gerhard Kegel (note 38), p. 50-59.

45 For references id., p. 59.

46 For references id., p. 60.

47 For references id., p. 62-66.

24

States have already seen and acknowledged the necessity to agree on common principles and rules in the affected matters.

2   The problems, however, of achieving a higher degree of common private law elements in the Member States of the European Community by treaties are evident when compared to legislation by regulations or directives. This can be seen clearly in an analysis of the disadvantages of conventions worked out by Ivo Schwartz some years ago.[48] The most important problems arise in the enactment and interpretation. As far as the enactment of a uniform statute is concerned there is no obligation of any State to take part in any treaty-project to harmonize the national private law with a model set of rules. In consequence, the composition of the group of participating States may vary from convention to convention, thereby creating a complex and badly arranged private law situation when looked upon from the viewpoint of a common private law in the Community. Moreover, as far as the interpretation of rules based on an international agreement is concerned, usually no mandatory judicial procedure is provided to guarantee a uniform interpretation and application of the principles and rules agreed upon in the treaty.[49]

[handwritten margin note: PROBLEMS]

[handwritten margin note: FRAGMENTATION OF TREATY RELATIONSHIP]

[handwritten margin note: NO JUDICIAL PROCEDURE FOR UNIFORM INTERPRETATION]

3   Common Private Law by 'Restatements'

3.1 The Method

Restatements are a method and phenomenon developed in the USA by the American Law Institute, which was organized in 1923. Restatements were originally conceived to show, in a systematic and statute-like way, the rules of a certain field of law as applied by the courts.[50] In a different and developed sense this method may also be used to formulate common legal rules for a certain field of law as found in statutes and court judgments of the different Member States in the European Community. The underlying idea of this approach is the assumption that a common core can be found or proposed in certain areas of the different national legal orders ('Gemeineuropäisches

[handwritten margin note: TRADITIONAL BASED ON PREEXISTING RULES]

[handwritten margin note: ASSUMPTION: EXISTING COMMON CORE]

---

48   See Ivo E. Schwartz, 'Wege zur EG-Rechtsvereinheitlichung: Verordnungen der Europäischen Gemeinschaft oder Übereinkommen unter den Mitgliedstaaten?', in: *Festschrift für Ernst von Caemmerer*, 1978, p. 1067 ss.

49   For this problem see already Otto Riese, 'Einheitliche Gerichtsbarkeit für vereinheitlichtes Recht', 26 *Rabels Zeitschrift* 604 ss (1961). However, a mandatory judicial procedure is provided for in the Brussels convention of September 27, 1966 (EUGVÜ) and in the Luxemburg convention of December 15, 1975 (GPÜ).

50   For that 'unique effort at systematization of case law which culminated in the Restatement of the Law' see as a survey E. Allan Farnsworth, *An Introduction to the Legal System of the United States*, 1963, p. 84-86.

Zivilrecht'[51]), at least in the way that a rule can be stated as the most common or advanced rule for a defined socio-economic problem, and that a different solution of the said problem in one state can be shown as a national peculiarity or deviation from this rule.

3.2 Fields of Applicability

The developed 'restatement' method can be applied to comparative work in all fields of civil law, though the chances of finding or proposing a most common or advanced rule will vary considerably with the problem in question, for example in the field of the formation of contracts as opposed to the laws of inheritance. In the United States, nine fields of law in which case law was dominant (agency, conflict of laws, contracts, judgments, property, restitution, security, torts, trusts) have become subject of restatements[52] (in the classical sense). In Europe, the Commission on European Contract Law deals with 'contract law' (see D).

3.3 Merits and Problems

1   The classical American restatement method was supposed to gain its merits in a different area than that of the achievement of a higher degree of common private law elements in the legislation of the different states. The idea of this endeavour was to repair two chief defects in American law as diagnosed by the American Law Institute: uncertainty and complexity.[53] Therefore restatements of law were conceived to create 'authoritative sources, making it unnecessary for each individual researcher to induce a rule from the increasingly unwieldy mass of case material'.[54] Obviously this would not be a proper objective in continental European States despite the increasing impact of court judgements on the development of law. In Europe, as it was said above, a developed 'restatement' method could rather serve the purpose of discovering and developing common rules in the different national legal systems than to overcome uncertainty or complexity caused by court decisions. At least one similar effect has been observed in the United States in so far as the reporter 'could resolve many of the

---

51   For this idea see Hein Kölz, 'Gemeineuropäisches Zivilrecht', in: *Festschrift für Konrad Zweigert*, 1981, p. 481 ss.
52   E. Allan Farnsworth (note 50), p. 85.
53   Report of the Committee on the Establishment of a Paramount Organization for the Improvement of the Law Proposing the Establishment of an American Law Institute, *Am. L. Inst. Proc.* 1 (1923)I 6.
54   Whitmore Gray, 'E pluribus unum? A Bicentennial Report on Unification of Law in the United States', 50 *Rabels Zeitschrift* 119 (1986).

conflicts only by making a choice between the various rules the courts had adopted',[55] thereby even creating rules and contributing to harmonization.

2   As Whitmore Gray noted, while the codes of the last century could be well viewed as being in some way the spiritual background of the restatements in the United States, there was no intention of the restatements being adopted by legislatures.[56] In this respect the classical restatement method also differs from the idea of model uniform codes created by the American Bar Association.[57] Thus the importance of the American restatements has to be seen in their persuasive authority for the courts as illustrated in the development of the doctrine of promissory estoppel.[58] In the continental Member States of the European Community the situation is fundamentally different. Wherever courts are bound by codes and statutes they can not decide against explicit provisions by simply referring to the 'persuasive authority' of a deviating rule contained in a 'restatement'. This would amount to violation of the principles of separation of public powers in general and the prerogative of the legislative in particular. Thus in such a constitutional context a 'restatement' designed by scholars or institutes could only exert legitimate harmonizing effects on different national jurisdictions in the frame of statutory general clauses that permit such an interpretation or by persuading national legislatures. In short, the developed 'restatement' method seems to be a very speculative way of achieving a higher degree of common private law elements in the reality of the different national legal systems in the European Community.

4 Common Private Law by UNIDROIT and the Commission on European Contract Law[59]

4.1 The Method

The method of achieving a higher degree of common private law elements in the Member States of the European Community, or at an even much larger scale, by the efforts of UNIDROIT and of the Commission on European Contract Law is not fundamentally different from the design of rules to be embodied in an international treaty. Neither UNIDROIT nor the Commission on

---

55   Id.
56   Id., p. 120.
57   As a survey of the record of passage of uniform and model acts, as of September 1, 1985 see Appendix id., p. 160-165; particularly for the U.C.C. see Braucher, 'The Legislative History of the Uniform Commercial Code', 58 *Colum. L. Rev.* 798 (1958).
58   See Hoffmann v. Red Owl Stores, Inc., 26 Wis. 2d 683, 133 N.W. 2d 267, 274 (1965).
59   Cf. Chapter 3, Hartkamp, 'Principles of Contract Law', in: *Towards a European Civil Code*, 1994.

NOT
BINDING
FORCE
(NOT A
LEGISLATIVE
ORGAN)

European Contract Law can create binding provisions themselves but only proposals to enact such binding provisions.

4.2 UNIDROIT

UNIDROIT
PROMOTE
UNIFORM
LEGISLATION
BY STATES

According to the original statute of UNIDROIT (Institut International pour l'Unification du Droit Privé), founded in 1926, its object is '(de) préparer graduellement l'adaption par les divers Etats d'une législation de droit privé uniforme'.[60] This is different from the 'restatement'-approach and somewhat similar to the Uniform-Code-method, in that UNIDROIT envisages an eventual legislation. Besides these tasks UNIDROIT is now also supposed to engage in comparative studies in private law.[61] In a similar way in the field of the law of international trade the United Nations Commission on International Trade Law

& UNCITRAL

(UNCITRAL), founded in 1968, has not only the task of preparing and of promoting the adaption of new international conventions, model laws and uniform laws, but also of promoting the codification and a wider acceptance of international trade terms, provisions, customs and practices.[62]

The efforts of UNIDROIT cover a variety of fields already, the most prominent being the international sale of goods and − methodically somewhat different and 'restatement'-like − the principles for international commercial law.[63] Their merits for the achievement of a higher degree of common private law rules parallel those of the traditional method of international treaties (or 'restatements') in principle, but have the chance of exceeding them as a consequence of the thorough and professional preparation extended to every single project. The shortcomings are basically the same as those of the treaty-method (see above B III 2) or the 'restatement'-method (see above C III 2).

4.3 Commission on European Contract Law

COMMISSION
ON EUROP.
CONTRACT
LAW

Similar to the UNIDROIT efforts the Commission on European Contract Law, installed in 1980, aims to propose private law rules, the main difference being

---

60 Article 2 of the original statute.
61 Article 1 (2)(c) of the statute of 1940; see Michael Joachim Bonell, 'Das UNIDROIT-Projekt für die Ausarbeitung von Regeln für internationale Handelsverträge', 56 *Rabels Zeitschrift* 275 (1992).
62 See *General Assembly Resolution* 2205 (XXI) of December 17, 1966.
63 See Michael Joachim Bonell (note 60) p. 274 ss; see also Michael Joachim Bonell, 'The Unidroit Initiative for the Progressive Codification of International Trade Law', 27 *Int. and Comp. L. J.* 413 (1978); Michael Joachim Bonell, 'A "Restatement" of Principles for International Commercial Contracts. An Academic Exercise or a Practical Need?', *RDAI* 1988, 873.

the limitation of the Commission to contract law.[64] The Commission is a non-governmental body of lawyers from the twelve Member States of the European Community. Its purpose is to provide Member States with non-binding recommendations of principles for their national contract law. Formal papers have not yet been released. Assessed by its potential contribution to achieving a higher degree of common private law elements in the European Community, its merits and problems may be rated basically as parallelling those of the UNIDROIT efforts. However, in view of its concentration on the Member States it may serve harmonization of private law in the Community more intensively and successfully.

MORE FOCUSED EFFORT THAN UNIDROIT

5 Conclusion

If the political will strives for a common private law in the European Community, directives are only second-best to coherent codification-like regulations, voluntary treaties no preferable alternative to Community law, and 'restatements' as well as proposals of model statutes and recommendations of uniform rules no convincing substitute to binding law. Nevertheless, recommendations of uniform rules, proposals of model statutes, 'restatements', voluntary treaties and directives constitute valuable elements for the development of a higher degree of common private law in the European Community.

---

64   See Ole Lando, 'Principles of European Contract Law', 56 *RabelsZ* 261, 273 (1992); see already Ole Lando, 'European Contract Law', 31 *Am. J. Comp. Law* 653 (1983).

Annex

Section 1: Council Directives

I   Private Law in general

- Council Directive (86/653/EEC) of 18 December 1986 on the coordination of the laws of the Member States relating to self employed commercial agents; OJ 1986 L 382/17
- Council Directive (85/374/EEC) of 25 July 1985 on the approximation of the laws, regulations and administrative provisions of the Member States concerning liability for defective products; OJ 1985 L 210/29
- Council Directive (85/557/EEC) of 20 December 1985 to protect the consumer in respect of contracts negotiated away from business premises; OJ 1985 L 372/31
- Council Directive (87/102/EEC) of 22 December 1986 for the approximation of the laws, regulations and administrative provisions of Member States concerning consumer credits; OJ 1987 L 42/48
- Council Directive (90/314/EEC) of 13 June 1990 on package travel, package holidays and package tours; OJ 1990 L 158/59
- Proposal for a Council Directive (91/C12/11) on the liability of suppliers of services (submitted by the Commission on 8 November 1990); OJ 1990 C 12/08; COM (90) 482 final SYN 308
- Proposal for a Council Directive (90/C 243/02) on unfair terms in consumer contracts (submitted by the Commission on 24 July 1990); OJ 1990 C 243/02; COM (90) 322 final SYN 285
- Proposal for a Council Directive (89/C251/04) on civil liability for damages caused by waste (submitted by the Commission on 1 September 1989); OJ 1989 C 251/03; COM (89) 282 final SYN 217

II   Law against Unfair Competition

- Council Directive (84/450/EEC) of 10 September 1984 relating to the approximation of the laws, regulations and administrative provisions of the Member States concerning misleading advertising; OJ 1984 L 250/17
- Proposal for a Council Directive (91/C180/15) concerning comparative advertising and amending Directive 84/450/EEC concerning misleading advertising (submitted by the Commission on 28 May 1991); OJ 1991 C 180/14; COM (91) 147 final SYN 343
- Council Directive (79/581/EEC) of 19 June 1979 on consumer protection in the indication of prices of foodstuffs; OJ 1975 L 158/19
- Council Directive (88/314/EEC) of 7 June 1988 on consumer protection in the indication of the prices of non food products; OJ 1988 L 142/19
- Council Directive (79/112/EEC) of 18 December 1978 on the approximation of the laws of the Member States relating to the labelling, presentation and advertising of foodstuffs for sale to the ultimate consumer; OJ 1979 L 33/1

III Protection of Industrial and Comercial Property

- Council Directive (87/54/EEC) of 16 December 1986 on the legal protection of topographics of semiconductor products; OJ 1987 L 24/36
- Council Directive (91/250/EEC) of 14 May 1991 on the legal protection of computer programmes; OJ 1991 L 122/42
- First Council Directive (89/104/EEC) of 21 December 1988 to approximate the laws of the Member States relating to trade marks; OJ 1989 L 40/01
- Proposal for a Council Directive (91/C53/04) on rental rights, lending rights, and on certain rights related to copyright (submitted by the Commission on 13 December 1990); OJ 1990 C 53/35; COM (90) 586 final SYN 319
- Proposal for a Council Directive (89/C 10/03) on the legal protection of biotechnological inventions (submitted by the Commission on 20 October 1988); OJ 1989 C 10/03; COM (88) 496 final SYN 159

IV Company Law

- First Council Directive (68/151/EEC) of 9 March 1968 on the coordination of safeguards which, for the protection of the interests of members and others, are required by Member States of companies within the meaning of the second paragraph of Art. 58 of the Treaty, with a view to making such safeguards equivalent throughout the Community; OJ 1968 L 65/08
- Second Council Directive (77/91/EEC) of 13 December 1976 on coordination of safeguards which, for the protection of the interests of members and others, are required by Member States of companies within the meaning of the second paragraph of Art. 58 of the Treaty, in respect of the formation of public limited companies and the maintenance and alteration of their capital with a view to making such safeguards equivalent; OJ 1977 L 26/01
- Proposal for a Council Directive (91/C8/04) amending Directive 77/91/EEC on the formation of public liability companies and the maintenance and alteration of their capital (submitted by the Commission on 13 December 1990); OJ 1991 C 8/12; COM (90) 631 final SYN 317
- Third Council Directive (78/855/EEC) of 9 October 1978 based on Art 58 (3)(g) of the Treaty concerning mergers of public limited liability companies; OJ 1978 L 295/36
- Fourth Council Directive (78/660/EEC) of 25 July 1978 based on Art 54 (3)(g) of the Treaty on the annual accounts of certain types of companies; OJ 1978 L 222/11
- Council Directive (84/569/EEC) of 27 November 1984 reviewing the accounts expressed in Directive 78/660/EEC; OJ 1984 L 314/28
- Council Directive (90/605/EEC) of 8 November 1990 amending Directives 78/660/EEC and 83/349/EEC on annual accounts and consolidated accounts as regards the scope of those directives OJ 1990 L 317/60
- Council Directive (90/605/EC) of 8 November 1990 amending Directive 78/660/EEC on annual accounts and Directive 84/349/EEC on consolidated accounts as regards the scope of those Directives; OJ 1990 L 317/60
- Amended Proposal for a Fifth Directive founded on Art 54 (3)(g) of the EEC Treaty concerning the structure of public limited companies and the powers and obligations of their organs (submitted by the Commission persuant to Art 149 (2) of the EEC Treaty on 19 August 1983); OJ 1983 C 240/02

31

- Second Amendement for the Proposal for a Fifth Council Directive (91/C7/05) based on Art 54 of the EEC Treaty concerning the structure of public limited companies and the powers and obligations of their organs (submitted by the Commission persuant to Art 149 (3) of the EEC Treaty on 20 December 1990); OJ 1990 C 7/4; COM (90) 629 final SYN 3
- Third Amendement for the Proposal for a Fifth Council Directive (91/C 321/09) based on Art 54 of the EEC Treaty concerning the structure of public limited companies and the powers and obligations of their organs (submitted by the Commission persuant to Art 149 (3) of the EEC Treaty on 20 November 1991); OJ 1991 C 321/09; COM (91) 372 final SYN 3
- Sixth Council Directive (82/981/EEC) of 17 December 1982 based on Art 54 (3)(g) of the Treaty, concerning the division of public limited liability companies; OJ 1982 L 378/47
- Seventh Council Directive (83/349/EEC) of 13 June 1983 based on Art 54 (3)(g) of the Treaty on consolidated accounts; OJ 1983 L 193/01
- Eighth Council Directive (84/253/EEC) of 10 April 1984 based on Art 54 (3)(g) of the Treaty and the approval of persons responsible for carrying out the statutory audits of accounting documents; OJ 1984 L 126/20
- Proposal for a tenth Council Directive (85/C 23/08) based on Art 54 (3)(g) of the Treaty concerning cross-border mergers of public limited companies (submitted by the Commission to the Council on 14 January 1985); OJ 1985 C 23/11; COM (84) 727 final
- Eleventh Council Directive (89/666/EEC) of 21 December 1989 concerning disclosure requirements in respect of branches opened in a Member State by certain types of company governed by the law of another State; OJ 1989 L 395/36
- Twelfth Council Company Law directive (89/667/EEC) of 21 December 1989 on single member limited liability companies; OJ 1989 L 395/40
- Proposal for a thirteenth Council Directive on Company Law (98/C 64/07) concerning the take over and other general bids (submitted by the Commission on 19 January 1989); OJ 1989 C 64/8; COM (88) 823 final SYN 186
- Amended Proposal for a thirteenth Council Directive on Company Law (90/C 240/09) concerning the take over and other general bids (submitted by the Commission on 14 September 1990 persuant to Art 149 (3) of the EEC Treaty); OJ 1990 C 240/07; COM (90) 416 final SYN 186

V Stock Market Law

- Council Directive (80/390/EEC) of 17 May 1980 coordinating the requirements for the drawing up, scrutiny and distribution of the listing of particulars to be published for the admission of securities to official stock exchange listing; OJ 1980 L 100/01
- Council Directive (79/279/EEC) of 5 March 1979 coordinating the conditions for the admission of securities to official stock exchange listing; OJ 1979 L 66/21
- Council Directive (82/121/EEC) of 13 February 1982 on information to be published on a regular basis by companies the shares of which have been admitted to official stock exchange listing; OJ 1982 L 48/26
- Council Directive (89/298/EEC) of 17 April 1989 coordinating the requirements for the drawing-up, scrutiny and distribution of the prospectus to be published when transferable securities are offered to the public; OJ 1989 L 124/08

– Council Directive (87/345/EEC) of 22 June 1987 amending Directive 80/390/EEC coordinating the requirements for the drawing up, scrutiny and distribution of the listing of particulars to be published for the admission of securities to offical stock exchange listing; OJ 1987 L 185/81

– Council Directive (88/627/EEC) of 12 December 1988 on the information to be published when a major holding in a listed company is acquired or disposed of; OJ 1988 L 348/62

– Council Directive (89/592/EEC) of 13 November 1989 coordinating regulations on insider dealing; OJ 1989 L 334/30

VI Banking Law

– First Council Directive (77/780/EEC) of 12 December 1977 on the coordination of laws, regulations and administrative provisions relating to the taking up and pursuit of business of credit institutions; OJ 1977 L 322/30

– Second Council Directive (89/646/EEC) of 15 December 1989 on the coordination of laws, regulations and administrative provisions relating to the taking up and pursuit of business of credit institutions and amending Directive 77/780/EEC; OJ 1989 L 386/1

– Council Directive (89/117/EEC) of 13 February 1989 on the obligations of branches in a Member State of credit institutions and financial institutions having their head office outside that Member State regarding the publication of annual accounting documents; OJ 1989 L 44/40

– Council Directive (86/635/EEC) of 8 December 1986 on annual accounts and consolidated accounts of banks and other financial institutions; OJ 1986 L 372/01

– Amended Proposal for a Council Directive (90/C42/06) on investment services in the security field (submitted by the Commission on 8 February 1990); OJ 1990 C 42/7; COM (89) 629 final SYN 716

– Council Directive (83/350/EEC) of 13 June 1983 on the supervision of credit institutions on a consolidated basis; OJ 1983 L 193/18

– Council Directive ((89/299/EEC) of 17 April 1989 on the own funds of credit institutions; OJ 1989 L 124/17

– Council Directive (89/647/EEC) of 18 December 1989 on a solvency ratio for credit institutions; OJ 1989 L 386/14

– Amended Proposal for a Council Directive (89/C36/01) concerning the reorganization and the winding-up of credit institutions and deposit guarantee schemes (submitted by the Commission on 11 January 1988); OJ 1988 C 36/01; COM (88) 4 final

– Council Directive (85/611/EEC) of 20 December 1985 on the coordination of laws, regulations and administrative provisions relating to undertaking for collective investment in transferable securities (UCITS); OJ 1985 L 375/03

– Amended Proposal for a Council Directive (87/C 161/04) on the freedom of establishment and the free supply of services in the field of mortgage credits (submitted by the Commission on 22 May 1987); OJ 1987 C 161/04; COM (87)255 final

– Proposal for a Council Directive (90/C 152/06) on capital adequacy of investment firms and credit institutions (submitted by the Commission on 18 April 1990); OJ 1990 C 152/06; COM (90) 141 final SYN 257

- Council Directive (91/308/EEC) of 10 June 1991 on presentation of the use of the financial system for the purpose of money laundring; OJ 1991 L 166/77

VII Insurance Law

- First Council Directive (73/239/EEC) of 24 July 1973 on the coordination of the laws, regulations and administrative provisions relating to the taking up and pursuit of direct insurance other than life insurance; OJ 1983 L 228/01
- Second Council Directive (88/357/EEC) of 22 June 1988 on the coordination of the laws, regulations and administrative provisions relating to direct insurance other than life insurance and laying down provisions to facilitate the effective exercise of freedom to provide services and amending Directive 73/239/EEC; OJ 1988 L 172/01
- Proposal for a third Council Directive (91/C99/02) on the coordination of the laws, regulations and administrative provisions relating to direct life assurance and amending Directives 79/267/EEC and 90/619/EEC (submitted by the Commission on 15 February 1991); OJ 1991 C 99/01; COM (91) 57 final SYN 329
- Council Directive (72/166/EEC) of 24 April 1972 on the approximation of the laws of the Member States relating to insurance against civil liability in respect of the use of motor vehicles and to the enforcement of the obligation to insure against such liability; OJ 1972 L 103/01
- Second Council Directive (84/5/EEC) of 30 December 1983 on the approximation of the laws of the Member States relating to insurance against civil liability in respect of the use of motor vehicles; OJ 1984 L 8/17
- Third Council Directive (90/232/EEC) of 14 May 1990 on the approximation of the laws of the Member States relating to insurance against civil liability in respect of the use of motor vehicles; OJ 1990 L 129/33
- Council Directive (90/618/EEC) of 8 November 1990 amending, particularly as regards motor vehicle liability insurance, Directive 73/239/EEC and Directive 88/357/EEC which concern the coordination of the laws, regulations and administrative provisions relating to direct insurance other than life assurance; OJ 1990 L 330/44
- Council Directive (84/641/EEC) of 10 December 1984 amending, particularly as regards tourist assistance, First Directive 73/239/EEC on the coordination of the laws, regulations and administrative provisions relating to the taking up and pursuit of business of direct insurance other than life assurance; OJ 1984 L 339/21
- Council Directive (87/344/EEC) of 22 June 1987 on the coordination of laws, regulations and administrative provisions relating to legal expenses insurance; OJ 1987 L 185/77
- Council Directive (87/343/EEC) of 22 June 1987 amending, as regards credit insurance and suretyship insurance, First Directive 73/239/EEC on the coordination of the laws, regulations and administrative provisions relating to the taking up and pursuit of business of direct insurance other than life assurance; OJ 1987 L 185/72
- First Council Directive (79/267/EEC) of 5 March 1979 on the coordination of laws, regulations and administrative provisions relating to the taking up and pursuit of the business of direct life assurance; OJ 1979 L 63/01
- Council Directive (90/619/EEC) of 8 November 1990 on the coordination of laws, regulations and administrative provisions relating to direct life assurance, laying down provisions to facilitate the effective exercise of freedom to provide services and amending Directive 79/267/EEC; OJ 1990 L 330/50

- Proposal for a third Council Directive (91/C 99/02) on the coordination of laws, regulations and administrative provisions relating to direct life assurance and amending Directives 79/267/EEC and 90/619/EEC (submitted by the Commission on 25 February 1991); OJ 1991 C 99/02; COM (91) 57 final SYN 329
- Proposal for a Council Directive (87/C 71/05) on the coordination of laws, regulations and administrative provisions relating to the compulsory winding-up of direct insurance undertakings (submitted by the Commission on 23 January 1987); OJ 1987 C 71/05; COM (86) 768 final
- Amended Proposal for a Council Directive (89/C 253/04) on the coordination of laws, regulations and administrative provisions relating to the compulsory winding-up of direct insurance undertakings (submitted by the Commission on 18 December 1989); OJ 1989 C 253/03; COM (89) 393 final SYN 80
- Council Directive (91/674/EEC) of 19 December 1991 on the annual account and consolidated accounts of insurance undertakings; OJ 1991 L 374/01
- Council Directive (78/473/EEC) of 30 May 1978 on the coordination of laws, regulations and administrative provisions relating to community co-insurance; OJ 1978 L 151/25
- Council Directive (64/225/EEC) of 25 February 1964 on the abolition of restrictions on freedom of Establishment and freedom to provide services in respect of insurance and retrosession; OJ 1964 L 64/878
- Council Directive (77/92/EEC) of 13 December 1976 on measures to facilitate the effective exercise of freedom of establishment and freedom to provide services in respect of the activities of insurance agents and brokers (ex ISIC Group 630) and, in particular, transnational measures in respect of those activities; OJ 1977 L 26/14
- Proposal for a Council Directive on the coordination of laws, regulations and administrative provisions relating to insurance contracts (submitted by the Commission on 10 July 1979); OJ 1977 C 190/02
- Amended Proposal for a Council Directive on the coordination of laws, regulations and administrative provisions relating to insurance contracts (submitted by the Commission on 30 December 1980); OJ 1980 C 355/30

VIII Labour Law

Labour Law Directives: see survey in Birk, Rolf: Textausgabe 'Europäisches Arbeitsrecht', Beck (ED.), Munich, 1990

Section 2: Agreements and Conventions of the European Council

- see general survey in Roth, Peter H.: 'World Treaty Index'; ABC Clio Information Services Oxford, GB; Santa Barbara, Cal., USA; 1981
- for Agreements and Conventions coordinating civil legislations of Member States of the European Council see IPraX 1985, S. 122
- for Patent Law:
Munich Convention on the European Patent (1973)
Luxemburg Convention on the Community Patent (1975)

Section 3: International Treaties

— see survey in 'Internationales Privatrecht' by Gerhard Kegel, Beck Editors, 6th edition, Munich 1987

Section 4: UNIDROIT Projects

— see 'Revue de Droit uniforme — Uniform Law Revue', edited by UNIDROIT (28, Via Panisperna, Rome), appearing yearly, which contains detailed information and reports on the particular harmonization projects

CHAPTER 3
Principles of Contract Law

Arthur Hartkamp

1 Introduction

Uniform law presents itself in numerous manifestations. There are the well known international Conventions, prepared by an international organisation, adopted at a diplomatic conference and afterwards hopefully ratified by a significant number of states. There are model laws, drafted with a view to being adopted by national legislators. Furthermore, there are legal guides, destined for use by private or public operators in the field of international trade. The next category are standard terms (general conditions), drafted either by an organisation of interested business people or by an international intergovernmental organisation, which only become law between the parties after having been adopted by parties to an individual contract. Again, within international organisations there may exist a particular type of machinery devised to produce other variants of law binding upon the Member-States or private actors (enterprises or individuals), such as the directives, regulations or court decisions within the framework of the European Communities. All these types of international instruments present their proper advantages and disavantages on which I do not have to dwell here.[1]

This chapter is concerned with yet another type of uniform law: the UNIDROIT Principles for International Commercial Contracts and the Principles of European Contract Law. Attention will be paid to the history of the activities and to the commissions that carry them out. After a discussion of the nature of the Principles and of their possible functions I will pass on to a brief survey of their contents. I will conclude with some comparative remarks on the work of both groups and with some suggestions for future work.

---

1   See Kropholler, *Internationales Einheitsrecht* (1975), p. 93 ff, Trompenaars, *Pluriforme unificatie en uniforme interpretatie* (1989), p. 55ff.

2 The Work on the Principles

2.1 UNIDROIT

It is fair to start with the UNIDROIT Principles because work on them started first, their international scope is wider, and they embrace — in the present stage — more subjects than the European Principles.[2]

UNIDROIT (Institut International pour l'Unification du Droit Privé) was founded in 1926 under the aegis of the League of Nations to promote the unification of private law. The Institute has its seat in Rome and currently includes 56 Member States, among which there are many European States, but also for example the United States of America, the Russian Federation and the People's Republic of China. The activities of the Institute are directed by a Governing Council consisting of 25 eminent lawyers from different Member States (mostly academics, some state officials) who are elected by the General Assembly every five years.

Until recently, the Institute directed its activities exclusively towards international conventions, its most renowned success being the 1964 Hague Uniform Laws on the International Sale of Goods which thereafter served as the key source of inspiration for the 1980 UN-Convention on the International Sale of Goods (CISG), which is already ratified by more than 30 states. However, as early as 1971 the Governing Council decided to embark upon the project of the 'Progressive Codification of International Commercial Law'. Since this name could give rise to misunderstandings as no decision had been taken as to the kind of instrument the Institute would eventually produce and, moreover, from the outset it was improbable that the outcome would be a codification in the proper sense of the word, the project was subsequently rechristened as the Principles for International Commercial Contracts.

After preparatory works were carried out by three well known comparatists representing three major legal systems (David from Aix/Marseille, Schmithoff

---

2   The UNIDROIT project has been described in several articles by its chairman Michael Joachim Bonell, Professor at Rome University 'La Sapienza' and legal adviser to the Institute. See 'The UNIDROIT initiative for the Progressive Codification of International Law', *ICQL* 1976, 413 ff; 'A "restatement" of principles for international commercial contracts: an academic exercise or a practical need?', *RDAI* 1988, p. 873-888; 'International Uniform Law in Practice — Or where the real trouble begins', *AJCL* 1990, p. 865-888; 'Das UNIDROIT-Projekt für die Ausarbeitung von Regeln für internationale Handelsverträge', *RabelsZ.* 56 (1992) p. 274-289; 'Unification of Law by Non-Legislative Means: The UNIDROIT Draft Principles for International Commercial Contracts, Draft Principles for International Commercial Contracts', *AJCL* 1992, p. 617-634. See also M. Fontaine, 'Les principes pour les contrats commerciaux internationaux élaborés par UNIDROIT', *Revue de droit international et de droit comparé 1991*, p. 25-40. Several issues presented by the Principles are discussed in *AJCL* 1992, p. 635-682 by U. Drobnig (Substantive Validity), Marcel Fontaine (Content and Performance), Dietrich Maskow (Hardship and Force Majeur), M.P. Furmston (Breach of Contract) and Denis Tallon (Damages, Exemption Clauses, and Penalties).

from Kent and Popescu from Bucharest) at the end of the seventies, a working group was formed which gradually was enlarged to a group of about 15 members originating from several European civil law countries, and in accordance with the universal vocation of the Institute, from other countries including Great Britain, USA, Canada, Australia, Russia, Japan, China and Ghana. Preliminary drafts for the separate chapters or sections were produced by members of the group and afterwards discussed in the group as a whole. Each chapter or section underwent at least two readings (one reading normally taking a session of a week's length). Decisions were normally taken by consensus, but sometimes, in exeptionally arduous cases, after long discussions this consensus was brought about by abiding to the outcome of an indicative vote.

The Principles are drafted as articles and are accompanied by both comments (including illustrations wherever deemed useful to illustrate their content and scope), and by references to other pertinent international instruments of unified law. The comments do not contain references to national legal systems, unless a specific rule or institution is borrowed from a national source and it is felt useful to indicate such origin; or, conversely, unless a rule intends — without expressly saying so — to exclude the application of a national rule, a notable example being the rule excluding any prerequisite for the conclusion of a contract like consideration or cause (see below, number 4.1.3).

It will be clear from what has been said, that the editorial presentation of the Principles resembles to a certain extent the American Restatements of the law. The main difference with the Restatements is that, whereas the latter in principle purport to set forth the existing law of the states of the Union as laid down by the courts basing themselves upon the common law, the Principles (and this is also true for the European Principles) cannot do so because of the divergencies in the laws of the nations of the world or even of the European Union.

Since 1980, the working group has met once or twice a year for a one week session. At the present moment the articles have reached their all but final redaction within the working group. The groups efforts are currently directed towards the finalisation of the comments and of the language versions (all documents are published in the two working languages of the Institute, English and French, but it is also hoped that other language versions will appear). The last word on the project must be given by the Governing Council, but due to the fact that a number of greatly debated questions has already been submitted to the Council for its consideration and advice over the preceding years, it is scheduled that the Council will be able to deal with the remaining issues in its 1994 session so that the Principles will be published later that year.

2.2 The Commission on European Contract Law

Much of what has been said above equally applies *mutatis mutandis* to the Commission on European Contract Law.[3] The Commission consists of some 17 members recruited from all the Member States of the European Communities, although the members are not selected by their governments and they do not represent their countries in an official capacity. They are mostly academics or practising lawyers (or both) who are free to make up their own minds without any instructions from their governments. Expenses are met partly by the European Commission, partly by other sources.

The form in which the Principles are laid down is the same as discussed above. They will soon be published in English and French. The activities of both groups are influenced reciprocally because they consist in part of the same scholars. The European group, too, started its work about 1980 and finished its work recently (after 14 weekly sessions). A major difference, however, is that the Commission dealt with only a part of the subject-matter of the UNIDROIT working group; I will return to this aspect below.

3 The Nature and Possible Functions of the Principles

Neither the UNIDROIT Principles nor the European Principles are meant to become binding law. On a world scale it would be totally unrealistic to hope for a codification of the general part of contract law to be brought about by an international convention within the foreseeable future. Not even the success of the UN-Convention on the International Sale of Goods, which partly contains rules that undoubtedly may be considered as such general rules, has brought such a codification within reach. On a European scale the idea of a codification, be it only of contract law, is hardly less unrealistic, strange though this may seem taking into account the official goals of an internal market unhampered by national economic or legal barriers. Private law is merely being dealt with on a

---

3   Here, too, various publications may be mentioned by the chairman of the group, Ole Lando, Professor at the Institute of European Market law, Copenhagen: 'European Contract Law', *AJCL* 1983, p. 653-659; 'A Contract Law for Europe', *International Business Lawyer* 1985, p. 17-21; 'Principles of European Contract Law', *Liber memorialis Laurent* 1989, p. 555-568; 'Principles of European Contract Law. An Alternative to or a Precursor of European Legislation?', *RabelsZ.* 56 (1992) p. 261-273; 'Teaching a European Code of Contracts', in De Witte/Forder (ed), *The Common Law of Europe and the future of legal education* (1992), p. 223-237; 'Principles of European Contract Law: An Alternative to or a Precursor of European Legislation?', *AJCL* 1992, p. 573-586; 'Is codification needed in Europe? Principles of European Contract Law and the relationship to Dutch law', *European Review of Private Law*, Vol. 1 (1993), p. 157-170. See also Oliver Remien, 'Ansätze für ein Europäisches Vertragsrecht', *ZVglRWiss* 87 (1988) p. 105-122, at p. 117ff; F.J.A. van der Velden, *Europa 1992 en het eenvormig privaatrecht*, Molengrafica 1990, p. 3-28, at p. 19ff; Ulrich Drobnig, 'Ein Vertragsrecht für Europa', *Festschrift Steindorff* 1990, p. 1141-1154, at p. 1149ff.

piecemeal basis, although it must be added that the pieces (product liability, general conditions) definitely tend to become more important. What then are the functions that the Principles are meant to achieve? These functions could be the following.

1   Since codification of private law, be it on a world or a European scale, is fragmentary, it is important to dispose of a general set of principles from which inspiration may be derived by national and international courts to interpret the provisions of the existing uniform law, to fill the gaps which it presents and to offer a background, however informal, for new law to be created. Within the European Communities the need for such general principles has particularly manifested itself. Incidentally, it is striking to note that not only on a national scale but also internationally, the part of the law most difficult to (re)form and therefore most commonly neglected by the legislature is the general part of private law.[4]

2   The Principles may serve as a model law that could inspire legislators who strive for law reform. In this respect, not only legislators in developing countries or in Eastern Europe, may find them relevant, but also states trying to modernize their existing legislations and wishing to be inspired by common international standards as they have recently emerged. It is clear that the 1964 Hague Uniform Laws and CISG have exerted such an influence on states with a codified system. The Principles may assume a comparable function in areas where CISG cannot be relied on.

3   The Principles (and their accompanying comments) may serve to enlighten parties negotiating a contract in order to single out the problems to be settled in their contract and, possibly, to find suitable rules to settle them. In this respect, the Principles could have the same function as *for example* the various legal guides drafted by UNCITRAL.

4   Parties to an international contract containing an arbitration clause could chose the Principles as the law applicable to their contract;[5] taking into account, of course, whether the law governing the arbitration (and preferably the law of the state where the arbitrary award will probably be executed) will permit such a reference.[6] Even in the absence of such an express reference arbitrators authorised to apply such notions like the

---

4   Cf. Hein Kötz, 'Gemeineuropäisches Zivilrecht', *Festschrift Zweigert* 1981, p. 481-500, at p. 483.

5   See for examples Ulrich Drobnig, 'General Principles of European Contract Law', in Sarcevic/Volen (ed.), *International Sale of Goods* (Dubrovnik Lectures), 1985, p. 305-333, at p. 309.

6   See e.g. Article 28 of the UNCITRAL Model Law on Commercial Arbitration: 'The arbitral tribunal shall decide the dispute in accordance with such rules of law as are chosen by the parties as applicable to the substance of the dispute [..] Failing any designation by the parties, the arbitral tribunal shall apply the law determined by the conflict of law rules which it considers applicable [...]'.

general rules of law, equity or the *Lex Mercatoria*, may resort to the Principles to find suitable solutions to the dispute at hand.[7]

5   The Principles will certainly have an important scholarly and educational value. Concerning the European legal scene, they will encourage the emerging trend to find the common denominator of the different private law systems in Europe in order to construct a new *ius commune Europae*.[8] Moreover, they will enhance the prospect of law schools introducing new curricula where European law is taught side by side with the national laws of their respective countries of residence. In the long run, this seems to be the most promising way to attain such a new *ius commune*.[9]

6   Finally, the Principles will, by the sheer fact of their existence, prove that a reasonable compromise between the various legal systems of Europe and beyond, can be reached. It seems probable that this will add weight to the voices of those who advocate the preparation of a European Civil Code.[10]

---

7   See e.g. Ole Lando, 'The Lex Mercatoria in International Commercial Arbitration', 34 *ICLQ* 1985, p. 752-768; Y. Derains, 'L'ordre public et le droit applicable au fond du litige dans l'arbitrage international', *Revue de l'Arbitrage* 1986, p. 375-413; Andreas Spickhoff, 'Internationales Handelsrecht vor Schiedsgerichten und staatlichen Gerichten', *RabelsZ*. 56 (1992), p. 116-141. For some examples of decisions of national courts upholding such an approach by the arbitrators, see Michael Joachim Bonell, 'Das UNIDROIT-Projekt für die Ausarbeitung von Regeln für internationale Handelsverträge', *RabelsZ*. 56 (1992) p. 287 Fn. 55.

8   See for a short survey Ulrich Drobnig, 'General Principles of European Contract Law', in Sarcevic/Volen (ed.), *International Sale of Goods* (Dubrovnik Lectures), 1985, p. 305-333. The concept of a European *ius commune* in a broader sense is discussed by Thijmen Koopmans, 'Towards a new "ius commune"', in De Witte/Forder (ed), *The Common Law of Europe and the future of legal education* (1992), p. 43-51.

9   This idea seems to be popular especially among scholars from Germany and the Benelux Countries. See e.g. Helmut Coing, 'European Common Law: Historical Foundations', in Cappelletti (ed.), *New Perspectives for a Common Law of Europe*, 1978, p. 31-44, at p. 44; R. Sacco, 'Droit commun de l'Europe, et Composantes du Droit', in Cappelletti (ed.), *New Perspectives for a Common Law of Europe*, 1978, p. 95ff, at p. 108; Hein Kötz, 'Gemeineuropäisches Zivilrecht', *Festschrift Zweigert* 1981, p. 481-500; Ewoud Hondius, *Nederlands Juristenblad* 1985, p. 1343; Ost/Van Hoecke, *Rechtskundig Weekblad* 1989-1990, p. 1001-1002; Verstegen, *Rechtskundig Weekblad* 1989-1990, p. 657ff; Helmut Coing, 'Europäisierung der Rechtswissenschaft', *NJW* 1990, p. 937-941; Arthur Hartkamp, *Wetsuitleg en rechtstoepassing na de invoering van het nieuwe burgerlijk wetboek* (1992), p. 18ff; Peter Ulmer, 'Vom deutschen zum europäischen Privatrecht?', *JZ* 1992, p. 1-8, at p. 7; Axel Flessner, 'Rechtsvereinheitlichung durch Rechtswissenschaft und Juristenausbildung', *RabelsZ*. 56 (1992), p. 243-260; Hein Kötz, 'A Common Private Law for Europe: Perspectives for the Reform of European Legal Education', in De Witte/Forder (ed), *The Common Law of Europe and the future of legal education* (1992), p. 31-41; Peter-Christian Müller-Graff, 'Common Private Law in the European Community', in De Witte/Forder (ed.), *The Common Law of Europe and the future of legal education* (1992), p. 239-254, at p. 252.

10   See (apart from the authors cited in the previous footnote), among others, Roger Houin, *Pour une codification européenne du droit des contrats et des obligations, Etudes juridiques offertes à Léon Julliot de la Morandière* (1964), 223-231; René David, 'Le droit continental, la common law et les perspectives d'un ius commune Européen', in Cappelletti (ed.), *New Perspectives for a Common Law of Europe*, 1978, p. 113-135; Winfried Tilmann, 'Zur

On the official European level those voices until now have only received support from the European Parliament which on 26 May 1989 passed a resolution requesting the Member States to make a start with the necessary work on drawing up a European Code of Private Law.[11] Eventually, they may end up — probably in a revised version taking into account scholarly criticisms, practical experiences and political negotiations — in the (partial) codification the absence of which has led to their coming into existence. Until then, like the old ius commune, they may only aspire to be applied not *ratione imperii*, but *imperio rationis*.[12]

4 The Contents of the Principles

4.1 The UNIDROIT Principles

The UNIDROIT Principles in their present, not entirely finalised state[13] consist of 7 Chapters: general provisions, formation, validity, interpretation, content, performance and non-performance. These Chapters together contain nearly 120 articles, ranging from statements of principle and flexible standards to more (but

---

Entwicklung eines europäischen Zivilrechts', *Fs W. Oppenhoff* 1985, p. 495-507; G.J.W.Steenhoff, 'Naar een Europees Privaatrecht? Impulsen vanuit de rechtsvergelijking', in *Recht als norm en als aspiratie* (1986), p. 85-101; Peter Mansell, 'Rechtsvergleichung und europäische Rechtseinheit', *JZ* 1991, p. 529-534; Peter Hommelhoff, 'Zivilrecht unter dem Einfluss europäischer Rechtsangleichung', *AcP* 192 (1992), p. 71-107.

11 In the preamble to the resolution it is said (sub E) that unification should be envisaged in branches of private law which are highly important for the development of the single market, such as contract law. See O.J.E.C. No. C 158/401 of June 26, 1989.

12 The phenomenon that legal texts drawn up in the form of draft articles have a greater persuasive force and tend to exert a stronger influence on courts and arbitrators than a discussion of legal principles in a text book, however clear that may be, can also be observed on a national scale. I refer to the gradual law reform by the Dutch Supreme Court between 1965 and 1992 effected through the so called 'anticipatory interpretation', *viz.* the interpretation of the existing texts of the old Civil Code on the basis of the drafts for the new Code. This was first noted by G.J. Scholten, 'Anticiperende interpretatie: een nieuwe interpretatiemethode?', *Weekblad voor Privaatrecht, Notariaat en Registratie* 5031 (1969), p. 111.

13 Text according to the publication in AJCL XL (1992), p. 703 ff. In July 1993, UNIDROIT has issued a working paper (Study L — Doc. 40, Rev. 11) which contains some minor modifications, mainly relating to the order of the rules. However, these are not relevant to the purpose of this article and I will refer to the principles as published in the AJCL. At the time I am writing, the comments have not yet been published.

never *very*) detailed provisions.[14] Some remarks about each chapter will be made.

4.1.1 General Provisions

The Principles open with the statement that they set forth general rules for international commercial contracts. These concepts are not defined in the Article. However, the comments indicate that 'commercial' is not to be understood in the sense of those legal systems whose codified law distinguishes between civil and commercial law, but is meant — following the example of CISG — to exclude the so called consumer contracts for which many states have specially legislated rules of a protective and mandatory character. On the other hand, this does not mean that according to the Principles in commercial contracts the principle of freedom of contract prevails without any restriction at all.[15] I refer to the provisions on general conditions and on gross disparity in the Chapter on Formation, to the rules on hardship in the Chapter on Performance, and to the rules on exemption clauses and on liquidated damages in the Chapter on Damages, to which I will return shortly.

Article 1.2 spells out some of the functions discussed above in Section 3.

The rest of the chapter formulates some general principles, including the principle of freedom of contract, the binding character of contract, the extent to which parties are bound to usages and the principle of paramount importance in international trade: good faith.[16] In fact, Art. 1.8 lays down that each party must act in accordance with good faith and fair dealing in international trade and that parties may not exclude or limit this duty. Throughout the Principles, rules may be found containing express or implicit elaborations of the principle of good faith. To my mind, the rule of Article 1.7 constitutes a marked improvement compared to Article 7 CISG which concedes to 'the observance of good faith in international trade' merely the function of one of the factors to which regard is to be had in the interpretation of the Convention.

4.1.2 Formation

Some ten articles concerning offer and acceptance closely follow the pattern offered by CISG. The other articles contain innovations, including confirmations in writing, contracts with terms deliberately left open, negotiations in bad faith

---

14 Especially at the international level Kötz' precept ('Taking Civil Codes Less Seriously', *Modern law Review* 50, 1987, p. 1-15, at p. 9) is valuable: '[...] the draftsman [...] must steer the best course available by finding language that strikes an apt balance between certainty and flexibility and facilitates the orderly development of the law without unduly fettering judicial creativity.'

15 Cf. the warning of Hein Kötz, 'Gemeineuropäisches Zivilrecht', *Festschrift Zweigert* 1981, p. 481-500, at p. 494.

16 According to Denis Tallon, 'Imprévision revisited: some remarks on the consequences of a change of circumstances on contracts', in Attila Harmathy (ed), *Binding force of contract*, Budapest 1991, p. 107-112, at p. 111 good faith 'may be the only undisputed rule of the evanescent Lex Mercatoria'.

(a party who has negotiated or broken off negotiations in bad faith is liable for losses caused to the other party), and the duty of confidentiality. Finally, there are several provisions on standard terms or general conditions, including a definition, a rule on the problem of the battle of the forms (standard terms not agreed upon bind the parties in so far as they are common in substance) and on surprising conditions (which shall not be effective unless expressly accepted by the other party).

4.1.3 Validity

The chapter on validity (which is clearly inspired by the 1972 UNIDROIT Draft Convention for the Unification of Certain Rules relating to the Validity of Contracts of International Sale)[17] deals with a subject-matter which is nearly entirely excluded from the scope of CISG, Article 4 of that Convention stating that it is not concerned with the validity of the contract or of any of its provisions.

Article 3.2 lays down the important rule that a contract is concluded, modified or terminated by the mere agreement of the parties, without any further requirement. The main purpose of this Article is to do away with the civil law notion of cause, and with the common law notion of consideration.

The rest of this Chapter is devoted to the so-called defects of consent. Not only mistake, fraud and threat are dealt with, but also 'gross disparity', namely the situation that the contract or an individual term unjustifiably gives a party an excessive advantage over the other party.

In the cases mentioned above, the contract may be avoided by the disadvantaged party by a notice to the other party which must be given within a reasonable time after the avoiding party knew or could not have been unaware of the relevant facts and became capable of acting freely. Avoidance may be partial and it has retroactive effect. The party who is entitled to avoid the contract may also claim damages (so as to put it into the same position it would have been in, if it had not concluded the contract) if the other party knew or ought to have known the ground for avoidance. In the cases of mistake and of gross disparity, it is possible for the other party to prevent the avoidance of the contract by a reasonable offer to modify the contract.

4.1.4 Interpretation

Chapter 4 deals with the interpretation of the contract, of the terms of a contract and of a party's statements or other conduct. A contract shall be interpreted according to the common intention of the parties, and if such an intention cannot be established, according to the meaning which reasonable persons of the same kind as the parties would give to it in the same circumstances. Moreover, there are also articles on the interpretation of unclear terms, on the *contra preferentem* rule, and on supplying an omitted term.

---

17 *Revue de droit uniforme* 1973, p. 60; also in *UNCITRAL Yearbook* VIII (1977), p. 104.

4.1.5 Content

Chapters 5 and 6 were for a long time combined under the heading of Performance. Finally, however, the Chapter was split in two and now Chapter 5 contains some provisions which were considered to touch on the content rather than on the performance of contracts. The Articles 5.1 and 5.2 elucidate the distinction between express and implied obligations. Article 5.3 requires each party to cooperate with the other party when such cooperation may reasonably be expected. The articles 5.4 and 5.5 describe the distinction between the duties to achieve a specific result and the duties of best efforts (while recognizing that an obligation may present the characteristics of both kinds), and specify a number of factors to which regard shall be had in determining the nature of a given obligation. Article 5.7 on price determination ensures that the contract is not invalid if it does not fix nor makes provision for determining the price: in that case a reasonable price will have to be paid. The same is true if the price is to be determined by one party whose determination is manifestly unreasonable.

4.1.6 Performance

This Chapter contains two sections, *Performance in general* and *hardship*.

The first section is devoted to many problems that are well known to lawyers familiar with a codification of private law: time of performance, order of performance, place of performance, payment by cheque or other instrument (a subject which as yet has found its way only into some national codes), currency of payment, imputation of payments and the like. A new topic is dealt with in Articles 6.1.14 ff, which are concerned with national public permission requirements affecting the validity of the contract or making its performance impossible. The rules state which party shall take the measures necessary to obtain the permission, and what will be the consequences of either the permission being refused or of it being neither granted nor refused.

The section on hardship begins by stating that if the performance of a contract becomes more onerous for one of the parties, it is nevertheless bound to perform his obligations. However, Article 6.2.2 allows for an exception in the case of hardship, described as the situation where the occurrence of events (specified in litt. a-d) fundamentally alters the equilibrium of the contract either because the cost of a party's performance has increased or because the value of the performance a party receives has diminished. In the case of hardship the disadvantaged party is entitled to request a renegotiation, to reach an agreement. In the event of a failure the court may, if reasonable, either terminate the contract at a date and on terms to be fixed, or adapt the contract with a view to restoring its equilibrium.

4.1.7 Non-performance

The last chapter is divided into 4 sections: general provisions, right to performance, termination, damages and exemption clauses.

Following the CISG-approach the Principles have adopted a unitary concept of 'non-performance' (Article 7.1.1): the term denotes any failure of a party to effect due performance, including late performance and defective per-formance.[18] The term has been preferred to the term 'breach' used in CISG, since the breach in the common law is restricted to non-performance which gives the other party the right to claim damages, whereas non-performance may also lead to the use of other remedies, such as termination of the contract and withholding performance, which are not conditioned upon the obligor committing a non-performance for which it is liable in damages. There is no such liability in the case of *force majeure*, namely when a party proves that the non-performance was due to an impediment beyond its control and that it could not reasonably be expected to have taken the impediment into account at the time of the conclusion of the contract or to have avoided or overcome it or its consequences (Article 7.1.7); but this does not preclude the other party from exercising the remedies mentioned above.

Section 2 relates to the right to claim specific performance. Not only the obligee of a monetary obligation disposes of that right, but also the obligee of a non-monetary obligation, unless one of the specific exceptions in Article 7.2.2 litt. a-e exists. To this innovation (a compromise between the civil law and the common law systems) is added in Article 7.2.4, authorising a court that orders a defaulting party to perform to direct that this party pay a penalty if it does not comply with the order; and that this penalty be paid to the aggrieved party unless mandatory provisions of the law of the forum provide otherwise.

Section 3 deals with the right to terminate the contract in the case of a fundamental non-performance; this concept is described in art. 7.3.1 para. 2 in a sligtly different manner to that contained in Article 25 of CISG. Similar to 'avoidance' in Chapter 3, the right to terminate[19] is exercised by a notice to the other party within a reasonable time. This Section also pays attention to anticipatory non-performance, to the effects of termination (which does not preclude a claim for non-performance) and, very briefly, to restitution.

Finally, the right to damages is set out in Section 4: the principle of full compensation (including compensation for non-pecuniary harm), certainty of harm, foreseeability of harm, mitigation of harm, the right to interest in case of failure to pay a sum of money. The section closes with two modern rules. According to Article 7.1.6, exemption clauses may not be invoked if it would be grossly unfair to do so, having regard to the purpose of the contract. Secondly a contractually specified sum to be paid in the case of non-performance may be reduced to a reasonable amount where it is grossly excessive in relation to the non-performance and the other circumstances.

---

18 See for a comparative survey Ole Lando, 'Harmonization of the rules on remedies for non-performance of contracts', in Attila Harmathy (ed), *Binding force of contract*, Budapest 1991, p. 69-79.

19 It should be noted that in CISG the term 'avoidance' is used in the sense in which 'termination' is used in the Principles.

4.2 The European Principles

The European Principles consist of four chapters: general provisions, terms and performance of the contract, non-performance and remedies in general, particular remedies for non-performance. Together the chapters contain nearly sixty articles, which like the UNIDROIT Principles, range from general statements and flexible standards to more detailed provisions. The survey of the chapters can be shorter than that of the UNIDROIT Principles, since there are many similarities between the two documents.

4.2.1 General Provisions
Article 1.101 paragraph 1. states that the Principles are intended to be applied as general rules of contract law in the European Communities. Contrary to the UNIDROIT Principles, they are not confined to international commercial contracts. The chapter enumerates general principles, such as some rules on interpretation, the principle of good faith and fair dealing, the duty to cooperate, the concept of reasonableness and the extent to which parties are bound to usages (a slightly more liberal rule than that in the UNIDROIT Principles).

4.2.2 Terms and Performance of the Contract
The chapter corresponds to the subject-matter of Chapters 5 and 6 of the UNIDROIT Principles. It, too, contains provisions on the determination of price (compare section 4.1.5), quality of performance, place of performance, time of performance, form of payment (including payment by cheque or other negotiable instrument), currency of payment, imputation of payments and change of circumstances (comparable to the hardship provisions, see 4.1.6). Moreover, there are provisions on *mora creditoris* (the creditor not accepting the property or the money due to him), contracts in favour of a third party and performance by a third party.

4.2.3 Non-performance and Remedies in General
The European Principles have adopted the same unitary approach as the UNIDROIT Principles; the general concept here being called the 'failure to perform' (Article 3.101). The concept of fundamental non-performance is defined in Article 3.103; and is more detailed than Article 25 CISG, but less elaborate than Article 7.3.1 of the UNIDROIT Principles. Article 3.104 gives the defaulting party the right to cure by offering a new tender conforming to the contract, provided that the time for performance has not yet arrived or the delay would not be such as to constitute a fundamental non-performance (Article 7.1.4 of the UNIDROIT Principles is more favorable towards the defaulting party). The Chapter also contains provisions on force majeure, and on clauses excluding or limiting liability which may not be invoked where the non-performance is intentional or grossly negligent.

4.2.4 Particular Remedies for Non-performance
The chapter is divided in five sections: right to performance, right to withhold performance, termination of the contract, price reduction, damages and interests.

Section 1 Article 4.102 contains a rule on specific performance of non-monetary obligations which is nearly identical to Article 7.2.2 of the UNIDROIT Principles.

Section 2 The same is true for Article 4.201 relating to the right to withhold performance; comp. art. 7.1.3 of the UNIDROIT Principles.

Section 3 Also the sections on termination are comparable, but the European Principles contain a more elaborate set of rules on restitution (Articles 4.306-309).

Section 4 Article 4.401 grants the party who accepts a tender of performance not conforming to the contract the right to reduce the price proportionally.

Section 5 on damages is comparable to Chapter 7, Section 4 of the UNIDROIT Principles. It also contains an Article (4.508) on liquidated damages and penalties that may be reduced when grossly excessive. Moreover this article states that the aggrieved party is not limited to the specified sum where the non-performance by the other party is intentional or grossly negligent.

5 Concluding Remarks

Comparing the two sets of principles it is striking to note the extent to which they resemble each other, not merely in the editorial form in which they (and the accompanying comments) are presented, but also in the solutions which have been chosen. Of course, the subjects which have been dealt with by the two Commissions coincide only partially, but within the framework of the subject-matter that does coincide (general provisions, terms of the contract, performance and non-performance) most topics have been treated in both documents, the most notable exceptions being the contract in favour of a third party (Article 2.115 European Principles), the rule on price reduction (Article 4.401 European Principles) and the duty to achieve a specific result versus the duty of best efforts (Article 5.4 and 5.5 UNIDROIT Principles). The solutions chosen by the groups mostly are closely comparable. Indeed, it is difficult to find any notable differences caused by the fact that the UNIDROIT group consisted of members recruited from countries all over the world, including countries with developing economies and socialist countries, whereas the European group was composed merely by representatives of Common Market Member States. Even taking into account the difference in the scope of the proposed rules (the UNIDROIT Principles being restricted to international commercial contracts, whereas the European Principles in principle are also intended to govern contracts on a national scale), such a result is remarkable and suggests that an international unification of the general part of contract law is not as unrealistic a prospect as many have considered it to be until now. It goes without saying that this is even more so when we limit our view to the European scene.

A second observation relates to the connection between the two sets of Principles on the one hand and CISG on the other. It is clear that both groups of drafters have followed to a large extent the solutions adopted by CISG, especially where the rules on formation and on non-performance are concerned. However there are also marked differences. The UNIDROIT Principles have not only broken new ground especially in Chapter 3 which deals with the validity of contracts; but also in respect of the subject-matter governed by CISG new rules have been elaborated in both sets of Principles, including the rules on good faith, general conditions, hardship, specific performance, exemption clauses and liquidated damages. Sometimes more liberal rules have been adopted, for instance with regard to a contract coming into existence without the price being determined (see Article 14 paragraph 1 and 55 CISG). Sometimes conceptual improvements have been achieved, such as the definition of the concept of fundamental breach. CISG offers an invaluable set of unified contract rules (it is to be hoped that this international character will be observed by the national courts when called upon to interprete the Convention!), but it is not perfect. Of course we already knew this but now for the first time CISG is being challenged on a comparable international level.

The UNIDROIT study group has all but finished its work. It remains to be seen what concrete results, if any, its endeavours will produce. To my mind, after some period for study and reflection has passed, it would be worthwile to consider resuming and continuing the work in UNCITRAL with a view to preparing an international convention on the general part of the law of contracts. The success of CISG, also in a sense a combined effort of both organisations, should produce the inspiration and the courage to undertake such a momentous, albeit arduous, enterprise.

The European group has merely finished the first part of its undertaking. It will continue its work on the remaining subjects tackled by the UNIDROIT Commission as well on other topics, such as agency and assignment and possibly some special contracts. In the future it will, I think, be inevitable to deal with the the law of securities on movable objects, which is an important corollary to contract law. The same is true for tort law, since a unification of the rules on non-performance is only partially succesful if for instance the producer or the seller of goods may be held liable in tort in a way which differs from country to country. As it is well known, the EC Directive on Product Liability does not infringe upon the national rules relating to the general part of the law of torts. Contract law certainly is not dead, but it is equally certain that tort law flourishes, and this should also be reflected in the efforts directed towards the unification of the law in Europe.

The Relation between Uniform Substantive Law and Private International Law

Ted M. de Boer

1 The Case of the Bale Compressor

On 25 September 1992, the Dutch Supreme Court (*Hoge Raad*) delivered a landmark decision highlighting the uncomfortable relationship between uniform substantive law and private international law.[1] Although the actual issue was about jurisdiction — specifically: the place of performance of a contractual obligation under Article 5(1) of the EEC Jurisdiction Convention — the ruling of the Supreme Court focused on the applicable law: which law applied to a contract of sale between a Dutch seller and a French buyer? The contract called for the delivery, assembly, and installation of a so-called 'bale compressor', a machine which is used in paper factories such as the French defendant's *papéterie*. Negotiations had taken place in France, by a French agent of the Dutch seller; all correspondence (offer, acceptance and the contract itself, including the seller's general conditions) had been in French, and the seller had duly delivered, assembled and installed the bale compressor in France. When the French *papéterie* refused to pay, the seller brought suit in a Dutch court.

The defendant company entered an appearance and contested the court's jurisdiction, claiming that the contract was governed by French law. According to Article 1247(3) of the *Code civil*, the purchase price must be paid '*au domicile du débiteur*', unless otherwise agreed. Since the parties had not stipulated, apparently, where payment should be made, only a French court should be allowed to hear the case, pursuant to either Article 2 or Article 5(1) of the Jurisdiction Convention. In response to this argument, the Dutch plaintiff maintained that the contract was governed by Dutch law, and that payment should have been made at the seller's place of business, which would bestow jurisdiction on the Dutch courts under the *forum solutionis* principle of the Jurisdiction Convention.

In first instance, the District Court of Almelo held that the contract was governed by French law, and, hence, that the Dutch courts had no jurisdiction to adjudicate. Although it did not expressly refer to it, the court had apparently relied on the Hague Convention on International Sales of 1986. While not in force in the Netherlands, it must have served the court as a source of choice-of-law inspiration,

---

1   HR 25 September 1992, *NJ* 1992, 750; *Ars Aequi* 1993, p. 207 (annot. De Boer).

a supposition which is borne out by the court's literal transcription of Article 8 of the Convention.[2]

The Court of Appeal of Arnhem reversed, on the grounds that the place of payment should be determined by Dutch rather than French law. Since the contract had been concluded before 1 January 1992, at which time the Netherlands substituted the 1980 Vienna Convention on the International Sales of Goods for the Uniform Sales Acts appended to the 1964 Hague Conventions on International Sales, the place of payment was determined according to Article 59 of the Uniform Sales Act rather than Article 57 of the Vienna Convention. The result would have been the same under either regime: payment should be made at the place of the seller's business. To arrive at the conclusion that the contract was governed by Dutch law, the Court of Appeal relied on Article 4(2) of the Rome Convention on the Law Applicable to Contractual Obligations of 1980, in which the place of business of the party carrying out the characteristic performance — *i.e.* the seller when we are dealing with a contract for the sale of goods — is deemed to indicate the most relevant connection between the contract and the legal systems involved. However, the contract had been concluded before the Rome Convention came into force in the Netherlands, and that meant that the court could only refer to it by analogy or in anticipation of ratification.

Before the Supreme Court, the complaint of the French buyer was based mainly on two grounds. French law rather than Dutch law should have been applied: (1) either under Article 8 of the Hague Convention of 1986, or (2) under Article 4(5) of the Rome Convention, or its equivalent in domestic Dutch conflicts law. The Supreme Court rejected both arguments, holding that (1) the choice-of-law rules laid down in Article 4 of the Rome Convention, unlike those of Article 8 of the Hague Convention, did not substantially differ from the rules that had previously been developed in Dutch case law, (2) ratification of the Rome Convention was well underway, while ratification of the Hague Convention was doubtful at best, and (3) there was no call for the appellate court to make an exception to the main rule of Article 4(2), as such an exception should only be used in extreme cases, in which the place of business of the party carrying out the characteristic performance is a specious contact that can have no bearing on the choice of the applicable law.

Apart from the intriguing question of whether the Supreme Court was right in positing that the Dutch judge-made conflicts rule for international contracts — referring to the place of business of the 'characteristic performer' and allowing

---

2   Article 8(1), based on the theory of the characteristic performance, refers to the law of the State where the seller has his place of business. This rule is subject to three exceptions, in which the law of the State where the *buyer* has his place of business must be applied: (a) if negotiations were conducted, and the contract [was] concluded by and in the presence of the parties, in that State; or (b) if the contract provides expressly that the seller must perform his obligation to deliver the goods in that State; or (c) if the contract was concluded on terms determined mainly by the buyer and in response to an invitation directed by the buyer to persons invited to bid (a call for tenders). The District Court came to the conclusion that French law applied on the grounds of Article 8(2)(a) and (b) combined.

very little room for a 'proper law escape' — can be equated with the open-ended formula of Article 4(1), 4(2) and 4(5) of the Rome Convention, the *Bale Compressor* case raises the more fundamental issue of whether private international law is still an adequate means to deal with international disputes, especially between European litigants. It could be argued that a system of uniform substantive law would obviate the need for choice-of-law rules, since the issue would be decided by the same substantive rules, regardless of the forum where the action is brought. If a uniform (sales) law were in force in all the jurisdictions concerned, the courts would not have to choose the applicable law anymore, for there is no point in applying the French rather than the Dutch version of a rule if their contents are the same.[3]

Where private international law has failed to secure decisional harmony in international civil litigation, uniform substantive law would appear to be the obvious means to achieve that elusive goal. If this is a valid assumption, the merits of (uniform) private international law vis-à-vis uniform substantive law[4] should be re-evaluated. We might come to the conclusion that private international law is destined to fade into legal history, as uniform substantive law progressively rules the world.

2 The *Raison d'être* of Private International Law

The need for rules of private international law originates from a dual reality: (1) the world consists of sovereign states, each having its own system of law; and (2) most people do not live in isolation but establish (legal) relations with one another, also — increasingly — beyond national borders. Differences between the national laws of the parties to an international legal relationship — whether marriage, contract, or tort — do not only give rise to the question by whose law their rights and duties should be determined, but they also cast doubt on the jurisdiction of domestic courts and evoke the specter of litigation abroad and the possibility of a 'limping' relationship if a foreign ruling is not recognized at home.

---

3   This principle of 'non-choice' has been postulated by H.U. Jessurun d'Oliveira, *De antikiesregel, een paar aspekten van de behandeling van buitenlands recht in het burgerlijk proces*, Deventer 1971, mainly for situations in which the rules of decision happen to be identical in all jurisdictions concerned. When it comes to uniform law, they are bound to be identical.

4   See generally: J.W. Westenberg, 'The Quest for Unification', in: *Forty Years On: The Evolution of Postwar Private International Law in Europe, Symposium in celebration of the 40th anniversary of the Centre of Foreign Law and Private International Law, University of Amsterdam, on 27 October 1989*, Deventer 1990, p. 195-217. Westenberg distinguishes four kinds of unification: unification of substantive law, unification of choice-of-law rules, unification through harmonization of law, unification by non-governmental or private organizations resulting in model contracts and restatements. Aware of the importance of the latter two varieties, I will focus on the two major sources of truly uniform law, as laid down in international conventions: private international law and substantive private law.

Private international law was designed as a means of coordination. The most common approach to choice of law purports to allocate an international legal relationship to one particular system of national law, generally the law of the country most closely connected with the parties, the event, or the property concerned. Essentially, this process of allocation transforms an international dispute into a domestic one, to be decided under the designated national law as if there never was an international context. Similarly, under the rules of international procedure, domestic courts will only assume jurisdiction over an international case if it is sufficiently connected with the state in which they sit. This implies that the plaintiff may have to bring his action in a foreign jurisdiction, or that he has a choice between courts in two or more states, not necessarily his own. Thus, private international law aims to distribute international jurisdiction, and to allocate a 'drifting' international controversy to the most appropriate legal system. The fruit of these coordinating efforts should be *'Entscheidungsharmonie'* (decisional harmony or uniformity of result): the choice-of-law decision — hence the application of the substantive rule of decision — should be the same wherever the case is adjudicated. As a result, a decision is bound to be recognized and, if necessary, enforced in another state, because that state has no reason to refuse recognition if its courts would have reached the same decision as the one actually taken by their brethren abroad.

UNIFORMITY OF RESULTS

Decisional harmony is most likely to be achieved if the rules of private international law are the same in each of the states with which an international case may be connected, so ultimately in each and every legal system of the world. Unfortunately, the divergences between national choice-of-law systems have never disappeared. Apart from a few time-honored standards — such as the *lex loci delicti* principle for torts, or the *lex rei sitae* rule for (real) property — there is very little concordance between conflicts rules, and in the field of jurisdiction the national laws still offer a variety of incongruent alternatives. Thus, resourceful forum-shopping will often influence the outcome of the case in terms of substantive law. Decisional *dis*harmony is the result.

It must be concluded, then, that private international law — as a branch of national law — has failed dismally to achieve its original objective: to facilitate international legal relations by a *'coördination des systèmes'*, producing uniform choice-of-law results and, consequently, identical substantive law decisions that could be recognized and enforced anywhere.

3 The Unification of Private International Law

That is why, ever since the end of the 19th century, efforts have been made to create uniform rules of private international law. The Hague Conference on Private

International Law was set up especially for this purpose.[5] Celebrating its centenary in 1993, this venerable organization has created more than thirty conventions, on jurisdiction, choice of law, recognition and enforcement, and procedural cooperation. The conventions in the latter category are the most successful ones in terms of ratification.[6] They are followed at some distance by the conventions on recognition and enforcement.[7] In the category of choice-of-law conventions, the convention on the form of testamentary dispositions (1961) has gained most ratifications, followed by the conventions on (child) maintenance of 1955 and 1973.[8] All other choice-of-law conventions have been ratified by less than ten member-states.[9]

Leaving aside the private international law conventions created by the *Commission Internationale de l'Etat Civil* (CIEC) and the Council of Europe,[10] we may turn directly to the achievements of the European Community in this field. The first EEC Convention on private international law is the one on jurisdiction and recognition, created in 1968 on the basis of Article 220 of the Rome Treaty. It has been amended several times, on the occasion of the accession of Denmark, Ireland and the United Kingdom (1978), Greece (1982), and Spain and Portugal (1989). The draft of its latest version has served as a model for the Lugano Convention of 1988, which is intended to be the main source of international procedural law in the Member-States of the EFTA. It is hoped that a system of uniform rules on

---

5   Its Statute expressly calls for the 'progressive unification' of private international law. See Article 1: *'La Conférence de La Haye a pour but de travailler à l'unification progressive des règles de droit international privé.'*

6   The Convention on Civil Procedure (1954), the Convention Abolishing the Requirement of Legalisation for Foreign Public Documents (1961), the Convention on the Service Abroad of Judicial and Extrajudicial Documents (1965), and the Convention on Civil Aspects of International Child Abduction (1980) have each gained endorsement by at least 24 states, the Convention on the Taking of Evidence Abroad in Civil or Commercial Matters (1970) by 21 states. These figures include accession by non-member states. The most successful convention is the one on Legalisation, with ratification or accession by 39 states. This was the status on 20 October, 1992.

7   The two conventions on recognition and enforcement of maintenance decisions (1958 and 1973) were adopted by 18 and 15 states respectively, the Convention on the Recognition of Divorces and Legal Separations (1970) by 14 states; status on 20 October 1992.

8   The 1973 maintenance convention replaces the one on child maintenance in 10 of the 13 states that have ratified the latter convention. Although the most successul choice-of-law convention is the one on the form of testamentary dispositions, now in force in 31 states, it could be argued that the nature of this convention is *procedural*: the formal validity of a will is likely to be at issue after the testator's death, in which case the choice-of-law rules of the convention operate as rules of recognition.

9   See generally: Th.M. de Boer, 'The Hague Conference and Dutch Choice of Law: Some Criticism and a Suggestion', *Netherlands International Law Review* 1993, p. 1-13.

10 Generally, the CIEC conventions cover matters that are relevant to the registry of personal data (births, deaths, marriages etc.), *e.g.* the Munich Convention on the Law Applicable to Surnames and First Names (1980). The subject-matter of the conventions by the Council of Europe ranges from human rights to information on foreign law; its main achievements in private international law are in the sector of family law, *e.g.* the Luxembourg Convention on Recognition and Enforcement of Decisions concerning Custody over Children and on Restoration of Custody of Children (1980).

international jurisdiction, recognition and enforcement will eventually be in force throughout Europe, based on the combined ratification of the two conventions.

The EEC's second contribution to the unification of private international law was the Rome Convention on the Law Applicable to Contractual Obligations of 1980. The preliminary draft (published in 1972) included provisions on non-contractual obligations as well, but these had to be left out for lack of consensus on a more suitable choice-of-law standard than the traditional *lex loci delicti* rule. The convention determines the applicable law for most types of contracts,[11] assignments and subrogation. While it leaves room for the application of choice-of-law rules laid down in other, more specialized conventions,[12] it does cover, in combination with the Jurisdiction Convention, most of the private international law issues that may arise out of an international contract: jurisdiction, choice of law, as well as recognition and enforcement of foreign decisions. In this respect, the unification of European private international law has made considerable progress.

4 The Unification of Substantive Law

In terms of progress, it is difficult to compare the unification of private international law with that of substantive private law. On both sides, there are numerous organizations dedicated to the cause of uniform law. On both sides, an inordinate amount of time and energy is spent on unification projects that are eventually shelved indefinitely, or fail to earn sufficient approval to make a real contribution to uniform law. On both sides, however, major achievements can be recorded as well. Scores of private international law conventions are in force, and numerous uniform substantive laws have been enacted. The difference between the two forms of unification, it would seem, is mainly in the subject-matter. Uniform choice-of-law rules have been created for most areas of private law − extending from marriage to traffic accidents, from succession to corporations − but as far as uniform substantive law is concerned, the range is considerably narrower. Here, the unification efforts have focused on various aspects of international commerce: securities, carriage of goods, sales, arbitration, and other topics that are of great importance to the international business community.[13] This limitation is usually

---

11   Excluded are: contractual obligations in the ambit of family law and succession, or arising from negotiable instruments, arbitration agreements and agreements on the choice of court, as well as questions governed by the law of companies, or regarding the position of third parties, the relationship between parties to a trust, evidence, procedure, and contracts of insurance covering risks situated within the EEC (Article 1).

12   Ratification is subject to the provisions of Articles 23 ff., requiring that other signatory states are informed on a member state's intention to become a party to such a convention.

13   See generally: B.W.M. Trompenaars, *Pluriforme unificatie en uniforme interpretatie, in het bijzonder de bijdrage van UNCITRAL aan de internationale unificatie van het privaatrecht,* Deventer 1989.

explained, on the one hand, by the need for legal certainty in the volatile world of international trade, and, on the other hand, by the feasibility of unification.[14]

While I wonder whether, in an international setting, businessmen have a greater need for uniform law than husbands and wives, parents and children, heirs, or victims of a tort, I fully agree with the feasibility argument. Organized in international trade associations, the business community can probably exert greater pressure on lawmakers than any other group. A smooth course of international commerce is not only in the interest of business itself but also to the benefit of the nations involved. It is not surprising, then, that the unification of commercial law is boosted by a spirit of cooperation that is less pervasive in other areas. Also, the subject-matter of uniform commercial law is less controversial than that of other branches of private law. Where national laws reflect a community's social, political or moral beliefs — particularly in the area of family relations, employment, consumer contracts, environmental protection, etcetera — it will be difficult to bring them into line with each other. Unification of choice-of-law rules may still be a feasible option here, but uniform substantive law is less likely to be accepted. The values underlying commercial law, however, are of a different nature. *Pacta sunt servanda*, expediency, certainty, equality, good faith are some of the catchwords in this sector, denoting universal standards that are most capable of being written into uniform law.

The best-known examples of recent substantive law unification are the Sales Conventions (LUVI and LUF),[15] prepared by the International Institute for the Unification of Private Law in Rome (UNIDROIT), and the Vienna Convention on the International Sale of Goods, a product of the United Nations Commission on International Trade Law (UNCITRAL). Although UNIDROIT, an intergovernmental organization, has a membership of some fifty states, the Uniform Sales Acts were adopted by only nine of them, three of whom have already repealed them in favor of the Vienna Convention. With more than thirty ratifications, the latter convention has fared much better, but this result can hardly be compared with that of other sources of uniform substantive law, such as the Brussels Convention on Collisions at Sea of 1910, adopted by more than seventy states, not to mention the Warsaw Convention or the Hague Rules.

5 The Effectiveness of Uniform Substantive Law

It may be true that the success of substantive law unification mainly depends on the needs of the international community, the nature of the subject-matter, and the

---

14   Cf. F.J.A. van der Velden, 'Europa 1992 en het eenvormig privaatrecht', in: D. Kokkini-Iatridou and F.W. Grosheide (eds.), *Eenvormig en vergelijkend privaatrecht 1990*, Molengrafica, Lelystad 1990, p. 3-28, at p. 24.

15   *Convention portant Loi Uniforme sur la (Formation des contrats de) Vente Internationale des objets mobiliers corporels*, The Hague 1964. By ratification, a Member-State takes on the obligation to incorporate the uniform acts, appended to the two conventions, into its national law.

acceptability of compromise. These factors affect the feasibility of all unification efforts, I suppose, whether they concern private international law or substantive law. But even if such obstacles are overcome, there is a limit to the effectiveness of uniform substantive law. There will always be gaps to be filled, and for that purpose we must still resort to private international law.

The first limitation of uniform substantive law is — in most cases — in its scope. Both the Vienna Convention and the Uniform Sales Acts, for instance, were conceived for *international* sales of goods. As a result, all Member-States have two sets of substantive rules on the sale of goods: uniform rules for international cases, and national rules for domestic situations. Furthermore, the Vienna Convention is based on reciprocity, requiring that buyer and seller each have their place of business or domicile in a Contracting State.[16] If not, their relationship will not be governed by uniform law, but by the law designated by the forum's choice-of-law rules. If the law thus found happens to be the law of a signatory to the Vienna Convention, its domestic law could be displaced again by the convention's uniform rules.[17] Similar limitations can be found in most other substantive law conventions. Unless their geographical purview is universal, a distinction must be made between cases within and outside of their scope of application. This is a choice-of-law decision in itself, triggered by the convention's provisions on its scope and subject-matter. If the facts do not meet the test, a further choice-of-law decision needs to be taken, now subject to the forum's 'ordinary' conflicts rules.[18] Such decisions would not be needed if there were no difference between uniform law and national law, and if uniform law were implemented in all states concerned.

But even if the substantive law of all concerned jurisdictions would be truly uniform — to the extent that no difference is made between international and domestic cases, let alone between reciprocity and non-reciprocity situations — even

---

16 The LUVI and LUF Conventions allow the Member-States to limit the scope of the Uniform Sales Acts to situations in which both parties are domiciled in a Contracting State. A declaration to this effect was made by the German Federal Republic, Gambia, the Netherlands, San Marino and the United Kingdom.

17 Czechoslovakia, the People's Republic of China and the United States of America have made the declaration of Article 95, which means that these states are not bound to apply the convention in the situation described in Article 1(1)(b). A rule similar to Article 1(1)(b) of the Vienna Convention can be found in the Uniform Sales Acts as enacted in the Netherlands pursuant to the LUVI and LUF Conventions, the difference with Article 1(1)(b) being that the Uniform Sales Acts would apply if *Dutch* law had been designated. The Vienna Convention must be applied whenever the chosen law is the law of a *Contracting State*. Curiously, this could lead to the result that, with regard to a contract of sale between an American seller and e.g. a Belgian buyer, a Dutch court would apply the Vienna Convention under Article 1(1)(b), whereas an American court, not bound to the Vienna Convention in this Article 1(1)(b) situation, is likely to choose American state law under its domestic choice-of-law principles. A Belgian court would not be bound to the Vienna Convention at all; under Article 3(1) of the Hague Convention on International Sales of 1955, it would probably apply domestic American law. Thanks to such reservations as the one laid down in Article 95, forum shopping can still be rewarding.

18 See also Article 7(2) of the Vienna Convention. This provision calls for application of the forum's choice-of-law rules, when the court needs an auxiliary source of substantive law to solve questions that are not covered by the convention.

then there is a limit to the effectiveness of uniform law. Let us assume that the European Union will adopt a 'European Civil Code', as some European jurists advocate. Does that obviate the need for a system of private international law? In my opinion, it does not. Unless we adopt a novel *lex fori* approach,[19] choice-of-law rules will still be needed to determine whether the 'European Civil Code' applies or not, especially in situations showing connections with states outside the Union. With a view to the parties' justified expectations and the ideal of decisional harmony, it may be more suitable to apply 'foreign' law instead of 'European' law, and that is another choice-of-law decision. The same can be said with regard to adjudicatory jurisdiction: if the case is in any way connected with a state outside Europe's *'espace judiciaire'*, there may be grounds for denying jurisdiction and leaving the adjudication to the courts of the 'foreign' state. Here is another decision that must be left to private international law rather than uniform procedural law. Thus, a second limitation of uniform law becomes apparent: as long as there are states that do not adhere to the standards of uniform substantive law, choices must be made, whether on jurisdiction, or the applicable law, or the recognition and enforcement of foreign decisions. Neither a European Civil Code, nor a European Code of Civil Procedure — unless they contain uniform private international law — will help us to decide where a Dutch plaintiff should bring an action on real property situated in Morocco, or what law governs the matrimonial property regime of an American couple living in Spain. Until uniform substantive law spans the whole world — a highly unlikely prospect, no matter how narrow the subject-matter — we still need private international law, uniform or not, to determine such choices.

A third factor reducing the effectiveness of uniform law — private international law and substantive law alike — is the possible disparity in interpretation. While the Supreme Courts of many countries were especially charged with safeguarding the unity of their law, there are few courts that have a final say on the interpretation of uniform law. The European Court of Justice and the Benelux Court have limited powers in this respect.[20] It must be feared, therefore, that uniform law is doomed to be 'nationalized' if its application is not supervised by an international court, or

---

19   This implies that national courts apply their own national law (*lex fori*), either as a matter of principle (as in Ehrenzweig's *'lex fori in foro proprio'* theory), or on the grounds that none of the parties has raised the choice-of-law issue (Flessner's *'fakultatives Kollisionsrecht'*). Neither approach has won favor with European conflicts scholars. I would prefer a facultative choice-of-law approach to the misconstructions of foreign law that can hardly be avoided under a procedural rule, prevailing in most continental European systems, that calls for an *ex officio* application of choice-of-law rules.

20   In principle, the European Court of Justice is authorized to rule on the interpretation of both the Jurisdiction Convention and the Convention on Contractual Obligations. However, unlike the Protocol accompanying the Jurisdiction Convention, the two Protocols on the interpretation of the Contracts Convention do not *oblige* the highest court in each Member-State to consult the European Court when in doubt about the meaning of the convention's provisions. Furthermore, the second of the latter Protocols will not enter into force until it has been ratified by all Member-States, which may take quite a while, if it happens at all.

if national courts are unwilling or unable to take judicial notice of foreign decisions and international scholarly sources.

6 National Law versus Uniform Substantive Law

In a democracy, the law may be deemed to reflect the values and beliefs of the society that lives by it. This explains some of the differences between national laws, especially in the area of family relations, where moral and/or religious principles pervade the law in most countries. Other differences can be traced to the geographical, demographic, economic, or social conditions prevailing in each state. For instance, in a crowded society, the protection of the environment may be of greater concern to the legislature than it is in a thinly populated country. Consumer protection is a luxury that only an affluent society can afford. Strict rules protecting the rights of tenants are needed less urgently if there is no housing shortage.

I am afraid that some advocates of uniform substantive law tend to overlook the ideological and factual differences that exist between national communities, even in Europe.[21] Although I am aware of the growing interdependence of today's community of nations, and the consequent need for international cooperation, I do not think that welding national laws into a global law, or — less ambitious — into a Common European Law, is either feasible or desirable. The limits of legal integration are marked by national idiosyncrasies and local circumstances. Like language, law is part of a community's cultural heritage. It is one of the factors that define a nation's identity. Unless we want to eradicate a tradition of centuries, we should be careful to retain those segments of national law that have particular value for the community in which such rules and principles developed. Unless we are ready to trade our national identity for a new cosmopolitan awareness, the unification of substantive law should be halted where it fails to acknowledge a single community's cultural values and specific needs.

In my opinion, the lawmakers of the European Union must leave room for the development of at least some pockets of private law in the individual Member-States, rather than try to bring about one uniform European private law. The process of European integration — expected to bring economic, political and even legal unity — need not go so far as to extinguish all the differences, including those in private law, that still mark the cultural identity of each Member-State.

As long as some elements of national private law survive, private international law must continue to serve as a means of system coordination, even in intra-community situations. In a united Europe without a fully unified private law, there will still be a need for a set of rules that allocate an interstate case to the legal system to which it is supposed to 'belong'.

---

21   *Cf.* Westenberg, *supra* note 4, p. 213 ff.

* WHAT ABOUT UNIFORM TRANSNATIONAL RULES AS DEFAULT RULES LETTING DOMESTIC JURISDICTIONS OPT OUT FOR INTERNAL CASES?

7 A Second Look at the Case of the Bale Compressor

What lessons can be learned from the *Bale Compressor* case on the relation between uniform private international law and uniform substantive law? Apart from the intertemporal difficulties the Dutch courts had to solve, due to the fact that neither the Vienna Convention, nor the Contracts Convention, nor the Hague Convention on International Sales were in force in the Netherlands at the time the contract was concluded, the decision highlights all the problems inherent in the unification of both substantive private law and private international law. First of all, the cause of uniform substantive law is not promoted by the co-existence of two sets of uniform rules covering the same subject. The Uniform Sales Acts were part of Dutch law, while France had adopted the Vienna Convention. In this particular case, both regimes led to the same result (payment at the seller's place of business), but if the issue had been different, the choice between the French and Dutch law on international sales would have been all-important. In the second place, decisional harmony could be frustrated by the co-existence, in each country, of different sets of substantive rules for domestic and international cases. If the contract had been concluded after the Vienna Convention entered into force in France, but before ratification by the Netherlands, the District Court's choice of French law would have entailed a further choice between the rules of the convention and French domestic law. While it stands to reason that the choice of French law implies application of the French rules for *international* sales — *i.e.* the Convention — rather than the *Code civil*, a state that is not a signatory to the Vienna Convention has no obligation to apply it. The Court of Appeal decided that the contract was governed by Dutch law, which implied a further choice between the Uniform Sales Act and the Dutch Civil Code. Thus, in a case in which only two states were involved, a choice had to be made between four competing sets of substantive rules: the Vienna Convention, the Uniform Sales Acts, the French *Code civil* and the Dutch *Burgerlijk Wetboek*.

If France and the Netherlands would not have had different rules on the place of payment, both Dutch and French courts would have been confronted with only one choice-of-law issue: the fact that the laws of the involved states were identical would support the conclusion that the case presented a 'no-conflict situation', in which there is no need to choose the applicable law.[22] It should be noted that even the decision *not* to choose the applicable law is based on a rule of private international law, not one of (uniform) substantive law. At any rate, the *Bale Compressor* case might not have reached the Dutch Supreme Court if there had been a European Civil Code that would have solved the issue, at least in this intra-community case. Yet, this is only true if the conventions on the international sale of goods would either be revoked by all states adopting the new Code, or if either

---

22   *Cf. supra*, note 3. However, in any legal system in which the highest court is not allowed to address issues of foreign law — see for instance Article 99(1) of the Dutch Judicial Organization Act — the parties may have an interest in an exact determination of the applicable law. Application of the 'non-choice' principle tends to ignore that interest.

one, preferably the Vienna Convention, would be in force in all of them. In the first case, the conventions' special regime for international sales would no longer be recognized; all domestic and intra-community cases would be subject to the Code, whereas other cases would be governed either by the new European law or by the law of a country outside the European Union, depending on the facts and the forum's choice-of-law criteria. If, on the other hand, the Vienna Convention were in force in all EC Member-States, domestic cases would be governed by European Union law (the new Code), intra-community cases by the convention, and all other cases either by the convention or by foreign law, depending on the place of business of the parties or on the forum's choice of law.[23] In terms of unification, the best solution would be the incorporation of the Vienna Convention into the European Code. Domestic cases and intra-community cases would then be subject to the same set of rules. The result would be a considerable facilitation of the judicial task, if only because there would be less need to explore unfamiliar foreign law.

The *Bale Compressor* case demonstrates similar problems with regard to the unification of private international law. Here, too, we are confronted with difficult choices between competing sets of rules. In the area of international sales, national courts must decide whether to apply the EEC Convention on Contractual Obligations or either one of the Hague Conventions on the International Sale of Goods.[24] If the contract is outside the scope of a convention — *e.g.* if it was concluded before the convention entered into force in the forum state — the court should decide whether to stick to its national choice-of-law principles, or to anticipate the ratification of a pertinent choice-of-law convention, as all three courts did in the *Bale Compressor* case — with different results. Even the existence of uniform rules of private international law does not guarantee the same outcome in different Contracting States. If a French court had ruled on the same issue,[25] it is equally conceivable that it would assume or deny jurisdiction under Article 5(1) of the EEC Jurisdiction Convention, depending on its interpretation of Article 4 of the EEC Contracts Convention.[26]

---

23 *Cf.* Article 1(1)(a) and 1(1)(b) of the Vienna Convention.

24 There are actually two Hague Conventions on the Law Applicable to Contracts for the International Sale of Goods, one dating from 1955 and in force in nine states, the other one created in 1986 and not yet in force.

25 If the Dutch plaintiff would have brought suit in France, the French court would already have jurisdiction under Article 2 of the Jurisdiction Convention. However, if the defendant had been domiciled in Spain, while all other facts of the *Bale Compressor* case remained the same, a French court could only assume jurisdiction as *forum solutionis*, or not at all.

26 In reality, a French court may not be prepared to apply Article 4, not even by anticipation, to a contract that was concluded before the Rome Convention entered into force.

8 Conclusion

Unification of either substantive law or private international law is not the final answer to the existing diversity of laws. Uniform substantive law is not only hard to achieve, but in some areas it is also undesirable. Where unification of substantive private law is feasible, its scope should not be limited to international cases; uniform law is most effective if it does not have to operate side by side with domestic law. As long as uniform substantive law has not replaced domestic law completely, there will remain issues of private international law that have to be solved by international or national standards. Since the 1960's, the unification of ✳ private international law has made considerable progress, if we measure its success by the number of conventions that have been drafted and the variety of their subject-matter. However, even the most successful private international law conventions — covering jurisdiction, choice of law, or recognition and enforcement — have been ratified by only a handful of states. When such conventions are based on reciprocity, they have less effect as a source of uniform law, as cases outside their scope of application are still subject to national rules of private international law. Unification of private international law is probably easiest to achieve in a relatively small, well-organized group of nations, such as the European Union, the Benelux or the EFTA. On the other hand, the smaller the number of participating states, the less impact unification will have. Conventions with a universal scope, clear-cut rules, and little room for result-selecting interpretation are probably the most effective means to achieve uniformity of result. However, one may well ask if such conventions deserve our endorsement if, for the sake of unification, the flexibility and subtlety of national law is supplanted by the rigidity of hard-and-fast rules.

Uniformity of result will never be achieved if there is no guarantee that uniform law, whether substantive law or private international law, will be interpreted in a uniform way. Based on pious hopes, in my opinion, are provisions such as Article 18 of the Contracts Convention, or Article 7(1) of the Vienna Convention, exhorting national courts to heed the 'international character' of the conventions and the 'desirability of achieving uniformity in their interpretation and application'. Without a supranational court to safeguard uniform interpretation, there are bound to be national divergences that will eventually defeat the purpose of unification. The way the Dutch Supreme Court applied Article 4 of the Contracts Convention in the *Bale Compressor* case is hardly in tune, I suspect, with the interpretation an English, or German, or French court would have put on it, in spite of Article 18. Without recourse to the European Court of Justice, there is little hope for a truly uniform law in Europe.

✳ NO, SEE NOTE P. 60

CHAPTER 5

Roman Law and European Legal Unity

Reinhard Zimmermann[*]

1 European Legal Unity

It is a self-evident characteristic of most sciences taught at a modern university that they are international in substance and outlook: this holds true from archaeology to medicine, from philosophy to chemistry. But it cannot be said of legal science. For the past 200 years or so there have been, in principle, as many legal systems in Europe as national states. To a large extent, the boundaries of legal science have become identical with the political borders. German lawyers apply the Bürgerliches Gesetzbuch, while French lawyers use the code civil. In England, the 'good old' common law still prevails. As a result, the doctrines of modern private law, the subject-matter of law courses, examination requirements and prerequisites for entry into the legal profession appear to be different in each country. In Germany, scores of legal writers continue their stern and unrelenting endeavours to beat a path through the dreaded third-party enrichment jungle;[1] to penetrate the mysteries of 'Fremdbesitzerexzeß' in the so-called 'Eigentümer-Besitzer-Verhältnis' and to draw ever finer distinctions between that consequential loss which is closely related to defective work and that which is not.[2] To an English lawyer this all seems just as confusing and exotic as the abracadabra of conditions, warranties and intermediate terms or the niceties of the so-called doctrine of consideration appear to us. Foreign literature is only rarely consulted in judicial decisions, academic posts in universities are occupied almost without exception by local lawyers; and because the regulations for legal education are orientated exclusively towards the law of the respective country, this particularization of legal science threatens to imprint itself also on the next generation of lawyer.[3]

---

[*] This is the text of a lecture delivered in October 1992 at the invitation of the Joachim Jungius Gesellschaft in Hamburg. It has been translated (and slightly adapted) at the request of the editors of the present volume and is published with the kind permission of the editor of the volume in which the German text has appeared (W. Ludwig (ed.), *Die Antike in der Gegenwart*, 1993).

[1] On this topic see the recent pithy comments of Horst H. Jakobs, Die Rückkehr der Praxis zur Regelanwendung und der Beruf der Theorie im Recht der Leistungskondiktion, in 1992 Neue Juristische Wochenschrift 2524 sqq.

[2] See e.g. Frank Peters, Reinhard Zimmermann, 'Verjährungsfristen', in: *Gutachten und Vorschläge zur Überarbeitung des Schuldrechts*, vol. I, 1981, 206 sqq.

[3] For another critical voice see Dietmar Willoweit, Bernhard Großfeld, 'Juristen für Europa', 1990 *Juristenzeitung* 605 sqq.

Even in his day and age, Rudolf von Jhering, who died just over 100 years ago in 1892, found this situation humiliating and undignified.[4] Today, it is also totally anachronistic. For in recent years, in the context of the European Community, we have experienced a process of legal unification, which has led to the uninhibited growth of new and specialized market-related subjects, but has also already affected (one could almost say infected) the classical core areas of private law.[5] Someone injured by the explosion of a faulty kitchen appliance can take legal recourse by way of the 'Produkthaftungsgesetz' [Product Liability Act] of 15 December 1989. A person who, in the course of a promotional leisure-time excursion, gets talked into buying the Encyclopaedia Britannica, may cancel the contract within a week in terms of the 'Haustürwiderrufsgesetz' [Cancellation of Front-Door Contracts Act] of 16 January 1986. Where someone purchases a new car by way of an instalment sale financed by a third party, he may raise as a defence even against the third party's claim for repayment of the instalments, that the accelerator pedal is defective; this is provided for in the 'Verbraucherkreditgesetz' [Consumer Credit Act] of 17 December 1990. All these pieces of legislation concerning that central transaction in everyday life, the sale, are based upon − or have been enacted in anticipation of[6] − European Community directives which have been implanted, in this or at least in similar fashion, into the national law of all EC member states. This process has, however, been unsatisfactory in that, until now, we have been faced merely with fragments of unified European law, inserted rather unorganically into the respective national legal systems; rather paradoxically, they have on occasion not only been sources of confusion and uncertainty but have also led to even greater fragmentation (within the national legal systems!).[7] One might even these days be tempted, without too much exaggeration, to warn of the danger of corrosion of our general private law. In view of this, the European Parliament has called for the unification of the entire private law on a European scale, in the sense

---

4   Rudolf von Jhering, *Geist des römischen Rechts auf den verschiedenen Stufen seiner Entwicklung,* vol. *I*, 8th ed., 1924, p. 15.
5   Cf. for example, the survey in Ernst A. Kramer, 'Europäische Rechtsvereinheitlichung', 1988 *Juristische Blätter* 477 sqq.; Peter-Christian Müller-Graff, *Privatrecht und Europäisches Gemeinschaftsrecht,* 2nd ed., 1991; Oliver Remien, 'Illusion und Realität eines europäischen Privatrechts', 1992 *Juristenzeitung* 277 sqq.; Uwe Blaurock, 'Wege zur Rechtseinheit Europas', in: Christian Starck (ed.), *Rechtsvereinheitlichung durch Gesetze − Bedingungen, Ziele, Methoden,* 1992, p. 90 sqq; Peter Hommelhoff, 'Zivilrecht unter dem Einfluß europäischer Rechtsangleichung', (1992) 192 *Archiv für die civilistische Praxis* 71 sqq. On the role of the courts see e.g. Ulrich Everling, 'Rechtsvereinheitlichung durch Richterrecht in der Europäischen Gemeinschaft', (1986) 50 *RabelsZ* 193 sqq.; on other non-legislative forms of legal unification cf. the contributions in (1992) 56 *RabelsZ* 215 sqq.
6   Cf., as far as the German 'Haustürwiderrufsgesetz' is concerned, Peter Ulmer, in: *Münchener Kommentar zum BGB,* 2nd ed., 1988, vol. III/1, p. 573 sqq.
7   For criticism, see e.g. Hein Kötz, 'Rechtsvereinheitlichung − Nutzen, Kosten, Ziele, Methoden', (1986) 50 *RabelsZ* 3 sqq.; Christoph E. Hauschka, 'Grundprobleme der Privatrechtsfortbildung durch die Europäische Wirtschaftsgemeinschaft', 1990 *Juristenzeitung* 523 sqq.; Peter Ulmer, 'Vom deutschen zum europäischen Privatrecht', 1992 *Juristenzeitung* 5 sqq.

of a code civil Européen.[8] But the time is by no means ripe for that. Without intensive scientific groundwork, a European codification of civil law is not realistically imaginable; nor is it desirable. First and foremost the juristic nationalism which still to a large extent characterizes our consciousness will have to be overcome; in its place, a comprehensive 'Europeanization' of legal science has to be brought about.[9]

2 The Re-Europeanization of Legal Science

This, of course, merely constitutes the roughest survey of the first aspect of my topic: European legal unity. Now what has Roman law to do with it? One could answer: nothing. For it is just about out of the question that the officials and politicians in Brussels, in the course of drafting their Directives and Regulations, have drawn their inspiration from Julian or Papinian, from Labeo or from Quintus Mucius Scaevola. Were this indeed the case, they would not, for example, rely so emphatically upon legislation as the high road towards establishing European legal unity. There are a variety of alternatives to legislative unification, which are even more typical of our Western legal tradition; among them particularly legal science. It offers a much more organic point of departure for transcending the national fragmentation of the law. Furthermore, the reference to legal science reminds us that instead of 'Europeanization', we should rather speak of a process of 're-Europeanization'. For a common European legal culture, centred around a common legal science and informed by the same sources, did once exist. Even today, despite the twohundred-year-long national fragmentation of our law, this tradition constitutes a unifying force of great potential; and anyone aiming to found a renewed European legal culture should use it to his advantage.

This 'old' European law, to which the rest of this paper will be dedicated, is known as the Roman-Canon ius commune.[10] It came into being as part of a dramatic and

---

8   Cf. for example Fritz Sturm, 1991 *Juristenzeitung* 555; in addition particularly the contribution of Winfried Tilmann, 'Eine Privatrechtskodifikation für die Europäische Gemeinschaft?', in a soon-to-be-published collection of conference proceedings, *Gemeinsames Privatrecht in der Europäischen Gemeinschaft*, edited by Chr.-P. Müller-Graff.

9   For programmatic statements see Helmut Coing, 'Europäisierung der Rechtswissenschaft', 1990 *Neue Juristische Wochenschrift* 937 sqq.; Filippo Ranieri, 'Der europäische Jurist, Rechtshistorisches Forschungsthema und rechtspolitische Aufgabe', (1990) 17 *Ius Commune* 9 sqq.; Reiner Schulze, 'Vom Ius Commune bis zum Gemeinschaftsrecht — das Forschungsfeld der Europäischen Rechtsgeschichte', in: Reiner Schulze (ed.), *Europäische Rechts- und Verfassungsgeschichte. Ergebnisse und Perspektiven der Forschung*, 1991, p. 3 sqq.; Reinhard Zimmermann, 'Das römisch-kanonische ius commune als Grundlage europäischer Rechtseinheit', 1992 *Juristenzeitung* 8 sqq.

10   Cf., in particular, Helmut Coing, *Die ursprüngliche Einheit der europäischen Rechtswissenschaft*, 1968; cf. the same author in various other publications, e.g. *Europäische Grundlagen des modernen Privatrechts*, 1986; *Von Bologna bis Brüssel — Europäische Gemeinsamkeiten in Vergangenheit, Gegenwart und Zukunft*, 1989.

far-reaching cultural upheaval: the so-called Renaissance of the 12th century.[11] First in Bologna, then also at other universities founded on the same model, lawyers began scientifically, using the scholastic method, to penetrate the most important body of Roman sources, the Digest (which had only recently been rediscovered) and to make it intellectually accessible. This was necessary, above all, because the Digest is not a systematically-structured piece of legislation or a textbook in the modern sense of the word, but rather a compilation of fragments from classical Roman legal writings, put together under Justinian in the 6th century AD. These writings themselves were full of controversy; furthermore, they originated from different stages of legal development. Nonetheless, the legal wisdom handed down in the Digest, the concepts, legal rules, systematic approaches and models of argumentation from Roman law proved superior to the contemporary customary laws. Thus the rationalization and scientific structuring of the law meant, to a significant degree, its Romanization; and over the following centuries Roman law, in the form imparted by Justinian and scientifically reworked by the lawyers of Bologna, conquered Europe. We call this process 'Reception'.[12] I would like to emphasize three aspects thereof which, in my opinion, are particularly characteristic.

3 The *ius commune*: a European Tradition

The first aspect is the truly European character of the tradition that was thus founded. Up until the time of the so-called usus modernus pandectarum in the 17th and 18th centuries, the whole of educated Europe formed a single and undifferentiated unit, not only in general cultural terms but also legally.[13] Lawyers who had received their education in one country could occupy a chair in another. The great French scholar Donellus, for example, was a professor at Heidelberg, Leyden and Altdorf; the Italian Alberico Gentili taught at Oxford, the German natural lawyer Samuel Pufendorf at Lund, the Spaniard Antonius Perezius at Leuven.[14] By the end of the 17th century, Hugo Grotius's work 'De jure belli ac pacis' had seen 40 editions in Germany, The Netherlands, Italy and Switzerland;[15] apart from that, there had been ten French, seven English and six German translations, as well as one into Italian. Heineccius's 'Elementa iuris civilis' was employed as a textbook at universities such as Halle, Pavia, Bologna, Cracow and

---

11 Cf., in particular, Harold J. Berman, *Law and Revolution. The Formation of the Western Legal Tradition*, 1983.

12 The authoritative account is by Franz Wieacker, *Privatrechtsgeschichte der Neuzeit*, 2nd ed., 1967, p. 45 sqq., 97 sqq.

13 This realization provides the point of departure for Helmut Coing's magnum opus *Europäisches Privatrecht, vol. I*, 1985.

14 Specifically on the Dutch professors of the 17th century cf. Reinhard Zimmermann, 'Roman-Dutch Jurisprudence and its Contribution to European Private Law', (1992) 66 *Tulane Law Review* 1715 sq.

15 These and the following figures are to be found in Coing, *op. cit.*, n. 10, p. 160 sqq.

Oxford. It appeared altogether in 75 editions in Germany, Italy, Switzerland, Austria, Belgium, France and Spain. In his Commentarius ad Pandectas, Johannes Voet[16] cited as a matter of course authors from Spain, Italy, France and Germany, right back to the 14th century. German students came on their peregrinatio academica to Italy or France in the same way as Scottish lawyers to Leyden or Utrecht. Law was not conceived of as a system of rules enacted for, and exclusively applicable in, a specific territory; rather it was recognized and applied on an international scale. Of course, this did not mean that the outcome of disputes would everywhere necessarily be the same . Whether an error of law, for instance, excludes the possibility of reclaiming what had been delivered without legal ground was (owing to the fact that the sources are entirely unclear on this point) answered totally differently by different lawyers at different times and in different parts of Europe.[17] Yet, all over Europe use was made of the same legal 'grammar': the dichotomy, in our example above, between error iuris and error facti; the fragmented system of the Roman condictiones which, over the centuries, formed the basis for the discussion of contested issues in enrichment law; and the prerequisites, generally agreed upon in principle, for the application of that most central of these enrichment actions, the condictio indebiti. Moving with the same cultural tides running through Europe,[18] and moored to a common educational[19] and scientific tradition, as well as to a common language, European legal science, in spite of many differences in detail, remained a unified intellectual world; and the international communis opinio doctorum was authoritative for its application and development.[20]

4 'Pure' Roman Law and *usus modernus*

The second aspect is Roman law's inherent flexibility and capability for development. What became the basis of our European common law was by no means pure Roman law, was not the law of Quintus Mucius or Papinian. Indeed, just the mention of these names shows that to speak of 'pure Roman law' would in any event be a fiction. Quintus Mucius Scaevola, the most important jurist of the truly creative epoch in Roman jurisprudence, lived around the turn of the first century BC; Aemilius Papinianus, the most brilliant representative of the late

---

16 About him see e.g. Robert Feenstra, C.J.D. Waal, *Seventeenth-Century Leyden Law Professors and their Influence on the Development of the Civil Law*, 1975, p. 35 sqq., 69 sqq.

17 For details, see Reinhard Zimmermann, *The Law of Obligations. Roman Foundations of the Civilian Tradition*, 1993, p. 849 sqq., 868 sqq.

18 Cf. Helmut Coing, 'Die europäische Privatrechtsgeschichte der neueren Zeit als einheitliches Forschungsgebiet', (1967) 1 *Ius Commune* 17 sqq.

19 This point of view is justly emphasized by Ranieri, (1990) 17 *Ius Commune* 9 sqq.

20 Cf. Gino Gorla, 'La "communis opinio totius orbis" et la reception jurisprudentielle du droit au cours des XVIe, XVIIe et XVIIIe siècles dans la "civil law" et la "common law"', in: Mauro Cappelletti (ed.), *New Perspectives for a Common Law of Europe*, 1978, p. 54 sqq., and Coing, *op. cit.*, n. 13, p. 124 sqq.

classical period, was praefectus praetorio under the Emperor Septimius Severus. Separating these two is a time-span of more than three hundred years, and if one also takes into account the time right back to the actual foundation of the Roman ius civile, the XII Tables, one is faced with a period of about seven hundred years, in the course of which the law was subjected to fundamental changes. In addition, the most important sources of this entire period were handed down to us in the form of a compilation, the above-mentioned Digest, which itself dates from the 6th century AD. At that stage, Rome was already in the hands of the Ostrogoths, while Constantinople was the new capital of the Empire. The Digest became the central component of a Byzantine law book, the Corpus Juris Civilis (as it was later called); and it was this work that was to determine the later view of Roman law and to become the basis of the common European legal science. The Digest itself can be described as a gigantic torso of Roman law, which contains a colourful mixture of case decisions, legal opinions and rules, commentary, disputes, and excerpts from textbooks and monographs. Altogether it contains fragments from about two thousand works. The overall character of the Digest is casuistic. Much of it reflects the contemporary position at the various stages of Roman legal history; other parts were altered to suit the requirements of the 6th century; and some parts simply contradict each other. A further 600 years later, the scholars in Bologna transplanted this complex sourcework into their present-day society, and sought in it answers to the legal problems of their time; they were followed by the Italian Commentators and all the subsequent law schools, right up to the representatives of the usus modernus pandectarum. The name for this — so far — last of the schools of a common European legal science, shows clearly what had happened in the meantime: a contemporary practice of Roman law had been developed, taking into account the changed requirements and value systems of the day. Documentary evidence of this practice is to be found in works such as Johannes Voet's great Commentary on the Digest and Simon van Groenewegen's Tractatus de legibus abrogatis et inusitatis, which lists all changes in the law in great detail. With that, a great task of integration, begun by Commentators such as Bartolus and Baldus, had been completed: the law which was actually practised, and which met the demands of the day (the 'consuetudines hodiernae'), had not become barren under a one-and-a-half century-old layer of law, but had rather, by way of Romanistic conceptualization and erudition, been made scientifically arable. How was that possible?

5 An Example: The General Concept of a Contract

Let us, for example, examine the law of contract. In the Rome of the Republic and Principate, its cornerstones were on the one hand the stipulation, an oral promise which was applicable in every situation but was form-bound, and on the other hand the consensual contracts, not affected by formal requirements but only available in limited number.[21] But even in the Corpus Juris, the conversion of the stipulation from contractus verbis to promise in written form was widely documented. This development continued during the Middle Ages. The 'writing obligatory' which was common in medieval commercial practice was really a degenerate descendant of the stipulation. Ultimately, however, the history of the stipulation ended in a cul-de-sac, for the application of contractual formalities had rapidly become an arcanum of notarial practice.[22] Instead of the stipulatio, it was the informal pactum that was destined to become the root of modern contract doctrine. A pactum had only been actionable in Roman Law if it could be classified as one of the four consensual contracts; otherwise the rule was: 'nuda pactio obligationem non parit'[23] — a naked pact begets no right of action. However, even in the post-classical period, one freezing pactum after another received a garment — though sometimes rather makeshift, and cut to many different patterns.[24] Thus, in this particular area, the Corpus Juris presented a somewhat confusing picture, marked by internal inconsistencies. However, a trend had become apparent, which was to set the tone for the ever-increasing erosion and ultimate abandonment of the principle 'ex nudo pacto non oritur actio'.[25] This development was driven on in the first place by the Canon lawyers, who had, charitably as could be expected of them, taken pity on the poor and naked pacts; and thus we find in the Decretals of Pope Gregory IX a sentence, which was to have far-reaching consequences: 'pacta quantumcunque nuda servanda sunt' — the direct root of our expression 'pacta sunt servanda'.[26] But international commercial practice also played an important role in this development; and many an author also took his inspiration from the supposedly Germanic[27] concept of good faith on which Tacitus had, somewhat unappreciatively, mused. Thereafter, from the 17th century onwards, the natural lawyers made it their business to fashion a single dress pattern for all pacts. At the same time the lawyers of the usus modernus finally overcame, for all practical purposes, the dogma of the unactionability of a naked pact.[28]

---

21 For details see Law of Obligations, *op. cit.*, n. 17, p. 68 sqq. (stipulation), p. 230 sqq. (consensual contracts).

22 Cf. Law of Obligations, *op. cit.*, n. 17, p. 546 sqq.

23 Ulp. D. 2, 14, 7, 4. See further Ulp. D. 2, 14, 7, 5; Ulp. D. 19, 5, 15; Paul. Sent. II, XIV, 1; C. 2, 3, 10 (Alex.) and Bruno Schmidlin, *Die römischen Rechtsregeln. Versuch einer Typologie,* 1970, p. 97 sqq. This rule was later formulated somewhat differently: 'ex nudo pacto non oritur actio'.

24 See for details Law of Obligations, *op. cit.*, n. 17, p. 508 sqq.

25 See Klaus-Peter Nanz, *Die Entstehung des allgemeinen Vertragsbegriffs im 16. bis 18. Jahrhundert,* 1985; Coing, *op. cit.*, n. 13, p. 398 sqq.; Law of Obligations, *op. cit.*, n. 17, p. 537 sqq. as well as the contributions of Bart, Birocchi and Feenstra in John Barton (ed.), *Towards a General Law of Contract,* 1990.

26 Lib. I, Tit. XXXV, Cap. I of the Liber Extra of the Corpus Juris Canonici.

27 Germania XXIV, 3 and 4; cf. e.g. Hugo Grotius, *Inleiding tot de Hollandsche Rechtsgeleerdheid, 1631,* III, I, 52.

28 See, most recently, Robert Feenstra, 'Die Klagbarkeit der pacta nuda', in: Robert Feenstra, Reinhard Zimmermann (eds.), *Das römisch-holländische Recht. Fortschritte des Zivilrechts im 17. und 18. Jahrhundert,* 1992, p. 123 sqq.

That contracts based on nothing more than formless consent are, as a rule, actionable, is recognized today in all Western European legal systems. This is one of those latent underlying principles of European contract law. And this principle, like many others, is in characteristic fashion Roman and non-Roman at the same time: it is Roman law in modern clothing, no longer in a toga or in a medieval coat of mail.

6 *Ius civile* in *iure canonico*

One word in this context on the role of the church. We have already referred to the Roman-Canon ius commune as the foundation of European legal unity.[29] What was taught at the medieval universities in the Middle Ages was indeed not only Roman law, but also Canon law. Hence the term 'ius utrumque' for contemporary legal science. Canon law is based upon a second large and also essentialy casuistic legal compilation, the 'Corpus Juris Canonici'. Its roots lie in the so-called Decretum Gratiani, which, not at all coincidentally, had also become the subject of scientific attention in 12th century Bologna. Now, of course, Roman and Canon law were by no means foreign or unconnected to one another. As the great English legal historian Maitland once charmingly put it: 'The imperial mother and her papal daughter were fairly good friends'.[30] The Popes could not, and did not want to, develop an intellectually independent legal system. Instead they depended to a large extent upon Roman legal rules and concepts, which thus, in a chasuble so to speak, not infrequently imprinted themselves on the development of European law. Contract doctrine provides a good example. 'Pacta quantumcunque nuda servanda sunt': this seminal sentence from the Corpus Juris Canonici (quoted above) did not only find its pivotal point in the Roman concept of pactum; it also unmistakably alludes to the glossatorial distinction between naked pacts and those clothed with actionability; and it subtly evokes the Roman praetor's promise contained in D. 2, 14, 7, 7: pacta conventa servabo'.[31] Furthermore, the canonists smoothed the transition from the Roman 'nuda pactio obligationem non parit' to the counter-rule 'ex nudo pacto oritur actio' by granting actionability only to those pacta which had been entered into by the parties 'serio animo et deliberate.' This then made it necessary to develop a criterion according to which serious agreements could be distinguished from those not seriously entered into. By using building stones hewn from the quarry of the Digest[32] and adding generous quantities of scholastic

---

29 In general on the significance of Canon law cf. recently Peter Landau, 'Einfluß des kanonischen Rechts auf die europäische Rechtskultur', in: Schulze, *op. cit.*, n. 9, p. 39 sqq.
30 Sir Frederick Pollock, Frederic William Maitland, *The History of the English Law Before the Time of Edward I.* 2nd ed., vol I, 1898, p. 116.
31 See Law of Obligations, *op. cit.*, n. 17, p. 508 sqq.
32 In particular Aristo/Ulp. D. 2, 14, 7, 2; Ulp. D. 2, 14, 7, 4; Ulp. D. 44, 4, 2, 3; further details in Law of Obligations, *op. cit.*, n. 17, p. 549 sqq.

mortar,[33] a suitable doctrine could be built up relatively quickly: only those agreements which rest upon a lawful causa[34] were actionable. This causa doctrine can still be found today, for example in art. 1131 code civil, and it also appears to be one of the roots of the famous English doctrine of consideration.

7 The Civilian Tradition Today

I now turn to the third important aspect: the characteristic — and thus fundamentally uniform — imprint which even our modern national legal systems have received from the tradition of the European Roman-Canon law. Of course this is particularly conspicuous where the continuity of the development has not been disrupted — or rather obscured — by the intervention of the legislator. In Western Europe, San Marino provides the only example known to me. Here the ius commune still applies, and law professors from Italian faculties, appointed as judges of appeal, base their decisions to the present day ultimately on the Corpus Juris Civilis.[35] The situation is similar in South Africa, where the Roman-Dutch law as imported by the settlers of the Dutch East India Company — that is, the Roman-canon ius commune in its Dutch variant — is still today applied.[36] Roman-Dutch law has always been a particularly vital branch of the civilian tradition, for during the 17th century, the northern Netherlands numbered not only politically, economically and culturally, but indeed also legally, amongst the leading European nations.[37] Thus, even today, the courts in Cape Town, Bloemfontein or Pretoria rely on authors of the 17th and 18th centuries such as Voet and Vinnius, Van Bynkershoek and Van Leeuwen, Grotius and Ulrich Huber; and, when required, they also venture back directly to the Roman sources. The most recent decision on the extent of a contractual exemption from warranty claims for latent defects in an object sold, to mention just one example, cites a string of fragments from title 21, 1 of the Digest ('de aedilicio edicto et redhibitione et quanti minoris') and includes then, inter alia, an almost three-page-long analysis of a passage from Johannes Voet's Commentary on the Pandects.[38] The position is similar in the neighbouring Roman-Dutch jurisdictions. In 1990 the Zimbabwe Supreme Court declared the Roman praetor's edictum de nautis, cauponibus et stabulariis to be

---

33 On the scholastic causa-doctrine cf., in this context, Alfred Söllner, 'Die causa im Kondiktionen- und Vertragsrecht des Mittelalters bei den Glossatoren, Kommentatoren und Kanonisten', (1960) 77 *Zeitschrift der Savigny-Stiftung für Rechtsgeschichte, Romanistische Abteilung* 183 sqq.

34 On the development of this doctrine see Law of Obligations, *op. cit.*, n. 17, p. 551 sqq.

35 Cf. Peter Stein, 'Civil Law Reports and the Case of San Marino', in: idem, *The Character and Influence of the Roman Civil Law*, 1988, p. 126 sqq.

36 Reinhard Zimmermann, *Das römisch-holländische Recht in Südafrika*, 1983.

37 See for a more detailed exposition Robert Feenstra, Reinhard Zimmermann (eds.), *Das römisch-holländische Recht. Fortschritte des Zivilrechts im 17. und 18. Jahrhundert*, 1992.

38 Van der Merwe v. Meades, 1991(2) 2 SA 1 (A). For further examples cf. 1992 *Juristenzeitung* 12 f.

applicable per analogiam to land transport.[39] And in last year's September edition of the South African Law Reports there appears a decision of the Namibia Supreme Court, which deals with the permissibility of pacta commissoria in the law of pledge.[40] All this may seem a little exotic. Geographically closer to us is Scotland, where the courts also still on occasion fall back on Roman law. For despite the Union of Crowns, Scotland has retained until today a legal system which is in principle independent and which owes its civilian flavour mainly to the institutional writers of the 17th and 18th centuries, the most prominent being Sir James Dalrymple, Viscount of Stair.[41]

Less obvious is the continuity of legal development in the modern codified legal systems. Since they came into force, the modern lawyer has limited his horizon with ever-increasing exclusivity to the codifications and the judgments based on them, and, at most, to the travaux préparatoires. At the same time legal history was imbued with a new humanistic spirit,[42] and thus the legal historian has increasingly come to regard himself as a pure historian, dealing with a special kind of source, and having, in the common perception, no impact on, and little responsibility for, the administration of modern law. Legal history and private law legal doctrine have parted company. This is unfortunate. For if we look into a code like the BGB, we see that many individual legal institutions have been preserved, either entirely unchanged or in a modernized form; and many rules of Roman law, in some or other codified version, still determine, for better or worse, the outcome of legal disputes at the end of the twentieth century.[43] Even where a new regime prevails, it has usually been introduced consciously or unconsciously in opposition to a rule of Roman law; and even in these cases, it is often only on the basis of a proper understanding of the Roman rule in question that one is able to appreciate, evaluate and understand the development. Even in defeat, therefore, Roman law retains a key function for any more than superficial comprehension of the modern law. And apart from that: such defeats have occasionally not been of a lasting character. The idea that a codification should be able entirely to cut off the continuity of historical development, has proved to be a rather simplistic illusion. Even in a codified legal system the re-appearance of ideas and solutions from the treasure-house of the ius commune is by no means a rare — although it is usually an unacknowledged — phenomenon. In the process, many of the jagged edges and

---

39   See Reinhard Zimmermann, 'Das römisch-holländische Recht in Zimbabwe', (1991) 55 *RabelsZ* 505 sqq.
40   Meyer v. Hessling, 1992 (3) SA 851 (Nm SC).
41   Cf. e.g. David M. Walker (ed.), *Stair Tercentenary Studies*, 1981.
42   On this neo-humanistic approach to legal history see Paul Koschaker, *Europa und das römische Recht*, 4th ed., 1966, p. 290 sqq.
43   Cf. e.g. Heinrich Honsell, 'Das rechtshistorische Argument in der modernen Zivilrechtsdogmatik', in: Dieter Simon (ed.), *Akten des 26. Deutschen Rechtshistorikertages*, 1987, p. 301 sqq., 305 sqq.

time-bound eccentricities of the German Civil Code got worn away.[44] But that is a topic for another lecture.

8 The European Character of English Law

I would like only to mention one other point which is particularly important for the question of European legal unity. It has to do with the position of the English common law, which continental jurists have always considered to be particularly strange and idiosyncratic. 'What have we here? Who is that savage?' a foreign jurist would ask, with no small wonder, if the writings of Sir Edward Coke, for example, were laid before him. 'Whence comes this wild man; naked, tattooed, painted ..., with rings and fantastic toys in his ears and nostrils, − from what island of the South Sea, or from what trackless forest? It cannot be that he was the Attorney-General of the King of England in an age of refinement − the contemporary of Cujacius ...'[45] This is how many German lawyers essentially still think today, when they are confronted with the casuistic nature of the English law, with its bizarre traditionality, or with the peculiar interlocking of common law and equity. Indeed, the English themselves like to cultivate the myth of their law as constituting an autochthonous national achievement. So, for example, in the third edition of the leading textbook on English legal history, which appeared in 1990, we can still read these clear and pithy words: 'And so English law flourished in noble isolation from Europe.'[46]

a) However, as we have just said, this is a myth.[47] For in reality England was never totally cut off from continental legal culture. Over the centuries, since the Norman conquest, there has been ongoing intellectual contact, which has left a definitive and characteristic mark on the English law. This becomes obvious wherever one looks. The agents of this continuous process of reception and adaptation of civilian ideas were, of course, the influential authors from Bracton in the 13th century[48] to Blackstone in the 18th[49] and Birks in the 20th century.

---

44   Cf. Theo Mayer-Maly, 'Die Wiederkehr von Rechtsfiguren', 1971 *Juristenzeitung* 1 sqq. as well as the references in 1992 *Juristenzeitung* 19 f.

45   Thomas J. Hogg, 'An Introductory Lecture on the Study of the Civil Law (1831)', printed in: Michael H. Hoeflich, *The Gladsome Light of Jurisprudence*, 1988, p. 96 sqq. (99 f.).

46   J.H. Baker, *An Introduction to English Legal History*, 3rd ed., 1990, p. 35.

47   For a more detailed discussion of what follows see Reinhard Zimmermann, 'Der europäische Charakter des englischen Rechts. Historische Verbindungen zwischen civil law und common law', (1993) 1 *Zeitschrift für Europäisches Privatrecht* 4 sqq.; also Richard H. Helmholz, 'Continental Law and Common Law: Historical Strangers or Companions?', 1990 *Duke Law Journal* 1207 sqq. and the same author in 1992 *Duke Journal of Comparative and International Law* 319 sqq.

48   Cf. e.g. Carl Güterbock, *Bracton and his Relation to Roman Law* (German translation by Brinton Coxe, 1866; reprinted in 1979); further Samuel E. Thorne (ed., transl., comm.), *Bracton on the Laws and Customs of England*, 1968, e.g. p. XXXIII, XXXVI.

Particularly instructive in this context were the 'treatise writers' of the late 18th and the 19th centuries.[50] This was the spirit in which they tackled their task (and I quote from the foreword to Sir William Jones's An Essay on the Law of Bailments, 1781): 'I propose to begin with treating the subject analytically, and, having traced every part of it up to the first principles of natural reason, shall proceed historically, to show with what perfect harmony these principles are recognized and established by other nations, especially the Romans, as well as by our English courts, when their decisions are properly understood and clearly distinguished'. Furthermore, the leading works of the continental natural law movement had, since the 18th century, been available in English translations. Pufendorf's 'De jure naturae et gentium' (together with Barbeyrac's gloss) had appeared, by 1730, in four editions;[51] by 1750, Grotius's 'De jure belli ac pacis' had been published six times in English.[52] Particularly important is the influence which the translations of Pothier's most important Traités had on the development of English contract law.[53] Furthermore, from about the middle of the 19th century, the views of the 'Historical School' gained currency in England,[54] particularly through translations of works by Thibaut, Savigny and Mackeldey. And John Austin discovered the model for his 'universal jurisprudence' in German pandect law.[55] But in tracing the influence in England of the continental civil law, one also stumbles very soon upon a succession of great judges in English legal history: Lord Holt, Sir Matthew Hale and Lord Mansfield number amongst the most prominent examples.[56]

---

49   On the systematic aspects of Blackstone's Commentaries on the Laws of England cf., in particular, John W. Cairns, 'Blackstone, An English Institutist: Legal Literature and the Rise of the Nation State', (1984) 4 *Oxford Journal of Legal Studies* 339 sqq.; Alan Watson, 'The Impact of Justinian's Institutes on Academic Treatises: Blackstone's Commentaries', in: idem, *Roman Law and Comparative Law*, 1991, p. 186 sqq.

50   A.W.B. Simpson, 'The Rise and Fall of the Legal Treatise: Legal Principles and the Forms of Legal Literature', (1981) 48 *University of Chicago Law Review* 632 sqq.

51   Sir William Holdsworth, *A History of English Law, vol. XII*, 1936, reprinted in 1966, p. 637.

52   P.G. Stein, in: A.W.B. Simpson (ed.), *Biographical Dictionary of the Common Law*, 1984, p. 219.

53   Generally on Pothier and on his influence on English law cf. (1985) 102 *Zeitschrift der Savigny-Stiftung für Rechtsgeschichte, Germanistische Abteilung*, 168 sqq., 176 sq., 178 sq., 188 sq., 201 sqq.

54   See Peter Stein, 'Continental Influences on English Legal Thought, 1600 - 1900', in: idem, *The Character and Influence of the Roman Civil Law*, 1988, p. 224 sq. Savigny's works 'were amongst the most frequently translated into English': Michael H. Hoeflich, 'Savigny and his Anglo-American Disciples', (1989) 37 *American Journal of Comparative Law* 19.

55   See Andreas B. Schwarz, 'John Austin und die deutsche Rechtswissenschaft seiner Zeit', in: idem, *Rechtsgeschichte und Gegenwart*, 1960, p. 73 sqq.; Stein, *op. cit.*, n. 54, p. 223 sq.; M.H. Hoeflich, John Austin and Joseph Story: 'Two Nineteenth Century Perspectives on the Utility of the Civil Law for the Common Lawyer', (1985) 29 *American Journal of Legal History* 36 sqq.

56   Cf. the overview by Daniel R. Coquillette, *The Civilian Writers of Doctors' Commons*, London, 1988, p. 215.

b) The church courts, too, were important bearers of the reception of Roman law.[57] Right up to the time of the Reformation they had exercised in England, just as on the continent, an extensive jurisdiction. It reached far into the affairs of every layman, for it stretched from the law of marriage to succession, from matters of defamation to breach of contract ('laesio fidei'). The Canon law was just as binding on the English ecclesiastical courts as it was on the church courts on the continent; and, as has already been mentioned, the connection between Roman and Canon law was very close. Thus, also in England, the ecclesiastical courts paved the way for the actionability of informal pacta, a principle which was quickly received by the common law courts, too.[58] The Court of Chancery, the source of that second layer of English law known as equity, must also be recorded as an influential channel for continental thought; after all, the Lord Chancellors serving in this court up to the time of Henry VIII were clergymen, usually well-versed in Canon law and Roman law. They had studied, predominantly, at Oxford University.[59] Right into the 19th century, Oxford and Cambridge remained the only English universities: their law faculties followed the continental model.[60] Although the teaching of Canon law was suppressed after the start of the Reformation, the study of Roman law has remained firmly and uninterruptedly entrenched at both universities. In a society known as 'Doctors' Commons', their graduates, the English 'civilians', kept the tradition of the learned laws alive.[61] They produced a rich literature, which corresponded to a great extent with the continental tradition.[62] The career opportunities of these learned jurists were by no means insignificant;[63] they monopolized legal practice before a string of specialized courts of law, from rather insignificant ones such as the High Court of Chivalry, dealing mainly with disputes over armorial bearings, through to, most importantly, the Court of Admiralty and the ecclesiastical courts. Moreover, they took up positions in the church administration, became bearers of clerical offices and benefices, served as judges in the courts which operated according to Roman-Canon procedure, and took posts in the diplomatic service and the government administration.

---

57   See, in particular, Richard H. Helmholz, *Roman Canon Law in Reformation England*, 1990; idem, *Canon Law and the Law of England*, 1987.

58   See Richard H. Helmholz, 'Contract and the Canon Law', in: Barton, *op. cit.*, n. 25, p. 59 sqq.

59   Cf. e.g. Helmut Coing, 'English Equity and the Denunciatio Evangelica of the Canon Law', (1955) 71 *Law Quarterly Review* 238; Baker, *op. cit.*, n. 46, p. 47, 115.

60   On the early history of legal development in Oxford cf. e.g. the contributions of Southern, Barton and Boyle, in J.I. Catto (ed.), *The History of the University of Oxford*, vol. I, 1984.

61   Cf. e.g. Coquillette, *op. cit.*, n. 56, p. 22 sqq.

62   Helmut Coing, 'Das Schrifttum der englischen Civilians und die kontinentale Rechtsliteratur in der Zeit zwischen 1550 und 1800', (1975) 5 *Ius Commune* 16 sqq.

63   See e.g. Brian P. Levack, *The Civil Lawyers in England 1603 — 1641*, 1973, p. 21 sqq.; idem, 'The English Civilians, 1500 — 1700', in: Winfried Prest, *Lawyers in Early Modern Europe and America*, 1981, p. 108 sqq.

c) The Court of Admiralty,[64] which was responsible primarily for maritime disputes, but also at one stage for all commercial contracts with a foreign connection, reminds us finally of a further source of European-inspired modernization of English law: the lex mercatoria, anglice Law Merchant. This is the term for the customs and rules, predominantly unwritten, but also partly laid down in statutes or legal compilations, which had developed since about the 17th century in connection with the blossoming trade around the Mediterranean, on the Atlantic coast and the Baltic Sea.[65] Although this common European law, specially applicable to merchants, constituted largely 'new' law, there were at least parts of it which took their inspiration from Roman law: the general average (derived from the lex Rhodia de iactu) or the bottomry loan (based on the foenus nauticum),[66] to mention two examples. Also in this respect, England belonged to Europe. Her economy was integrated into the European trade system, and so the international lex mercatoria was bound to spread across the Channel. Its development followed exactly the same pattern as in the rest of Europe. What had emerged in the Middle Ages as customary commercial law and was applied by special merchants' courts became, from about the 16th century, increasingly the subject of scientific examination.[67] This classical period of a European science of commercial law was followed from around the middle of the 17th century by the incorporation of this body of law into the developing national legal systems. The above-mentioned Lord Mansfield, a judge of Scottish descent who had, moreover, studied Roman law at Oxford, was of paramount importance in this respect.[68] 'The law of nations', he declared,[69] 'in its full extent [is] part of the law of England, ... [and is] to be collected from the practice of different nations, and the authority of writers'; this explains the hundreds of quotations from continental legal records and legislation, as well as from treatises on the lex mercatoria, on natural law, Roman law and its usus modernus, which are to be found in Mansfield's judgments.[70]

---

64   See, in summary, Sir William Holdsworth, *A History of English Law*, vol. *I*, 7th ed., 1956, p. 544 sqq.; William Senior, *Doctors' Commons and the Court of Admiralty*, 1922, p. 14 sqq., 84 sqq.; Baker, *op. cit.*, n. 46, p. 141 sqq.

65   Cf. e.g. Berman, *op. cit.*, n. 11, p. 333 sqq.

66   For an overview, see Coing, *op. cit.*, n. 13, p. 519 sqq.

67   See Coquillette, *op. cit.*, n. 56, passim.

68   Cf. Sir William Holdsworth, *A History of English Law*, vol. *XII*, 1938, p. 464 sqq., 493 sqq., 524 sqq.; Stein, *op. cit.*, n. 55, p. 220 sqq.; also, more recently, Christopher P. Rodgers, 'Continental Literature and the Development of the Common Law by the King's Bench, c. 1750 - 1800', in: Vito Piergiovanni (ed.), *The Courts and the Development of Commercial Law*, 1987, p. 161 sqq.; Michael Lobban, *The Common Law and English Jurisprudence 1760 - 1850*, 1991, p. 98 sqq.

69   Triquet v. Bath, (1764) 3 *Burrow's Reports* 1478 (1481).

70   For details see Rodgers, *op. cit.*, n. 68, p. 166 sqq.

d) In view of these manifold and centuries-old connections, it is not surprising that large areas of English law (in particular the law of contract[71]) were inspired, characterized or at least influenced by the ideas and concepts, the rules and institutions as well as the general intellectual undercurrents of the European ius commune. This is not infrequently even true of those doctrines which we generally regard as typically English. The doctrine of consideration (which states that promises are only legally enforceable if they are given in return for some counterprestation from the promisee) provides an example: for it is the specifically English variant of the medieval causa-doctrine.[72] In many cases, of course, the Roman impetus led to rather un-Roman results.[73] Thus, for instance, we read in the most famous of the so-called 'coronation cases':[74] 'The real question in this case is the extent of the application in English law of the principle of the Roman law which has been adopted and acted on in many English decisions'. This principle, which provided the point of departure, is the civilian rule 'debitor speciei liberatur casuali interitu rei':[75] the debtor is relieved of his duty to deliver the object if it has been destroyed through no fault of his own. In about the middle of the 19th century, English judges began to read this rule into the parties' agreement.[76] For this purpose they availed themselves of a construction which also originated in Roman law: the introduction of a (tacit) resolutive condition.[77] As a consequence, however, the entire contract had to be taken to have been dissolved in the event of fulfilment of the condition (i.e. when the object of the contract was destroyed). This principle was then carried over to cases in which the performance was not impossible, but in which merely the purpose for which the parties had entered into the contract had been frustrated. This occurred in the case of that

---

71 On this topic see, as far as the 19th century is concerned, in particular A.W.B. Simpson, 'Innovation in Nineteenth Century Contract Law', (1975) 91 *Law Quarterly Review* 247 sqq.; P.S. Atiyah, *The Rise and Fall of the Freedom of Contract*, 1979, p. 139 sqq., 405 sqq.; Philip A. Hamburger, 'The Development of the Nineteenth Century Consensus Theory of Contract', (1989) 7 *Law and History Review* 241 sqq.; James Gordley, *The Philosophical Origins of Modern Contract Doctrine*, 1991, p. 134 sqq.

72 Cf. the overview in Law of Obligations, *op. cit.*, n. 17, p. 549 sqq. as well as 1992 *Juristenzeitung* 16 sqq.

73 This is emphasized by Helmholz, 1990 *Duke Law Journal* 1207 sqq., (1218).

74 Krell v. Henry, [1903] 2 *Law Reports, King's Bench Division* 740 (747 f.). See e.g. R.G. McElroy, Glanville Williams, 'The Coronation Cases', (1940) 4 *Modern Law Review* 241 sqq.; (1941) 5 *Modern Law Review* 1 sqq.

75 Cf. e.g. Hermann Dilcher, *Die Theorie der Leistungsstörungen bei Glossatoren, Kommentatoren und Kanonisten*, 1960, p. 185 sqq.

76 Taylor v. Caldwell, (1863) 3 *Best and Smith's Reports* 826 sqq. See e.g. Max Rheinstein, *Die Struktur des vertraglichen Schuldverhältnisses im anglo-amerikanischen Recht*, 1932, p. 173 sqq.; Barry Nicholas, 'Rules and Terms — Civil Law and Common Law', (1974) 48 *Tulane Law Review* 965 f.; G.H. Treitel, *Unmöglichkeit, 'Impracticability' und 'Frustration' im anglo-amerikanischen Recht*, 1991.

77 For a more detailed exposition of this whole field, see Reinhard Zimmermann, '"Heard melodies are sweet, but those unheard are sweeter ...". Conditio tacita, implied condition und die Fortbildung des europäischen Vertragsrechts', (1993) 193 *Archiv für die civilistische Praxis* 121 sqq.

faithful royalist who had hired an apartment situated on the route of the planned coronation procession of King Edward VII. But then the procession had to be cancelled because the monarch had contracted peritonitis. Did the rental have to be paid nonetheless? Vaughan Williams, L.J., relying on Roman law, answered this question in the negative. We refer today to the 'doctrine of frustration of contract'. It corresponds functionally to the civilian doctrine of clausula rebus sic stantibus[78] which had likewise been constructed of Roman building stones, although as such it was also unknown to Roman law: a contract need not be performed if there has been a fundamental change of those circumstances which were decisive for its conclusion.

9 Prospects

'Roman law and European legal unity': this is a programmatic topic. It should, however, not induce the modern Roman lawyer to turn back the clock of legal development by two thousand years. In the pointed words of Maitland: '... any one who really possesses what has been called the historic sense must, so it seems to me, dislike to see a rule or an idea unfitly surviving in a changed environment. An anachronism should offend not only his reason, but his taste'.[79] The vital contribution the legal historian is able to render today lies in fostering an awareness that a common legal tradition (which has indelibly been imprinted by Roman law) still informs our modern national legal systems; in carving out their common systematic, conceptual, dogmatic and ideological foundations, which are hidden under the debris piled up in the course of the legal particularization over the last two hundred years; and in restoring the intellectual contact between his discipline on the one hand, and comparative law and doctrinal legal scholarship on the other — a contact which has largely been disrupted by the modern codifications.[80] The unification of European law should not be left to an institutionalized Europe which merely reacts to specific needs and aims at implementing economic policies: otherwise, the keyword 'Brussels' would quickly gain a negative connotation also in legal circles. European legal unification is in the first place a task for legal science — a science which could almost be described as a revived 'Historical School' of jurisprudence; and which therefore, 'progressing organically' (Savigny) from the common roots of the modern European legal systems, once again sets out

---

78 For an overview, see Law of Obligations, *op. cit.*, n. 17, p. 579 sqq.; since then Ralf Köbler, *Die 'clausula rebus sic stantibus' als allgemeiner Rechtsgrundsatz*, 1991, p. 23 sqq.; Michael Rummel, *Die 'clausula rebus sic stantibus'*, 1991.

79 H.A.L. Fisher (ed.), *The Collected Papers of Frederic William Maitland, vol. III*, 1911, p. 486.

80 See, in this regard, the agenda of the new *Zeitschrift für Europäisches Privatrecht*, 1993, p. 1 sqq., edited by Jürgen Basedow, Uwe Blaurock, Axel Flessner, Reiner Schulze, Reinhard Zimmermann. Cf. also Zimmermann, 1992 *Juristenzeitung* 8 sqq., as well as Carlo Augusto Cannata, 'Usus hodiernus pandectarum, common law, diritto romano olandese e diritto comune europeo', (1991) 57 *Studia et documenta historiae et iuris* 383 sqq. and Hein Kötz, 'Was erwartet die Rechtsvergleichung von der Rechtsgeschichte?', 1992 *Juristenzeitung* 20 sqq.

to design a ius commune Europaeum around the core of the general private law — and in so doing may or may not level the ground for unificatory legislation. For this purpose, knowledge of Roman law and its influence on the formation of the European legal mind is still today indispensable.

CHAPTER 6

Procedural Consequences of a Common Private Law for Europe

Marcel Storme

1 The Question

The question which is examined in this collection of essays is whether the unification of private law in Europe influences procedural law. More particularly, the question can be raised whether the unification of substantive law requires or produces the unification of procedural law.

This contribution is not the correct place to discuss the relationship between private and procedural law in its full entirety.

This contribution's point of departure, distinct from that of Binder[1] in his time, is that the body of private law and the body of law relating to the protection of legal rights does not form a complete unity. Not only do the repercussions of private law arise out of legal proceedings, legal proceedings can also create rights which did not exist before the trial.

Substantive law and procedural law must be distinguished which does not naturally mean that either they are independent of each other or they do not influence each other.

With reference to this relationship, it is possible to perceive two important phenomena.

The first phenomenon is that there are federal states where private law is unified whilst the states themselves continue to have their own procedural law. Switzerland is the most significant example of this situation where the law of obligations (Obligationenrecht, (O.R.)) and the rest of private law (Zivilgesetzbuch, (Z.G.B.)) are unified but every canton has its own procedural law. This situation confirms the point of departure for the reasoning of this contribution.

The second phenomenon is that rules of conflict of laws can require judges to apply foreign substantive law whereas judges can never be compelled to apply a foreign procedural law.[2] Therefore, procedural law has a stronger national identity than substantive law.

Nevertheless, the distinction between substantive law and procedural law does not make the question, of the consequences for procedural law of a (planned) unification of private law in Europe, any less relevant.

---

1   J. Binder, *Prozess und Recht*, Leipzig, 1927.
2   In the Babcock case (Cass., 9 October 1980, R.W., 1981-82, 1471) it was expressly held, for the first time, that the applicable foreign law must be interpreted in accordance with the interpretation given by the courts and scholars in the foreign state.

To my mind, it seems quite evident that a unified procedural law could better guarantee a unified application of a unified private law. It is worth mentioning in this respect that the Swiss Constitution explicitly states that the entire law of procedure should be dealt with *sensu lato* by the legislatures of the cantons, '*wie bis anhin*', (Article 64, Abs. 3, BV), which alludes to possible federal interference.

However, it may be added that a unified private law can sometimes lead to necessary adjustments being made to procedural law and this occurred in a remarkable case in European Community law when the European Court of Justice held that an efficient protection of rights requires the possibility to award provisional and urgent measures.[3]

It also seems clear to me that a unified procedural law, in a way prepares the law for the reception of a unified private law. It is not difficult to accept that a unified law related to the attachment order would bring about the unification of the law relating to property and securities.

As a preliminary conclusion I would like to make the following two points. The first point is that the unification of private law by itself does not necessarily require the unification of procedural law. However, the unification of procedural law is desirable either to provide adequate assistance to the unification of private law if it is already happening, or to prepare for a future unification of private law. The second point is, however, that I would like to emphasize most strongly, that the unification of procedural law has become imperative due to the creation of the European internal market and this will form the subject of the following section.

2 The Need for Unification or, where Appropriate, Harmonization of European Procedural Law

2.1 General Need for World-wide Approximation

Although comparative law had for a whole century been considered an established method for achieving unification of various legal systems, it can hardly be claimed that a comparative study of procedural law was a realistic proposition.

This approach changed radically as people in all parts of the world became increasingly aware of the urgent need to improve access to justice. There was a

---

3   E.C.J., 19 June 1990, 'The Queen v. secretary of state ex parte factor tame limited e.a.'. This does not prevent judges from being inspired by foreign law when introducing new concepts into their own procedural law. In this way the concept of *référé-provision* (a provisional amount to pay in cases in a *kort geding*) was introduced into Belgium by referring to the French Civil Code of Procedure — similarly England the *saisie-conservatoire* when introducing the Mareva injunction.

universal desire for a system of procedural law which would enable justice to be administered promptly, cheaply and properly.[4]

This concern had already been expressed earlier in international agreements. However, it was not realized at the time exactly what an explosive train of events would be set in motion by these agreements, more particularly through the case law which was developed not only by the international courts, but also at the domestic level. This applies to both the ECHR of 1950 and the ICCPR.[5] The first-named of these instruments was given its main impulses in the seventies by the decisions of the Strasbourg Court, whereas the second, by virtue of the precedence accorded to international law over domestic law, achieved a breakthrough via the case law of the national courts in those countries in which the ICCPR had been given legal effect.

However, it was the Treaty of New York (1958) in particular which, more than the general principles of the proper court procedure as expressed in the two aforementioned international treaties, achieved a real degree of uniformity in the field of procedural law.

Although this treaty concerns international arbitration, where the need for unification is particularly marked in the business world-scale[6] unification.[7]

True unification was subsequently achieved on a very broad regional — i.e. not on a global — scale in Europe and in Latin America.

In Europe, the European Enforcement of Judgments Convention was signed and its territorial scope has continued to widen.[8]

In Latin America, a model code was adopted in the shape of the Codigo tipo ibero-americano (1988). Although this code had no binding force, its text is a model for any reforms in procedural law in Latin America.[9] This can be illustrated by the new Codigo General del Proceso in Uruguay (November 1989).[10]

---

4   In his book *Judges, Legislators and Professors* (Cambridge, 1987), R.C. Van Caenegem sets out the eight characteristics of good law; naturally these include 'accessible justice' (o.c., p. 157 et seq., spec. p. 162-163).

5   Treaty made in New York on 19 December 1966.

6   The Treaty was subsequently ratified in nearly 100 States.

7   For further comments, see Van den Bergh, J., The New York Arbitration Convention of 1958, Deventer, 1981.

8   The Brussels Convention of 1958 entered into force on 1 February 1973, was amended in 1982 and 1989, and is currently in force in every Member State.

9   See in this connection: *El codigo procesal civil modelo para Iberoamerica. Historia, antecedentes, exposicion de motivos, texto del Anteproyecto.* Ed. preparada por E. Vescovi Montevideo, 1988; see also on this subject the excellent lecture delivered by Carlos de Miguel y Alonso, *Hacia un proceso civil universal*, Valladolid, 1991.

10   Vescovi, E., and del Carmen Rueco, M., *Los primeros resultados de la Reforma de la Justicia en Uruguay, Un balance a los dieciochi meses de la entrada en vigencia del Codigo General del Proceso*, Montevideo, 1991.

At this point it is appropriate to reflect on the status of unification of procedural law, its scope and its limitations.[11]

Any unification project must meet a particular need and at the same time be feasible.

In an area of law which is particularly oriented towards legal practice, it appears to us that unification must be dictated by the requirements of the practitioner.

If such unification is to be attained, it should preferably be set about in areas which are linked both geographically and by legal culture. Hence the reason why in the following passages we shall devote our attention largely to the European internal market.

2.2 What is Needed in the European Community

2.2.1 Requirements Specific to Procedural Law

A particularly important point which can be made at the outset and which highlights the need for a unified system of procedural law is this: the courts may apply the substantive law, but not the procedural law, of another country.

Consequently, it is possible for all the courts in Europe to apply Italian substantive law on the basis of the rules of international private law, but none of them may apply any rules of procedural law other than those which are applicable in the judge's own country.[12]

Many rules of procedural law are such that they are capable of cross-frontier application, and therefore require an international or uniform system — for example, the rules relating to jurisdiction, evidence, exequatur, and enforcement.

In international relations within the European internal market, the question as to which procedural law applies to a legal dispute will be important from aspects such as the gathering of evidence, any clause in the contract which makes provision for arbitration proceedings or for determining the court which shall have jurisdiction, or the creation of legal persons having the required capacity to act in court proceedings.

Unification could prevent surprises from occurring in many of these areas.

However, uniformity could also be required in the context of purely national disputes, i.e. where the systems of procedural law in question are in permanent contact with each other.

This is certainly the case within the European internal market: the interpenetration of European law firms, the mobility of persons and enterprises, the constant problem of disparate rules of procedural law — these are factors of a kind

---

11　See on this subject the excellent contribution by K. Kerameus, 'Procedural Unification: the Need and the Limitations, in: *International Perspectives on Civil Justice, Essays in honour of Sir Jack I.H. Jacob*, London, 1990, p. 47 et seq.

12　See Kerameus, K., *o.c.*, p. 49, with extensive references under footnote 10.

which call for approximation, or even unification, of the procedural law systems in question.

2.2.2 Requirements Specific to the Internal Market

In general terms, it can be said that any form of integration requires a certain form of procedural law unification: 'Procedural unification goes hand in hand with overall unification.'[13]

The need for legal certainty has — for well-known reasons — increased exponentially. European citizens and enterprises will require extensive legal protection within the European internal market, not only in their own countries but frequently also in one or more Member States of the European Community.

Confidence in the institutions, and in particular the judiciary, is a major component of the foundations of the European edifice.

Reinforcement of such confidence can only be accomplished if the citizen is fully aware that throughout Europe there exist equal, analogous and/or equivalent judicial procedures which give citizen and enterprise alike equal access to a system of procedural law which operates as straightforwardly, swiftly, efficiently and economically as possible.

Fundamental confidence in European justice must be gradually built up by setting the Community's sights, as from 1993, on harmonization and progressive unification of procedural law.

However, more is obviously required in order to stimulate a desire for unification of procedural law in Europe.

More particularly, there are two specific classes of needs which stand out in this context, i.e. economic and legal. In addition, there are a number of impending dangers which make this unification process a matter of urgency.

Both the aforementioned types of needs are examined more closely below.

2.2.2.1 The Internal Market and its Need for More Harmonized Procedural Law from an Economic Standpoint

(a) It is common knowledge that the world of international business requires an effective and transparent system of procedural law. This is becoming all the more necessary with the multiplication of transnational contacts. Unification will be ineluctable as soon as such commercial contacts assume a permanent character. In Europe, internal barriers have been removed from the internal market; all the greater, then, is the expectation of potential litigants that a judicial system will be created which is available to them on more or less equal terms, wherever they may be.

---

13   Kerameus, K., *o.c.*, p. 66.

(b) On analysing more closely the various systems of procedural law in Europe,[14] one is struck not only by their diversity but also by the disparate nature of the results obtained with respect to the three vital questions which must precede any litigation:

(1) What will it cost?

(2) How long will it take to complete?

(3) What benefit will I get from it or what will I be required to pay in the way of compensation?[15]

Cost, duration and inefficiency form the 'three-headed hydra' to which Sir Jack Jacob refers in connection with present-day court proceedings.[16]

We could reply to these questions by providing detailed analyses of the various procedural systems in operation. However, this is not a comparative dissertation.

Since the cost of litigation is the most sensitive area from an economic standpoint and since, moreover, it lends itself best to a comparative analysis, we set out below the most striking differences:

a   Interest fixed by the court ranges from 4% (Germany) to 34% (Greece).

b   Legal aid is available to those whose incomes falls below a threshold which varies from 3,800 ECU (England and Wales) to approximately 22,000 ECU (Denmark).

c   The remuneration to which lawyers are entitled (lawyers' fees) is laid down by statute (Germany), assessed by the courts (England and Wales) or left to the reasonable discretion of the lawyers themselves.

d   In some countries it is the client who has to pay either the major part (Belgium) or the full amount (Luxembourg) of the lawyer's remuneration, whereas in others it is the losing party who has to bear either the major part (England and Wales: 'if proper and necessary') or the full amount of such remuneration.

e   In most EC countries, the 'contingency-fee system' is prohibited, although in some of them a debate is in progress on this issue; this system is, however, authorized in exceptional cases (Germany, The Netherlands) or permitted up to a certain percentage (Greece, where the relevant proportion is 20%).

f   Court costs vary considerably from country to country; they are determined on either a flat-rate or a percentage basis.

Anyone who peruses only this — moreover, very brief — overview will be forced to admit that serious differences (Article 101 of the EEC Treaty) exist in European procedural law. They have the effect of distorting conditions of competition.

---

14   Actually, there are 14 such systems, when account is taken of the marked procedural differences between England and Scotland and the minor differences between England and Northern Ireland.

15   See in this connection the study commissioned from a number of European law firms by the Tokyo Marine and Fire Insurance Company: Loudou, 1991.

16   Jacob, J., Justice between man and man, in: *Current legal problems*, 1985, 211 ff, spec. 226.

Such inequality of access to the courts not only results in wrongful discrimination but will also encourage firms, under the expert guidance of their legal advisers, to engage in forum shopping, and therefore also in market shopping.

Thus any foreign firm — whether or not European — will give its preference to trading with or investing in a country whose system of procedural law offers greater advantages in terms of time, cost and efficiency than those of other countries.

2.2.2.2 The European System of Law and the Techniques Specific to Community Law Similarly Call for Unification of Procedural Law

a   The preliminary ruling procedure (Article 177 of the EEC Treaty) already demonstrated the extent to which this procedure differs from Member State to Member State in terms of structure, treatment and implications.

b   No legal system can afford to tolerate internal disparities in procedural law. This applies a fortiori to the European Community.

Three examples can be adduced to illustrate this point: proceedings *in absentia*, orders for payment and the consequences of forming appeal.

A defendant can conduct his/her defence in a number of ways. However, he/she must realize that if he/she chooses not to put forward any defence, the decision will be awarded against him/her. In some countries this will be by means of proceedings *in absentia*; in others, subject to certain conditions, the case will be dealt with by proceedings with full hearing on both sides.[17]

In Belgium, appeal proceedings suspend the enforcement of the decision appealed against unless it is provisionally enforceable.

In England and Wales, an appeal does not operate automatically as a stay of execution, but a stay can be granted by the court.

It is therefore quite conceivable for one and the same creditor to be faced with different rules on proceedings *in absentia*, payment orders or appeal, depending on the Member State in which the case was brought.

It has already emerged from the foregoing that the differences in the rules relating to costs can also constitute an infringement of the equality of arms principle.

c   The Francovich decision of the European Court of Justice dated 19 November 1991 adds a further dimension to arguments which seek to justify the necessity for harmonization of procedural law.

According to this decision, European citizens will be able to claim compensation from their national authorities on the grounds of failure to implement a European directive or to implement it within the prescribed time-limit.

---

17   The recently introduced Belgian law of 3 August 1992 stipulates that any party who has appeared once and presented his/her pleadings once shall have his/her action settled after a full hearing of both parties, even if he/she failed to appear at a subsequent hearing. On the subject of the marked differences as regards proceedings in absentia, see Kerameus, K., *o.c.*, p. 63-64.

This means that where the directive in question contemplated the creation of a compensation fund for all employees in the event of closure of a firm, equal treatment in all Member States is jeopardized on two counts: one under substantive law and one under procedural law.

The substantive differences in the legal basis and scope of the rules relating to the civil liability of the authorities for their actions could give rise to disparate results; however, this is not our concern for the time being.

Our concern is rather with the manner in which these disputes are brought before and settled by the State courts.

How will a case be brought before a court? Is it possible for the court to deliver a provisional remedy by way of provisional measures? Can the State be ordered to establish a compensation fund subject to payment of a civil penalty? What is the influence of an appeal proceeding?

Are the procedural deadlines the same, and are they calculated on the same basis?

The conclusion is that any national system of procedural law could cause a distortion of the principle of equal — and therefore more or less uniform — access to a civil liability action before the national courts of any of the Member States.

This procedural aspect threatens to strike a severe blow at the authority of the leading decision in the Francovich case.

2.2.2.3 Harmonization of Procedural Law is Becoming a Matter of Urgency on Account of the Impending Danger of Persistent Differentiation

Procedural law is currently in a state of considerable ferment, because throughout the world, but in particular in Europe, efforts are repeatedly being made to achieve better functioning of the judicial machinery.

In most cases, these efforts are following two courses: the traditional course of legislation designed to improve the rules governing procedure; and the most recently developed course, called Alternative Dispute Resolution.

Both trends have resulted in still greater diversity, and therefore Community-wide action in the field of European procedural law is a matter of urgency.[18]

2.2.2.3.1 Ever-increasing Reforms of Procedural Law

The problem is not only that the existing codices are quite disparate. In recent years, a number of EEC countries have carried out reforms which may give rise to still greater distortions.

Belgium was the first country in the second half of the 20th century to break away from the old procedural law — in casu, the French Code de procédure civile,

---

18 Here we have ignored an additional danger, outside the European Community, namely that of fragmentation, in which more and more countries in smaller areas adopt the course of separate bodies of procedural law: small and beautiful procedures!

dating from 1806 — by introducing a *complete* new Judicial Code (1967). Since then, new laws have brought about a number of changes to this Code,[19] the most recent being that of 18 July 1991 concerning the selection and appointment of judicial officers and that of 3 August 1992 concerning the actual proceedings involved.

2.2.2.3.2 Alternative Dispute Resolution

To provide an answer to the vexing problem inherent in the explosive increase in disputes (*litiges*) and lawsuits (*procès*) and the mounting backlog of court cases, recourse is being had on all sides to alternative dispute resolution, i.e. settlement by persons and institutions other than the officially appointed judge.

This, while possibly not a regrettable development in itself, is something to be deplored in the context of European Community law. The point can best be illustrated by taking the optimum form of alternative dispute resolution, namely resolution by arbitrators.

Arbitration proceedings have in fact been marked by a refusal to link up with Community law, in two matters of principle.

On the one hand, it was argued that under the preliminary ruling procedure set out in Article 177 of the EEC Treaty the arbitrator is unable to obtain access to the Court of Justice.[20] On the other hand, it was decided that the EEX Treaty is likewise inapplicable in arbitration proceedings — pursuant to Article 1 of the Treaty — even in cases brought before the officially appointed judge and relating to an arbitration procedure.[21]

What applies to arbitration procedures applies *a fortiori* to all other alternative forms of dispute resolution (mediation, conciliation, rent a judge, etc.).[22]

Thus a great many cases have been excluded from the uniform functioning of European Community law.

This trend can be curbed only if more or less uniform rules of procedure are introduced in Europe which ensure equal and straightforward access to the judge in all Member States.

2.2.3 The Administration of Justice

There is also a need for judicial institutions which work well from a technical standpoint.

---

19   From 1967 to 1982, i.e. over a period of 25 years, nearly 150 amended laws were passed in Belgium. If swift action is not taken to harmonize a number of procedural rules, further separate development of procedural law in the Member States will accentuate the existing differences.

20   CJ, Nordsee, 23 March 1982, C 102/81; for commentary, see Goffin, L., Arbitrage et droit, Liber amicorum A. Fettweis, p. 159 seq.

21   CJ, 25 July 1991, C 190/89 Marco Rich.

22   See Storme, M., 'Contractuele vormen van geschillen-beslechting', in: *De overeenkomst vandaag en morgen*, Antwerpen 1990, 565 seq.

By this is meant that, apart from the specific needs of the internal market citizens in Europe cherish the hope that Community policy will not be confined to Euro-jam and Euro-juice but will also recognize the necessity of a properly functioning 'fabric of justice.'[23]

Confidence in the courts will be a significant factor in the internal market. Citizens must accordingly have the feeling that those in authority will constantly be bending their minds to the pursuit of a harmonizing policy in the field of procedural law.

Now that the full authority of the Court of Justice is being recognized and appreciated, the second stage is obvious: absolute respect by and for all European Community judges through constant heed to European procedural law.

For the sake of completeness, it should be added that unification, although not automatic, can also contribute to the improvement of the national procedural law of each of the Member States.[24]

For instance, it is clear that the uniform introduction of the periodic penalty payment in many of the Member States would be an improvement in the field of enforceability of judgments which do not go so far as to impose payment of a sum of money (enforcement of non-money judgments by way of an 'astreinte').

2.2.4 Procedural Law as the Embodiment of European Values

From time immemorial, European law has been characterized as a set of instruments which can be used to fulfil socio-political aims; needless to say, it can also introduce or stress certain values.

First and foremost, adequate legal protection for the European citizen constitutes a major value as such. When it is considered what a tremendous influence Article 6 of the European Convention on Human Rights (ECHR) (fair trial) has had on the case law of the Council of Europe countries, it can also be readily imagined that, for instance, the value of equal access to justice is a European value *in itself.*

Equal access thus also means increased access, in which efforts are made to abolish all exceptions hampering procedure, which would assuage the lamentations expressed by Lord Devlin:

'Where injustice is to be found is not so much in the cases that come to Court, but in those that are never brought there. The main field of injustice is not litigation but non-litigation, and the prime cause of non-litigation is two-fold: first, the incompleteness and obscurity of the law that prevents or deters action, and secondly, the appalling cost. The two together have turned litigation, which ought to be a gentle solvent of disputes, into a thing of horror.'[25]

---

23   The term has been taken from Sir Jack Jacob, *The Fabric of English Civil Justice*, London 1987.
24   It was Kerameus who underlined the fact that quality does not always go hand in hand with unification; 'unification on the practical level is deprived of any quality aspiration' (*o.c.*, p. 49). I do not subscribe to this far too radical pronouncement.
25   Lord Devlin, 'Who is at Fault when Injustice occurs', in: Michael Zander (ed.), *What's wrong with the law?*, B.B.C. 1970, 72.

Next, an approximation of the rules of procedural law can undoubtedly lead to a common legal culture for Europe. Thus, by way of example, in such a legal culture more value could be attached to decisions under public law than to decisions under private law.

In my opinion what is still more important is the fact that in Europe aims can be pursued which lie beyond the proper administration of justice.

Examples come readily to hand:

1   Adequate protection of the consumer, and of the environment, postulates a European judicial system for dealing with complaints in these sectors. For instance, class action in all Member States would be a particularly valuable instrument.[26]

2   Uniform rules on confidentiality of correspondence between lawyers (barristers and practising consultants) could excercise a salutary influence because that would make it easier to settle disputes amicably.

3   Uniform rules on court costs would be a remarkable achievement. In such a context, cost-free proceedings, to take an example, can be formulated as a principle. Again, the contingency-fee system can be either confirmed or rejected as a common rule. Furthermore, a general rule can be postulated which states that lawyers' fees must be paid by the losing party.

4   Victims of *délits* (more serious offences) in general and traffic accidents in particular would have to be able to obtain compensation for damage in a single concentrated action. This is an action in which the criminal conviction and the award of damages are pronounced at the same time.

From these few examples, it can be seen that new social and/or ethical values can be framed through the medium of uniform procedural law.

The conclusion, then, is that there must be a widening of the scope, at least in Europe, for the 'quest for justice'. Deliberation on and preparation of the way for a harmonized procedural law can provide the necessary impulses.

3 Conclusion

It is apparent that there is a need for a unification, or in any case a harmonising of procedural law in Europe; the only remaining question is how such a unification could be achieved.

---

26   Goyens, M. and Vos, E.I.L., 'Transborder consumer complaints', *European Consumer Law Journal*, 1991, p. 193 et seq.; see also Storme, M., The legal authority of the European Community to intervene in the matter of group actions for consumers and the choice of legal instrumentation, in Group actions and consumers protection, Louvain la Neuve, 1992, p. 179 seq.

My personal conviction is that the unification of the law can generally be realised in several ways: either by legislative intervention (in the form of a treaty, single act, directive) or by case law.[27]

However, the best way of achieving a unification is to combine these two methods. More specifically, for the unification of procedural law the best way is slightly different because the use of legislation is the most appropriate form of legal intervention due to the requirements of legal certainty which is fundamental to procedural law.

This was also the opinion of the working party, over which I had the honour to preside, which in 1988, had been asked to undertake a study of the harmonisation of procedural law within the European internal market and also to prepare for such a harmonisation.

The report of this working group has been submitted to the Commission and also to the Council of Ministers and to the European Parliament.[28] It contains by way of a draft directive proposals for the approximation of procedural law in Europe, especially on the following subjects:

1   Conciliation
2   Commencement of the proceedings
3   Subject matter of litigation
4   Discovery
5   Evidence
6   Technology and proof
7   Discontinuance
8   Default
9   Costs
10 Provisional remedies
11 Order for payment
12 Execution of judgments or orders for the payment of money
13 Astreinte
14 Miscellaneous provisions
     A. Computation of time
     B. Nullities
     C. Rules related to the judge and the judgment

It is my personal belief that there is a very urgent need for approximated procedural laws in Europe especially for the following procedures: astreinte, *Mahnverfahren*, summary proceedings and provisional remedies, computation of time and nullities. It is also my hope that there will be in the near future an initial attempt to experiment with common procedures in the European Union. Neither

---

27   See Storme, M., Lord Mansfield, Portalis of Von Savigny, T.P.R., 1991, 849 seq.; Storme, M., Rechtsvereinheitlichung in Europa, Rabels Z., 1992, 290 seq.
28   This report is published by Kluwer, Antwerp and Martinus Nijhoff. The Hague: Storme, M., (ed.), *The approximation of judiciary law in Europe*.

nationalism nor subsidiarity can stop this unavoidable and absolute trend, which is dictated by the needs of practical life in the internal market.

However, it seems useful to remind ourselves of the basic ways to achieve the unification of procedural law.[29]

1   The diversity of the twelve[30] legal systems of procedural law can be maintained and, where it seems necessary, a properly functioning international procedural law can be extended. This situation already exists in Europe because of the Brussels Convention of 1968.

2   A dual track model can be followed in which a common system is created from transnational conflicts in addition to the national procedural law of every Member State.

This situation exists in the United States and Switzerland.

3   When using a model code, it can be hoped that the quality of the drafting is such that it is incorporated either entirely, or partially, into the national codes. Examples of using model codes can be found in the Codigo-typo-ibero-americano of 1989 and also in the UNICITRAL model law for international arbitration (1985).

4   Attempts can be made to try and find a common framework for some specific procedures, within which these specific procedures can be co-ordinated. This last technique can be applied by means of using a Community Directive.

5   The final way, but this can only be dreamed about, is to create a uniform procedural law which would be identical in every country, although this is currently neither desireable nor feasable.

---

29   See also Stürner, R., 'Das Europaïsche Zivilprozessrecht — Einheit oder Vielvalt?', in *Festschrift F. BAUR*, Tübingen, 1991.
30   Actually 13 or 14 systems (if we include Scotland and Nothern Ireland).

CHAPTER 7

The Sources and Backgrounds of European Legal Systems

Carlos Bollen and Gerard-René de Groot

1 Introductory Remarks

The aim of this chapter is to give some information on the legal systems of European countries, to see which laws in the field of the law of contracts, torts and property could be of influence on a European Civil Code in the future. Moreover this information will be useful since it will complement the other chapters of this book where many references to the legal systems of various European countries have been made.

The remarks in this chapter regard the legal systems in Western and Central Europe. Until recently it was common to divide the European legal systems in five groups, so-called 'legal families'. Many authors distinguished on the continent a) the French legal family, b) the German legal family, c) the Nordic legal family and d) the Socialist legal family. Furthermore, the British Isles and Ireland were described as countries belonging to e) the Anglo-American legal family.[1] However, some authors have stressed that — especially in comparison with the other legal families — there exist so many similarities between the first three mentioned legal families, it would be better to speak about a Romano-Germanic legal family with three sub-families. It goes too far to discuss this difference of opinion in this contribution.[2] After the developments in Eastern Europe in 1989 and 1990 the former socialist legal systems are in a transitory period. Many new statutes influenced by regulations and ideas from other continental European legal systems are gradually enacted in the former socialist countries and in a couple of years they probably will not constitute a separate legal family anymore. In this chapter no remarks will be made about the codifications still in force during the actual transitory period in these countries. It should be underlined as well, that a division of legal systems in legal families mainly has a didactical function. It gives some information about the general orientation of a legal system in a certain field of law.

---

1   See for instance Konrad Zweigert/Hein Kötz (translated by Tony Weir), *An Introduction to Comparative Law*, vol. I, Clarendon Press, Oxford 1987.
2   See for instance Peter de Cruz, *A modern approach to Comparative Law*, Deventer 1993, 27-40.

Even though some remarks will be made about procedural law, this introduction will primarily focus on civil and commercial law.[3] Studying European legal systems in the fields of the law of contracts, torts and property, one should realise that all legal systems are largely influenced by Roman law. These influences are obvious in the continental European systems. Some rules can be traced back to regulations of the Corpus iuris civilis of Emperor Iustinian. But it should also not be forgotten that the English and Irish law have on some points been influenced by the way of thinking of Roman law, mainly caused by the fact that during the middle ages judges often had an ecclesiastical background and were educated in the principles of canonic law, which is largely influenced by principles of Roman law.

One should also bear in mind that the law of the European Communities, in the form of the treaty, council regulations and directives, today plays a large role in the legal systems of the Member States, especially in the area of commercial law. European Community law also indirectly influences the commercial law of non-Member States, since most of these states are members of the European Free Trade Association (EFTA), which has concluded an important treaty with the European Community on this matter, the European Economic Area Treaty.

2 The French Group

2.1 General Remarks

After the French Revolution a committee for the preparation of codifications on several fields of law to be introduced on the whole territory of the French Republic was established. Until that time a strong Roman law orientated system of law was in force in the southern part of modern France (pays de droit écrit), whereas in the northern part many different systems of customary laws with less Roman law influences existed (pays de droit coutumier). The committee prepared three important codes in the field of civil law, which were later enacted: a Civil Code (Code Civil, 1804), a commercial code (Code commercial, 1807) and a code of civil procedure (Code de procedure civile, 1804). The Civil Code was divided in three books: 1) law of persons and family; 2) law of property; 3) law of obligations including the law of inheritance and matrimonial property.

One has to realize, that these codes came into force at the moment that the French Republic, under the leadership of Napoleon, covered an important part of

---

3   Compare for short descriptions of the procedural laws of the member states of the EC: Maurice Sheridan/James Cameron (ed.), *EC legal systems; an introductory guide*, Butterworths, London 1992.

Western Europe. Therefore, these codes were immediately enforced on the territory of Belgium, Luxembourg, the southern part of the Netherlands and parts of Germany as well. In other countries of Western Europe, under the influence of France, similar codes were introduced, for example the Civil Code for the Kingdom of the Netherlands which was enacted during the reign of King Louis-Napoleon, a brother of the French Emperor.

After the decline of the French empire in 1814, the codes of the Napoleonic area stayed in force in France, but partly also in countries which formerly belonged to France or were under French influence. This was caused by the fact that it was quite generally accepted that it was valuable to have some central codifications on the most important fields of law instead of different local laws, which existed before in most European countries.

2.2 France[4]

After the liberation of France in 1945 the Civil Code of 1804 was so out of date that a revision was necessary. A commission to revise the code was established, but this was dissolved in 1958 when the Gaullist Fifth Republic was realized. It was decided that the existing code was not to be replaced by a new one and instead it was decided it should be updated to meet the requirements of the modern times. The area of family law, in particular, underwent considerable change, the major reforms being the matrimonial regimes acts from 1965 and 1985 (Loi du 13 juillet 1965 et 23 décembre 1985 sur les régimes matrimoniaux), the Filiation Act from 1972 (Loi du 3 janvier 1972 sur la filiation) and the divorce act 1975 (Loi du 11 juillet 1975 sur le divorce). These acts have all been incorporated in the Civil Code. In 1975 the code de procédure civile has been replaced by the nouveau code de procédure civile (new code of civil procedure) but some provisions of the old code remained in force since the new code was not, and still is not, completed. This has led to the situation that two codes of civil procedure exist side by side. The commercial code from 1807 still exists but it has been eroded since its main regulations have been replaced by special acts. From the original 648 sections only 140 still remain. In the fields of trading companies, commercial registers, seaborne trade, bankruptcy and the procedure before the Court of Appeal, the code has been substituted by specific acts.

---

4   Xavier Blanc-Jouvan/Jean Boulouis, France, in: *International Encyclopedia of Comparative Law*, Volume I (June 1972); Alfred Rieg, Frankrijk, in D. Kokkini-Iatridou, *Een inleiding tot het rechtsvergelijkende onderzoek*, Kluwer, Deventer 1988, 311-349; Martin Weston, *An English reader's guide to the French legal system*, Berg Publishers, Oxford 1991; Andrew West/Yvon Desdevises/Alain Feet/Dominique Gaurier/Marie-Clet Heussaff, *The French legal system: an introduction*, Fourmat Publishers, London 1992.

2.3 Belgium[5]

At the Congress of Vienna in 1815 the territory of Belgium and the territory of the former Republic of the United Netherlands were united as the Kingdom of the Netherlands. In the new kingdom the preparations for new independent codifications after the French model started, but before these new codes came into force the territory of Belgium was separated from the Netherlands after a revolt in the year 1830 and the Kingdom of Belgium was created. The Napoleonic codes remained in force. During the nineteenth and twentieth century these codes were modified on many points, mainly to adapt the regulations to the changing patterns of social life. Nevertheless, many of the core articles on the law of obligations and property still have the original text of the French Code Civil. Belgian court decisions and doctrine are still evidently influenced by French developments. Until 1961 only the French text of the Civil Code was authentic, since then the Dutch translation (Burgerlijk Wetboek) has authentic value as well. There still is a distinction between civil and commercial law in Belgium. Commercial law is mainly regulated by the Code de commerce (Wetboek van koophandel). This code is also still the Napoleonic one from 1807 but it has been revised in all its sections. From the original text almost nothing has remained in the contemporary version. The code on civil procedure was replaced by a new Code judiciaire (Gerechtelijk Wetboek) in 1967.

2.4 Italy[6]

In parts of Italy, the Napoleonic codes were introduced during the French rule at the beginning of the past century. After the fall of Napoleon these codes were repealed again. One has to recall, that in these days several independent states existed within the territory of modern Italy. Some of these states introduced codes after the French model in the first part of the nineteenth century. Immediately after the unification of Italy in 1861 uniform codes were enacted (Codice civile (Civil Code) 1865, commercial code 1865, code of civil procedure 1865). These codes were only partly translated copies of the French ones. In 1882 the commercial code was replaced by a new one. In the nineteen twenties a Franco-Italian committee began to draft provisions in the field of the law of obligations and contracts. The aim of this committee was to enact

---

5   Jan Limpens/Guy Schrans, Belgium, in: *International Encyclopedia of Comparative Law*, Volume I (December 1972); Hans van Houtte, Belgie, in D. Kokkini-Iatridou, *Een inleiding tot het rechtsvergelijkende onderzoek*, Kluwer, Deventer 1988, 212-220.

6   Mauro Cappelletti/Pietro Rescigno, Italy, in: *International Encyclopedia of Comparative Law*, Volume I (January 1972); Roberto Sacco, Italië, in: D. Kokkini-Iatridou, *Een inleiding tot het rechtsvergelijkende onderzoek*, Kluwer, Deventer 1988, 393-403; Mauro Cappelletti/John Henry Merryman/Joseph M. Perillo, *The Italian legal system: an introduction*, Stanford University Press, Stanford California 1967; G. Leroy Certoma, *The Italian legal system*, Butterworths, London 1985.

uniform law of contracts in both countries. This project was not realised, although this was in part due to the political developments in Italy. A whole new Italian Civil Code, which was partly based on the proposals of this committee, was drafted and enacted in 1942. The 'French' tradition is still manifest in regard to many regulations in this code, but on several points the solutions of the code were influenced by provisions and theories from other European countries, especially by regulations of the German and Swiss Civil Code and the Swiss code of obligations. An important feature of the Italian Civil Code is the fact that civil and commercial law are integrated in one single code. Italy does not have a separate commercial code anymore. The Civil Code contains six books, namely: persons and family, succession, property, obligations, labour, and the protection of rights. The Italian Civil Code of 1942 was modified several times (especially in 1944/1945 after the liberation of Italy) but it is still in force. The rules on civil procedure are given by the code on civil procedure of 1942 which replaced the previous codification on procedural law.

2.5 Luxembourg[7]

The Grand Duchy of Luxembourg was created at the Vienna Congress of 1815. The first Grand Dukes of Luxembourg were the Kings of the Netherlands of the House of Orange-Nassau. However, the legislation of the Netherlands was not enforced in Luxembourg and the Napoleonic legislation stayed in force even after the Netherlands introduced new codes in the field of civil law on its own territory in 1838. In 1890 after the death of King William III of the Netherlands, the personal union with the Netherlands ended. From that time onwards the Grand Dukes descended from another branch of the House of Nassau. Luxembourg never realised new codifications in the field of private law, but many smaller modifications of the codes were enacted. Nevertheless the main part of the codes still contain the original text of the Napoleonic times. The modifications of the codes were generally inspired by legislative precedents in France or Belgium. In this context one should recall that Belgium is also strongly influenced by French legal models.

---

7   Pierre Pescatore, Luxembourg, in: *International Encyclopedia of Comparative Law*, Volume I
     (March 1973).

2.6 Netherlands[8]

Since the southern provinces of the Netherlands were part of the French empire in this period, the Napoleonic legislation came into force in 1804 in these provinces. The northern provinces of the country constituted the Kingdom of Holland from 1806 to 1810 under King Louis-Napoleon. In this kingdom codes following the French model were introduced. A Civil Code (Wetboek Napoleon voor het Koningrijk Holland) came into force in 1809. In 1810 the whole territory of the modern Netherlands became part of the French empire and in 1812 the French codes came into force in the whole country. These codes remained provisionally in force with minor modifications in the Kingdom of the Netherlands (created at the Congress of Vienna) until separate codifications were enacted. On the field of private law the new Dutch codes were introduced on 1 October 1838 (Burgerlijk Wetboek (Civil Code), Wetboek van Koophandel (commercial code) and Wetboek van Burgerlijke Rechtsvordering (code of civil procedure)). The structure of the Civil Code differed from the French Code Civil, although many of the provisions were mere translations of the French original. Only in some matters the codes followed its own, more traditional Dutch solutions, like in the field of matrimonial property law and the law regarding the transfer of ownership. After an unsuccesful attempt in the nineteenth century, a project to recodify private law was started in 1947. In that year Professor Meijers was entrusted with the official task to make a draft for a new Civil Code. In 1970 the first book of this new code (on the law of persons and family) came into force, followed by a second book on the law of legal entities in 1976. In 1991 book 8 on the law of transport was put into force. Finally the core of the new code (book 3: general part of patrimonial law; book 5: law of property; book 6: law of obligations; parts of book 7: specific contracts) came into force on 1 January 1992. Book 4 (law of succession) and the other parts of book 7 will follow in the near future. Many provisions of this code still show the descendence of the French tradition, but on various points influences from other traditions are obvious. The code was prepared after

---

8   Arthur S. Hartkamp, Civil Code revision in the Netherlands 1947-1992/ La révision du code civil aux Pays Bas 1947-1992, in: P.P.C. Haanappel/ Ejan Mackaay, *Nieuw Nederlands Burgerlijk Wetboek/ Het Vermogensrecht* (New Netherlands Civil Code/ Patrimonial Law; Nouveau Code Civil Néerlandais/ Le Droit Patrimonial), Kluwer, Deventer 1990, XIII-XLVI; J.M.J. Chorus/ P.H.M. Gerver/ E.H. Hondius/ A.K. Koekkoek (ed.), *Introduction to Dutch Law for Foreign Lawyers*, Kluwer, Deventer 1993; Jan M. Hebly, *The Netherlands Civil Evidence Act 1988 and related provisions of the Netherlands Law of Evidence*, Kluwer, Deventer 1992; Elena Ioriatti, *Il nuovo codice civile dei Paesi Bassi, fra soluzioni originali e circulazione dei modelli*, Trento 1991; Thijmen Koopmans, Netherlands, in: *International Encyclopedia of Comparative Law*, Volume I (December 1971); Steven R. Schuit/ Marcel Romijn/ Gerrit H. Zevenboom, *Dutch Business Law, Legal, Accounting and Tax Aspects of Doing Business in The Netherlands*, Kluwer, Deventer, loose-leaf; H.C.S. Warendorf/ R.L. Thomas, *Companies and other legal persons under Netherlands Law and Netherlands Antilles Law*, Kluwer, Deventer, loose-leaf.

thorough comparative research and the Swiss, Italian and German codes, in particular, influenced the solutions chosen by the legislator in the Netherlands. On certain topics even Anglo-American theories influenced it. Like the Italian Civil Code the new code of the Netherlands integrates civil and commercial law. When all parts of the new code are in force the commercial code will be abolished.

2.7 Portugal

Portugal introduced a commercial code in the French tradition in 1833, which was totally revised in 1888 and strongly influenced by the Italian and Spanish commercial codes. In 1867 a Civil Code prepared by Professor Seabra of Coimbra University came into force. This code was on many points influenced by the French one, but the style and structure were different. The Portuguese code was more academic and contained many abstract definitions. In 1967 a new Civil Code was enacted, again in the French tradition, but also influenced by the German, Italian and Swiss codifications. Portugal maintained the division of civil law in two separate codes: the civil and the commercial code. In this sense the Portuguese code is very traditional. The structure of the Civil Code follows the German code, including the choice to start with a General Part. The code has been modified several times since 1967. The most drastic change took place in 1977 after democracy had been restored in Portugal. The content of the code was brought into agreement with the new constitution, while the opportunity was utilized to adjust the text of the code on many other places as well.

2.8 Spain[9]

Codes in the Napoleonic tradition were introduced during the rule of Joseph, a brother of Napoleon. After his decline these codes were abolished again. Nevertheless Spain tried to realise new codifications in the French style during the nineteenth century. A commercial code came into force in 1829 and was modernised in 1885. But Spain did not succeed in introducing an own Civil Code until 1889. In that year the Codigo civil of 1888 came into force. This code, which is still in force, is highly influenced by the French Civil Code. An important characteristic of the Spanish system is the fact, that next to the Civil Code some parts of the country have their own regulations in the field of civil

---

9   Diego Espin Canovas/Justino Duque Dominguez, Spain, in: *International Encyclopedia of Comparative Law*, Volume I (December 1986); Vincente L. Simo Santonia, Spanje, in: D. Kokkini-Iatridou, *Een inleiding tot het rechtsvergelijkende onderzoek*, Kluwer, Deventer 1988, 512-530; Thomas W. Palmer Jr, *Guide to the law and literature of Spain*, Hyperion Press, Westport Connecticut 1979.

law, the so-called derechos forales (compilation of local customary laws). Therefore, Spain has a pluralistic system of civil law.

Civil procedure is regulated by the Ley de enjuiciamiento civil (Code of Civil Procedure) of 1881.

3 The German Group

3.1 General Remarks

The reception of Roman law which has taken place since the Middle Ages had an important influence on the legal systems which belong to the German group. This was caused by the fact that there did not exist a central power; local landlords and cities held most of the power. Even though there was an emperor, the court was not fixed in one place, it moved from town to town. Contrary to the situation in for instance France or England, no centre where lawyers and legal academics were educated was developed. Due to this situation the easiest way to develop an own legal system was to update Roman law. Furthermore, the German emperors considered themselves as direct successors of the Roman emperors (compare the German expression: Römisches Reich deutscher Nation). Especially in Germany the so-called Pandectists tried to elaborate a scientific system of private law based on the principles of the Digestae (or Pandects) of the 'corpus iuris civilis' of the Roman-Byzantian emperor Iustinian. This school tried to transform the old Roman law into a contemporary legal system. A good example of these attempts was the important treatise of Friedrich Carl von Savigny on the system of modern Roman law ('System des heutigen römischen Rechts') published since 1840. In particular this treatise and the works of Puchta and Windscheid influenced the content of the legal systems of the German group and the commentaries written on the Civil Codes, which continue the tradition of the Pandectists. The consequence of this tradition is that the codes of the German group are much more systematic than the codification within other groups. Moreover, the 'general principles' play a considerably more important role.

3.2 Germany[10]

Before 1870 Germany did not exist as one state, and several independent states existed on the territory of Germany. Some of these states had Civil Codes in the

---

10 Dieter Medicus, Federal Republic of Germany, in: *International Encyclopedia of Comparative Law*, Volume I (December 1972); Ulrich Drobnig, Bondsrepubliek Duitsland, in: D. Kokkini-Iatridou, *Een inleiding tot het rechtsvergelijkende onderzoek*, Kluwer, Deventer 1988, 221-237.

French tradition (Baden; Rhineland), others knew codifications of another older tradition like Prussia (Allgemeines Landrecht 1794; General Land Law) or Bavaria (Codex Maximilianus Bavaricus 1756), again other states had no codification and the recepted Roman law was applied next to local statutes (usus modernus pandectarum). In the beginning of the past century there has been a discussion on the advantages and disadvantages of a codification of private law for the whole territory of Germany (Thibault and Von Savigny). Uniform Commercial Code (Allgemeines Deutsches Handelsgesetzbuch) was already created in 1861, before the establishment of the German empire in 1870. This code was replaced by a new one on 1 January 1900. In 1877 a Code on Civil Procedure (Zivilprozessordnung) and a law on bankruptcy (Konkursordnung) were put into force, followed by a Civil Code (Bürgerliches Gesetzbuch) on 1 January 1900. This code was highly influenced by the recepted Roman law.

After the decline of the German empire in 1918 the Civil Code remained in force during the period of the Weimar republic and the subsequent Third Reich. After the Second World War two separate German states arose on the territory of Germany, the Federal Republic of Germany and the German Democratic Republic. The Civil Code remained in force in both states, until an independent Zivilgesetzbuch was enacted in the German Democratic Republic in 1975, which came into force on 1 January 1976. After the reunification of Germany in 1990 the Civil Code came into force on the whole territory again.

A special feature of the German Civil Code is the fact that it has a 'General part' as first book, giving rules applicable on the matters regulated by all following books. The structure of the Bürgerliches Gesetzbuch is definitely more systematic than the structure of the French Code Civil. It is not surprising, that many commentaries in Germany follow the order of the articles of the Civil Code. In France this would be impossible from systematic point of view.

3.3 Austria[11]

The Civil Code of Austria (Allgemeines Bürgerliches Gesetzbuch; General Civil Code) came into force on 1 January 1812 and therefore it belongs to the oldest codes still in force in Europe. The preparation of the code began in 1753 with the appointment of a committee, by Empress Maria Theresia, given the task to draft a Civil Code. The committee had to compile existing law and fill in the gaps according to 'right reason'. A first draft (known as the Codex Theresianus) was presented to the empress in 1767, but was rejected because it contained too many provisions and it stayed too close to Roman law. Therefore a new draft

---

11   Fritz Schwind/Herbert Zemen, Austria, in: *International Encyclopedia of Comparative Law*, Volume I (October 1971).

had to be prepared. In 1786 a draft statute on the law of persons and family was presented to Emperor Joseph II and it was enacted with minor modifications in 1787 as Josephinisches Gesetzbuch. In 1790 Emperor Leopold II appointed a new committee under supervision of Von Martini who were to process the other parts of the Codex Theresianus. In 1796 this committee presented a draft (known as the Martini draft) which was put into force in Galicia in 1797 as an experiment. Based on the Martini draft and the experiences in Galicia a new committee under the leadership of Von Zeiller adopted the final text of the code. The new Civil Code came into force on 1 January 1812. It was slightly influenced by the code of Prussia; the French Civil Code did not influence the regulations of the Austrian code. The code is mainly based on principles of Roman law with strong influences from natural law doctrine. Although the Austrian code is much older than the German, Austria is generally included in the countries with a 'German' tradition. The reason for this is the fact that German doctrine influenced the interpretation of the Austrian code on many points. This is caused by the intensive exchange of academic scholars between Austria and Germany. Many Austrian specialists on private law were teaching in Germany and vice versa. Since 1900 many revisions of the Austrian Civil Code were influenced by German models, especially the important revisions of the code during the years 1914, 1915 and 1916. From 1938 until 1945 Austria was a part of Germany, but the Austrian Allgemeines Bürgerliches Gesetzbuch stayed in force. During this period the German Commercial Code (Handelsgesetzbuch) was put into force in Austria and it remained in force after the new independance in 1945.

3.4 Greece[12]

Even during the time of the Turkish domination Roman-Byzantinian law was applicable in Greece. This situation was maintained after the country became independent in the beginning of the nineteenth century. During that century several statutes, influenced by Austrian, French and German law, were enacted. Gradually, the German school of Pandectists gained influence in Greece, partly caused by the fact that a Bavarian prince became king of Greece. Since the first half of the nineteenth century committees were working on the preparation of a new Civil Code. A draft was published in 1878, but never enacted. A text of a Civil Code was not promulgated until 1940, which came into force on 23 February 1946. The Greek Civil Code has a Roman-Byzantinian basis and is largely influenced by the German code, whose structure it follows. It takes into account many rules given by German courts based on the German Civil Code.

---

12 Charalambos Fragistas, Greece, in: *International Encyclopedia of Comparative Law*, Volume I (February 1976); Konstantinos D. Kerameus, Griekenland, in: D. Kokkini-Iatridou, *Een inleiding tot het rechtsvergelijkende onderzoek*, Kluwer, Deventer 1988, 350-364; Konstantinos D. Kerameus/ Phaedon J. Kozyris (ed.), *Introduction to Greek Law*, Kluwer, Deventer 1988.

Furthermore, some provisions are inspired by the Swiss, French and Italian codes. Commercial law is regulated by a Commercial Code which is an official translation of the French commercial code of 1807. The translation was published in 1835 but it has since been modified by many enacted statutes. The rules regarding civil procedure are laid down in a Code of Civil procedure, which came into force on 16 September 1968.

3.5 Switzerland[13]

In the nineteenth century almost all of the Swiss cantons introduced their own codes in the field of private law. Some cantons followed the model of the French Code Civil, others were inspired by the Austrian Civil Code, again others were influenced by the German school of Pandectists. In 1881, a federal code of obligations (Obligationenrecht) was enacted. This unification was made possible by the enactment of the Federal Constitution of 1874, which allowed federal legislation in all legal matters related to commerce and movables. After an amendment of the constitution, allowing federal legislation on all of the other matters of civil law as well, a Civil Code (Zivilgesetzbuch, which covers the law on persons and family, the law of succession and the law of property) was enacted in 1907. It was put into force in 1912. The time between the enactment and coming into force of the new Civil Code was utilized to carry out a partial revision of the code of obligations of 1881 (first and second divisions (General part and Specific contracts), Art. 1-551), which became the fifth part of the Civil Code. The provisions of this fifth book remained numbered separately. Another important revision of the code of obligations took place in 1936, when the third division (Commercial Companies and Co-operatives) of this code was revised. Switzerland does not know a real distinction between civil and commercial law, it does not have a separate commercial code. The code of obligations covers many topics which are regulated in the commercial codes in several other continental European countries. The Swiss Civil Code was mainly the work of one single man, Eugen Huber, who based his draft, inter alia, on his comprehensive comparative study of the civil laws of the cantons.[14] The rules on civil procedure are mainly given on the level of the cantons, only in cases directly brought before the Federal Tribunal the procedural law is regulated on federal level.

All Swiss legislation is published in three of the national languages of Switzerland: German, French and Italian.

---

13   Walter Stoffel, Switserland, in: *International Encyclopedia of Comparative Law*, Volume I (March 1987); Fritz Sturm, Zwitserland, in: D. Kokkini-Iatridou, *Een inleiding tot het rechtsvergelijkende onderzoek*, Kluwer, Deventer 1988, 642-656.
14   Eugen Huber, *System und Geschichte des Schweizerischen Privatrechts, 1886-1889.*

4 Nordic Countries

4.1 General Remarks

An important number of similarities exist between the legal systems of the Nordic countries. In the first place the general impact of Roman law was less than in other parts of the European continent. In the second place similarities are caused by the fact that there were quite a lot of political unions between the Scandinavian countries in the past. Through the Union of Kalmar in 1397, the Nordic kingdoms were united under Danish domination: Queen Margareta of Denmark, who was already Queen of Norway and the Norwegian dependencies of Iceland and Greenland since 1380, became the Queen of Sweden (including the territory of Finland, which was occupied by the Swedish in the twelfth century) as well. In 1523 Sweden (with Finland) reacquired independence (under the House Wasa). At the peace together conference of Frederikshamm (1809) Sweden had to cede Finland to the Russian empire. Finland got the status of a Russian Grand Duchy with considerable autonomy in legal affairs. After the Russian October Revolution Finland declared its independence in 1917. At the peace treaty of Kiel in 1814 Denmark had to cede all its rights on Norway to Sweden, but it did not give up its rights to the old Norwegian dependencies of Iceland, the Faroes and Greenland. Within the Swedish kingdom Norway had a certain autonomy and in 1905 Norway obtained independence. Last but not least, similarities are caused by a close co-operation in legislation between the Nordic countries. This co-operation started with 'de nordiska juristmotene' (Congress of Nordic lawyers), which met for the first time in 1872 and which has met then every three years from then. On the initiative of this association, several co-ordinated statutes were enacted in the Nordic countries, in the beginning mainly in the field of commercial law, later in the field of contracts and family as well. In 1953 a Nordiska Rad (Nordic Council) was founded with the goal to develop new initiatives on the field of legislative co-ordination and supervision on the implementation of co-ordinated legislation by the governments of the Nordic countries. An important legal basis for this co-operation is an Agreement between Finland, Denmark, Iceland, Norway and Sweden Concerning Co-operation, signed at Helsinki on 23 March 1962.[15] The legal co-operation between the Nordic countries is facilitated by the fact that the Scandinavian languages are closely related. An exception is of course Finnish, but the legal system of Finland is bilingual Finnish-Swedish.

---

15   434 UNTS 182-197 for the English and French texts of this agreement.

4.2 Denmark[16]

In 1683 King Christian V brought into force a comprehensive code for the whole of Denmark, the so-called Danske Lov (Danish Law). This code covered the entire private, criminal and procedural law and abolished all previous legislation. It was very casuistic and contained very few general principles. The Danske Lov was never totally repealed, but only few of the original provisions are still in force, like the regulations on vicarious liability. Nowadays, important parts of Danish private law are mainly case law. Furthermore, statutes prepared by inter-Nordic committees play an important role. Important statutes on the area of private law are the Tinglysningsloven (Land Registration Act) of 31 March 1926, the Lov om aftaler og andre retshandler på formuerettens område (Law on Contracts and other transactions within the field of property law) of 8 May 1917 and the Kobeloven (Sale of Goods Act) of 6 April 1906.

Commercial law is not regarded as a separate branch of the law. The principles of judicial procedure in civil matters are regulated by the Retplejelov (law on civil procedure) of 11 April 1916.

4.3 Finland[17]

Finland was part of Sweden from the beginning of the thirteenth century until the beginning of the nineteenth century. From 1809 until 1917 it was an autonomous Grand Duchy within the Russian empire. Finland's legal system has been greatly influenced by Swedish law, especially by the Sveriges Rikes Lag (Swedish General Code) of 1734. This code covered both private, criminal and procedural law. It did not cover all of the law on these areas but only those parts which were considered suitable for legislative action, so it was very pragmatic. Certain parts of the code are still in force in Finland, like the chapter on succession, which was totally revised in 1965, and the chapter on procedure. The main part, however, has been repealed and replaced by legislation prepared by the inter-Nordic committees, especially on the field of private and commercial law, like the laws on marriage (1929), contracts (1929), instruments of debt (1947), conditional sales (1966) and patents (1967).

---

16 Mogens Koktvedgaard, Denmark, in: *International Encyclopedia of Comparative Law*, Volume I (March 1972); Torben Svenné Schmidt, Denemarken, in: D. Kokkini-Iatridou, *Een inleiding tot het rechtsvergelijkende onderzoek*, Kluwer, Deventer 1988, 247-255.

17 Heikki Jokela, Finland, in: *International Encyclopedia of Comparative Law*, Volume I (December 1972); Tore Modeen, Finland, in: D. Kokkini-Iatridou, *Een inleiding tot het rechtsvergelijkende onderzoek*, Kluwer, Deventer 1988, 303-310.

4.4 Iceland[18]

Iceland was settled in the ninth century by the Nordic Vikings. In 1262 the Icelanders swore allegiance to the King of Norway. Iceland came, together with Norway, under Danish domination in 1380. At the Treaty of Kiel in 1814, Denmark had to cede Norway to Sweden, but it was explicitly decided that Iceland, Greenland and the Faroe Islands remained under the Danish crown. In 1918 Iceland became a completely independent state, united with Denmark solely by the monarchy and a common foreign policy. When the Germans occupied Denmark in 1940, the Islandic government took over all functions, including those previously conducted by the king or the Danish foreign office. In 1944 the Republic of Iceland was proclaimed.

Iceland always had its own laws. Norwegian and Danish law was never directly enforced in Iceland but it enjoyed considerable influence, especially in the eighteenth and nineteenth centuries. The separate identity of Islandic law was underlined in 1874 when the Islandic parliament (Althing) got legislative power in internal affairs. An independent law school was established in 1908. Nevertheless Islandic laws are closely related to the laws of other Nordic countries. Many statutes on the field of private law have been drafted by inter-Nordic committees and then enacted in the Nordic countries with minor modifications. Especially in the field of property and obligations Islandic law is very simular to Danish and Norwegian law. Differences exist regarding the land registration, mortgages and the ownership of real estate. The Icelandic statute on contracts (7/1936) is almost literally identical to the Danish statute of 1917, and the Sale of Goods Act (39/1922) is practically the same as the Danish statute of 1906.

Commercial law is considered to be an integral part of private law. Procedural law is regulated by an Act of 1936 and follows the example of the Danish law on civil procedure.

4.5 Norway[19]

Since the Kalmar Union (1397) Norway remained in a union (ultimately as a province) with Denmark until 1814. It is therefore not surprising that the Danish code of 1683 (Danske Lov) was brought into force in Norway in 1687 as Norske Lov (Norwegian Law). It has been modified innumerable times since

---

18 Thór Vilhjálmsson, Iceland, in: *International Encyclopedia of Comparative Law*, Volume I (December 1972).

19 Peter Lodrup, Norway, in: *International Encyclopedia of Comparative Law*, Volume I (May 1972); C.C.A. Voskuil, Noorwegen, in: D. Kokkini-Iatridou, *Een inleiding tot het rechtsvergelijkende onderzoek*, Kluwer, Deventer 1988, 454-480.

then. Norway does not make a distinction between civil law and commercial law, the latter is an integrated part of private law. In the field of private law many statutes are prepared by inter-Nordic committees. Therefore, many similarities exist with statutes in other Nordic countries. An important feature of Norwegian law is its anti-conceptualistic character: few terms and concepts are of a general nature or application. In the field of private law some statutes should be mentioned explicitly: the statute on the sale of goods of 1907, the statute on contracts of 1918 and the statute on tort claims of 1969. The rules on civil procedure are regulated by a statute of 1915.

4.6 Sweden[20]

During the fourteenth century, the law in Sweden was unified in two different codes: the Stadslag for the towns and the Landlag for the rest of the country. These medieval codes were not directly influenced by Roman law, but the influence of Canonic law was obvious. In 1734 a codification for the whole country was realised, known as Sveriges Rikes Lag (Swedish general code). This code covered all legal fields, including private law, criminal law and the law of procedure. It was casuistic and not very systematic. It contained nine books, known as *balkar*. Since its enactment Sveriges Rikes Lag was modified innumerable times. Only few provisions of the original text are still in force, but the formal framework of the code and its structure still exist. Many *balkar* are replaced by new statutes, also called *balkar*. Several of these *balkar* are the result of Nordic co-operation in legal affairs. But also outside of the framework of Sveriges Rikes Lag many statutes regulate private law matters. Important *balkar* and other statutes are: the Jordabalk (law on immovables) of 1970, the Avtalslag (Law of Contracts) of 1915, the Köplag (Sale of Goods Act) of 1905, the Skuldebrevslagen (Law on Promissory Notes) of 1936 and the Skadeståndslag (law on the compensation for damages) of 1972. Commercial law is not regarded as a separate discipline, a special commercial code does not exist. The principles of civil procedure are regulated by the Rätgångbalk (procedural code) of 1942.

---

20 Åke Malmström, Sweden, in: *International Encyclopedia of Comparative Law*, Volume I (June 1983); Michael Bogdan, Zweden, in: D. Kokkini-Iatridou, *Een inleiding tot het rechtsvergelijkende onderzoek*, Kluwer, Deventer 1988, 635-641; Stig Strömholm (ed.), *An introduction to Swedish law*, Norstedts Förlag, Stockholm 1988.

5 The Anglo-American Group

5.1 General Remarks[21]

The countries belonging to this family are the countries with a Common Law system, as opposed to the countries belonging to the Civil Law system, which contains all legal systems based on Roman law. The distinction between common law and civil law can also be summarized by the distinction between judge made law and statute law. Generally speaking these distinctions are correct but one has to bear in mind that they tend to be too rigid since the common law has indirectly been influenced by Roman law. Furthermore, there is a tendency in these countries to codify certain areas of law.

The origins of the common law can be dated back to the Battle of Hastings (1066), when the Normans under the leadership of William Duke of Normandy conquered England. From this period on the administration of law, previously in the hands of local sheriffs, became centralised in the king and his court. Former customary law, which varied from district to district, was gradually replaced by the common law as developed by the king's court (Curia regis) from which later special courts derived: the Court of Exchequer, primarily entrusted with tax cases, the court of King's Bench, dealing with cases in which interests of the Crown were involved and the court of Common Pleas, dealing with disputes between civilians. The administration of law was very casuistic. This led to a strong emphasis on procedures; if there ought to be a remedy in a specific case, there ought to be a right. A procedure could only be started if a so-called writ was issued, a kind of summons issued by the king or his Chancellor on the request of the plaintiff. From the end of the twelfth century the writs became standardized and for each type of action a writ was developed, like the writ of trespass, debt or right. All these writs were collected in the Register of Writs. Each writ embodied a particular form of action, a sort of scenario for the trial. If the plaintiff chose the wrong writ he lost the case. If no appropriate writ was available one could petition the king to issue an action. These petitions were frequently dealt with by the king's Chancellor, who was his main advisor and 'keeper of the King's conscience'. Gradually this resulted in a Chancery Court with a separate jurisdiction from and complementary to the common law courts. Thus two separate legal systems developed side by side, the common law and equity. One important distinction between them is that in the common law system personal circumstances and personal behaviour do not play a role, the judge can only decide on the basis of facts, while in equity the Chancellor has

---

21 Kenneth R. Simmonds, United Kingdom, in: *International Encyclopedia of Comparative Law*, Volume I (January 1975); Edgar Bodenheimer/John Bilyeu Oakley/Jean C. Love, *An introduction to the Anglo-American legal system*, West Publishing co., St. Paul, Minnesota 1980; J.H. Baker, *An introduction to English legal history*, Butterworths, 1990.

to decide upon personal circumstances and natural equity (fairness). This led to the development of two different kind of remedies, the common law remedies and the equitable remedies. The rules of common law and equity developed independently from each other in different courts. In the beginning of the seventeenth century this led to growing rivalry between these courts, finally resulting in the rule that on the one hand equity follows the law, on the other hand equity prevails; equity only comes into action if a common law verdict is unfair in its specific result, but if a verdict has been given by an equity judge common law judges have to respect it. Due to the inefficiency of the existence of two separate legal systems a reform at the end of the nineteenth century led to the Judicature Acts (1873-1875), in which all existing courts were fused into one Supreme Court of Judicature, consisting of a High Court and a Court of Appeal. This court could apply either system, also since the system of writs had been abolished in 1852 (Common Law Procedure Act). In case of a conflict between the rules of common law and equity, the latter prevails.

Another special feature of the common law system is the doctrine of precedent (stare decisis). All judges are bound by the decisions of the superior courts. Principles arising from earlier cases have to be applied by judges, even if this principle was developed years ago. The superior courts themselves felt bound by their own precedent as well, until in 1966 the Lord Chancellor declared that the House of Lords, the highest court, would not feel bound by its own decisions anymore if it was of the opinion that upholding such decision would not be just. The Court of Appeal, however, remains bound by its own decisions.

In the nineteenth century there was a growing tendency to more legislation, but on the overall view this still was very marginal and judge made law remained the main source of law. Nevertheless, the call for codification remains and is even getting louder, also due to the social changes that have occured over the last hundred years. As a result a Law Commission for England and Wales and one for Scotland were installed in 1965, given the task to keep 'under review all the law... with a view to a systematic development and reform, including in particular the codification of such law, the elimination of anomalies (and) the repeal of unnecessary enactments'.[22] But due to the fact that the legislator does not accept any general rules or broadly described principles only legislation on very specific topics has proved realizable. On the field of the law of obligations three important acts exist, the Sale of Goods Act (1979) which consolidates with some amendments the original Sale of Goods Act (1893), the Supply of Goods and Services Act (1982) and the Unfair Contract Terms Act (1977), a consumer protection act. On the field of family law there has been a lot of codification but this has not been brought together in a systematic code. Nevertheless this

---

22   Law Commission Act 1965 (c.22) s.3, as cited in Kenneth R. Simmonds, United Kingdom, in: *International Encyclopedia of Comparative Law*, Volume I (January 1975), U-73.

codification is known as the Family code. The most important acts on this area are the Guardianship of Minors Act (1971), the Matrimonial Causes Act (1973), the Children Act (1975), the Matrimonial and Family Proceedings Act (1984) and the Family Law Reform Act (1987).

5.2 England, Wales and Northern Ireland[23]

The English system as described above was implemented in Wales in 1536, when the unification of England and Wales was completed. All former Welsh laws, mainly deriving from customary law (like the laws of Hywel Dda), were abrogated. In 1830 England and Wales became one unified jurisdiction when procedures were assimilated. The Act of Union of 1800 united Great Britain with Ireland. In 1921 Ireland parted into Northern and Southern Ireland and only Northern Ireland remained united with Great Britain. The Irish legal system and its courts remained to exist, but there is hardly any difference with the English system, also due to the fact that most of the Irish lawyers received their vocational training in England.

5.3 Ireland[24]

Ireland became an independent state in 1921 after a liberation war against England. Since the seventeenth century the English common law system completely ousted the original Irish legal system. This situation was maintained after Ireland became independent. Irish civil and commercial law is in essence similar to English law, in both statute and common law. The law of contracts, for example, is almost entirely based upon precedents. Since 1960 Ireland has tried to bring Irish law closer to the legal rules prevailing on the continent of Europe. It codified the principles for civil liability for accidents in 1961, succession law was totally codified in 1965, land ownership was regulated by the registration of title act of 1964. The family law of the Republic of Ireland is influenced by the opinion of the Roman Catholic church in family matters.

---

23 J.G. Sauveplanne/G.J.W. Steenhoff, Engeland, in: D. Kokkini-Iatridou, *Een inleiding tot het rechtsvergelijkende onderzoek*, Kluwer, Deventer 1988, 256-302.

24 Paul O'Higgins, Ireland, in: *International Encyclopedia of Comparative Law*, Volume I (July 1972).

5.4 Scotland[25]

The Scottish legal system was originally based on feudal and customary law, to be administered by sheriff courts. In 1532 the Court of Session was established as a permanent court of justice. Due to the political situation in the period from the fourteenth to the seventeenth century (Scotland fought lenghty wars with England), Scottish law has been greatly influenced by Roman law since many lawyers went to the continent for their judicial education. In 1603 James VI, King of Scotland, took up the English crown after the death of Elizabeth I and thus he became James I of England. The merger of the English and Scottish crowns led to a political unification in 1707 in the Treaty of Union, when the State of Great Britain was created. The separate parliaments were abolished and one parliament was established. But even after the Union the Scottish legal system evolved separately from the English system, no assimilation of the two legal systems took place. After the Union the independence of the Court of Session was protected, thus preserving the own face of the Scottish legal system. But Scottish law has been influenced by English legal ideas since then and the influence of Roman law has gradually declined. As in England, there was a tendency towards codification in the nineteenth century, especially on the fields of property and commercial law. In 1965 the Law Commission for Scotland was set up and, one of its tasks was, the investigation of the possibilities of codification of the law. At the moment there is a strong awareness of an own identity in Scotland, which also influences the ideas of the Scottish legal thinking.

5.5 British European Dependencies[26]

The British European dependencies are not a part of the United Kingdom, but they are British Crown dependencies. These dependencies consist of the Channel Islands and the Isle of Man. The Channel Islands, the main ones being Jersey and Guernsey, have been attached to the British Crown since 1066. The legal system of the islands can be traced back to Norman customary law, the Ancienne Coutume de Normandie. Even though the legislation and administration are in the hands of the British Crown, the English common law system was not implemented here. The Isle of Man has its own legislation and

---

25 Kenneth R. Simmonds, United Kingdom, in: *International Encyclopedia of Comparative Law*, Volume I (January 1975); David M. Walker, *The Scottish legal system*, W. Green & Son Ltd, Edinburgh 1981; Enid A. Marshall, *General principles of Scots law*, W. Green & Son Ltd, Edinburgh 1982; David M. Walker, *Principles of Scottish Private Law*, Claredon Press, Oxford 1982-1983 (3 volumes).

26 Kenneth R. Simmonds, The British Islands, appendix to United Kingdom, in: *International Encyclopedia of Comparative Law*, Volume I (January 1975).

administration, but the legal system of the isle is substantially similar to English law.

Part 2 – Substantive Law

A – Law of Contract

CHAPTER 8
The Formation of Contracts

Sjef van Erp*

1 Introduction

When discussing the common core of European private law, the law of contract is one of the most clear examples of the existence of a more or less 'common' law. These common aspects of European law, as Lipstein[1] would prefer to call them, are no doubt based upon a shared legal heritage. However, a critical remark should be made at the outset. The feeling that when one looks at the principles and rules of contract law and finds it surprisingly easy to recognise familiar principles and rules in a foreign legal system, might very well prove to be, what Schlesinger in his famous work on Formation of Contracts, has called a 'booby-trap'.[2] As will be seen later, it has now − in the light of all the research done in this field by, among others, the United Nations Conference on International Trade Law (Uncitral) and the International Institute for the Unification of Private Law (Unidroit)[3] − become relatively less of an effort to describe the formal rules of the formation of a contract. Essentially, a contract comes into existence after the sequence of offer and corresponding acceptance. However, the formal rules do not give a complete picture of legal reality. Their application differs from one legal system to another. To give one striking exam-

---

*   The research and writing for this chapter was done during a stay as a vacation visitor of Wolfson College, University of Cambridge (UK) and as a visiting scholar at the University of California, School of Law (Boalt Hall), Berkeley (USA).

1   Lipstein, 'European legal education in the future: teaching the "common law of Europe"', in: De Witte/Forder (eds.), *The common law of Europe and the future of legal education/Le droit commun de l'Europe et l'avenir de l'enseignement juridique* (Deventer, 1992), p. 255 ff.; see also Kötz, 'A common private law for Europe: perspectives for the reform of European legal education', *ibid.*, p. 31 ff., Müller-Graff, 'Common private law in the European Community', *ibid.*, p. 239 ff. See also for Germany Ulmer, 'Vom deutschen zum europäischen Privatrecht', 47 *Juristen Zeitung* 1 (1992), Zimmermann, 'Das römisch-kanonische ius commune als Grundlage einer europäischen Rechtseinheit', *ibid.*, p. 8 ff., Hommelhoff, 'Zivilrecht unter dem Einfluß europäischer Rechtsangleichung', 192 *Archiv für die civilistische Praxis* 71 (1992) and cf. for the Netherlands Van Erp, 'Europees privaatrecht in ontwikkeling?', in: Franken/Gilhuis/Peters (eds.), *Themis en Europa, een opening van nieuwe grenzen?* (Zwolle, 1989), p. 61 ff.

2   Schlesinger, *Formation of contracts, A study of the common core of legal systems, Conducted under the Auspices of the general principles of law project of the Cornell Law School, Vol. I*, p. 56 (Dobbs Ferry, N.Y., 1968).

3   Cf. the (United Nations) Vienna Sales Convention and its history, documented by Honnold, *Documentary history of the Uniform Law for International Sales, The studies, deliberations and decisions that led to the 1980 United Nations Convention with introduction and explanation* (Deventer, 1989) and the *Principles for international commercial contracts*, drawn up by a special working group of Unidroit.

ple: the English common law does not recognise any duty to negotiate in good faith, as was recently decided in a unanimous, single speech, decision by the House of Lords.[4]

In the following pages the more substantive aspect of the formation of contracts will be briefly considered, after a short review of the formal rules of contract formation.

2 Formation: Offer and Acceptance

All the Member States of the European Community share the economic view that a market economy will, at the end, result in the most efficient and fair distribution of labour, goods, services and capital. However, the type of market economy, might differ from one country to another as some Member States favour state interference in certain areas of economic life, where others would oppose it fiercely. Consequently, privatisation and deregulation have gone further in some countries than in others. Still, the basic private law freedoms related to a market economy are shared by all and are the basis of the economic integration within the European Community. In the words of Müller-Graff,[5] 'the existence of compatible institutions of private law such as freedom of contract, the freedom of competition, the freedom of association and the guarantee of property rights as well as the existence of equivalent basic ideas in legal reasoning concerning conflicts in private relations such as the principle "pacta sunt servanda", liability in torts or protection of property' are used as an already existing common legal basis for economic integration within the EC.

Given that when describing the formation of contracts the starting-point is the freedom to enter (or not to enter) a contract as well as the freedom to decide about its content, the question arises of when this freedom is being surrendered and consequently when a binding relationship comes into existence. Since the end of the 19th century, it can be quite accurately stated that all legal systems in Western Europe demand a rather formal procedure for this surrender of freedom. There has to be a sequence of an offer followed by a corresponding acceptance of this offer and only through this formal sequence can a contractual relationship ensue. Of course there are divergencies in the further elaboration in areas for example, of what consitutes an offer, when an offer (or, as the case may be, an acceptance) can be withdrawn, under what circumstances an offer will be irrevocable, but basically the mechanism is clear.[6] The whole purpose of

---

4   Walford v. Miles [1992] 2 W.L.R. 174; cf. Van Erp, 'Good faith: A concept "unworkable in practice"?', 1 *Tilburg Foreign Law Review* 215 (1992), with erratum in 1 *Tilburg Foreign Law Review* 406 (1992).

5   Loc. cit. p. 239/240.

6   A good example of this mechanism can be found in the new Dutch Civil Code. Cf. for the English and French translation of the relevant provisions of the code (articles 3:32 ff. on juridical acts, 6:217 ff. on the formation of contracts and 6:232 on general conditions),

this mechanism is to ensure certainty. It should be clear exactly when a contract comes into existence, so that the line between freedom and being bound to someone else is unambiguous. This means that, in principle, pre-contractual dealings do not result in any legally binding relationship and that — generally speaking — between negotiating parties no general duty of disclosure as to essential information exists. It also means that, once being bound, the law will enforce the contract even under unforeseen circumstances. However, this rigidity in its extreme form no longer exists, although some legal systems are still more rigid in this respect than others. It is being increasingly realized that a contract is an ongoing relationship, with for example, a duty to co-operate,[7] which develops itself in time.[8]

In civil law systems, the softening of the mechanism of offer and acceptance as the exclusive test for the formation of a contract, took place by the development of the duty to perform and enforce a contract in good faith towards an overall duty to act in good faith once a legally relevant relationship had come into existence. This also meant that the negotiating parties could be bound by this duty.[9] As a consequence of this overall duty to act in good faith a duty of disclosure can arise — at least in certain specific situations — to provide the other party with highly relevant information, necessary for the conclusion of a contract by informed consent. The requirement of informed consent can be seen as the modern expression of the freedom of contract.

Haanappel/Mackaay, *Nieuw Nederlands Burgerlijk Wetboek, Het vermogensrecht/New Netherlands Civil Code, Patrimonial law/Nouveau Code Civil Néerlandais, Le droit patrimonial* (Deventer/Boston, 1990). A brief discussion of the new Dutch Civil Code, especially in the area of contract law, can be found in Whincup, 'The new Dutch Civil Code', 142 *New Law Journal* 1208 (1992).

7   Cf. Bateson, 'The duty to co-operate', *The Journal of Business Law* 1960, p. 187, Honnold, *Uniform law for international sales under the 1980 United Nations Convention*, p. 407/8 and p. 430/1 and Legrand, 'Information in formation of contracts: a civilian perspective', in: 'Essays in honour of Jacob S. Ziegel', 19 *Canadian Business Law Journal/Revue Canadienne du Droit de Commerce* 318 (1991), p. 331.

8   Cf. Van Erp, *Contract als rechtsbetrekking, Een rechtsvergelijkende studie/Contract as a form of legal relationship, A comparative study* (doctoral thesis; Zwolle, 1990) where some of the developments which will be described later in this chapter are also discussed with further references, to which can be added Bridge, 'Does Anglo-Canadian contract law need a doctrine of good faith?', 9 *The Canadian Business Law Journal/Revue Canadienne du Droit de Commerce* 385 (1984), p. 417 ('To the extent that contract transcends its written expression, agreement can no longer be regarded as an event: it must be seen as a process.')

9   There is some circularity in reasoning to be detected here. The very moment that the step is taken that contracting parties, by the fact of their contract negotiations, enter into a legally relevant relationship, good faith is their basic norm of behaviour. See Hoge Raad (Netherlands Supreme Court) 15 November 1957, *Nederlandse Jurisprudentie* 1958, 67 (Baris v. Riezenkamp). On the other hand, their relationship can be said to be legally relevant, because good faith governs their pre-contractual dealings. See Hoge Raad 18 June 1982, *Nederlandse Jurisprudentie* 1983, 723 (Plas v. Valburg).
Cf. for German law, Loges, 'Die Begründung neuer Erklärungspflichten und der Gedanke des Vertrauensschutzes' (*Schriften zum Bürgerlichen Recht*, Band 136; doctoral thesis; Berlin, 1990), p. 80 ff.

Surrender of freedom has to be free itself and this can only be so where one knows what is being given up and which legal ties are being established. Again some legal systems demand in this respect more than others, as will be briefly discussed hereafter.

3 The Rules of Offer and Acceptance Relating to an International Sales Contract as a Starting-point for European Principles of Contract Formation

The rules of offer and acceptance, rather straightforward as they seem to be, hardly need any further elaboration from a comparative-technical point of view, taking into consideration the research already done by UNCITRAL and currently being undertaken by UNIDROIT.[10]

To give one example: one of the main traditional differences between common law and some civil law countries is in the revocability of an offer, which has been solved by the Vienna Sales Convention in Article 16, stating that '(1) Until a contract is concluded an offer may be revoked if the revocation reaches the offeree before he has dispatched an acceptance. (2) However, an offer cannot be revoked: (a) if it indicates, whether by stating a fixed time for acceptance or otherwise, that it is irrevocable; or (b) if it was reasonable for the offeree to rely on the offer as being irrevocable and the offeree has acted in reliance on the offer'. The Convention certainly proposes in this respect a workable compromise, taking a middle-course between those countries which consider an offer as, in principle, revocable (for example England, France and the Netherlands)[11] and those which consider an offer as, in principle, irrevocable (for example Germany).[12] In doing this, the Vienna Sales Convention reflects the present more general European attitude to shift emphasis from applying absolute rules towards having recourse to more flexible standards. This changing approach shows itself very clearly in the area here under discussion. The legal systems which take the revocability of an offer as their starting-point quite often counterbalance this in some way. To illustrate this let me give two examples. In English law, whilst an offer as such is revocable, equity may prevent its withdrawal; similarly French law accepts that, although an offer as

---

10   As the principles for international commercial contracts are still being discussed within UNIDROIT I will not go into detail about how certain problems will be solved in the UNIDROIT proposals.

11   Cf. for English and Dutch law: Rinkes and Samuel, *Contractual and non-contractual obligations in English law, Systematic analysis of the English law of obligations in the comparative context of the Netherlands Civil Code* (doctoral thesis; Nijmegen, 1992), p. 113 ff. and for French law, Ghestin, *Traité de droit civil, Les obligations, Le contrat; formation* (Paris, 1988), p. 226 ff.

12   Cf. Larenz, *Allgemeiner Teil des deutschen bürgerlichen Rechts* (Munich, 1989), p. 515 ff., Brox, *Allgemeiner Teil des Bürgerlichen Gesetzbuchs* (Cologne/Berlin/Bonn/Munich, 1990), p. 88 ff. and Palandt, *Bürgerliches Gesetzbuch* (Munich, 1991), § 145 ff.

such is revocable, it may nevertheless bind the offeror within a reasonable period.[13]

Another traditional comparative law problem in the area of contract formation — distinguishing common law from civil law — is the English doctrine of consideration: no contract without '*do ut des*'. Again the Vienna Sales Convention offers a workable way out of this quandary. Under the Convention consideration is no longer a prerequisite for the formation of a contract, given that a sales contract will always be based on an exchange of promises.[14]

A final example of comparative-technical difficulties, this time originating in German law, is the legal meaning of the so-called '*kaufmännisches Bestätigungsschreiben*' (merchant's confirmation or writings in confirmation). This type of confirmation is usually sent after the conclusion of a contract and may include slightly different terms than agreed upon orally. In such a case, the questions which may then be asked are: which terms will govern the contract, and whether the contract terms can be concluded by silent acquiescence from one of the parties.[15] This problem about formation of contracts by inaction, is closely related to the question of: under which conditions a so-called modified acceptance can determine the contents of a contract.[16] As such this type of problem no longer proves to be an obstacle to a European harmonisation effort, as is being shown — once more — by the Vienna Sales Convention.[17] Also related to the problem of a merchant's confirmation, is the question of when a contract is governed by general conditions and, particularly important in a commercial context, whose general conditions will apply in a case where both parties refer to their own conditions in their exchange of offer and acceptance (the so-called 'battle of forms'). How to decide about a reference, for example, in a merchant's confirmation to one's own general conditions, without any previous discussion about whose general conditions will apply? Again I would like to mention the research done by UNCITRAL and UNIDROIT trying to solve these matters in a generally acceptable way.[18]

Considering this growing agreement on a comparative-technical level, it seems to me at this moment more useful to examine the formation of contracts from a more general comparative perspective. The resulting observations will focus on the — very regrettable — seemingly growing gap between English law on one hand and the laws of the other Member States of the European

---

13 See Ghestin, *loc. cit.*, p. 228 and 234.
14 Cf. Honnold, *Uniform law for international sales under the 1980 United Nations Convention*, p. 282 ff.
15 See Sandrock, *Handbuch der internationalen Vertragsgestaltung, Ein Leitfaden für den Abschluß von Verträgen im internationalen Wirtschaftsverkehr, Vol. 1*, p. 278 ff.
16 See e.g. articles 19 and 9 Vienna Sales Convention and article 6:225 new Dutch Civil Code.
17 Cf. for the Vienna Sales Convention Honnold, Uniform law for international sales, p. 220/1.
18 Cf. Honnold, *ibid.*, p. 227 ff.

Community[19] on the other. These observations will be preceded by some preliminary remarks.

4 Formation of Contracts: a More General Comparative Perspective

The idea behind a European Civil Code, or what I would prefer to call a European private law Restatement,[20] should be to state the basic principles or standards applicable in general to any type of contract, whether it is a contract which is inter (Member) State, or strictly domestic.[21] This necessarily means that these principles must be fairly abstract and general, in order to encompass, as much as possible, the different legal traditions in Europe (common law, civil law and the law of the Nordic countries). However, I am very much afraid that it will prove to be extremely difficult to avoid stating principles which are so general that they might lose any meaning althogether in legal reality. A technique which could avoid this hazard is to counterbalance the openness of the standard by formulating guiding (policy-weighing) factors. This is a technique which is at present widely used in the case law throughout the European Community.[22]

How would these standards, with regard to the formation of contracts, look like? As mentioned above, both the Vienna Sales Convention and the UNIDROIT principles for international commercial contracts, can be taken as a solid base to build upon. Unfortunately, this foundation requires further rethinking. The rules concerning the formation of contracts as for example laid down in the Vienna Sales Convention are — obviously — meant for international commercial contracts, and not for purely domestic contracts or for consumer con-

---

19 And also, I might add, for that matter American law.

20 Cf. Remien, 'Illusion und Realität eines europäischen Privatrechts', 47 *Juristen Zeitung*, p. 277 ff. (1992) and Schulze, 'Allgemeine Rechtsgrundsätze und europäisches Privatrecht', 1 *Zeitschrift für Europäisches Privatrecht*, p. 442 ff. (1993).

21 In this way an attempt might be made to avoid the intricacies of private international law, although I doubt if this attempt can ever be successful. Even if European private law would apply in the general way as is here advocated, its standards will be of such a general nature that the national laws of the member states by sheer necessity will have a forceful supplementary role to play. Thus revitalizing the old conflict of laws questions.

22 Cf. Remien *ibid*, p. 281.
    From an English perspective even the acceptance of a European restatement would clearly mean a considerable step towards their European counterparts. Traditionally, English lawyers are not in favour of abstract principles. Besides Walford v. Miles, already referred to, this can be seen in Murphy v. Brentwood District Council [1990] 3 W.L.R. 414, a case in the area of the tort of negligence.
    For an American view see Llewellyn, *The case law system in America* (Gewirtz, ed., translated from the German by Ansaldi; Chicago/London, 1989), p. 84 ff., discussing certainty and clarity in American law (§ 60) and legal compendiums and legal certainty (§ 61).

tracts.[23] In addition, these are rules for contracts for the sales of goods, and not for other types of contract or even for sales of immovables.[24] Moreover, and perhaps even more important than what has just been mentioned, it should be pointed out that the formation of a contract can take place without offer and acceptance. After lengthy and complex negotiations, it is sometimes almost impossible to trace the final offer and/or the final corresponding acceptance. Then there are situations where contracts come into existence by the sole fact that people behave as if there was a contract: what in German law is called, the 'faktische Vertragsverhältnisse' (de facto contractual relations).[25] Finally, the 'neat divisions of offer, acceptance and invitation to treat'[26] are not really that applicable in cases of a multipartite agreement or in efficiently explaining the potentially binding nature of a contract with respect to third parties. Of course it can be argued, and to a certain extent rightly so, that the basic model of offer and acceptance will apply in most of the above mentioned situations. Yet it might still make a difference whether these provisions would be applied, let us say, in a strictly commercial setting or in a consumer context. Therefore, one important aspect when formulating European private law should be to take the internationally accepted model of offer and acceptance as a starting-point before a further elaboration of principles for the different types of situations just specified. This would create abstract standards, which could be exemplified according to the type of contract, by formulating various applicable guiding factors.[27] American experience preceeds us, as was pointed out by Lücke:[28]

'(...) the United States legal system has some special characteristics which make it necessary for lawyers to embrace broad principles and policies, deeper reasons, abstract approaches and ethical terminology. The United States Bill of Rights is itself expressed in such terms. Moreover, it is probably only by attention to broad principles that some degree of unity can be achieved for the United States legal system with its huge and relentless flow of reported cases and its many separate systems of common law. Also, a homogenous society will find it easier to leave basic assumptions unspoken than does a multicultural one like that of the United States. The comparative method has proved

---

23   As to the distinction between civil law and commercial law it can very well be argued that it no longer proves to be as strict as it originially was. Cf. for a comparative analysis Kozolchyk, 'The commercialization of civil law and the civilization of commercial law', 40 *Louisiana Law Review* 3 (1979).

24   This remark does not apply to the UNIDROIT proposals, as these contain general principles for international commercial contracts.

25   Examples are boarding a bus, or parking one's car in a car park Cf. Larenz, *Allgemeiner Teil des deutschen Bürgerlichen Rechts*, p. 534 ff., Brox, *Allgemeiner Teil des Bürgerlichen Gesetzbuchs*, p. 86 ff. (with further references), esp. p. 96/7 and, for English law, Atiyah, *The rise and fall of freedom of contract* (Oxford, 1979, reprint 1985), p.693 ff., esp. 734 ff.

26   Bridge, 'Does Anglo-Canadian law need a doctrine of good faith?', 9 *The Canadian Business Law Journal/Revue Canadienne du Droit de Commerce* 385 (1984), p. 418.

27   Different guiding factors might also be formulated for the different legal systems as such.

28   Good faith and contractual performance, in: Finn (ed.) *Essays on contract* (Sydney, 1987), p. 155 ff, p. 156.

useful in meeting that undoubted need, as have other factors such as the strong influence of the "national" law schools and the associated flow of high quality academic writing.'

If these remarks by Lücke are true for the United States, where the law in the respective states (except Louisiana) is primarily based on the common law as the shared legal tradition, they should be even more true for Europe where a prevailing legal tradition does not exist. What Lücke writes here is also a clear *caveat*. We should not let ourselves be deceived by the *prima facie* similarities in formal rules on offer and acceptance. Divergence in legal tradition, related to a divergence in legal atmosphere or, in other words, a different social, economic and political climate, does influence ideas as to the role of, in our case, the law on the formation of contracts.[29] The result of this divergence are the deep-seated conflicting modes of thought in the different European traditions and these will not change the very moment a European restatement will be published.[30]

To illustrate this I will give two examples, which will be discussed in the next paragraph: firstly the legal consequences of negotiating in contradiction with the requirements of good faith and secondly, closely related to this problem area, the acceptance of a general duty of disclosure during contract formation. It seems that the current approach of these questions on the one hand of English law and on the other hand, Dutch, French and German law, can almost be classified as antagonistic. It therefore appears to me to be an impossible task to discuss all the national legal systems of Europe. Instead, a comparison will be made between four European Member States to illustrate my earlier remarks.[31]

---

29 Cf. the discussion between Bridge and Tancellin about the introduction of good faith' in Anglo-Canadian law, 9 *The Canadian Business Law Journal/Revue Canadienne du Droit de Commerce* 385 ff. and 430 ff. and cf. Lord Goff of Chievely, 'Opening address' (second annual Journal of Contract Law conference in London in September 1991), 5 *Journal of Contract Law* 1992, 1. See also the book review by Hooley of O'Connor's book 'Good faith in English law' (Dartmouth, 1990), 49 *The Cambridge Law Journal* 515, referring to the already mentioned article by Bridge.

30 On the other hand, it might very well be that after the introduction of a European Civil Code or Private Law Restatement the differences in legal attitude gradually change. This phenomenon was noted by Frier, 'Interpreting codes', 89 *Michigan Law Review* 2201 (1991), as one of the long term consequences of the introduction of the UCC in the United States.
Cf. in this respect for a view on developments in English legal practice Bingham, L.J., '"here is a world elsewhere": the changing perspectives of English law', 41 *International and Comparative Law Quarterly* 513 (1992).

31 Although in the legal areas on which this chapter will focus among others the law of the United States would also offer a most rewarding object of comparative study, this legal system cannot be further discussed for the reasons mentioned in the text.

5 Pre-contractual Dealings: the (non-)Existence of a Duty to Negotiate in Good Faith and a General Duty of Disclosure

5.1 The Duty to Negotiate in Good Faith

Traditionally, one of the basic distinctions between continental legal systems and the English legal system has been the absence in English law of both academically and judicially developed general concepts, like good faith. It was argued that because English law had known a constant case by case evolution rooted in judicial practice, which had only at a fairly late stage been rationalized by academic legal scholars, common law meant practical law to solve practical problems, and not speculative law to solve theoretical problems. Speculative law to solve theoretical problems was to be found on the continent, where academic legal writing, strongly influenced by moral concepts based on canon law and general precepts based on roman law, had shaped legal practice, which had to suffer a further practical setback when even more theoretical codes were introduced. As has clearly been shown by others, this picture of the differences between English law and other legal systems is, remarkably enough, itself rather theoretical and incorrect. English law is far more influenced by Roman law than is sometimes admitted,[32] continental legal systems are far more practice oriented than might seem[33] and English law did develop general concepts in equity.

Let us elaborate further on the last mentioned point, in order to clarify what is meant. A reference might be made here to the discussion of the so-called 'maxims of equity' in the first (1868) and the twenty-eighth edition (1982) of Snell's Principles of equity. In the first edition Snell mentions eleven such maxims, arguing[34] that the 'ingenuous student will find no difficulty in tracing almost every maxim or head of equity to that great maxim, the keystone of the whole arch, — "Equity suffers no wrong without a remedy"'. In the 28th edition, Baker and Langan mention twelve maxims ('equity acts in personam' is added) and defend[35] that 'it would not be difficult to reduce them all under the first and the last, "Equity will not suffer a wrong to be without a remedy", and

---

32 See Gorla and Moccia, 'A "revisiting" of the comparison between "continental law" and "English law" (16th-19th century)', 2 *The Journal of Legal History* 143 (1981), Moccia, 'English law attitudes to the "civil law", *ibid.*, p. 157 ff., Gordley, *The philosophical origins of modern contract doctrine* (Oxford, 1991) and also 'Common Law und civil law: eine überholte Unterscheidung', *Zeitschrift für Europäisches Privatrecht*, p. 498 ff. (1993).

33 Cf. Frier, 'Interpreting codes', 89 *Michigan Law Review* 2201 (1991). He points out (p. 2213/4), as was said earlier, that a code (like the continental codes or the American Uniform Commercial Code) results in what he calls an 'expanded interpretive community': the judiciary, the bar and (academic) legal authors.

34 *Loc. cit.* p. 12.

35 *Loc. cit.* p. 28.

"Equity acts on the person"'.[36] It is also quite revealing to read what Jessel M.R. said in the case of *Re Hallet's Estate*,[37] acknowledging that equity was invented by judges.[38] In his own words: '... it must not be forgotten that the rules of the Courts of Equity are not, like the rules of the Common Law, supposed to have been established from time immemorial. It is perfectly well known that they have been established from time to time — altered, improved, and refined from time to time. In many cases we know the names of the Chancellors who invented them. No doubt they were invented for the purpose of securing the better administration of justice, but still they were invented.' Of course I do realize that equity developed into a system of rules, laid down in precedents, with its own specific character next to the common law. The point I am trying to make, nevertheless, is that English law is able to transform general norms[39] into workable rules, not unlike a continental judge's ability to transform good faith into workable 'sub-regulations', as has been described for example by Alpa.[40] The fact that a code system uses (even must use) open ended principles and standards does not necessarily mean that it is unable to produce practical solutions or that the judges who have to apply these principles and standards are hampered in their creativity. For that reason I cannot but disagree with Bridge[41] when he argues: 'General principles, such as good faith, can serve the purposes of innovation and creativity in a civil law system that are carried forward by a more creative judiciary in the common law tradition.' My first reaction to this statement would be to say that judicial creativity can be limited to the same extent by the binding nature of precedents as by the binding nature of a statute, as a code essentially is.[42] But foremost I would reply that I strongly believe that a discussion about whose judges are more creative is an unnecessarily negative as well as an unproductive approach which tends to move

---

36   See for a brief historical practice note on the maxim 'he who comes into equity must come with clean hands' Starke, 63 *The Australian Law Journal* 854 (1989).

37   (1880) 13 Ch. D. 696, 710.

38   Cf. also Gardner, *An introduction to the law of trusts* (Oxford, 1990), p. 34 (note 34).

39   Snell (first edition, 1868), even describes a maxim of equity as an 'active and comprehensive aphorism'. (*Loc. cit.* p. 12.)

40   Italian report about precontracual liability, in: Hondius (ed.), *Precontractual liability, Reports to the XIIIth congress International Academy of Comparative Law* (Montreal, Canada, 18-24 August 1990)(Deventer/Boston, 1991), p. 195 ff., p. 200.

41   'Does Anglo-Canadian contract law need a doctrine of good faith?', 9 *The Canadian Business Law Journal/Revue Canadienne du Droit de Commerce* 385 (1991), p. 414.

42   I refer to a feeling expressed by Lord Goff of Chievely, already mentioned, that in English law the introduction of a good faith principle in contract law is beyond the powers of the English judiciary. Cf. Lord Goff of Chieveley, 'Opening address', *ibid.*, p. 4. Reflecting upon this submission I cannot help but feeling intrigued by the fact that in Germany (and later in the Netherlands) the most influential force in developing good faith as a general norm applying to the whole of the contractual process was — remarkably enough for a code system — not the legislature, but on the contrary, the judiciary.

analysis away from a more fundamental discussion of good faith in a comparative context.[43]

Why this, perhaps at first sight somewhat provocative, introduction to the subject which we are discussing in this paragraph? Although it only until recently seemed likely that the above mentioned traditional distinction between English law and continental legal systems was gradually disappearing, this proved to be a deceptive impression. A first illustration of this at first converging, then diverging development in the area of good faith is being offered by a case about the incorporation of a general condition into a contract, Interfoto picture library Ltd. v. Stiletto visual programmes Ltd.[44] In this case Bingham L.J. said this, 'English law has, characteristically, committed itself to no such overriding principle (i.e. that in making and carrying out contracts parties should act in good faith, J.v.E.) but has developed piecemeal solutions in response to demonstrated problems of unfairness.' However, he added,[45] 'The tendency of the English authorities has, I think, been to look at the nature of the transaction in question and the character of the parties to it; to consider what notice the party alleged to be bound was given of the particular condition said to bind him; and to resolve whether in all the circumstances it is fair to hold him bound by the condition in question. This may yield a result not very different from the civil law principle of good faith, at any rate so far as the formation of the contract is concerned.' Developments like this case led the legal writer O' Connor amongst others, in a book published in 1990, to defend the thesis that English law had come very close to introducing a general good faith concept.[46] Prior to O'Connor, Lücke[47] also had defended the introduction of good faith in the common law. However there were also other voices. Lücke wrote partly as a reaction to an, already mentioned, article written by Bridge, 'Does Anglo-Canadian contract law need a doctrine of good faith?'.[48] The answer which Bridge gave to this question was distinctively negative: introduction of good faith as a general norm of behaviour in contract law would disrupt the 'complex amalgamation of doctrine, case law and legislation, which is beyond the realistic

---

43 A discussion about whose language is better equiped for comparative law analysis runs the same risks. Cf. for an attempt to avoid this unproductive type of discussion about legal languages Remien, 'Rechtseinheit ohne Einheitsgesetze? — Zum Symposium "Alternativen zur legislatorischen Rechtsvereinheitlichung"', 56 *Rabels Zeitschrift* 300 (1992), p. 307.

44 [1989] 1 Q.B. 433 (1987), 439.

45 *Ibid.* p. 445.

46 O'Connor, *Good faith in English law* (Dartmouth, 1990), critically reviewed by Hooley, 49 *The Cambridge Law Journal* 515 (1990).

47 'Good faith and contractual performance', in: Finn (ed.), *Essays on contract* (Sydney, 1987), p. 155 ff. See for the role of good faith in Australian contract law, which seems to be more receptive to this concept than English and Anglo-Canadian law, Carter/Harland, *Contract law in Australia* (Sydney, 1991), p. 11 and Starke, 'Current topics, The current activities of Unidroit', 64 *The Australian Law Journal* 685 (1990), 686. Starke mentions that UNIDROIT will incorporate good faith into its principles for international commercial contracts and that Australian contract law is no longer hostile to this idea.

48 9 *The Canadian Business Law Journal/Revue Canadienne du Droit de Commerce* 385 (1984).

range of instant human achievement.' He did see a role for good faith 'in articulating contract theory and in defining the goals that our contract law is harnassed to serve'. However, legislative adoption along the lines of United States law or continental codes would be 'an abuse of the comparative legal method', it would fail 'to address the role and function of good faith in differently constituted societies',[49] which would result in the introduction of a 'highly selective legal transplant without regard to the whole of a country's legal tradition'.[50] Another English author, Cartwright, writing in 1991 also disagreed with O'Connor and basically agreed with Bridge: 'There is no general rule in English law that a party has to bargain in good faith, or to comply with a principle of fair and open dealing.[51] However, he continued, even if English law does not enforce a rule of fair dealing, it does take account of *un*fair dealing.'

Less than two years after the publication of O'Connor's book and one year after the publication of Cartwright's book, it appears that the latter was right after all, at least as far as the non-recognition of good faith is concerned. The House of Lords made it unequivocally clear that the introduction of good faith in English contract law would, and even could not happen. The case, already mentioned earlier, in which this was decided is Walford v. Miles.[52] The case is about the legal consequences, if any, of a contract to negotiate and the final breakdown of negotiations. In a single speech by Lord Ackner, the following was said about the possible acceptance into English law of a duty to negotiate in

---

49 Bridge, *ibid.* p. 426. Cf. the comments to this paper by Farnsworth and Tancellin, *ibid.* p. 426 ff. and p. 430 ff. See also Hassan, 'The principle of good faith in the formation of contracts', 5 *Suffolk Transnational Law Journal* 1 (1980)

50 *Loc. cit.* p. 414. See also Klapisch, 'Der Einfluß der deutschen und österreichischen Emigranten auf contracts of adhesion und bargaining in good faith im US-amerikanischen Recht, Zugleich eine Darstellung der vorvertraglichen Haftung in den USA' (*Arbeiten zur Rechtsvergleichung*, Schriftenreihe der Gesellschaft für Rechtsvergleichung, Band 152) (Baden-Baden, 1991), esp. p. 157 ff. Here the author discusses the reasons why American law did not develop a doctrine of culpa in contrahendo as it is known in German law.

51 *Unequal bargaining, A study of vitiating factors in the formation of contracts* (Oxford, 1991), p. 224/5, referring in a footnote to the already mentioned case of Interfoto v. Stiletto Visual Programmes.

52 [1979] 2 W.L.R. 174. Looking at English history, bearing in mind that English law is being seen as an uninterrupted continuing flow of cases, one cannot but be surprised by this categorical denial of good faith as a general concept in contract law. Nevertheless good faith, or even the utmost good faith the principle of *uberrimae fidei*, has always been accepted as a fundamental norm of behaviour in insurance law. The historical landmark is the case of Carter v. Boehm (1766) 3 Burr. 1905. Here Lord Mansfield even remarked: 'The governing principle (i.e. that a concealment will avoid a policy, J.v.E.) is applicable to all contracts and dealings. Good faith forbids either party by concealing what he privately knows, to draw another into a bargain, from his ignorance of that fact, and his believing the contrary. But either party may be innocently silent, as to grounds open to both, to exercise their judgment upon.'

good faith, 'A duty to negotiate in good faith is as unworkable in practice as it is inherently inconsistent with the position of a negotiating party.'[53]

In sharp contrast with English law is Dutch law,[54] following the direction as indicated by French and more in particular by German law.[55] The Dutch Supreme Court (Hoge Raad) decided in 1957[56] that the precontractual stage was a legal relationship governed by good faith. Then in 1982[57] it was decided that the negotiating process could be divided into three stages: an initital stage, where determining negotiations would not lead to any claim for damages, an intermediate stage where negotiations might be determined under the condition that the other party's reliance expenses were paid, and an ultimate stage where it was no longer in accordance with good faith when the negotiations would be ended and the other party's expectation damages had to be paid where no contract ensued after all. This third stage has not only attracted some attention in the Netherlands, but also abroad.[58] A first remark which should be made in this respect is that until now there were no cases decided by the Supreme Court in which this third stage apparently was reached and has led to the payment of expectation damages. A second remark concerns the test to decide if this ultimate stage is reached. In 1982 the test was formulated as follows: 'if the parties, from both sides, could trust that some contract would, in any case, ensue from the negotiations'. This test has recently been rephrased. The only thing which is relevant now is the reliance by the party who is being confronted by a party who determines the negotiations. As a consequence of this reformulation

---

53   The words that good faith is a concept 'unworkable in practice' might refer to a remark by the Canadian author Waddams, 'Pre-contractual duties of disclosure', in Cane/Stapleton (eds.), *Essays for Patrick Atiyah* (Oxford, 1991), p. 237 ff., p. 254: 'It is true that the law, in its general objectives, represents a community sense of morality, but actual legal rules must also be fair and *workable in practice* with a reasonable degree of regularity, and reasonably inexpensive to apply. Justice is the general objective of the law, but the search for justice is not advanced by the adoption of rules that are so expensive to apply that they put its attainment out of practical reach.' (Italics mine, J.v.E.) Adding (ibid.): 'What is needed is a set of rules sufficiently in conformity with the community sense of morality not to produce results perceived as outrageous, while at the same time preserving sufficient content to be workable and reasonably inexpensive of regular application, and maintaining a fair degree of security, of property transfers.'

54   Cf. Van Dunné, 'Dutch report' in: Hondius (ed.) *Precontractual liability, Reports to the XIIIth congress International Academy of Comparative Law* (Montreal, Canada, 18-24 August 1990), p. 223 ff. and the 'general report' by Hondius, *ibid.*, p. 1 ff., p. 23.

55   Cf. for French law Ghestin, *loc. cit.*, p. 249 ff. and for German law Esser/Schmidt, *Schuldrecht, Band I, Allgemeiner Teil* (Heidelberg, 1984), p. 435 ff., Larenz, *Lehrbuch des Schuldrechts, Erster Band, Allgemeiner Teil* (Munich, 1987), p. 106 ff., Brox, *loc. cit.*, p. 193 and Loges, *loc. cit.*, p. 39 ff.

56   Hoge Raad 15 November 1957, *Nederlandse Jurisprudentie* 1958, 67 (Baris v. Riezenkamp).

57   Hoge Raad 18 June 1982, *Nederlandse Jurisprudentie* 1983, 723 (Plas v. Valburg).

58   Farnsworth, 'Precontractual liability and preliminary agreements: fair dealing and failed negotiations', 87 *Columbia Law Review* 217 (1987), p. 221.

of the reliance test it is no longer necessary that both parties relied on a positive outcome of their precontractual dealings.[59]

5.2 The Duty to Disclose Essential Information

Reflecting upon the non-acceptance of a general duty to negotiate in good faith and the reasons given by the House of Lords as well as several common law authors, the question then arises what causes this abrupt change in the process from convergence to divergence. Does the present trend perhaps indicate − it is for the time being only tentatively suggested − that there is a growing desire to preserve (or even to re-establish) an historically evolved feeling of self-identity as a case law system? Before answering this question it is useful to look at another example of the present trend in English contract law to move away from other legal systems: the refusal to accept a general duty of disclosure in the pre-contractual stage. The present position of English law is quite clear, as was recently affirmed in the case of Banque Keyser Ullmann S.A. v. Skandia (U.K.) Insurance Co. Ltd. and Bank of Nova Scotia v. Hellenic Mutual War Risks Association (Bermuda) Ltd.[60] Basically, with an exception for example to insurance contracts, the principle as laid down in Smith v. Hughes[61] still applies.[62] In the words of Cockburn C.J.,[63] 'I take the true rule to be, that where a specific article is offered for sale, without express warranty, or without circumstances from which the law will imply a warranty − as where, for instance, an article is ordered for a specific purpose − and the buyer has full opportunity of inspecting and forming his judgment, if he chooses to act on that judgment, the rule caveat emptor applies.' Or, as Blackburn J. put it in even

---

59 It is interesting to note that this change in emphasis from the reliance of both parties to the reliance of the party who has to face that someone else breaks down the negotiations in fact means a change in emphasis from an examination of the parties' mind to a questioning of one party's behaviour. A comparable trend away from the state of mind of the victim of an error or fraud to an examination of the other party's behaviour can also be seen in French law. Cf. Legrand, 'Pre-contractual disclosure and information: English and French law compared', 6 *Oxford Journal of Legal Studies* 322 (1986), p. 337 and Legrand, 'Information in formation of contracts, Essays in honour of Jacob S. Ziegel', 19 *Canadian Business Law Journal/Revue Canadienne du Droit de Commerce* (1991) 318, p. 332/3.

60 [1991] 2 A.C. 249, [1990] 3 W.L.R. 364, H.L. (E.) and [1991] 2 W.L.R. 1279, H.L. (E.). Both of these decisions concern a duty to inform in the case of an insurance contract.

61 (1871) LR 6 QB 597.

62 See also Cartwright, *Unequal bargaining, A study of vitiating factors in the formation of contracts* p. 90 ff.
    Two more recent decisions underlining the approach taken by the House of Lords are Barclays Bank Plc. v. Khaira [1992] 1 W.L.R. 623 (Chancery Divison; the Court of Appeal struck out a notice of appeal) and Barclays Bank Plc. v. O'Brien [1992] 3 W.L.R. 593, C.A. In the latter case, Purchas L.J. on the one hand refused to categorise the existing caselaw in this area, but on the other hand did rephrase the authorities by putting forward what he called "propositions" (*ibid.* p. 635/6).

63 Smith v. Hughes, *ibid.* p. 603.

stronger words:[64] '(...), whatever may be the case in a court of morals, there is no legal obligation on the vendor to inform the purchaser that he is under a mistake, not induced by the act of the vendor.'

In very much the same way as we saw whilst looking at non acceptance into English law of a general contractual standaard of good faith, we see here that English and Anglo-Canadian authors are supportive of the approach taken by the House of Lords. Nicholas, although realizing the gap between English law and French law, certainly seems to be sustaining the English piecemeal acceptance of a duty of disclosure.[65] Also Waddams[66] similarly favours the incremental approach, based on the further development of existing situations where a duty to disclose has been accepted. This approach 'has more to recommend it than the revolutionary.'

Looking at French and German law, one cannot but conclude that there is an unmistakably different attitude to be found. It is argued by authors like Ghestin and Legrand[67] that a general duty of disclosure of essential information necessary for an informed consent to contract does exist in French law. Ghestin summarizes French law in the following way,[68] 'To sum up, a party who was or (having regard especially to any professional qualification) ought to have been aware of a fact which he knew to be of determining importance for the other contracting party is bound to inform the latter of that fact, provided that he was unable to discover it for himself or that, because the nature of the contract, the character of the parties, or the incorrectness of the information provided by the other party, he could justifiably rely on that other to provide the

---

64   Smith v. Huges, *ibid.* p. 606/7.

65   'The pre-contractual obligation to disclose information', 2: 'English report', in: Harris/Tallon, *Contract law today, Anglo-French comparisons* (Oxford, 1989), p. 166 ff.

66   *Loc. cit.* p. 256. See also Waddams, 'Precontractual duties of disclosure', 19 *Canadian Business Law Journal* 349 (1991) (a summary of his contribution to the Essays in honour of Patrick Atiyah) and the comments on Waddams' article by Farnsworth, 19 *Canadian Business Law Journal/Revue Canadienne du Droit de Commerce* 351 (1991). Also, as was the case with the introduction of a general concept of good faith, it seems that Australian contract law is more receptive towards a general duty of disclosure than its English and Anglo-Canadian counterparts. Cf. Finn, 'Good faith and nondisclosure', in: Finn (ed.), *Essays on torts* (Sydney, 1989), p. 150 ff.

67   Ghestin, *Traité de droit civil, Les obligations, Le contrat; formation*, p. 502 ff., Ghestin, 'The pre-contractual obligation to disclose information', '1:French report', in: Harris/Tallon (eds.), *Contract law today, Anglo-French comparisons* (Oxford, 1989), p. 151 ff., p. 166; Legrand, 'Pre-contractual disclosure and information: English and French law compared', 6 *Oxford Journal of Legal Studies* 322 (1986), p. 337 and also 'Information in formation of contracts, Essays in honour of Jacob S. Ziegel', 19 *Canadian Business Law Journal/Revue Canadienne du Droit de Commerce* 318 (1991), p. 332/3. See also for a comparison of French-Canadian with American law Legrand, 'De l'obligation pré-contractuelle de renseignement: aspects d'une réflexion métajuridique (et paraciviliste)', 21 *Ottawa Law Review/Revue de droit d'Ottawa* 585 (1989, discussing inter alia the opposite of a duty of disclosure: the right to remain silent about certain secrets).

68   *Ibid.* p. 166.

information.' A conclusion which, no doubt, could also have been formulated for German law.[69]

How this gap between English law and other legal systems might be bridged, in spite of the seemingly antagonistic approach, will be suggested in the next paragraph.

6 Final Remarks: How to Bridge the Gap between English Law and the Other European Legal Systems?[70]

English law and continental legal systems seem, as was remarked earlier, no longer to converge but to diverge. Nicholas[71] has put forward the view that the basic distinction between English and French law is that English law departs from an economic viewpoint and French law from a moral viewpoint, at the same time referring to the difference in conceptual structures between the two legal systems. Adding to this analysis, reference can be made to what Finn has said[72] about the common law as inclined to cherish virtues like individual responsibility and self-reliance and to what was remarked by Farnsworth[73] namely that the common law traditionally favoured the goals of finality, certainty and practicality by generally not requiring disclosure. Legrand, in contrast, has characterized French law, comparing it with English law, as positive (it accepts an obligation of information), altruistic (acceptance of a duty to share certain information between partners) and concrete (it is not as much the nature of a contract which is decisive if a duty of disclosure will be accepted, but the character of the parties: 'professionel' versus 'profane').[74] He considers this approach as the legal reaction to a 1950's society in which the liberal classical economic model of (enlightened) *laissez-faire* was replaced by the welfare model of the mixed economy, where the community and individuals share responsibilities, creating what Legrand calls an 'esprit de solidarité'. Another aspect of this changed society is that it has become highly technological, thus causing a division, already suggested, between 'experts' (those who possess knowledge and are able to use it) and 'profanes', namely their counterparts, those who do not possess knowledge and even if they would, do not know

---

69 Cf. Larenz, *Lehrbuch des Schuldrechts*, loc. cit., p. 110 ff. and the (critical) study by Loges, passim.
70 Or, so might be asked, 'how to tunnel the channel?', to refer to a successful, albeit costly, attempt to bring England and the continent closer together.
71 *Loc. cit.* p. 184; cf. also the conclusions, *ibid.* p. 187 ff.
72 *Loc. cit.* p. 159.
73 'Comments on Professor Waddams' "precontractual duties of disclosure", Essays in honour of Jacob S. Ziegel', 19 *Canadian Business Law Journal/Revue Canadienne du Droit de Commerce* 351 (1991), p. 352.
74 *Pre-contractual disclosure*, loc. cit., p. 349; *Information in formation*, loc. cit., p. 346.

how to use it to its maximum. Finally, this changed society is more concerned about consuming than about the improvement of producing.[75]

Considering all this, the impression slowly starts to build up that somehow there might be more to the differences in development of English law compared to other legal systems than meets the eye. Perhaps it is too straightforward simply to presume that the background of conceptual diversity at least partly can be explained by a desire to preserve a feeling of self-identity. It could very well be that Bridge is right after all when he characterizes (common law) Canada — and probably England — as 'differently constituted societies' in comparison to French law Canada, the (mostly common law, but partly French law) United States, (common law) Australia and countries with a (French, German or Swiss type) code system, arguing that this is the cause of conceptual diversity. A diversity that would make it 'an abuse of the comparative legal method' to introduce a general concept of good faith in England and (common law) Canada. It is not altogether clear to me what Bridge exactly means by societies which are 'differently constituted', but my submission is that the socio-economic phenomena, as tentatively described by Legrand, indeed might be close to the heart of the problem. Perhaps England and common law Canada did develop their own particular legal system because of the type of society which existed at the time. In England, certainly, the feudal system did influence legal concepts to a large degree. But are England and common law Canada — both modern, democratic societies with a free market economy, like all the other countries in Western Europe as well as the United States and Australia — really so different from other societies even to the present day? If the answer is yes (but the answer would require a study of far more length and depth than is possible here), this would mean that legal harmonization within Europe desperately needs the development and short term implementation of a common social, economic and technological policy, in order to establish the common extra-legal basis for a European private law.

This does not mean that for the time being harmonization as to the requirement of good faith in negotiation and formation, as well as to a general duty of (precontractual) disclosure would be impossible. It only means that it can absolutely not be done in the form of a code. This would prove to be too compelling for in particular England. Principles, on the other hand, might work well, because they leave more interpretive freedom than rules. They would allow both English and other judges to opt either for an implementation by incremental development (using the principles as background notions) or for an acceptance as such (in the way as now happens in for example Dutch, German and French law). Therefore, I would support the principles as to be proposed by

---

75 *Pre-contractual disclosure*, loc. cit., p. 330, *Information in formation*, loc. cit., p. 331.

UNIDROIT, which on one hand include good faith behaviour in general and on the other hand more specifically exclude bad faith behaviour in negotiations,[76]

'(Article 1.8, Good faith and fair dealing)
(1) Each party must act in accordance with good faith and fair dealing in international trade.
(2) The parties may not exclude or limit this duty.'

'(Article 2.14, Negotiations in bad faith)
(1) A party is free to negotiate and is not liable for failure to reach an agreement.
(2) However, a party who has negotiated or broken off negotiations in bad faith is liable for the losses caused to the other party.
(3) It is bad faith, in particular, for a party to enter into or continue negotiations intending not to make an agreement with the other party.'

Let us hope that by the end of this century, the harmonization effort in the area of European private law might have proved to be far less of a burden than it is now beginning to appear. For this hope to be realized it is however a *conditio sine qua non* that comparative research does not end where it unveils conceptual divergency, but that it also attempts to overcome otherwise seemingly insuperable obstacles to harmonization by including in its analysis a thorough study of social, economic and political factors relevant to the functioning of a legal system.

---

76   Tenth consolidated version. Cf. about good faith in international commercial sales law also Honnold, *Documentary history of the Uniform Law for International Sales, The studies, deliberations and decisions that led to the 1980 United Nations Convention, with introduction and explanation* (Deventer, 1989), p. 369/370; the same author, *Uniform law for international sales under the 1980 United Nations Convention* (Deventer/Boston, 1991), p. 146 ff. and Ercüment Erdem, *La livraison de marchandises selon la Convention de Vienne, Convention des Nations Unies sur les contrats de vente internationale de marchandises du 11 avril 1980* (Travaux de la faculté de droit de l'Université de Fribourg, Suisse, no. 101; Fribourg, 1990), p. 51 ff.
An interesting development in the area of consumer protection which should be mentioned here is the EC Council Directive 93/13 on Unfair Terms in Consumer Contracts, dated 5 April 1993, O.J. L 95/29. In this directive consumers will be given protection against so-called 'unfair contract clauses'. These are clauses which have not been individually negotiated and which, against the requirements of good faith, create a significant divergence between the rights and duties for the parties to the contract.

CHAPTER 9

Defects of Consent and Capacity in Contract Law

Madeleine van Rossum

1 Introduction

The issue under consideration in this chapter is whether common principles throughout Europe concerning defects of consent and capacity in the law of contract actually exist which may be capable of yielding suggestions for a uniform concept of law in this area and to discover the major obstacles.

I will therefore examine the substantial elements of the subject of defects in consent and capacity and try to discover some overall characteristics which lie at the root of the national legal systems to be analysed and which can constitute the underlying conditions towards a unification of European rules on the subject alloted to me.[1]

I will confine myself to the capacity of natural persons and I will not deal with the problems of the capacity of corporations as this is a subject evoking many specific questions which go beyond the scope of this essay.

In order to obtain a more general and representative view, I will examine the common law tradition, as represented by English law, the civil law tradition, as represented by French law for the Roman law system and German law for the German law system[2] and Dutch law as an illustration of new legislation. I am fully aware that every restriction with respect to the choice of the legal systems under review contains a certain arbitrariness and incompleteness. Notwithstanding this limitation, the size allowed for this chapter makes it possible to give only a bird's-eye view of the legal systems and therefore an elaboration of case law and jurisprudence has been omitted. Instead I will confine myself to glean from these sources only the salient features.

After this survey I will compare the national legal systems referring to defects of consent and capacity and finally come to the crucial point of whether some general rules can be obtained which can ultimately lead towards harmonization. This will be a difficult and risky enterprise but also a challenge.

---

1   For the rationales of comparative studies see for example D. Kokkini-Iatridou, 'De rechtsvergelijking resp. de infrastructuur van de rechtsvergelijking' in: D. Kokkini-Iatridou et. al., *Een inleiding tot het rechtsvergelijkende onderzoek* (1988) p. 3-42, resp. p. 78-93; Hugh Collins, 'Methods and aims of comparative contract law', *Oxford Journal of Legal Studies* (1991), p. 396-406.

2   In accordance with K. Zweigert and H. Kötz, Translated by Tony Weir, *An introduction to Comparative law* (1992), p. 76-285.

I will focus particularly on the subject of error and undue influence as they prove to be of great importance in legal practice.

2 The Common Law Tradition on the Subject of Defects of Consent and Capacity in Contract Law

2.1 The Common Law System, as Represented by English Law

2.1.1 Defects of Consent: Mistake and Misrepresentation (Error), Duress and Undue Influence

A IN GENERAL

Mistake, misrepresentation, duress and undue influence concern the formation of the contract and refer to the intention of the parties to create legal relations. Because of the common law tradition, these legal concepts are not *prima facie* considered as defects of will or consent and the elements of *consensual agreement* and *will* play a less important role than in the civil law tradition. However the alien doctrine of mistake was incorporated into English law in the 19th century on the false assumption that the English law of contract, as with French contract law, was based upon consent and agreement.

In cases of mistake the emphasis is placed on the misconception of the party in error whilst in cases of misrepresentation, duress (threat) and undue influence, the (unlawful) behaviour of the other party is emphasized. The main rule in common law is that a mistake renders the contract void. However in equity, the contract may be held to be voidable at the option of one or both parties. Referring to misrepresentation, duress and undue influence the contract can be rescinded by the party who has been induced to enter into the contract. When the contract has been concluded under the influence of negligent or fraudulent misrepresentation, duress and undue influence the injured party also has a claim for damages.

The concepts of mistake, misrepresentation, duress and undue influence involve a rather complex mixture of common law, equity and statute law (The Misrepresentation Act 1967). Because of the casuistic approach of the Anglo-American law system as represented by English law it is difficult to find some general rules on this topic.

B MISTAKE AND MISREPRESENTATION[3]

The effect of a mistake on an otherwise apparently valid contract is rather difficult both to define and to regulate. This is further complicated by the fact that the rules

---

3   On this subject see for example S.J. Stoljar, *Mistake and misrepresentation* (1968); P.S. Atiyah, *An introduction of the law of contract* (1981) p. 218-288; D.K. Allen, *Misrepresentation (1988)*, *Chitty on Contracts, vol. I, General Principles* (1989) paras 331-401, 411-493: M.H. Whincup, *Contract law and practice, The English system and continental comparisons* (1992).

are entirely a product of case law and thus somewhat fragmentary and difficult to predict, next to the fact that there are two quite different approaches to the problem — that of common law and of equity.

With mistake the main emphasis is on the misapprehension of the mistaken party. In English law one usually distinguishes between unilateral and bilateral mistake. Most instances of unilateral mistake concern cases of 'mistaken identity' also called 'mistake as to the person' and entail the doctrine of 'documents mistakenly signed'. Bilateral mistake occurs when *both* parties have misapprehended the basic contents of the contract. Bilateral mistake is subsequently divided into common mistake (both parties share the same misapprehension) and mutual mistake (either party holds a different view of the subject matter of the contract).

In common law the mistake renders the contract completely void. There is no half-way solution. In equity however, the contract may be held to be voidable at the option of one or both parties, and the court has the discretion to adapt and modify the contract or to impose certain terms on the contracting parties.

The concept of misrepresentation concerns a statement of fact made by one party (the representor) to the other (the representee) which is false and is one of the reasons that induced the representee to enter into the contract. Thus the misrepresentation must be material to make it actionable. In respect of the doctrine of misrepresentation the representee's duty to investigate for himself is applied restrictively because in general on a representation concerning a substantial element of the contract one may have been relied.

English law recognizes three categories of misrepresentation: fraudulent misrepresentation (deceit), negligent misrepresentation stemming from negligence, and innocent misrepresentation where the misrepresentator has justifiable reason to believe his representation to be correct. All three categories of misrepresentation can lead to a rescission of the contract. Damages, however, can only be claimed in cases of fraudulent or negligent misrepresentation.

Thus in the case of *Howard Marine* v. *Ogden*[4] a barge owner declared the capacity of his boats as 1, 600 tonnes, based on information derived from the Lloyds Register. However the correct figure, which was stated in the shipping documents, was only 1,055 tonnes and the barges proved to be unfit for the work involved. The hirers refused to pay and successfully sued for negligent misrepresentation, and damages were consequently awarded. Under English law the duty to make correct precontractual statements is very broad.

In *Howard Marine* v. *Ogden* the Court of Appeal indicated that the onus of proof immediately passes to the representor to prove that he had reasonable grounds to

---

4   [1978] 2 ALL ER 1134. Other cases relating to the doctrine of misrepresentation include Ridge v. Crawley [1959] EG 959, Brown v. Raphael [1958] 2 ALL ER 79, Chess v. Williamson [1957] 1 ALL ER 325, Bentley v. Smith [1965] 2 ALL ER 65, JEB Fasteners Ltd v. Marks, Blooms & Co [1983] 1 ALL ER 583, Esso Petroleum v. Mardon [1976] 2 WLR 582, Royscot Trust Ltd v. Rogerson and another [1991] 3 WLR 57, Morgan Crucible Co. v. Hill Samual Co [1991] 2 WLR 655, East v. Maurer [1991] 2 ALL ER 733.

believe the facts represented to be true. In the words of Bridge L.J.: 'In the course of negotiations leading to a contract the statute [that is to say The Misrepresentation Act 1967, MvR] imposes an absolute obligation not to state facts which the representor cannot prove he has reasonable ground to believe'.

English law basically recognizes no duty of disclosure. Mere knowledge of vital facts which might influence the other's party decision on whether to enter into the contract or not, does not in and of itself amount to misrepresentation.[5] However there are several exceptions to this rule, for instance in the case of contracts *uberrimae fidei*, in connection with a fiduciary relationship between the parties or in case of sales of land, certain defects in the vendor's title must be disclosed.[6]

Misrepresentation emphasizes the false precontractual statement of fact or the failure to disclose information to the other party whereas mistake accentuates the error of the mistaken party.

C   DURESS (THREAT) AND UNDUE INFLUENCE (ABUSE OF CIRCUMSTANCES)[7]

In English law a contractor can annul a contract on the ground of duress if he entered into it under threat of physical injury or by some other evil, for example blackmail. Duress is a concept of the common law which takes a narrow view as to the facts which would constitute the pressure. At common law duress consists of only actual or threatened violence or imprisonment. In equity however the courts have administered the wider doctrine of undue influence.

In cases of undue influence there is an abuse of a personal relationship of confidence and care or, even without such relationship, a domination of one party by another. Thus the equitable doctrine of undue influence covers both cases of abuse of circumstances owing to a particular relationship, as well as cases of coercion, domination or pressure outside these special relationships and is therefore less narrowly defined as duress.

A leading case in this area is *Lloyds Bank* v. *Bundy*,[8] where an elderly farmer had mortgaged his property to stave off the bankruptcy of his son's business after the father had received a visit from the son's bank manager.

The Court of Appeal set the agreement aside, emphasizing the fiduciary relation-ship between the bank and the farmer. The Court of Appeal indicated that the relationship was one to which the doctrine of undue influence applied and required that the weaker party had independent advice prior to entering into the transaction.

---

5   On this subject see for example the leading case of Bell v. Lever Brothers Ltd [1932] AC 161.
6   B. Nicolas, 'The precontractual obligations to disclose information. English report', in: D. Harris and D. Tallon (eds.), *Contract Law today: Anglo-French comparisons* (1991), p. 166-193; C. Harpum, 'Selling without title: a vendors duty of disclosure', *LQR* (1992) p. 1280 et seq.
7   *Chitty on Contracts, vol. I, General Principles* (1989) paras 501-521, 522-542; K. Zweigert and H. Kötz, *op. cit.* n. 2, p. 440-458.
8   [1975] QB 326. On this subject see for example also the classic case of Tate v. Williamson [1866] 2 Ch App 55.

In recent years the courts seem to have cautiously recognized the possibility of economic duress which may blur the traditional distinction between the classic concept of duress and undue influence. Economic duress may occur when the coercive nature of the threat to the other party's economic interests is so powerful that it leaves him with no other realistic alternative but to contract. Yet there is a very narrow dividing line between economic duress and normal thrust of business.

So in *North Ocean Shipping Co Ltd* v. *Hyundai Construction Co Ltd*,[9] shipbuilders who were building a ship under a contract for the purchasers, without any legal jusitfication threatened to terminate the contract unless the purchasers agreed (within a few days) to an increase in the price of 10 per cent. Given the purchasers' great need for the vessels, and the likely consequences of a termination by the builders, the purchasers reluctantly acquiesced to this demand, but under protest.

The Privy Council, confirmed by the House of Lords, considered that the threat exceeded the normal commercial pressure and this amounted to a case of economic duress.

Closely related to economic duress is the doctrine of the restraint of trade. In this concept a promise is in the restraint of trade if its performance would limit competition in any business or restrict the exercise of a gainful occupation.

Under English law it is not quite clear how to treat the legal rules relating to duress and undue influence. When the judicial nature of duress and undue influence — in accordance with the civil law tradition — is conceived as resting on the absence or the deviation of consent, the terminology is confusing. It is questionable if the party who was subject to duress or undue influence was incapable of making a free choice or acting voluntarily, or that duress and undue influence did not literally deprive the person affected of all choice but that he intended to do what he did, but did so unwillingly. In the latter case, the contract procured by the coercion is not void but voidable at the discretion of the party subject to the coercion. Once this view is accepted, and there is a tendency in English law towards this option, it follows that it is the nature of the influence and the behaviour of the other party which becomes all-important.

2.1.2 Capacity[10]

The common law system does not have a general concept for a person's capacity to contract. Casuistical as always, it has been concerned with identifying the types of cases in which some categories of individuals are subject to a degree of contractual incapacity. These categories are minors, mentally disordered persons, and drunken persons. The law will protect those whose mental powers are

---

9   [1979] QB 705. See also the cases of Occidental Worldwide Investment Corporation v. Skibs A/S Avanti [1976] Lloyd's Rep. 293, Universe Tankships of Monrovia v. International Transport Workers Federation [1983] AC 366, and the article by Roger Halson, 'Opportunism, economic duress and contractual modifications', *LQR* 1991, p. 649-678.

10   *Chitty on Contracts, vol. I, General Principles* (1989) paras 551-626; K. Zweigert and H. Kötz *op. cit.* n. 2, p. 372-380.

underdeveloped by preventing them from doing harm to themselves as a result of their legal actions.

Since the Family Law Reform Act 1969 the age of capacity for the purposes of the law of contract which was 21, was reduced to 18. The general rule in common law is that all minor's contracts are optionally voidable, apart from contracts for necessaries and contracts of apprenticeship, education and service. Necessaries can be defined as goods or services suitable to the young person's social position and actual needs.

English law makes a distinction between those contracts made by lunatics (as identified by a judge) and those contracts made by people who are mentally disordered or intoxicated. If the mental disturbance has been judicially ascertained, the contracts of these 'lunatics so found' are held void. Except in cases of contracts other than for necessaries the basic rule is that a mentally disordered or an intoxicated person is bound by his contract unless he can show that he was not responsible for his actions at the time of making the contract and that the other party was aware of this incapacity.

3 The Civil Law Tradition on the Subject of Defects of Consent and Capacity in Contract Law

3.1 The Roman System, as Represented by French Law

3.1.1 Defects of Consent: erreur (Error), dol (Fraud) and violence (Threat)

A   IN GENERAL

Article 1109 of the French Civil Code states that contractual consent is vitiated by error, fraud or threat. Contracts affected by these so-called *vices du consentement* can be annulled. Defects of consent can be defined as certain circumstances or conditions which alter the formation of the will in his conscience or freedom. They do not destroy the will completely but only 'deflect' it. Gradually these defects of consent changed in character and the element of the will became less predominant. The courts have interpreted *erreur, dol and violence* with great ingenuity. Although the '*vice du consentement*'-approach has not been left, the good faith-approach has gained prominence and the stress has shifted from the misconception of the mistaken, deceived or threatened party, to another's behaviour, in whose context the justifiable reliance of the parties becomes increasingly important.

The defects of consent can lead to a rescission of the contract at the discretion of the person whose judgment has been influenced by error, fraud or threat. When the other party has acted wrongfully a claim for damages can also be awarded next to or instead of the rescission of the contract. The basis for the claim for damages is article 1382 CC (the liability for unlawful acts).

B *ERREUR* (ERROR (MISTAKE))[11]

Under French law an error resulting in a *vice du consentement* nullifies a contract. Article 1110 of the French Civil Code distinguishes between two different kinds of mistake namely an error as to the substantial matter of the contract *l'erreur sur la substance* and an error as to the person *l'erreur sur la personne*. Mistake as to the substance concerns the essence or identity of the thing which is the object of the contract *qualités substantielles*. Mistake as to the person annuls a contract only if the particular qualities of that person — physical, intellectual, moral or legal— are the basis of the contract. Under French law an error may only be taken into account if it is a principle motivation in concluding the contract, *motif principal ou déterminant*. An error constitutes the determining motivation if the mistaken party would never have entered into the contract but for the mistake.

Although the error is primarily concerned with the quality of the mistaken party's consent, French law accords increasingly weight to the conduct of the other party and the influence which this conduct has exercised on the mistaken party's consent. Gradually the emphasis is now placed not on the state of mind of the mistaken party, but on the behaviour of the other party, and a solution is sought which fits in the perspective of a reasonable allocation of risk. This of course *a fortiori* holds true for fraud (see sub section c), but also in case of error it is generally accepted that the other party can be obliged to give his contracting party such information as will allow him to enter into the contract with sufficient knowledge of the facts. This obligation of disclosure has its source in the inequality of the information available to the parties.[12] In this respect the *status* of the parties seems to play an important role, such as between a layman and a professional.

The *Tribunal de Grande Instance de Paris 4-3-1980, D 1980, somm. 262* has imposed a duty of disclosure on a professional vendor of a house who did not tell the purchaser about an unusual restriction to build, this omission evoked the error.[13]

It is also agreed — although the French Civil Code says nothing on this point — that an error is only relevant in so far as it is excusable. In deciding whether an error is excusable or not the courts attach great importance to the professional qualifications or abilities of the mistaken party and any bad faith on the other side. The principle instance of an inexcusable and therefore irrelevant mistake occurs when the party in error has the means or capacity of informing himself of the true state of the facts before entering into the contract.

---

11 Jacques Ghestin, *Traité du droit civil, Les Obligations, Le contrat; formation* (1988) paras 368-415; René Rodiere (ed) *Les Vices du consentement dans le contrat* (1977); K. Zweigert and H. Kötz, *op. cit.* n. 2, p. 440-458.

12 Jacques Ghestin, 'The Pre-contractual Obligation to Disclose Information' in: *Contract Law Today: Anglo-French comparisons* (1991) p. 151-166.

13 For the duty of disclosure in French law see Yves Boyer, *L'Obligation de renseignements dans la formation du contrat* (1978), especially p. 373-408, TGI d'Argentan 15 oct. 1970, D 1971, JPR 719, Cour de Paris 22 Jan. 1953, JCP 1953, II 17435, TGI Paris ('Poussin — case') 13 Dec. 1972, D 1973, JPR 410, TGI Brest 5 Nov. 1974, D 1975, JPR 295, Cour de Rennes, 9 July 1975, D 1976, JPR 417, TGI Paris 6 March 1985, D 1984, JPR 457.

Together with cases concerning an error as to the subject matter of the contract and an error as to the person, French law recognizes cases of *'l'erreur obstacle'*, when the consent of the contracting parties is totally lacking because of an error as to the expression or the transmission of the will, for example when parties talk at cross-purposes.[14]

C   *DOL* (FRAUD) AND *VIOLENCE* (THREAT)[15]

Under French law there is a close connection between being mistaken and being deceived. The difference is that in cases of an error, the emphasis is primarily laid on the misconception of the mistaken party while in cases of fraud the misbehaviour of the other party is accentuated. However, the dividing line between the two has gradually been drawn less sharply because in cases of mistake the behaviour of the party who causes the error becomes increasingly important.

Fraud can vitiate consent to a contract when one's party deceptive manoeuvres are such that the other party would not otherwise have entered into the contract (article 1116 of the French Civil Code). The deceitful acts consist of lies or other artifices. The burden of proof is laid on the person who pretends to be injured. Silence may constitute fraud only when one contracting party has a duty to give the other information he cannot discover for himself.[16] French law seems to insist that the fraud has been caused by a party to the contract whose bad faith is demanded. Under French law duress consists of physical violence which effects the will of the threatened party and induces him to enter into the contract (article 1112 of the French Civil Code). Duress may be exercised by the other party to a contract and by third parties, even when the other party is not aware of the threat. In France it is not the physical violence itself which deflects the will but the fear it inspires. The victim of the violence has to prove the existence of the illegitimate pressure.

Economic duress as a ground for the rescission of the contract is strictly defined: the economic pressure must be essentially untrue and illegal to fall within the scope of this rule.

Although French law does not embrace *stricto sensu* a doctrine of undue influence it does recognize some fiduciary relationships where 'utmost good faith' is required, such as between parent and child (article 1114 of the French Code Civil), guardian and ward (article 907 of the French Code Civil), doctor and patient (article 909 of the French Code Civil). In those situations a mental predominance of one party over another is presumed and when this circumstance is abused, a parallel may be drawn with the cases of undue influence. The underlying principle is the protection of justifiable reliance. Furthermore, there is a tendency in French

---

14   Jacques Ghestin, *op. cit.* n. 11, para 373.
15   Jacques Ghestin, *op. cit.* n. 11, paras 416-442, 443-454; Jacques Ghestin, *op. cit.* n. 12; René Rodiere, *op. cit.* n. 11; K. Zweigert and H. Kötz, *op. cit.* n. 2, p. 440-458.
16   Jacques Ghestin *op. cit.* n. 11, paras 430-436, Cass. civ. 3e Jan. 1971 JCP 1971, IV 43, D 1971, Cass. com. 21 March 1977, JCP 1977, IV 135 Cass. com. 13 Oct. 1980, D 1981, IRP 309, Cass. civ. 20 July 1981, JCP 1982, Ed.N. no 8367, p. 437, Cass. civ. 3e, 25 Febr. 1987, Bull. civ. III no. 36, p. 21.

law to broaden the scope of this rule in situations where the relationship between the parties is based on confidence and reliance or is characterized by a distinct inequality of bargaining power especially in case of contracts of adhesion.[17]

It must be mentioned that the lines between the various defects of consent have become less defined.

3.1.2 Capacity[18]

The age of majority in France is 18. The general rule is that a minor cannot make a valid contract unless his parents or guardian have approved of it (article 423 of the French Code Civil). However to establish that the contractor was a minor at the time the contract was made is not enough to rescind the contract. Moreover the minor must establish that the transaction was disadvantageous for him.

Some important transactions, such as sales of land, cannot be concluded by a minor himself even if they are profitable, because only the minor's statutory representative could make the contract on his behalf by complying with certain formal requirements. On the other hand, the transactions of daily life which minors usually conclude are generally binding on a minor as they are seldom disadvantageous.

The protection of adults suffering from some incapacity is nowadays regulated by the statute of 3rd January 1968. This protection can be accomplished by the court by rescinding lesionary transactions or by giving them only limited effects, or by setting up a tutorship *tutelle* when a person needs constant representation or a curatorship *curatelle* when a person only needs supervision. This person under care can conclude the normal daily transactions but needs consent of his curator for other affairs.

The policy of the rules relating to capacity is to protect those persons whose abilities are (supposed to be) limited.

3.2 The Germanistic System, as Represented by German Law

3.2.1 Defects of Consent: Irrtum (Error), arglistige Taüschung (Fraud), wider-rechtliche Drohung (Threat)

A IN GENERAL

Under German law the manifestation of the will, *Willenserklärung* can be defective on different grounds. German law distinguishes between a defect in the *formation* of the will *Willensbildung* in case of an error of motive *Motivirrtum*, fraud *arglistige Täuschung* and threat *widerrechtliche Drohung*, and a defect in the *declaration* of the will *ein Mangel in der Erklärungshandlung*, which arises for example when the representor says something different from which he intends to say, this constitutes an *Erklärungsirrtum*. The mistaken party can rescind the

---

17   Yves Boyer, *op. cit.* n. 13, p. 322-349, Jacques Ghestin *op. cit.* n. 12, p. 164-165.
18   Jacques Ghestin, *op. cit.* n. 11, para 194; K. Zweigert and H. Kötz, *op. cit.* n. 2, p. 372-380.

contract, regardless of the behaviour of the other party. However the other party has a claim for the harm he has suffered if he has justifiably relied on the promise now rescinded.

The contract can also be vitiated in case of the so-called fundamental error *Grundlage Irrtum*, when the error effects the essence of the contract.

Relating to fraud and threat, German law assumes that the deceived or threatened party was incapable of making a free choice because his will has been completely 'overthrown'. Thus the victim is deprived of any will and on that basis he can annul the contract. Furthermore the deceived or threatened party has a claim for damages. In that respect he can require to be put in a position as if the contract were never concluded, this is called *Ersatz des Vertrauensschadens*.

B *IRRTUM* (ERROR)[19]

Basically German law distinguishes between *an error in the transaction Erklärungsirrtum*, which effects the contract and *an error of motive Motivirrtum*, which does not effect the contract (paragraph 119 BGB). The distinction between these two categories is rather subtle. It is a material error in the transaction when the contractor has formed his intention quite correctly but has made a mistake in declaring it, while in case of an error of motive, the intention itself is incorrectly formed.

However the question as to whether the error is one in the transaction or one of motive is of no great importance under German law, while pursuant to paragraph 119 sub 2 BGB a contractor may also rescind for errors of motive if they concern qualities of the person or the thing which are, according to standard business practice, regarded as essential. So the circumstances which fall under the scope of paragraph 119 BGB and which may allow a party to set the contract aside because of mistake include situations.of slips of the tongue or the pen, and the use of ambiguous terms or expressions, as well as misunderstandings about the essential elements of the contract.

Apart from paragraph 119 BGB a contract can be annulled because of a fundamental error when both parties share the same misconception about the subject matter of the contract. In cases of this so-called fundamental error *Grundlagenirrtum*, the error concerns a particular feature of the contract which, according to good faith and normal commercial practice, is contemplated as the necessary foundation of the contract. In the absence of a specific statutory provision, this concept is based on the broad principle of good faith (*Treu und Glauben*), (paragraph 157, paragraph 242 BGB). The courts regarded it as unreasonable if the contract is upheld when both parties are mistaken about the underlying assumption of the contract *Geschäftsgrundlage*, which in fact does not exist. The courts have a great discretion to determine whether or not an error is fundamental.

---

19   Karl Larenz, *Algemeiner Teil des deutschen Bürgerlichen Rechts*, 1989, p. 362-397; K. Zweigert and H. Kötz, *op. cit.* n. 7, p. 372-380.

Under German law *Irrtum* is a defect of consent in *optima forma*. As already mentioned, the party in error can rescind the contract irrespective of how it was evoked. As a rule the behaviour of the other party is irrelevant except to his claim for damages after the rescission of the contract if he has justifiably relied on the promise now rescinded. However througout German contract law gradually more attention is paid to the behaviour of the contracting parties in accepting a duty of disclosure which can take precedence over the duty to make one's own investigations.[20]

Furthermore in contracts of sale, German law particularly imposes on the vendor a duty to inform the other party about qualities of the subject matter of the contract in case of material and juridicial defects (paragraph 434 ff BGB, paragraph 459 ff BGB), in which situations may resemble cases of error. It is the general opinion in case law and jurisdiction that these rules relating to material and juridicial defects prevail over the rules concerning error.

The underlying principle for the duty of disclosure is to protect the reasonable expectations and the justifiable reliance of the contracting parties in the context of a reasonable allocation of risk.[21]

C *ARGLISTIGE TAÜSCHUNG* (FRAUD) AND *WIDERRECHTLICHE DROHUNG* (THREAT)[22]

Also under German law the relationship between being mistaken and being deceived is emphasized. In case of fraud however, the accent is specifically laid on the objectionable behaviour of the other party.

According to paragraph 123 BGB, fraud under German law requires a deliberate deception, which induced the misled party to enter into the contract. It is assumed that the free will of the deceived party has been fully destroyed and thus his private autonomy, which is a basic element of contract law, is at stake and this gives him the right to invalidate the contract. It seems to be necessary that the party who invokes the fraud has acted on purpose. A failure to speak only constitutes fraud when there is a duty to speak according to the principle of good faith and taking into account all the circumstances of the individual case.

The *Bundesgerichtshof* has held a party liable for fraud in case where the vendor of land had concealed a notice of the local authority and in another case where the vendor of a building did not disclose the fact that an extension to the building was built illegally.[23]

When the deceit is practised by another than the contracting party rescission is only granted when the contracting party himself was aware or should have been

---

20 For example BGH, NJW 1974, 1975, A G Köln NJW 1978, 2603, BGH NJW 1978, 41, BGH, NJW 1978, 2546, BGH NJW 1979, 1707.

21 Jürgen Lauer, *Vorvertragliche Informationspflichten (insbesondere gegenüber Verbrauchern) nach schweizerischem, deutschem und französischem Recht* (1983), Stephan Breidenbach, *Die Voraussetzungen von Informationspflichten beim Vertragsschluss* (1989).

22 Karl Larenz, *op. cit.* n. 19 p. 397-406; K. Zweigert and H. Kötz *op. cit.* n. 2, p. 440-458.

23 Respectively BGH, WM 1976 401 and BGH, NJW 1979, 2243. See also BGH, NJW 1971, 1795, BGH, NJW 1977, 1055, BGH; NJ 1979, 1707.

aware of the deception or if the third's party behaviour is attributable to him (paragraph 123 BGB).

In case of threat *widerrechtliche Drohung* the threatened party acts under an illegitimate pressure and therefore can annul the contract. It seems that a person under threat has a greater claim to annul the contract than in the case of fraud and the threat even can be established against a contractor who was in good faith and innocent to the threat.

There is neither a general rule which allows the person acting under an economic pressure to rescind the contract nor a general concept of undue influence. However under paragraph 138 BGB a contract is void, if a fiduciary relationship exists and one party abuses another's poverty, dependency, irresponsibility or inexperience, which resembles cases of economic duress and undue influence.[24]

Recently the *Bundesgerichtshof* has extended the scope of paragraph 138 BGB in a case where a brewery lent money to a couple in order to furnish their café. The terms of the loan were very onerous. The couple were obliged to sell only the brewery's products for a period of 10 years and they did not receive any protection against the brewery supplying another café in the area where they operated. Moreover, after expiration of the contract they had to hand over all the clients without any compensation whilst another clause prevented them subsequently operating in the same line of business. Thus the couple was bound hand and foot. It was held that the contract was void refering to paragraph 138 BGB.[25] In this context a parallel may be drawn with the Anglo-American 'restraint of the trade-doctrine' in which the competition of any business would be limited or the promisor would be restricted in the exercise of a gainful competition, which is closely related to situations of economic duress.

3.2.2 Capacity[26]
Under German law the basic rule is that every person who reaches the age of majority — which since the 1st of January 1975 has been fixed at 18 years — is capable of performing juristic acts except for persons suffering from severe mental illness and persons under restraint. German law distinguishes between incapacity and limited capacity. A child under 7 is lacking any contractual capacity (paragraph 104 BGB sub 1), just like an adult who in consequence of lunacy, madness or similar circumstances totally lacks the capacity to act in a normal way (paragraph 104 BGB sub 2). The legal position of a mentally disturbed person is not quite clear under German law. A compromise is sought between the protective aim which underlies the policy of incapacity and the needs of business.[27]

Contracts with minors aged between seven and eighteen are valid only if their legal representatives have approved of them (paragraph 105-107 BGB). However

---

24 Michael Kempermann, *Unlautere Ausnützung von Vertrauensverhältnissen im englischen, französischen und deutschen Recht*, 1975, p. 104-119.
25 BGH, NJW-RR 1987, p. 628.
26 Karl Larenz, *op. cit.* n. 19, p. 88-128; K. Zweigert and H. Kötz, *op. cit.* n. 2, p. 372-380.
27 Karl Larenz, *op. cit.* n. 19, p. 100-101.

when a contract has purely a legal advantage to the minor, he is bound by his declaration of intention (paragraph 107 BGB) but this exception is narrowly defined. The mere fact that the contract would have a beneficial effect on the minor's estate is not sufficient; the contract must not impose even the slightest obligation on the minor, which illustrates the paternalistic approach of German law.

A minor's contract is also valid if he can execute the contract with means specifically or generally provided by his legal representative or by another party with the representative's consent. This so-called pocket money paragraph *Taschengeldparagraph* (paragraph 110 BGB), concerns particularly situations where parents have given their minor child an allowance or have given him a provision for travelling to and from school or college.

Generally the BGB gives a minor a great protection but on the other hand restricts severely the independence of the minor by requiring the legal representative to ratify the contract even when the obligations for the minor are trivial and even if that would be reasonable to do so according to all the circumstances.

The legal capacity of an adult can totally or partly be removed by way of a judicial order, *Entmündigung*, on grounds of lunacy, mental derangement, extravagance, dipsomania or addiction to drugs (paragraph 6 BGB). In cases of lunacy, the person under interdiction is entirely without contractual capacity. If a person under interdiction is still capable of any judgment or whose interdiction is based on other grounds than lunacy, his contractual capacity is only limited and he is treated as a minor with an age of over 7 years (paragraph 114 BGB).

4 New Codifications, as Represented by Dutch Law

4.1 Defects of Consent: *dwaling* (Error), *bedreiging* (Threat), *bedrog* (Fraud) and *misbruik van omstandigheden* (Abuse of Circumstances)

A IN GENERAL

Under Dutch law error (*dwaling*), threat (*bedreiging*), fraud (*bedrog*), and abuse of circumstances (*misbruik van omstandigheden*) are considered vices of consent or defects of will (*wilsgebreken*). Threat, fraud and abuse of circumstances are to be found in section 3:44 of the new Dutch Civil Code and are generally applicable to all juridicial acts whereas error is placed in section 6:228 of the new Dutch Civil Code and primarily concerns contracts.

In case of a defect of consent there is *a consensus ad idem* between the contracting parties and the agreement has been expressed correctly but the underlying will has been formed in a defective way. On this ground a party can rescind the contract and under certain circumstances can claim for damages. Concerning threat, fraud and abuse of circumstances, the unlawful behaviour of the other party is emphasized which induced the victim to enter into the contract. Moreover in cases of mistake and misrepresentation both in the case law and under the new legislation, the stress has shifted from the error of judgment of the mistaken party to the misstatement or omission by the other party in whose context the interaction between the duty to inform and the duty to make one's own investigations is of great importance.

To claim damages under Dutch law it is usually required that liability should arise in tort (section 6:162 of the new Dutch Civil Code). Yet liability may also be based on the concept of good faith/reasonableness and fairness which is a leading principle throughout Dutch law (section 6:2 and 6:248 of the new Dutch Civil Code).

Furthermore there is under Dutch law some room left for common mistake, to be found in section 6:228 sub 1c of the new Dutch Civil Code, when both parties share the same misconception about the subject matter of the contract, so both parties are in error.

B *DWALING* (ERROR)[28]

'*Dwaling*', like the other defects of consent, plays a role in the formation of the contract and concerns the intention of the contracting parties to create legal relations. The concept of *dwaling* under Dutch law has been developed from a traditional defect of consent where the main emphasis is on the misrepresentation of the mistaken party, to a legal concept with the accent on the false precontractual statement of fact made by the other party or his failure to disclose information. Formerly *dwaling* was primarily controlled by the notion of the *zelfstandigheid der zaak*, that is to say the subject matter of the contract. After the leading cases on this subject *Baris* v. *Riezenkamp (1957), NJ 1958, 67* and *Van der Beek* v. *Van Dartel (1973), NJ 1974, 97*, dwaling is now placed within the legal context of the duty to make true statements of fact in the course of precontractual negotiations, the duty to disclose information and the duty of the representee to make his own inquiries before concluding the contract.

Thus in the case *Baris* v. *Riezenkamp* a purchaser bought the equipment for the production of auxilary motors after a misrepresentation of the vendor concerning the calculation of the cost price. The purchaser was allowed to rescind the contract because the *Hoge Raad* assumed that generally a party could justifiably rely on the correctness of a representation of the other party which turned out to be false, and which induced him to enter into the contract.[29]

In the case of *Van der Beek* v. *Van Dartel* a duty to disclose relevant information was accepted where the vendor of a house had 'forgotten' to tell the purchaser that the local authority had the intention to claim the occupation of the house unless — within two months — a reasonable proposal for the occupation of the house would be received. The *Hoge Raad* held that there is a duty of disclosure

---

28 Asser-Hartkamp II, *Verbintenissenrecht, Algemene leer der overeenkomsten* (1993) no 173-198; M.M. van Rossum, *Dwaling in het bijzonder bij koop van onroerend goed* (1991) p. 9-53; E.H. Hondius, *Consumentenrecht*, Mon. Nieuw BW A-8, p. 21-23.

29 On this subject see also for example the case of Booy v. Wisman (1966), *NJ* 1966, 183.

which prevails over the duty to make one's own investigations.[30] However under Dutch law, the perception of *dwaling* as a defect of consent has not been discarded, although the emphasis has shifted.

The new Dutch Civil Code came into force on 1st January 1992 and the concept of *dwaling* is contained in section 6:228. Although the nature of *'dwaling'* has changed from the original Dutch Civil Code it remains a defect in consent. Whilst the new emphasis is placed on the precontractual statement of fact made by the representor or his failure to disclose, some room for common mistake remains.

So far, for an action based on *dwaling* to be succesful it is necessary that the false precontractual statement of fact or the failure to disclose is of such importance that without this behaviour, the party in error would not — or at least not on the same terms — have entered into the contract. In case of common mistake the error of both parties must similarly be of substantial importance.[31]

Furthermore in section 6:228 sub 2 of the new Dutch Civil Code some restrictive conditions referring to *dwaling* are laid down. The error cannot be based therefore on future circumstances, and sometimes the error is not excusable merely because there is a predominant duty for the mistaken party to make his own inquiries before entering into the contract, especially when he is an expert or a professional party. Thus the concept of *dwaling* under the new Dutch Civil Code is situated within the context of a justified allocation of risk.

C *BEDROG* (FRAUD), *BEDREIGING* (THREAT), AND *MISBRUIK VAN OMSTANDIGHEDEN* (ABUSE OF CIRCUMSTANCES)[32]

Under Dutch law fraud and error are closely connected. It is the fraud which causes the error and it is not the fraud itself that constitutes the defect of will but the misconception of the deceived party which is effected by the fraud. Fraud exists if a representee is induced by another party to enter into the contract by deliberately providing him with false information, by intentionally concealing any fact he was obliged to tell, or by any other trick. For fraud, as contrasted with error, the intention to mislead the representee is of critical importance. General recommendations, notwithstanding the fact that they may not be true, cannot constitute fraud.

Threat occurs where one party induces another party to conclude a contract by unlawfully coercing him or a third party, with harm to his person or his property (for example by blackmail). The threat must be of such a nature that a reasonable person would be influenced. For the rescission of a juristic act it is necessary that the threat has an illicit character.

---

30 Other cases include Van Hensbergen v. Gemeente 's-Gravenhage (1979), *NJ* 1980, 290, Van Lanschot v. Berthe Bink (1990), *NJ* 1991, 759, Van Geest v. Nederlof (1990), *NJ* 1991, 251.

31 See M.M. van Rossum, 'The concept of dwaling under the new Civil Code compared to the doctrine of misrepresentation', *NILR* (1992) issue 3, p. 303-331.

32 Asser-Hartkamp II, *op. cit.* n. 28, no. 199-204, no. 205-209, no. 209-216; Van Rossum, *op. cit.* n. 28, p. 55-74.

Furthermore the new Dutch Civil Code recognizes a fourth defect of consent with the abuse of circumstances. A person who acts under special circumstances, such as a state of necessity or dependency, inexperience or mental crisis, can rescind the contract if the other party induces him to enter into the contract although what the other party knows or ought to have known should have prevented him from concluding the contract. In most of the cases involving the abuse of circumstances the other party acts from a mental or economic dominance.

Thus in the case of *Van Elmbt* v. *Feierabend (1964) NJ 1965, 104* an elderly widow who had sold her house which she was very fond of, to a man who she considered as the person who would help her out of her financial problems and who she trusted blindly. The man knew that keeping of her house was of crucial importance to the widow. The *Hoge Raad* held that the contract was void in view of her state of mind and her dependency.[33]

When the threat, fraud or abuse of circumstances is evoked by a third party, the juristic act can only be annulled when the other party has been aware of it. Under Dutch law economic duress is applied restrictively.[34]

4.2 Capacity[35]

Under Dutch law every natural person is capable of performing juristic acts except where the law provides otherwise (section 3:32 of the new Dutch Civil Code). Minors and persons under guardianship *curatele* are considered not capable of performing judicial acts. The function of the rules relating to incapacity is basically protective: those persons whose mental faculties are underdeveloped should be stopped from doing themselves harm by their legal acts. According to this policy only the minor or his legal representative can rescind the contract. However a unilateral juristic act of an incapable person is void when it is not addressed to one or more specifically determined persons.

The age of majority is 18. Yet a minor is capable of performing legal acts when he has acted with the consent of his parents or with funds which the parents have put at his disposal for the cost of living or study (section 1:234 of the new Dutch Civil Code). This provision is conceived broadly and encloses situations where the minor himself has the disposal of his own wages.

An adult can be put under guardianship for reasons of mental disturbance, extravagance or addiction to drink (section 1:378 of the new Dutch Civil Code). The rules concerning minors and persons under guardianship are valued so highly that they take precedence over the needs of business.

It should be mentioned that in case the mental deranged person is not under guardianship, Dutch law gives a special provision in section 3:34 of the new Dutch

---

33   Recently on this subject Van Meurs v. Ciba-Geigy BV (1992) *NJ* 1992, 377.

34   For example the case of Brandwijk v. Brandwijk (1979), *NJ* 1980, 249, Wirtz v. A.S.Z. (1987), *NJ* 1987, 989, Donkelaar v. Unigro (1990), *RvdW* 1990, 117.

35   Asser-Hartkamp II, *op. cit.* n. 28, no. 87-96.

Civil Code, which differentiates from the rules relating to incapacity. If it is established that a person as a result of mental disturbance has no free will, the legal act is voidable but for the fact that the other party did not know or should not know that the mental deranged person did not act voluntarily.

5 Conclusion

5.1 Comparison of the Various Legal Systems.
Towards a European Civil Code?

In this concluding paragraph the legal systems concerned will be compared with each other in order to find out if they have some basic principles in common which may serve as a starting point for obtaining some general uniform European rules on the subject of defects of consent and capacity and to encounter the main oppositions. However it should be kept in mind that the preparation of some general rules relating to a specific subject is something quite different from the drafting of a whole European Civil Code. In the latter case the concept of defects of consent and capacity should be placed in a broader perspective and should be enclosed in the whole system of the law of obligations.

Referring to the subject of defects of consent in general the main problem for the preparation of some general uniform rules seems to be that the common law tradition as contrasted with the civil law tradition does not primarily regard error, fraud, duress and undue influence as defects of consent, owing to the fact that in England the theory of intention has attracted much less thought than on the Continent. In the Anglo-American system the courts have always attached great importance to reliance and external appearance rather than to the subjective intentions of the parties in the framework of the construction of legal transactions. The function of English law has always been not to seek some elusive mental element but to ensure, as far as possible, that the reasonable expectations of the parties are not disappointed.[36] However, throughout the legal systems there seems to be a tendency to emphasize the (unlawful) behaviour of an other party. Increasingly a solution is sought that corresponds with the concept of a justifiable allocation of risk.

Drafting a uniform rule concerning error will not be easy because the conditions constituting error differ considerably within the legal systems under

---

36 P.S. Atiyah, *The rise and fall of freedom of contract* (1979), p. 716-778, elaborated in: 'The binding nature of contractual obligations, the move from agreement to reliance in English law and the exclusion of liability relating to defective goods', in: D. Harris and D. Tallon (eds.) *op. cit.* n. 6, p. 21-38; K. Zweigert and H. Kötz, *op. cit.* n. 2, p. 83-93; Chitty on Contract, *op. cit.* n. 3, part one. The formation of the contract; G. Samuels & J. Rinkes: *Contractual and non contractual obligations in English law* (1992) p. 113-129; Anne de Moor, 'Intention in the law of contract: elusive or illusory?', *LQR* (1990) p. 632-655.

review. Notwithstanding this fact, the new Dutch Civil Code proves that a symbiosis of these various approaches is not impossible, and that throughout the legal systems, the duty of disclosure and the duty to make one's own investigations before entering into the contract become increasingly important. The basis for these obligations is the justifiable reliance which the parties may have in one another.[37]

The conditions of the other defects of consent differentiate less than in *the case of error* within each legal system and accentuates the misbehaviour of another party. Although undue influence is not specifically recognized as such in all these legal systems, they all pay special attention to legal relationships founded on reliance and confidence, resulting in the protection of a weaker party.[38]

In cases of incapacity all the legal systems under review contain rules which protect minors and those whose mental powers are deranged although differ considerably in the exceptions to and the elaboration of this principle.[39]

A solution must be found which protects the interests of those whose mental powers are underdeveloped or deranged and which also takes into account the needs of business.

To reach a harmonization of European rules concerning defects of consent and capacity will not be an easy task. Sometimes the legal systems under review differ considerably in their attitude to these subjects but they share enough common elements to justify a uniform approach. These commonalities may be illustrated by some examples and the congruent approach of the subjects throughout the legal systems under review.

EXAMPLE I

— Suppose a purchaser had bought a painting, represented as having been painted by an old master. The purchaser subsequently discoveres that in fact he has not bought a genuine old master but in fact a copy.
Can the purchaser claim rescission of the contract?

— It is clear that the error is evoked by a false precontractual statement concerning the subject matter of the contract. All legal systems under review agree on the requirement that in order to rescind the contract the error must refer to a substantial element of the contract.
In English law particularly the misstatement of the party which evokes the error is emphasized, however in French and in Dutch law, the behaviour of the

---

37 See M.M. van Rossum, *op. cit.* n. 31; G. Samuel & J. Rinkes, *op. cit.* n. 36, p. 138-146. See also Mattias Drexelius, *Irrtum und Risiko, Rechtsvergleichende Untersuchungen und Reformvorschläge zum Recht der Irrtumsanfechtung* (1964); J.B.M. Vranken, *Mededelings-, informatie- en onderzoeksplichten in het verbintenissenrecht* (1989); A.G. Castermans, *De mededelingsplicht in de onderhandelingsfase* (1992).

38 See also Michael Kempermann, *Unlautere Ausnützung von Vertrauensverhältnissen im englischen, französischen und deutschen Recht* (1975), and R.P.J.L. Tjittes, 'Economische bedreiging I and II', *WPNR* 6090 and 6091.

39 See also Karl August Deynet, *Die Rechtstellung des Nasciturus und der noch nicht erzeugten Person im deutschen, französischen, englischen und schottischen bürgerlichen Recht* (1960); K Zweigert and H. Kötz, *op. cit* n. 2, p. 372-380.

party who causes the error also becomes increasingly important, although the perception of the error as a defect of consent is not discarded.

In German law, the error is primarily concerned with the quality of the mistaken party's consent, and the mistaken party can rescind the contract irrespective of the behaviour of the other party. However in German law after rescission of the contract the behaviour of the parties becomes relevant. If the mistaken party was at fault himself, the other party will be able to claim damages. In cases where the error is evoked by the other party this will be a rare occurence. In Dutch law and in French law and to a lesser extent in English law, in order to rescind the contract, the error must be excusable. Under certain conditions, the party in error is obliged to make his own investigations. This duty to investigate depends on all circumstances of the case, such as the purchase price, the conditions under which the sale took place, the availability of a certificate of authenticity, and the knowledge and the status of the parties.

Thus all the legal systems are akin to accord weight to some degree of the behaviour of the parties and the justifiable reliance they may have in one another and in finding a solution which can be placed within the context of a reasonable allocation of risk.

EXAMPLE II

— Suppose the seller of a second-hand car concealed from the purchaser the fact that the car was involved in a serious car accident. After the conclusion of the contract, an inspection of the car proved that the damage was badly repaired and that the car was in fact a potential 'death trap'.

The question then arises as to whether or not the purchaser can rescind the contract.

— The casus must be placed in the legal framework of the duty to give information and the obligation to make one's own investigations.

The duty of disclosure has its source in the inequality of the information available to the parties, but that is not enough to impose a duty of disclosure. Furthermore it is demanded in the interests of justice that the ignorance of the mistaken party justifies the existence of this duty.

There is, throughout the legal systems concerned, an increasing acceptance that the private consumer's reliance is justifiable and that there is a correlative obligation of disclosure upon the professional.

In England as a rule, the mere knowledge of essential facts which might influence the other party's decision as to whether or not to conclude the contract, does not in itself lead to an obligation to disclose the relevant information. However occasionally some English cases seem to gradually invoke a duty to warn of a specific danger to the buyer.[40]

---

40 See on this subject for example Hurly v. Dyke [1979] RTR 265.

The continental law systems are more generous in recognizing a duty of disclosure, provided that the mistaken party was unable to discover the information for himself. Some guidelines for the existence of a duty of disclosure are: the nature of the contract (including those contracts which have a personal or a confidential character), the quality of the parties (for example between a professional and a layman) and their safety.

Thus when the seller of the car was a professional dealer, he probably ought to have revealed the defects to the (lay) purchaser, notwithstanding the fact that the purchaser did not inspect the car before entering into the contract. In this situation the duty to inform prevails over the duty to make one's own investigations.

EXAMPLE III

—   Suppose A persuaded B to sell him land at half of its value concealing the fact that A had learned from a geological survey that the land contained valuable minerals. He knew that B was unaware of this and did not enlighten him. Is A under the duty to disclose to B these facts?

—   It can be assumed that there is an inequality of information available to the parties.

The crucial point is whether or not the purchaser's conduct to conceal the facts is a failure to behave in good faith and in accordance with reasonable standards of fair dealing, and whether or not the ignorance of the vendor is excusable.

The answer to the question depends on all the relevant circumstances of the case which might include the knowledge of the purchaser and the efforts he had made to obtain the information, the nature of the subject matter of the contract and whether or not it is difficult to check the truth, the status of the parties and the relationship that exists between them.

The situation changes considerably therefore wherever a confidential or fiduciary relationship exists between the parties. Thus when the parties stand in such a relation to one another that one party has necessarily placed confidence in the other which is abused, or the influence which comes out of that confidence is exerted to obtain an advantage at the expense of the confiding party, the person so availing himself of his position will not be permitted to conceal the facts or at least must recommend that the purchaser seeks for independent advice.[41]

All legal systems concerned are akin in seeking ways to protect the interests of the weaker party against his opponent who acts out of a mental, moral or economic predominance which is abused.

---

41   See on this subject for example Lloyds Bank v. Bundy [1975], *QB* 326, Barclays Bank PLC v. O'Brien [1992], *QB* 109, HR 1 juni 1990, *NJ* 1991, 759 (Van Lanschot/Berthe Bink).

EXAMPLE IV
— Suppose an elderly widow, without consulting a legal adviser, charged her property to her bank by way of guarantee for the debts of her son's company. It was obvious that she was relying upon the bank manager for advice. Can she annul the contract?
— In this situation a confidential relationship arises and when this confidence is abused, undue influence can be asserted. Throughout the legal systems concerned there is a tendency to protect the weaker party against a party who acts out of a mental, moral or economic domination.
As the bank manager neither fully explained to the widow the company's position to that of her son nor recommended that she should seek independent advice, she could set the contract aside.
The legal systems under review generally seem to be reluctant in recognizing mere economic pressure as a ground for nullifying the contract.
Only in the Common law system does the doctrine of economic duress and the closely related doctrine of the restraint of trade seem to be cautiously accepted.[42]
In German law too there is a trend towards the protection of a debtor whose excercise of a gainful business is too heavily restricted in accordance with good faith and fair dealing.[43]
Besides there is no sharp demarcation between economic and mental predominance and also the lines between error and undue influence are often vague.
The key for an equitable solution must be found in a reasonable allocation of risk in which the justifiable reliance of the parties in one another together with the interaction of the duty to inform and the duty to make one's own inquiries have become increasingly important.

I want to conclude this chapter with a suggestion for a uniform European rule referring to the subject of error and undue influence.

5.2 Suggestion for a Uniform Rule

5.2.1 Concerning Error
Section 1 A party can rescind the contract by reason of *error* when he has entered into the contract under a misconception about the subject matter of the contract, and the behaviour of the other party which evokes the error is not in accordance with the principles of good faith and fair dealing: this may occur if the mistaken

---

42 See the cases of Pao On v. Lau Yiu Long [1979], 3 *All ER* 65, North Ocean Shipping Co Ltd v. Hyundai Construction Co Ltd [1979], *QB* 705, Universe Tankship of Monrovia v. International Workers Federation [1981], *ICR* 129. B§S Contracts § Design Ltd v. Victor Green Publications Ltd [1984], *ICR* 419.
43 For example BGH, NJW-RR 1987, p. 628.

party is induced to enter into the contract by a material misrepresentation of the other party or by the latter's failure to disclose essential information.

Section 2 Where both parties share the same misconception relating to the subject matter of the contract, the contract can be annulled in so far as this is reasonable according to good faith and normal commercial practice.

Section 3 The contract cannot be rescinded by the mistaken party where the error is inexcusable in view of all the circumstances of the case and where he has the duty to make his own investigations before entering into the contract.

5.2.2 *Concerning Undue Influence*
A party can rescind the contract by reason of undue influence, when he is induced to enter into the contract by the other party because:
1 a confidential relationship between the parties exists and the influence which comes out of that confidence is abused by the other party or
2 the other party acts out of a mental, moral or economic domination which is abused, unless the other party gives a full explanation of the relevant facts or suggests for independent advice to the other contracting party.

Bibliography

For the *English law*
— *Chitty on Contracts, vol. I, General Principles* (1989)

For the *French law*
— Yves Boyer, *L'Obligation de renseignements dans la formation du contrat* (1978)
— Jacques Ghestin, *Traité du droit civil, Les obligations, le contrat; formation* (1988)

For the *German law*
— Stephan Breidenbach, *Die Voraussetzungen von Informationspflichten beim Vertragsschluss* (1989)
— Karl Larenz, *Algemeiner Teil des deutschen Bürgerlichen Rechts* (1989)

For the *Dutch law*
— Asser-Hartkamp II, *Verbintenissenrecht, Algemene leer der overeenkomsten* (1989)
— A.G. Castermans, *De mededelingsplicht in de onderhandelingsfase* (1992)
— M.M. van Rossum, *Dwaling in het bijzonder bij koop van onroerend goed. Beschouwingen over inhoud en betekenis van de dwaling in het contractenrecht, toegespitst op koop van onroerend goed, in vergelijking met het Engelse recht.*
— J.B.M. Vranken, *Mededelings-, informatie- en onderzoeksplichten in het verbintenissenrecht* (1989)

Comparative studies:

- Karl August Deynet, *Die Rechtsstellung des nasciturus und der noch nicht erzeugten Person im deutschen, französischen, englischen und schottischen bürgerlichen Recht* (1960)
- Matthias Drexelius, *Irrtum und Risiko, Rechtsvergleichende Untersuchungen und Reformvorschläge zum Recht der Irrtumsanfechtung* (1964)
- D. Harris and D. Tallon (eds), *Contract law today, Anglo-French comparisons* (1991)
- Michael Kempermann, *Unlautere Ausnutzung von Vertrauensverhältnissen im englischen, französischen und deutschen Recht* (1975)
- D. Kokkini-Iatridou c.s., *Een inleiding tot het rechtsvergelijkende onderzoek* (1988)
- Jürgen Lauer, *Vorvertragliche Informationspflichten (insbesondere gegenüber Verbrauchern) nach schweizerischem, deutschen und französischen Recht* (1983)
- René Rodière (ed), *Harmonisation du droit des affaires dans les pays du marché commun, Les Vices du consentement dans le contrat* (1977)
- G. Samuel & J. Rinkes: *Contractual and non contractual obligations in English law, Systematic analysis of the English Law of Obligations in the comparative context of the Netherlands Civil Code* (1992)
- M.H. Whincup, *Contract law and practice, The English system and continental comparisons* (1992)
- K. Zweigert and H. Kötz, Translated by Tony Weir, *An Introduction to Comparative Law* (1992).

CHAPTER 10
The Validity and the Content of Contracts

Matthias E. Storme

1 Introduction

1 VALIDITY OF CONTRACT APPEARS TO BE RESISTANT TO HARMONISATION
The validity of contracts is not the most obvious of subjects under the heading
'Europan private law'. If there is any aspect of contract law which is resistant to
harmonisation, it is probably this one. Symptomatic of this phenomenon is Article
4 of the C.I.S.G., which states explicitly that the Convention 'is not concerned with
the validity of the contract or of any of its provisions or of any usage,' even though
the Convention regulates both the formation of contract and the rights and
obligations of the parties arising from it! The Unidroit Principles contain a chapter
on substantive validity, which is precisely intended to fill this gap,[1] but in
substance only deals with matters affecting the consent of the parties (if we assume
for the time being that 'gross disparity' (inadequate consideration) can be deemed
to come under this heading). The draft Principles of European Contract Law
(PECL) are consistent with this trend, even though they contain rules concerning
unfair contract terms. On the other hand, the only existing body of EC-law
concerning the general law of contracts in the strict sense of the term is the
Directive on unfair terms in consumer contracts,[2] which therefore deals with one
particular aspect of the validity of contracts. However minimal may be the degree
to which this Directive harmonises this subject, it forms an appropriate starting
point, since a common market in this area is obstructed to a much greater extent
by mandatory rules on the validity of contracts or on specific contract clauses than
by the diversity of non-binding rules.

2 THE ISSUE OF VALIDITY IS LINKED TO THAT OF CONTENT AND FORMATION
There is another reason why validity of contracts is a difficult subject area. It is
possible to devise but very few rules on the validity of contracts in general. It is
rarely appropriate to refer to the validity of contracts without explaining what type
of obligations have been affected − i.e. created, modified or terminated − by the
contract. It is therefore more sensible to examine what types of obligation, and
what terms, may be validly created, modified and/or terminated by means of a
contract (which will provisionally be defined as a transaction between the parties),

---

1   This Chapter is based on the Unidroit Draft Convention on the Validity of International sales
     Contracts, *Rev. droit uniforme* 1973, p. 60; VIII. *Uncitral Yearbook* 1977, p. 104.
2   Council Directive 93/13/EEC of 5 April 1993, *OJ* 21-4-1993 n° L 95/29.

as well as the conditions in which they may do so. Therefore this Chapter will be explicitly restricted to 'obligational contracts' (contracts dealing with obligations) and will not deal with agreements where they have direct implications for the property relationships involved (e.g. the transfer of property or creation of limited rights of ownership).

Similarly, it is very difficult to separate the question of the validity of contracts, which ultimately comes down to the question of the binding nature of obligations created by contracts from the issue of the formation of contracts (and the creation of obligations thereunder). Not only the matters which affect the consent of the parties, which will be dealt with elsewhere in this book, but also the question whether consideration and/or acceptance is necessary on the part of the creditor for the undertaking to be binding, demonstrates the close relationship which exists between those two subject. Even the question of unfair contract clauses is linked to that of formation, since the rules tend to differentiate between standard clauses and individually negotiated clauses.

Taking these difficulties into account, the question to be dealt with in this chapter can provisionally be summarised as follows: provided there is a communication or conduct which seeks to create, alter or terminate obligations, what are the conditions — except consent and capacity — which need to be met in order to derive legally enforceable obligations from this act and how should the content of such obligations be determined?

In Part 2, I will endeavour to outline the main issues involved, without any specific reference to existing rules or concepts. Part 3 will deal with the main issues arising from the diversity of specific rules or concepts as they appear in the main legal systems of the EC (i.e. the domestic rules). The remainder of the chapter concerns the various technical questions which must be solved in order to establish a set of common rules in this field.

2 Main Issues

3 THE SCOPE OF THE FREEDOM TO CONTRACT S.S.

All European legal systems do recognize *the freedom of persons which have the capacity to act at law in order to regulate their (mutual) legal relationships —* subject to certain restrictions, to be discussed later — *by means of undertakings (promises and/or contracts) which will be binding upon them* (this binding nature being subject to more specific rules on non-performance, termination, etc). Would it therefore not be sufficient to embody this principle in a European Code of Contract Law, merely adding certain specific rules on matters affecting the consent of the parties and the capacity to act at law, as well as a general rule on the limits of the freedom to contract, these limits being expressed in terms of 'illegality and/or immorality'? Such an approach would, in my opinion, soon prove to be inadequate.

A mere glance at the rules of domestic law and the proposed uniform principles relating to matters affecting the consent of the parties, particularly those on mistake, would clearly show that the question of the *formation and validity of contracts cannot be reduced to a mere meeting of the minds* within some general limits traced by law. The many cases which concern the contractual liability for obligations not truly agreed upon (obligations arising from reliance, clauses supplemented by mandatory and even non-mandatory rules, etc.) in my opinion only serve to increase the number of question marks on this issue. In addition, some elementary but unbiased reflection on this question leads to the conclusion that the freedom to contract as such — as a principle of public law rather than private law — cannot by itself explain why parties are no longer free to change their minds unilaterally, whereas the binding nature of promises or contracts will be of no use as long as long as the parties fail to change their minds. Thus we need to draw a distinction between, *on the one hand, the problem of the freedom of the parties in relation to the public authorities and/or third parties,[3] and, on the other hand, the question of their mutual (contractual) liability.* As long as legal rules do nothing more than rendering certain promises or contract clauses unenforceable, without prohibiting their performance, it is not the hallowed principle of the freedom to contract which is at stake, but precisely the opposite, namely subjecting one of the parties to a power which the other party claims to exercise over the former. Such powers, if they are to be allowed or recognized by law, must be legitimised by other means than merely relying upon the freedom to contract.

4 THE MINIMUM CORE OF COMMON RULES
On the other hand, it is not necessary to carry this reflection to the ultimate conclusion of denying promises any specific legal significance whatsoever, and of allowing the law of contracts to be subsumed into the mainstream law of torts. In my opinion, the attempts to draw a body of general principles of contract law, such as the Unidroit Principles or the PECL, are too much based on the 'classical' theory of contracts.[4] We must certainly not elevate the distinction between contract and tort, or the parallel distinction between a positive (expectation) interest and negative (reliance) interest to the status of an absolute principle; nor is it necessary to do so in order to establish that *it is at least useful to 'stake out an enclave within the general domain of tort'[5]* in the sense of establishing a separate set of rules on the obligations arising out of promises and the specific content of such obligations in legal terms. All European legal systems identify in at least some cases involving

---

3   The problems which concern the involvement of specific third parties in contracts — e.g. the *actio Pauliana* — are not dealt with in this chapter, but are featured in the chapter on Contracts and Third Parties.

4   Cf. the criticism made by, *inter alia*, J.H. van Erp, 'Europees privaatrecht in ontwikkeling', in: *Themis en Europa*, Tjeenk Willink, Zwolle 1989, p. (61) 65, directed against, *inter alia*, U. Drobnig, 'General principles of european contract law', in: *International sale of goods. Dubrovnik lectures* (P. Sarcevic & P. Volken, eds.) Oceana Publications, New York 1986, p. (305) 311-312.

5   This expression is used by G. Gilmore, *The death of contract*, Ohio State University, Columbus 1974, p. 87.

contracts, or in certain types of contract, a contractual liability which cannot be completely reduced to the rules of tort law, and where the test of liability is not purely the enforcement of a 'negative interest'.

All these systems have in common that contractual liability, or, if you prefer, the binding nature of contractual obligations, is to a certain extent — subject to restrictions based on the public interest or on the interests of third parties — based on *a mixture of a certain notion of autonomy and a certain notion of legitimate expectation or of reliance,* although opinions may differ on such matters as the conditions of legitimacy of the expectation or reliance.[6] However, these differences do not necessarily follow national lines, and can also be found among leading authors operating within the same legal system.

5 REFORMULATION OF THE PROBLEM
The two main issues in this chapter can thus be rephrased as follows:

—   Under what conditions, and to what extent, are expectations created by a promise or a commitment[7] made by another party protected by law, especially where they are not matched by voluntary performance.

—   Given the basic principle of freedom to contract by the parties in relation to the public authorities (and/or third parties), what are the restrictions placed on the freedom to contract and/or the obligations imposed by considerations of public policy or the public interest (and/or the interests of third parties).

It is in this light that the various tools used under the domestic legal systems will be analysed shortly, in order to explain their function.

3 Main Concepts Used in the Different Legal Systems which Obstruct the Harmonisation of Contract Law

6 CAUSE
The main problem with the notion of 'cause', as used mainly in French-based legal systems, is not so much its uselessness, as many would claim, than *the confused manner in which several functions have been merged into one concept* — the majority of these aspects concerning private interests but some of which also

---

6   Roughly speaking, these vary from, on the one hand, the requirement of an equivalent quid pro quo, to, on the other hand, the mere acceptance of the promise in the reasonable belief that a statement or conduct constitute a promise of a certain tenor made to him.

7   'Commitment' is the term used by J. Köndgen, *inter alia,* in: *Reconstructing promissory obligation: From Status to Contract to Quasi-Contract,* precisely in order to broaden the concept of promise in order to include any communicative behaviour which brings about some sort of obligation.

involve considerations of public policy. Roughly speaking, it is possible to distinguish between at least three different functions of this notion in the law of obligations where this notion is regarded as a requirement for the validity of a contract (the fourth function, which concerns the transfer of property, is not discussed here).[8]

The first function is *to distinguish between binding promises or commitments on the one hand, and unenforceable ones* on the other hand, the term 'binding' being understood as creating a liability which may exceed the scope of tortious liability (in traditional terms: a liability according to the expectation interest which may possibly exceed a liability according to a mere reliance interest). Viewed in this light, the term 'cause' is a 'causa obligationis', a reason for conferring a claim on the promisee, and must be vested with the promisee. This function more or less corresponds to the 'consideration' under the common law, and could thus be viewed as a problem relating to the formation of contracts. However, unlike consideration, this concept has been extended, and therefore diluted to such an extent — whether deliberately or by misunderstanding — that it seems to have disappeared altogether from the continental legal systems as an actual requirement as distinct from consent and acceptance. In any case, this problem will be discussed in full under 5. infra. In French law, it could be said to have an effective function as a device for solving certain problems which arise after the conclusion of a contract. This aspect will be discussed later (4. infra).

The second function of the cause of a contract is *to give relevance to certain assumptions made by one or both of the parties which do not give rise to any possibility of avoidance based on mistake* in accordance with the relevant rules on mistake (a relevance which is denied where the promise is considered to be 'abstract' in a certain relationship). Viewed in this light, the cause is not the 'causa obligationis', but the cause of the promise (or of any other legal transaction) (the concept is precisely not restricted to acts creating obligations), sought on the part of the promisor. In the French Civil Code, it is expressed by the term 'fausse cause'. However, the term is not restricted to French-based legal systems, but is also found in provisions such as § 812 BGB. Originally, it was used only to give relevance to the typical assumption concerning the legal situation or the effects of the act, and the number of causae (Rechtsgründe) was limited: namely, a promise could be made *credendi* or *adquirendi causa* (on the assumption that a reciprocal claim or property right would be obtained), *solvendi causa* (on the assumption that one will be freed from a lawful debt or obligation), in order to guarantee the performance of an obligation assumed to be valid, or *donandi causa* (assuming no debt or reciprocal claim, except for some expression of gratitude). It was thus able to solve the problem of 'erreur sur l'efficacité juridique de la cause'. However,

---

8   This passage owes so much to the analysis made by G. Gorla, *Il contratto, problemi fondamentali trattati con il metodo comparativo e casistico*, Giuffré, Milano, 1954, that there is probably little point in giving more specific references to his work.

where the assumption made relates to facts or to law existing when the promise was made or the contract concluded, it was, and is, possible to achieve this with the concept of mistake. Given that the articles of the Unidroit Principles and of the PECL relating to mistake give relevance to assumptions of this kind — as long as they relate to facts or to law existing when the promise was made or the contract concluded — where the general conditions for avoidance based on mistake have been met,[9] this notion of cause has to be discussed, in the light of a common law for Europe, only insofar as it also gives relevance to assumptions relating to the facts or the law as they arose after the conclusion of the contract. This is precisely the manner in which this concept is currently relevant in French law, owing to a very extensive interpretation of the term cause as meaning any *decisive motive* or purpose entertained by the parties[10] which has been frustrated or not been fulfilled. As will be discussed under 4. infra, however, this problem can, in our view, no longer be regarded as a problem of validity, but as one which concerns (non-)performance. On the other hand, the rules on performance and non-performance form part of the contents of a contract, to be determined in accordance with certain principles which will be discussed under 8. — this notion of cause could very well play a part there, since one cannot in principle exclude the possibility that such assumptions could be regarded as implied terms on which the contract could be terminated or as defeasance clauses.

The third function of the notion of 'cause' can be found in the notion of *'unlawful cause'*. The 'unlawful cause' concept is used especially in order to invalidate contracts hich have no illegal or immoral 'contents' in the strict sense of the term. The question whether the notion of cause can be of assistance here will be discussed under No. 15 and 35. Here again, the cause must be found with the creditor, and this concept is used to invalidate promises whose performance or enforcement is not illegal in principle, but could become illegal in the light of the performance made or promised in consideration of that promise.[11] In this sense, it is also used in order to protect one party against any excessive or unfair advantages stipulated by the other party; however, this problem is not discussed in this chapter, since our European private law tends to view it as a matter affecting the validity of the consent, i.e. as taking unfair advantage of circumstances.

7 CONSIDERATION

The 'consideration' requirement, on the other hand, is a typical common law concept, whose functions only coincide in part with those of the 'cause' — namely with the first mentioned function. Although it is considered as an issue relating to the

---

9   Cf. in particular Articles 3.4 and 3.5 Unidroit Principles and Article 6.101 PECL.

10   On this development, cf. in particular G. Gorla, *Il contratto* § 22c.

11   In spite of the authoritative nature of Zweigert and Kötz, *An Introduction to comparative law*, II, p. 54, I do not consider such distinctions to be artificial or useless. Rules such as § 134 and 138 BGB or Article 3:40 NBW could be too general precisely because they fail to draw an adequate distinction between possible cases and causes of illegality.

formation of contracts rather than to their validity, it also falls within the scope of this chapter. An examination of the common law doctrine on this subject can, moreover, reveal to us the close relationship between problems which have traditionally been treated as totally separate issues on the Continent, such as cause, form and acceptance.

8 OBJECT

Like the 'cause', the 'object' of a contract is, in French-based legal systems, considered to constitute a requirement for its validity, and like the notion of 'cause', it is *a mishmash of various issues*, most of which can hardly be regarded as being fundamental requirements for the validity of a contract.[12] Also, like the cause, the object of a contract and the object of the obligations arising from it (or altered or terminated by it) have also become mixed up in this concept. It is also necessary, in our view, to have separate rules on invalidity based on private interests on the one hand, and invalidity based on considerations of public policy on the other hand.

The first question is that of *ability to determine the content* of the contract, or rather of the obligations arising from it. The ability to determine the contents of a contract could be regarded as being a requirement for any contract, but not as a requirement for its validity which is separate from the act of promising, or from the agreement itself. A promise is invariably a promise to do something, an agreement is always an agreement on something, and an obligation is at all times an obligation to do something. Therefore proposed rules of European private law on this subject obviously state that a contract is only concluded where the terms are sufficiently definite, either by agreement between the parties, or because they can be determined under the law (cf. Articles 5.101 and 5.103 PECL), and these rules have rightly been inserted in the chapter on formation. Therefore, what is needed is not a separate requirement for the validity of a contract or obligation, but a set of rules laying down the circumstances in which the terms can be determined by objective standards and the methods for determining a term which can be lawfully chosen by the contracting parties. These rules will be specified when we discuss the determination of the contents of a contract under 8., No. 28.

The second issue concerns the question whether any lawful obligation arises where its *performance was impossible from the outset* (i.e. at the time of concluding the contract). Whether or not this is a question of validity will be discussed under 4. *infra*.

This question will also be discussed in relation to many other cases in which the theory of *the 'unlawful object'* of a contract manifests itself, such as the case where

---

12 Once again, I am indebted for this view to G. Gorla, 'La teoria dell'oggetto del contratto nel diritto continentale (civil law)', *JUS* 1953, p. 289 et seq. Compare also Zwiegert / Kötz, *An introduction to comparative law*, II, p. 7.

(a) performance of the obligation is in itself unlawful (illegal or immoral) from the outset, (b) performance of such an obligation is not absolutely unlawful, but infringes property rights or other subjective rights of third parties, and is therefore unlawful if done by the promisor, (c) performance is not unlawful by itself, but must be done in such a way as to comply with certain mandatory rules, (d) performance is not unlawful by itself, but can not be binding on the performing party, in the sense that it can never be enforced, and can thus not be the subject-matter of any obligation, or (e) where it may not only not be enforced, but is also not owing and thus subject to restitution.

Finally, as is the case with the 'cause' concept, the 'object' notion is applied in order to resolve certain problems which arise after the conclusion of the contract, and which amount to what is known as *the discontinuation (the 'falling away') of the object*. However, in our view these problems can no longer be regarded as problems of validity, but merely as problems of (non-)performance, although here again, the possibility cannot in principle be excluded that assumptions concerning the object of the obligations can be regarded as implied cancelling terms.

9 TYPES OF INVALIDITY

A further difficulty as regards the harmonisation of the rules on validity can be found in the various types of invalidity applied by the various legal systems. Thus, the German-based legal systems draw a distinction between the nullity (Nichtigkeit) and the avoidability (Anfechtbarkeit) of contracts, whereas French law distinguishes between 'absolute nullity' and 'relative nullity'. Here again, we must examine the possible differences in the legal effects in order to make an informed choice amongst these types. The French tradition considers that the question whether the invalidity can be relied upon by anyone, or whether it can be relied upon only by the protected party (or by the third party) is the crucial issue, and bases almost all the other differences on this one.[13] The German-based tradition tends to take as its starting point the question whether the contract is void or null *ipso iure*, or whether it has to be avoided (nullified) first, being provisionally valid in the meantime. I agree with the fear expressed by R. Zimmermann that, unless the category of persons who may rely upon the invalidity is used as the relevant test, 'seeking to attribute substantive significance to (this) distinction (...) like blind men looking in a dark room for a black cat which wasn't there.'[14] Given that present-day law tends to make general use of the possibility of avoidance merely by declaration by the person who is entitled to rely upon the voidable circumstance,

---

13   The relative nullity provided under French law has to be distinguished from the 'inopposabilité' (inability to rely upon the contrct against third parties). In the first case, the nullity has to be invoked by the protected party; if he does so, the contract is avoided *erga omnes*. In the latter case, if the protected party 'avoids' the contract, it remains valid as between the parties and in relation to other third parties.

14   R. Zimmermann, *The law of obligations. Roman Foundations of the Civilian Tradition*, Juta Cape town, 1990, p. 678.

and no longer requires the intervention of a court, the main question cannot be whether the invalidity must be relied upon — what is the meaning of the term 'automatic (ipso iure) nullity' if no-one ever relies upon it? — but who is entitled do so. This is also the case because, where a dispute arises, it will always be a court which will ultimately settle the issue, and here again, it is more important to establish who is entitled to rely on the cause of invalidity in court, than to establish whether, *a posteriori*, the contract was always void or had been annulled retroactively, with exactly the same legal effect. I have no objection whatsoever against the use of the term 'nullity' on the one hand, and the term 'avoidability' on the other hand, but only if *the distinction between the two is based on the purpose of the invalidating rule (the ratio legis), and more specifically the category of persons protected by this rule.* Thus certain causes of invalidity which are regarded as a nullity in German law, but which only protect private interests, will merely be treated in this chapter as a cause of avoidance (e.g. unilateral legal transactions committed by minors, BGB § 111 and comparably Article 3:32 (2), 2nd sentence NBW; transactions not concluded in the legally prescribed form which only protects private interests, BGB § 125, Article 11 Swiss Obligationenrecht, Article 3:93 NBW; abuse of circumstances, BGB § 138, in this respect different from Article 3:44 NBW, etc.).

10 VARIATIONS IN THE EFFECTS OF ESTABLISHED INVALIDITY
As regards the qualification to be given to the effects of invalidity, once it has been established, be it a nullity or an avoidance, the differences between the legal systems on this point are based less on different conceptions than on purely substantive grounds. The partial invalidity of contracts, the conversion of invalid transactions, the confirmation, convalescence or regularisation of invalid transactions, etc., are more readily accepted in some domestic legal systems than in others, or they may be accepted under different conditions. The concluding sections of this chapter will deal with some of these effects.

The specific issue of restitution will not be discussed in this chapter, but in the chapter on restitution and unjust enrichment. The question of the legal effect of the invalidity of contracts on a subsequent transfer of property and the manner in which *bona fide* third parties are protected, will be dealt with in the chapter(s) on the law of property.

11 THE VARIOUS MEANINGS OF THE TERMS INTERPRETATION AND BONA FIDES
Finally, harmonisation is also obstructed by the variety of concepts used in order to determine the contents of contracts and the different meanings or extended interpretations given in certain legal systems to some of these concepts, such as interpretation, equitableness and *bona fides*. The main questions here, however, once again concern the substantive differences in the use of identical, or very similar, concepts in the various legal systems, rather than the use of totally different concepts or the use of the same concept to indicate different functions. Therefore we do not need to analyse this function in this part of this chapter.

4 The Scope of the Issue of Validity and that of the Issue of (Performance and) Non-performance

12 THREE QUESTIONS

From our analysis of the concepts used in relation to the problems of the validity of contracts, three questions arise in order to determine the field to be covered by the rules on validity:

— we must decide which problems which have arisen at the moment of concluding the contract (whether known to the parties or not), other than the relevant matters which affect the consent of the parties, may cause the obligation to be held invalid, and which ones only lead to the application of rules on (non-) performance, especially termination or modification effected in accordance with these rules;

— we must decide whether an obligation can become invalid because one of the conditions for its validity ceases to apply at a later stage, after its conclusion;

— finally, we must point out certain rules on the effects of the invalidity of one obligation on the validity of the other obligations arising from the same contract.

We can simplify matters by dealing with the second question first, because a clear answer on this second question is available and renders certain developments on the first question redundant.

13 VALIDITY TO BE DETERMINED AT THE TIME OF CONCLUDING A CONTRACT

The first fundamental rule of European common private law is that *circumstances which arise after the time of concluding the contract cannot render a valid obligation or contract invalid, but can only lead to the application of the rules on performance or non-performance.* This rule cannot be found explicitly in the PECL or Unidroit Principles, but is implicit in some of their other rules, e.g. the definition of 'mistake' in the Unidroit Principles and PECL,[15] or the rule in Article 3.7. of Unidroit.[16] For this reason, it is is unfortunate that the CISG uses the term 'avoidance' for certain circumstances where contracts are terminated (Cf. Articles 26, 49, 64, 81-84 CISG).

This rule implies that subsequent developments, which in some domestic legal systems are regarded as a reason for the discontinuation ('falling away') of the cause or object of the obligation or contract, can no longer be regarded as problems of validity. Whether this discontinuation will have retroactive effect or not will thus depend on the rules relating to the effects of termination or the effects of the

---

15 Article 3.4. Unidroit: 'Mistake is an erroneous assumption relating to facts or law existing when the contract was concluded'; Article 6.101 PECL: 'A party may avoid a contract for mistake of fact or law existing when the contract was concluded if ...'; compare Article 6:228 (2) NBW and § 119 BGB *et al.*

16 'A party is not entitled to avoid the contract on the ground of mistake if the circumstances on which that party relies afford, or could have afforded, it a remedy for non-performance'.

fulfillment of a condition subsequent (cf. e.g. Article 4.305 et seq. PECL). I am unsure as to whether the rules which have already been drawn up on non-performance take these cases sufficiently into account, since they are not necessarily cases where the performance becomes more onerous or less valuable, as is required under, for example, Article 2.117 PECL (Change of circumstances).

Where circumstances which arise after the conclusion of a contract cannot render invalid a valid obligation or contract, the opposite is not necessarily the case. Invalid contracts can sometimes become valid retroactively by the subsequent fulfillment of a condition for their validity.

Moreover, the abovementioned rule contained in Article 3.7. Unidroit excludes the possibility of the concurrent application of the rules on non-performance on the one hand, and mistake on the other hand, since the possibility of avoidance on grounds of mistake is excluded not only where the circumstances on which the party relies provide that party with a remedy for non-performance, but also when they could have provided him with such a remedy.

14 IMPOSSIBILITY FROM THE OUTSET
Viewed in the same light, many problems which are present at the time of concluding the contract, whether known by the parties or not, do no necessarily lead to the obligation or contract being invalid.

This is the case where there is an impossibility of performance of an obligation from the outset. There is no reason why the fact that performance was already impossible at the time at which the contract was concluded should necessarily render the contract invalid, especially where the promisor was aware of this impossibility, or accepted the risk. On the contrary, many legal systems tend nowadays to consider any information relating to the object of the contract as a promise or a warranty, precisely in order to make a promisor contractually liable if the information he provided turns out to be incorrect. In many such cases, however, performance is impossible — for example, whenever the contract concerns a specific thing which lacks a quality which has been attributed to it. Such cases also fall within the scope of the concept of non-conformity of the goods as laid down in the Uniform Law on Sales (CISG). Although it is true that incorrect information should not invariably impose contractual liability (for full damages), and that in certain cases the promisor might be allowed to avoid the contract on grounds of mistake, this serves to demonstrate that in European private law:

'the mere fact that at the time of the conclusion of the contract the performance of the obligation assumed was impossible does not affect the validity of the contract'
(Article 3.3 (1) Unidroit Principles, a similar rule being laid down in the PECL).

In other words: *possibility of performance is not a requirement for the validity of an obligation.* However, it could be made a condition precedent, but there again, this is a question which concerns the determination of the contents of a contract.

15 Unlawfulness from the Outset

A similar principle must also apply where, at the time of the concluding the contract, one of the parties was not entitled to dispose of the assets to which the contract relates — Article 3.3 (2) Unidroit Principles expressly provides that this does not affect the validity of the contract, although this could be regarded as a form of unlawfulness from the outset. This rule thus lays down that unlawfuless (illegality or immorality) of performance from the outset does not necessarily affect the validity of the obligation or contract. In a more general sense, it could be said that 'relative unlawfulness' does not in itself render a contract invalid, 'relative unlawfulness' being unlawfuless in relation to the person of the promisor or the debtor, which is not, however, 'absolute' in the sense that no-one could lawfully perform the obligation. This rule follows from the generally accepted principle that performance by a third person is normally valid (e.g. Article 2.116 PECL).[17] It also covers those obligations whose performance could be unlawful under domestic law of one part of Europe, but lawful in other parts, if performance could validly take place in the latter. In all such cases, there is no problem of validity, but only a possible problem of (non-)performance.

It is more difficult to find a general rule on cases of 'absolute' unlawfulness which exists at the moment at which the contract is concluded. There are, however, several arguments in favour of restricting the circumstances leading to invalidity. First of all, it could be possible for the performance to become lawful (legal or morally acceptable) at a later stage; in such cases, the validity of the obligation or contract should not be affected, unless the parties actually agree to perform it in an illegal or immoral manner. Nor should a contract be held on grounds of illegality or immorality if the obligation has been entered into subject to the performance becoming lawful and morally acceptable. Whether a party will be contractually liable if he fails to perform the obligation in a legal (and morally acceptable) way will then amount to a question of the interpretation or contents of the contract.

In the remaining cases, two approaches are possible on the question whether performance of the obligation will necessarily be illegal or immoral.

The first only takes account of the purpose of the (statutory) rule infringed. Nevertheless, the contract will be invalid, unless the infringed rule does *not* purport to render contracts which are contrary to it invalid (see Article 3:40 (2) NBW and § 134 BGB). If the purpose of the rule is met by rendering the contract only partially invalid, the invalidity will only be partial, unless the contract is indivisible according to the interpretation given to it. In the remaining cases of illegality or immorality, the party who was unaware, and should not have been aware, of the illegality or the immorality receives no protection arising from the contract; the

---

17   Comp. Article 1236 French Civil Code, § 267 BGB, Article 6:30 NBW; R. Zimmermann, *The law of obligations,* p. 752.

liability of the party who was aware, or should have been aware, of the illegality or immorality is restricted to a liability in tort or a pre-contractual liability.

In the context of a common private law, a more radical approach should, in my opinion, be adopted, which would *restrict the cases of invalidity on grounds of illegality or immorality to contracts where both parties to a contract were aware, or should have been aware, that performance was necessarily illegal or immoral and did not subject the obligation to a condition of subsequant legality.* In a European perspective, where many domestic legal systems are capable of prohibiting performance of certain obligations and purport to invalidate contracts containing such obligations, the other party cannot be deemed to have knowledge of all such legal systems; unless the mistake relating to validity was commonly known (and thus gave rise to the possibility of avoidance), he should therefore be protected on a contractual basis (positive interest) where he was unaware, or should not have been aware, that performance was necessarily illegal or immoral. Such an approach would be more in line with the principle of equivalence, as explained in 9., No. 34 *infra*. Moreover, it is possible to ask the question whether there are many obligations whose performance is absolutely illegal or immoral, as:

‘the determination of what is contrary to the so-called "policy of the law" necessarily varies from time to time. Many transactions are upheld now by (our) courts which a former generation would have avoided as contrary to the supposed policy of the law.’[18]

In any case, in such circumstances it is difficult to imagine a case where a party should not have been aware of the illegality or immorality.

The rules thus developed should, *mutatis mutandis*, also apply to cases of illegality or immorality where it is not the performance itself which is illegal, but the bargaining, in particular the stipulating of a price or of an unfair advantage for services which may not be appraised in such terms, or promising a price or an unfair advantage for services which may not be rendered in return for financial or other rewards (the so-called cases of ‘unlawful cause’). However, in such circumstances it will once again rarely be the case that a party should not have been aware the illegality or immorality. For that reason, invalidity will normally be the outcome.

If it is not the performance itself which is illegal, but the binding nature of the promise or its enforcement (especially obligations restricting fundamental freedom or liberties), the result must not be the total invalidity of the contract, and the unenforceable performance will be converted into a condition precedent instead of an obligation, as the invalidity may not extend any further than is necessary for the purpose or *ratio legis*. If there is a voluntary performance, the other party will be

---

18   *Evanturel v. Evanturel*, (1874) L.R. 6 P.C. 1, p. 29, cited by Zweigert / Kötz, *An introduction to comparative law*, II, p. 52.

bound to pay the agreed price for it (compare the offer calling for an act, not for acceptance, or so-called unilateral contract under english law).

16 Financial or Patrimonial Nature

Another condition which cannot be imposed for the contract to be valid is the financial ('patrimonial') nature of performance. The ability to value the (performance of the obligation) in monetary terms may be relevant to the damages in case of non-performance, but this is a different matter from that of the validity of an obligation.

Certain legal systems, such as that of Italy, apply a broader concept as a condition for the validity of contracts, namely the 'social or economic function' of the contract. This objective is, however, one of the theories surrounding the cause requirement, used in order to distinguish legally binding promises from non-binding promises, which is an issue discussed under 5. *infra*.

17 Insulation or Abstraction of Promises

An issue which is in my opinion unrelated to invalidity, but is at times confused with it, since it deals with the notion of cause in the sense of an assumption on the part of the promisor (*supra* No. 6), is the problem of 'abstract' promises. This is not an issue concerning the validity of a promise or contract, but one which relates to the possibility of pleading certain defences (including the defences of nullity and avoidance), or the exclusion of such a possibility where 'abstract' promises have been made. The question is not whether an 'abstract' promise is valid, but whether it is really 'abstract'. It is widely accepted nowadays that a defence cannot be excluded in the relationship between the parties which gave rise to it, or rather, that such an abstraction is only formal, i.e. a reversal of the burden of proof: *qui petit quod redditurus est, dolo agit*. On the other hand, it is accepted just as widely that the parties are free to exclude the use of certain defences in their relationship with third parties who are not deliberately acting in fraud of the debtor's rights, as is the case, for example, with letters of credit. Although such a letter is obviously not invalid for want of cause, I prefer to say so explicitly, since some domestic courts — although they may bear the title 'supreme' — wrongly consider this to be an exception to the cause requirement.[19]

---

19   E.g. Belgian Cass., 13-11-1969, *Pas.*, 1970, I, 234, *R.C.J.B.*, 1970, 326; Belgian Cass., 5-11-1976, *Pas.*, 1977, I, 267, *R.W.*, 1977-78, 440; Belgian Cass., 17-5-1991, *Pas.*, n° 480.

5 General Requirements, other than Consent and Capacity to Act at Law on the Part of the Promisor, to get Protection when Expecting the Performance of a Promise

18 TWO OPPOSING VIEWS

As has been stated earlier (cf. No. 3 in fine), the fact of subjecting the promisor / debtor to the power of the promisee / creditor has to be legitimised by other means than simply invoking the freedom of contract, since the freedom to contract does not in itself explain why the expectations of the disappointed party will be protected if the other party changes his mind. Obviously, the autonomy of the parties plays an important role, but not, perhaps, in its usual sense. Since the law is concerned with relationships between persons, the ideas of autonomy and the (protection) of reliance or legitimate expectation must also be viewed in a relational manner. The required autonomy is the autonomy on the part of the promisor, but it must be seen in relation to the promisee. *The question is not so much whether the will of the promisor was defective or not, but whether the promisee did respect the right of self-determination of the promisor and did not unduly influence it.* Since I have dealt with this subject elsewhere[20] and since matters affecting consent are discussed in another chapter of this book, I will not elaborate on this idea here. However, I will give some thoughts on the other element, being its reverse, namely the element of 'confidence' (legitimate expectation or reliance). The 'confidence' required is the confidence on the part of the promisee, but this must also be seen in a relational manner. There, the question is *whether the promisor did sufficiently cause the promisee to rely on the promise, to expect its performance.* It is this question of adequate cause which is addressed in traditional doctrines such as the doctrine of consideration or of cause (causa obligationis): is not the price to be paid by the promisee, i.e. the reliance which is bargained for, the most convincing reason for keeping the promisor to his promise? And, in the absence of such a reliance bargained for, is there a better criterion available than the fact that the promisee is in possession of a promise which is materialised or realised, such as a deed supplied to him, or the delivery of the thing promised, as is the case in the manual gift *inter vivos* or gratuitous loan (loan without interest)?

On the other hand, these standards are too narrow and have been justifiably criticized. Present-day law, including current attempts at enacting a European private law, applies — at least in theory — a different criterion, namely *the intention to be legally bound, which is to be determined from the promisor's statement and conduct as they were reasonably understood by the promisee* (cf. Article 5.102 PECL). In order to exclude the need for consideration, cause, performance (in the so-called 'real' contracts) or formality as a general requirement for the validity of

---

20 'De bindende kracht van de overeenkomst', in: *Beginselen van vermogensrecht, BW-krant jaarboek 1993* (M.E. Franke, J.P. Jordaans, J.M. Smits & W.L. Valk, Eds.), Gouda Quint, Arnhem 1993, p. 117 et seq.

contracts, the Unidroit Principles and the PECL expressly state that there is no further requirement for the formation of contracts:

'A contract is concluded, modified or terminated by the mere agreement of the parties, without any further requirement' (Unidroit Article 3.2.)

c.q.

'A contract is concluded if a) the parties intend to be legally bound and b) they agree on terms which are sufficiently definite, without any further requirement'(Article 5.101 PECL).[21]

19 SOME LESSONS TO BE LEARNED FROM THE SOCIAL SCIENCES

However, I would like to express some doubt about such a criterion, as well. Contract law deals with the protection of legitimate expectation caused by the conduct of the other party, regardless of the actual detriment caused by the reliance on these expectations and conduct.[22] This is legitimate to the extent that it' is reasonable for the promisee to entertain such expectations, to expect performance (or expectation damages) from the promisee. To take the appearance of the intention to be bound as the criterion for the reasonableness of these expectations presupposes *the anthropological view that men who promise and carry out their promises are* not primarily prompted by a multitude of egoistic and altruistic motives, such as the obtention of material benefits, or the opportunity to do so, the stabilisation of mutual relationships, the granting of rewards, the fact of earning gratitude, praise, honour, etc., but *primarily by one single motive, i.e. to affirm one's identity by living up to previous representations made of one's self.* Certainly, the last-named motive is an important human motive, and provides us with the best possible way of legitimising the classical doctrine of contracts,[23] and does so far better than the rather nonsensical traditional explanations. However, it would certainly be going too far to consider it to be the main, or even the sole, reason for issuing promises and for carrying them out. However important the quest for identity may be to human beings, it will not continue to prompt him to conform to his representation of himself if the fact of his *carrying out his promise is not sustained by any reciprocity.* Reciprocity must, however, be understood in a much wider sense than that which is used under the traditional doctrine of consideration.[24]

---

21 Compare Article 29 (1) CISG: 'a contract may be modified or terminated by the mere agreement of the parties'.

22 Restricting contractual protection to cases of actual detrimental reliance would constitute a strong incentive to overrely. Compare J. Köndgen, *Reconstructing promissory obligation: From Status to Contract to Quasi-Contract.*

23 I have been assisted enormously in developing my awareness of this by J. Köndgen, *Reconstructing promissory obligation: From Status to Contract to Quasi-Contract.*

24 *Ibid.*

20 THE HIDDEN REQUIREMENTS

Moreover, when we take a close look at the classical doctrine of contracts, we will notice that a mere promise with the intention to be legally bound, without any other element of formality or consideration, hardly ever constitutes an adequate reason for enforcing performance, regardless of any actual reliance on it. In the French-based legal systems, gratuitous contracts were traditionally enforceable only if they were surrounded by certain formalities (e.g. donation) or if the performance had already started (manual gift *inter vivos*, real contracts). In the German-based legal systems, an additional requirement was constituted by (1) the requirement that the — gratuitous — contract be in written form, as in the case of donations, and (2) the need to accept the promise, even in the case of unilateral contracts, this being a requirement which can not be explained if the intention to be bound constituted the sole criterion for the binding nature of a promise,[25] and which is not applied by all European legal systems.[26] In the Unidroit Principles and the PECL, it is explicitly stated that these Principles do not make the conclusion of a contract subject to any requirement as to form (Article 1.2 Unidroit; Article 5.106 PECL). But they do not try to get away with the existing mandatory rules, applicable according to the Rome Convention on the law applicable to contractual obligations (*infra* 6.). On the other hand, the PECL provide that *promises intended to be legally binding without acceptance are binding without acceptance and are treated mutatis mutandis like contracts* (see Article 5.108 PECL).

The simplicity of the 'mere agreement' rule is, however, still quite deceptive, when it is considered that a complete separation of the questions of formation and validity of contract on the one hand, and on the rules of (non-)performance on the other hand, obscures that there is no such thing as *the* binding character of the contract, but that there exist only *various degrees to which a contract binds the parties*. The latter depend, *inter alia*, on the benefit, or disadvantage (detriment) or reciprocity *sensu lato* of the transaction. No system of contract law enforces contracts without consideration with the same degree of severity as reciprocal promises, especially if such contracts have not been concluded in the course of business.[27] The interpretation of such gratuitous promises is also different: it is often accepted that the decisive motive of such promises constitutes an implied term, even if it was not the motive of the promisee — in reciprocal contracts, this must be a motive common to both parties. The measure of their enforcement is also different and is probably closer to that which prevails under the law of torts.

---

25 Cf. in particular G. Gorla, 'Il dogma del consenso', *Rivista di diritto civile*, 1956, p. 923, also in: *Diritto compararo e diritto comune europeo*, Giuffré Milano 1981.

26 U. Drobnig, 'General Principles of European Contract Law', in: *International sale of goods. Dubrovnik lectures 1986*, p. (305) 314. The author concludes that no common principle can be found on this point.

27 See G. Gorla, *Le contrat dans le droit continental et en particulier dans le droit français et italien*, Institut universitaire d'études européennes Torino 1958, § 11-12; recently A.C. van Schaick, 'Affectionis causa', in *In het nu wat worden zal. Opstellen Schoordijk*, Kluwer Deventer 1991, p. 223 et seq.

175

Exemption clauses will be judged more liberally in relation to gratuitous services. Reciprocity certainly plays a part in the balance of rights and obligations of the parties, which may not be disturbed to the consumer's detriment contrary to the requirement of good faith (cf. Article 3 EC Directive on unfair terms in consumer contracts).[28] More qualifications could be added, but since these are more appropriate in a chapter on non-performance, or in the examination of the question of interpretation (cf. 8. *infra*), I will not elaborate on this subject here.

21 CONCLUSIONS

My conclusion is not that we should necessarily expect a promise to meet some other requirement in order to be binding, but that the ideas which underlie concepts such as cause or consideration must be taken into account when interpreting promises and determining their contents and conditions. I do not consider the intention to be legally bound as being an appropriate criterion for distinguishing between binding and non-binding promises; however, rules of interpretation such as the one contained in Article 5.102 PECL, which states that a party's intention must be deduced from that party's statements or conduct as they were reasonably understood by the other party, make this criterion a workable one. It must be reasonably apparent to any promisee that something like an intention to be legally bound does not exist as an abstract concept, but is invariably conditioned by the type of transaction and the relevant circumstances, especially the degree of reciprocity involved. It is also reasonably apparent to the promisee that certain types of statement and conduct, especially if it assumes a written form, indicate a more serious intention to be legally bound than others.

On the other hand, I also agree that the requirement that the promise be accepted cannot be upheld. *Acceptance adds nothing* decisive to the extent to which the other party intends to be legally bound, to the reasonable appearance assumed by the promise, or to the degree of reliance which must be protected.

6 Specific Formal Requirements as regards Contractual Obligations

22 GENERAL RULES
Article 1.2 of the Unidroit Principles (and Article 5.106 PECL) states that:

---

28 Although 'assessment of the unfair nature of the terms shall relate neither to the definition of the main subject matter of the contract nor to the adequacy of the price and remuneration, on the one hand, as against the services or goods supplied in exchange, on the other (...)' (art. 4 (1) of the Directive) (Compare e.g. Article 6:231 NBW; ABGB § 879, 3; German AGBGesetz § 8), the unfairness of any other contractual terms 'shall be assessed taking into account the nature of the goods or services (...) and by referring to (...) all the other terms of the contract (...)' (art. 4 (2) of the Directive), thus taking into account the price or the remuneration.

'Nothing in these Principles requires a contract to be concluded in or evidenced by writing. It may be proved by ane means, including witnesses.'

However, this provision cannot hide the fact that, as far as more specific formal requirements are concerned, no attempts have as yet been made to draw up uniform or harmonised general principles on this subject, owing to the mandatory nature of formal requirements in domestic laws.

On the other hand, a certain degree of *favor validitatis* has already been introduced by Article 9 (1, 2 and 4) and 14 (2) of the Rome Convention on (the law applicable to) Contractual Obligations. These rules could be considered as the first major breakthrough of the *doctrine of equivalence* of the laws of the different member states of the EC, well-known from the case law on the free movement of goods (although the Rome Convention obviously goes further, since it does not only concern intra-Community contracts). These rules must be understood as meaning that even the mandatory rules of the forum cannot invalidate a contract once the formal requirements of one of the legal systems indicated have been met, even though these may produce other legal effects — except in the field of specific types of contracts, for which a more rigid rule is contained in Article 9 of the Rome Convention.

In my opinion, it is not necessary to enact any further general rules governing the formal requirements themselves and their applicability — save for the exceptions laid down in Article 9, which are yet to be examined (cf. infra) — even though further harmonization may be desirable for certain specific contracts. However, it should be possible for a common european legal system to formulate common rules on the effects of the failure to comply with formal requirements and the possibility of abusing such requirements by invoking non-compliance with such formalities in such a way as to breach the principle of good faith.

Although many formal requirements may also be inspired by considerations of public policy, it is rarely necessary to invalidate the contract as between the parties in order to satisfy these considerations, invalidity being normally intended as a penalty which protects only private interests. There are therefore no grounds for considering such invalidity to be 'absolute', since it is for the protected party (or parties) to plead it, and since they may also waive the right to do so. In addition, the protected party should not be allowed to avoid the contract once he has voluntarily started the process of performance. This rule is reflected in the various legal systems, although under different names (abuse of right, infringement of the principle of good faith, venire contra factum proprium or estoppel, etc.).[29]

---

29 Cf. *inter alia* H. Merz, 'Auslegung, Lückenfüllung und Normberichtigung dargestellt an den Beispielen der unzulässigen Berufung auf Formungültigkeit und des Mißbrauchs der Verjährungseinrede', 163. *AcP* 1963, p. 305 et seq.

23 EXCEPTIONS

In addition to the rare categories of specific contracts which are subject to uniform rules throughout Europe,[30] the Rome Convention itself lays down or implies certain exceptions to Article 9 in relation to certain specific contracts. On the one hand, certain consumer contracts specified in Article 5 (1 and 2) of the Rome Convention are, certainly as far as their formal requirements are concerned, governed by the law of the consumer's habitual residence (Article 9 (5) Rome Convention), on the other hand, contracts concerning real property ('immovable property') are subject to the formal requirements of the lex rei sitae if that law imposes those requirements regardless of the law governing the contract. The second exception causes greater disruption, concerning as it does an area of the law which appears to be impervious to any attempt at harmonisation, but its scope is extremely limited. The first exception causes less disruption, since consumer protection is precisely the only area of civil law in which the EC has made a serious attempt at achieving harmonisation. The exclusive applicability of the law of the consumer's residence (at least as far as formal requirements are concerned) loses a great deal of its importance in that those formal requirements are gradually harmonized by means of EC Directives. It could be argued, however, that this exclusive application of the formal requirements laid down by the law of the consumer's residence in those cases where no harmonisation has yet been achieved is contrary to the principle of the equivalence between the various institutions of the member states of the EC, and to the obligation to give effective recognition to these institutions especially in the areas covered by the free movement of goods or services. As a result of this doctrine, especially financial services supplied from one EC-country to consumers in another EC-country should be recognized if they meet the requirements imposed by the member state of origin, and a refusal to recognise its validity would interfere with the free movement of services.[31] Where this rule applies, it takes precedence over the Rome Convention by virtue of Article 20 of the latter.

Other exceptions can be found in contracts which fall outside the scope of the Rome Convention, such as the choice of forum clauses (governed by Article 17 of the Brussels Convention), arbitration clauses and insurance contracts.

In a certain sense, restrictions on the contents of general conditions included in a contract could also be considered as constituting formal requirements, in that these restrictions do not apply to individually negotiated clauses. Instead, the manner in which the clause has been imposed rather constitutes an element to be taken into account in assessing whether or not the imbalance caused by the clause is contrary

---

30   In most cases, only the rules on international contracts have been harmonised.
31   Compare M. Worlf, 'Privates Bankvertragsrecht im EG-Binnenmarkt. Auswirkungen der II. Eg-Bankrechts-Richtlinie auf privatrechtliche Bankgeschäfte', *Wertpapier-Mitteilungen (ZfWirtschuBankR)*, 1990, (1941) 1943-1944.

to good faith, and thus whether or not it is a valid part of the contract. This question will therefore be dealt with below (No. 32 *infra*).

7 Errors of Expression or of Communication, Misunderstandings, etc.

24 ERRORS OF EXPRESSION OR
OF COMMUNICATION TREATED AS MISTAKES
Ever since F.C. von Savigny's time, the leading authors have endeavoured to draw a distinction between mistake as a matter affecting consent on the one hand, and errors of expression, communication or understanding, which actually prevent consent, on the other hand. The Netherlands Civil Code has treated both these issues as completely separate matters, the former in Article 6:228, the latter in Article (3:34 and) 3:35. However, an examination of the relevant of case law shows that this distinction never had any real chance of success in the case law, and that errors of the second type have almost invariably been treated as mistakes.[32] The italian Civil Code has codified this existing practice in Article 1433, and a similar rule is found in Article 3.6 of the Unidroit Principles: '*An error occurring in the expression or transmission of a declaration is considered to be a mistake from the person from whom the declaration emanated*'— and probably also in the PECL.

25 IMPLIED PRINCIPLES OF INTERPRETATION
Although mistake on the one hand, and misunderstanding or errors of communication on the other hand cannot always be clearly distinguished from each other, there exist clear examples of both types which have little in common. An error made in the transmission of a statement cannot be defined as 'an erroneous assumption relating to facts or law existing when the contract was concluded' — as the element of mistake has been defined. It is merely 'considered to be a mistake'. Equality of treatment is therefore not evident, but implies more than that which appears at first sight — namely, it implies certain principles on the interpretation of contracts.

This equality of treatment is, in my opinion, only possible where *the interpretation of a contract is not based on the 'common intention' of the parties* — precisely this element is missing where an error of communication or a misunderstanding arises — *but on an objective interpretation of the statements, or conduct, of the parties* — leaving aside for the moment the question whether such an interpretation should be based on the grammatically normal meaning of the terms or from their socially normal meaning, i.e. their reasonable meaning — in other words, the question

---

32   Cf. R. Sacco & G. di Nova, *Il contratto*, in: *Trattato di diritto privato* diretto da Pietro Rescigno, T. X, 2, Torino, UTET 1983, p. 113 et seq. Compare also G. Rouhette, 'La force obligatoire du contrat, rapport français', *Le contrat aujourd'hui. Comparaisons franco-anglaises,* Paris, L.G.D.J. 1987, (27) 30 n° 4 c., translated as 'The obligatory force of contract in French law', in *Contract Law Today. Anglo-French Comparisons*, Clarendon Oxford 1989.

whether the principle of good faith forms part of the process of interpretation or only comes into play afterwards. Adopting such a starting point does not prevent us from giving relevance to a possible different common intention of the parties, if such a common intention can be established — bearing in mind the rule of *falsa demontratio non nocet*. However, it is a necessary one for the purpose of explaining that *a party can be bound in cases where there is no common intention*, since this is the case where the possibility of avoidance is limited — this possibility indeed being limited by the Italian Civil Code, the Unidroit Principles and the PECL in precisely the same way as it is the case in relation to other errors or mistakes. More precisely, according to Article 3.5 of the Unidroit Principles and Article 6.101 of the PECL, such an error may give rise to avoidance only where this mistake was (a) caused by (information provided by) the other party, or the other party was aware, or ought to have been aware, of the mistake, and it was contrary to the principle of fair dealing to leave the mistaken party in error,[33] and (b) sufficiently important, subject to the additional condition (stipulated in the PECL) that this importance was known, or should have been known, to the other party.

The last-named condition implies that *the intention of one party forms part of the contract* — more specifically the intention to consider something as constituting an important element —, *even if it is not the common intention of the parties, as long as the other party knows or should know, that this was the intention of the former.* This rule cannot at present be restricted to the question whether a certain assumption is relevant or not, but must constitute a general rule of interpretation. This rule could be worded as follows:

'Where one of the parties commits an error of expression or in transmitting a statement, or uses a word intending to convey a meaning which it would not normally have, (or fails to make clear its intention on certain terms of the contract which he considers to be essential) and the other party is aware of this error (or substantial omission), and fails to point it out, but knows, or should know, what the first-named party intended, the other party shall be treated in the same way as if the statement had correctly (and fully) expressed the first-named party's intended meaning.'

or:

'If it is established that one party intended the contract to have another meaning and at the time the contract was made the other party could not have been unaware of the first party's intention, the contract is to be interpreted in the way intended by the first party.'

---

33   The third ground for avoidance based on mistake, i.e. shared mistake, is irrelevant where the error in question is an error in communication or transmission — if both parties 'share' in this error, this means that they both used a word according to a meaning which is different from its normal meaning; in this way, a common understanding has been reached.

Indeed, a rule along this line is currently being discussed by the CECL.[34] Should it apply, the result will no longer be the avoidance of the contract, but the validity of the contract in the wording apparently intended by the other party. This indicates that not only the question whether it is possible to avoid the contract — namely on the ground of mistake —, but also the interpretation of promises and other statements shall be determined by *balancing the duties to examine against the duties to disclose* of the parties involved. This subject is discussed in greater detail in chapter 8, dealing with the formation of contracts (by J.H. van Erp).

These rules also correspond to the principle, examined earlier, which is embodied in Article 5.102 of the PECL, i.e. that a party's intention to be legally bound is determined by that party's statements or conduct as they were reasonably understood by the other party (cf No. 21 *supra*).

8 Fundamental Principles for the Construction or Determination of Contractual Obligations. Some Specific Problems

26 TWO OPPOSITE VIEWS — AGAIN

Earlier we saw that certain rules of interpretation have been developed to deal with the question as to what intention of the parties is relevant in cases where that intention is not entirely shared by both parties. We have left aside the question whether the interpretation of contracts can be restricted to interpretation of the parties' intentions or whether it should also be guided by other principles, such as the *bona fides* principle. This issue, which forms the substance of this section, concerns the relationship between the various sources which are traditionally accepted as determining the contents of a contract, i.e. clauses, implied intentions, custom and practice, statutory provisions, and reasonableness and/or equitableness.[35] Whether we apply a broad or a narrow view of what contitutes interpretation, the contents of a contract are invariably determined by combining, or 'integrating', these different sources, usually on the basis of a certain hierarchy between them.

These elements determine many aspects of contractual obligations — not only the object of the various obligations, especially the performance to be expected from

---

34   Many members consider that this rule goes too far if the other party, who is aware of the error, does not know what the first party actually intended, but should have known it. However, to restrict this rule to cases where the other party knew the intention would be inconsistent with the rule of Article 6.101 PECL on mistake ('if the other party knew or should have known that the mistaken party, had he known the truth, would not have entered the contract or would have done so only on essentially different terms').

35   Most, or all, of these elements are found in the various domestic or international codifications. Cf. e.g. Article 7-9 CISG, Article 1.7, 1.9, 4.8 and 5.2 Unidroit Principles, Article 1.101, 1.106-1.108, 2.101 and 7.008 PECL, Article 1135 French and Belgian Code Civil.

the debtor, but also its detailed conditions, or 'modalities' (time and place of performance, quality of performance, conditions precedent or subsequent attached to the obligation), as well as the rules concerning non-performance and contractual liability — and therefore also the extent to which the obligation is binding —, the terms on which the debtor is released from its obligation or may terminate or modify it, etc. The entire range of rules relating to performance and non-performance form part of the substance of the contract, to be determined on the basis of these elements.

When reassessing the prospect of a common European system of contract law, we should ask the question whether it is possible to devise a principle — or rather a perspective — on the basis of which the integration of these various sources of the contents of a contract can be understood.

Here again, the traditional view is that to determine the contents of a contract, one should start from the interpretation of the statements and conduct of the parties in the psychological sense of the term, namely from the intention of the parties to be legally bound as expressed in these statements and conduct. However, such a principle will be even less capable of explaining the manner in which the contents of contracts are determined than it was capable to explain its validity 'by mere agreement of the parties' (cf. *supra*, under 5.). *The intention of the parties can only explain a small proportion of the contents of a contract* (these contents include the rules on performance and non-performance, the implied terms and conditions, etc.). It provides no explanation for the mandatory rules which protect private interests of the parties (usually the so-called weaker party) and only gives a fictitious or artificial idea of non-mandatory rules (by explaining them as an expression of the implied intention of the parties).

Certainly, on a very broad range of human activities, the parties to a contract are, in principle, free to regulate their mutual relationships, in the sense that the public authorities will not interfere as long as the parties still agree, except by virtue.of certain rules and restrictions dictated by the requirements of public policy and public morality. They are free to carry out their promises and other acts claimed by the other party. But here again, this freedom to contract fails to solve the problems which arise where parties no longer are in agreement.[36] It is nonsensical to claim that it is the notion of autonomy of the will which prompts us to compel a person to perform that which he once intended, but now no longer wishes, to perform. The basic issue of contract law is to determine what expectations of the parties have to be protected by law, and to what degree they must be thus protected, when they are not being voluntarily fulfilled. Once again, the intention of the parties to be (legally) bound is in my opinion an unsatisfactory criterion for

---

36 Compare in particular G. Rouhette, 'La force obligatoire du contrat, rapport français', *Le contrat aujourd'hui*, translated as 'The obligatory force of contract in french law', in *Contract Law Today. Anglo-French Comparisons.*

establishing this. In reality, our law of contracts — and our private law in general — does not decree that one must *in all circumstances* be as good as one's word, but rather that one must act *as a reasonable man*, taking into account the legitimate interests of the other party; these two criteria are often, but not always, the same. The expectation which is protected by law, and therefore also the contents of a contractual obligation, is precisely that the other party should act as a reasonable man.

This prospect on the law of contracts, and on private law in general, has, ever since the heyday of Roman law, been symbolized by the notion of *bona fides* (good faith) — or, in its procedural expression, the *exceptio doli generalis*.[37] Therefore good faith is not so much a rule on the same level as other rules, but rather the principle on the basis of which the various elements enabling us to determine the contents of contractual obligations need to be integrated. This notion of *bona fides* is also contained in the Unidroit Principles and the PECL.[38] A rather far reaching notion of good faith is also implied by the EC Directive on unfair terms in consumer contracts (cf. Article 3 (1)).

27 DEFINING *BONA FIDES*

Obviously the fact that the principle of good faith takes precedence over the various elements of the contents of a contract tells us nothing yet about the practical meaning of this concept. The object of this concept is precisely not to convey a clear-cut meaning, but *to dispel the creeping danger of fossilisation to which the law is always vulnerable*.[39] Thus the prevailing trends in society on the concepts of fairness and reasonableness can come into play.

---

37 See Beck, 'Zu den Grundprinzipien der bona fides im römischen Vertragsrecht', *Aequitas et bona fides, Festschrift zum 70. Geburtstag von August Simonius*, Helbing, Basel 1955, p. 18 et seq.; C. Zevenbergen, *Aard en werking der goede trouw in het romeins verbintenissenrecht*, Tjeenk Willink, Zwolle, 1931; F. Baert, 'De goede trouw bij de uitvoerig van overeenkomsten', *R.W.* 1956-57, p. 487 et seq.; L. Nanni, 'L'uso giurisprudenziale dell'exceptio doli generalis', *Contratto & impresa* 1986, p. 197 et seq.; Wendt, 'Die exceptio doli generalis im heutigen Recht oder Treu und Glauben im Recht der Schuldverhältnisse', *AcP* 1906 II, p. 1 et seq.; R. Zimmermann, *The law of obligations*, p. 668, 674.

38 For more details, cf. the chapter by O. Lando, 'Performance and remedies in the Law of Contracts'. Compare my *De invloed van de goede trouw op kontraktuele schuldvorderingen*, Story, Brussel 1990.

39 Compare the resistance by many authors to giving too concrete an expression ('herunterkonkretisieren') of the principle of good faith, e.g. G. Teubner, 'Die Geschäftsgrundlage als Konflikt zwischen Vertrag und gesellschaftlichen Teilsystemen, zur Fragwürdigkeit ihrer Re-Dogmatisierung', *ZHR* 1982, p. 625 et seq., and in *Alternativkommentar zum BGB*, '§ 242'; H. Schoordijk, 'Typologiseren en moduleren in de rechtsvinding', in *Rechtsvinding, Opstellen J.M. Pieters*, Kluwer, Deventer 1970, p. 235 et seq.; W. van Gerven & A. Dewaele, 'Goede trouw en getrouw beeld', in *Liber amicorum Jan Ronse*, Story, Brussel 1986, p. (103) 111; Comp. H. Merz, 'Die Generalklausel von Treu und Glauben als Quelle der Rechtsschöpfung', *ZsR* 1961, p. (335) 344; S. David-Constant, 'Des vivants et des morts dans le droit des obligations', *J.T.* 1977, p. 651.

Certainly the prevailing view has been that reasonable behaviour consists of nothing more than keeping to one's word in all circumstances, or at least to keep to one's word in the manner (commonly) intended by the parties. Coming from the pen of Domat, who formulated the rule contained in Article 1134 of the Civil Code, this principle probably translated his Jansenist view that man, as a sinful being, was only capable of receiving divine grace by keeping his promises at all cost. These moralistic views also corresponded to certain trends and needs in society, which was avid for security after a century of civil and religious wars. This conception survived the age of industrialism and capitalism virtually unscathed, although one major change which occurred was the much greater degree of freedom to determine the contents of contracts; the rather extreme view taken of their binding nature reflected an attitude which viewed all contracts as an exercice in risk-allocation. This idea remains very much alive today in the rules which govern international commercial contracts, since usually they continue to be viewed as such an exercice.

However, in many respects *our anthropological perceptions have changed, and with them our interpretation of the notion of good faith.* On the one hand, the definition of the price and other subject-matter of contracts for the exchange goods or services has been liberalised to an unprecedented extent — mainly on the account of the development of competition law. On the other hand, the allocation of risks in case of non-performance is considered to be primarily a matter of collective decision-making. More particularly there is a 'growing recognition that the opportunity to change one's mind is itself a valuable right which often outweighs the desirability of holding parties bound to some futur arrangement.'[40] More generally, the idea of the autonomy of the will is changing radically. The basic metaphor used by Grotius, which held a promise to be a partial surrender or alienation of one's freedom,[41] is gradually becoming unacceptable in present-day thought, which is taking the notion of the inalienable nature of fundamental rights much more seriously. The elevated moral notion of the autonomy of the human person is probably better served by a legal system which emphasises the duty to respect the right to self-determination of others, even if they fail to keep their promises, than by a legal system which imposes strict liability for the non-performance of promises.

Clearly, the notion of reasonable behaviour continues to imply that the normal situation is for a person to keep to his word. It remains part of our anthropological perception that a person affirms his identity by living up to the manner in which

---

40 P.S. Atiyah, *The Rise and Fall of the Freedom of Contract*, Clarendon, Oxford 1979, p. 756.

41 H. Grotius, *Inleidinge tot de hollandse rechtsgeleerdheid*, III.1.12. Cf. the Comments made by G. Gorla, 'Il potere della volontà nella promessa come negozio giuridico', *Rivista di diritto commerciale* 1956, I, p. 18, reprinted in *Diritto compararo e diritto comune europeo*, Giuffré Milano 1981; M. Diesselhorst, *Die Lehre des Hugo Grotius vom Versprechen*, Böhlau, Köln/Graz 1959, p. 34 et seq.

he has presented himself before, to the image which one has created of oneself; moreover, this idea is well entrenched in both the law of torts and the law of contracts. However, reasonable behaviour cannot be seen to be determined solely by such a quest for identity, and not also by other human motives, such as obtaining material benefits, stabilising mutual relationships, granting rewards, earning gratitude, praise or honour, etc. Many of these motives are considered to be equally reasonable, and law must take that into account.

As a result, the notion of *good faith* is no longer understood as conveying the simple idea that one should keep to one's word, but rather *as a combination of a number of elements or principles to be balanced against each other*. The most important of these elements or principles can be summarized as (a) *responsibility for the expectations one has created*, not only by making promises, but also by making other types of statement, by conduct, or even by remaining silent, as long as the promisee placed a reasonable interpretation on these elements and did not understand them as an unconditional intention or a creation of strict liabilities; (b) *due respect for the right of self-determination*, free from any undue influence; (c) the maintenance of a degree of *proportionality between the advantages and the disadvantages which any action can cause to the parties involved* (d) determining the rights and obligations of the parties taking into account their *reciprocity* — to be understood in a broad sense, and thus including elements such as past consideration, goodwill, etc., and not only the reliance bargained for (consideration), and (e) *the fair allocation of risks*, taking into account the possibilities of the parties to avoid or shift or spread them. These ideas form the basis of most of the more specific rules of the law of contracts, but the precedence which the notion of good faith has over these rules guarantees the possibility that they might be rebalanced, when the more specific rules will have become inappropriate in the changed social or economic climate. It transforms the system of contract law to a dynamic system, under which the relative value of the various elements need to be assessed continuously, and shifted gradually.

The Netherlands *Hoge Raad* has developed a style in its grounds of judgment on the subject of the notion of good faith which can be regarded as a model of its kind.[42] It compels the courts to take into account a comprehensive 'check-list' of elements, and to include in their grounds of judgment the reason why, in the light of these elements, the principle of good faith requires a certain interpretation, or

---

42   The first clear example of this style is found in the decision of the Hoge Raad dated 19-5-1967, in which it was applied when discussing the validity, under the good faith principle, of an exemption clause (W. Saladin t. Hollandse Bank Unie, *NJ* 261 note G.J. Scholten, p. 16. *Ars Aequi* 214 note P. Stein). The Hoge Raad stipulated the following elements: the degree of negligence, related to the nature and the seriousness of the interests involved, the nature and remaining contents of the contract, the social position of, and mutual relationship between, the parties, the manner in which the clause was made and the level of awareness by the parties of its purpose. Similar checklists have been used in cases concerning many other types of clause, as well as cases concerning misunderstanding, mistake, interpretation of terms and clauses, etc.

conditions in a certain manner the rights or obligations of the parties. It provides certain — but not many — indications regarding the relative value of these elements. It introduces some rules of thumb, which may be overruled, but only for convincing reasons.

28 INDETERMINATE TERMS

It is obviously not possible to trace in this chapter the possible influence of the principle of good faith in all aspects of the law of contracts. Suffice it to draw your attention to certain rules which could be applied to certain specific problems which have, to my knowledge, not been dealt with specifically elsewhere in this book.[43]

The first question concerns the rules on the determination of indeterminate elements which are essential for the adequacy of an agreement, or hich have been deliberately left open by the parties, whether by reference to a decision by one of the parties or not. The PECL includes a number of rules on this subject.

The first rule solves the problem as to *how to determine the contents of a contract where one of the terms has not been fixed and the method of determining it has not been specified.* As we have already noted, no contract can be concluded if its terms cannot be determined by the law.[44] Whether or not a contract has been concluded could thus depend on the opportunities for determination provided by our law of contracts. Article 55 CISG (and equally Article 5.7 Unidroit Principles) already states that in the absence of an express or implied specification of the price, the parties, in the absence of any indication to the contrary, are deemed to have impliedy made reference to the price normally charged at the time of the conclusion of the contract for goods such as the ones in question sold, given comparable conditions, in the trade concerned. Article 2.101 of the PECL provides that the parties must be deemed to have agreed on a reasonable price. It adds that the same rule applies to the mode of performance of the contract. The rule should be deemed to apply to any other term except the main subject matter of the contract. However, the main subject matter of a contract, other than the price of goods or services, will only be determinable if the parties have performed, or started to perform, the obligation concerned.

Other rules should determine *the validity and consequences of clauses which allow the terms to be determined by one of the parties.*[45] In such cases, the other party should be protected against the arbitrariness of the first-named party, whether this takes the form of pitching the obligation at too high a level where its determination

---

43 I will not deal with the specific problem of changes of circumstances, which is considered by O. Lando in the chapter of performance and non-performance.

44 Cf. Article 5.101 j° 5.103 PECL.

45 Cf. D. Tallon (dir.), *La détermination du prix dans les contrats, étude de droit comparée*, Institut de droit comparé Paris II, 1989; M.E. Storme, 'De bepaling van het voorwerp van een verbintenis bij partijbeslissing', *TPR* 1988, p. 1259 et seq.

is left to the creditor, or of fixing the price to be paid at too low a level, where its determination is left to the debtor of that payment. Article 2.102 PECL lays down a uniform rule:

'where the price or any other contractual term is to be determined by one party whose determination is grossly unreasonable, then notwithstanding any provision to the contrary a reasonable price or other term shall be substituted.'

Article 1 (1) of the Annex to the EC-Directive on unfair terms in consumer contracts has introduced an even stricter rule in relation to consumer contracts, where it lays down that may be regarded as unfair, terms which have the object or effect of:

'providing for the price or goods to be determined at the time of delivery or allowing a seller of goods or supplier of services to increase their price without in both cases giving the consumer the corresponding *right to cancel the contract if the final price is too high* in relation to the price agreed when the contract was concluded.'

The substitution of a reasonable term and/or right of termination by the other party also implies a rule on the so-called '*condition potestative*'. In certain legal systems this type of condition — and therefore the whole contract — is invalid as it would render the obligation unenforceable; however, this is no reason for invalidating the entire contract. Here, the problem is situated at a different level. It once again concerns a question of protecting the other party against the arbitrary attitude of the first party, who could force the other one to perform its part of the contract by offering him only a laughable price or no price at all. The solution to this problem is not to invalidate the contract, but once again to substitute the term and/or to grant the other party the right to terminate the contract. This in my opinion also results from Article 1 (c) of the Annex to the EC-Directive on unfair terms in consumer contracts, which refers to terms which have the object or effect of:

'making an agreement binding on the consumer whereas provision of services by the seller or supplier is subject to a condition whose realization depends on his will alone.'

This article should not apply where the entire contract — or its performance — is subject to a condition whose realisation depends on the will of one of the parties (in this case, the seller or the supplier) alone. This is the essence of any option contract, which is a perfectly valid type of contract. However, unless the duration of this contract is fixed, it may be terminated by the other party subject to reasonable notice. In these circumstancs, no 'condition potestative' can be qualified as unfair.

29 IMPLIED TERMS AND CONDITIONS — GENERAL

One of the most difficult questions to resolve is the extent to which implied conditions or other such terms should be accepted and construed. It is possible to draw a distinction between generally implied conditions and terms on the one hand,

187

and terms and conditions implied through the specific circumstances of the case on the other hand.

As to the first-named type of implied terms, our common european system of law will, as is the case with most domestic systems, determine the substance and terms of contractual obligations on the basis of (mandatory and non-mandatory) *legal rules, custom and practice, and judge-made expressions of good faith (reasonableness and equitableness)*. Many of these rules can be found in the chapters on performance and non-performance, e.g. the place of performance (Article 2.106 PECL, Article 31 and 57 CISG), the time of performance (Article 2.107 PECL, Article 33 and 58 CISG), absence of liability for lack of conformity which the buyer knew or could not be unaware of at the time of the concluding the contract (Article 35 (3) CISG), excuse due to an impediment or based on supervening circumstances (Article 3.108 PECL which more or less corresponds to *force majeure* rules), the right to withhold performance (Article 4.201 PECL, which embodies the *exceptio non adimpleti contractus*), the right to terminate a contract for non-performance (Article 4.301 PECL), the duty to examine performance within a short period and give notice of lack of conformity (Article 38-39 CISG), etc. Many of these rules saw the light of day as expressions of the general principle of good faith, and gradually became traditional rules, often codified. However, their codification must not be allowed to arrest the further development of similar rules based on good faith — e.g. the rule on changes of circumstances which do not fall within the scope of Article 3.108; this rule is enshrined in Article 2.117 PECL and discussed in this book by O. Lando.

30 IMPLIED TERMS AND CONDITIONS — SPECIFIC APPLICATIONS

In more specific terms, however, we must ask the question of the extent to which our common European system of law should give relevance to certain *particular expectations — which differ from ordinary or average expectations — concerning the object of or the terms governing performance or the conditions of a contract* (in particular defeasance clauses or 'resolutive conditions') which have not been expressly made known or which are not shared by the other party. Most European legal systems have developed a number of rules to give relevance to some of these expectations, but on the basis of very different theories and criteria, some of them in the disguise of concepts such as the cause or object in French-based legal systems,[46] or tacit assumption (Voraussetzung) or *Geschäftsgrundlage* in German-based and Scandinavian legal systems.

---

46 As we mentioned earlier, the 'falling away' of the object or cause ('caducité') of a contract cannot invalidate it. This occurrence is only relevant if it can be construed as an implied defeasance clause which gives rise to a right to terminate the contract. Compare P.A. Foriers, 'L'objet', in: *Les obligations en droit français et en droit belge. Convergences et divergences*, ed. P. Jestaz & F. Glansdorff, Bruylant/Dalloz, Bruxelles/Paris 1993, n° 22.

In my opinion, it would be inconsistent to solve this question by using specific devices. We must instead apply, *mutatis mutandis*, the rules developed in relation to mistake, error of communication, and misunderstanding. I have therefore implicitly proposed a solution for this problem where, earlier (No. 25 *supra*), I proposed the following rule:

'Where one of the parties (...) fails to make clear its intention on certain terms of the contract which he considers to be essential, and the other party is aware of this (...) substantial omission and fails to ask any questions or to refuse to accept it, although he knows, or should know, what the first-named party intended, the other party shall be treated in the same way as if the statement had (...) fully expressed the first-named party's intended meaning.'

Where those expectations concern the object of terms of performance, this rule can already be found in Article 35 (2) b CISG, requiring goods to be:

'fit for any particular purpose (expressly or) *impliedly* made known to the seller at the moment of conclusion of the contract, except where the circumstances show that the buyer did not rely, or that it was unreasonable to rely, on the seller's skill and judgment.'

Although legal systems are traditionally much more hesitating where the implied term does not relate to a particular quality or a term of performance, but rather to a condition, in particular a defeasance clause or 'resolutive condition', there is no reason for refusing to apply a similar rule. Certainly it is not sufficient that the other party knows, or should know, about the expectation: it is necessary that he knows, or should know, that this expectation is essential or determining as far as the other party is concerned, and that it was, in his opinion, part of the contents of the contract. Once again, the interpretation of promises and other statements is to be determined by balancing the duty to examine against the duty to disclose on the part of the parties involved.

As is the case with other aspects of interpretation and determination of the contents of a contract, the reciprocal or gratuitous nature of a promise will play a definite role here. Implied terms and conditions must be accepted more readily where they have determined the act of the promisor, or in other words his duty to disclose will be judged more liberally and the duty to examine on the part of the promisee more severely.

31 PROMISES IMPLIED IN STATEMENTS OF FACT

A further more specific question in relation to implied terms concerns the *legal effect of statements of fact* made by a party during the negotiations for a contract, or those made afterwards, and relating to the contract. Do they amount to a contracual commitment that the statement is true, giving rise to remedies for non-performance if it is not realised, or do they only give rise to the possibility of avoidance for mistake by the other party? In the first case, the possibility of avoidance is excluded under Article 3.7 of the Unidroit Principles.[47] The question is important, if only because the criterion for measuring the damages would be different (positive or expectation interest v. negative or reliance interest).

There is no single answer to this question, and it is quite difficult to find a criterion which will enable us to distinguish between cases where the first solution prevails on the one hand, and cases in which the second applies. Certainly, a statement of fact is not a promise and vice-versa, but this does not prevent us from treating them alike, since they can both be considered as being a type of 'commitment'.[48] In many cases, statements made by a supplier of goods or services, relating to these goods or services, will thus be treated as a promise to deliver goods or services which have the qualities presented by the supplier.[49] This is all the more the case where the statements are made in the course of advertising, unless any guarantee as to the truth of a specific statement has been expressly excluded — in such cases, liability for misleading advertising will not yet be excluded by this fact.

In the CECL, agreement has been reached on an Article 8.101 along the following lines:

'8.101 Statements giving rise to contractual obligations.
(1) A statement by one party is to be treated as a contractual (undertaking) (warranty) as to the contents of the statement if, (in the light of the circumstances, including) (among other things):
(a) the apparent importance of the statement to the other party,
(b) whether either party was making the statement in the course of business, and
(c) the relative expertise of the parties,
the other party reasonably understood that a (warranty) (promise/undertaking) was being made to him.
(2) A statement (by one party) is to be treated as a contractual (warranty) (undertaking) as to the contents of the statement if a professional supplier gives information about the quality or use of services, goods or other property, when marketing (or advertising) them or otherwise before the contract (for them) is made, unless it is shown that the other party knew or could not have been unaware that the statement was incorrect. (...)'

32 Unreasonable or Unfair Terms
The third category of problems concerns the validity or invalidity of specific clauses. Here again, it is not possible to separate the question of the validity of the

---

47 'A party is not entitled to avoid the contract on the ground of mistake if the circumstances on which that party relies afford, or could have afforded, it a remedy for non-performance.'
48 The basic similarity between a promise and an intentional representation is stressed in the aforementioned article by J. Köndgen, *Reconstructing promissory obligation: From Status to Contract to Quasi-Contract.*
49 Cf. in particular § 2-313 of the Uniform Commercial Code. A similar position is implied in Article 7:18 NBW. For a comparative viewpoint, cf. P.S. Atiyah, 'Misrepresentation, warranty, estoppel', in *Essays on Contract*, Clarendon Oxford 1986, p. 275 et seq.

contract from its contents. However, a distinction can, in my opinion, be drawn between clauses which are invalid because they are unreasonable to the other party and clauses which are invalid because they are considered to be contrary to public policy or morality. The latter category will be dealt with in the following section (9.). The first question will be dealt with here, since the concepts of unreasonableness or unfairness on the one hand, and of good faith on the other hand, are closely linked.

It is not possible to qualify our contract law as constituting a common system of law for Europe if, on the question of validity of specific clauses, one is completely referred to domestic law. Although on the basis of the principle of subsidiarity and the other elements of the division of powers, the regulation of certain specific contracts can be left to domestic law (e.g. landlord and tenant agreements, certain areas of labour law, contracts related to family law, etc.), this should not be the case for the general principles applicable to all contracts or a very considerable category of contracts, such as consumer contracts.

Thus the PECL thus contain *certain Articles which may not be excluded by a specific clause*, such as Article 3.109, which lays down that liability may not be excluded or limited where non-performance is intentional (or reckless, see Article 1.105 (c)) or the restriction or exclusion unreasonable; see also Article 4.508 (2) which lays down that:

'despite any agreement to the contrary, the specified sum (for non-performance) may be reduced to a reasonable amount where it is grossly excessive in relation to the loss resulting from the non-performance and the other circumstances.'

As to the other clauses, these Principles merely refer to the general obligation of the debtor and the creditor to act in accordance with the requirements of good faith and fair dealing (apart from the rule on unfair general conditions, discussed later). Since the meaning of the principles of good faith and fair dealing could be open to a variety of constructions by the various domestic courts, even without any reference to specific local circumstances or customs justifying such differences, our common European system of contract law must lay down some specific, although not too rigid, criteria as to which clauses will be considered unreasonable.

A further step in this direction was made by the *EC-Directive on unfair terms in consumer contracts*, particularly in Article 3 which provides that:

'a contractual term which has not been individually negotiated shall be regarded as unfair if, contrary to the requirement of good faith, it causes a significant imbalance in the parties' rights and obligations arising under the contract, to the detriment of the consumer,'

as well as the Annex, which contains an indicative and non-exhaustive list of those terms which may be regarded as unfair. The connection with the notion of good

191

faith has clearly been made in this Directive. This is apparent not only from Article 3 (1), but also from Article 4 (1), which provides that:

'(...) the unfairness of a contractual term shall be assessed, taking into account the nature of the goods or services for which the contract was concluded and by referring, at the time of conclusion of the contract, to all circumstances attending the conclusion of the contract and to all the other terms of the contract (...).'

The last-named Article does not prevent us from considering as contrary to the principle of good faith the exercising of a contractual right by one of the parties, even if the term conferring this right could not be considered unfair at the time of conclusion of the contract; however, such invalidity will no longer be based on the existing EC Directive. The same applies to individually negotiated clauses – although this is certainly an important circumstance which must be taken into account when assessing whether the clause is unfair or not,[50] they can still be considered to be unfair if a sufficient number of the other elements prompt this conclusion. The PECL will contain a rule copied from Article 3 of the Directive, but not restricted to consumers and thus covering all clauses not individually negotiated (Article 6.110 PECL).

An important element in our common European system of law (and in the current rules which apply in many domestic systems) regarding the validity of specific clauses in the light of requirements of good faith is *the exclusion of the possibility that the substance or main subject matter of the contract (i.e. the price, goods or services) could be invalidated or adjusted,* except in the context of avoidance or adjustment on grounds of abuse of circumstances, which should be considered as a matter affecting consent.[51] This element is emphasised in particular in Article 4 (2) of the Directive on unfair terms in consumer contracts.[52] Although this does not exclude the possibility of examining the adequacy or inadequacy of the main obligations of the parties outside this context, this will only be the case when it comes into assessing the fairness or unfairness of *other* terms of the contract. The doctrine of *justum pretium* thus remains buried, and this is of fundamental

---

50   The EC Directive on unfair terms in consumer contracts considers that 'particular regard shall be had to the strength of the bargaining position of the parties (...) whereas the requirement of good faith may be satisfied by the seller or supplier where he deals fairly and equitably with the other party whose legitimate interests he has to take into account'.

51   Cf. e.g. Article 6.108 (1) PECL: 'A party may avoid a contract if, at the time of the making of the contract, (a) he was dependent on or had a relationship of trust with the other party, was in economic distress or had urgent needs, was improvident, ignorant, inexperienced or lacking in bargaining skill, and (b) the other party knew or ought to have known of this and, given the circumstances and the purpose of the contract, took excessive or unfair advantage of it'. The Unidroit Principles on the other hand are not yet in tune with this position (cf. Article 3.10 'gross disparity', where abuse of circumstances is only one of the elements to be regarded in order to judge the excessive character of the advantage unjustifiably given to that party by the contract or term).

52   Compare e.g. Article 6:231 NBW; ABGB § 879, 3; AGBGesetz § 8.

importance to the functioning of the market economy. Accordingly, our common European system of law should also restrict the opportunities for imposing maximum prices for any marketable goods or services to temporary situations of market failure — but as this is not directly a problem relating to the law of contracts, I will not dwell on this point at this juncture.

In my opinion, these applications of the principle of good faith should not be regarded as matters which concern public policy (the public interest); they only protect (one of) the parties to the contract (e.g. the consumer); the invalidity of unfair clauses will therefore be a 'relative' one,[53] and the penalty imposed will be avoidance. However, this is without prejudice to the possibility of government or class action against sellers or suppliers who continue to use unfair terms in contracts concluded with consumers, as required by Article 7 of the EC Directive. However, such actions form part of competition and trade law rather than of the law of contracts. There are many other cases where the violation of a rule is penalised even by the criminal law, and parties still have the opportunity to compromise on their mutual rights which arise from a contract in violation of such rules (e.g. in labour law).

33 UNFAIR DOMESTIC LEGISLATION
The Directive on unfair terms also raises the question whether this implies a minimal degree of protection of the consumer, even in cases where the terms of the contract do not depart from the domestic law, because the latter itself does not provide that protection which cannot be set aside by not individually negotiated clauses. Even when viewed in the light of our common European system of contract law, the question remains relevant, since a common system of general contract law does not yet exclude the existence of a variety among domestic laws on certain types of specific contract. On the basis of the object of the Directive, as expressed in its recitals, some leading authors have argued that this implies that in consumer contracts, those rights which cannot be restricted or excluded by clauses which have not been individually negotiated are also incapable of being excluded by domestic legislation in relation to specific contracts.[54] Only in this way can a common degree of minimum protection of consumers be guaranteed.

34 APPLICATION OF PRIORITY RULES ALONGSIDE CONFLICT OF
LAW RULES OR EQUIVALENCE OF DOMESTIC RULES
The final issue to be dealt with in this section concerns the application of mandatory rules which protect particular interests beyond the scope of application of the common European system of contract law. Within the EC, European

---

53   Compare Article 3:40, 2 NBW: 'If the provision is intended solely for the protection of one of the parties to a multilateral juridical act, the act may only be avoided'.
54   E.g. P. Hommelhoff, 'Zivilrecht unter dem Einfluß europäischer Rechtsangleichung', 192. *AcP* 1992, (71) 83-84.

Community law clearly takes precedence over the conflict of law rules,[55] and therefore we have to examine the extent to which EC law, including our common European system of contract law, prevents the applicability of domestic mandatory rules — whether applicable on the basis of the rules on conflicts of law contained in the Rome Convention, or priority rules (règles d'application immédiate) — within the territory of the EC.

Until now, the drafters of common principles, whether Unidroit or the CECL, have failed to take any steps in order to restrict the applicability of mandatory rules applicable under the relevant rules of private international law; on the contrary, these principles provide that they do not restrict any such applicability.[56] Nevertheless, other areas of EC law may do so already, either now or in the future. Particularly important for the question of applicability of domestic mandatory rules is the doctrine of the equivalence of the protection given by the various domestic laws, as developed by the Court of Justice in the Cassis de Dijon case,[57] and in other decisions on the free movement of goods. It has been argued that not only rules of administrative law, but also rules of private law, insofar as they restrict the free movement of goods or services to an economically important extent, must be subjected to the treble test of legitimate purpose, relevance for this purpose and proportionality, before they can exclude the applicability of the rules of another Member State. *De lege lata*, this viewpoint has been defended in relation to the free movement of goods (direct effect of Articles 30 and 36 EEC Treaty) but also in the field of financial services, on the basis of the object of the 2nd Banking Directive.[58] The trend is also discernible in the Directives on insurance law, even though still to a limited extent.[59] As a result of this doctrine, the private law institutions of all Member States of the EC must be recognised by the other Member States, insofar as such recognition is necessary in order to liberalise the

---

55   This is also implied by Articles 20 and 21 of the 1980 Rome Convention on Contractual Obligations.
56   Cf. in particular Article 1.4 Unidroit Principles.
57   C.J.E.C. Case 120/78, dated 20-2-1979, Rewe-Zentrale v. Bundesmonopolverwaltung für Branntwein (1979) *ECR* 649.
58   Cf. in particular M. Wolf, 'Privates Bankvertragsrecht im EG-Binnenmarkt. Auswirkungen der II. Eg-Bankrechts-Richtlinie auf privatrechtliche Bankgeschäfte', *Wertpapier-Mitteilungen (ZfWirtsch-uBankR)*, 1990, (1941) et seq. This radical conclusion is not accepted by many other authors, e.g. P. Hommelhoff, 'Zivilrecht unter dem Einfluß europäischer Rechtsangleichung', 192. *AcP* 1992, (71) 100; G. Brüggemeier & C. Joerges, 'Europäisierung des Vertrags- und Haftungsrechts', Tagung *Gemeinsames Privatrecht in der Europäischen Gemeinschaft*, Trier 2-4 IV 1992.
59   Cf., *inter alia* , the 5th recital and Article 7 of the 2nd Directive on Non-Life Insurance of 22-6-1988; the 5th recital and Article 4 of the 2nd Directive on Life Insurance of 8-11-1990; Article 28 of the 3rd Directive on Non-Life Insurance of 18-6-1992 and Article 24 of the 3rd Directive on Life Insurance of 10-11-1992; J. Basedow, 'Das neue internationale Versicherungsvertrags-recht', *NJW* 1991, p. 785 et seq.; D. Lorenz, 'Das auf grenzüberschreitende Lebensversicherungs-verträge anwendbare Recht', *ZGsVersWis 1991*, p. 121 et seq.; G. Brüggemeier & C. Joerges, 'Europäisierung des Vertrags- und Haftungsrechts', Tagung *Gemeinsames Privatrecht in der Europäischen Gemeinschaft*.

market completely, unless the application of the mandatory rules of the Member State where the activity is taking place, rather than the rules of the other Member State, is considered to be strictly necessary in safeguarding a purpose of public interest, such as public morality, public security, public health, etc., or in securing fair trade or consumer protection (Article 36 EEC Treaty). The various legal systems of the Member States are deemed to give an equal degree of protection, subject to evidence to the contrary.

In my opinion, our common European system of contract law should extrapolate this doctrine and formulate a more radical rule of recognition. The wording of such a rule could be as follows:

'These principles restrict the applicability of mandatory rules (applicable in accordance with the relevant rules of private international law) to cases where their applicability is necessary for the purpose of safeguarding a purpose of public interest, such as public morality, public safety, public health, fair trade or consumer protection, in the sense that no equivalent protection will be afforded without their applicability , taking into account all the other applicable rules as well as the terms of the contract.'

9 'Essential Validity' (Illegality, Immorality)

35 PUBLIC POLICY AND PUBLIC MORALITY VIEWED IN A EUROPEAN CONTEXT
The main point which I wished to make on the question of the illegality or immorality of contracts has already been stated in Nos. 31 and 33, since, in my opinion, the same considerations apply to those cases where the illegality or immorality protect not only private interests, but the 'public interest' or public policy.

Here again, it is the common European system of contract law which has to determine the general rules on illegality and immorality, leaving the domestic làw the option to add other prohibitions, as long as these remain within their jurisdiction and their rules are not contrary to EC law. In a European perspective, we should do more than Unidroit, where the latter states that its 'Principles do not deal with invalidity arising from illegality or immorality.'[60]

As has been argued elsewhere (*supra*, No. 15), a general rule governing 'absolute' invalidity arising from immorality or illegality should be restricted to cases where (a) the contract incites a party (or third parties) to commit acts which are, in objective terms, contrary to public policy or public morality, or (b) the contract promises or stipulates a price for — or otherwise remunerates — acts which should not give rise to any reciprocal performance or to any reward, even if the act itself is perfectly legal and morally justified. In addition to these cases, it is superfluous

---

60   Article 3.1. Unidroit Principles.

to accept a doctrine of *fraus legis* if we only use sensible rules for the interpretation of law, e.g. by not restricting objective illegality to acts which use the same legal denomination as used by the rule, but extending it to acts which are not in any way distinct from the prohobited act, except its legal denomination, unless such an extension were contrary to the *ratio legis* of the rule concerned. The intention to infringe the law, however, is in my opinion an irrelevant and even dangerous criterion, since it inevitably leads to 'a trial of intentions'.

The notions of public policy and public morality are themselves in part given substance by EC-law (in particular EC competition law), and could also be given substance by domestic law, as long as Community law — including the European Convention on Human Rights — is observed in the process. As has been discussed earlier, the application of mandatory rules must — on the basis of Community law, and therefore also restricting the scope of Article 7 e.a. of the 1980 Rome Convention — be limited to those cases where their application is necessary — in the sense of the Cassis de Dijon decision — to an objective of public interest, such as public morality, public safety, public health, workable competition, etc.

10 Implications of 'Relative' Invalidity or Avoidability c.q. 'Absolute' Invalidity

36 FUNDAMENTAL DIFFERENCE
The last issue to be dealt with in this chapter concerns the effects of invalidity. Here, I will concentrate on the differences, in terms of their effects, between the two fundamental types of invalidity, i.e. 'relative invalidity' or avoidability on the one hand, and 'absolute' nullity on the other hand. The distinction itself and the criteria on which it is based have already been discussed supra, under No. 9. It has been decided to base this distinction on the type of interest protected by the invalidating rule, reserving the penalty of absolute nullity to those cases where public policy, and not just the interests of private parties, is at stake.

The fundamental difference between these two categories is that *in cases of relative nullity, the protected party may waive its right to invalidate the contract,* whereas this option is excluded in cases of absolute nullity. Apart from the procedural differences, which are not discussed here, the fundamental difference consists mainly in the following.

37 CONFIRMATION
The first difference is that the possibility of avoidance (but not absolute nullity) is excluded 'if the party who is entitled to avoid the contract expressly or impliedly confirms it after he knows or ought to have known of the ground for avoidance, or

becomes capable of acting freely.'[61] Unreserved voluntary performance must be equated with implied confirmation, according to the fundamental rules on interpretation, examined supra, under No. 25.

I see no reason for excluding this rule in cases where formal requirements have been imposed for the protection of the private interests of (one of) the parties, since the condition that he should have known the ground for avoidance, or that he becomes capable of acting freely before confirmation can be validly given, affords adequate protection. Certainly if the protective measure involved consists in allowing some time for reflection, within which the contract may be avoided,[62] no confirmation is possible within that period. However, such rules introduce a — mandatory — suspensive condition rather than a formal requirement.

38 TIME LIMIT FOR AVOIDANCE

The second difference is that the possibility of avoidance is limited in time, whereas the period in which absolute nullity may be relied upon is in itself not limited (although actions for restitution, etc., will be subject to time limits). In the Unidroit and PECL proposals, this limitation is construed as a 'Verwirkungsfrist' rather than as a prescription, and a precise length of time is not provided:[63]

'(1) Notice of avoidance must be given within a reasonable time, with due regard to the circumstances, after the avoiding party knew or ought to have known the relevant facts or became capable of acting freely.
(2) Where an individual term of the contract may be avoided by a party (...), the period of time for giving notice of avoidance begins to run when that term is asserted by the other party.'[64]

No indication is given as to the 'strong' or 'weak' character of this limitation, i.e. whether the ground for avoidance may still be relied upon as a defence against any action based on the contract. Most of the legal systems in the EC tend to adopt the 'weak' solution as expressed by the adagium *'Quae temporalia sunt ad agendum, perpetua ad excipiendum.'*[65] There are indeed sound arguments for defending the view that a party should not be obliged to avoid a contract as long as there is no actual reason to do so, especially where the contract (or clause) remains dead letter.

On the other hand, the 'weak' character of the limitation, the vague nature of the 'reasonable time' requirement, and the fact that this limitation does not necessarily

---

61 Article 6.205 PECL. Compare Article 3.12 Unidroit, which is very similar.
62 E.g. Article 5 Directive 85/577 of 20 December 1985, *OJ* 1985 L. 372/31; Article 11 Draft Directive 92/C 156/05, *OJ* C 156/14 on Distance Sales.
63 A similar period is used in several provisions concerning the remedies for non-performance. Compare also Article 39 CISG.
64 Article 6.204 PECL and Article 3.15 Unidroit, which is very similar.
65 Cf. more generally K. Spiro, *Die Begrenzung privater Rechte durch Verjährungs- Verwirkungs- und Fatalfristen*, Stämpfli Bern 1975, e.g. § 47 and 422; F. Glansdorff, 'Le caractère imprescriptible des exceptions', *R.C.J.B.*, 1991, p. 267 et seq.

apply to contracts invalidated on another basis than a factor affecting consent (e.g. on the basis of formal requirements), make it necessary, in my opinion, to lay down a rule along the lines of Article 3:55 (2) NBW- which could read as follows:

'The possibility of avoidance shall also be excluded if, once the party entitled to avoid the contract knows, or should have known, the ground for avoidance, or becomes capable of acting freely, a directly interested party serves notice on that party requiring the latter to choose, within a reasonable period, between confirmation and avoidance, and no choice has been made within that period.'[66]

39 CONCESSIONS EXCLUDING THE POSSIBILITY OF AVOIDANCE, PARTIAL INVALIDITY, CONVERSION OF VOID TRANSACTIONS

The third rule excluding the possibility of avoidance in certain cases is found in Article 6.206 PECL:[67]

'If a party is entitled to avoid the contract for mistake but the other party declares itself willing to perform or actually does perform the contract as it was understood by the party entitled to avoid it, the contract is to be treated as if it had been concluded as the mistaken party understood it. The other party must make such a declaration or render such performance promptly after having been informed of the manner in which the party entitled to avoid it had understood the contract and before that party has acted in reliance on any notice of avoidance. After such declaration or performance the right to avoid is lost and any earlier notice of avoidance is ineffective.'

Such a rule could prevent certain forms of abuse by a party entitled to avoid the contract. As such, the rule can only accomodate mistakes of communication and misunderstandings. For other matters affecting consent, similar considerations favour the exclusion of the possibility of avoidance if an offer of adjustment is made to the party entitled to avoid which will adequately remove the disadvantage. Since the possibilities of adjustment may differ according to the various factors which may affect consent, they are not gone into in any detail here.

There is also an analogy between this case and the possibility of 'converting' a void tranaction into a valid one, if it contains the necessary elements for this purpose, since this rule also prevents certain forms of abuse of nullity by one of the parties.

The same applies to the principle which restricts the penalty of avoidance and nullity to a partial invalidity, if only part of the contract, or a particular term, is

---

66   Such a rule is also inspired by comparable rules in the field of remedies for non-performance (Article 48 (2) CISG, Article 6:88 NBW, BGB § 355 and 466 and Article 26 Scandinavian sales law) and in the field of unauthorised agency (Article 3:69 (4) NBW, BGB § 177 (2) and Article 38 Swiss Obligationenrecht).

67   Also, a very similar rule in Article 3.13 of the Unidroit Principles.

affected. These rules will therefore be found in the Unidroit Principles as well as in the PECL.[68]

40 RETROACTIVITY

Finally, it could be considered as a common principle in our contract law that nullity and avoidance take effect retroactively.[69] The CECL, however, prefers not to use this term, as it could give rise to certain misunderstanding, especially in the common law countries which are unused to a clear dividing line between the obligations of a contract and its implications under the law of property. The PECL merely state the most important effects of avoidance, especially in the field of restitution, and lay down rules favouring the separate nature and validity of a choice of the forum, an arbitration clause, etc. To prevent any possible misunderstanding, however, it may be be sufficient to clarify that the retroactivity of avoidance takes effect without prejudice to the rules of property law concerning the things or rights transferred or constituted on the basis of the invalid obligation or contract.

11 Concluding Remark

41 The issues of the validity and contents of contracts under a common European system of contract law certainly cannot be dealt with in anything more than a very superficial manner in one single chapter. I have merely endeavoured to indicate the fundamental differences between the legal systems which impair the process of harmonisation, the choices to be made, and some elements of the background and/or implications of these choices. Most of the questions dealt with in this chapter are technical matters, and those aspects which would be most appropriately illustrated by specific cases have been dealt with in other chapter. What remains is a somewhat 'academic' study which, however, I hope still constitutes a helpful contribution towards the study of the harmonisation of the law of contract in Europe and its attendant problems.

---

68 Article 6.203 PECL: 'If a ground of avoidance affects only a particular term of a contract, the effect of an avoidance is limited to those terms unless, giving due consideration to all the circumstances of the case, it is unreasonable to uphold the remaining contract' (Article 3.16 Unidroit Principles is very similar).

69 Article 3.17 (1) Unidroit Principles: 'avoidance takes effect retroactively'.

CHAPTER 11

Performance and Remedies in the Law of Contracts

Ole Lando

1 Introduction

1.1 The Subject Matter

The contract terms which the parties agree upon will generally govern their relationship. Some contracts contain many and elaborate terms, some do not. A contract for the construction of an off-shore oil rig will generally contain hundreds, if not thousands of pages of contract terms. A contract whereby a buyer merely faxes the seller: 'Send me 1000 bales of cotton', which the seller then does, contains few terms. In the first contract almost everything is settled. The contract terms describe in great detail the quality of the performance and the terms of payment. They stipulate how to solve unforeseen contingencies, such as unexpected sea-bed or stream conditions, and technical improvements, which may call forth changes in the performance. There are even terms on non-performance by one party and its consequences. In the second case, the sale of cotton, the contract only provides the quantity and type of the commodity. The law or usages will tell the parties how much cotton there must be in a bale, and which qualities the cotton must have. Legal rules or usages will also provide the terms and place of delivery, and the terms of payment. They will prescribe the conditions and consequences of non-performance.

This chapter will contain proposals for the adoption of two principles on performance of contracts in a European Civil Code. The first principle is that of good faith and fair dealing which, although not confined to the performance of contracts, will have its main field of operation in their performance. The second is a rule on hardship (French: imprévision) as either cause for the termination of a contract or for a modification of its performance.

Furthermore, the chapter will set forth a system for non-performance of contracts to be adopted in the general part of the law of contract of a European Civil Code, and, to the extent this is possible in a general part, some principles regarding the remedies for non-performance such as damages.

The rules which will be proposed will be compared to those existing in the common law of England and the United States and in the civil law countries, notably France, Germany, the Nordic countries and the Netherlands. The rules proposed are inspired by the Principles adopted by the Commission on European Contract Law (hereinafter PECL) and the Unidroit Principles for International Commercial Contract (hereinafter UNIDROIT Principles) both examined by Arthur S. Hartkamp in chapter 3 above.

The rules on performance and non-performance to be dealt with are, as mentioned, to be provided in the general part of the law of contracts. Before dealing with these rules we will discuss briefly whether, today, it is meaningful to maintain a general part of the law of contracts, and, if so, what impact the contract for the sale of goods will have on this general part.

1.2 The Utility of a General Part

Contracts exist in a great variety of forms: sales, leasing, employment, transport, insurance, construction of buildings, agency, etc. In fact, there is no such thing as a 'general contract'. The rules of the general part of contract law will always apply to a specific contract.

For each specific contract there are separate rules on what is required for due performance and on the remedies for non-performance. A sales contract and an insurance contract do not have many rules on these issues in common. In modern times the types of contract have increased, and so have the kinds of contract within each type. For several contracts such as transport, insurance, employment and lease of immovables, the legislature has provided rules which are aimed at protecting the weak party or at safeguarding the public interest, rules which also bear upon the performance and non-performance of these contracts. The variety of contracts and policies have limited the scope of the general rules on performance and non-performance. Against this background some writers have argued that it is no longer meaningful to operate with a general contract law.

One of the critics of 'pure contract law' is Laurence M. Friedmann.[1] He sees this law linked to the 'completely free market', a law for parties of equal bargaining power, a deliberate attempt to avoid any restriction of party autonomy. This criticism, it is submitted, does not hold true any longer.[2] The 'pure contract law' contains several restrictions on the parties' freedom to contract. Friedmann also sees the difficulties of applying general contract rules to a great variety of contracts and situations, but this is not his main point.

The best way in which to measure the utility of a general part of contract law is to look to experience. Most of the countries with 'old' codes, such as France,

---

1   E.g. Friedmann in *Contract Law in America* 20 (1965).
2   See *Farnsworth on Contracts*, 1990 Vol. I Chapters 4 and 5, and Zweigert and Kötz, *An Introduction to Comparative Law*, 2d ed. 1987 Vol. II 8 ff.

Belgium, Luxembourg, Spain and Germany, have provided general rules of the law of obligations also covering torts and unjust enrichment and so have the countries with more or less 'new' codes, like Greece, Italy, Portugal and the Netherlands.

The Nordic countries have no codes in the continental sense of the word, and therefore no codified general part of the law of obligations. However, the general part is found in the text books and other legal writing and is taught in the law schools. It lives in the minds of the lawyers, and is practiced almost as much as in the countries with codes.

This also holds true of the common law countries. They operate with a mainly unwritten general part of the law of contracts, which has a great practical importance. In the worlds of teaching and academic debate, it seems to have more importance than has the writings on the law of the specific contracts.

In legal practice, the general part of the law of obligation is as important in the law today as it was in the last century. It is applied in courtrooms and in the attorney's 'cabinets' as much as it was before. Text books and commentaries on the general part are published and consulted as much as before.

The utility of a general part of the law of contracts has also been the credo of the UNIDROIT and the Commission on European Contract Law in their efforts to draft Principles of Contract Law.[3] The UNIDROIT Principles cover formation, interpretation, validity, contents, performance and non-performance of contracts in general. The Commission on European Contract Law has until now drafted general principles on effects, performance and non-performance of contracts. Provoked by the above-mentioned doubts of the value of a general part, the Commission has examined how the drafted rules would operate upon a number of specific contracts such as leasing, long time supply and requirement contracts, transport contracts in general, charterparties, documentary credit, banking contracts, financial services, agency and distributorship contracts, supply of services in general, and the transfer of technology and know-how. It was found that on the whole the Principles were well suited for these specific contracts.[4]

However, providing general rules on contract law has never been unproblematic. As we shall see, such rules, if they are made precise, will not be apt to meet the needs of many of the specific contracts. If they are to cover all contracts many of them must be vague rules.

---

3   See Hartkamp, *Principles of Contract Law, supra* chapter 3 and Lando in *RabelsZ* (56) 1992, 261.
4   See also Farnsworth (*op.cit.* note 2) p. 40.

1.3 Importance of the Sales Contract

The sale of goods has always been considered the paradigmatic contract. In the European Codes the general provisions on the law of obligations have paid particular attention to this contract. In the Nordic countries several of the statutory provisions on sales have been regarded as general principles of contract law,[5] and so have in the United States many of the sales provisions in Article 2 of the Uniform Commercial Code.[6]

The United Nations' Convention on Contracts for the International Sale of Goods (CISG) is becoming world law. More than 40 countries have now ratified it including Denmark, Finland, France, Germany, Italy, The Netherlands, Norway, Sweden and the USA. This will probably have far reaching consequences. The first consequence is that it has already encouraged the efforts to harmonize the general contract law of the world. Both the Commission on European Contract Law and the UNIDROIT[7] have taken the rules of CISG as their startingpoint when drafting rules on the performance and non-performance of contracts. When visualising the effects of their general principles they have often resorted to the sales paradigm. In fact, both in the Commission and in the UNIDROIT the members have frequently felt it necessary to remind each other that they were not drafting rules solely for the sales contract.

The second consequence is that although CISG is only applicable to international and not to domestic contracts it will probably influence the general contract law of the Member States as it has already affected the new Sale of Goods Acts in Finland, Norway and Sweden.

1.4 Plan

In the following sections we will examine some aspects of the effects and performance of contracts, notably the principle of good faith and the hardship rule (section 2) and the conditions of and remedies for non-performance (section 3). The purpose of this is to examine whether, in the light of the experience gained in UNIDROIT and the Commission on European Contract Law, there are any prospects for a unification or harmonisation of terminology, system and rules.

---

5   Ussing, *Obligationsrettens Almindelige Del*, 1964 p. 9.
6   Farnsworth (*op.cit.* note 2) p. 45.
7   See Bonell in *RabelsZ* (56) 1992-274.

2 Performance of the Contract

2.1 Contents and Performance

The UNIDROIT Principles and PECL have made several of the rules of the CISG on the contents and performance of the sales contract into general contract rules. This applies to the time and place of performance of money obligations and obligations other than money obligations, on the quality of performance, the duty to receive performance and the determination of the price to be paid. Furthermore, the two sets of principles contain provisions on the form and currency of money obligations and with appropriation of a performance. A few other issues are also examined in the chapters on contents and performance.[8]

On two controversial issues the UNIDROIT and the Commission on European Contract Law have deviated from CISG. One issue is the adoption of the principle of good faith and fair dealing, and the other the rule on the modification and termination of the contract in case of hardship.

2.2 Good Faith

2.2.1 Survey of the Law of the European Communities
The principle of good faith and fair dealing is known as a guideline for contractual behaviour in all EC countries. There is, however, a considerable difference between the legal systems as to how far and how powerful the penetration of the principle has been. At one end of the spectrum is a system where the principle has revolutionized the contract law (and other parts of the law as well) and added a special feature to the style of that system (Germany). At the other end we find systems which do not recognize a general obligation of the parties to conform to good faith in the performance of a contract, but which in many cases reach the results which the other systems have reached by the principle of good faith, by specific rules (England and Ireland).

The other systems within the EC range between these two opposites. They recognize a principle of good faith and fair dealing as a general clause, but have not given it the importance as it has in German law.

2.2.2 Germany[9]

2.2.2.1 In General
In Germany § 242 BGB has been used to make possible what one author calls a

---

8   See Hartkamp *supra* chapter 3.
9   See Zweigert & Kötz (*supra* note 2) 156.

'moralization' of contractual relationships in Germany.[10] § 242 states in general terms that everyone must perform his contract in the manner required by good faith and fair dealing (Treu und Glauben) taking into consideration the general commercial practice.

This provision has been used to qualify a rigorous individualism of the orginal contract laws of the BGB. It has operated as a 'superprovision' which may modify the effect of other statutory provisions. Based on § 242 BGB, the German courts have developed new concepts (see 2.2.2.2. below) and have created a number of obligations to ensure a loyal performance of a contract such as a duty of the parties to cooperate, to protect each others' interests, to disclose information, and to submit accounts.

There is, however, one important limitation to the operation of the good faith principle. It does not permit the courts to establish a general principle of fairness and equity. A court may not replace the effects of a contract or of a statutory provision by an outcome which it believes to be more fair and equitable.[11]

2.2.2.2 The Institutions
Among the institutions created by the courts relying on the good faith principle the following should be mentioned:

— A change of circumstances (*Wegfall der Geschäftsgrundlage*) which makes the performance of the contract extremely onerous for one party and may lead to the modification or termination of his contractual obligation, see below 2.3 on grounds of hardship.

— A party's right may be limited or lost if enforcing it would amount to an abuse of right. An abuse of right is found in the following typical cases: (1) A party cannot acquire a right through dishonest behaviour (*exceptio doli specialis*); this rule bears some resemblance with the concept of 'unclean hands' in English doctrine of equity.[12] (2) A party will lose a right by breach of his own duty (*Verwirkung* — equitable estoppel). (3) A party cannot claim a performance which he will soon have to give back to the obligor (*dolo facit, qui petit, quid statim redditurus est*). (4) A party may not pursue an interest which is not worth protecting. (5) A party may not rely on a behaviour which is inconsistent with his earlier conduct (*venire contra factum proprium*).

— Ending of contractual obligations which extend over a period of time. These obligations may be ended for compelling reasons (*wichtiger Grund*) even though this is not supported by a statutory or contractual provision. The right

---

10   *Idem* 156.
11   See Soergel-Siebert, *Bürgerliches Gesetzbuch* 11 ed. 1978 § 242 N. 4.
12   See Palandt, *BGB* 46 ed. 1987 § 242 N 4 C.a.

to end these obligations may be limited by the contract, but it may not be completely excluded.[13]

2.2.3 England

As was mentioned above under 2.2.1, the common law of England does not recognize any general obligation to conform to good faith and fair dealing in the performance of a contract.

However, many of the results which in other legal systems are achieved by requiring good faith in performance have been reached under English and Irish law by more specific rules. For example, the courts have limited the right of a party who is the victim of a slight breach of contract to terminate the contract on that ground when the real motive appears to be to escape a bad bargain.[14] Conversely, the victim of a wrongful repudiation is not permitted to ignore the repudiation, complete his own performance and claim the contract price from the repudiating party, unless the victim has a legitimate interest in doing so.[15] There are many examples of the courts interpreting the terms of a contract in such a way as to prevent one party using a clause in circumstances in which it was probably not intended to apply. The clearest examples of this occur in relation to exclusion clauses[16] but other terms have been construed similarly (e.g. *Carr v JA Berriman Pty Ltd.* (1953) 27 AJLR 273 (High Court) where it was held that an architect under a construction contract could not exercise a power to order work to be omitted simply in order to give the same work to another contractor, who was prepared to do it for less). Thus to some extent the good faith principle merely articulates trends already present in English law. But the English approach based on the construction of the agreement is a weak one as it cannot prevail against clear contrary provisions in the agreement.[17]

2.2.4 The Other EC Systems

2.2.4.1 Sources

Statutory provisions laying down a principle of good faith in the performance of the contract are to be found in: France, see Civil Code Article 1134 (3); the Netherlands, NBW book 6: Article 2 and Article 248; as well as in several other European codes, see Article 1375 and Article 1175 of the Italian Civil Code.

---

13 See *BGH* 4 April 1973, 'Betriebsberater' 1973, 819.
14 See *Hoenig v Isaacs* [1952] 2 All ER 176 (CA) and *Hong Kong Fir Shipping Co Ltd v Kawasaki Kisen Kaisha Ltd* [1962] 2 QB 26 (CA).
15 See *Attica Sea Carriers Corp. v Ferrostall Poseidon Bulk Reederei GmbH* [1976] 1 Lloyds Rep. 250 (CA).
16 See Treitel, *Law of Contract* (8th ed, 1991) p. 202-223 and Coote [1970] *Cambridge LJ* p. 221.
17 See *Photo Production Ltd. v Securicor Transport Ltd* [1980] AC 827 (HC), exclusion clauses, or even clear implication for the circumstances *Bunge Corporation v Tradax* SA [1981] 1 WLR 711 (HC): right to terminate for breach which might not have any serious consequences.

In the Nordic countries, this principle is recognized by the courts and the legal writers. Although the principle has not been expressed in the statutes in the same general terms as it has in the countries mentioned above, several statutory provisions presuppose its existance, see for instance Article 36 of the Contract Act.

2.2.4.2 Degree of Penetration

It is not easy to measure and compare how deeply into the contract law the good-faith principle has been integrated into the various legal systems.

The Dutch NBW Article 6.2 uses powerful language. Good faith will not only supplement obligations arising from contract but may also modify and extinguish them. Under Article 6.2 (1) which applies to all obligations, the obligor and obligee must act in their mutual relationship in accordance with the requirements of reasonableness and equity. Under Article 6.2 (2) a rule which binds the parties by virtue of law, usage or legal act shall not apply to the extent that under the circumstances this would be unacceptable under the standards of reasonableness and equity. Article 6.248 (1) which applies to contracts, provides that a contract has not only the effect agreed to by the parties but also those which according to the nature of the contract result from law, usage and the requirements of reasonableness and equity. Article 6.248 (2) has the same rule for contracts which Article 6.2 (2) provides for obligations.

Before the NBW came into force some institutions similar to those developed in Germany had been established by the Dutch courts. Having created a leading principle of reasonableness and equity, the new Code will probably encourage the courts to develop these institutions further.[18]

In France, the courts have not given the rule expressed in Article 1134 (3) cc the same importance as it had in Germany and the other above mentioned countries. However, similar results have often been reached without a reference to good faith, for instance by using the well established theory of an abuse of right. In the last two decades the courts have openly used the good faith principle in the determination of the parties' obligations. The writers invoke this principle in order to impose upon the parties a duty of mutual loyalty, of information and co-operation, and to restrict the operation of clauses exempting a party from liability for breach of contract.[19]

2.2.5 CISG, PECL and the UNIDROIT Principles

This century has witnessed the principle of good faith gain in importance. The courts have attached a growing importance to it. In most of the EC countries it is a general clause, expressing the court's sense of justice, a feeling which often

---

18 See Hartkamp in *Nieuw Nederlands Burgerlijk Wetboek*, 'Het Vermogensrecht' (1990) XXI.
19 See Malaurie & Aynès, *Droit civil, Les Obligations*, 2.ed. Paris 1990, no 614, Marty & Raynaud, *Droit civil, Les Obligations I*, Paris 1988, no 246.

cannot be categorized. This has also created uncertainty and its value has been questioned by those who cherish certainty. When given a wide scope of application it will sometimes be misused. When applied to cases governed by international conventions there is a danger that the national courts will let their own traditions and legal values influence its application, and thereby distort the desired uniformity in the application of the convention. This was reflected in the deliberations leading to Article 7 of CISG. As a *via media* between the protagonists and antagonists of the principle it was agreed that good faith should operate in the interpretation of the rules of the convention. However, good faith was not mentioned as a factor which determines the interpretation of a contract governed by CISG.

In spite of this compromise, several writers have argued that good faith must also govern the interpretation and implementation of the contract.[20] It is not possibe to maintain a distinction between the interpretation of an article of the Convention and the interpretation of a contract governed by the Convention without creating antinomies. If the distinction is maintained, good faith would govern the interpretation of the *'force majeure'* rule in Article 79 of CISG but not the interpretation of a *force majeure* clause in a contract.

In the Commission of European Contract Law and in UNIDROIT, the good faith principle was established. The UNIDROIT Principles provide that 'each party must act in accordance with good faith and fair dealing in international trade'. This principle applies to all the subjects covered by the Principles. The PECL which have hitherto dealt only with the performance of the contract provides that 'in exercising his rights and performing his duties each party must act in accordance with good faith and fair dealing'.

2.3 Hardship

2.3.1 Force Majeure

It is genereally accepted that a party is bound to fulfil his obligations even if performance has become more onerous: *'Pacta sunt servanda'*.

In most European countries this principle is abandoned only in case of what is here compendiously called *force majeure*. *Force majeure* is not a uniform concept in the legal systems but it has the following main features.[21]

---

20   See Honnold, *Uniform Law for International Sales* 2d ed. 1991 no 94; von Caemmerer & Schlechtriem, *Kommentar zum einheitlichen Kaufrecht*, 1990 Art. 7, RN. 15-18 (-Herber); Bianca-Bonell, *Commentary on the International Sales Law*, 1987, 83f (Bonell); Enderlein, Maskow, Stargard, *Kaufrechtskonvention der UNO*, 1985, Art. 7. Anm. 5; Lando, *Udenrigshandelens Kontrakter* 4. ed. 1991, 13, but see Schlechtriem, *Einheitliches UN Kaufrecht*, 1981, 25.

21   See Zweigert & Kötz (*op.cit.* note 2) vol II chapter 14.

a   A party is excused from performing his obligations if performance has become impossible in fact or in law. Some of the legal systems also accept quasi-impossibility; performance is not physically impossible but has become so onerous that it amounts to the same as impossibility.

b   The impossibility or impediment is one which the obligor could not 'be expected to have taken into account.

c   The impossibility must have occurred outside of the control of the obligor. He is supposed to have control of himself, his employees and others whom he has entrusted to perform, and of his own equipment and inventory. He is not supposed to control the sources of supply outside of his enterprise.

d   Force majeure ends the contract. There is no room for renegotiation with a view to modifying its terms.

A rule as the one treated above was provided in CISG, PECL and the UNIDROIT principles all of which provide rules similar to CISG Article 79.

2.3.2 The need for a More Lenient Rule

In many business circles the strict pacta sunt-servanda rule has been considered to be too severe, especially in contracts of duration such as contracts for the continous supply of goods and services, and long lasting construction contracts. For these and for several other contracts a more lenient hardship rule is needed to meet unforeseen contingencies, notably in times of depression and unrest. Hardship clauses have been inserted into many contract documents, but experience has shown that the parties often do not remember or do not find it necessary to insert a hardship clause. It has been argued that in such cases the party who is exposed to hardship must bear the consequences of his forgetfulness or lack of care. However, the hardship which a party suffers is often out of proportion to the fault made in forgetting or omitting to take care.

Some legal systems have therefore relieved the obligor from all or part of his obligations when performance, though not impossible, has either become excessively onerous (Italy)[22] or so burdensome that the economic basis upon which the contract has been made must be considered to have disappeared (Germany: Wegfall der Geschäftsgrundlage).[23] A similar principle is found in Dutch law, see NBW at 6:258 and in French administrative law.[24]

2.3.3 PECL and UNIDROIT

CISG has not included cases of hardship in its rule on changed circumstances, see Article 79.[25]

---

22   Ital. c.c. art. 1467.

23   Zweigert & Kötz (op.cit. note 2) p. 211.

24   See Rodière & Tallon (ed), Les modifications du contrat en cours de son exécution en raison de circonstances nouvelles, Paris 1985.

25   See Honnold (op.cit. note 20) p. 583.

As its starting point PECL Article 2.117 (1) states that *pacta sunt servanda* is to be observed even when the cost of performance has increased and when the value of the performance has diminished.

Article 2.117 (2) states that if performance of the contract becomes excessively onerous because of a change of circumstances, the parties are bound to enter into negotiations with a view to adapting the contract or terminating it, provided that

a   the change of circumstances occurred after the time of conclusion of the contract, or had already occurred at that time but was not and could not reasonably have been known to the parties;
b   the possibility of the change of circumstances was not one which could reasonably have been taken into account; and
c   the risk of the change of circumstances is not one which, according to the contract, the party affected should be required to bear.

The hardship rule differs from the force majeure rule in the following respects:

a   Performance need not be impossible but 'only' excessively onerous.
    Thus, there is hardship when an enterprise has undertaken to supply water to a hospital for 'times ever after' at a fixed price which has become derisory due to inflation. There is also hardship when a gas company has promised to deliver gas to a city for a period of 30 years at a fixed tariff and when during that period the price of coal used to produce gas increases by four times due to shortages of coal caused by war.

b   The contract is not ended but may be modified by the parties renegotiating the contract.
    The duty to renegotiate the contract is imposed upon the parties because they are generally the best judges of their situation. The renegotiation must be concluded in good faith and must deal with all the issues caused by the hardship. Very often the contract may be adapted to the new situation so that a reasonable solution is found. The parties may also agree to end the contract if no other solution is practical because of the fact that under the force majeure rule the circumstances creating the hardship must not have been such which the party suffering hardship should have taken into account when the contract was made, and they must have occurred outside of his sphere of control.

PECL Article 2.117 (3) deals with the situation where the parties fail to reach agreement within a reasonable time.

The court or the arbitrator may then

a   terminate the contract at a time and on terms to be determined by the court; or
b   adapt the contract in order to distribute between the parties in a just and

211

equitable manner the losses and gains resulting from the change of circumstances; and

c   in either case, award damages for the loss suffered through the other party refusing to negotiate or breaking off negotiations in bad faith.

3 The Failure to Effect Performance

3.1 ULIS and CISG

CISG's Part 3 covers what it calls 'Sale of Goods'; where in fact it only deals with the obligations of the seller and the buyer, and the remedies for non-performance of these obligations.

It is the latter, 'the remedies for breach of contract' on which we will try and set up a structure and terms. The purpose is to use a neutral language and a simple structure. In doing this we have been guided by two main considerations. The first consideration is to have a structure which is compatible with that of the CISG. The second consideration is to use one which may apply to contracts other than those of the sale of goods.

The terms and the structures of the national legal systems differ considerably.[26] When preparing the first drafts of the 'Uniform Law for the International Sale of Movable Goods' Ernest Rabel[27] and his fellow draftsmen established a system which was modelled upon the common law and the law of the Scandinavian Countries, notably their Sale of Goods Act from 1905-07. This system has roughly been followed in later drafts, in the Uniform Law of the International Sale of Goods from 1964 (ULIS) and in the CISG.

3.2 The Fact Situations

Let us recall the situations we are dealing with. Most contracts set a time for their performance. If the contract has not fixed a time, the law will do it. Furthermore, it is expressed or implied that the performance must have a certain quality and quantity. If the person who is to perform — the obligor — has to deliver goods, these goods must be free from any rights and claims of a third party. The contract may contain other obligations such as a duty not to disclose information received

---

26   See Zweigert & Kötz (*op.cit.* note 2) Vol II, Chapter 13, Treitel, *Remedies for Breach of Contracts*, Oxford 1987, passim.

27   See Rabel, *Das Recht des Warenkaufs, I-II* (Tübingen 1957 and 1958), Vol I, 118 ff, 329 ff, 380 ff, Vol II 368 ff, hereinafter cited as *Rabel I & II*, Schlechtriem 1981 *op.cit.* note 20) 1, 7, 65, 76 and Schlechtriem/Huber 1990 (*op.cit.* note 20) Art. 45 Anm. 1-17.

from the other party, or not to engage in certain competitive activities.

If the contract is not performed in accordance with these express or implied terms the failure to perform may be due to the obligor's fault; or it may have causes for which he cannot be blamed, but for which he nevertheless must bear the risk. The failure to effect due performance may also have been caused by the person who is to receive performance — the obligee — either by his fault or by other causes for which he bears the risk.

The legal systems will allocate detrimental consequences to the defaulting party if that party is in fault or carries the risk. The failure to perform may give the other party — the aggrieved party — certain rights against the defaulting party. The aggrieved party may claim damages for the loss he suffers from the other party's failure to effect due performance; in some cases he may reduce his own performance. Furthermore, he may withhold his own performance until the other party makes a due performance. Under certain conditions he may terminate the contract, that is to say choose not to perform his own obligations and not to claim performance by the other party.[28] The aggrieved party may finally have a right to specific performance, that is to claim that the contract be performed as agreed. All these rights are called remedies here.

3.3 The Failure to Perform and the Non-performance

The remedies are given to the obligee when for reasons for which the obligor carries the risk the latter fails to effect due performance. If, for instance, the seller of scrap iron does not deliver it, the buyer may terminate the contract, buy the iron from another seller, and claim damages from the first seller for the loss he has suffered. The same remedies may also be accorded to the obligor when the obligee fails to receive performance. If a buyer of scrap iron refuses to receive it, the seller may terminate the contract, sell the iron to another purchaser and claim damages from the first buyer for the loss he has suffered.

The situations where there is a failure to effect due performance which gives the aggrieved party one or more remedies we call situations of *non-performance*.[29]

In the case of the scrap iron we face a problem of terms. The seller who has a duty to deliver the iron also has a right to get rid of it. The buyer who has a right to get the iron also has a duty to remove it or receive it. Both parties are therefore 'obligors' and 'obligees' in relation to the same performance, and there is non-

---

28 Sometimes termination has the consequence that each party must return what he has received from the other party, see e.g. CISG art. 81 (2).

29 Schlechtriem/Huber 1990 (*op.cit.* note 20) use the word 'Vertragsverletzung', see art. 45 RN 10. CISG uses 'breach of contract', 'contravention au contrat', see art. 25.

performance if they fail to perform their duties.

Sometimes a party's failure to receive performance or to contribute in other ways to the obligor's performance will not entitle the obligor to avail himself of any remedies. In some cases the failure of the obligee to receive performance − or to help the obligor to perform − (*mora creditoris*), does not give the obligor any of the remedies described above. The effect of the failure is that the obligee does not get his performance at the time stipulated or of the quality he has contracted for, but the obligor who is prevented from effecting due performance, cannot force his performance upon the obligee, nor can he terminate the contract or claim damages. He can claim his counter-performance as stipulated in the contract but that is not a remedy for failure to perform. Thus, if a pianist who has been engaged to come and play in the bride's home at a wedding party, is dismissed because the couple has decided not to marry, the pianist can claim his fee, but he cannot force the couple to listen to his performance, nor can he − under normal circumstances − claim damages because he was denied the opportunity to perform. The refusal of the couple to admit him to play in the bride's home causes a failure in his performance, but since it does not give him any remedies caused by that failure we will not call it a non-performance, neither on his part nor on the part of the couple.

There are other circumstances where the obligor's failure to perform gives the party who is to receive performance no rights or remedies. Thus where identified goods are to be delivered and they perish before delivery but after the risk has passed, due to a contingency for which the seller is not liable, the buyer who has to pay the price has no remedies. Performance is not made but there is no non-performance since there is no remedy.

3.4 Excused Non-performance

The obligor is not always liable in damages for non-performance.

Under some rules he is liable only if the obligee can show that the obligor's failure to perform was due to his fault or the fault of those for whom he was responsible. Other rules provide that the obligor is exonerated if he can prove that the non-performance was not due to his or his assistant's fault. Yet other rules will only exempt the obligor from liability if he can show that the extraordinary supervening circumstances made performance impossible or impracticable. This strict liability has been adopted by CISG, see Article 45, 61 and 79. A party is then only free from liability if performance becomes impossible or impracticable due to an impediment which is beyond his control. For instance, the seller is not liable in damages if after the conclusion of the contract, an unexpected embargo is placed on scrap iron which prevents the seller from delivering it to the buyer's country.

In all the cases where the aggrieved party cannot claim damages for non-performance from the defaulting party he cannot, as a rule, claim specific performance from him either[30] The *non-performance* is *excused*. However, the aggrieved party may still withhold his own performance, in this case his payment of the purchase price. If the non-performance becomes substantial, where for example the embargo persists, the aggrieved party may terminate the contract. He may then refuse to receive the iron even if, after the embargo is lifted, the defaulting party wishes to deliver it. In this respect, the defaulting party carries the risk for the non-performance.

Thus non-performance may be divided into two categories: the *excused* and the *non-excused*. In the former case the aggrieved party may neither claim damages nor specific performance but he may have the other remedies; in the latter cases he may well have all the remedies.

3.5 The Proposed Structure

There are now the following categories:

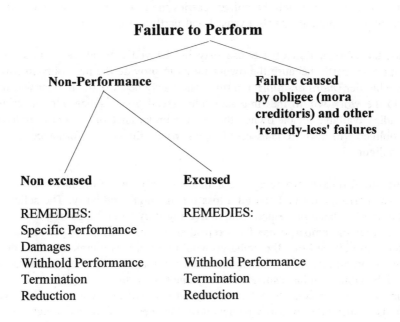

Failure to Perform

Non-Performance

Failure caused by obligee (mora creditoris) and other 'remedy-less' failures

Non excused

REMEDIES:
Specific Performance
Damages
Withhold Performance
Termination
Reduction

Excused

REMEDIES:

Withhold Performance
Termination
Reduction

---

30   It is not conceivable why CISG art. 79 has retained this right in cases of the excused non-performance, see art. 79(5), Schlechtriem, 51, and Tallon in Bianca & Bonell, *Commentary on the International Sales Law*, Milan 1987, 588, but see Schlechtriem/Stoll 1990 (*op.cit.* note 20) art. 79 Rn. 58.

It is to be noted that the obligee's failure to receive performance may be a non-performance on his part. However, the failure to receive performance may also be 'remedy-less'. The division between the non-performance and the other cases of a failure to perform goes between the failures which give the aggrieved party a remedy and the 'remedy-less' failures.

In CISG the terms 'remedies' ('moyens') (title of chapters 2 and 3, section III) and 'rights' ('droits') (Article 79 (5)) are used for what is called remedies here. CISG uses the word 'breach' ('contravention') (title of section III) where we use the word non-performance. However, in CISG 'breach' is not linked to the remedy of damages. In the common law there is breach when and only when the aggrieved party has a right to damages. As in CISG this is not the case in our system. Non-performance is not tied to damages only, and therefore non-performance has been preferred to the term breach.

3.6 Mixed Situations

There are situations where a failure to perform is partly due to *mora creditoris*, partly to causes for which the obligor carries the risk, and there are cases of non-performance which are partly excused and partly not-excused.

Thus, the construction of a house may be delayed beyond the time set for its completion, partly because the owner failed to provide the necessary instructions to the builder (*mora creditoris*) in time, and partly because the builder was unable to do the work within the time schedule agreed upon. When administering the remedies available for the owner, the relative importance of the *mora creditoris* of the obligee will have to be assessed together with the non-performance caused by the obligor.

There are also cases where a *force majeure* is only one of the factors which have delayed performance and caused a loss for the aggrieved party. The seller of the scrap iron has been prevented from delivering it by an embargo of short duration. When after the embargo has been repealed the buyer asks for performance, the seller who believed that the embargo would persist was unable to effect delivery with a short notice. As a result of these two contingencies the buyer suffered a loss which he would not have suffered if only one had occurred. Also in these cases the court will have to consider whether the non-performance which was not excused is in itself sufficient to justify an award of damages. Such mixed situations do not disturb the structure.

3.7 The Structure and Some Legal Systems

3.7.1 The Non-performance

The system which the Common Law and the Nordic laws apply and which is proposed here covers all the 'breaches'. It covers the delays in performance, which comprise the definitive failure to perform, the defective performance (lack of conformity), the lack of title and the non-performance of other duties assumed by a party to the contract.

This system differs from that of the German Civil Code, which has no unitary concept of non-performance and which is only concerned with impossibility and delay as 'breach' of contract.[31] After the Code was enacted German writers and courts introduced the socalled 'positive breach of contract' (positive Vertragsverletzung). This covers cases where a performance is rendered in due time, but where the obligor violates other duties. A seller, for instance, does not keep a promise he has made not to deliver to others in the buyer's district; a physician treats his patient negligently; goods delivered cause damage to the buyer's property, etc. To this 'positive breach' some of the rules in the Civil Code on delay have been made applicable. Defects in specific goods and lack of title for which the Civil Code has made special provisions are not covered by the general provisions of non-performance in the Civil Code.[32]

Also the French use a different terminology. In France 'inexécution' covers the 'breaches' and includes the delivery of non-conforming goods. There is also 'inexécution' if the seller has delivered goods which have a 'hidden defect' or if he lacked title in the goods, but as in Germany special rules on 'guarantee' apply. On the other hand 'inexécution' covers a failure to perform for which the obligee carries the risk. It is 'inexécution' when the obligee prevented the obligor from performing the contract, see on the example of the pianist who could not play, no. 3.3 supra.

Under the Nordic systems[33] and the system which we propose the term non-performance is used to describe the situations where the obligor carries the risk for the failure to perform. That he does so is shown by the existence of a remedy.

It is helpful to reserve the term non-performance for the situations where one party's failure to perform triggers a remedy for the other party. The rules under

---

31 See Zweigert & Kötz (*op.cit.* note 2), 177, 199 and Schlechtriem/Huber (*op.cit.* note 20) Art. 45 Rn. 9a-9c.

32 Zweigert & Kötz, *ibidem*. A proposal to amend German law has been made recently, see 'Abschlussbericht der Kommission der Überarbeitung des Schuldrechts', *Bundesanzeiger* 1992.

33 See Ussing, *Obligationsrettens Almindelige Del*, 4 ed 1964, 50 f, Gomard, *Obligationsret*, 1 Del 1989, 31, Rohde, *Lärobok i Obligationsrätt*, 4 ed 1975, 75 f.

which the obligee may claim damages etc. if due performance did not occur, does not cover the situation the obligee himself carries the risk for the failure to perform. An example of this would arise where the obligee has prevented performance by his own acts or omissions. It would be redundant to provide for each remedy that it does not operate in these cases of 'inexécution'.

The terminology here used is in fact implied in CISG.[34] Article 80 provides that a party cannot rely on the failure of the other party to perform to the extent that such failure was caused by the first party's act or omission. Therefore, when CISG Article 45 provides the remedies which the buyer may exercise 'if the seller fails to perform any of his obligations under the contract of this Convention' it is understood that these remedies are not available for the buyer if the seller's failure to perform was due to contingencies for which the buyer carries the risk. Thus the remedies do not operate if a buyer who has bought goods on FOB. conditions does not provide the ship on which the goods are to be carried. In this case the seller has no obligation to deliver the goods on board a ship.

The conceptual framework of the Dutch NBW is close to that of CISG and the Nordic countries. The 'neutral' term for all situations of failure to perform is called 'niet-nakoming'. The failure which gives the aggrieved party a remedy (non-performance) is called 'tekortkoming in de nakoming'. When there is 'tekort-koming' the aggrieved party may claim damages, terminate the contract, and withhold his own performance, see Articles 6:74, 6:265 and 6:262ff.

Failure to perform (*niet-nakoming*) which is caused by the obligee excludes the obligee from the right to terminate, see Article 6:266 and the obligor from coming in 'default', see Article 6:61. This means that a failure to perform caused by the obligee will prevent him from exercising any remedy.

Several legal systems, and among them the French and the English, treat the events which exempt a party from liability and which are here compendiously called '*force majeure*' as circumstances which destroy the foundation of the contract. The failures they cause are therefore not treated as a 'breach' or 'inexécution'.[35] The effect of '*force majeure*' is that the contract is extinguished and that none of the parties need to make a declaration to that effect.

CISG, like the Nordic countries, take a different attitude. If a party is exonerated under Article 79 (1) or (2) this will affect the other party's right to claim damages only. The aggrieved party may still 'exercise any right other than damages', see Article 79 (5). This means that CISG, although it does not expressly say so, treats '*force majeure*' as a 'breach', i.e. a non-performance, and that the aggrieved party

---

34   See Schlechtriem/Huber (*op.cit.* note 20) art. 45 Rn 12-17.
35   France: Weill & Terré, *Droit civil, les obligations*, Paris 1986, no. 414, England: Treitel, *The Law of Contract* 7ed, 1987, p. 702.

who wishes to terminate the contract must give notice to the other party.

Some '*force majeure*' situations may affect only part of the performance and some, such as strikes and embargoes, may be temporary. It may be uncertain whether an impediment is total or partial, definitive or temporary. The rules in CISG on notice of termination for breach are well fitted for such situations. As long as the goods are not delivered the buyer will not loose his right to terminate, see Article 49 (2). When it becomes apparent that the delay is or will be a fundamental one, the aggrieved party may give notice of termination, and if the defaulting party asks him whether he wishes to uphold the contract, he will have to inform the latter if he wishes to terminate, see Article 26.

3.7.2 The Remedies

3.7.2.1 The Concept
In the Common Law the term remedy is sometimes used to describe the reliefs which an aggrieved party can obtain in case of a breach of contract. These reliefs may be the very performance he contracted for or something in substitution of the promised performance. They cover specific performance, damages and restitution.[36] Other authors use the term remedy for other rights of an aggrieved party as well, for instance the right of an aggrieved party to withhold his own performance and to terminate the contract.[37] As was mentioned above breach presupposes liability for damages. There is no breach unless the aggrieved party would be entitled to claim damages.

In the present system non-performance is used for cases where the aggrieved party has at least one remedy. This may be damages or another remedy. Most of the remedies are described in CISG Articles 45 ff and 61 ff, which mention specific performance, termination, which in CISG is called avoidance, reduction of the aggrieved party's own performance, and damages (see the titles of section III of Chapter II and Section III of Chapter III). The party's right to withhold his own performance until the other party performs his obligation is provided for in Article 58, which is located in Section II of Chapter III, and which is not reckoned among the 'remedies for breach of contract'.

3.7.2.2 Remedies not Covered by CISG
In the national legal systems remedies exist which are not mentioned in CISG. A party who has undertaken an obligation not to do an act, and who nevertheless does it or threatens to do it, may be enjoined by a court from doing the act. In some legal systems a party, notably an unpaid seller, can be reinstalled in the possession

---

36 *Farnsworth on Contracts*, III, 152.
37 Beale, *Remedies for Breach of Contract*, London 1980, 152.

of goods sold to a buyer who does not pay in time (action en revendication).[38]

Some legal systems have introduced a penalty which a court may impose upon a defaulting party as long as he does not perform his obligations (astreinte).[39] The UNIDROIT principles introduce this remedy. Under Article 7.2.4 a court which orders a defaulting party to perform may also direct this party to pay a penalty, if he does not comply with the order. The penalty is to be paid to the aggrieved party unless mandatory rules of the law of the forum country provides otherwise. Payment of a penalty to the aggrieved party does not exclude any claim for damages. The Commission on European Contract Law also considered to introduce a rule similar to the UNIDROIT rule but gave it up. It feared that the application of the 'astreinte' would lead to difficulties in those EC countries which do not know it. Furthermore, it seemed to be incompatible with the public policy of the common law countries to let the aggrieved party pocket a penalty for 'contempt of court' especially if it is ordered paid in addition to damages.

3.7.3 Remedies and Imputation

German law only provides remedies for delay, impossibility and 'positive Vertrags-verletzung' if these contingencies can be imputed to the obligor. They are not imputed to him if he shows that they were due neither to his fault, nor to the fault of those persons whom he had entrusted performance nor to lack of economic means. In case he has to provide generic goods the obligor is only excused in case it is not possible to deliver any of the species and in case of a 'Wegfall der Geschäftsgrundlage', see section 2.3 above.

French law makes a distinction between obligations involving a duty to achieve a specific result and obligations involving only a duty of best efforts, between 'obligations de résultat' and 'obligations de moyens'. In the former case the failure to procure the result is a non-performance. In the latter case a failure to procure the result envisaged by the contract will only be a non-performance if the obligor has not made those efforts which would be made by a reasonable person of the same kind under similar circumstances. A seller's duty to deliver conforming goods at the right time is a duty to achieve a specific result, and if he fails he is strictly liable. A doctor's attempt to cure his patient is to be made at his best efforts. If he has made his best efforts there is due performance, and the doctor is not liable if the patient is not cured.[40]

The duty to use best efforts in performing an 'obligation de moyens' also comprises persons to whom the obligor has entrusted the performance.

---

38 French Civil Code Art. 2104 (4) 2d paragraph, see Mazeaud & Mazeaud, Leçons de droit civil III 2.1, Partie, Vente & Échanges, 1984 no 1008.
39 See on French law of 5 July 1972, Weill & Terré, (op.cit. note 35) no 834.
40 Weill & Terré (op.cit. note 35) no 396 ff.

Under the Dutch system the aggrieved party has a remedy in case of non-performance, see above. The aggrieved party may terminate the contract and withhold his performance even though the non-performance cannot be imputed to the defaulting party and even in case of 'force majeure'. This, as was mentioned above, are principles which Dutch and Nordic law have in common with CISG.

In NBW the rules on liability for damages are to be found in Article 6:74 ff. Article 6:74 provides that the obligee cannot claim damages if the non-performance cannot be attributed (toegerekend) to him. Article 6:75 provides that a non-performance cannot be attributed to the obligor if it does not result from his fault, and if he cannot be held liable for it by the rules of law or by legal act, or prevailing opinion in society or in the particular trade.[41] The obligor is excused in case of force majeure and cannot be held liable. 'Force majeure' will also in practice prevent the obligee from claiming specific performance of a synallagmatic contract. The typical example of liability following from a legal act is the assumption of liability by a contract clause. The term 'prevailing opinion' refers to legal rules laid down by the courts before the NBW. It covers a variety of situations arising in the various specific contracts, some of which have received some general application. Thus the courts have applied the French distinction between the 'obligations de résultat' under which the obligor was strictly liable for non-performance, and 'the obligations de moyens' which only contained an obligation to use best efforts. However, when performing an 'obligation de moyens' the obligor is liable for the fault of his servants and employees and others whom he had entrusted performance, see Article 6:76, and generally for the tools he has used in performance, see Article 6:77.

The Nordic laws are close to the Dutch law. The main rule regarding liability for damages still seems to be that the non-performance must be imputed to the obligor. The distinction between 'obligations de résultat' and 'obligations de moyen' — though noted by a well known Swedish author[42] has not been adopted in practice, but the rules provide similar results.

The prevailing opinion in the Common law is that contract liability is strict liability.[43] Only frustration of the contract will free the obligor. If in other cases the contract is not performed there is breach which gives rise to damages and which may give the aggrieved party a right to terminate the contract and — in special cases — to claim specific performance. There are, of course, contracts under which the obligation is not to achieve a specific result but to use one's best efforts — such as employment and services contracts. This duty does not seem to have been treated very differently from the way it has been in France and the Netherlands. General rules on this subject do not seem to exist.

---

41 See art. 3:12 on what is prevailing opinion.
42 Knut Rodhe (op.cit. note 33) 27f.
43 *Restatement of the Law, Second, Contracts*, 1981 Vol II 309.

CISG's system is close to that of the Common law. However, as was mentioned earlier 'breach' (non-performance) is not tied to the remedy of damages. Even in case of an excused non-performance the aggrieved party may terminate the contract. As far as damages are concerned the fact that CISG only operates with *'force majeure'* (Article 79 (1)) as an excuse for non-performance means that the seller's and the buyer's obligations are treated as *'obligations de résultat'*. Further grounds for excuse than *'force majeure'* are not considered.

PECL has the same system as CISG. However, this system may be modified if the Commission, as planned, is to draft principles covering specific contracts such as services contracts. The UNIDROIT principles also follows the CISG pattern. However, they have made the distinction between *'obligations de moyens'* and *'obligations de résultat'*.

Whereas it is possible to establish a system which divides excused and non-excused non-performance it is doubtful whether it is feasible to provide rules for all contracts, which lay down under which conditions the liability for non-performance is strict, and under which conditions there is liability only when the non-performance may be imputed to the obligor.

4 Closing Remarks

It is possible to establish a system for non-performance and a terminology accompanying this system. However, it has proved impossible to provide general rules on performance and remedies for non-performance of contracts which have any great precision. Rules aimed at meeting all the contracts and all the contract situations must have a vague character. The same holds true for rules on good faith and on hardship. It will be for the courts to develop further guidelines and 'institutions'. Several situations will be cases of first impression and some of them will remain so. The value of such vague principles is the way in which they direct the courts. Like Moses' Commandments their exact scope will be uncertain but the core of the message they bring should always be understood.

CHAPTER 12
Breach of Contract and
Reparation of Damage

Denis Tallon

Towards a European Civil Code ... an ambitious project and a strong challenge for all the jurists of Europe, but something which cannot be achieved with a wave of a magic wand. At the outset, it is obvious that this will need a lot of hard work. Unification of the law does not bear improvisation. In this kind of work, there is no greater danger than a superficial consensus masking fundamental oppositions, which have not been detected or which have been discretely swept under the carpet.[1] Included, at this initial stage, before daring to suggest uniform solutions,[2] the major tasks are the discovery of the fundamental oppositions and the listing of the points at issue.

A difficult task, of course, which is illustrated by the subject allotted to me: breach of contract and reparation of damage. From the beginning, one can wonder if this subject means the same thing to a Dutch, an English or a French lawyer. Therefore, the subject requires a careful analysis of its terms.

'Failure in performance' or '*manquement dans l'exécution*' (the words used in the translation of the NBW)? O. Lando has proposed (see chapter 11) a subtle distinction between failure to perform and non-performance, more or less inspired by Scandinavian law, but not easily compatible with most European laws. For my purpose, it is easier to start with the simple definition in NBW 6:74 and 6:75. There is a (so called) breach of contract whenever the obligee does not get what the obligor[3] has promised. Hence the importance to determine the scope of the promise and the role played in this respect by the distinction between '*obligations de moyens*' and '*obligations de résultat*'.[4] [5] A

---

1   The Vienna Convention offers examples of such a situation. On the ease with which common lawyers and so-called civil lawyers may talk at cross-purposes, see my article: 'L'harmonisation les règles du droit privé entre pays de droit civil et de common law, contribution au 13e Congrès international de droit comparé' (Montréal 19-24 août 1990), published in *Rev. Internat. droit comparé*, 1990, p. 513-523.
2   This book should offer advanced students a plethora of subjects for theses, dissertations and articles.
3   I use the terms obligor/obligee rather than creditor/debtor (as in the NBW translation), because at common law these two words apply to the parties to a monetary obligation only.
4   See *NBW* 6:27, to be compared with Article 1137(1) of the French Civil Code as both provisions contain a duty of care within the obligation to deliver. Article 1137(1) has been one of the bases on which the theory of *obligation de moyens* and *obligation de résultats* has been elaborated by authors and subsequently upheld by the courts. Malaurie & Aynes, *Droit civil,*

remedy is offered to the obligee unless 'The failure in performance cannot be imputed to the (obligor)'. This distinction between imputable and non-imputable non-performance is fundamental as it is only in the case of non-imputable non-performance that the damage caused by non-performance may be compensated.

Whatever the function of the concept of fault may be in this process, it is of non-impact for our purpose. In any event, it is a very controversial question which would need lengthy elaboration.[6]

My topic is restricted to remedies after a breach, emphasizing the reparation of damage (or loss),[7] as a result of this breach. In the new Dutch Civil Code this subject is to be found within Book 6 of NBW Articles 74-94 concerning: The effects of the non performance of an obligation — and to Article 6:277 NBW concerning termination. In French law, the subject matter is covered by Section III, Chap. III, Titre III, livre III French Civil Code: Articles 1146-1155, *Des dommages-intérêts résultant de l'inéxecution de l'obligation*, and also Articles 1142-1145 (*de l'obligation de faire ou de ne pas faire*) and Article 1184, a fundamental text, but uncomfortably placed under the heading '*des obligations conditionnelles*'.[8] However, the German BGB is more dense and less structured: Book II, Section I, Subsection I: Obligation of performance contained in § 241-304, and § 346-361 on termination. In the new Quebec Civil Code,[9] the relevant Articles 1605-1619, are placed under the heading, '*de l'exécution par équivalent*' which I will discuss later. See also the Italian Civil Code, Articles 1218-1229 and the Swiss Code of Obligations, Articles 108 and 109. In all of these texts one can find more or less detailed rules on 'reparation of damages'. Of course, the matter is dealt with in English law by complex and sometimes uncertain case-law.

Les obligations, no. 816-825, 2e éd., Paris 1990.

5   Here again there is a problem of translation: either a literal translation, 'obligation of means/of result' or more descriptive, 'duty to achieve a specific result/duty of best efforts', used in the UNIDROIT project. However, the term 'best efforts' may be confusing, as expressing more than the normal standard of diligence of the *bonus paterfamilias*.

6   Between the extremes of the no-fault principle of the Common law and the openly fault based systems of *BGB* (§ 276) and *NBW* (art. 6:75), the French system is difficult to assess. (For a rather one-sided view: Treitel, *Remedies*, no. 8 *et seq*) The general texts do not refer to fault and it could be argued that a fault is no more than an imputable non-performance.

7   Here is another source of confusion: is damage the same as loss, at least in English law? see G. Samuel & J. Rinkes, *op.cit.*, p. 228. I shall use the term damage in its general meaning of '*préjudice*' (in French, of course ...). It may be useful to remind the reader that damage (in the singular) corresponds to *préjudice* and damages (in the plural) are *dommages-intérêts*.

8   Very few of these articles have been modified since 1804.

9   There are two major reasons why reference should be made to this Code. Firstly, together with the NBW, it is the most recent Civil Code in the world (accepted by Parliament in 1991 but not yet in force). Secondly, it is bilingual and both versions (French and English) have the same legal value.

According to NBW 6:103, reparation of damage is made in money; exceptionally, the court may award reparation in another form. However, this allocation of damages largely depends upon what other remedy the obligee resorts to. It is thus necessary, in Section I, to fix the place of the system of reparation in the general system of remedies in case of non-performance. Then we shall look at the regime of this reparation in Section II.

I will leave aside the reparation of damage in cases of the non-performance of a monetary obligation (*dette de somme d'argent*).[10] This does not mean to say that the elaboration of such rules in a European Code would be easy[11], but it is inspired by specific reasons.

I The Place of Reparation of Damage in the General System of Remedies for Breach

When the obligee does not receive what was promised to him, in most systems — but not all — the law provides a choice of remedies, one of which being monetary compensation. Is monetary compensation just a remedy among several others or a privileged one? The answer to this question is an initial issue (Section A), which is related to the way the reparation of damage finds its place within the general system of remedies (Section B).

A Damages Versus Specific Performance

Two radically different approaches are to be found, that of the civil law[12] (1) and that of the Common law (2). A choice will have to be made between the two for an eventual European Civil Code (3).

1 The civil law solution is simple. Several options are available to the aggrieved party who, as a rule, may freely choose which one he would like. Article 1587 of the Québec Civil Code provides a perfect example:

'An obligation confers on the creditor the right to demand that the obligation be performed in full, properly and without delay.

---

10 *NBW* Articles 6:119 and 6:120, *BGB* § 288 and *HGB*, § 352; French Civil Code 1153 and 1153-1; Italian Civil Code: art. 1224; C.O.: art. 104-106 C. Civ. Quebec: art. 1615 and 1617.

11 At least two main difficulties arise: the determination of the rate of interest (fixed or variable); and the granting of supplementary damages and the conditions thereof.

12 The expression 'civil law'is ambiguous (civil law as opposed to commercial law?) and even wrong (civil/roman law is not the only basis of the *système romano-germanique*, to use the better adapted terminology of René David). But this expression is convenient and short and should not mislead a comparatist.

Where the debtor fails to perform his obligation, without justification on his part, and if he is in default, the creditor may, without prejudice to his right to the performance of the obligation in full or in part by equivalence,

(1) force specific performance of the obligation;
(2) obtain, in the case of a contractual obligation, the 'resolution' or termination of the contract or the reduction of his own correlative obligation;
(3) take any other measure provided by law to enforce his right to the performance of the obligation'.

The new Dutch Civil Code, in Article 6:87, gives the option between performance and damages; under Article 3:296, the court is entitled to order the obligor to perform his obligation 'unless the law, the nature of the obligation or a juridical act produce a different result' and Article 6:265 gives the obligee the right to set aside the synallagmatic contract under certain conditions. According to French law (Article 1184 C.civ. see also Article 1, L.9 juillet 1991, on the reform of enforcement of rights (*procédures civiles d'exécution*)) the obligee may either terminate the contract with damages,[13] or enforce the contract (notwithstanding the apparent terms of 1142 cc, which will be discussed later). Article 1453 (1) of the Italian Civil Code provides a similar solution, whereas section 241 BGB entitles the creditor of an obligation to claim performance from the debtor, as a first remedy.

The idea is the same everywhere, that a contract is made to be performed: *pacta sunt servanda*. To repudiate a contract is to breach one's word, a moral fault according to the canonist tradition. The PECL-rule is inspired by the same idea: Article 4:102.

This performance in nature may be obtained through different means: for obligations not to do (*obligation de ne pas faire*), by destroying what has been done: NBW 3:296 and 3:299 (2), French Civil Code, Article 1143, and the Québec Civil Code, Article 1599 or by performance by a third person, at the expense of the obligor (French Civil Code Article 1144).

Individual liberty, however, limits the scope of direct enforcement. Since the second half of the XIXth century, a new instrument has been used by the courts in France: the *astreinte*,[14] or judicial penalty. After much discussion, and despite strong criticism (the *astreinte* is a windfall for the obligee, who receives the liquidated amount of the *astreinte* in addition to the damages allowed to

---

13 Résolution judiciaire. Another linguistic pitfall, both in English: 'to set aside', 'to terminate', 'to cancel', even the very bad 'to avoid' of CISG, and in French: 'résoudre' or 'résilier' ... v. G. Cornu, *Vocabulaire juridique*, 2e éd. 1990, V^{bis} 'Résiliation and Résolution'.
14 On *astreinte*: Malaurie & Aynes, *Droit civil, les Obligations*, 2e éd, 1990, no. 1016-1019; D. Tallon, *Contract law Today*, p. 268; in *Belgian law*: S. David-Constant: 'La fin d'une disgrâce: l'avènement de l'astreinte en droit belge', Mélanges A. Weill, 1983, p. 184.

him) the technique has been recognized by statute, (currently, L. 9 juilliet 1991, Articles 33 to 37) and is widely used in France. It has also been adopted by the Benelux countries by a uniform law of 1974 (see: Dutch Code of Civil Procedure, Articles 611.a-611.1). In short, specific enforcement is a fundamental right of the obligor and when this cannot be obtained, the other remedies, such as reparation of damages, are called *exécution par équivalent*[15] or performance by equivalence. Performance by equivalence can be found in the Quebec Civil Code in Title of § 6 of Section II, Chapter VI, of the 1st Title of Book V: Obligations and also in Article 6:87 NBW and is used in civil law literature. Monetary compensation is still performance, if only by equivalence.

2 The Common law has taken quite a different standpoint. For the Common law, at least from the extreme position taken by Holmes,[16] the obligor may choose between performance and compensation. It is a kind of alternative obligation (*obligation alternative*). To the moral approach of civil law is substituted the economic rationale.[17] This explains why English and American authors speak of the repudiation of the contract – almost a sin for civil lawyers – and elaborate strange theories inspired by the doctrine of Law and Economics, such as the concept of efficient breach.[18] Conversely, specific performance is strictly limited. It is only possible where damages are not an adequate remedy and even then it is submitted to very restrictive conditions.[19] Thus, instead of a broad range of remedies, we have here a hierarchy at the top of which are damages, and far below is termination (not always considered as a remedy) and specific performance. Hence the reparation of the damage caused by a breach of contract occupies a greater place in the common law and this also accounts for the repulsion felt by English jurists towards the *astreinte*.

Two remarks may be made by way of conclusion:
The first remark is the strange formula in Article 1142 cc: '*Toute obligation de faire ou de ne pas faire se résout en dommages et intérêts, en cas d'inexécution de la part du débiteur*'.[20] It is very similar to the Holmes formula. Yet, irrespective of the antecedents of this article and the evolution of its interpretation by the courts,[21] it may be said that its meaning is now

---

15 Cf. The *Ersatz in Geld* of German law.

16 *Contract law Today*, p. 386.

17 *Loc.cit.*, p. 385.

18 For a brilliant discussion of this theory, see B. Rudden & P. Juilhard, 'La théorie de la violation efficace', *Rev. internat. dr. comparé*, 1986, p. 1011.

19 See A. Ogus, in *Contract law Today*, p. 254 et s.; The hopes entertained here for a more liberal approach do not seem to have been fulfilled: G.H. Treitel, *The law of Contract*, 8th ed. 1991, 902.

20 Art. 1143 (right to destroy) and 1144 (performance by third person) being the exceptions, which need the authorization of the court.

21 Malaurie & Aynes, *op.cit.*, no. 1015; D. Tallon, *Contract law Today*, p. 284-285. The courts refer to physical, and more interesting, to moral impossibility to enforce performance.

completely reversed and that specific performance is now always available unless there is a physical or moral impossibility. Because of the widespread use of *astreinte* in French law[22] performance *in natura* is at the forefront of remedies.

The second remark is the paradox which is to be found in English law, where court orders such as a decree of specific performance have a very efficient sanction (civil and even criminal contempt of court)[23] and yet they are so seldom used.

3 In the face of such opposition, what is the best rule for European Civil Code? The first solution is to abandon all hope of unification. This is what has been done by the Vienna Convention, where according to Article 28 CISG a court is not bound to enter a judgment for specific performance unless the court would do so under its own law.

The second solution is to try to find a compromise, such as the one adopted by the EEC rules in Article 4:102, which affirms the right to specific performance but lays down a number of exceptions which are somewhat wider than those admitted in Civil law systems. Of course, these exceptions may not be interpreted in the same way by an English court or a Civil law court. In such a situation uniformity cannot be reached from the origin but instead shall be the result of converging efforts by the courts.

Now that we know that except in the Common law, reparation of damage is one remedy among others, we must now look at the way it combines with these other remedies.

B Choice and Combination of Remedies

In cases of 'imputable non-performance' a variety of remedies exists, some of which tend to procure the obligee what he had contracted for, whilst other remedies aim to compensate the damage caused by non-performance (namely performance which is partial, defective, or delayed).

Except at Common law where damages are the main remedy, the aggrieved party has a free choice;[24] for instance he may opt for specific performance, for termination and damages, for accepting of performance together with a reduction

---

22 Especially as termination needs the intervention of the court: art. 1184 C.civ. francais.

23 *Astreinte* is powerless *vis-à-vis* an insolvent defaulting party, but not criminal contempt of court.

24 See Article 1587 C.civil de Quebec which is the best expression of this free choice. See also Article 45 (2) *CISG*; EEC rules, Articles 3:101 and 3:102.

of the price. He may also cumulate the compatible remedies.

There are exceptions to this however, the major one being in German law where § 325 BGB gives the obligee the choice between damages and termination (*Rücktritt*), with no opportunity to cumulate — a much criticized solution.

There are also certain limitations: all remedies are subject to restrictive conditions, which of course must be met. Some of these limitations are quite important.

One limitation, even in non-Common Law systems, is that specific performance must not infringe upon individual freedom, for example in the performance of certain personal obligations. Then, as a rule, termination requires a serious breach[25] and there are many ways of ensuring that the breach is sufficient to justify the death of the contract (fundamental breach;[26] distinction between condition and warranty in English law; *Nachfrist* procedure of German law; prior (*a priori*) control by the court in French law).[27]

Moreover, courts may exercise a degree of control not only on a particular remedy, but also on the way the obligee exercises his choice. This is a characteristic feature of French law, which tends to submit all remedies to a strict control, at least *ex post facto*. The trial judge has the discretion 'to determine the mode of adequately compensating the damage' and does not have to give specific reasons to support his decision. Control by the Cour de cassation is therefore minimal.[28]

In this context, how does the reparation of damage operate? Everything depends on the result of the breach and on the choice made by the obligee. If, one way or the other, he gets what he has contracted for, he may obtain damages for delay (*dommages et intérêts moratoires*) if performance *in natura* has taken too much time — for instance if there has been a late cure by the obligor, or if he has resisted and has only given in under the pressure of a *astreinte*. He may also ask for compensation for the supplementary expenses he may have incurred (for example, where there has been performance by a third party, at a higher cost).

If the obligee does not receive what he has contracted for and opts for '*exécution par équivalent*', he will usually receive '*dommages et intérêts compensatoires*'. These damages aim at compensating what he did not obtain,

---

25   *NBW* 6:265 (1) in fine.
26   Article 25 *CISG*.
27   Treitel, *Remedies*, p. 349-381.
28   D. Tallon, in *Contract law Today*, p. 286-288 and the references quoted in the text. The court may even change the choice of the obligee, for instance substitute an award in damages to the claim of specific enforcement. The reverse is more doubtful.

after a partial or defective performance if he accepts this performance. Of course, there will also be '*dommages et intérêts moratoires*' in cases of late performance. Alternatively, if the contract has been terminated, and with the exception of German law, the damages compensate the loss arising from the ending of the contract which is imputable to the obligor. If loss has been caused partly by the obligee, there will be a diminution or even a suppression of damages.[29]

Thus it has been shown that there are various ways to repair the damage in case of breach, and that the damages depend on the basic choice made by the obligee, espacially on the choice whether he decides to enforce or to terminate the contract.

What remains to be shown is how damages are assessed.

II The Assessment of Damages

Monetary damages are the normal way of effecting the reparation of damage: NBW 6:103. I shall leave aside the exceptional reparation in a form other than the payment of a sum of money. For other reasons, I will not enter into discussion on two difficult questions which do interfere in the award of damages: the obligee's participation to the harm (*fait du créancier*) and the mitigation of damage. Their discussion would need a separate study.[30]

The way these damages are assessed varies very much according to the different European laws. A European Civil Code will eventually require a choice being made between these systems. Such a choice can only be made if one is well aware of the contrariness in the basic principles of the assessment (A) and of the variety of the modalities of assessment (B).

A The Basic Principles of Assessment

Two major issues to be settled in the perspective of a European Code: 1) a common set of rules for all kinds of reparation or two sets, one for tortious

---

29 French case-law has even elaborated a curious theory of '*résolution aux torts réciproques*', inspired by the rules of divorce ... D. Tallon, *La résolution aux torts réciproques, Mélanges en l'honneur de C. Freyria*, forthcoming.

30 Incidentally, the common lawyer attaches a lot of importance to the rule of mitigation and is very surprised that other European laws do not know of it as such. Common lawyers give much less attention to the *fait du créancier* than the civil lawyers. On these two questions: *EEC* Article 4:504 concerning loss attributable to aggrieved party, regrettably covers both questions under the same heading.

liability and one for contractual liability, being admitted that in the case of a dualist system, there is by necessity a considerable overlap. 2) A more or less rigid system of full compensation, or a *pouvoir modérateur* by which the judge may openly make equitable (in the ordinary mearing) adjustments to the reparation.

1 The questions of a unique or dual set of rules to govern damages has a theoretical basis. For some authors,[31] there is a general theory of civil liability (*responsabilité civile*) with two more or less linked divisions: tortious and contractual liability (responsabilité délictuelle et contractuelle). In some systems, such as the Common law, the two are (nearly) completely separate and damages obey to different rules (as regards for instance economic loss or foreseeability). In some others, there is only one set of rules for damages, under the heading: non-performance of obligations (NBW Article 6:95 to 5:100; BGB § 249-253; CO: 99-3). In French law, there are no special rules on tortious damages. The general rules of Article 1146 to 1155 C.civ.[32] have been written with an eye on contractual liability and the courts have used them, whenever possible, in torts.[33]

A first choice has to be made. But even if it is made in favour of unity — which appears to be the modern trend (NBW; C.civil Québec), it might be advisable to ponder on the necessity of having some specific rules for contractual damages, for instance when they are linked to other remedies for breach of contract or when it depends on the proper nature of contractual relationship. I am thinking specifically of the rule according to which the loss must have been foreseeable at the time of the conclusion of the contract in order to be compensated. The comparative picture on this point is rather confusing. Certain national laws have no such rule (German law, Switz law and the NBW) and seem to do very well without it.[34] It exists both at Common law (the rule in Hadley v. Baxendale[35] and in many Civil Codes (Article 1150 French Civ.c.; 1225 Italian Civ.c.; 1611 Québec Civ. code) and has been retained in the PECL (Article 4.503). But even then, there is great difference between these texts and Common law. At Common law, foreseeability is just a test to assess remoteness of harm: is too

---

31 For instance, for French law, G. Viney, whose imposing treatise on 'La responsabillté' (volume I: conditions, 1982, volume II: effets, 1998) in the *Traité de droit civil, sous la direction de J. Ghestin*, is the necessary reference.

32 The general rules on obligations in the French Civil Code are given for contractual obligations, considered as the model of all obligations.

33 The 3d Title of book 3 is entitled: *Des contrats ou les obligations conventionnelles en général*, and the Section on damages: *Des dommages et intérêts résultant de l'inexécution de l'obligation*.

34 Foreseeability may play an indirect role by being considered as an element of causality between breach and harm; for instance for the application of art. 6:98 *NBW*. For a similar use of the foreseeability test, art. 6:96, 2, at least according to the French translation.

35 (1854) 9 Ex. 341.

remote — and outside compensation — the harm which could not have been foreseen by a reasonable man at the time of conclusion of the contract. In French law, foreseeability is a separate condition for compensation: the harm must be both *direct* (that is not too remote) and foreseeable. This derives from the exception of Article 1151 C.civ. as interpreted by the courts: in case of intentional or grossly negligent[36] non-performance, '*les dommages et intérêts ne doivent comprendre ... que ce qui est une suite immédiate et directe de l'inexécution de la convention*'.[37] This is an excellent example of how a superficial analysis may lead to serious misunderstanding: it is not enough to decide in favour of the foreseeability rule, one must also choose the way the rule should operate.

2 Another dubious issue is the power to be given to the court in the assessment of damages. The traditional principle to be found in many codes is the full compensation principle. What must be considered the whole of the direct damage, no more and no less, regardless of the behaviour of the obligor. This condemns punitive damages.[38] But first the Swiss Code of Obligations, then the NBW (Article 6:109) have conferred upon the Courts a '*pouvoir modérateur*', that is to say the right to reduce the full reparation according to the circumstances 'including the nature of the liability, the juridical relationship between the parties and their financial capacity'.[39] In any case, this power exists everywhere even if it is not officially recognized. There cannot be a rigid assessment of damages (NBW Article 6:98 confesses the fact) and the Court always has a certain discretion, specially as regard some kinds of harm (*prejudice moral* for instance). And some laws, such as the French, accept that the judge makes a lump appreciation, without having to give a detailed motivation of his assessment. It is perhaps better to be more frank and to give openly this power of reducing in equity the amount required by full compensation.

B The Modalities of Assessment

In discussing this very large question, I shall privilege two lines of reflexion, well aware that there are many other important questions to be settled.[40]

---

36 In Italian law, grossly negligent non-performance is not assimilated to intentional non-performance.

37 For a further discussion: D. Tallon, *Contract law To-day*, p. 275-277.

38 Which have been retained by the Québec Civil Code: art. 1609. But it does not concern *astreinte*, which is different from damages.

39 The *NBW* adds that 'this reduction may not exceed the amount for which the debtor has covered his liability by insurance or was obliged to do so' — a rule which will please those authors who insist on the impact of insurance on the law of liability.

40 For instance liquidated damages and penalty clauses, where there is a strong opposition between common law and 'civil law' (with some exceptions, as Belgian law).

1 The first is a matter of drafting policy. How detailed should be the section devoted to damages? Here again, we have different models, from the very short texts of the French Civil Code to the much more detailed rules of NBW (Article 6:108 on reparation in case of death being a good example of this minute and precise drafting) — to say nothing of the Common law where precedents are numerous and sometimes rather uncertain. Too many details impair the action of the judge and require imperatively a *pouvoir modérateur*. Too few give an excessive freedom to the court and, in countries where there are many courts of first instance or courts of Appeal, may lead to a great disparity in the awards.

It may be useful to make at least a distinction between patrimonial and other than patrimonial harm; such a distinction is to be found in the NBW.[41]

Much depends, any way, on the general approach concerning assessment of damages.

2 Here again we have two different traditions. One is to be found in Article 1149 French Civ.c. which has been influenced by the civil law tradition: '*les dommages et intérêts ... sont, en général, de la perte qu'il a faite et du gain dont il a été privé*': *damnum emergens* and *lucrum cessans*, also to be found in Article 1222 Italian Civil Code, Article 1609 Québec Civil Code, Article 47 CISG, and NBW Article 6:96, (1); it appears also in the EEC rules: Article 4.502. And the French case-law explains this formula as intended to put the aggrieved party in the situation he would have been if the '*acte dommageable*' had not occurred (that is to say the breach of contract or, in tortious liability, the fault or other cause of the damage).

The other approach is based on the interests protected; this concept, developed under the influence of Ihering, is used in Germany and in Swiss law. But it has mainly prospered in the United States, after the resounding article of Fuller and Purdue in 1936[42] and it exercises a growing influence on English law.[43] These interests are the expectation interest (*Erfüllungsinteresse*; *intérêt positif*) where the court has to place the aggrieved party in the same situation as if the contract had been performed; the reliance interest (*Vertrauensinteresse*; *intérêt négatif*) when the situation is to be envisaged as if there had been no contract; and the restitution interest, which takes into account the performance already rendered.[44]

---

41 For an excellent Anglo-French comparison: G. Viney & B. Markesinis, *La réparation du dommage corporel — essai de comparaison des droits français et anglais*, Paris 1986.

42 'The Reliance Interest in Contract Damages', 46 *Yale L.J.*, 52, 373 (1936); Restatement 2d Contracts, § 347 and 349.

43 A. Ogus, *Contract Law Today*, p. 247-28; summary of discussion, p. 292 where it is shown that an equivalent notion in the *intérêt négatif* may exceptionally be found in French law.

44 Which, in some systems, is dealt with under unjust enrichment.

It is difficult to compare these two approaches,[45] and it is uncertain if they lead to very different results. It would be very helpful to deal with this knotty problem in order to find formulas which could be acceptable to all participants in the drafting of a European Civil Code.

Conclusion

These few and incomplete remarks confirm the initial observation that the elaboration of a European Civil Code is a difficult task, and that its achievement will take a long time. Those who will undertake it will have to beware of two dangers: excessive optimism, which could lead to a surface harmonization and retain underneath the major oppositions, and an excessive pessimism, which makes a mountain of these oppositions and breeds resignation or despondency.

The experience of the EEC Commission on European Contract law shows that goodwill and obstinate labour can overcome most of the apparently insuperable obstacles.

But drafting a whole Civil Code (even if limited to Obligations and Property. – and perhaps, a general part) is quite a different affair from the preparation of isolated rules on contract. The treatment of contract in a Civil Code requires to take into account the environment of contract law: as a part of the law of Obligations, and, as regards the reparation of damage, the link with tortious liability.

One must insist on the importance of agreeing upon the basic concepts ... for instance on the notion of contract.[46] Then, one shall have to tackle the question of language. The choice of a working language is not innocent: it gives an unconscious preference to the legal system expressed in this language. Therefore, it is better, as far as possible, to have several working languages and to draft simultaneously in these languages.

Yes, indeed, the preparation of A European Civil Code is a difficult task, But how fascinating!

---

45 It has been done excellently by B. Nicholas, *French law of Contract*, 2e ed., 1991, p. 226; also Treitel, *Remedies*, p. 82 and f.

46 See for instance G. Samuel & J. Rinkes, *op.cit.*, no. 73 ff; D. Tallon: 'The Notion of Contract: A French Jurists Naive Look at Common Law Contract', in *Comparative and Private International law, Essays in Honor of John Henry Merryman on his Seventeeth Birthday*, 1990, p. 283-290.

Bibliography

Comparative studies:

- K. Zweigert and H. Kötz, Introduction to comparative law, 2nd ed. 1987, translation by T. Weir, vol II, p. 157-228 (the Performance of Contracts)
- G.H. Treitel, *Remedies for Breach of Contract, a comparative account*, 1988.

Bilateral studies:

- D. Harris & D. Tallon: *Contract law Today, Anglo-French Comparisons*, 1989.
  Version francaise: *Le contrat aujourd'hui: comparaisons franco-anglaises*, 1987.
- G. Samuel & J. Rinkes: *Contractual and non contractual obligations in English law, Systematic analysis of the English law of obligations in the comparative context of the Dutch Civil Code*, 1992.

For an external view point:

- R. David and D. Pugsley, *Les contrats en droit anglais*, 2e éd. 1985.
- B. Nicholas, *French law of Contract*, 2e éd., 1991.

N.B. The EEC Rules on Contract are still in a mimeographed version. They should be published in 1994. I have derived much profit from the national notes written by Hugh Beale (English law), Joachim Bonell (Italian law), Ulrich Drobnig (German law), Frans van der Velden (Dutch law).

CHAPTER 13

Contract and Third Parties

Bas Kortmann and Dennis Faber

1 Introduction

The doctrine of *privity of contract* is the basis of law of contract not only in the Netherlands, but also in neighbouring countries, whether their legal systems are codified or based on common law. What the principle essentially means is that a contract is only binding upon the contracting parties, i.e. the persons who have entered into the contract. In principle, a contract cannot confer rights upon third parties, nor can it impose obligations upon them. The various legal systems allow a number of exceptions or mitigations to the doctrine of privity of contract. However, the ways in which they do so vary considerably. In some cases, the third party is actually deemed to be a party to the contract, whereas in others, he is not a party to the contract but is brought within its scope in some other manner. Such exceptions or mitigations may be statutory, or again they may be based on case law. This article will discuss some of the main general exceptions and mitigations to, and restrictions on, the doctrine of privity of contract. Although the main frame of reference will be Dutch law,[1] brief comparisons will also be made with Belgian, French, German and English law.

2 The Doctrine of Privity of Contract

Contracts[2] only apply to the contracting parties. This principle of contract law was laid down in Articles 1351 and 1376 of the former BW, in force prior to 1 January 1992. The same principle is still found in Article 1165 of both the BW/CC and the CC, and § 241 of the BGB is based on the same notion.[3] Although no longer explicitly stated in the new BW,[4] the principle continues to

---

1   In references to Dutch law, the abbreviation BW (Burgerlijk Wetboek) refers to the new Civil Code, the central part of which came into force on 1 January 1992. Where reference is made to the Civil Code that was in force before this date, the words 'former BW' are used.
2   Only contracts that create an obligation will be discussed in this article.
3   The abbreviations CC (Code civil) and BGB (Bürgerliches Gesetzbuch) refer to the French and the German Civil Code respectively. The bilingual abbreviation BW/CC is used for the Belgian Civil Code in order to distinguish it from its Dutch and French equivalents.
4   Former BW Articles 1351 and 1376 have not been maintained in the new BW, since they might seriously impede the development of law in allowing the privity principle to be waived (see *Parl. Gesch. Boek 6*, pp. 916-918). Articles 6:213, 6:248 and 6:261 of the new BW are, however, based on the same notion.

apply. The basic rule remains that only the contracting parties have a mutual obligation to fulfil the terms of the contract which they have entered into, and that a contract cannot in principle confer rights, or impose obligations, upon a third person who is not a contracting party.

Within certain limits, any person is free to decide *whether* he wishes to enter into a contract and, if so, *with whom* and *on what terms*. Freedom of contract is an essential element of the law of contract. A person who uses his freedom to enter into a contract with someone else is then bound by that contract. However, only the contracting parties are so bound. No third party is involved in the contractual relationship between the parties. Any other conclusion would be incompatible with freedom of contract and with the third party's freedom of action. From the third party's point of view, the doctrine of privity means that the contracting parties cannot sue him on the contract. Nor can they be sued on the contract by the third party. From the point of view of the contracting parties, the principle means that they only have contractual obligations and rights in respect of the other party. On the other hand, the doctrine of privity does not mean that the existence of a contract is of no concern to third parties. Indeed, a contract may well have implications for non-contracting parties. For example, in order to determine the extent of a plaintiff's disability, the defendant may refer to a contract between the plaintiff and the latter's employer. The existence of an insurance contract between the insurer and the defendant may affect the plaintiff's entitlement to claim (for example, cf. BW Article 6:109, paragraph 2). The fact that the plaintiff is insured, may also affect the extent of the defendant's liability.[5] In 1909, the possibility of invoking the existence of a contract was expressed by the Belgian Court of Cassation[6] in the following terms:

'Attendu que si les conventions n'ont d'effet qu'entre les parties contractantes, ce principe ne règle que les droits et obligations qui découlent des contrats; qu'il ne met pas obstacle à ce que ceux qui y sont demeurés étrangers constatent l'existence de conventions avouées ou légalement prouvées et tirent argument du fait de cette existence non pour réclamer à leur profit l'exécution des obligations qu'elles stipulent, mais pour

---

5   For another example in which a contract may have implications for non-contracting parties, see, *inter alia*, HR 11 November 1937, *NJ* 1937, 1096, nt. EMM; HR 23 December 1955, *NJ* 1956, 54; HR 19 February 1960, *NJ* 1960, 473, nt. HB; HR 11 March 1960, *NJ* 1960, 261; HR 13 January 1961, *NJ* 1962, 245; HR 12 January 1962, *NJ* 1962, 246, nt. HB; HR 27 April 1962, *NJ* 1962, 254, nt. HB; HR 3 January 1964, *NJ* 1965, 16, nt. GJS; HR 26 June 1964, *NJ* 1965, 170; HR 18 December 1964, *NJ* 1965, 171, nt. GJS; HR 4 June 1965, *NJ* 1965, 381; HR 26 May 1967, *NJ* 1967, 331, nt. GJS; HR 17 November 1967, *NJ* 1968, 42, nt. GJS; HR 18 June 1971, *NJ* 1971, 408; HR 28 June 1974, *NJ* 1974, 400, nt. GJS; HR 12 October 1979, *NJ* 1980, 117, nt. GJS; HR 17 May 1985, *NJ* 1986, 760, nt. CJHB and WMK; HR 27 January 1989, *NJ* 1990, 89, nt. CJHB; *AA* 1989, p. 572 *et seq.* and p. 800, nt. SK; HR 8 December 1989, *NJ* 1990, 217 and HR 1 November 1991, *NJ* 1992, 423 and 424. Under certain circumstances, a third party to a contract, taking advantage of a party's non-compliance with that contract, may be sued for damages by the injured party.

6   See Court of Cassation, 27 May 1909, *Pasicrisie belge* 1909, I, 272.

en déduire, eu égard aux liens et aux droits qui en découlent, les conséquences favorables ou défavorables pour les parties que les événements ou les agissements des tiers ont entraînées pour elles.'

(Whereas, although agreements are only binding on the contracting parties, this principle only governs the rights and obligations arising from contracts, and does not prevent strangers thereto from noting the existence of avowed or legally proven agreements and from using such existence, not in order to require the performance for their own benefit of the obligations specified therein, but to infer, in the light of the duties and rights arising therefrom, such beneficial or adverse consequences as the circumstances or acts of third parties have entailed for the contracting parties.)

The fact that the existence of a contract may be of relevance to third parties does not constitute an exception to the doctrine of privity. On the other hand, an exception to the principle can be said to exist where third parties are — directly or indirectly — bound by obligations imposed under, or can invoke rights conferred by, the contract. In discussing such extension of contracts to third parties, a distinction needs to be made between extension *for the benefit* of third parties and extension *to their detriment*. Both kinds of extension to third parties may be expressly provided for by statute, or again may be based on case law.

According to the prevailing opinion, any extension of contracts to third parties is deemed to be an exception or a mitigation to the doctrine of privity of contract. However, it should be noted that the doctrine can also be approached more flexibly. Such an approach will involve determining whether — in the light of all the circumstances of the specific case — the autonomy of the contracting parties and/or the autonomy of the third party can truly be said to have been infringed. If this is not found to be the case, the doctrine of privity of contract does not apply. An example of this arises in connection with the third-party stipulation (cf. item a of Section 4 below). A right stipulated by the stipulator in his contract with the promisor on behalf of a third party cannot be imposed on the third party *peremptorily* and *against his will*. There is no infringement of the third party's autonomy, since, in Dutch law, the third party acquires the right only upon accepting the third-party stipulation (up to that point he merely has a right of volition), and on doing so he becomes a party to the contract between the stipulator and the promisor. In the law of neighbouring countries, the third party acquires the right without having first to accept the third-party stipulation, but may repudiate the acquired right, in which case he is deemed never to have acquired it. Nor is there any infringement of promisor's autonomy, since the promisor consents to the third party's acquisition of a right in respect of him. There is therefore no question of an exception to the (qualified) doctrine of privity of contract.[7] In this article we shall, for simplicity's sake, keep to the prevailing opinion that any extension of contracts to third parties is an exception or a mitigation to the doctrine of privity of contract.

Before examining the extension of contracts to third parties more closely, let us take a look at the meaning of the terms *party, third party, persons acquiring rights by general title* and *persons acquiring rights by particular title*.

3 Contracting Parties, Third Parties, and Persons Acquiring Rights by General and Particular Title

The parties to a contract (the contracting parties) are generally defined as those who have entered into the contract, whether in person or through an agent, together with those who have become a party to the contract as a result of the succession by general title to the rights and obligations of either of the contracting parties. Anyone else is a third party. The convenience of these definitions lies in their simplicity. Third parties, however closely they may be involved in the contract and irrespective of the extent to which they may be considered to have an interest (including an economic interest) in the contract, are deemed in law not to be parties to the contract.[8] On the basis of this distinction between contracting parties and third parties, persons acquiring rights by particular title from either of the contracting parties may be deemed to be third parties.[9] A person acquiring rights by particular title succeeds to one or more parts of his legal predecessor's patrimony, but does not become a party to any contract which the latter entered into with the other party and from which the acquired right has resulted.[10] The position of persons acquiring rights by general title is different; they succeed to all of their legal predecessor's patrimony or to a proportion of it.[11] They may be considered third parties to the contract between the legal predecessor and the other party *as long as legal*

---

7   For the more flexible approach to the doctrine of privity of contract referred to in the text, cf. C. E. du Perron, '"Hadden wij dan iets afgesproken? Ik ken u niet", Rechtsbeginselen en de derdenwerking van overeenkomsten', *AA* 1991, p. 848/132 *et seq.*, and S.C.J.J. Kortmann, 'Res inter alios acta, aliis neque nocere, neque prodesse potest', in: *Beginselen van vermogensrecht, BW-krant jaarboek 1993*, Arnhem 1993, p. 137 *et seq.*

8   Cf., *inter alia*, HR 25 March 1966, *NJ* 1966, 279, nt. GJS; HR 7 March 1969, *NJ* 1969, 249, nt. GJS; HR 12 January 1979, *NJ* 1979, 362, nt. ARB; HR 20 June 1986, *NJ* 1987, 35, nt. G and HR 9 June 1989, *NJ* 1990, 40, nt. JLPC.

9   Cf. HR 3 March 1905, *W* 8191. Cf. also HR 9 February 1940, *NJ* 1940, 302, nt. EMM, in conjunction with former BW Article 1376a.

10   A person acquiring a right by particular title can nonetheless become a party to the contract by taking the contract over (or by acceding to the existing contract).

11   The only ways in which property may be acquired by general title are specified in the law: inheritance, fusion of patrimonies and succession to the patrimony of a legal person which has ceased to exist. Cf. BW Article 3:80, paragraph 2.

succession has not taken place. However, where rights are transferred by general title, the acquirer will — except in certain specified cases[12] — take over all his legal predecessor's rights and obligations and will become a party to any contracts entered into by the latter.[13]

4 Extension of Contracts *for the Benefit* of Third Parties

Exceptions to, or restrictions upon, the main rule that a contract can only be binding upon the contracting parties, and that it cannot confer contractual rights or impose contractual obligations upon third parties, are more likely to be allowed where a right is conferred than where an obligation is imposed upon the third party. Extension of contracts for the benefit of third parties presents less of a problem than extension to their detriment. However, the conferral of rights upon third parties is also subject to restrictions. Rights or other benefits must not be imposable on the third party against his will.[14] Of the instances in which contracts are extended for the benefit of third parties, we will examine in turn the third-party stipulation, the extension of defences for the benefit of servants and other third parties, and the transfer of qualitative rights.[15]

a The Third-party Stipulation
The third-party stipulation is a vital legal concept. Examples can be found in the much-used perpetual clauses (in Dutch: *kettingbedingen*), contracts of carriage, insurance contracts for the benefit of third parties, maintenance provisions for the benefit of third parties, etc.[16] One of the contracting parties (the stipulator) stipulates that the other (the promisor) will perform a service for the benefit of a third party, or that the third party can otherwise invoke the contract between the promisor and the stipulator.[17] In Dutch law prior to 1 January 1992, the scope

---

12 For exceptions to the rule that, in the case of transfer by general title, rights and obligations are transferred to the legal successor, see, *inter alia*, BW Articles 7:409, 7:410, 7:422, 7:438, 7A:16391, 7A:1648 and 7A:1683. Similar exceptions are allowed in the neighbouring countries. For statutory provisions on fusion of patrimonies, see BW Article 1:93 *et seq.*

13 Cf. BW Article 6:249 and former BW Article 1354. Cf. also HR 3 March 1905, *W* 8191; HR 4 June 1965, *NJ* 1966, 469, nt. JHB; HR 8 December 1972, *NJ* 1973, 496, nt. KW and HR 28 November 1980, *NJ* 1981, 440, nt. WMK. For French and Belgian law, cf. CC Article 1122 and BW/CC Article 1122.

14 This notion recurs at various points in the new BW, including Article 6:5, paragraph 2, Article 6:160, paragraph 2, Article 6:251, paragraph 3, Article 6:253, paragraph 1, Article 6:253, paragraph 4 and Article 7A:1703 *et seq.* See also BGB § 333, § 516 II and § 1942 I.

15 Other examples of extension of contracts for the benefit of third parties will not be discussed. Cf. for instance BW Article (7:424 together with) 7:420 and Article 8:63, paragraph 2.

16 For other examples, cf. *Asser-Hartkamp II*, Zwolle 1993, No. 420, with references to jurisprudence and literature.

17 The stipulator will include such a stipulation in his contract with the promisor in order to fulfil a civil or natural obligation towards the third party or to benefit the third party by making him a gift. The third-party stipulation may be explicitly made or be implicit in the contract between

for making third-party stipulations was restricted. The stipulator was also required to make some stipulation for his own benefit or to make a gift to the promisor. Accordingly, not all contractual links between the stipulator and the promisor were deemed compatible with a third-party stipulation.[18] These restrictions have not been maintained in the new BW.[19] Under the law as it now stands, a third-party stipulation may be the sole content of a contract between the stipulator and the promisor.

German law on this point is essentially the same as current Dutch law.[20] In France and Belgium, third-party stipulations often remain subject to restrictions. Thus, for example, BW/CC Articles 1119 and 1121 lay down the same restrictions as applied in the Netherlands before the new BW came into force.[21] However, pronouncements by the courts have relaxed these restrictions to such an extent that it is now considered sufficient for the stipulator to have some personal interest in the third-party stipulation that he wishes to make. The same applies in French law.[22] In some recent French literature, the view is expressed

---

the stipulator and the promisor.

18 Cf. former BW Article 1353. See also HR 26 June 1914, *W* 9713, nt. EMM, *NJ* 1914, p. 1028; HR 15 November 1918, *W* 10387, *NJ* 1919, p. 39; HR 29 January 1920, *W* 10555, *NJ* 1920, p. 225; HR 13 February 1924, *W* 11211, *NJ* 1924, p. 711; HR 17 December 1926, *W* 11620, *NJ* 1927, p. 257; HR 29 May 1931, *W* 12332, *NJ* 1931, p. 1585, nt. PS. Prior to 1914, interpretations were generally less strict.

19 Cf. BW Article 6:253, paragraph 1. In this connection, see TM, *Parl. Gesch. Boek 6*, p. 948, and MvA II, *Parl. Gesch. Boek 6*, p. 956.

20 Cf. Karl Larenz, *Lehrbuch des Schuldrechts*, Band I, Allgemeiner Teil, 14. Auflage, Munich 1987, § 17 II; Hans Brox, *Allgemeines Schuldrecht*, 20. Auflage, Munich 1992, Rdnr. 364 *et seq.*; Wolfgang Fikentscher, *Schuldrecht*, 8. Auflage, Berlin and New York 1992, § 37; Esser and Schmidt, *Schuldrecht*, Band I, Allgemeiner Teil, Teilband 2, 7. Auflage, Heidelberg 1993, § 36, and Dieter Medicus, *Schuldrecht I*, Allgemeiner Teil, 7. Auflage, Munich 1993, § 66. Cf. also Heinrichs, *Münchener Kommentar zum Bürgerlichen Gesetzbuch*, Band 2, Schuldrecht, Allgemeiner Teil (§§ 241-432), 2. Auflage, Munich 1985, p. 1003 *et seq.*; Soergel, *Bürgerliches Gesetzbuch*, Band 2, Schuldrecht I (§§ 241-432), 12. Auflage, Stuttgart, Berlin and Köln, 1990, p. 1521 *et seq.*; Jauernig, *Bürgerliches Gesetzbuch*, 6. Auflage, Munich 1991, p. 355 *et seq.*; Erman, *Handkommentar zum Bürgerlichen Gesetzbuch*, 1. Band, 9. Auflage, Münster 1993, p. 795 *et seq.*, and Palandt, *Bürgerliches Gesetzbuch*, 53. Auflage, Munich 1994, p. 412 *et seq.*

21 Cf. E. Dirix, *Obligatoire verhoudingen tussen contractanten en derden*, dissertation at the University of Antwerp, Antwerp and Apeldoorn 1984, p. 97 *et seq.*, and the authors and jurisprudence which he cites. Cf. also Pierre Jadoul, 'La stipulation pour autrui', in: *Les effets du contrat à l'égard des tiers*, sous la direction de Marcel Fontaine et Jacques Ghestin, Paris 1992, p. 408 *et seq.*

22 Cf. Alex Weill and François Terré, *Droit civil*, Les Obligations, Paris 1986, Nos. 530 and 531; Jean Carbonnier, *Droit civil*, 4 - Les Obligations, Paris 1988, No. 57; Gabriel Marty and Pierre Raynaud, *Droit civil* Les obligations, Tome 1, Les sources, 2ᵉ édition, Paris 1988, No. 283; Christian Larroumet, *Droit civil*, Tome III, Les obligations, Le contrat, 2ᵉ édition, Paris 1990, No. 806; Henri and Léon Mazeaud, Jean Mazeaud and François Chabas, Leçons de *Droit civil*, Tome II, premier volume, Obligations, Théorie générale, 8ᵉ édition, Paris 1991, Nos. 774 and 780; Jacques Flour and Jean-Luc Aubert, *Droit civil*, Les obligations, 1 — L'acte juridique, 5ᵉ édition, Paris 1991, No. 464; Philippe Malaurie and Laurent Aynès, *Cours de Droit civil*, Les

that a third-party stipulation may be the sole content of a contract between the stipulator and the promisor. A stipulator's personal interest in the third-party stipulation is no longer considered a requirement for the validity of the third-party stipulation, or is considered only a formality.[23] French jurisprudence on the subject still seems to be somewhat stricter.

Unlike the law in continental countries, English law has always been very wary of the concept of third-party stipulations. In England, the guiding principle is still *nemo alteri stipulari potest (res inter alios acta, aliis neque nocere, neque prodesse potest)*.[24] A third-party stipulation is often deemed inadmissible by virtue of the doctrine of privity and the consideration requirement. The consideration requirement, which is unknown in continental legal systems, means that contracts other than those made in a prescribed form, are only binding if the parties have provided or promised one another 'something of value in the eye of the law.'[25] Current English jurisprudence rejects the concept of the third-party stipulation.[26] In Dunlop Pneumatic Tyre Co. Ltd. v. Selfridge & Co. Ltd.,[27] Viscount Haldane gives the following quite explicit opinion on the subject: 'In the law of England certain principles are fundamental. One is that only a person who is a party to a contract can sue on it. Our law knows nothing of a ius quaesitum tertio arising by way of contract.'

An essential point when making a third-party stipulation is that it should be the parties' intention to confer a personal right upon the third party. Whether this is so depends on how the contract is interpreted.[28] If the third party is merely a 'payee' and does not acquire a personal right in respect of the debtor, there can be no third-party stipulation. In that case, the debtor is only under an obligation towards the other contracting party, not towards the third party, to perform the

---

obligations, 3ᵉ édition, Paris 1992, No. 671, and Jacques Ghestin, *Traité de Droit civil*, Les obligations, Les effets du contrat, Paris 1992, No. 835 *et seq.*

23   See previous note.

24   For detailed historical reflections on this principle, cf. R. Zimmermann, *The Law of Obligations, Roman Foundations of the Civilian Tradition*, Deventer and Boston 1992, pp. 34-45.

25   See C. Æ. Uniken Venema, *Law en equity*, Zwolle and Antwerp 1990, p. 255. For general information on the consideration requirement, see Cheshire Fifoot & Furmston, *Law of Contract*, Twelfth Edition, London, Dublin and Edinburgh, 1991, pp. 7-9 and 70-110, and G.H. Treitel, *The Law of Contract*, Eighth Edition, London 1991, pp. 63-148.

26   Cf. Tweddle v. Atkinson (1861) 1 *B & S* 393; Dunlop Pneumatic Tyre Co. Ltd. v. Selfridge & Co. Ltd. [1915] *AC* 847, and Beswick v. Beswick [1968] *AC* 58, [1967] 2 *All ER* 1197.

27   See previous note.

28   Cf. BGB § 328 II, § 329 and § 330. In principle, the intention of conferring on the third party a personal right in respect of the promisor is not presumed. German law does occasionally depart from this principle. Cf. BGB § 330. The presumption that the third party does *not* acquire a personal right in respect of the promisor can be found in BGB § 329.

service.[29] In fact, it is not necessary for the identity of the third party to be known at the time that the third-party stipulation is made. It is deemed sufficient that the identity of the person for whose benefit the third-party stipulation is made should be *capable of being ascertained*. Nor, in principle, are there any restrictions on the form of a third-party stipulation. However, where the law requires the contract between the stipulator and the promisor to be in any particular form, the third-party stipulation will automatically conform to this.

Once the legal validity of the third-party stipulation has been established, either the third party or the stipulator may, in principle, require compliance with the stipulation for the third party's benefit.[30] This is explicitly stated in BW Article 6:256 and BGB § 335. In France[31] and Belgium,[32] it is taken for granted. The third party may oppose any requirement by the stipulator that the promisor comply.[33] It is also possible that, under the terms of the contract between the stipulator and the promisor, the stipulator cannot require compliance.[34] In the event of failure to comply, not only can the third party claim damages, but the stipulator can also, in principle, claim damages on the third party's behalf.

BGB § 334 explicitly states that the promisor can invoke against the third party any defence which he is entitled to invoke against the stipulator under the terms of his contract with the latter.[35] Dutch law has not generally adopted this rule, since, although it may be deemed just in many cases, it is not always so. In the parliamentary discussions on the subject, there is an example of a third-party

---

29   Even the German *Vertrag mit Schutzwirkung für Dritte* (contract with third-party protection), which is recognized within fairly strict limits as a means of avoiding the restrictions of extra-contractual liability law (in particular BGB § 831), does not entitle the third party to require performance of the primary service, although it does entitle him to bring a claim for damages which is similar to a contractual action. This is not a third-party stipulation in the true sense of the term. In this connection, see Larenz, *op. cit.*, § 17 II and III; Brox, *op. cit.*, Rdnr. 376 *et seq.*; Fikentscher, *op. cit.*, Rdnr. 260 *et seq.*, and Medicus, *op. cit.*, § 67. Cf. also Heinrichs, *op. cit.*, § 328, Rdnr. 60 *et seq.*; Soergel, *op. cit.*, Anhang zu § 328; Jauernig, *op. cit.*, § 328, Anm. III; Erman, *op. cit.*, Vor § 328, Rdnr. 9, and § 328, Rdnr. 11 *et seq.*, and Palandt, *op. cit.*, § 328, Rdnr. 13 *et seq.* In this case, BGB § 278 applies in place of the more restrictive § 831.

30   Cf. HR 11 March 1983, *NJ* 1983, 585, nt. PAS.

31   Cf. Weill and Terré, *op. cit.*, Nos. 540 and 541; Carbonnier, *op. cit.*, No. 57; Marty and Raynaud, *op. cit.*, No. 289; Larroumet, *op. cit.*, No. 815; Mazeaud, Mazeaud and Chabas, *op. cit.*, No. 789; Flour and Aubert, *op. cit.*, No. 473; Malaurie and Aynès, *op. cit.*, No. 679, and Ghestin, *op. cit.*, Nos. 861 and 863.

32   Cf. E. Dirix, *op. cit.*, Nos. 110-112, where other authors are cited.

33   Cf. BW Article 6:256.

34   Cf. BW Article 6:250 together with Article 6:256.

35   Cf. Larenz, *op. cit.*, § 17 I b; Brox, *op. cit.*, Rdnr. 373; Fikentscher, *op. cit.*, Rdnr. 248 and Rdnr. 258; Esser and Schmidt, *op. cit.*, § 36 III 2, and Medicus, *op. cit.*, § 66 III 3. Cf. also Heinrichs, *op. cit.*, § 334, Rdnr. 1 *et seq.*; Soergel, *op. cit.*, § 334, Rdnr. 1 *et seq.*; Jauernig, *op. cit.*, § 334, points 1 and 2; Erman, *op. cit.*, § 334, Rdnr. 1 *et seq.*, and Palandt, *op. cit.*, § 334, Rdnr. 1 *et seq.*

stipulation intended to provide the third party with a guarantee that the stipulator will perform an obligation. In cases such as this, the promisor cannot be allowed to invoke against the third party all the defences arising from his relationship with the stipulator.[36]

Until the third-party stipulation has been accepted by the third party, it may be revoked by the stipulator,[37] and — where stipulated — by the promisor or the stipulator and the promisor acting jointly.[38] To safeguard the possibility of revoking the third-party stipulation — whether or not for a specified period — the stipulator and the promisor may agree that the third-party stipulation can still be revoked after the third party has accepted it,[39] or that the third party may accept the stipulation only after a specified period has lapsed. They may also agree that designation of the beneficiary will be postponed until later. In German law, it is usually held that the stipulator, or the stipulator and the promisor acting jointly, can reserve the power to revoke or to vary the third party's right.[40] It is not necessary for this right to be explicitly stated in the contract between the parties; it can also be inferred from the circumstances of the case and from the parties' intention in drawing up the contract.

Where the third-party stipulation is without effect with respect to the third party in question, the stipulator may — in principle (cf. BW Article 6:250 together with Article 6:255) — designate either himself or another third party as the beneficiary.[41] In Dutch law, where the promisor has given the stipulator a reasonable period within which to make such designation and the stipulator has not done so within that period, the stipulator is deemed — except where otherwise stipulated — to have designated himself as the beneficiary.[42]

In the Netherlands, it is usually held that the third party's right only takes effect when he accepts the third-party stipulation.[43] This is known as the doctrine of

---

36   Cf. TM, Parl. Gesch. Boek 6, p. 961, where reference is made in turn to *Suijling II*, 1, No. 129, p. 227.
37   Cf. BW Article 6:253, paragraph 2. A contract between the stipulator and the promisor may produce a different result. Cf. BW Article 6:250. Cf. also by analogy BW Article 6:219. in conjunction with MvA II, *Parl. Gesch. Boek 6*, p. 960. For revocation of a third-party stipulation in French and Belgian law, cf. CC Article 1121 and BW/CC Article 1121.
38   Cf. BW Article 6:250 together with Article 6:253, paragraph 2.
39   Cf. BW Article 6:250, in conjunction with BW Article 6:253, paragraph 2.
40   See BGB § 328 II, § 331 II and § 332, and also VVG (Gesetz über den Versicherungsvertrag) § 166.
41   Cf. BW Article 6:255, paragraph 1 and BGB § 332 for explicit statements of this.
42   Cf. BW Article 6:255, paragraph 2.
43   Cf. BW Article 6:253, paragraph 1. See also MvA II, *Parl. Gesch. Boek 6*, p. 957, and *Asser-Hartkamp II*, Zwolle 1993, Nos. 422-424. According to HR 13 February 1924, *W* 11211, nt. SB, *NJ* 1924, p. 711, the same was true under earlier legislation. There are no exceptions to the rule that the third party's right only takes effect upon acceptance. See BW Article 6:250 together with Article 6:253, paragraph 1 and MvA II, *Parl. Gesch. Boek 6*, p. 959.

statement of acceptance of rights (in Dutch: *de leer van de rechtverkrijgende verklaring*).[44] Until the third party has accepted the third-party stipulation, his only right is a right of volition, namely the right to give the third-party stipulation legal validity by accepting it. An offer does not need to be made to the third party. It is enough for the third party to have become aware in any way of the third-party stipulation made for his benefit and then to have notified one of the parties that he accepts it.[45] Although acceptance of the third-party stipulation is not retrospective,[46] the third party may, provided this does not conflict with the intent of the stipulation, derive from it rights over the period prior to its acceptance.[47] This may, for example, be relevant where the stipulator has stipulated in his contract with the promisor, on behalf of the third party, that the latter may invoke an exemption clause contained in their contract.[48] Acceptance of such a clause will usually take place only after the damage for which the third party may be liable has already occurred and the third party has subsequently become aware of the exemption clause made, *inter alia*, for his benefit.

In German, French and Belgian law, the third party's right to claim takes effect — except where otherwise stipulated — as soon as the contract is concluded between the stipulator and the promisor, without the third party needing to be involved. This is known as the doctrine of statement of confirmation of rights (in Dutch: *de leer van de rechtbevestigende verklaring*).[49] However, the third

---

44   An irrevocable stipulation which, with respect to the third party, has been made by gratuitous title, is deemed to have been accepted if it has come to the attention of the third party and he has not rejected it without delay. See BW Article 6:253, paragraph 4.

45   Cf. TM, *Parl. Gesch. Boek 6*, p. 950; VV II, *Parl. Gesch. Boek 6*, pp. 955-956; MvA II, *Parl. Gesch. Boek 6*, pp. 957 and 960, and *Asser-Hartkamp II*, Zwolle 1993, No. 422. In certain cases, the third party must notify *both* parties to the contract, upon pain of liability for damages towards the unnotified stipulator or promisor. Cf. TM, *Parl. Gesch. Boek 6*, p. 950; MvA II, *Parl. Gesch. Boek 6*, p. 959, and *Asser-Hartkamp II*, Zwolle 1993, No. 423.

46   Cf. MvA II, *Parl. Gesch. Boek 6*, pp. 957-959.

47   Cf. BW Article 6:254, paragraph 2 and MvA II, *Parl. Gesch. Boek 6*, p. 958. See also HR 13 February 1924, *W* 11211, nt. SB, *NJ* 1924, p. 711. Contractual derogations from BW Article 6:254, paragraph 2 are permissible. Cf. BW Article 6:250.

48   For an example regarding perpetual clauses, see *Asser-Hartkamp II*, Zwolle 1993, Nos. 423 and 413.

49   For German law, cf. Larenz, *op. cit.*, § 17 I a; Brox, *op. cit.*, Rdnr. 372; Fikentscher, *op. cit.*, Rdnr. 247; Esser and Schmidt, *op. cit.*, § 36 II 1; Medicus, *op. cit.*, § 66 III 1; Heinrichs, *op. cit.*, § 328, Rdnr. 1, 2 and 23, and § 333, Rdnr. 1; Soergel, *op. cit.*, Vor § 328, Rdnr. 6 *et seq.*, § 328, Rdnr. 1, 36 and 117, and § 333, Rdnr. 1 *et seq.* (where a different view on the subject is expressed by Hadding); Jauernig, *op. cit.*, § 328, Anm. II 3 a aa; Erman, *op. cit.*, § 328, Rdnr. 7, and § 333, Rdnr. 1, and Palandt, *op. cit.*, Einf. v. § 328, Rdnr. 6, and § 333, Rdnr. 1; for French law, Weill and Terré, *op. cit.*, Nos. 534-538; Carbonnier, *op. cit.*, No. 57; Marty and Raynaud, *op. cit.*, Nos. 286 and 290-293; Larroumet, *op. cit.*, Nos. 807, 810 and 818; Mazeaud, Mazeaud and Chabas, *op. cit.*, Nos. 791-793, 795-796 and 801; Flour and Aubert, *op. cit.*, No. 476; Malaurie and Aynès, *op. cit.*, No. 677, and Ghestin, *op. cit.*, Nos. 843, 853, 857 and 862; and for Belgian law, *inter alia*, E. Dirix, *op. cit.*, No. 123 and P. Jadoul, *op. cit.*, pp. 417-418 and 423-424, both with references to other literature.

party may repudiate the right that has been 'imposed' upon him, by making a statement to that effect to the promisor.[50] In that case, the right is deemed retrospectively not to have been acquired. The right can no longer be repudiated in this way if the third party has explicitly accepted it, or if his acceptance of it can conclusively be inferred from his conduct.

In Dutch law, if a third party accepts a stipulation made for his benefit — which he may do either explicitly or tacitly[51] —, he is then deemed to be a party to the contract between the stipulator and the promisor.[52] Acceptance of a third-party stipulation thus turns a bipartite contract into a tripartite one. In Germany, France and Belgium, this is not the case. Similarly, under Dutch law prior to 1 January 1992, a third party who accepted a third-party stipulation was not considered to have thereby become a party to the contract.

Finally, it should be mentioned that in principle the third party's right depends on the continued existence of the contract between the stipulator and the promisor. Invalidity or annulment of the contract usually makes the third-party stipulation void.[53] The question of whether, conversely, invalidity or annulment of the third-party stipulation makes the entire contract void must be assessed in the light of the circumstances of the case.[54]

b Extension of Defences to Benefit Servants and Other Third Parties
Defences which a party to a contract may invoke under the terms of that contract may, under certain circumstances, be extended to benefit a third party. In that case, the third party may, if sued, invoke that particular defence against his opponent. Defences may be extended for the benefit of third parties by means of a third-party stipulation as discussed above.[55] In fact, however, there is no need to resort to this. The new BW expressly states that, where a contracting party can derive a defence from the contract against the other party to shield him from contractual or extra-contractual liability for conduct by his servant, the servant may — if sued by the other party on the basis of this

---

50   In German law this is explicitly laid down in BGB § 333.
51   Cf. BW Article 6:253, paragraph 3 together with Article 3:37, paragraph 1. Cf. also HR 15 May 1964, *NJ* 1964, 472 and HR 19 March 1976, *NJ* 1976, 407, nt. PZ.
52   Cf. BW Article 6:254, paragraph 1. For the provisions of the law pertaining to contracts between more than two parties, see BW Article 6:213, paragraph 2 and Article 6:279. See also, in this connection, *Asser-Hartkamp II*, Zwolle 1993, Nos. 427 and 428. A contract between the stipulator and the promisor may derogate from BW Article 6:254, paragraph 1. Cf. BW Article 6:250.
53   Cf. *Asser-Hartkamp II*, Zwolle 1993, No. 429.
54   Cf. *Asser-Hartkamp II*, Zwolle 1993, No. 430.
55   This is in keeping with both the wording and the intent of BW Article 6:253, paragraph 1. See Rapport aan de Koningin, *Parl. Gesch. Boek 6*, p. 952; MvA II, *Parl. Gesch. Boek 6*, p. 957, and MvT, *Parl. Gesch. Boek 6* (*Inv.* 3, 5 and 6), pp. 1823-1824.

conduct − invoke the same defence as if he were a party to the contract.[56] This rule is of relevance not only to exemption clauses, but also to any other contractually stipulated or statutory defences which limit liability. However, only exemption clauses will be discussed here.

A party to a contract who is confronted with an exemption clause must be prevented from suing the other party's financially more vulnerable servant for damages. Indeed, were such an unjust action to be allowed, the exemption clause would generally become fairly meaningless, since the servant, having paid the damages, could then recover them from his employer under the terms of their employment contract.[57] An employer who imagined he had protected himself against claims for damages by the other party could thus end up having to pay damages after all. In order to prevent injured parties from circumventing exemption clauses in this way, BW Article 6:257 allows a servant to invoke against the injured party an exemption clause contained in a contract between the latter and the servant's employer.[58] Where the injured party is not a party to the contract with the employer, but − under the circumstances referred to in item a of Section 5 below − must nevertheless allow the exemption clause to be invoked against him (extension of defences to the detriment of third parties), we believe it must be accepted (even though BW Article 6:257 makes no reference to this) that the employee will also be able to invoke the said exemption clause against the injured third party (extension of defences for the benefit of a third party and to the detriment of another third party).[59]

However, it needs to be remembered that the rule laid down in BW Article 6:257 only applies if the exemption clause exempts the employer from claims

---

56 Cf. BW Article 6:257. Under Dutch law prior to 1 January 1992, this was usually taken for granted. Cf. *Asser-Hartkamp II*, Zwolle 1993, No. 435, with references to other literature. Under the law as it previously stood, acceptance of an implicit third-party stipulation or interpretation of the agreed exemption clause made it possible to achieve a result comparable with BW Article 6:257. BW Article 6:257 cannot be waived: BW Article 6:250 explicitly states that there may be no derogations by contract from BW Article 6:257.

57 Here and in the remainder of the text, the term 'employer' must be interpreted broadly. It includes not only those who direct others to carry out work for them under the terms of an employment contract, but also government bodies who appoint civil servants. The term 'servant' (in Dutch: *ondergeschikte*) is to be interpreted in accordance with BW Article 6:170.

58 For the rationale behind BW Article 6:257, see also VV II, *Parl. Gesch. Boek 6*, p. 917; MvA II, *Parl. Gesch. Boek 6*, p. 964; Eindverslag I, *Parl. Gesch. Boek 6*, pp. 964-965, and MvA II, *Parl. Gesch. Boek 6* (Inv. 3, 5 and 6), p. 1825. Provisions similar to BW Article 6:257 are to be found, for example, in the law pertaining to carriage. Cf. BW Article 8:365, which (by virtue of BW Articles 8:31, 8:71, 8:91, 8:116, 8:531 (together with Article 8:880), 8:559, 8:880, 8:991, 8:992, 8:994 and 8:1081) is stated to be applicable mutatis mutandis to other contracts of carriage (or similar agreements). Cf. also BW Article 8:72.

59 The same view is expressed by R. Zwitser, 'De verpersoonlijking van het zakenrecht', in: *Quod Licet* (Kleijn-bundel), Deventer 1992, p. 496, and *Asser-Hartkamp II*, Zwolle 1993, No. 436. Cf. also BW Article 8:365, mentioned in the previous note, in conjunction with BW Articles 8:362-364.

for damages for unlawful conduct *by his servant*.[60] If the employer has only stipulated that he is exempted from liability for his *own* failing or unlawful conduct, BW Article 6:257 is not applicable: it is generally held that both the employer and the servant can then be sued for damages caused by the servant's unlawful conduct.[61] It should also be remembered that this problem will not arise if the employer stipulates not only that *he* is exempted from liability for his own or his servant's conduct, but also that his *servant* is exempted from liability. This can be done with the help of a third-party stipulation on behalf of the servant. One further restriction should be pointed out. An exemption clause can be circumvented if the servant has caused injury to the other party through either malice or gross negligence. This can be inferred from the phrase 'as if he were a party to the contract' in BW Article 6:257. If the servant himself had entered into the contract with the other party, he could not have invoked the exemption clause, since it is generally held that no-one can, in principle, be legally exempted from liability for malice, gross negligence or conscious recklessness.[62] In principle, only the employer can invoke the exemption clause in such cases;[63] the servant cannot. The reverse is equally conceivable. If the employer has himself acted with malice (or gross negligence) but the servant is only slightly at fault — or if the employer does not or cannot invoke the exemption clause for any other reason —, the servant remains free to invoke the exemption clause. This is because BW Article 6:257 does not require the employer to invoke, or to be able to invoke, the clause in order to be exempted from liability *for his own conduct*; it merely prescribes that the employer must be able to derive from the contract a defence in respect of his liability *for the conduct of one of his servants*.[64]

The previous qualifying remarks regarding the applicability of BW Article 6:257 apply *mutatis mutandis* where the servant causes injury to a third party who is

---

60 In general, exemption clauses are broadly framed, in that they are usually intended to exclude an employer's liability for a servant's unlawful conduct as well as for his own failing and unlawful conduct.

61 Cf. BW Articles 6:170 and 6:162.

62 In this connection, cf. Asser-Hartkamp I, Zwolle 1992, No. 341 *et seq.*, and the other literature cited there. For French, German, English and Belgian law, cf. Laurent Aynès, Joachim Schmidt-Salzer, Hugh Beale and Pierre van Ommeslaghe, *Les clauses limitatives ou exonératoires de responsabilité en Europe*, Actes du Colloque des 13 et 14 décembre 1990, sous la direction de Jacques Ghestin, Paris 1991, p. 5 *et seq.*, p. 43 *et seq.*, p. 153 *et seq.*, and p. 229 *et seq.* Apart from being void as explained here, there are all kinds of other reasons why an exemption clause should remain inapplicable or cannot be invoked in practice. Such cases will not be discussed here.

63 Exemption from liability for malice or gross negligence by servants is in principle held to be permissible. Cf. HR 26 March 1920, *W* 10592, *NJ* 1920, p. 476; HR 3 June 1938, *NJ* 1938, 920, nt. EMM; Asser-Hartkamp I, Zwolle 1992, No. 343; *Asser-Hartkamp II*, Zwolle 1993, No. 269, and the other literature cited there. The qualification should perhaps be added that such exemption will fail if the servant in question is in a senior position.

64 Cf. MvA II, *Parl. Gesch. Boek 6*, p. 964, and *Asser-Hartkamp II*, Zwolle 1993, No. 437.

not a party to the contract with the employer but who must, under certain circumstances, allow the exemption clause included in the contract to be invoked against him. The question of whether the employer and/or the servant will be able to invoke the exemption clause must be settled in the light of the circumstances of the specific case, in accordance with the foregoing. There are several alternative situations. It is conceivable that neither the employer nor the servant will be able to invoke the exemption clause. It is also conceivable that, in a specific case, both the employer and the servant will be able to invoke the exemption clause. Finally, it is possible that only the employer, or only the servant, will be able to invoke the exemption clause against the third party.

BW Article 6:257 does not apply to non-servants.[65] A number of specific cases are regulated by statutory provisions.[66] Where there are no such provisions, a similar result may nonetheless be achieved by other means. A non-servant may derive a defence from a contract to which he is not a party, provided he has accepted a third-party stipulation made to this effect on his behalf. Such a stipulation may either have been explicitly made or be implicit in the contract. If a third-party stipulation has been made, the third party becomes a party to the contract as soon as he accepts the stipulation, and BW Article 6:257 then becomes applicable to *his* servants, at least in cases where the non-servant who has accepted the third-party stipulation is able to derive from the contract to which he has become a party a defence in respect of not only his *own* behaviour, but also the behaviour *of his servants*.

Neighbouring countries have no provisions similar to BW Article 6:257. There are no statutory provisions on the subject. However, in most countries a more or less similar result is achieved for servants by various different means.

---

65 The legislator does not consider a general rule of the kind formulated for servants to be either practicable or desirable in the case of independent (self-employed) contractors. Cf. Eindverslag I, *Parl. Gesch. Boek 6*, pp. 964-966; VV II, *Parl. Gesch. Boek 6 (Inv.* 3, 5 and 6), pp. 1824-1825, and MvA II, *Parl. Gesch. Boek 6 (Inv.* 3, 5 and 6), pp. 1825-1826. However, we believe that jurisprudence may eventually develop a similar rule for cases other than those referred to in BW Article 6:257. Cf. also MvA II, *Parl. Gesch. Boek 6* (Inv. 3, 5 and 6), p. 1826; S.C.J.J. Kortmann, *'Derden'-werking van aansprakelijkheidsbedingen*, dissertation at the University of Nijmegen, Deventer 1977, pp. 163-173; *Asser-Van der Grinten I (De vertegenwoordiging)*, Zwolle 1990, No. 118, and *Asser-Hartkamp II*, Zwolle 1993, No. 435.

66 E.g. BW Article 7:608, paragraph 1 (together with paragraph 4) and paragraph 3 together with paragraph 2 (and paragraph 4), on sub-depositaries, and also certain provisions of the law pertaining to carriage. See, for instance, BW Article 8:363, which (by virtue of BW Articles 8:31, 8:71, 8:91, 8:116, 8:531 (together with Article 8:880), 8:880, 8:991, 8:992, 8:994 and 8:1081) is stated to be applicable mutatis mutandis to other contracts of carriage (or similar agreements). Cf. also BW Article 8:364. Caution is required when applying the provisions of the aforementioned articles by analogy to contracts other than contracts of deposit or carriage (c.a.). See MvT, Parl. Gesch. Boek 7 (Inv. 3, 5 and 6), p. 407, with references to MvA II, *Parl. Gesch. Boek 6*, p. 918, and Eindverslag I, *Parl. Gesch. Boek 6*, pp. 964-965.

In Belgium, there is less need for liability clauses to be extended for the benefit of third parties, owing to the quasi-immunity enjoyed by independent agents and the similar protection provided for employees.[67] In cases where there *is* a need for exemption clauses to be extended, this can only be done with the help of a third-party stipulation.[68]

In German law, too, the extension of exemption clauses for the benefit of third parties must always be based on the contract between the stipulator and the promisor. An exemption clause cannot operate for the benefit of third parties solely by virtue of the third-party stipulation. In order for there to be a third-party stipulation in the true sense of the term, BGB § 328 requires *a right to claim* to be conferred on the third party. However, it is inferred from the principle implicit in § 328 that the parties can make a '*pactum de non petendo* for the benefit of third parties'. In more recent pronouncements and legal writings, it is often assumed that the debtor intended his servants and independent agents to be protected by the exemption clause. This is then related to the doctrine of '*Verträge mit Schutzwirkung für Dritte*' (contracts which protect third parties).[69] According to this doctrine, contracting parties owe a particular duty of care to certain third parties involved in the contract. A corollary of this doctrine is that third parties involved in a contract who are sued by one of the contracting parties should also be afforded the protection of the exemption clause.

In England, especially in the past, the notion of extending exemption clauses for the benefit of third parties was rejected. In Scruttons Ltd. v. Midland Silicones Ltd., for instance, the stevedore employed by the carrier could not invoke the exemption clause contained in the contract between the carrier and the plaintiff.[70] Present-day English law recognizes two other means whereby

---

67 For quasi-immunity of agents, cf. in particular Court of Cassation, 7 December 1973, *RW* 1973-1974, p. 1597, nt. Herbots; Court of Cassation, 3 December 1976, *RW* 1977-1978, p. 1303, nt. Van Oevelen, and Court of Cassation, 8 April 1983, *RW* 1983-1984, p. 163, nt. Herbots. For the similar protection provided for employees, cf. Article 18 of the Arbeidsovereenkomstenwet (Employment Contracts Act). Cf. also E. Dirix, *op. cit.*, Nos. 129 *et seq.*, 276 *et seq.*, 303 and 304, and E. Dirix, *Exoneratiebedingen*, TvP 1988, pp. 1189 and 1195 *et seq.*

68 There is no presumption that such a clause has been made. Cf. Court of Cassation, 27 September 1974, *Arr. Cass.* 1975, 125.

69 Cf. U. Blaurock, *Haftungsfreizeichnung zugunsten Dritter*, ZHR 1982, p. 238 *et seq.*; Larenz, *op. cit.*, § 17 II; Brox, *op. cit.*, Rdnr. 380, and Esser and Schmidt, *op. cit.*, § 36 V. Cf. also Heinrichs, *op. cit.*, § 328, Rdnr. 17 and Rdnr. 94 *et seq.*; Soergel, *op. cit.*, § 328, Rdnr. 90, and Anhang zu § 328, Rdnr. 42 *et seq.*; Jauernig, *op. cit.*, § 328, Anm. IV 2 b ee, and § 328, Anm. III 3 c; Erman, *op. cit.*, § 328, Rdnr. 18, and Palandt, *op. cit.*, § 276, Rdnr. 60, Einf. v. § 328, Rdnr. 8, and § 328, Rdnr. 20. Cf. also BGH, *NJW* 62, 388.

70 See House of Lords [1962], *AC* 446, [1962] 2 *All ER* 1. In a dissenting opinion, Lord Denning advocates extension for the benefit of the stevedore. Lord Denning is among those who take the view that third-party stipulations should be allowed.

exemption clauses may be extended to a certain degree for the benefit of third parties: the assumption of an 'implied contract' between the third party and the other party to the contract with the exemptor, and the concept of 'agency'.[71] The latter is based on the concept of representation.[72] In jurisprudence, agency is the main concept used to extend exemption clauses for the benefit of third parties. The decisive case in this connection is The Eurymedon.[73] Here the stevedore — who was a third party to a contract between the carrier and the plaintiff — was held to be protected by the exemption clause contained in the contract of carriage.

In France, the prevailing opinion in recent decades has been that an extra-contractual action cannot be brought against a contracting party who has caused injury to a contractually involved third party.[74] The consequence of this view is that, in the case of *linked contracts*, an injured party wishing to sue a contractually involved third party — e.g. the other party's servant or independent agent — rather than the other contracting party, must sue for breach of contract rather than unlawful action. In recent years, this interpretation has been repeatedly confirmed in judgments by the French Court of Cassation.[75] The defendant in such a contractual action may invoke exemption clauses contained in the contract.[76] However, in a recent pronouncement dated 21 July 1991, the Plenary Assembly of the Court of Cassation appears to have halted this development whereby the third-party liability was considered a purely contractual matter.[77] On this occasion the Court of Cassation held that a customer could not bring a contractual action for damages against a subcontractor whose work was shoddy. According to the Court of Cassation, there was no contractual link between the subcontractor and the customer. Recognition of a subcontractor's contractual liability towards a customer would conflict with CC Article 1165, in which the doctrine of privity is codified. In

---

71 Cf. G. H. Treitel, *op. cit.*, pp. 552-558, and Cheshire, Fifoot & Furmston, *op. cit.*, pp. 165-172.

72 However, agency is not quite the same as the continental concept of representation. For agency, see C. Æ. Uniken Venema, *op. cit.*, No. 55.

73 See New Zealand Shipping Co. Ltd. v. A. M. Satterthwaite & Co. Ltd., The Eurymedon [1975], *AC* 154, [1974] 1 *All ER* 1015, discussed by G. H. Treitel, *op. cit.*, p. 554 *et seq.*, with references to other jurisprudence and literature.

74 This view has become particularly prevalent since 1975. See B. Teyssié, *Les groupes de contrats*, Paris 1975, Préface J.-M. Mousseron, Nos. 492-495 and 564-572; J. Huet, *Responsabilité contractuelle et responsabilité délictuelle*, thèse Paris II, 1978, 2ᵉ partie; J. Neret, *Le sous-contrat*, Paris 1979, Préface P. Catala, 2ᵉ partie; F. Bertrand, *L'opposabilité du contrat aux tiers*, thèse Paris II, 1979, No. 277 *et seq.*; M. Espagnon, *La règle du non-cumul de responsabilités contractuelle et délictuelle*, thèse Paris I, 1980, No. 188 *et seq.* See also G. Durry, *La distinction de la responsabilité contractuelle et de la responsabilité délictuelle in Cours McGill*, Montreal 1986, Nos. 120-128.

75 See Cass. Civ. 1ʳᵉ, 21 June 1988, *La Semaine Juridique 1988*, Éd. G, II, 21125, and Cass. Civ. 1ʳᵉ, 31 October 1989, *La Semaine Juridique 1990*, Éd. G, II, 21568.

76 In this connection, see Christian Larroumet, *La Semaine Juridique 1988*, Éd. G, I, 3357.

77 See Cass. Ass. Plén., 12 July 1991, *La Semaine Juridique 1991*, Éd. G, II, 21743.

such cases, then, the customer must bring an extra-contractual action for damages. French law rarely if ever permits exemption from extra-contractual liability. It is generally held that CC Article 1382 *et seq.* can never be waived.[78] The result is that a third party — whether a servant or an independent agent — who is sued on an extra-contractual basis cannot invoke an exemption clause contained in a contract to which he is a third party.

c Qualitative Rights

A further exception to the principle that contracts cannot confer rights upon third parties is the legal transfer of qualitative rights to successors by particular title. Where a right *susceptible of transfer* and *resulting from a contract relates to property*[79] *belonging to the creditor in such a fashion that he only retains an interest in that right as long as he retains the property*, the right is automatically transferred to the person who acquires the property by particular title (cf. BW Article 6:251, paragraph 1).[80] Not only contractually stipulated rights, but all rights arising out of a contractual legal relationship — including for example rights in respect of failure to fulfil an obligation — are covered by this article. However, a qualitative right can be transferred to the successor by particular title only if it is susceptible of transfer[81] and if there is a close enough link between the property to be transferred and the right in question. If there is no such link — i.e. if the right is not qualitative —, the parties may still confer the right on the successor by particular title by cession or by making a third-party stipulation.

In Dutch law prior to 1905, it was held that not only qualitative rights, but also obligations, were transferred to successors by particular title together with the property.[82] This was inferred from former BW Article 1354. However, ever since HR 3 March 1905, W 8191 (Blaauboer/Berlips), this article has been interpreted in a narrower sense: only qualitative rights are transferred to successors by particular title, and obligations are not.[83] Under Dutch law as it

---

78 Cf. Court of Cassation, 3 January 1933, D 1933, 113, and Court of Cassation, 11 December 1952, D 1953, 317, nt. Savatier. Cf. also G. Viney, T*raité de droit civil V*, Les obligations, La responsabilité: effets, Paris 1988, No. 213 *et seq.*, with reference to other literature.

79 The term *property*, as used in this article, must be interpreted broadly. A *universitas rerum distantium* (a set of goods and liabilities that belong together), including an enterprise, is to be considered as property within the meaning of BW Article 6:251, paragraph 1. Cf. *Asser-Hartkamp II*, Zwolle 1993, No. 397, and MvA II, *Parl. Gesch. Boek 6*, pp. 932-933.

80 Transfer of qualitative rights is governed by BW Article 6:142 *et seq.*

81 The creditor and debtor may have limited or excluded the transferability of the right, or the right itself may be of such a nature as to be untransferable (cf. BW Article 3:83). Strictly personal rights are not transferred to a successor by particular title.

82 Cf., *inter alia*, HR 28 January 1841, W 157, and HR 24 April 1884, W 5031.

83 Cf. *Asser-Hartkamp II*, Zwolle 1993, Nos. 396a, 402 and 403a, with references to other literature. See also HR 16 April 1982, *NJ* 1982, 580, nt. WMK, and HR 17 May 1985, *NJ* 1986, 760, nt. CJHB and WMK.

now stands, this rule is no longer so relevant as it was (cf. qualitative obligations, discussed below in Section 5).

BW Article 6:251, paragraph 1 offers ample scope for establishing qualitative rights. In neighbouring countries, the scope for this is more limited. Earlier interpretations — since 1905 — of former BW Article 1354 by the Dutch Supreme Court match current interpretations of CC Article 1122 by the French Court of Cassation and of BW/CC Article 1122 by the Belgian Court of Cassation. However, the scope for the transfer of qualitative rights appears to be more restricted in those countries than it used to be in the Netherlands.[84]

BW Article 6:251, paragraph 2 prescribes that, where a service has been agreed to in exchange for the qualitative right, the obligation to perform that service is also transferred to the successor by particular title, at least to the extent that it pertains to the period following the transfer. Together with the acquirer, the alienator remains liable towards the other party (solidarily liable — cf. BW Article 6:6, paragraph 2), except to the extent that the other party can, after the transfer, release himself from his obligation by rescinding or terminating the contract in the event of non-performance of the service.[85] A contract between the alienator and the other party may produce a different result than described above.[86] It may be agreed that the obligation to perform the service in exchange will not be transferred to the person who acquires the property by particular title, or that, by derogation from BW Article 6:251, paragraph 2, the alienator will not be solidarily liable in addition to the acquirer.

The acquirer of the property can be released from the transferred obligation by making a statement to the debtor whereby he repudiates the transfer of the right. In that case, neither the qualitative right nor the obligation to perform the service in exchange are transferred to him.[87] The debtor may give the acquirer a reasonable period within which to make such a statement.[88] If the acquirer fails to do so within that period, both the qualitative right and the associated obligation to perform the service in exchange are definitively transferred. In

---

84   For French law, cf. Weill and Terré, *op. cit.*, No. 511; Carbonnier, *op. cit.*, No. 59; Marty and Raynaud, *op. cit.*, No. 265; Larroumet, *op. cit.*, No. 780 *et seq.*; Mazeaud, Mazeaud and Chabas, *op. cit.*, No. 752 *et seq,*; Flour and Aubert, *op. cit.*, No. 436 *et seq.*, and Malaurie and Aynès, *op. cit.*, No. 660 *et seq.*

85   In this connection, cf. *Asser-Hartkamp II*, Zwolle 1993, Nos. 402-403a; TM, *Parl. Gesch. Boek 6*, p. 928, and MvA II, *Parl. Gesch. Boek 6*, p. 934. For the other party's right to rescind the contract or to suspend performance, see BW Article 6:261, paragraph 2, in conjunction with BW Article 6:265 *et seq.* and BW Articles 6:262-264.

86   Cf. BW Article 6:250 together with Article 6:251, paragraph 2.

87   Cf. BW Article 6:251, paragraph 3. If the statement is made after the right has been transferred, both the right and the associated obligation are deemed never to have been transferred. See TM, *Parl. Gesch. Boek 6*, p. 928.

88   Cf. TM, *Parl. Gesch. Boek 6*, p. 929, and MvA II, *Parl. Gesch. Boek 6*, p. 935. This is an application by analogy of the more general BW Article 6:248.

fact, in addition to a statement by the acquirer (or a contract between the acquirer and the alienator; cf. BW Article 6:250, in conjunction with BW Article 6:251, paragraph 1), the actual juridical act whereby the property is transferred may have as its result that no transfer of the qualitative right and of the obligation to perform the service in exchange will take place.[89]

Prior to 1 January 1992, as we have seen, the situation in Dutch law was the same as in current French and Belgian law. The benefits were transferred to the successor by particular title, but — apart from certain statutory exceptions — the accompanying burdens were not. There was in fact no particular difficulty about this, as long as it was accepted that the debtor could suspend his obligation (towards the acquirer of the property and the qualitative right) to perform a service until the other party (the alienator of the property) had himself performed the agreed service, and that his contract with the other party could, if necessary, be rescinded. In both France and Belgium, this is fairly generally accepted. The debtor is not required to perform as long as it is uncertain whether the other party will do so.

The German BGB includes no provisions governing the transfer of qualitative rights to successors by particular title. Nor, as far as we can tell, is there any reference to this matter in German legal writings.

The issue of qualitative rights is similarly disregarded in English law and in English legal writings.

5 Extension of Contracts *to the Detriment* of Third Parties

The extension of contracts to the detriment of third parties is less readily accepted than extension for their benefit. Nevertheless, there are a number of instances in which the extension of contracts to the detriment of third parties is allowed. Below we will discuss two such instances: defences invoked against third parties, and transfer of qualitative obligations.[90]

a Defences Invoked Against Third Parties
We have already discussed cases in which a third party can invoke a defence — particularly by invoking an exemption clause — on the basis of a contract to which he is not a party. Here, the reverse applies. In certain circumstances, contractual defences which apply between contracting parties can also be used

---

89   Cf. BW Article 6:251, paragraph 4.
90   Other examples of extension of contracts to the detriment of third parties will not be discussed here. Cf. for instance BW Article (7:424 together with) 7:421. For other examples, cf. A. S. Hartkamp, *Compendium van het vermogensrecht volgens het nieuwe Burgerlijk Wetboek*, Deventer 1990, No. 370, and *Asser-Hartkamp II*, Zwolle 1993, No. 385.

against third parties. Once again, exemption clauses are a good example. We will also discuss the right of retention. Other types of defence will not be considered here.[91]

The question of whether exemption clauses contained in a contract may be invoked as defences against persons who are not parties to the contract has been the subject of numerous pronouncements by the courts. It is difficult to lay down general rules on the subject. In HR 20 June 1986, NJ 1987, 35, nt. G; *AA* 1986, p. 775, nt. SK (Deka-Hanno/Citronas), the Dutch Supreme Court affirmed the basic principle that contracts are only binding upon the contracting parties. Exceptions to this principle may be allowed in certain cases, but only if sufficiently justified by the nature of the specific case. The Supreme Court states three circumstances (the list is not exhaustive) which are of relevance when deciding whether an exemption clause should be allowed to operate to the detriment of a third party in a specific case. These relevant circumstances include the assumption by the party invoking the clause (A), in the light of the conduct of the third party (C), that he will be able to invoke the clause in respect of goods entrusted to him by the other contracting party (B), as well as the nature of the contract and of the particular clause, together with the particular relationship of the third party to the party invoking the clause.[92] At the same time, account must be taken of statutory arrangements, especially if statutory provision is made for certain specified types of contract to be extended to third parties within certain limits and if the case concerned falls within the scope of these arrangements. In this particular case, the Supreme Court did not allow extension, nor did it do so in its judgment HR 9 June 1989, *NJ* 1990, 40, nt. JLPC, (Vojvodina/ECT).[93] All Supreme Court decisions on cases involving extension of exemption clauses to third parties have been based on

---

91 Cf., *inter alia*, BW Article 6:11, Article 6:107, paragraph 2, Article 6:108, paragraph 3 and Article 6:145.

92 In this connection, the Supreme Court refers to its judgment of 7 March 1969, *NJ* 1969, 249, nt. GJS, in which extension was allowed, and its judgment of 12 January 1979, *NJ* 1979, 362, nt. ARB, in which an exemption clause was likewise allowed to operate to the detriment of a third party.

93 For extension of exemption clauses to third parties, cf. also HR 25 March 1966, *NJ* 1966, 279, nt. GJS, and HR 30 June 1978, *NJ* 1978, 694, nt. GJS. See also *Asser-Van der Grinten I (De vertegenwoordiging)*, Zwolle 1990, No. 117, and the literature cited in *Asser-Hartkamp II*, Zwolle 1993, No. 386. For statutory provisions on extension of exemption clauses and other types of defence to the detriment of third parties, cf. BW Article 7:608, paragraph 2 (together with paragraph 4), on depositaries, and BW Article 7:608, paragraph 3 together with paragraph 2 (and paragraph 4), on sub-depositaries, as well as various provisions of the law pertaining to carriage. See, *inter alia*, BW Articles 8:71, 8:72 (together with Article 8:71), 8:490, 8:569, 8:955, 8:1132, 8:1154 (together with Article 8:1132) and 8:1197. Cf. also BW Article 8:364. Caution is required when applying the provisions of the aforementioned articles by analogy to contracts other than contracts of deposit or carriage (or similar agreements). See MvT, *Parl. Gesch. Boek 7 (Inv. 3, 5 and 6)*, p. 407, in connection with MvA II, *Parl. Gesch. Boek 6*, p. 918.

reasonableness together with the specific circumstances of the case concerned. It is therefore difficult to lay down general rules for this kind of extension. In order to determine whether a liability clause should be extended to the detriment of the third party (C), we believe it is essential to determine whether the other contracting party (B) was empowered, in his relationship with the third party (C), to enter into contracts with A that related to things belonging to the third party (C) or to C's interests, and that contained liability clauses binding upon the third party. In this context, the term 'empowered' is to be interpreted as including any apparent empowerment which A was justified in assuming.[94]

Thus, where an intermediary (B), acting on C's instructions, enters into a contract with A in his own name, A will often be able to invoke against C an exemption clause contained in the contract between A and B. However, A will not be able to do so if he was not entitled to assume that B was empowered to enter into a contract stipulating such an exemption in respect of C's interests. If A has entered into the contract with B as B's servant or independent agent, he will not normally be able to invoke against C the exemption clause contained in the contract between A and B. In such cases, the conditions under which the work is to be carried out will be determined by the principal contract between C and B. In principle, B is not empowered to enter into a contract with his agent A whereby additional limitations of A's liability are made 'binding' upon C.

In French law, we have already seen that contracts cannot, in principle, include exemption clauses in respect of liability in tort (i.e. extra-contractual liability). Statutory provisions under the law of tort cannot be waived. Accordingly, if an extra-contractual action for damages is brought against contracting party A by third party C, an attempt by A to invoke against C the exemption clause contained in his contract with B will fail. Since the end of the last century, the French Court of Cassation has recognized the right of a non-contractually involved third party (the *penitus extraneus*) to bring an action in tort.[95] As already explained under item b of Section 4 above, the Court of Cassation has in recent years, in a number of cases involving linked contracts, held that a contractually involved third party (C) could only bring a contractual action against the injuring party (A). In view of the Court's change of course in its aforementioned 1991 judgment, it seems safe to conclude that a contractually involved third party C can henceforth bring a tort (and not a contractual) action. If only because it is held that such claims can never be set aside, the injuring party A will not be able to invoke the exemption clause. Accordingly, the question of extension to third parties does not arise.

---

94   This fits in with BW Article 7:608, paragraph 4 and MvT, *Parl. Gesch. Boek 7 (Inv.* 3, 5 and 6), pp. 406-407. Cf. also BW Article 3:291, paragraph 2 and MvA II, *Parl. Gesch. Boek 3*, pp. 884-885; MO, *Parl. Gesch. Boek 3*, p. 886, and NvW, *Parl. Gesch. Boek 3*, pp. 887-888.
95   See Court of Cassation, 23 February 1897, S. 898, I, 65.

In Belgium, unlike in France, liability in tort can be limited or excluded. In cases where the injuring party (A) is a servant or an independent agent, the question of extension to third parties does not arise, since agents (whether servants or 'executive agents') are afforded quasi-immunity. In other cases where a tort action *is* allowed, there is no evidence that the Belgian courts permit exemption clauses to be extended to third parties.

As in the Netherlands, the German courts have acknowledged the extension of exemption clauses to third parties in a number of cases. In the case of linked contracts, the injured third party C may bring both a contractual and a tort action against the injuring party A. Pronouncements by the courts indicate that exemption clauses may be extended to third parties even in tort actions.[96] In German literature, such extension is often explained in terms of the theory of the *'Vertrag mit Schutzwirkung für Dritte'* (contract which protects third parties). Though not always explicitly, the German Federal Court bases extension of exemption clauses to third parties on the principle laid down in BGB § 334. A notable pronouncement in this connection was that made by the Imperial Court on 25 November 1911.[97] The case concerned a contract of carriage under which the carrier (B) had employed an agent (A) to transport goods from the quayside to the ship. A's liability was limited under the terms of his contract with B. The goods were subsequently damaged by A, who was sued for damages by the plaintiff C. The Imperial Court held that A could not invoke against C the exemption clause contained in his contract with B. This judgment is in accordance with what we stated earlier about Dutch law with regard to exemption clauses stipulated by servants or independent agents.

In England, the doctrine of privity opposes the extension of exemption clauses to third parties. However, extension is possible in certain circumstances, on the basis of 'agency', 'implied contract' or 'bailment'. However, both the English courts and English legal literature remain wary of the notion.[98] It appears that extension of exemption clauses to third parties is usually only accepted in the case of bailment. Bailment is only possible in the case of moveables, which must actually be surrendered. An example is where the owner of goods takes them to a repairer and allows him to send the work out to a subcontractor.

The second type of defence which we will discuss here is the right of retention, i.e. the power of a creditor to suspend the performance of an obligation to surrender a thing to his debtor until payment of the debt.

---

96   See, for example, *HansGZ* 1902, 208; 1912, 165, 167; *RGZ* 66, 363; 70, 174, 176 *et seq.*; 75, 169, 172; *BGHZ* 17, 214, 217; 64, 355; 46, 140, 142; BGH, *NJW* 79, 2148.
97   See *RGZ* 77, 317, 320 *et seq.*
98   See G. H. Treitel, *op. cit.*, p. 558 *et seq.*, and J. Visser, *De werking van contractuele bepalingen ten nadele van derden*, Post Scriptum Reeks, Deventer 1987, Ch. VIII.

The BW contains general statutory provisions on the subject.[99] There are a number of cases in which the right of retention may be invoked against a third party. It may be invoked not only against the debtor, but also against the latter's creditors.[100] It may likewise be invoked against third parties who have acquired a right to the thing *after* the creditor's claim has arisen and the thing has come under his control.[101] Finally, it may also be invoked against third parties with a *prior* right, but only if the creditor's claim results from a contract which the debtor was empowered to enter into in respect of the thing, or if the creditor had no reason to doubt the debtor's empowerment to do so.[102]

The French CC and the Belgian BW/CC contain no general provisions on the right of retention, but they do include provisions regulating the right of retention in specific cases. Through pronouncements by the courts, this has evolved into a more general legal concept. Broadly speaking, the prevailing view in France is that the right of retention can be invoked against non-contracting parties in the same instances as in Dutch law.[103] In Belgium, there is uncertainty regarding the extension of the right of retention to third parties. The courts have made few pronouncements on the subject, and the literature is by no means unanimous.[104] Extension to third parties appears to be less readily admitted in Belgium than in the Netherlands or France. The prevailing doctrine in Belgium is that the right of retention can be invoked against ordinary creditors as well as

---

99   See BW Section 3.10.4. This section is very closely related to the provisions on the right to suspend performance in BW Section 6.1.7. For special statutory provisions on the right of retention, see, *inter alia*, BW Articles 8:30, 8:69, 8:489, 8:510 (together with Article 8:489), 8:954, 8:980 (together with Article 8:954) and 8:1131.

100   Cf. BW Article 6:53 together with BW Articles 6:52, 6:57 and 3:290.

101   Cf. BW Article 3:291, paragraph 1 and MvA II, *Parl. Gesch. Boek 3*, p. 883.

102   Cf. BW Article 3:291, paragraph 2 and MvA II, *Parl. Gesch. Boek 3*, pp. 884-885; MO, *Parl. Gesch. Boek 3*, p. 886, and NvW, *Parl. Gesch. Boek 3*, pp. 887-888. For Dutch law prior to 1 January 1992, see HR 16 March 1933, *NJ* 1933, 790, nt. EMM; HR 1 May 1964, *NJ* 1965, 339, nt. JHB; HR 13 May 1988, *NJ* 1989, 201, nt. WMK, and former BW Article 1576o.

103   See Court of Cassation, 31 March 1851, *D* 1851, 1, 65; Court of Cassation, 13 May 1861, *D* 1861, 1, 328; Court of Cassation, 8 December 1868, *D* 1869, I, 76, and Court of Cassation, 22 May 1962, D 1965, 58, nt. Rodière. See also Gabriel Marty, Pierre Raynaud and Philippe Jestaz, *Droit civil, Les sûretés, La publicité foncière*, 2ᵉ édition, Paris 1987, No. 49 *et seq.*; Henri and Léon Mazeaud, Jean Mazaud and François Chabas, *Leçons de Droit civil*, Tome III, premier volume, Sûretés, Publicité foncière, 6ᵉ édition, Paris 1988, No. 126 *et seq.*; Philippe Simler and Philippe Delebecque, *Droit civil, Les sûretés, La publicité fonciaire*, Paris 1989, Nos. 401 and 419-421; Michel Cabrillac and Christian Mouly, *Droit des sûretés*, Paris 1990, No. 563 *et seq.*; C.C.J. Aarts, *Het retentierecht*, Arnhem 1990, No. 400 and Ch. 14A, especially Nos. 644 and 645, and Philippe Malaurie and Laurent Aynès, *Cours de Droit civil*, Les sûretés, La publicité foncière, 5ᵉ édition, Paris 1993, No. 447, all with references to other literature and jurisprudence. Cf. also J.E. Fesevur, *Retentierecht*, Serie Recht en Praktijk No. 49, Deventer 1988, pp. 154 and 184-185.

104   See C.C.J. Aarts, *op. cit.*, No. 401 and Ch. 14B, especially Nos. 660-664, whith references to literature and jurisprudence.

against the debtor, and also against the receiver in cases of bankruptcy.[105] According to De Page, these are the limits of extension of the right of retention to third parties.[106] A number of writers go somewhat further and assume that, under certain circumstances, the right of retention may also be invoked against preferential creditors, such as mortgage lenders or creditors with privileged claims on specific property or on all property. However, opinions differ as to the circumstances under which this would be possible.[107] There is also disagreement as to whether the right of retention may be invoked against the person acquiring the retained thing by particular title.[108] In recent literature there have been suggestions that the right of retention should be very broadly extended to third parties. Dirix and De Corte, for example, take the view that the right of retention may be invoked against all third parties, including preferential creditors, the third-party owner with a prior right and the person acquiring the retained thing by particular title.[109]

Like Dutch law, German law contains general provisions on the right of retention (known in German as *Zurückbehaltungsrecht*).[110] It also provides for a separate right of retention in connection with commercial transactions (known as *kaufmännisches Zurückbehaltungsrecht*).[111] The general right of retention cannot be invoked against a third-party owner with a prior right or against a third-

---

105 Cf. Court of Cassation, 7 November 1935, *Pasicrisie belge* 1936, I, 38, and L. Lamine, *Het retentierecht*, Reeks Recht en Praktijk No. 3, Antwerp 1982, No. 269, with references to other literature and jurisprudence. For a different view see, *inter alia*, J. Berten, *Le droit de rétention et ses effets à l'égard des tiers*, JT 1956, 112-113, and — with an explicit rejection of the aforementioned judgment of the Court of Cassation — Kh. Bergen, 18 September 1978, *BRH* 1979, 88.

106 See H. de Page and R. Dekkers, *Traité élémentaire de droit civil belge*, Brussels 1948-1974 (10 Volumes), VI, Nos. 824-827.

107 For various different views, cf., *inter alia*, A. Clerens, *Het recht van terughouding en het voorrecht van de vervoerder op het nationaal en internationaal plan*, RW 1957-1958, p. 1277; P. van Ommeslaghe, *Observations sur les effets et l'étendue du droit de rétention et de l'exceptio non adimpleti contractus, spécialement en cas de faillite du débiteur*, RCJB 1963, p. 82-83, and RPDB, Tw. Rétention, Nos. 162 and 163. Cf. also L. Lamine, *op. cit.*, No. 291, and C.C.J. Aarts, *op. cit.*, Nos. 661 and 662.

108 L. Lamine, *op. cit.*, No. 296, takes the view that it may. Cf. also Kh. Antwerpen, 21 May 1931, *Jur. Anvers* 1931, 169, and Kh. Namen, 12 December 1946, *Jur. Liège* 1946-47, 180. De Page, *op. cit.*, No. 827, takes the opposite view. Cf. also Kh. Antwerpen, 3 August 1953, *Jur. Anvers* 1954, 53. For the question of whether the right of retention may be invoked against a third-party owner with a prior right, cf. L. Lamine, *op. cit.*, Nos. 302-304, and C.C.J. Aarts, *op. cit.*, No. 664.

109 See E. Dirix and R. de Corte, *Zekerheidsrechten*, Reeks Recht en Praktijk No. 17, Deurne 1992, No. 419. See also Nicole Verheyden-Jeanmart and Nathalie Lepot-Joly, 'L'opposabilité des contrats à l'égard des tiers et assimiles', in: *Les effets du contrat à l'égard des tiers*, sous la direction de Marcel Fontaine et Jacques Ghestin, Paris 1992, pp. 245-248.

110 See BGB § 273 and § 274. See also BGB § 1000 *et seq.*

111 Cf. HGB (German Code of Commercial Law) § 369 *et seq.* It is conceivable that both the commercial right of retention and the general right of retention may be invoked in specific cases. Cf. RG, *JW* 34, 2971.

party creditor, but may be invoked against the person acquiring the retained thing by particular title.[112] It currently remains unclear whether, and if so to what extent, the courts can be induced to take a more flexible view. The overriding principle remains that the right of retention can only be invoked against a contracting party. In principle, this also applies to the commercial right of retention. However, for extension of the commercial right of retention to third parties (such as the subsequent owner, usufructuary or pledgee of the retained thing), see the text of HGB § 369 II, in conjunction with the relevant provisions of the BGB.[113]

English law recognizes a concept of possessory lien which — to a certain extent — resembles the continental concept of right of retention.[114] A possessory lien may be particular or general. A particular lien gives the possessor the right to retain goods until a debt arising in connection with those goods is paid. A general lien gives him the right to retain goods not only against debts arising specifically in connection with them, but also against other debts owed by the owner of the goods. General liens arise by express agreement or by trade usage, as in the case of factors, bankers and solicitors. The law favours particular rather than general liens. The extension of possessory lien — particular as well as general — to third parties is not systematically discussed in English legal literature. To the extent that extension of specific forms of possessory lien to third parties is discussed at all, the discussion is generally confined to a brief comment. This usually concerns the possible extension of possessory lien to a third-party owner with a prior or posterior right. Such extension to third parties is admitted under certain circumstances. No general indication can be given of the extent to which extension of possessory lien to third parties is admitted in English law. At the same time, it would not be practicable, in the context of this article, to embark on a detailed discussion of the various forms of possessory lien.

---

112 Cf. J. E. Fesevur, *op. cit.*, pp. 154 and 185; C.C.J. Aarts, *op. cit.*, Nos. 401, 404 and 413, and E. B. Rank-Berenschot, *Over de scheidslijn tussen goederen- en verbintenissenrecht*, dissertation at the University of Leiden, Deventer 1992, p. 282. For invocation of the right of retention against a person acquiring the retained thing by particular title, cf. BGB § 986 II together with *BGHZ* 64, 122, 124 and BGH, *NJW-RR* 86, 282. In case of a third-party stipulation, the promisor can invoke the right of retention against the stipulator as well as the third party. Cf. BGB § 334 and BGH, *NJW* 80, 450.

113 In this connection, cf. Baumbach, Duden and Hopt, *Handelsgesetzbuch*, 28. Auflage, Munich 1989, § 369, point 4; Karl-Hermann Capelle, *Handelsrecht*, fortgeführt von Claus-Wilhelm Canaris, 21. Auflage, Munich 1989, § 28 II 4 a and § 28 III 2; Heymann, *Handelsgesetzbuch (ohne Seerecht)*, Band 4, Viertes Buch, Berlin and New York 1990, § 369, Rdnr. 33 *et seq.*, and Hans Brox, *Handelsrecht und Wertpapierrecht*, 10. Auflage, Munich 1993, Rdnr. 322.

114 Possessory or common law lien needs to be distinguished from maritime lien and equitable lien. Other than with possessory lien, maritime lien and equitable lien do not depend upon possession. These various forms of lien also differ in other respects, which will not, however, be discussed here. For lien in general, cf. Alfred H. Silvertown, *The law of lien*, London and Edinburgh, 1988.

b Qualitative Obligations

We have already seen that, under the new BW, obligations may, within certain limits, automatically be transferred to a person acquiring property by particular title. This applies to the qualitative obligations specified in BW Article 6:252, as well as to the contractually agreed obligation to perform a service in exchange for a qualitative right (see item c of Section 4 above). There are also certain specific statutory exceptions to the rule that obligations are not transferred when property is transferred by particular title.[115]

A *contract* may stipulate that the obligation of one of the parties to *tolerate* or *not to do* something in respect of his *registered property* will be transferred to those who will acquire the property by particular title, and that the stipulation will also bind those who will acquire from the title-holder a right to use the property (cf. BW Article 6:252, paragraph 1). The scope of BW Article 6:252 is limited: it is only intended to apply to the obligation to tolerate or not to do something.[116] In the case of an obligation *to do* something, only a perpetual clause is in principle possible.[117] A further restriction lies in the fact that this article only refers to obligations in respect of registered property, i.e. property the transfer or creation of which requires entry in the public registers provided for that purpose. BW Article 6:252, paragraph 5 also prescribes that the article does not apply to obligations which (under the terms of a contract) limit a title-holder in his power to alienate or encumber the property.[118]

---

115 Cf. BW Article 7A:1612 and Article 34 of the Pachtwet (Agricultural Holdings Act). Both articles assume the legal transfer of rights and obligations under a lease from the alienator of the property to the acquirer. Following the transfer, the lessee can invoke his rights in respect of the new lessor and is also bound with respect to the latter. With reference to leases, cf. also BW Articles 3:217 and 5:94. See also, *inter alia*, BW Articles 7A:1635, 7A:1639aa *et seq.*, 8:375 and 8:894.

116 Cf. TM, *Parl. Gesch. Boek 6*, p. 936, and MvA II, *Parl. Gesch. Boek 6*, pp. 943-944, as well as *Asser-Hartkamp II*, Zwolle 1993, No. 407. Where there is a penalty clause reinforcing the obligation to tolerate or not to do something, the obligation under that clause is transferred to the legal successor, to the extent that the penalty has not yet been forfeited at the time of transfer. Cf. also BW Article 6:157, paragraph 4 and MvA II, *Parl. Gesch. Boek 6*, pp. 582 and 944. It is likewise arguable that an obligation to do something which may be deemed a subsidiary obligation to the principal obligation to tolerate or not to do something, and which at the same time is conducive to a satisfactory exercise of the right and does not impose a disproportionate burden upon the debtor, may be transferred to the successor by particular title together with the principal obligation. Cf. *Asser-Hartkamp II*, Zwolle 1993, No. 407.

117 Within certain limits, an obligation to do something may also be part of a servitude. Cf. BW Article 5:71. In this connection, see *Asser-Beekhuis II Zakenrecht*, Zwolle 1990, Nos. 207, 213, 214, 241 and 242. On the differences between qualitative obligations, perpetual clauses and servitudes, see Asser-Mijnssen-De Haan, Zwolle 1992, Nos. 44 and 49-54, and *Asser-Hartkamp II*, Zwolle 1993, Nos. 411-413, which both refer to other literature.

118 Cf. MvA II, *Parl. Gesch. Boek 6*, pp. 944-945 and 947, as well as MvA II, *Parl. Gesch. Boek 6 (Inv. 3, 5 and 6)*, pp. 1822-1823. See also EV II, *Parl. Gesch. Boek 6 (Inv. 3, 5 and 6)*, p. 1823, and Nota II, *Parl. Gesch. Boek 6 (Inv. 3, 5 and 6)*, p. 1823.

However, the aforementioned contract in BW Article 6:252, paragraph 1 is not sufficient; such a contract only binds the contracting parties. In order for it to be extended to third parties, a *notarial deed* must be drawn up of the contract between the parties, and it must then be *entered in the public registers*.[119] Where the creditor no longer has a reasonable interest in the performance of the obligation and it is unlikely that this interest will revive, the court may, at the debtor's request, modify the effects of the contract or rescind all or part of it.[120] The same applies if at least ten years have lapsed since the contract was entered into and the unmodified continuation of the obligation is contrary to the public interest.[121]

Where a service has been agreed to in exchange for the qualitative obligation, the right to that service is also transferred upon the transfer of the obligation, to the extent that it pertains to the period following the transfer and that the stipulation with respect to the service has also been entered in the public registers.[122] Where the right has already lapsed, the question of its transfer obviously no longer arises.

In Dutch law prior to 1 January 1992, there was no rule of the kind now laid down in BW Article 6:252, nor is such a rule to be found in neighbouring countries. In French and Belgian law, for example, qualitative obligations are not transferred to successors by particular title, barring certain statutory

---

119 Cf. BW Article 6:252, paragraph 2 and MvA II, *Parl. Gesch. Boek 6* (*Inv.* 3, 5 and 6), p. 1821. Even if public registration has taken place, BW Article 6:252, paragraph 3 prescribes that the clause cannot be invoked against (a) persons who, prior to registration, have acquired by particular title a right to the property or a right to use it, (b) the seizor of the property or of a right encumbering it, if the registration had not yet taken place at the time of registration of the minutes of seizure, or (c) persons who have acquired their right from a person who, by virtue of the provisions of sub (a) or (b), was not bound by the stipulated obligation. For provisions concerning receivers, cf. Article 35a of the Faillissementswet (Bankruptcy Act). Finally, cf. also BW Article 7:15, paragraph 2.

120 Cf. BW Article 6:259, paragraph 1, sub b, and Article 6:260.

121 Cf. BW Article 6:259, paragraph 1, sub a, and Article 6:260. For qualifications regarding the ten-year period, see BW Article 6:259, paragraph 2. BW Article 6:259 also applies to perpetual clauses. Cf. TM, *Parl. Gesch. Boek 6*, pp. 980-981, and MvA II, *Parl. Gesch. Boek 6*, pp. 984-985.

122 Cf. BW Article 6:252, paragraph 4. In this connection, see TM, *Parl. Gesch. Boek 6*, p. 937, and MvA II, *Parl. Gesch. Boek 6*, pp. 946-947. Cf. also BW Article 6:250. As in BW Article 6:251, paragraph 2, the benefits and burdens are linked. Transfer of the right to the service agreed to in exchange for the qualitative obligation is governed by BW Article 6:142 *et seq.*

exceptions.[123] Similarly, qualitative obligations are not recognized in German law.[124]

6 Conclusion

The doctrine of privity of contract applies in each of the legal systems that we have discussed. Exceptions or mitigations to the principle are allowed not only in the Netherlands, but also in the other countries studied. Here we have merely discussed a few important general exceptions. Such a limited investigation cannot reliably indicate whether it is realistic to expect a European Civil Code to reconcile the existing differences between the various legal systems with regard to contract and third parties. We will confine ourselves to the following comments:

- The doctrine of privity of contract is admitted in all five of the countries which we have examined. In England – at least when it comes to pronouncements – the principle is adhered to far more strictly than in the other countries.
- The extension of a contract *for the benefit* of third parties appears to raise fewer problems than its extension *to their detriment*. Third-party stipulations are allowed in each of the countries studied, except England, where similar results may be achieved in certain cases with the help of the concepts of 'implied contract' and 'agency'. Both concepts originate in Anglo-American law and do not readily fit into the continental legal system. At the same time, the vast majority of English legal practitioners appear to have great difficulty in accepting the continental concept of third-party stipulations.
- The cases which we have discussed point to fairly considerable differences regarding the extension of contracts to the detriment of third parties. Where such extension is allowed, the theoretical arguments used in support of it differ.
- The issue of extension of contracts to third parties arises in a wide variety of contexts, many of which we have not discussed, such as take-over of debts, take-over of contracts, cession, subrogation, subordination, and what is known in German as *'Drittschadensliquidation'* (liquidation of third-party damage). In order to incorporate the doctrine of privity of contract and the

---

123 For Belgian law, cf. BW/CC Article 1122, as well as Court of Cassation, 6 February 1913, *Pasicrisie belge* 1913, I, 93, and Court of Cassation, 16 September 1966, *Arr. Cass.* 1967, 67, *JT* 1967, 59. For French law, cf. CC Article 1122. See also Weill and Terré, *op. cit.*, Nos. 512 and 513; Carbonnier, *op. cit.*, No. 59; Marty and Raynaud, *op. cit.*, No. 266; Larroumet, *op. cit.*, No. 788; Mazeaud, Mazeaud and Chabas, *op. cit.*, No. 755; Flour and Aubert, *op. cit.*, No. 446 *et seq.*, and Malaurie and Aynès, *op. cit.*, No. 662. It remains unclear whether the French and Belgian courts can be induced to take a more flexible view on the subject.

124 Nevertheless, a system with somewhat similar results can be found in BGB § 1090 *et seq.* (*beschränkte persönliche Dienstbarkeiten*).

exceptions and mitigations to it into a uniform European system, a central part of European law of contract would need to be codified, together with some adjacent areas of patrimonial law. We are by no means convinced that such an exercise would succeed.

B — Extra-Contractual Liability

CHAPTER 14

Restitution and Unjust Enrichment

William John Swadling

1 Introduction

There is no doubt that, as a matter of commercial expediency, the harmonization of the law of restitution or unjust enrichment in the Member States of the European Community is a desirable objective. Professor Hartkamp has already pointed out that a unification of the rules of contract law would be only partially successful if, for example, the tortious liability of a producer of goods varied from one country to the next. The same can equally be said for the law of restitution. A harmonisation of the rules of contract would also be in vain if the various domestic laws of restitution provided different responses to such questions as whether moneys paid under a contract of sale which was frustrated before delivery of the goods must be returned to the purchaser or whether a vendor who, in breach of contract, sold the contract goods to a third party was liable to disgorge the profits made from his breach.

This chapter will examine whether such a codification is possible. A European-wide codification would of course necessitate an assimilation of the civil and common law rules of restitution. Given the Roman antecedents of the law of restitution evident in both the common law and the civil law, one might be forgiven for assuming that the two systems were essentially the same. Nothing, however, could be further from the truth. This is not to say that the two systems will never reach the same result in a given case. Although they often do achieve similar results, *albeit* via different routes, important differences remain.

The essay will take as examples typical of civil law systems the laws of Germany and France and ask how the German, French and English legal systems handle the various types of restitutionary claims.[1] Where appropriate, reference will also be made to the provisions of the new Dutch Civil Code. We begin, however, with an examination of the basic structure of restitutionary claims in each of the three jurisdictions.

---

1   For an excellent account in English, see K Zweigert & H Kötz, *An Introduction to Comparative Law* (2nd ed, 1984), vol II, 229-287. See also B Dickson, 'The Law of Restitution in the Federal Republic of Germany: A Comparison with English Law', (1987) 36 International & Comparative Law Quarterly 751 and R. Zimmerman, *The Law of Obligations — Roman Foundations of the Civilian Tradition* (1990), pp 834-901.

2 The Structure of Unjust Enrichment Claims

For a continental lawyer, the most notable feature of the English law of restitution, which is almost entirely judge-made, is its lack of a general enrichment action. As Lord Diplock noted in *Orakpo* v. *Manson Investments Ltd*:

'...there is no general doctrine of unjust enrichment recognised in English law. What it does is to provide specific remedies in particular cases of what might be classified as unjust enrichment in a legal system that is based on civil law.'[2]

Although those cases in which English law does allow an action for restitution may be said to be based on a general *principle* against unjust enrichment,[3] in the sense that it 'constitutes a unifying legal concept which explains why the law recognises, in a variety of distinct categories of case, an obligation on the part of a defendant to make...restitution for a benefit derived at the expense of a plaintiff',[4] it is important to stress that in English law there is no general *doctrine* of unjust enrichment. For a restitution action to succeed in England, the plaintiff must be able to point to some specific factor which makes the receipt of wealth by the defendant 'unjust'. It is not simply a case of showing that the defendant has no legitimate reason to retain the enrichment. And the process of finding an 'unjust factor' does not give to the judge a power to 'assert a judicial discretion to do whatever idiosyncratic notions of what is fair and just might dictate'.[5] As one of the leading English exponents of this branch of the law has noted, the 'unjust factor' must 'look downwards to the cases'.[6] In other words, the 'unjust factor' must be found to exist in the case-law of the subject, with the consequence that a plaintiff who is unable to fit his or her cause of action into one of the recognised heads of restitutionary claim will be unable to recover. Thus, there is in English law a *numerus clausus* of restitutionary causes of action, and one of the main tasks of the common-law restitution scholar is the elucidation of the factors which come within that list.

---

2   [1978] AC 95, 104.

3   For many years the English courts laboured under the mistaken view, taken from a mistranslation of the words *quasi ex contractu*, that the obligation to make restitution rested on an implied contract to repay: see Peter Birks & Grant McLeod, 'The Implied Contract Theory of Quasi-Contract: Civilian Opinion Current in the Century Before Blackstone' (1986) 6 Oxford Journal of Legal Studies 46. This had the unfortunate inhibiting effect of denying restitutionary claims in circumstances in which an express contractual claim could not be made. The implied contract heresy was, however, firmly put to rest by the Australian High Court in *Pavey & Matthews Pty Ltd* v. *Paul* (1987) 69 ALR 577, and, with rare exceptions, no longer forms the basis of judicial reasoning in this area.

4   *Pavey & Matthews* v. *Paul* (1987) 69 ALR 577, 604, *per* Deane J.

5   *Ibid.*

6   Peter Birks, *An Introduction to the Law of Restitution* (1989) p 22.

French and German law, by contrast, do have general enrichment actions. In France there are a number of instances of specific restitutionary liability provided for in the *Code Civil*, the most important of which concern payments not due (*paiement de l'indu*) and management of another's affairs (*gestion d'affaires*), provisions contained in arts. 1371 ff of the Code. However, the narrowness of these codal provisions led the French courts in the late nineteenth century[7] to develop a more general action of '*enrichissement sans cause*' to operate as a supplement to the specific codal provisions. In applying this general enrichment action the methodology adopted by the French courts is to ask first, whether the plaintiff has suffered an impoverishment and the defendant a corresponding enrichment and secondly, whether there is any reason, *eg* that the payment was made pursuant to a contract or some other legal duty, which legitimises the defendant's retention of that enrichment. The main factors which limit such a claim are first, that there is no other legal basis on which the plaintiff might ground his or her claim (the principle of *subsidiarité*) and second, in order to preserve the institution of gifts, that the plaintiff did not transfer the wealth voluntarily under a duty of honour or morality.

The Unjust Enrichment sections of the new Dutch Civil Code are clearly influenced by the French model. Title 4 of Book 6 is headed, 'Obligations from sources other than tort and contract.' It contains three sections, the first (article 6:198) dealing with management of another's affairs, the second (article 6:203) with performances not owed, and the third (article 6:212) with unjustified enrichment. Although prior to this there were codal provisions on *negotiorum gestio* and *solutio indebiti*, the Hoge Raad had denied the existence of any general enrichment action,[8] an omission now remedied with the enactment of the code. The only remaining difference between France and the Netherlands is that in the latter the supplementary enrichment action appears expressly in the code, whereas in the former it is judge-made. What is not clear, however, is why, given that the code enacts a general enrichment action, it was thought necessary to retain specific provisions on *negotiorum gestio* and *solutio indebiti*.

In German law a general enrichment action exists as a result of a specific provision of the Bürgerliches Gesetzbuch (BGB), *viz* §812, which provides that:

'A person who without legal justification obtains anything from a person at his expense, whether by transfer or otherwise, is bound to give it up to him. This obligation also arises if the legal justification subsequently ceases to exist or if the transfer does not have the effect envisaged in the transaction.'

---

7   In the *Boudier* case (15th June 1892, DP 1892.I.596).
8   HR 30 January 1959, NJ 1959 no 548.

That general principle is then qualified by the ten articles which immediately follow §812. As with French law, payments made voluntarily or in performance of a moral duty cannot be recovered (§814). Limits are also placed on the recovery of payments which were either illegal or contrary to public policy (§817). But by far the most important qualification on recovery is that contained in §818 para 3, which provides that 'The obligation to surrender or to restore value is excluded insofar as the receiver has ceased to be enriched.'

3 The Grounds of Restitution

English law divides the grounds for restitution (the 'unjust factor') between, on the one hand, *Autonomous Unjust Enrichment*, and, on the other, *Restitution for Wrongs*.[9] The first category, which we might call the substantive part of the subject, contains those restitution-generating facts which are independent of any other branch of the law. The factor which in this class of case makes the transfer of wealth from the plaintiff to the defendant 'unjust' is generally that the plaintiff had no intention or at best an impaired intention to give in the events which happened.[10] Two classes of case are comprised within this category: in the first the plaintiff had no intention to give at all (vitiated intention); in the second he did intend to give but only on a certain basis, which basis has failed to come about (qualified intention). In the category of vitiated intention are cases of transfers through ignorance, mistake and duress, while in that part called qualified intention are included such things as payments made under a contract which is subsequently frustrated or a gift made in contemplation of a wedding which never takes place, cases which in Roman law would fall within the *condictio causa data causa non secuta*. The second category, *Restitution for Wrongs*, is purely remedial in character. The 'unjust factor' here is not to be found within the law of restitution itself. It will instead consist of a breach of a duty laid down in some other part of the law. A typical case is the one where a defendant breaches a duty of confidence owed to a plaintiff and thereby makes a profit for himself.[11] Is the plaintiff confined to an action for the actual loss he himself has suffered (which might be nominal) or can he recover the enrichment which the defendant made at his expense, the term 'at his expense' being used in the sense of 'by doing a wrong to him'? This is, at present, one of the most contentious issues in the English law of

---

9   The scheme which follows is that described in Birks, n 1.
10   There are two further categories of autonomous unjust enrichment. First, there is the much disputed category of 'free acceptance' and second, there are those cases, such as *Woolwich Building Society* v. *Inland Revenue Commissioners (No 2)* [1992] 3 All ER 737 (recovery of taxes paid pursuant to an *ultra vires* demand), where restitution is given for reasons of public policy, in this case respect for the constitutional principle enshrined in the Bill of Rights 1688 that there should be no taxation by the Crown without Parliamentary consent.
11   *Attorney General* v. *Guardian Newspapers (No 2)* [1990] AC 109.

restitution. There is no doubt that some wrongs do generate a restitutionary remedy; the example of breach of confidence posited above is one. What is in doubt is exactly which wrongs do and which do not yield a restitutionary remedy.

As we have already seen, the grounds for restitution in France and Germany are more widely drawn than in England. Both French and German law start with a *prima facie* right on the part of the plaintiff to recover payments made *sans cause* and focus their enquiry on whether the defendant's retention of the benefit is legitimate. English law, by contrast, directs its attention to the plaintiff and asks whether, from his point of view, the receipt of the benefit by the defendant was 'unjust', the word 'unjust' signifying a *numerus clausus* of restitution-yielding events. Two examples, one from French law and one from English law, will suffice to demonstrate the radical difference such an approach can make.

In the case which provides the genesis of the general enrichment action in France, the *Boudier* decision, the plaintiff supplied fertiliser to a tenant farmer who used it on his crops. The lease was then terminated and the tenant and his landlord agreed that the latter should take the crops in part payment of outstanding rent, the valuation of the crops being made so as not to include the cost of the fertiliser. The plaintiff had never been paid for the fertiliser but instead of suing the tenant, who in any event was now insolvent, he instead brought an action against the landlord. The Cour de Cassation allowed the plaintiff's claim, on the ground that the benefit received by the defendant could not be justified by any *cause légitime*.

Such a result would be anathema to an English lawyer.[12] Why, it would be asked, should the plaintiff acquire the benefit of another debtor simply because of the fortuitous occurrence that the benefit which he contracted to sell has ended up in the hands of a third party? Is it not the case that in a contractual setting, the contracting parties alone should each bear the risk of the other's insolvency?[13] This, however, never becomes an issue in English law, the reason being that the *Boudier* facts would fail to generate a restitutionary action at all. Looking down the list of 'unjust factors', the plaintiff would certainly have *a* restitutionary cause of action, namely failure of consideration. The benefit which he conferred on the tenant was on the basis of a contract which we must assume had been terminated on account of the tenant's repudiatory breach. The basis of that transfer having failed, the plaintiff would be entitled to a restitutionary action *against the tenant*. But he would not be entitled to a similar action against a third party to whom the tenant gave the benefit for either of two reasons. First, English law insists that in a claim based on failure of consideration, the basis upon which the benefit was

---

12   A German lawyer would agree, but solve the problem through the requirement of 'directness of transfer' (*Unmittelbarkeit der Vermögensverschiebung*), discussed below.

13   Zweigert & Kötz, n 1, p 235.

conferred should at least have been known to the defendant in the action. *Vis à vis* the defendant, a plaintiff cannot transfer wealth on a secret basis and then demand its return if that secret basis fails. Secondly, although the defendant landlord was enriched, it could not be said that the enrichment came from the plaintiff, with the result that the plaintiff has no standing to claim what the defendant received. The reason is that the fertiliser became the property of the tenant when it was received by him, so that when he passed it on to the landlord he was passing on his own property.[14] There was thus no transfer of wealth from plaintiff to defendant and hence no possibility of a restitutionary action.

The second example is provided by a recent decision of the House of Lords. In *Woolwich Building Society* v. *Inland Revenue Commissioners (No 2)*[15] the plaintiff, under protest, paid £57,000,000 in tax, claiming that it had been demanded under delegated legislation which was invalid. In separate proceedings for judicial review the plaintiff later successfully impugned the validity of the relevant legislation. It then demanded the return of the money paid under what was therefore an unlawful demand. Although the money was eventually repaid, it became important to determine whether repayment was due as of right or was merely a matter for the discretion of the revenue authorities. The plaintiff argued that it had a right to repayment but the difficulty it faced was that it could not fit itself within one of the usual heads of restitutionary liability. It had made no mistake (even if it had, it was a mistake of law),[16] nor could it say that it had acted under duress. The claim failed at first instance precisely on the ground that no cause of action could be made out.[17] It did, however, succeed before the House of Lords, but only because the House was prepared to recognise a special head of liability peculiar to public bodies. No such difficulty would, of course, have faced a French or German plaintiff which had at its disposal a general enrichment action for payments made without cause.

Given the generality of their unjust enrichment actions, it is not surprising that both French and German law cover broadly all those areas covered by English law. Both have a part which would roughly equate with the section known in English law as *Autonomous Unjust Enrichment*. Thus, all three systems provide a remedy for the mistaken payor, although English law currently refuses restitution where the

---

14   *Cf Lipkin Gorman* v. *Karpnale* [1991] 2 AC 548, discussed below. In that case too property
        passed to the intermediary, though the plaintiffs seem to have retained the power to revest it in
        themselves whenever they wished. The reasoning of the House of Lords on this point is perhaps
        the most difficult point of this important case. See further, Peter Birks, 'The English Recognition
        of Unjust Enrichment', [1991] Lloyd's Maritime and Commercial Law Quarterly 473, 476-481.
15   [1992] 3 All ER 737.
16   Mistake of law is not a restitution-yeilding event in English law. See further, below.
17   [1989] 1 WLR 987.

mistake was one of law rather than fact,[18] a restriction not found in either France,[19] Holland or Germany.[20] Again, the person who transfers wealth on a conditional basis which fails to materialise may have redress in all three jurisdictions. Such a claim is specifically catered for in §812 BGB[21] and falls within the general enrichment action in France.[22]

In Germany, the claims so far discussed would be known as *'Leistungs-kondiktionen'* (action based on plaintiff's act), by which is meant those cases where the benefit was deliberately conferred by the plaintiff on the defendant but for one reason or another, *eg*, mistake, the plaintiff wants it back. The question we must ask is whether there is a direct correspondence between this category and the English category *Autonomous Unjust Enrichment*? The answer is, not quite. Apart from the fact that the German category is, as explained above, in some respects wider, it may also be narrower in that it fails to take account of the English category called 'ignorance', typified by the recent case of *Lipkin Gorman* v. *Karpnale*.[23] There a solicitor spent money stolen from the plaintiff, a firm of solicitors of which he was a partner, on gambling at the defendant's casino. The plaintiff sought and the House of Lords granted restitution of the moneys so received.[24] Since the plaintiff's property was appropriated without its consent, a German lawyer would simply say that there was in that case no 'transfer' from the plaintiff to the defendant and that it was a case for the law of property rather than the law of restitution. The difference is crucial because, as we shall see, English law has now introduced a defence of change of position in respect of restitutionary claims. But that defence does not exist so far as property or tort claims are concerned. This means that it has now become essential for English law to decide whether a case such as *Lipkin Gorman* is restitutionary or proprietary. It may in the end turn out that the German model is to be preferred and the category of 'ignorance' expunged from the English law of restitution.

---

18   *Bilbie* v. *Lumley* (1802) 2 East 469. The rule was recently abolished in Australia by the decision of the High Court in *David Securities Pty Ltd* v. *Commonwealth Bank of Australia* (1992) 66 ALJR 768; noted Birks (1993) 109 LQR 164. It has suffered a similar fate in Canada (*Air Canada* v. *British Columbia* (1989) 59 DLR (4th) 161) and South Africa (*Willis Faber Enthoven (Pty) Ltd* v. *Receiver of Revenue* 1992 (4) SA 202 (A)).

19   A mistaken payment in France would, of course, come within the specific provisions of the code mentioned above.

20   Zweigert & Kötz, n 1, p 261.

21   Above.

22   See, for example, Dijon 7 Feb 1928, Gaz Pal 1928 I 501.

23   [1991] 2 AC 548.

24   The defendant's otherwise valid plea of bona fide purchase for value failed, the House of Lords holding that since this was a gaming contract which was rendered null and void by statute, no value had been given in exchange for the money. A partial defence of change of position was, however, allowed. See further, below.

Before leaving the area of autonomous unjust enrichment we should take note of another respect in which both French and German law, at least at first sight, differ from English law. It is often said that the common law knows nothing of the Roman institution of *negotiorum gestio*,[25] under which one who intervenes in a situation of emergency to preserve another's property is entitled to reimbursement or remuneration. Such a right is expressly conferred on the intervenor by the codes of Holland, France and Germany, the *quid pro quo* in each case being that he or she must exercise due care in the management and will be liable for any losses they cause. The dominant position in England is summed up in the following words of Bowen LJ in *Falcke* v. *Scottish Imperial Insurance Co*:

'The general principle is, beyond all question, that work or labour done or money expended by one man to preserve or benefit the property of another do not according to English law create any lien upon the property saved or benefited, nor even, if standing alone, create any obligation to repay the expenditure. Liabilities are not to be forced on people behind their backs any more than you can confer a benefit upon a man against his will.'[26]

There are, however, many exceptions to this rule, so much so that the validity of Bowen LJ's general principle is probably nowadays open to question.[27] Certainly, were the common law to acknowledge a *negotiorum gestio* principle, it would do well to study the refinements made to it in civil law systems.

We turn now to the other major division in the English law of restitution, *Restitution for Wrongs*. Again, there is no doubt that both French and German law here cover much of the same ground as English law. It will be recalled that §812 BGB talks of a defendant being enriched 'by transfer *or otherwise*'. The largest group of claims in which the enrichment arises 'otherwise' than by transfer are those in which the defendant simply *takes* the enrichment from the plaintiff without his or her consent, claims known to German lawyers as cases of *Eingriffskondiktion* (action based on interference). So, for example, a person who makes an unauthorised use of the plaintiff's property must pay for the cost of his or her user, regardless of the fact that the plaintiff suffered no actual loss, because, for example, there was no market for the goods.[28] And in France it has been held that if a waterworks uses the plaintiff's pipes for distributing water to its customers it must

---

25 See generally the excellent comparative treatment by S J Stoljar of *negotiorum gestio* in Chapter 17 of Vol X of the *International Encyclopedia of Comparative Law*, (1980).
26 (1886) 34 Ch D 234, 248-9.
27 See generally, Lord Goff of Chieveley and Gareth Jones, *The Law of Restitution* (3rd ed, 1986), pp 331-366. To the cases cited by Goff & Jones should also be added cases in equity such as *Boardman* v. *Phipps* [1967] 2 AC 46 (wrongdoer who improved his own as well as the plaintiff's position entitled to reasonable remuneration for his services) and *Re Berkeley Applegate (Investment Consultants) Ltd* [1988] 3 WLR 95 (liquidator of trust company entitled to remuneration for his services out of assets held for third parties).
28 RGZ 97, 310.

pay for this use.[29] Exactly the same position obtains in English law. In *Strand Electric & Engineering Co* v. *Brisford Entertainments*[30] the defendants returned forty-three weeks late some theatre-lighting equipment they had hired from the plaintiff. The plaintiff sued the defendant for the wrong of conversion and sought, as damages, the cost of hire for the period in question. Although the defendant was able to show that during the period in question the plaintiff had more equipment than they could hire out and had therefore suffered no loss the Court of Appeal allowed the plaintiff's claim.

There are, however, a number of differences between the civil law and the common law in this area. The first is that the restitutionary claim at common law is based on the commission by the defendant of a *wrong* to the plaintiff, while in the civil law systems it is triggered by an interference by the defendant with a *right* of the plaintiff. Thus, even an interference which does not amount to a wrongdoing will found a claim in Germany or France, whereas it will not in England. This difference should not, however, be exaggerated. In civil law systems fault is generally a requirement of wrongdoing, with the consequence that an innocent interference with the plaintiff's rights will not be classed as wrongful; nevertheless, it will still yield restitution. In England liability for interference with the property of another is, by contrast, strict; an innocent interference will be wrongful and may therefore, just as in France or Germany, give rise to a restitutionary remedy.

Secondly, as mentioned above, not all wrongs in English law will generate a restitutionary remedy, although it has to be admitted that those concerned with property generally do and might legitimately be described as the English equivalent of the *Eingriffskondiktion*.

Thirdly, and most importantly, there are some wrongs which do yield restitution but which would not seem to be catered for by the civil law systems under review. These are the many cases of restitution in which there has been no subtraction of wealth from the plaintiff, by transfer or otherwise, but rather a 'pure profit' to the defendant. Take, for example, the case of *Boardman* v. *Phipps*.[31] A solicitor to a trust used information received in that capacity to make a profit for himself. In so doing he committed a breach of the fiduciary duty which he owed to the beneficiaries of the trust fund. The House of Lords ordered him to pay to the beneficiaries the profits which he made 'at their expense' (used here in its other sense of 'by doing a wrong to')[32] despite the fact that no wealth had ever left the

---

29   Req 11 Dec 1928, DH 1929, 18.
30   [1952] 2 QB 246.
31   [1967] 2 AC 46.
32   See generally, Peter Birks, *The Independence of Restitutionary Causes of Action* (1990) 16 Queensland University Law Journal 1.

beneficiaries. So too in *Attorney General* v. *Guardian Newspapers (No 2)*.[33] A government employee in the security services, the infamous Mr Peter Wright, made a vast fortune from the wrongful sale of his memoirs, wrongful because its publication was in breach of the duty of confidence which he owed to his employer. The House of Lords held that had he been physically within the jurisdiction of the court he would have been liable to pay over all the profits he made from the breach to his employer, the state. Once again, restitution was ordered despite the fact that no wealth could be said to have passed from plaintiff to defendant.[34] The category of *Eingriffskondiktion* seems to be confined to cases in which the defendant is made to pay for the use he has made of the plainiff's rights. This focus of attention on 'user' cases demonstrates that German law is concerned solely with instances of subtractive enrichment. Cases of pure profit, in which there has been no subtraction from the plaintiff, although often successful in English law, would seem to be beyond the reach of the German law of unjust enrichment altogether.

This would not, however, seem to be the case in Holland. Article 6:104 of the new code gives to the judge a power to assess damages for an unlawful act or a failure to perform an obligation according to the amount of profit derived by the debtor from that act or failure, a provision clearly not confined to the unlawful use of another's property. In fact, it may go further than even the common law in this area in that, like Isreali law,[35] it allows a profits-based remedy for breaches of purely contractual obligations, something currently denied by the English courts.[36]

4 The Principle of Directness

We have already said that the principle objection to the decision of the Cour de Cassation in *Boudier* was that it had the totally fortuitous and undeserved effect of giving a supplier of goods another debtor should the immediate purchaser of the goods prove unable to pay for them. We also saw that English law, because of its lack of a general enrichment action, would not have allowed such an action to succeed. German law also avoids this result, though by another route. Although, as in France, German law contains a general enrichment action, it has one very important limiting factor, namely, the principle of directness of transfer (*Unmittelbarkeit der Vermögensverschiebung*). The rule applied by the German courts, but which is not to be found anywhere in the BGB, provides that the loss

---

33   [1990] AC 109.

34   For a comparable American decision, see *Snepp* v. *United States* 100 S Ct 763 (1980).

35   *Adras Ltd* v. *Harlow Jones GmbH* (1988) 42(1) PD 221, noted by Friedmann (1988) 104 LQR 383.

36   *Surrey County Council* v. *Bredero Homes Ltd* [1993] 3 ALL ER 705.

of the plaintiff and the benefit to the defendant must result from one and the same transaction.[37] But even with this directness principle in play, the German general enrichment action will still generate more instances of restitution than its English counterpart, as the continuing denial by English law of recovery of payments made under a mistake of law illustrates.

5 The Principle of Subsidiarity

There is present a tendency, which always needs to be guarded against, for an overinclusive law of restitution to undermine established doctrines to be found in other parts of the law. To take a simple example, a contractor might underestimate the cost of some work. Should he be allowed to bring an unjust enrichment action for the 'extra' benefit which he confers on his employer? A law of restitution which allowed him to do so would clearly be insensitive to the contractual allocation of risk and would thereby virtually demolish the law of contract. All three systems are alive to this problem and would deny the contractor a restitutionary claim. English law does so by saying that on the facts as stated there is simply no 'unjust factor' and so no restitutionary claim, while German law would say that since the benefit was provided under a valid contract it was not one which was received 'without legal justification'. French law attempts to solve the problem in a different way. The courts have qualified the general enrichment action by the addition of a proviso to the effect that such a claim will only be available where there is no other legal basis on which the plaintiff can ground his or her claim, the principle of *subsidiarité*. However, they have not in the process overruled the *Boudier* decision itself. The principle of *subsidiarité* only applies where the other cause of action lies against the defendant to the restitutionary action itself. No such principle has yet received express recognition in English law, though there are many cases which can best be explained as denying restitution precisely on the ground that to do otherwise would be to outflank a deliberate policy of the law. Cases where full restitution is denied in cases of loans to minors and other bodies incapable of borrowing money provide the best examples.[38]

6 Defences

What must never be forgotten when dealing with any question relating to the law of restitution is the legitimate and competing concern of the defendant in the

---

37   Zweigert & Kötz, n 1, p 235.
38   *R Leslie Ltd* v. *Sheill* [1914] 3 KB 607 (loan to minor); *Sinclair* v. *Brougham* [1914] AC 398 (ultra vires loan to corporation).

security of his receipt. A payee has an interest in knowing how much wealth at any one time he has to spend. It would be intolerable if he had forever to be making provision for the possibility of a claim against him for the return of benefits received. And that individual interest becomes a public interest when it is realised that insecurity of receipt spread across the whole population would bring the economy to a standstill.

The task of protecting the defendant's security of receipt can be approached in one of two ways. One is by limiting the grounds on which a plaintiff may claim restitution in the first place. Another would be to give plaintiffs a liberal enrichment action but at the same time provide defendants with liberal defences on which they might rely. The latter approach is the one adopted by German law, the general enrichment provision of §812 BGB being counterbalanced by §818 para (3), which provides that 'The obligation to surrender or to restore value is excluded insofar as the receiver has ceased to be enriched'.[39] So, for example, an employee who is mistakenly overpaid his salary and who spends the money to maintain a higher standard of living than that to which he would ordinarily be accustomed, will have a complete defence to a claim for restitution by his employer.[40]

Until recently English law took exactly the opposite approach.[41] In *Baylis* v. *Bishop of London*[42] the plaintiffs over a number of years mistakenly paid tithes to the church in respect of property they no longer owned. Although the money was spent on the spiritual needs of the parish the church was unable to resist a claim by the plaintiffs for the full amount of the overpayment. It was no defence to the restitutionary claim that the recipient of the mistaken payments was no longer enriched.[43] In England, however, the categories of mistake which will generate a restitutionary claim are more limited than in Germany. The most obvious difference, as we have seen, is that the mistake must be one of fact rather than of law before restitution will follow.[44] It used also to be thought that the

---

39 For an excellent account in English, see Dawson, *Erasable Enrichment in German Law* (1981) 61 Boston University Law Review 271.

40 RG JW 1911, 323. French law, by contrast, restricts the defence of change of position to non-money cases, the argument being that 'since money may be used in so many different ways the recipient must be taken to have benefited from the mere fact that he once had the money to dispose of as he thought fit': Zweigert & Kötz, n 1, p 276. This was also the position adopted by Roman law: *ibid.*

41 As Zweigert & Kötz astutely note, so long as the underlying basis of a restitutionary claim in English law was an implied contract to repay, as in the case of an express contract to repay, it was simply irrelevant that the payee was no longer enriched: Zweigert & Kötz, n 1, p 277.

42 [1913] 1 Ch 127.

43 It may well be that the case would still be decided the same way today, on the basis that the defendant would still have made the same expenditures, regardless of the receipt of the mistaken payment.

44 This was also to some extent the position in classical Roman law and in pre-codification Germany: see Zimmerman, n 1, pp 868-871.

mistake of fact had to amount to a 'liability mistake',[45] that is, that the payor's mistake led him to make a payment which he would have been liable to make had his view of the facts not been mistaken.[46] Although the restriction of restitution to liability mistakes has now been discarded, it is still the case that not every mistake of fact will yield restitution.[47] What underlies all these restrictions on the types of mistake which will generate restitution is the law's fear of too much restitution.[48] Indeed, the main justification for excluding restitution for mistakes of law given by Sir James Mansfield in *Brisbane* v. *Dacres*[49] was the injustice recovery would cause to the recipient: 'For see how it is! If the sum be large it probably alters the habits of his life, he increases his expenses, he has spent it over and over again, perhaps he cannot repay it all or not without great distress: is he then, five years and eleven months after, to be called upon to repay it?'. Such thinking would clearly find approval in a German court.

In this respect, however, the approach of the English courts may now be set to change. In 1991 the House of Lords, in *Lipkin Gorman* v. *Karpnale*,[50] introduced for the first time a general defence of change of position, by which a defendant will have a defence to any restitutionary claim to the extent that 'he will suffer an injustice if called upon to repay or to repay in full'.[51] Applying that defence to the facts of the case, a casino at which a thief gambled away money drawn from the plaintiff's bank account was able to deduct from the amount they were forced to repay the winnings they had in good faith paid over to the thief. Barely a year later, and perhaps not entirely fortuitously, the High Court of Australia in *David Securities* v. *Commonwealth Bank of Australia*[52] abolished the mistake of law doctrine. Although (as at the date of writing) the rule still survives in England, the introduction of the defence of change of position may mean that its days may be numbered in this country too.

It could be argued that English law is gradually moving towards the German model of a general enrichment coupled with a defence of change of position. That may well be the case, though of course only time will tell. But before we proclaim that

---

45   *Aiken* v. *Short* (1856) 1 H & N 210.

46   Also the position in Roman law: Zimmerman, n 1, p 868.

47   The question currently taxing English restitution lawyers is whether the mistake must be a 'fundamental' mistake, or whether it is merely one which is 'causative' of the payment.

48   Birks, n 6, p 148-9.

49   (1813) 5 Taunt 143.

50   [1991] 2 AC 548.

51   *Ibid*, at p 579, *per* Lord Goff.

52   (1992) 175 CLR 353. The effect which the introduction of the defence of change of position might have on the grounds of restitution was expressly noted by Lord Goff in *Lipkin Gorman* itself. He described the recognition of the defence as beneficial for the reason, *inter alia*, that it would enable a more generous approach to be taken to the recognition of the right to restitution: see [1991] 2 AC 548, 581.

the two systems are in harmony and ripe for assimilation, we should notice two crucial differences which remain. The first is that so far as the English version of the change of position defence is concerned, it is not likely — nor indeed desirable — that the courts will allow it to become so liberal as to be wholly unpredictable or inexplicable. It has been argued that there must be a causally related consumption of the enrichment, not merely fortuitous bad luck.[53] This should be contrasted with the very liberal régime in Germany where the plaintiff 'is made to bear the risk of all events which adversely affect the economic benefit accruing to the recipient',[54] a factor which has been described as the characteristic 'weakness' of unjustified enrichment claims in that jurisdiction.[55]

The second difference, already adverted to, is illustrated by the decision in *Lipkin Gorman* itself. The facts of that case were peculiar in that the plaintiff was a firm of solicitors and the thief a partner in that firm. As a partner, he had authority to draw on the firm's account with the consequence that by English law the sums he withdrew, though they were for the purposes of gambling, became his property.[56] He thus gambled with his *own* money rather than with the money of the firm. This had the important consequence that the casino could not be held liable for the wrong of conversion, a wrong of strict liability in which innocent receipt is no defence, and which would normally be committed where a thief gambled with another's property. It should also be noted that liability in the tort of conversion does not depend on the continued retention by the defendant of the plaintiff's property. There is no defence of change of position in the English law of torts and it was only the unlikely fact of the thief's relationship with the plaintiff that prevented the case being decided in the law of wrongs, with the consequence of liability being determined by value received rather than value remaining.[57] German law, by contrast, has no tort of conversion. It has only what an English lawyer would recognise as an action for detinue,[58] the equivalent of the Roman *vindicatio* by which the defendant is ordered to return the plaintiff's goods or pay their value. Although it will be no defence for a wrongdoer to assert that he no longer holds the goods, such a plea will in Germany avail an innocent recipient, who will only have to compensate the plaintiff to the extent that he or she still has the property in question. And where an innocent defendant has sold the property he or she will be liable to a restitutionary claim for the sale price received, but

---

53   Birks, *Restitution — The Future* (1992), pp 123-147.
54   Zimmerman, n 1, p 896.
55   Axel Flessner, *Wegfall der Bereicherung* (1970), p 2.
56   *Union Bank of Australia Ltd* v. *McClintock* [1922] 1 AC 1; *Commercial Banking Co of Sydney Ltd* v. *Mann* [1961] AC 1.
57   One part of the case was actually decided on this basis. As well as drawing money from the account, the thief also endorsed over to the casino a banker's draft made payable to his firm. This he had no authority to do so that the mere fact of the casino's receipt of the draft meant that they committed the tort of conversion in respect of it and were liable for its full value.
58   Still present in English law but now subsumed within the tort of conversion.

again subject to the defendant still having that value in his or her estate. As might be expected, the German law of property is thus in complete harmony with the German law of restitution. This is not the case in English law. Most cases of stolen property will be decided as conversion cases and not as restitution cases, with the result that a defence of change of position will not be available. In this respect the difference between the property laws of England and Germany means that their respective restitution laws will inevitably be at variance with one another as well.

7 Conclusion

These are stimulating times for restitution lawyers in England. Having thrown off the shackles of the implied contract theory,[59] the many difficulties inherent in this branch of the law can now be squarely faced. Cases of great moment coming before the courts are gradually supplying answers to some of these questions, but many more remain. For example, English law has, as we have seen, yet to develop any coherent theory regarding the recovery of the profits of wrongdoing.[60] Another difficulty which awaits resolution is the liability of a recipient of property taken by a third hand from one who was ignorant of the transfer, a difficulty compounded by the peculiarly common law[61] divide between law and equity. Where it is the plaintiff's legal property which comes into the defendant's hands then liability is strict. Where, however, the plaintiff is merely deprived of his equitable ownership liability is sometimes strict[62] and sometimes fault-based.[63] No rational defence of this dichotomy has yet been produced, and one of the most pressing issues for the English law of restitution is the removal of this anomalous state of affairs.[64] We have also adverted to the rule barring recovery for benefits conferred under a mistake of law. Should that rule now be changed? Finally, there is the novel defence of change of position, which the House of Lords has

---

59   See above, n 3.

60   A very rough and totally arbitrary demarcating factor seems to revolve round the jurisdictional nature of the wrongdoing in question. Where the 'wrong' is one which originates in the courts of Equity, recovery of profits will generally be allowed. Where, however, the 'wrong' is one which arises from the Common law, recovery of profits will generally be denied. The application of this random test would seem to be the only basis on which the recent decision in *Surrey County Council* v. *Bredero Homes Ltd* [1993] 3 All ER 705 (no restitutionary damages for breach of contract) was decided.

61   Used in this sense in contradistinction to civilian systems developed from Roman law.

62   As in *Re Diplock* [1948] Ch 465.

63   To complicate matters still further, some decisions have held that liability will be triggered by negligence on the part of the recipient (*Agip (Africa) Ltd* v. *Jackson* [1990] Ch 265), while others have held that only dishonest receipt will suffice (*Re Montagu's Settlement Trusts* [1987] Ch 264).

64   Liability in other areas of restitution, eg, mistake, is strict. A plaintiff need never show that the recipient knew that the payment was mistaken. Why, it is then asked, should he need to show knowledge on the defendant's part in the case of a payment made in ignorance?

deliberately left unformed, preferring it is to be developed on a case by case basis.[65] These and other factors which space does not permit to be discussed show that the English law of restitution has a long way to go before any attempt at codification can be made.

But even were the English law sufficiently developed to be susceptible of codification it is doubtful whether any assimilation of the common law and civil law in this area could be made. As we have seen, the two systems approach the question of unjust enrichment from completely different angles, the civil law from the perspective of a general enrichment action with limiting factors and the common law from a standpoint of a *numerus clausus* of restitutionary causes of action. While this fundamental difference of approach remains a European-wide codification would seem impossible. Moreover, there are some cases, most notably profits from (rather than user for) breach, where the common law of restitution goes further than its civil law counterparts. Equally, as the *Boudier* case shows, there are cases where the exact opposite will apply. There is, in addition, the question whether 'pure profits' made at another's expense are ever recoverable in civil law systems. Also problematic, as we have noted, is the different treatment by the two legal families of the receipt of another's property springing from the absence of a strict liability tort of conversion in civil law systems. This difference will prove significant when it comes to applying a defence of change of position.

And it is not only differences in the law of property which make comparison difficult. Fundamental differences in the laws of contract of civil and common law systems will also have an inevitable knock-on effect on their respective laws of restitution. To take just one example, in England certain events might occur which will cause a contract to be frustrated and so bring to an end the contractual obligation to perform. If any benefits have been conferred on either party to the contract restitutionary remedies may then become available to the conferring party. If, however, the same facts amounted to a case of *force majeure* in French law, a French court might vary or reduce the content of the promisee's obligation to take account of the reduced obligations of the promisor.[66] The court can, in other words, rewrite the contract, something which an English court could never do. A related difficulty will be the fact that English law has no general defence of *force majeure*, so that what may amount to a breach of contract in England may be excused in France. Until we have a European law of contract there is little hope for assimilation of an area of law which spends much of its time plugging the gaps caused by failures of the contracts. At present the gaps are in different places.

---

65   [1991] 2 AC 548, 558 (Lord Bridge), 568 (Lord Ackner) and 580 (Lord Goff).
66   Nicholas, *The French Law of Contract* (2nd ed, 1992), p 207.

This is not to say that the two systems have nothing to learn from each other. There is no doubt that in its development of a defence of change of position the English courts should turn to the experience of their German counterparts who have, after all, been busy developing and refining it for the best part of a century. And were it considered expedient to move to a general enrichment action in England, the various limiting devices in use on the continent, *eg*, the principle of *subsidiarité* in French law and that of 'directness of transfer' in German law, would also repay examination. The same is true in respect of the law relating to *negotiorum gestio*. In this respect, perhaps the most constructive route to unification would be the urgent completion of chapter X (Restitution — Unjust Enrichment and Negotiorum Gestio) of the *International Encyclopedia of Comparative Law*,[67] for only a detailed examination of the law in each jurisdiction will reveal the common problems we face, and, more importantly, the best solutions on offer.

---

67   Under the editorship of Ernst von Caemmerer and Peter Schlechtriem.

CHAPTER 15

General Theory of Unlawful Acts

Basil Markesinis

1 Introductory Remarks

An invitation *tout court* to contribute a chapter on the 'General Theory of Unlawful Acts' in a book entitled *Towards a European Civil Code* is bound to strike both a Common lawyer and a Civil lawyer as, at best, a formidable intellectual challenge and, at worst, an impossible if not even a dangerous task. For the Common lawyer is not only likely to start from a position of hostility towards codes;[1] he is also likely to feel extreme discomfort with the drafting techniques that his continental counterparts would expect to be applied to an enactment such as a code. Additionally, the Common lawyer is, rightly I think, likely to balk at the magnitude of the task of synthesis and compromise that such a truly European task calls for. As the arch English Euro-sceptic observed 'consensus is the absence of principle and the presence of expediency';[2] and though this was uttered in a political context, the same reluctance to abandon or modify well-tested concepts and legal institutions might be present *unless* one could show that either the foreign institutions were not as different as they were thought to be or that, though different, they were both better *and* transplantable into the different historical and procedural context of the Common law. To put it simply: the burden of persuading one system (be it the English, German, or any other) to alter its rules must be discharged by those who advocate reform.

The same concern for such an ambitious project might be voiced by a continental lawyer though its immediate target would not be the feasibility of the exercise nor even, perhaps, its desirability,[3] but the lack of planning and co-

---

1 Thus, soon after its creation in 1965, the Law Commission put the codification of the law of contract on top of its priorities. The enthusiasm did not last long and by 1973 the decision was taken to suspend work on this project. See *8th Annual Report* 1972-73, Law Com. No. 58, paras. 3-4. One can find some penetrating observations on the English attitude towards codes in Professor B. Rudden's 'A Code too Soon' in *Essays in Memory of Professor F.H. Lawson* (1986), pp. 101 et seq. For further discussions of the more recent English attempts see: Anton, 'Obstacles to Codification' (1982) *Jurid. Rev.* 15; North, 'Problems of Codification in a Common Law System' (1982) 46 *Rabels Zeitschrift* 490; Kerr, 'Law Reform in Changing Times' (1980) 96 *LQR* 515.

2 Lady Thatcher in an interview with *Newsweek* 27 April 1992, p. 15.

3 Among the many misconceptions that Common lawyers have about modern civilian lawyers is the belief that the latter still have a passion for codes. That they do not is testified by some recent literature among which one should consult, Irti, *L'età della codificazione (1979)*; De Cupis, 'A proposito de codice e decodificazione' (1979) II *Rivista di diritto civile* 47 et seq.; Sacco, 'La codification, forme dépasse' de législation?' in *Rapports nationaux italiens au XI Congrés International de Droit Comparé à Caracas 1982* (1982), 85 et seq.; Kübber, 'Kodifikation und Demokratie' (1969) *JZ* 645; Esser, 'Gesetzesrationalität im Kodifikationszeitalter und heute' in

ordination necessary before the tort section can take its shape as part of a rationally devised and coherent system. On this score, perhaps, the Common lawyer, less accustomed to a systematic and inter-related development of the various parts of the law in general (and the law of obligation in particular), might feel less inhibited in expressing his views or, even, attempting a first draft. Once again, therefore, the differences in mentality must loom large.

So we come to the comparatist who can afford to go where Common and Civil lawyers alike may fear to tread. Changing spectacles can change one's vision of the world; and though I have always advocated that the comparatist must have an intensely-focused view of the specific institutions he wishes to study (which does not mean that he can ignore the background against which these institutions operate), I think he can, on occasions such as the present one, stand back from his position as a national lawyer, take a broader view of a particular branch of the law, and suggest ways in which the unbridgeable might be bridged. At the end of the day, however, even if this attempt to find a *via media* among the rich diversity of European approaches fails, the contributors to (and, perhaps, the readers of) this volume should be grateful to its editors. For the exercise of reducing massive case law to brief principles may, at the very least, hold out some *academic* value as numerous Oxford students discovered when the late Professor Lawson (along with the late Sir Kenneth Wheare) would invite them to attempt to draft a British Constitution.[4] What follows, therefore, must be seen more in this light than as a credible attempt to discover the fundamental ingredients of this imaginary European Civil Code. That would require a much more *combined* intellectual effort than the one that has gone into the writing of this chapter.

2 The Models

It has not always been particularly profitable to over-emphasise some systems over others, to attempt to classify them in particular ways, for example on the basis of their private law, or to ignore mixtures that have emerged from conscious or unconscious legal borrowings and dilutions of one's original starting point. Yet our imaginary European draughtsmen would, almost certainly, have to consider a number of basic issues which are handled differently by the major systems of the Western World before he got down to his drafting task seriously. Before considering these issues, however, let us, very briefly, look at four important models.

Vogel and Esser, *100 Jahre oberste deutsche Justizbehörde* (1977). Contra, Schmidt, *Die Zukunft der Kodifikationsidee* (1985). For a lucid comparative discussion see Kötz, 'Taking Civil Codes less seriously', 50 (1982) *MLR*, 1.

4 See B. Nicholas, Frederick Henry Lawson, *Proceedings of the British Academy*, 76, 473 at 479. Professor Lawson in fact twice wrote on this subject. Thus, see: 'A Common Lawyer Looks at Codification' and 'Further Reflections on Codification' both reprinted in his *Selected Essays* (1977) vol I, *Many Laws*, 48 and Vol II, *The Comparison*, 96.

2.1 The Common Law of Tort

This does not exist in codified form in its country of origin, but a fairly elaborate presentation of its basic rules can be found in the *American Restatement (Second) on Torts*. This, one must remind the reader, does not have the force of law; but it can, at least, give to a Continental lawyer some idea of how the basic Common law rules might look if reduced to article form. Even in this form, however, the tort rules only reveal the barest outlines of the subject since the bones fully make sense only when fleshed out by the rich case law and various specific statutory rules. Indeed, as far as the *English* Common law is concerned it must be admitted that, notwithstanding the richness of the case law, its modernisation has come about by means of many and often complicated statutes.[5] An informed and most readable summary of English (and American) law and, indeed, of the Germanic and Romanistic systems, can be found in Zweigert and Kötz *An Introduction to Comparative Law*,[6] the best textbook on comparative law currently in print, and need not be repeated here. For present purposes suffice it to highlight three features of the English Common law which are likely to strike a foreign observer as particularly noteworthy.

First, English law still bears the mark of the medieval forms of action. Text books still reflect the nominate tort divisions; and, to continental eyes, the inability or reluctance to synthesise the casuistic rules of yesterday must seem remarkable.[7] Thus, the oldest tort — that of trespass — is still (understandably, perhaps,) divided into three chapters or headings: trespass to land, trespass to goods, and trespass to the person, while the last of the three torts (less understandably), instead of having been synthesised under some kind of declaration that any intentional interference with the human person is unlawful if not done with a lawful excuse, is still taught under the separate headings of assault, battery, false imprisonment, and the residuary rule of *Wilkinson v Downton*.[8] Such fragmentation/compartmentalisation would, of course, have to go if the proposed code were ever to see the light of day.

Secondly, though the ambit of English tort law is growing (and, indeed, is in one sense wider than continental tort law since it has always included protection of land

---

5   The contrast with the *American* Common law of torts is, in this respect, striking. For an excellent discussion of this different approach see J. Fleming *The American Tort Process* (1988), ch. 3. See, also, my article 'The Destructive and Constructive Role of the Comparative Lawyer' in 51 (1993) *RabelsZ*,438.

6   Vol. II 2nd edn. (1987), translated into English by Tony Weir.

7   Professor Rudden's recent study 'Torticles', 6/7 *Tulane Civil Law Forum* 105 (1991-2) makes this point very clearly.

8   [1897] 2 QB 57. For further details see B.S. Markesinis and S. Deakin *Tort Law* 3rd edn. (1994), chapter 4, especially p. 353-368.

and reputation within its scope), the growth is remarkably incremental[9] as, indeed, is the retraction from legal solutions which turn out to be unsatisfactory; and it still has gaps in the range of protected interests and relationships which are important when compared to continental law. England has thus not experienced the kind of growth that we find in the case law of article 1384 of the French Civil Code, or in the development of the general right of personality in Germany; nor has it been willing to entertain liability for pure omissions. Overall it could even be said that, contrary to the prevailing myth, English judges, in the area of tort law at least, have been less adventurous than their civilian counterparts.[10]

Thirdly, English law has followed a dynamic pattern of Hegelian dialectics with dramatic antitheses following imaginative theses. The tort of Negligence offers the best illustrations. The retractions that follow often unexpected expansions can be piecemeal and take place within the lifetime of a standard text book which makes it imperative for a foreign observer to strive to remain up-to-date with such developments; they can also leave our law lacking in internal consistency and systematic quality.[11] The current phase of conservatism that prevails in our tort law, prompted largely by an understandable (but, at times, also misplaced) fear of increased litigation, may thus not prove long-lived. But English xenophobia – often explicable in the light of the undoubted effectiveness of numerous legal institutions and the unequalled prestige of English judiciary – is likely to make the average English lawyer react cooly towards the idea of a European Code.

2.2 The Romanistic Systems

The French is the obvious model in this category and it tends to create mixed feelings to outsiders. Thus, to the Germanic lawyers its literary style is likely to be seen (often rightly) as hiding terminological impreciseness.[12] To the Common lawyer its terseness must appear as an unacceptable invitation to judicial legislation and litigation. Finally, to the modern codifier its old age (and general arrangement of its material) is obvious in more ways than one. Yet its vagueness has been

---

9 Lord Goff of Chieveley, one of England's most distinguished Law Lords, calls this the principle of 'gradualism' and has defended it extra-judicially in his articles 'Judge, Jurist and Legislature' (1988) 2 *Denning L. Journal*, 79 and 'The Search for Principle' (1983) 69, *Proceedings of the British Academy*, 169.

10 On this see my Inaugural Address to the Royal Belgian Academy entitled 'The Destructive and Constructive Role of the Comparative Lawyer' 51 (1993) *Rabels Zeitschrift*, p. 438-448.

11 Continental doctoral theses, which show an admirable and growing interest in English and American law, often miss the significance of quoting from the latest edition of leading text books; and even that is often insufficient for the purposes of informing the foreign observer of the current state of English law. For a criticism of the tendency to alter the law in a gradual and an unplanned manner see B.S. Markesinis and S. Deakin 'The Random Element of their Lordships' Infallible Judgment' 55 (1992) *MLR*, p. 619-646.

12 See, for example, the observations of Zweigert and Kötz *An Introduction to Comparative Law* Vol. I (1987) p. 92-93.

transformed by the judiciary into flexibility; and despite its lack of legal sophistication (at any rate when compared to the German codification) the simple division of its tort section into liability for one's acts, liability for the acts of persons for whom one is responsible and, finally, liability for one's animals and inanimate objects, has proved resilient as the new Dutch Code (Book 6, Title 3, Section 2) — which still largely follows it — clearly attests.

2.3 The Germanic Systems

While the significance of the previous legal family cannot be denied, it remains equally indisputable that in intellectual terms the German Civil Code (BGB) still gives rise to great admiration and not inconsiderable problems (many of which can be explained by reference to the real or misunderstood Roman past).[13]

The tort section of the German Code — halfway between the English nominate torts and the French manifesto provisions — represents a mixture of specific rules (some extremely narrow or nowadays archaic)[14] and three general provisions — paras. 823 I, II and 826 BGB — all of which make unlawfulness their key concept. But though the Roman concept of *injuria* survives into modern times, it receives a different definition in each of the three provisions: narrow in the first, where it is made to depend on the violation of one of the carefully enumerated and protected interests; wider in the second, where it turns on the purview of the violated statute which gives rise to a civil remedy; and almost amorphous in the third, where it is defined by reference to the prevailing *boni mores*.

To the Common lawyer the modern German law of tort presents two further notable characteristics. First, like French law, the law in practice has much departed from the law originally set out in the Code, so that the modern German law of torts can only be discovered through a careful study of the rich case law. Secondly, while trying to evade the strictures of a carefully-drafted Code which is full of closely interrelated provisions, German lawyers have come up with theories and constructions which fully justify both the widespread admiration for their dogmatic analyses and the suspicion towards their excessive theorising.[15] The room for *abstract* comparative observations is virtually limitless once the barest outline of these systems is grasped; but, on the whole, the utility of such exercises is limited

---

13   The unfortunate para. 831 BGB is one example; the codal regulation of breach of contract is, arguably, another. The Pandectist structure of the Code also presents serious drawbacks.

14   Para. 825 BGB is an obvious example.

15   The development of the 'complex structure' theory in the context of damage *to* products can be seen as a device to allow tort recovery for pure economic loss despite the strictures of para. 823 I BGB. Professor J. Fleming — in (1989) 105 LQR 508 — shares this interpretation; and the rich and complicated case law and literature is reviewed by, among others, Hager, 'Zum Schutzbereich der Produzentenhaftung', ACP 1984, 413; Steffen, 'Die Bedeutung der "Stoffgleichheit" mit dem "Mangelunwert" für die Herstellerhaftung aus Weiterfresserschäden', VersR 1988, 977; Kullmann, 'Die Rechtsprechung des BGH zum Produkthaftpfichtrecht in den Jahren 1989/90', NJW 1991, 675.

since it only accentuates conceptual differences between the systems and helps conceal their considerable convergence in practical solutions.

2.4 New Codifications

Legal eclecticism is the characteristic of these enactments among which the recent Dutch Code must hold a special position. For here, while the overall structure echoes the original French model, Germanic ideas are also clearly interspersed and at the same time concession is also made to new problems (or, rather, problems that modern technology has aggravated) like manufacturer's liability and liability for dangerous substances. For the Common lawyer, however, what is most notable about the Dutch law of torts (including, of course, the pre-codification law) is the relative absence of case law and the paucity of literature on a whole range of topics that have given him much cause for concern. Among them one could mention the question of liability for economic loss, accountants' liability towards third parties, liability for nervous shock, and wrongful life and wrongful birth actions. More about this, however, later on.

3 Approaching the Problem of Codification

Even from the little said in the preceding paragraphs, our hypothetical supra-natural legislator will have realised the formidable task that faces him. At the very outset, and before going into the detailed regulation of specific aspects of delictual liability, he thus has to make some basic decisions. Here are some:

3.1 How general or specific must his text be? Too detailed (and legalistically-phrased) and the danger of ossification could loom ahead. On the other hand, a broad formulation of principles, which would undoubtedly ensure flexibility, might be seen as unworkable by some, as an invitation to judicial legislation by others. The English tendency towards specificity, imbued by the draughtsman's desire to be concrete and anticipate, as far as possible, likely problems,[16] may be equally unsatisfactory. Thus it has important critics in England[17] and would clearly, if followed, lead to a Code that could rival in size the Prussian Code of 1792. For,

---

16   This imperative to be scientifically precise and complete is mentioned by, among others, Kerr, op. cit. note 1 above, at p. 527-8 and Sir Charles David, Legal Adviser to the House of Commons Select Committee on European Secondary Legislation, in his evidence to the Renton Committee, Cmnd. 6053, para. 52. Contrast, however, Sir William Dale's prescriptions in *Legislative Drafting: A New Approach* (1977), 335.

17   Professor Tony Honoré has severely criticised English drafting techniques; and he has attributed this in part to the absence of 'a genuine legal culture'. *The Quest for Security: Employees, Tenants, Wives,* Hamlyn Lecture 1982, 119. English law is also perceptively criticised by Kötz, 'Taking Civil Codes Less Seriously' (1987) 50 *MLR* 1 et seq.

if it takes 27 lines to describe the legal consequences of killing or injuring a dog worrying livestock,[18] one shudders at the eventual size of a full Civil Code!

Not all English statutes can be described as verbose. The Sales of Goods Act 1893 (as amended) must, surely, be a model of codification of a relatively narrow but important part of the law of obligations; and other areas of tort law — e.g. the Occupiers' Liability Acts 1957 and 1984 — have shown that a relatively complete regulation of a section of tort liability can be achieved and, with a minimum of effort, it could be abridged further.[19] True, these Acts still remain 'expansive' in form if compared with European Codes. One must, however, note two things. First is the similar tendency towards detailed drafting found in modern French and German enactments such as the German Law of Travel, (*Reisevertragsgesetz* of 1979 now paras. 651 et seq. BGB), the General Conditions of Business (*Allgemeine Geschäftsbedingungen Gesetz* of 1977), the French law of Traffic Accidents of 5 July 1985, and the German law regulating products liability of 15 December 1989, incorporating into municipal law the basic outlines of the relevant EEC Directive of 1987. That some (though not all)[20] of these enactments have now even been incorporated into their respective Codes despite their expansive form demonstrates that the classic tendency for terse and broadly-phrased principles seems less favoured these days, no doubt in part because of the complexity of the new topics that are being regulated. Secondly, one must not ignore the tendency of the English legislator to confer on judges very wide discretionary powers. Section 11(1) of the Unfair Contract Terms Act 1977 (introducing the 'reasonableness test' which determines the validity of an exemption clause), section 33 of the Limitation Act 1980 (allowing judges the right not to apply pre-determined time limits of limitation), and section 54(1) of the Employment Protection Act 1978 (enshrining the right against unfair dismissal) are as wide in their phrasing as any general clause one might find in the German Civil Code. The differences in legislative drafting techniques could thus be exaggerated by those whose real aim was to defeat the declaration of tort rules common to most European countries.

In my view, therefore, and in view of the above, there is some room here for a compromise of styles, especially if one were to proceed on the basis proposed later in this paper of a regulation of the basic tort rules in the Code, along lines stylistically similar to the modern Dutch Code, but accompanied by a series of statutes of strict (or no-fault) liability, dealing with oft-litigated areas which have been shown to call for less litigious-oriented ways of resolution. Accidents at work, traffic accidents, and medical accidents are some of the areas that spring to mind.

---

18   Section 9 of The Animals Act 1971.

19   Professor Kötz, op. cit. note 17 above at p. 4-5, gives some excellent examples of unnecessary legislative prolixity and others could be added to his list.

20   Non-incorporation in the Civil Code may not, necessarily, indicate a general decline in interest in codes but may be the result of pragmatic considerations on behalf of the promoters of the new legislation.

3.2 Our codifier must next decide as to the proper place of fault in the modern law of torts. No doubt the 19th century emphasis on fault will be diluted — the comparison of article 162-3 of the New Dutch Code with articles 1382 CC and 823 I BGB must, surely, underline the contemporary belief that whereas true faults should, other factors being satisfied, lead to liability, the absence of fault is no longer a reason for denying such liability. Having said this I would, for a number of reasons, prefer to focus on the general part of our imaginary Code on the principle that intentional and negligent acts form the core of the law of tort and then add that liability irrespective of fault may also arise where statute, expressly or by compelling analogy, otherwise dictates.[21] I would leave it to these statutes to determine whether the liability thus imposed was strict or whether they introduced, (preferably perhaps) a genuine no-fault scheme allowing victims to be compensated from a fund set up for this purpose. Finally, I think one would have to consider the possibility of these statutes setting monetary maxima that could be claimed in cases covered by them. By fixing these sums at reasonable levels and, unlike current German law, allowing analogical extension 'in compelling cases', I would hope to remove from the courts the bulk of litigation concerning the matters regulated by such statutes.[22] As stated, prime subjects for such treatment would be accidents at work, on the road, and injuries resulting from medical treatments. I would accompany the removal of this traditional tort material from the main core of tort law by a 'tightening' of the meaning of intention and, above all, negligence which I would equate with moral blameworthiness and thus separate from the kind of regrettable and unavoidable errors which one finds in many modern accidents and for which our imaginary Code would anticipate separate regulation.

My above-mentioned personal preferences lead me to the next issue which I think is even more important and which even modern legislators have, in my view, inadequately explored. I take it almost as axiomatic — even if it is not necessarily convincing — that for financial reasons European systems are likely to continue treating differently accident and disease.[23] What, however, they must do is to acknowledge openly and regulate accordingly the inter-relationship between tort remedies and other sources of compensation, mainly those emanating from the State. The parallel and separate development of these two worlds has for too long produced much confusion in all European systems and our imaginary Code should,

---

21   This is the position in Austrian law (e.g. OGH 10 Sept. 1947, SZ xxi 46; OGH 20 Feb. 1958, SZ xxxi 26; OGH 18 March 1953, SZ xxvi, 75; OGH 30 Aug. 1961, SZ xxxiv 111) which I prefer to the stricter approach adopted by German courts since the beginning of this century (RGZ 78, 171).

22   Again, in deviation from German law, I would be inclined to remove (or, at any rate, reduce) the availability of the defence of contributory negligence which I see in many cases as an excuse for insurers to delay making prompt and adequate offers of compensation. The innovations brought about by the French traffic accident law of 1985 and its effects on litigation rates and insurance premiums would thus deserve to be studied closely.

23   The unfairness and illogicality of the distinction has been clearly shown by J. Stapleton's *Disease and the Compensation Debate* (1986).

having resolved a number of related ideological issues, take a clear position about this relationship, the possible evaluation of awards, and the possibility of subrogation actions. Every reader will realise the immense complexity that these few lines conceal but I am willing to state my own guiding principle which, in most cases, would aim for rapid and cheap compensation outside the gladiatorial tort system even if this meant that the award was not as full as that obtainable after successful litigation along traditional tort lines. In colloquial terms I would thus envisage tort law reduced to dealing with genuinely 'bad' conduct and place a premium on the rapid resolution of disputes.

3.3 The aims of the tort rules given in the general part should, I think, be clearly set out not only in order to exclude the idea of punishment and punitive awards which I would prefer to leave to other breaches of the law, but also in order to make plain that the compensatory element — which I regard as crucial in tort litigation — can be taken to refer both to the plaintiff's loss but also the defendant's gain. This would, incidentally, have the advantage of re-drawing somewhat the boundaries of the subject — a topic which, in England at least, has given rise to difficulties and also to some unacceptable results.[24]

3.4 Finally, I think some indication should be given in our Code of the range of protected interests. This is no matter of mere detail since considerable differences currently do exist between the major systems which would have to be brought together under our hypothetical Code. A few illustrations can be given along with some brief suggestions on how the existing divergencies might be bridged.

a Personal injuries lie at the core of tort law and receive the widest and fullest compensation. This should, of course, continue. There are, however, certain types of 'physical injury' which have raised varying degrees of difficulty in the different systems of Western Europe and whose compensation seems to depend on 'consequentialist' judicial arguments or the ideological positions that particular systems have taken in other parts of their internal law.

Characteristic of the first is the problem of nervous shock — hardly litigated in the Netherlands under the old regime, but of great significance in both German and English law.[25] Our imaginary Code need not, I think, attempt to regulate whether its compensation be limited to 'close relatives' of the immediate victim; nor should it attempt to fossilise the law by imposing the kind of requirements of temporal and spatial proximity between the plaintiff (victim of nervous shock) and the immediate

---

24 For some difficulties that English law has had to face in this context see P. Birks, 'Civil Wrongs: A New World', *Butterworths Lectures* 1990-91 (1992) p. 55 et seq.

25 For a brief comparative discussion of these two systems see B.S. Markesinis *The German Law of Torts* 3rd edn. (1994) ch. 2 with rich references to further literature.

victim of the tortious act. In my opinion it would be sufficient to clarify that 'medically recognised' physiological or psychological consequences are included in the system's understanding of the term physical injuries and leave it to the case law to develop the remaining modalities. The absence of juries in civil litigation in Europe, the free appreciation of evidence by the judge, and the cost of litigation would, I think, act as a sufficient barrier against the usually feared increase of litigation that might ensue if the rule of thumb (which, for example, is adopted by English law) was abandoned.

Wrongful life and birth claims are also new causes of action — indeed unknown where the system refuses to sanction abortion except in the most extreme of cases.[26] American courts, which have blazed the trail,[27] are currently seeing their work undercut by the (usually inactive) legislatures no doubt prompted by current political pressures from lobbies that oppose abortion.[28] Whether our Code was liberal on abortion or not, the actions should, I think, be recognised; and the study of American case law could provide some helpful hints on the question of which should be the permissible headings of damages.[29]

b The compensation (through tort) of pure economic loss is another troublesome topic which — in theory at least — rigidly separates German and Anglo-American law on the one hand and the Romanistic systems on the other. The reasons why English and German law have opposed in a blanket manner this heading of damages are well known but, in my opinion, are becoming less and less convincing. As a result of this one can see in some systems (e.g. the German) a trend to come up with immensely complicated devices in order to avoid the traditional rule. Our Code should, I think, adopt the more liberal Romanistic rule and leave it to practice to develop its own limiting devices. These could vary from the kind of 'preliminary investigations by specialised bodies' — such as we find in the Netherlands on the question of accountants' liability — which could attempt to discover 'what went wrong' and then, indirectly, encourage the parties to a settlement;[30] or it could be combined with tighter regulation of obligatory insurance which would, in practice, set the upper limits of potential legal liability. Finally, it should not be too readily assumed that legal costs and other extra-legal

---

26 Countries like Ireland and Belgium seem to fall into this category.

27 For references to case law and academic literature see my *German Law of Torts* 3rd edn. (1994) ch. 2 and accompanying translated cases.

28 See Note 'Legislative Prohibition of Wrongful Birth Actions', 44 *Wash. and Lee L. Rev.* 1331 (1987). Comparison with Germany may, again, be instructive. For, despite the decision of the *Bundesverfassungsgericht* of 28 May 1993 (EuGRI 1993, 229) declaring abortion illegal in principle, the signs are that the Bundesgerichtshof will hold its ground in the context of an unwanted birth of a handicapped (and, perhaps even, healthy) child. See BGH Az: VI ZR 105/92 discussed in the *Süddeutsche Zeitung* of 18.11.1993.

29 *Procanik v Cillo* 478 A. 2d. 755 (1984) is a very instructive case.

30 The Dutch position is sketched out in Jansen, 'Enkele Aspecten van beroepsaansprakelijkeid Recht op een scheve schaats' (essays edited by F.H.A. Arisz, 1991); Bertrams, 'Aansprakelijkeid van accountants jegens derden', 1991 *De Naamloze Vennootschap*, 198-205.

factors (e.g. adverse publicity from litigation) would not also act as a brake against the risk of enhanced litigiousness that some fear might follow the liberalisation of the rules.

c Finally, the protection of reputation and privacy would also pose special problems to our hypothetical legislator.

The growing 'de-criminalisation' of defamation law, always favoured by English law, seems increasingly *en vogue* on the Continent of Europe and should, I think, be encouraged further. The protection of privacy on the other hand may well be best achieved by a combination of civil and criminal measures. The inclusion of both interests in our Code is, I think, essential; but it will pose two significant difficulties. The first is one of substance: how one should attempt to regulate the conflict between privacy and reputation on the one hand and free speech on the other. The second is, largely, one of drafting techniques, further complicated by a host of technical statutes that regulate the subject matter in England. Neither should one forget the constitutional regulation of the matter which, in countries such as Germany, exercises a significant influence on the development of the purely private law.

Out of deference to both the importance and complexity of the subjects (defamation and privacy) and in recognition of the fact that in some systems (such as England) there already exists a corpus of statutory law that could not be wiped out at a stroke, I would favour the barest treatment of the subject in the Code and leave the regulation of details to national legislation with the request that it (a) paid due regard to the importance of maintaining a balance of the competing interests and (b) devised ways to expedite disputes out of court. Along with this, I would abolish the English distinction between written and oral defamation, I would adopt American ideas in placing on the plaintiff the burden of proving the falsity of the allegations, I would favour monetary compensation only in cases of provable damage in the event of intentional or reckless defamation and, otherwise, consider rectification of the calumny 'in appropriate manner' as the most obvious remedy. At first instance, the law should leave this to the parties to work out. Likewise, in the case of privacy, I would proclaim the need to maintain a balance between human privacy and free speech and leave it to particular statutes to define how to achieve this goal through a correct combination of civil and criminal sanctions. Much of the material contained in the Calcutt Report[31] I would regard as providing useful guidance in the achievement of the main aim.

---

31 Report on the Committee on Privacy and Related Matters, Cmnd 1102 (1990) briefly discussed by me in *Festschrift für Werner Lorenz zum siebzigsten Geburtstag* (1991) pp. 717 et seq. See, also, more recently the Lord Chancellor's Consultation Paper 'Infringement of Privacy' July 1993 where a general right of privacy is proposed.

4 Other Matters to be Regulated by the Code

This title does little justice to the importance of the remaining topics that, in my opinion, would have to be treated in the Code. Again, due to lack of space, I mention four by way of illustration.

4.1 Liability for Breach of Statutes

I regard para. 823 II BGB as succinctly formulating a number of relevant rules and, even though the full extent of the purview of this article cannot be discovered without examining the rich case law, I would favour its adoption. The advantages of the German model, apart from its succinctness, are mainly two. First, it unambiguously states that breach of a *protective* statute gives rise to a civil remedy and does not leave it to the judge to discover — as is the case in England — whether the legislator 'envisaged' such an additional remedy. Secondly, the German model makes this *additional*, civil, remedy available only where fault has been proved. Given the proliferation of strict liability statutes I think this restriction is desirable; but it is also in keeping with my proposal to focus the codal regime mainly in the direction of true faults.

4.2 The treatment given to vicarious liability in the new Dutch Code (articles 170-171) seems clear and, I suspect, would be broadly acceptable to most systems. Equally desirable is article 170.3 of the Dutch Civil Code (which roughly accords with the law that prevailed in Germany until fairly recently) and excludes the master's right to seek a contribution or an indemnity from the tortfeasor/servant save in those cases where the damage was the result of the latter's intentional conduct. Parallel to vicarious liability one should, of course, also provide for the master's primary liability in the type of circumstances that English law describes as cases of 'personal non-delegable duties'. Here, then, I would attempt to blend the best features of English and German law.

4.3 The same is true of the treatment of torts committed by those 'under age', the potential liability of their custodians, and the questions of contribution between joint tortfeasors. The provisions of the new Dutch Code provide, I think, good starting points for possible further elaboration of all these subjects. Finally,

4.4 I would include in the Code the regulation of *ricochet* damage in the context of fatal accidents. The richness of the solutions offered by the various legal systems must be noted[32] and, hence, it would not be surprising if divergent views were to arise as to (a) who should be entitled to claim in such cases and (b) what should be claimable (moral damage as well as economic losses?) These are some of the points that would have to be discussed at the more detailed sessions that would precede the drafting of the Code, but here I confess I prefer the Romanistic and more liberal approach to the more rigid though, admittedly, more certain German solutions. I would, however, expressly exclude from such claims insurers (and other payers who had otherwise 'compensated' the primary victim) as well as employers claiming for the loss of key employees and vice versa.

5 Matters not Expressly Dealt With in the Code but Which Should, however, Be Linked to the General Codal Treatment of Unlawful Acts

I have already expressed my preference that certain great litigators — e.g. accidents at work, traffic accidents, medical accidents, product liability — should be regulated outside the Code through strict or, preferably perhaps, no-fault liability regimes. To this list, I think one might add liability arising from toxic substances.

As stated, many of these topics have considerable autonomy and may have already been the subject of E.C. intervention. Handling them in this way would thus not only have a greater chance of eventually reaching concordant regulations on these topics; but it could also be done in the greater detail they seem to require and which might not be appropriate to a Code. This should not, however, mean that they should be totally ignored by the Code (a) because I feel that there is here, too, a need to co-ordinate their specific schemes with social security and other state-funded compensation and (b) because it may not be desirable to exclude totally the fault-based system of the Code where (i) the compensation provided by the specific schemes is inadequate *and* (ii) the potential victim is willing to undertake the risks of an additional fault-based litigation process. In practice, however, this should be truly exceptional; and an adequately-fixed compensation ceiling through the proposed special statutes would, in my opinion, achieve this result.

6 Concluding Remarks

I have throughout this paper expressed serious doubts about the feasibility of this project in the near future by, inter alia, referring to the proposed European Code as 'our hypothetical Code'.

By focusing on the difficulties I have mentioned I have deliberately avoided discussing (other than incidentally) the wider issue of the desirability or relevance

---

32 For more details see H. McGregor, 'Personal Injury and Death' in *International Encyclopedia of Comparative Law* vol XI ch. 9 (1969).

of codes on the eve of the twenty first century. This, however, does not mean that I do not value, especially as an academic lawyer, the advantages of 'order, form, and structure' that codes can bring to a legal system. All that it means is that, for the time being, my common law environment persuades me that these commendable aims can be best pursued through text books, not codes and a reform of the academic curriculum; and that the main 'battle' that the advocates of a more rationally ordained system have on their hands is in persuading judges to consult such works more frequently before their slide into the 'wildness of simple instances'.[33]

As far as substance is concerned, I have made it clear that the requisite degree of harmonisation is more likely to be achieved through EC Directives such as those we have seen on products and services soon, I hope, to be followed by one dealing with the problems of traffic accidents and the case law of the Court of the European Communities as it systematically fleshes out the articles of the Treaty of Rome.[34] In my opinion, this step-by-step method of regulation is not only the one most likely to achieve the degree of harmonisation that would be needed before the drafting of a European Code could even be contemplated. It would also enable a more detailed regulation of these complicated subjects which, I suspect, unlike the general principles of the law of obligations, are incapable of being reduced into the terse formulation of principles one finds in civil codes such as the French *Code Civil*. It would, finally, leave our Code to deal with the residue of intentional and (truly) negligent acts (and some incidental problems) on which, I suspect, agreement could eventually be reached once it was realised that the protection currently afforded by the different systems of Western Europe is, broadly, similar.

Even if my pragmatic approach were adopted as the blue-print for producing the European Code, I still feel that the academic exercise embarked upon by all those who have contributed to this book would take years to come to fruition. The emergence of the New Dutch Civil Code must surely attest to the correctness of this prediction;[35] indeed, it must also indicate that a slow process of interchange between academics, E.C. initiatives, and court decisions would benefit, not hinder, this task of gradual moulding of the common basic principles. For this to happen, however, both national universities and national courts must play their part. On the whole, it must be admitted that both these institutions — at any rate in my country

---

33   Stoljar, 'Codification and the Common Law' in *Problems of Codification* (1977), 8. Views similar to those expressed in the text above can be found in Professor Kötz's 'A Common Private Law for Europe: Perspectives for the Reform of European Legal Education' in *The Common Law of Europe and the Future Legal Education* (ed. B. de Witte and C. Forder) 1992, 31, especially p. 41.

34   'Article 119 [for example] provides an excellent example of the way in which Community law can have an impact on English law' Lord Slynn, *Introducing a European Legal Order* the Hamlyn Lectures, 43rd series (1992), 127. See, also, *The Gradual Convergence. Foreign Ideas, Foreign Influences, and English Law on the Eve of the 21st Century* (a collection of essays - gen. ed. B. Markesinis, 1994).

35   See Professor A.S. Hartkamp's observations in *New Netherlands Civil Code Patrimonial Law*, P.P.C. Haanappel and E. Malay (editors) (1990) p. xxix et seq.

— have not been quick to appreciate these new perspectives. Intellectual conservatism is, arguably, the main reason for academic inertia despite a latter-day enthusiasm for half-baked Erasmus-type schemes. Lack of time and expertise may be the root cause for the reluctance of national courts to add the comparative method to their existing armoury though in my country judges such as Lords Goff and Mustill, Lord Justice Bingham and Lord Justine Steyn are openly championing judicially and extra-judicially the use of the comparative method. At the end of the day, however, transnationally-minded lawyers, whether in the classroom or the courtroom, cannot force the pace of legal harmonisation if politicians (and electorates) are — understandably I believe — proceeding at a more cautious pace. And if the history of existing European civil codes teaches us anything, it is that legal codification seems to follow — not precede — economic and political unification. And on this front the picture is not clear; or, as our French colleagues would say, *on verra*!

CHAPTER 16
Vicarious Liability in a European Civil Code

Gerrit van Maanen*

1 Introduction

If we were to draft a European Civil Code on the subject of liability for other persons, a number of questions would need to be considered before we could embark on such an ambitious project.[1][2] I will limit myself to employers' liability, leaving other forms of vicarious liability, such as that of parents and agents, aside for the moment. In view of the objects of the common European market, parental liability does not require regulation.

The first question that needs to be answered is whether vicarious liability of employers should be strict liability, since it is conceivable that a system could be chosen in which the employer has the option of raising an exculpatory defense.
A second question would be whether the requirement that the employee had committed a fault should be incorporated, or whether the mere fact that damage was caused would be sufficient.
Considering the various types of liability we should adopt a clear model. The model of vicarious liability that is the clearest seems to be the one in which there is no statutory option for the person liable to exculpate himself from liability for the faults of others. Such a form of vicarious liability corresponds best with the existing rules in the various European countries. Elsewhere in this book, Markesinis also feels that 'treatment given to liability in the Netherlands Code would be broadly acceptable to most systems.'[3]
As for the style of the provisions, I would endorse Markesinis' suggestion of opting for the French style of formulating general rules where the basic rules governing tortious liability are concerned, as was done for the 1992 Netherlands Code. However, with regard to the specific subareas, such as (liability for) traffic accidents and medical errors, I would opt for a series of special statutes governing these subjects in more detail.

---

*   I am deeply indebted to Louise Rayer for the translation of this chapter.
1   See in general on this topic Peter-Christian Müller-Graff, Common Private Law in the European Community, in: *The Common Law of Europe and the Future of Legal Education*, Deventer (Kluwer) 1992, p. 239 ff.
2   I will not go into the question as to whether and why we need a European codification of civil liability law.
3   *Towards a European Civil Code*, General Theory of Unlawful Acts (B.S. Markesinis), Chapter 15.

Unlike Markesinis, I feel that in this new European codification not only should be laid down rules governing liability for intentional and negligent acts, but that strict liability should be included as well. I therefore propose that a number of very general liability rules based on strict liability rather than on fault, should also be drafted. Neither do I see why liability should be limited to specific maximum sums of money.[4]

I will first provide a survey of the regulation of employers' liability in the major European countries. Subsequently, I will asses whether a common denominator can be found under which a European rule is feasible. Dutch law will be described in somewhat more detail, providing a broader background for describing the other legal systems.

2 Vicarious Liability in the Netherlands

The system of the 1992 Netherlands Civil Code incorporates in Chapter One of Title 6.3 (*onrechtmatige daad* [civil wrongs]) a number of general provisions relating to (individual) liability for one's own wrongful acts. The second chapter contains provisions governing liability for both persons and (corporeal) property.

2.1 Liability for Servants

Every employer knows that he is responsible for the faults of his staff. When a roofer is careless in joining layers of bitumen, which results in the entire factory building being reduced to ashes, the employer knows that he had better call his insurance company. More precisely, but rather intricately, put in the language of the law:

'A master in whose service a servant performs his tasks is liable for damage caused to a third person through the fault of that servant, where the probability of such fault was increased by the servant's assignment to perform the work and where the master, by virtue of the legal relationship between them, had control over the conduct from which the fault originated' (art. 6:170, s.3 Civil Code).

The requirement for employer liability is therefore that the employee (the 'servant') has committed a 'fault'. In the 1992 Netherlands Civil Code this means an attributable wrongful act, in other words it should also be possible to hold the employee himself liable. A further requirement — as in the pre-1992 law — is the employer's control over the employee's conduct which caused the fault. Not only do traditional workers fall within this category, but also such officers as the factory

---

4   F. J. de Vries' study clearly demonstrates this: *Wettelijke aansprakelijkheid*, Zwolle 1990. See also my comments on the subject in *TVVS* 1991, p. 330-332.

manager and the director of a privately held limited liability company (*B.V.*). Public authorities are also liable for the faults of their public servants on the grounds of this provision. In cases of temporary staff, both the employer in fact (the hirer) and the employer in law (the temporary employment agency) are liable on the basis of Article 170 of the Netherlands Civil Code. The degree of control is decisive. Where control ceases, there is no longer liability for the (legal) employer.

In the Code it is defined as: 'increasing the probability of fault'. In employing such a definition the legislator has indicated that there has to be a distinct relation between the wrongful act and the task assigned. If a plumber drops his heavy tool kit on an antique drawing room table which subsequently collapses, it is obvious that the risk of this fault is related to the job assigned. Even if the plumber were to return at night to pick up some fine silverware, this might lead to liability of the employer.

This broad criterion, however, only governs professional employers who, within the scope of the practice of a profession or the carrying on of a business, are responsible for their staff. If the person is employed by a natural person, as is the case, for instance, with maids or cleaning ladies employed by a private person, there is a more limited criterion. In such cases, for the employer to be liable the requirement is that the servant acted 'in the discharge of the task assigned to him' when committing the fault (art. 6:170, s.2 Civil Code).

The Code also contains rules for the question of who in the end will have to pay the damage if a claim for damages was laid against the employer and the employer was ordered by the court to pay. The principal rule is that in ordinary cases the employer carries the financial burden; only in exceptional cases, — in the Code the phrase: 'intent or conscious recklessness' is used — may the employer recover from his employee. In former times, bus drivers were held accountable by their employers, where the former had caused damage. The prevailing view today is that the financial consequences of faults that are bound to be made by any employee at a given time must be borne by the employer.

2.2 Subcontractors and Other Non-Servants

Under the 'old' Dutch Civil Code, where there was no control over the conduct of another, there was no liability for those who had assigned that other person to perform certain work. In the 1992 Netherlands Civil Code, an action for damages may be brought against the general employer for the faults of subcontractors or the latter's employees. In Anglo-American law, there have been provisions for such liability of 'independent contractors' for some time. Contractors' liability is limited to 'activities necessary in the carrying on of a business'. A private person who contracts a piano tuner to do work for which he is professionally qualified, cannot be held liable where the piano tuner — being overworked — assaults a visitor upon the latter's remark about the tonal purity of the F sharp.

2.3 Agents

According to Article 6:172 Civil Code, where an agent's conduct, in the execution of the powers granted to him as an agent, constitutes a fault against others, the principal himself is also liable with regard to that third person. At first sight this provision seems to have a broad scope. Upon a closer look, this proves not to be the case; the provision does not apply to all those agents, who as 'representatives' (*vertegenwoordigers*), are employed by a company, since they are governed by the general rule of Article 170: vicarious liability of the employer for his employee. Nor does the provision apply to the director of a privately held limited liability company (*B.V.*) empowered to represent his company, inasmuch as his acts are deemed to be acts by the juristic person he is representing. Those who remain are those agents who are not in service, but who are, for instance, empowered on the basis of an agency agreement to enter into specific contracts in the name of the company. An example of such an agent is the intermediary in assurance. But legal representatives such as the guardian, the trustee in bankruptcy and the liquidator also belong to this category.

3 Germany[5]

The development of vicarious liability for employees in German law clearly shows the difficulties that may arise from an employers' liability rule, if such liability is based on a — refutable — fault of the employer, as is the case in German law.[6]

The principle of 'no liability without fault' was based on the pandectist preoccupation believed to be supported by Roman law, that each form of liability, including vicarious liability should be contingent on whether any personal fault by a superior contributed to the damage caused by staff. This principle is laid down in article 831 BGB, although in this rule there is the presumption of fault on the part of the employer. It is the employer who has to prove that he has taken all generally required precautions in selecting and training his servant (*Verrichtungsgehilfe*).

This leads to the rather odd situation that in case of an accident in which an employed truck driver is involved, the debate does not concentrate on the question of whether the driver was at fault, but on whether the employer took the necessary precautions in hiring and training the driver. The exculpatory evidence put forward

---

5   A clear and concise survey of vicarious liability in German law can be found in Zweigert/Kötz, *An Introduction to Comparative Law*, Oxford 1987, Vol. II, Ch. 18: Liability for Others. An excellent treatment of the subject was written (in Dutch) by Oldenhuis. F.T. Oldenhuis: *Aansprakelijkheid voor onrechtmatige daden van anderen*, Deventer 1985 (diss. Groningen), p. 143 ff.

6   See Ernst von Caemmerer, Reformprobleme der Haftung für Hilfspersonen, *Zeitschrift für Rechtsvergleichung*, 1973, p. 241 ff.

by the employer will be based on facts the plaintiff is not cognizant of prior to the trial. The outcome of such a trial is therefore rather unpredictable.

This is one of the reasons why German judges have been trying to lessen the effect of article 831 BGB,[7] by constructing, for example, a contractual claim for the plaintiff in which case the defendant is deprived of the possibility of an exculpatory defense under article 831 BGB. By extending the notion of contract to situations in which negotiations have just begun, or where the defendant, without intention to enter into an agreement, just happened to be in the plaintiff's shop (*culpa in contrahendo*), the courts extended contractual liability. Another way of reducing the undesired effects of the rule of exculpatory proof has been the very strict requirements which the courts set for exculpatory proof. However justified the outcome of this development, the price to be paid for all this, of course, is that situations which should be governed by the law of civil wrongs ('tort') are now dealt with through contractual concepts. Efforts to reform the rule of article 831 BGB have resulted in a draft statute which reads: 'A person who appoints another to perform a function is bound along with that other person to indemnify a third party for the harm caused by an intentional or negligent tort committed by that other person in the execution of his task.'[8]

In this draft, we clearly see the preconditions for employers' liability:

— The employer or the person in charge of a business must have appointed someone to perform a task. Normally, this is the case with salaried and wage-earning employees.
— Furthermore, the 'servant' must have caused the damage in the exercise of the duties assigned to him ('in the execution of his task').
— Unlike the present situation in German tort law, the draft proposal does not mention the possibility of exculpatory evidence that may be submitted by the superior; instead it imposes strict liability on him for the events in which the servant is at fault in the execution of the duties assigned to him.

---

7   Article 831 BGB reads: '*Wer einen anderen zu einer Verrichtung bestellt, ist zum Ersatze des Schadens verpflichtet, den der andere in Ausführung der Verrichtung einem Dritten widerrechtlich zufügt. Der Ersatzpflicht tritt nicht ein, wenn der Geschäfsherr bei der Auswahl der bestellten Person und, sofern er Vorrichtungen oder Gerätschaften zu beschaffen oder die Ausführung der Verrichtung zu leiten hat, bei der Beschaffung oder der Leitung die im Verkehr erforderliche Sorgfalt beobachtet oder wenn der Schaden auch bei Anwendung dieser Sorgfalt entstanden sein würde. Die gleiche Verantwortlichkeit trifft denjenigen, welcher für den Geschäfsherrn die Besorgung eines der im Absatz 1 satz 2 bezeichneten Geschäfte durch Vertrag übernimmt.*'
8   Translation from Zweigert/Kötz, op. cit., Vol. II, p. 330.

4 The Liability Laws of Switzerland and Austria

Swiss law very much resembles German law in this respect. Article 55 of the Swiss *Obligationenrecht* is drafted in the same fashion as article 831 BGB.[9] In Swiss law, there also are very strict requirements for exculpatory proof. The employer allegedly liable must not only prove that he fulfilled the required duty of care when hiring and supervising his employee, but also that he exercised the necessary care in the case at issue. In practice, such liability of the employer approximates strict liability in which an exculpatory defense is allowed in exceptional cases only. Also in Swiss law, there must be a clear functional link between the damage-causing act and the work assigned.[10] Hence the use of the term *Kausalhaftung* in this respect.

Austrian law departs from the same principle as German and Swiss law. Where the employer himself is at fault, he is liable according to the rule laid down in article 1315 ABGB. But contrary to Swiss and German law, the burden of proof is on the victim.[11]

5 French and Belgian Liability Law

The liability of the *maître* for his *préposé* is conveniently summed up by Oldenhuis and by Zweigert/Kötz.[12] Article 1384 French Civil Code starts out with the statement that a person is responsible for the harm caused by an act of another for whom he is responsible. In section 5 of the same article, it is laid down that the employer (*maître*) and the *commettant* are responsible for the damage caused by their servants and employees in the exercise of their duties.[13] Since 1804, this liability has evolved into genuine strict liability.[14] Initially, the legal basis for this liability was found in either bad choice of staff or inadequate supervision of staff. This legal basis of the *culpa in eligendo* meant that for Article 1384, section 5 *Code civil* to apply, there was to be *choix libre*, the employer's free choice in selecting his employees.

These days, the predominant requirements are: the state of subordination (*subordination*); the damage must have been caused in the exercise of the task

---

9   See Keller, *Haftplichtrecht*, Basel und Frankfurt am Main, 1985, p. 157 ff.

10   See Guhl, *Das Schweizerische Obligationenrecht*, Zürich 1980, p. 179 ff.

11   See Zweigert/Kötz, op. cit., Vol. II, p. 326.

12   F. T. Oldenhuis, op.cit., p. 134 ff, and Zweigert/Kötz, op. cit., Vol. II, p. 330 ff. Of the French reference books I mention: Viney, *Traité de droit civil. Les Obligations. La responsabilité*, vol. IV., Paris 1982, p. 866 ff.; Mazeaud/Chabas, *Leçons de droit civil*. Tome II, Premier Volume, 1991, p. 491 ff.

13   Article 1384 *Code civil* reads: '*On est responsable non seulement du dommage que l'on cause par son propre fait, mais encore de celui qui est causé par les faits der personnes dont on doit répondre (...). Les maîtres et les commettants, du dommages causé par leurs domestiques et préposés dans les functions auxquelles ils les ont employés.*'

14   See: André Tunc, *Jalons*, Paris 1991, p. 259 ff.

assigned; and a fault must have been committed by the subordinate (*préposé*) himself, in other words, the subordinate must be accountable as well.

The requirement of subordination is broadly construed. There must be, in particular, a power of command. Independent craftsmen and doctors do not satisfy this criterion. The required causal relationship between the damage inflicted and the task assigned is also broadly construed. There is a certain tendency, however, which manifests itself especially in the decisions of the *Chambre civile*, to demand a closer link between the task and the damage inflicted. The *Chambre criminelle*, which often also deals with the civil consequences of criminal offenses, stuck to the traditional view and accepted liability of the employer even in cases where the servant misused his employment (*abus de fonctions*). In 1983 the *Cour de Cassation* held that the employer was not liable, because the employee, contrary to his assignment, had caused the damage by contaminating a water basin at his own initiative.[15]

As to the requirement that the subordinate himself must have committed a fault, it should be noted that Article 489, section 2 *Code civil* means that inflicting damage under the influence of a mental defect, may still lead to liability of the person who caused the damage. This implies that, providing other requirements are met, the employer may also be held liable for such damage.[16]

Belgian vicarious liability law is in essence the same as that of France. Article 1384 of the Belgian *Code civil* was also originally viewed primarily as based on an irrefutable presumption of fault. In the course of time, the emphasis has gradually shifted to the master's function of guarantor vis-à-vis the injured party.[17] There is equally the prerequisite in Belgian law that the person employed (*aangestelde*) be a subordinate. This requirement notwithstanding, in practice, also pharmacists and doctors in the service of a clinic are qualified 'subordinates.'

Of course, Belgian liability law also requires that there was a fault on the part of the subordinate and that there is a specific relationship between that fault and the tasks assigned. In case law, this criterion is broadly construed, *e.g.* damage caused by employees during their lunch break is for the account of the employer.[18]

---

15 Cass. plénière, 17 juin 1983, J.C.P. II. 20120.
16 Oldenhuis' view on the matter is too sophisticated, I feel. See also Viney, op. cit, p. 899. Zweigert/Kötz, op. cit., Vol. II, p. 333, are erring here, since they clearly overlooked the amendment of 3 January 1986, amending Article 489-2.
17 See F.T. Oldenhuis, op. cit., p. 139.
18 For a more detailed treatment of this topic, see Kruithof, *Aansprakelijkheid voor andermans daad*. RW 1978-1979, p. 1394 ff. and Cornelis, *Beginselen van het Belgische buitencontractuele aansprakelijkheidsrecht*, Deel I, p. 361 ff.

6 Italian, Spanish and Portuguese Liability Law

The provisions of Article 2049 Italian *Codice civile* are similar to the French provisions on vicarious liability law.[19] At the time this code was introduced, the ratio was also found in the presumption of fault on the part of the employer in selecting and controlling the employee. Nowadays, the premise is that the employer is strictly liable for the employee, which derives from the idea that if one makes use of others for reasons of self-interest, one must also act as guarantor for the damage caused as a result of such employment of others. In other words, he who profits from the employment of others, must also bear the burden of responsibility for these others. Furthermore, it is held that the aggrieved person must be protected against the possible insolvency of the actual wrongdoer.

As in French law, Article 2049 of the Italian Civil Code prescribes that the employer himself must be at fault. There is a tendency among authoritative Italian writers to also assume liability of the employer where it is not possible, in the context of the complex modern corporate structure, to blame individual employees for the damage inflicted on third parties.[20]

The Spanish equivalent of this type of liability is laid down in Article 1903 *Código civil*.[21] Equally, at its inception, the presumed fault of the employer in selecting and/or employing the employee formed the legal foundation for this type of liability[22] But in Spanish law, there is also a gradual movement towards more severe forms of strict liability of the employer no longer based on the presumption of fault.[23] In Spain, authoritative writers also tend to accept liability of the employer where there is no fault on the part of the employee.[24]

Article 491 of the Portuguese *Codigo civil* contains a rule similar to the Spanish one described above.

7 Common Law/Scots and Irish Law

Anyone wanting to hold a master liable must prove that the actual wrongdoer was a servant, as opposed to an independent contractor; that the servant committed a wrongful act (a 'tort'); and that he committed the tort 'in the course of his employ-

---

19 Article 2049 *Codice civile* reads: '*I padroni e i committenti sono responsabili per i danni arrecati dal fatto illecito dei loro domestici e comessi nell'esercizio delle incombenze a cui sono adibiti.*'
20 Geri/Busnelli/Breccia/Natoli, *Diritto civile. 3. Obligatione e contratti.* Torino 1990, p. 738.
21 Article 1903 *Código civil* reads: '*Lo son igualmente [responsables] los dueños o directores de un establecimiento o empresa respecto de los perjuicios causados por sus dependientes, en el servicio de los ramos en que los tuvieren empleados, o con ocasión de sus funciones.*'
22 Yágüez, *La responsabilidad civil*, Bilbao 1989, p. 116.
23 Idem, p. 119.
24 Idem, p. 135.

ment'.[25] This liability is not dependent on any fault by the master, the employee's fault automatically being imputed to the master by operation of law.[26]

It is difficult to describe in a few words in which cases there is a master/servant relationship. In each decided case on the matter we encounter subtle differences. The traditional criterion for distinguishing servants from independent contractors is the degree of and the right to control. This criterion, however, originated in the nineteenth-century situation in which there was unskilled labour and the employer himself instructed the unskilled labourer in detail on the manner in which the work was to be performed. In most cases, there is no longer such a relationship. In the case of skilled and specialized staff (e.g. doctors), the employer no longer exercises control over the work performed. Nowadays, the courts take into account a variety of tests to determine the nature of the relationship between the wrongdoer and his employer.[27]

Where the damage is caused by someone who can be qualified as an independent contractor, rather than as a servant, in principle only the independent contractor can be sued for damages. There are, however, many exceptions to this rule. Particularly where the duties are 'personal non-delegable duties', often the master can be sued for damages, since he has a duty of care with regard to the person aggrieved.[28] Zweigert and Kötz formulate this as follows: not only is there 'a duty to take care', but there is also 'a duty that care is taken.'[29] In addition, there are cases in which the master authorizes the commission of a wrongful act, in which case he is liable as a joint tortfeasor along with the independent contractor. Although this is not vicarious liability, the effect is the same. This gives rise to the fact that, in many cases, a master must stand guarantor for the damage caused by the independent contractor contracted by him.

At common law the rule is also that the servant himself must be at fault. The employee must have caused the damage by means of a tort. The view that a master is liable by virtue of his having committed a tort himself has been rejected. At present, the prevailing view is that vicarious liability is indeed 'vicarious' and that a master can only be held liable provided his servant commits a tort.[30]

The requirement that the servant must have committed a tort in the course of his employment, is difficult to describe in more detail. Courts often appear to find less difficulty than writers, who keep striving 'to reconcile the irreconcilable', as Dias and Markesinis put it.[31] Whether an act falls within or outside the scope of his employment, is a question of fact. It has been decided, for instance, that an employee who causes an accident on his way to work, does not act in the course

---

25 Dias and Markesinis, *Tort law*, Oxford 1989, p. 379.
26 Zweigert/Kötz, op. cit., Vol. II, p. 333.
27 Dias and Markesinis, op. cit. p. 384.
28 See G. Samuel and J. Rinkes, *Contractual and non-contractual obligations in English law*, Nijmegen 1992, p. 202 ff.
29 Zweigert/Kötz, op. cit., Vol. II, p. 335.
30 Dias and Markesinis, op. cit., p. 387.
31 Dias and Markesinis, op. cit. p. 389. See on the rather complex matter of specific torts: Bernard Rudden, Torticles, *Tulane Civil Law Forum*, 1991-1992 (Vols. 6/7), p. 105-129.

of his employment, whereas the opposite is the case, where the employer assigns him to perform his tasks at a certain location and the employee, on his way to the assigned site, causes an accident. There is a tendency to liberally construe 'course of employment.'

Vicarious liability in Scots law is similar to common law vicarious liability in England and Wales.[32] The same holds true for vicarious liability under Irish law.[33]

8 Greece

Article 922 Greek Civil Code prescribes strict liability for the master for the damage done to another through the fault of the servant.[34] The ratio behind this strict liability is the fact that the master benefits from the servant's work.

9 Conclusion

Which conclusions can be drawn from our rather summary survey of vicarious liability[35] in the Common Market countries? There are three questions that spring to mind: Why should we want to harmonize or unify the various regulations?; how should we go about this?; and: what are the chances of success?

As to the first question, it is helpful to bear in mind the words of Fleming on the justification of vicarious liability. In his view, this type of liability is justified from the point of economically sound cost-allocation, because it represents production costs which should be reflected in the price of goods or services charged to the customers of the enterprise.[36] This may be a valid reason for working towards an EC directive on vicarious liability, because there is a direct link with production costs which may vary depending on the severity of the liability in question.[37]

---

32 See on this: David M. Walker, *Principles of Scottish private law*, Volume II, Oxford 1975, p. 1036 ff.
33 See McMahon and Binchy, *Irish law of torts*, Oxon, 1981, p. 97 ff.
34 See Panos Kornilakis, *Auf dem Wege zu einem Europäischen Haftungsrecht. Der Beitrag Griechenlands*. Saarbrücken 1986, p. 20 ff. (Vorträge, Reden und Berichte aus dem Europa-Institut (Nr. 73)).
35 See Geneviève Viney, *Vers la construction d'un droit européen de la responsabilité civile. Les apports possibles du droit français*, Saarbrücken 1986 (Vorträge, Reden und Berichte aus dem Europa-Institut (Nr. 59)).
36 John G. Fleming, *An introduction to the law of torts*, Oxford 1985, p. 163.
37 See from a 'law and economics' point of view: Faure and Van den Berg: *Objectieve aansprakelijkheid, verplichte verzekering en veiligheidsregulering*, Antwerpen (Maklu) 1989, no. 195.

I can think of no good reason why the EC should promote a directive on liability for services rendered on the one hand, and not one on vicarious liability on the other.[38]

How then are we to draft a proposal for a European code regulating vicarious liability? I agree with Zweigert and Kötz[39] that the rules of vicarious liability in the civil and common law tradition correspond on essential points. At this moment, only the German provisions of article 831 BGB are at variance. But the new draft version of this article will bring it into line with the rules in the rest of Europe (leaving Austria and Switzerland aside for the moment).

In the common law family, there is no clear distinction, in my view, between situations in which there is a master/servant relation and the ones in which there is an independent contractor. For the sake of having a clear ideal type of liability for others and for reasons of cost allocation, I would prefer to place both situations under the same vicarious liability regime. For this purpose, I propose to extend the rule of vicarious liability for employees to vicarious liability for independent contractors. As to the exact formulation of such a rule, I would suggest to follow the draft statute on Article 831 BGB, or the text of Article 6:170 Netherlands Civil Code (leaving out the rather subtle differentiation made in the second section of Article 6:170 NCC): 'The master in whose service a servant fulfils his duties is liable for damage done to another by the fault of that servant, if the likelihood that a fault would be committed has been increased by the order to perform the duties of the servant.'[40]

As said earlier, I would rather see this liability extended to independent contractors. Departing from the Dutch Article 6:171, I suggest the following: 'Where, for the purpose of the carrying on of a business by another person, an independent contractor who performs work at that other person's orders, is liable towards a third person for a fault committed in the course of those activities, that other person is also liable to the third person.'[41]

What are the chances of success? On a short-term basis, I would say very slim. But in the long term, the chances are better. Since we have product liability all over Europe (and nobody seems to complain about that) and we are working towards liability for services (which everybody complains about), it is not so big a step towards regulating vicarious liability, considering the differences between the existing regulations are in fact rather small.

---

38 See for a more general survey of the question: Müller-Graf, Common private law in the European community, in: Bruno de Witte and Caroline Forder (ed.), *The common law of Europe and the future of legal education*, Deventer (Kluwer) 1992, p. 239 ff.
39 Zweigert/Kötz, op. cit., Volume II, p. 337.
40 Translation Haanappel/Mackaay, *New Netherlands Civil Code*, Deventer/Boston, 1990, p. 302. I prefer to leave out the requisite of control over the conduct of the servant, inasmuch as this control test is of limited application to specialists and experts in most situations.
41 This translation is partly based on Haanappel/Mackaay, op. cit., p. 303.

CHAPTER 17
Product Liability

Geraint Howells

The creation of the European Community, and the recent establishment of a broader European Economic Area, has brought with it the need to create a greater degree of harmonisation among the trading laws of European countries. Much of the harmonising legislation to-date has been of a technical, regulatory nature, but such activity was bound to cause lawyers to question whether it is desirable and practicable also to harmonise the basic private law of obligations which after all form the background rules within which regulatory rules operate. The continental mind instinctively thinks of the possibility of a grand European Civil Code — hence this book.

A common lawyer must approach the task of discussing the possibilities of establishing a European Civil Code with some trepidation, for common lawyers — at least of the anglicised variety — are unaccustomed to the concept of a 'Code'. Our prime sources of law are the principles espoused by the judges on a case by case basis, and legislation has traditionally been narrowly interpreted and certainly has not been seen as a source of general principles of law. Therefore common lawyers may have some difficulties in understanding the status of a Code. An English lawyer can probably never completely understand all the nuances and subtleties of a Code. It is also probably all too easy for the English lawyer to acquaint himself with one civil law legal system and then arrogantly to assume that the 'Code' has the same status in all civil law countries. To guard myself against such criticisms I will set out my understanding of what a European Civil Code should be. My conception of a European Civil Code is of a set of basic principles governing the laws of civil liability which can be both agreed upon *and* also consistently applied by members of the European legal community. The second limb of this definition is important, for it is not sufficient that countries agree on the formal wording of the Code, that wording must also be understood as having the same content in the different legal systems.

The task of writing the chapter on product liability carries with it a particular responsibility, because product liability was the first major area of 'private law' to be subjected to the EC harmonisation process and hence has potentially a great deal to teach us about the possibilities for the creation of a European Civil Code. This harmonisation process was set in motion by a 1985 EC directive[1] which was to be implemented by member states by July 1988. The United Kingdom, Italy and Greece were the only member states to comply with this deadline. Seven other member states have since brought their domestic law into line with the directive, but France and Spain are still in default. Meanwhile, Austria, Finland, Norway and

---

1   Directive 85/374/EEC, O.J. L 210/29, 7.8.1985.

Sweden have all created laws based on the directive, even before they were compelled to do so by the European Economic Area Agreement.

The extent to which the product liability laws of Europe have been successfully harmonised might be taken as a gauge to the possibility of success in other areas and hence shed some light on whether the concept of a European Civil Code is feasible. Of course even if the harmonisation of product liability laws can be considered a success this does not necessarily mean that the success can be repeated in other areas of civil law. There may be special factors at play in the area of product liability: to pre-empt subsequent discussions a little, this may have been an area ripe for harmonisation, as convergence might already have been taking place due to the need of all developed countries to meet a common social phenomenon. Equally the establishment of similar formal liability rules may belie the real extent of harmonisation of product liability laws for two reasons. First, as alluded to earlier the practical application of the rules may differ giving them a different *de facto* content in different legal systems. Second, liability rules form only part of product liability law, in practice more cases turn on questions of causation than liability and also damage laws are of the greatest importance.

The structure of this chapter will therefore be as follows:

1   to ascertain the essential features of the product liability directive;
2   to consider the extent to which these factors had been present in European legal systems prior to the directive;
3   to evaluate the likely success of the EC directive as a harmonising measure and to consider the lessons product liability harmonisation can teach us about the prospects for the successful creation of a European Civil Code.

1 Product Liability Directive

Codes are about establishing basic legal principles. Therefore, I shall restrict myself to asking certain basic questions about the directive in order to establish (i) whether these were to be found in the pre-existing laws of member states and (ii) have they been successfully harmonised. The following issues appear to be pertinent.

1 What is the Scope of the Directive, i.e. How is Product Defined?
Art. 2 of the directive provides that 'product' means all moveables, even when incorporated into another moveable (i.e. component parts) or an immovable (i.e. fixtures) and it expressly provides that electricity is to be included within the definition of a product. The directive however excludes primary agricultural produce and game, by which is meant 'the products of the soil, of stock-farming and fisheries' which have not undergone initial processing.

2 Who is Liable?

The basic principle is that the 'producer' should be liable.[2] The term producer covers those one would naturally think of as being so described, i.e. the manufacturer of a finished product or component part and the producer of any raw material. It is however extended to cover 'own-branders' i.e. those who by putting their name, trademark or other distinguishing feature on the product present themselves as being its producer. In addition, liability is placed on the importer of goods into the European Community. Suppliers are only liable if they fail to respond to a request from an injured person to inform him of the identity of his supplier or the producer/importer.

3 When Does Liability Arise?

Liability arises when a defective product is shown to have caused injury. It should be noted that proof of causation remains an essential element of a product liability action. The biggest change the directive was intended to have produced was a change from fault to strict liability. As we shall see in practice many legal systems had in effect already made their product liability laws much 'stricter', and doubts can also be raised about just how strict the product liability directive's standard really is.[3] Thus the key to understanding the directive lies in its definition of defect. Art. 6 provides that:

'A product is defective when it does not provide the safety which a person is entitled to expect, taking all circumstances into account, including:
   (a) the presentation of the product;
   (b) the use to which it could reasonably be expected that the product would be put;
   (c) the time when the product was put into circulation.'

The directive has various defences,[4] the one which most obviously affects the liability standard is the so-called development risks defence. Art. 7(e) provides the producer with a defence is he proves that 'the scientific and technical knowledge at the time when he put the product into circulation was not such as to enable the existence of the defect to be discovered.' The directive gives member states the option of removing this defence from their implementing legislation.

4 What Damages Are Recoverable?

The directive covers damages caused by death or personal injury. However it leaves the question of recovery for non-material damage to national provisions and

---

2   Art. 3.
3   See G. Howells, *Comparative Product Liability*, (Aldershot : Dartmouth, 1993) p. 35-39 and J. Stapleton, 'Products Liability Reform — Real or Illusory' (1986) 6 *OJLS* 392.
4   I.e. that the defendant did not put the product into circulation; that the defect did not exist when the product was put into circulation; that the product was not commercially manufactured or distributed in the course of a business; that the defect was due to compliance with regulatory standards or in the case of a component manufacturer that the defect was due to the design of the end product or to instructions given by the manufacturer of the end product (art.7).

gives member states the option of imposing a ceiling of not less than 70 million ECU on damages resulting from a death or personal injury caused by identical items with the same defect.

Recovery for property damage is more tightly controlled. The *damaged* property must be both of a type ordinarily intended for private use or consumption and actually used by the injured person mainly for his own private use or consumption. Also the first 500 ECU of property damage is not recoverable.

From this brief survey of the directive it is clear that there remain some areas of debate about the basic features of the product liability regime. Most obviously this is true of the matters on which member states have been given an option: the inclusion of primary agricultural produce and game; the development risk defence and the ceiling on personal injury damages.

2 The Trends in European Product Liability

If the European legal systems were already converging around certain common principles then this might allow us to speculate that the time was ripe for the creation of some common European principles. Product liability might then either be seen as a special case, or the supporters of a European Civil Code could argue that similar convergences of legal principles to meet common social phenomena either are taking place in other areas or, at least, ought to be occurring.

Regarding the scope of existing laws it is fair to say that no European county had a liability regime which was specifically designed to cover all products. Germany did have a special regime for drugs and insurance based regimes existed for drugs in Sweden and Finland.[5] The Spanish Consumer Protection Act 1984 did introduce a form of strict liability for products and services which are likely to be dangerous, and specifically extended to foodstuffs, hygiene and cleaning products, cosmetics, pharmaceuticals, health, gas and electrical services, home appliances, lifts, means of transport, motor vehicles, toys and other products for children. The notion of a special product liability regime had however been widely canvassed in European countries most notably in the United Kingdom by the Pearson Royal Commission[6] in France by the Calais-Auloy Commission[7] and had been canvassed in German legal literature by academics such as Diederichsen and Lorenz.[8] However, equally the conventional product liability laws of sale of goods and tort apply to all products without exception. Therefore the exclusion of primary agricultural produce and game in the directive could be said to go against the trend of European laws, and the *Ghestin* committee set up to consider reform of the

---

5   See G. Howells, 'Drug product liability in West Germany and Sweden' in G. Howells (ed.), *Product Liability, Insurance and the Pharmaceutical Industry* (Manchester: MUP, 1991).
6   *Royal Commission on Civil Liability and Compensation for Personal Injury*, Cmnd. 7054, 1978.
7   See J. Calais-Auloy, *Vers un nouveau droit de la consommation*, (Paris: La documentation française, 1984).
8   See G. Howells (1993), op. cit. p. 126-128.

French law, in the light of the directive, seems to have persuaded the French Government that agricultural produce should be included in the new product liability regime. The fundamental point to note however is that the idea of a distinct product liability regime was not unknown in Europe and in any event as the new regime is only likely to be a stricter version of the general law, which already applied to products there should be no problem with creating a distinct product liability regime: as of course the adoption of the product liability directive confirms.

Leaving aside the novel liability of own-branders and importers,[9] and the subsidiary liability of suppliers who fail to disclose their suppliers or to identify the producer/importer, the underlying policy of the directive is to trace responsibility back to the producer, i.e. the manufacturer. Many European legal systems were already developing their laws in this way prior to the directive. This was not only true of the special product/pharmaceutical liability regimes mentioned above, but was also true of the general law. This is perhaps most clearly seen in countries such as France, Belgium, Luxembourg by the creation of an 'action directe' between the consumer-purchaser and higher links in the distribution chain[10] and in Austria by the notion of contracts having protective effects for third parties.[11] Equally however the inclination of many countries to reject contract as a way of resolving product liability disputes in favour of tort laws, underlines the point that increasingly the law was recognising that the person responsible for the quality and safety of products is the producer, rather than the retailer, who is the party the consumer has the contractual nexus with. Although tort law can apply to all suppliers it is most obviously directed against the manufacturer, who is most likely to be to blame for the defective nature of the product. A good example of tort law aimed explicitly at the manufacturer is the French case law based on art. 1384.1 of the Civil Code which, inter alia, makes a person liable for things in their keeping. Goldman was concerned that the product user was being unfairly made the insurer of the product's quality.[12] He therefore drew a distinction, which has been accepted by the courts, between '*garde de la structure*' (the product's design) and '*garde du comportement*' (how the product is used): whilst the user was responsible for damage caused by the latter, the manufacturer remained liable for the '*garde de la structure*'.[13]

---

9   A 1979 German case ([1980] *NJW* 1219) is significant in this respect. It concerned liability for defective bicycles. The Court held that no extra duties should be imposed by virtue of the fact that the distributor was an importer. The court did however feel that it was relevant that the goods had been imported from one of the six original member states of the European Community − suggesting that it might have taken different considerations into account if the goods had been imported from other countries.

10   See Cass. com. 27 April 1971, *JCP* 1972, II, 17280 and Cass. civ. 1, 9 March 1983, Bull civ. 1, no. 92, p. 81: see Howells (1993), op. cit., p. 106-108.

11   This was based on academic writings such as those of F. Bydlinski, 'Vertragliche Sorgfaltspflichten zugunsten Dritter', (1960) 82 *JB* 359.

12   *La détermination de gardien responsible du fait des choses inanimées.* (Paris: Sirey, 1947).

13   See e.g. Cass. civ. II, 5 June 1971, *Bull. civ.* II, no 204, p. 145.

317

Germany is the country which has most strongly, in the 'chicken-pest' case,[14] rejected an extension of contract in product liability in favour of stronger tort laws. The 'chicken-pest' case saw a reversal of the burden of proof being introduced for manufacturing defects, which was extended to design defects in the 'brake' case[15] and recently in the 'Milupa' case,[16] to warning defects (but not to post-marketing warnings).

There is obviously a certain push to place the primary responsibility for damage caused by the product on the producer, and this is a trend reflected in the product liability directive. The above discussion also hints at the fact of a move towards stricter product liability laws. In those countries which took the contractual route this was achieved by retaining the strict liability principle of contractual liability, whilst removing the barrier of privity. Those which took the tortious route tended to strengthen their liability laws. As we have seen Germany is the prime example, but across Europe tort laws were being strengthened so that certainly it became fairly straightforward in most countries to recover for manufacturing defects,[17] whilst producers were being placed under stringent obligations to keep up to-date in order to satisfy their duty of care, i.e. lack of fault, in relation to product design. To what extent is the directive's chosen liability standard — one based on consumer expectations — to be recognised in the pre-existing European legal systems?

In the Netherlands, even before the directive was implemented the Courts were able to claim their law included a consumer expectation standard. In the Halcion case, concerning a sedative, the Court of Appeal upheld by the Supreme Court held that 'a drug is defective if it does not provide the safety which a person is entitled to expect, taking all the circumstances into account.'[18] More generally the point can be made that there is little difference between a consumer expectation defectiveness standard and a negligence liability standard. They can be viewed as providing the same answer to two similar questions that have been posed in a slightly different manner. The consumer expectation test answers the question of whether the product is of the appropriate standard, whilst negligence standards question the actions of the producer. In reality the two tests will turn on similar factors: the economic and technical feasibility of undertaking further research or providing more adequate warnings and the amount of risk which is acceptable given the benefits the product brings. Of course this is rather controversial for it seems to equate strict liability with negligence, but this need not be the case for the difference might lie in the timeframe in which the judgments are made — time of marketing in negligence, time of injury or trial in strict liability — and this is a point which is returned to below. Contract law does of course have different juridical roots based around the notion of a bargain, but nevertheless traces of

---

14   BGHZ 51,91.
15   *BB* [1970] 1414.
16   *JZ* [1992] 633.
17   I.e. defects occurring during the production process or by the use of faulty materials.
18   [1989] *Int'l Bus Lawyer* 390.

consumer expectation test reasoning are to be found in the implied terms such as those of merchantable quality and *vice caché* for the fitness of the product is judged against what consumers should have been entitled to expect in the circumstances.

The rationale for strict liability ought to be to impose liability regardless of fault, particularly for risks which only became known subsequent to the marketing of the product, in the interests of compensating the unfortunate injured person and spreading the cost among all consumers. Regrettably the directive does not seem to have adopted this strong version of product liability for the level of safety which can be expected of a product is to be judged according to 'the time when the product was put into circulation' and of course the development risks defence is available unless member states have chosen to exclude it. Nevertheless more optimistically it could be noted that the directive's development risk defence is very stringent — it places the burden of proving the defence on the producer and is drawn very narrowly so that the producer would fail to establish the defence if the defect was technically discoverable, even though it had not actually been discovered.[19] In fact it is interesting to note that European legal systems had been adopting a similar stringent approach to such questions — in some cases being even stricter than the directive.

In English contract law development risks defence are of no relevance. If the product fails to meet the required standard there is liability notwithstanding any lack of fault on the part of the producer. In France the position is somewhat different for the *vice caché* doctrine depends in theory upon the seller knowing of the hidden defect if consequential damages are to be recoverable. However the case law has developed an irrebuttable presumption that the professional seller knew of the defect and this applies even if it was impossible for him to have known of the defect.[20]

In assessing manufacturer's behaviour the courts in some European legal systems have not been very receptive to argument smacking of development risks type arguments. Thus in England the defendants in *Vacwell v B.D.H. Chemicals*[21] were held liable for failing to provide and maintain a system for carrying out adequate research into the scientific literature. They had in fact studied four modern texts on the subject, including the standard work on the industrial hazards of chemicals, none of which had mentioned the explosive qualities of boron tribromide, when it came into contact with water. The English courts have also been very demanding as regards the applications to which they expect defendants to apply known knowledge. In *IBA v EMI (Electric) Ltd and BICC Construction Ltd*[22] the defendants were held liable for failing to take account of the effects ice would have when it accumulated on the stays of a television mast. In similar vein the German courts, in a case involving a recyclable lemonade bottle, talked in

---

19   But see discussion, below, of the scope of the defence in English law.
20   Cass. com. 15 Nov 1971, D. 1972, p. 211.
21   [1971] 1 *QB* 88.
22   (1981) 14 *BLR* 1.

terms of the producer going to the limits of what is 'technologically feasible and economically reasonable.'[23]

The heads of damages which are recoverable under the directive are as regards property damage subject to some quite novel conditions. The limitation to consumer property and the exclusion of the first 500 ECU of damage are not to be found elsewhere in the domestic laws of member states. The directive's provision regarding recovery for damages for personal injury and death on the other hand do illustrate divergent trends in the member states. Some countries, such as Germany, have a tradition of combining strict liability with a ceiling on damages and this explains why member states are permitted the option of including a ceiling on personal injury damages of not less than 70M ECU. Equally European legal systems have different rules about both the availability and extent of damages for non-material damage (i.e. pain and suffering and loss of amenity) and the directive is expressly said to be subject to national provisions on this point.

3 The Directive as a Harmonising Measure — the Prospects for a Civil Code

The fact that the key elements of the product liability directive — the placing of liability on the producer and adoption of strict liability — reflects trends which were already discernible in the major European legal systems boded well for the harmonisation of European product liability laws. Equally the fact that a system defined in scope by the concept of a product was, if not familiar, then at least something not unknown or opposed by the existing legal systems again augured well for the harmonising measure. Equally the types of damage the directive hoped to compensate were familiar, even if there were some novel features. All these elements suggest that harmonisation (or the establishment of the principles of product liability for a European Civil Code) should be possible. Indeed the agreement of the member states to the directive underlines this point. Prior convergence of laws is not of course a pre-requisite for a harmonisation programme, but it clearly increases the chance of success both in negotiating an agreement and in implementing the resulting agreement. Familiarity with the legal terms used in the harmonising instrument is likely to be an important factor in determining how well it is received into the domestic legal systems of the European states.

As a first attempt at harmonising European private law — dare one suggest as the first stage in the creation of a European Civil Code — the product liability directive is in many ways a remarkable success. By removing the 'level playing field' argument the Community was able to press through a measure of consumer protection, which industry had seemed able to persuade national legislators it was not in the national economic interest to adopt. However the scars of battle between

---

23   [1988] *NJW* 2611.

the various legal traditions and the pressure exerted by lobby groups are also evident. Legal traditions explain the option to have a ceiling on personal injury damages and the leaving to national legal system matters appertaining to non-material damages and the right of contribution or recourse. Lobby pressure explains why the inclusion of development risks and primary agricultural produce and game are left to the option of member states. The aim of the directive was of course to 'approximate' the laws — not to make them uniform — and whether this is acceptable is a matter for debate, although it should be noted that the directive might be viewed as only a first stage since it has built in review procedures. Would such differences be tolerated in a European Civil Code? A distinction could perhaps be drawn between matters such as whether primary agricultural produce and game should be included which is an essentially technical matter and the issue of whether development risks should be included, which is a far more fundamental matter of principle. Similar concern could be expressed about the lack of uniformity concerning rights of contribution and recourse and particularly about the lack of a common approach to personal injury damages, both in relation to the ceiling on damages and non-material damages. This relates to a broader point about the range of legal rules and principles involved in product liability cases, which will be returned to below.

Of course the possibility of divergent implementation is not a problem if in practice countries choose to adopt similar laws. How then has the directive been implemented? With regard to the three options:

1 only Luxembourg has included primary agricultural produce and game, although France is likely to follow suit;
2 again only Luxembourg has removed the development rules defence, although Spain is considering not applying the defence to medicines and food and some such risks may be included within the German pharmaceutical liability regime which is excluded from the scope of the implementing legislation; and,
3 a ceiling for personal injury damages is to be found in the German, Greek and Portuguese implementing legislation and is likely to be included in the Spanish legislation.

The experience of the implementation process of the directive also reveals some further difficulties facing the drafters of a European Civil Code. The new German law, for instance, does not allow recovery of non-material damages: these must be sought in traditional tort law. The United Kingdom's Consumer Protection Act 1987 not only provides for a development risks defence but provides for an apparently more generous defence than the directive allows: it introduces the concept of *expectation* of discovery of defects and judges producers against the standard reflecting norm of what could be expected of producers of the same type of product.[24] The proposed French law would make it the sole source of legal rights for people injured by products who suffered damages which fall within the scope of its application.[25] As regards product liability harmonisation this is not particularly dangerous — it might even be seen as advantageous for the existence of other domestic sources of remedies in product liability cases can maintain divergent levels of consumer protection. For the prospects of a European Civil Code however it poses a clear warning. It shows fundamental differences between the legal psyche of the European countries. The French desire clear boundaries between sources of liability, whereas the common law tradition, in particular, is happy to find the solution to a case from whatever legal instruments can be made to apply. What this brief survey of the implementation of the directive shows however is that member states give effect to their own national wishes and traditions when giving effect to the agreed principles.

Only in future years will we know whether the harmonisation which has been achieved around a consumer expectation defectiveness standard is merely symbolic or has substantive content. This is because of the possibility that whilst the laws can formally be the same in different countries, nevertheless the content of the rules may vary significantly when it comes to their application. Will the consumer expectation standard, and where applicable the development risks defence, be applied uniformly across Europe, even given that the rules are enacted with the same or similar wording? This of course turns upon how much discretion the judge is given in determining the substantive content of the standard. One way of circumscribing this discretion is to structure the discretion by providing strict guide-lines so as to define its content. The directive tries to achieve this with regard to the defectiveness standard by directing that the presentation of the product, the use to which it could be expected to be put and the time when it is put into circulation should all be taken into account. However this guidance is quite general and not specific on either the question of what bearing these factors should have on the defectiveness standard or what weight should be given to the various factors. Similarly the development risk defence leaves it to the judge to determine both what the relevant state of scientific and technical knowledge is and whether that was such as to enable the existence of the defect to be discovered. Even if the European Court of Justice were to lay down further guidance the judge trying the case is likely to retain a large area of discretion. This is inevitable given the standard reflecting norm based on consumer expectation which was chosen. To the extent that this allows the content of the standard to develop overtime this may be advantageous. The problem arises if the standard is interpreted differently in different legal systems *at the same time*. This could easily happen within Europe for consumer expectations are the result of both social and economic conditions.

---

24   S. 4(1)(e) of the Consumer Protection Act 1987 provides a defence where 'the state of scientific and technical knowledge was not such that a producer of products of the same description as the product in question might be expected to have discovered the defect if it had existed in his products while they were under his control'.

25   The legality of this approach is questionable: see Howells (1993) op. cit., p. 114-115, 197-198.

In this context social conditions can be equated with the degree to which a society is prepared to allow its citizens to take risks. This can be illustrated by looking at road traffic regulation: is the wearing of a helmet compulsory for motor cyclists? Do cars have to be fitted with front and/or rear seat belts? Must passengers wear them? Just as these regulatory issues are subject to different laws across Europe, so might judges take differing views on consumer expectations, reflecting local preferences as to risk-taking. The economic conditions within Europe are fairly homogeneous when viewed in global terms, but nevertheless significant disparities exist particularly between the North and South of Europe. Lower economic conditions tend to reduce consumer expectations of safety as poor consumers are willing to trade off safety for lower price and hence the greater affordability of products.

So far the product liability experience has been used to illustrate two problems facing the drafters of a European Civil Code: (i) the tendency for legal systems to cling on to their own legal traditions and (ii) the difficulty of ensuring that laws which are commonly agreed upon are not, nevertheless, applied in different ways in the various European legal systems. The final point which will be noted relates to the fact that product liability cases — like most legal problems — involve a complex range of legal issues. To use the example of product liability, there is little practical impact in harmonising liability standards if both the rules on causation and damages remain in the province of national laws.[26] In practice most product liability cases are more likely to be decided on causation than liability grounds and the question of damages often remains the key to forum shopping. Thus the point can be made that product liability law has only been partially harmonised by a directive which concentrates on the question of liability, and even then does not cover post-marketing defects. In one sense this points to the need for a European Civil Code so that all the relevant matters can be dealt with. On the other hand the danger is raised that a European Civil Code could fail to meet its objectives if its scope is not wide enough. There is clearly a danger that national policy makers will agree to a European Civil Code, but wish to exclude certain sensitive areas.

4 Conclusion

Private law is in many ways the soul of a legal system. Any infringement upon it is viewed with suspicion by lawyers steeped in their own legal tradition. Yet if a case can be made out for harmonisation of regulatory rules, the same logic and policy must dictate a need to harmonise the private law rules which form the background within which the regulatory rules operate. Thus the project to create a European Civil Code is beginning to be discussed.

26　I have limited my discussions to substantive law principles: procedural differences such as access to justice questions and rules on discovery are also likely to play important roles in product liability litigation. Equally other substantive law principles can inter-relate with those covered by the directive.

Product liability was one of the first areas of private law to be harmonised by the European Community. This experience has some lessons for the broader European Civil Code project about (i) the difficulties of overcoming national legal traditions, (ii) the danger that laws which are formally harmonised may differ in their application in the various legal systems and (iii) limited utility of the exercise if all aspects of the legal problem are not harmonised.

The experience relating to product liability suggests that those who want to take the European Civil Code project on further have at least one important set of questions to answer and one important lesson to learn.

First, it is important to decide just what degree of consensus the Code is seeking to achieve. Must there be complete uniformity or is it sufficient that certain key principles be harmonised with other matters being left to national laws? Is it viable to allow states to choose between a range of options on certain issues? Equally is it satisfactory that common principles are established even if their application differs in practice in the various legal systems?

Second, the would be codifier must learn to be patient. The product liability directive had a long gestation period and the criticisms that have been made of the directive must be judged against the difficult task the drafters faced. Future reviews of the directive, the possibility for which are provided for within the directive, may well serve to eradicate the majority of the present flaws.

The rush to create the internal market perhaps provided the necessary political impetuses for the harmonisation process. It did however create an impression that in Europe if something cannot be achieved immediately it is not worth achieving. Particularly with the European Civil Code project, however, long and serious deliberations are essential. This is both because of the complex issues involved, and because the result is likely to have a fundamental impact on the laws of the member states for a significant time to come. One suspects that if the project is to succeed its guardians will have to be peculiarly gifted with both idealism and pragmatism — but are they not the trademarks of all great jurists?

CHAPTER 18
Traffic Accident Compensation

André Tunc

1 Traffic accident compensation should be an important chapter of a European Civil Code. Traffic crossing the frontiers is permanently increasing and, with it, the number of traffic accidents occurring in a foreign country.

It is unfortunate for the victims to find themselves under an unknown system of compensation and to regret not having taken a voluntary insurance which would have usefully complemented it. It is even possible that a number of persons may be reluctant to go and drive in foreign countries from the fear that an accident might occur, the consequences of which are unknown.

Furthermore, while complaints about the present systems of compensation are heard in many countries, a unification of the systems would be an opportunity for both reform and improvement of the law.

Finally, unification would be beneficial to the insurance companies, which, in this important field, would work on surer grounds, and would more easily offer insurance in foreign countries.

2 Very wisely, the contributors to the second part of this volume are asked, 'to give a brief description of their specified subject as regulated in the new Dutch Civil Code and in various other European countries'.

The present contributor, however, would like to be excused from this directive. He had tried, some years ago, to make a survey of the various system of traffic accident compensation.[1] Few developments seem to have occurred since that time in Europe.

a The most important one is the enactment, in France, of a statute of the 5 July 1985, *tendant à l'amélioration de la situation des victimes d'accidents de la circulation et à l'accélération des procédures d'indemnision*. This statute is the result of a compromise.[2] It leaves compensation of the drivers under the fault regime. But the other victims (pedestrians, cyclists and mere passengers of a motor vehicles) benefit from a quasi-no-fault compensation regime. They are entitled to compensation, unless, being between 16 and 70 years of age, they have committed an 'inexcusable fault' which is the only cause of the accident. After fierce resistance and attacks, the new law is now accepted and many commentators regret that it does not give a better cover to drivers. It has increased the number of victims who receive compensation and reduced the time taken to reach a settlement. It has greatly reduced litigation. In Spring 1991, the rate of litigation

---

1   Traffic Accident Compensation: Law and Proposal, Ch. 14 of Vol. XI (Torts) of the *International Encyclopedia of Comparative Law* (1970 and Supp., 1980).

2   Within a vast literature, see mainly Geneviève Viney, *L'indemnisation des victimes d'accidents de la circulation*, 1992.

for personal injury involving permanent disability or death, which was, before the reform, 28%, had already fallen to 12% (11% for mutual companies); if all personal injury cases are considered, the figures are, respectively, 20% and 8%.
b The new Dutch Civil Code contains no specific provision on traffic accidents. Liability in the case of a car accident is governed by Article 31 Wegenverkeerswet (Road Traffic Act). Recently, the Hoge Raad (Dutch Supreme Court) on the basis of this Article, formulated new rules which link up the system of liability for car-accidents with the general, more risk-oriented, system of liability of the new Dutch Civil Code. To properly understand the new rules, it has to be remembered that every car in the Netherlands has to be covered by liability insurance for the driver. The following summary of the case-law holds true only for accidents where the victim is either a pedestrian or a cyclist.

The new case-law[3] makes a distinction between cases in which the victim of a car accident is a child under 14 years old (who cannot, according to Article 6:164 new Dutch Civil Code, be held liable for its actions in tort) and cases in which the victim is 14 years old or above. The new case-law is relevant to two distinct subjects.

The first subject is the imputation of the accident to the driver. Whatever the age of the victim, the driver is only considered not to be at fault if he has made no mistake whatsoever. Faults of other participants in traffic which are not completely unforseeable are imputed to the driver if he has not altered his conduct to the possibility of the occurence of these faults. Furthermore, where the victim is under 14, the driver will only be exempted from liability if the sole cause of the accident is an intentional or reckless, bordering on intentional, act of the victim. Mere faults of a victim under 14 are imputed to the driver. If the victim is over 14, this rule does not apply.

The second subject is the division of damages in case of contributory negligence. According to Article 6:101 of the new Dutch Civil Code, damages are divided 'in proportion to the degree in which the circumstances which can be imputed to [the victim and the person who has the obligation to repair the damage], have contributed to the damage.' This division can be altered if equity so requires. On the basis of equity, the Hoge Raad has formulated the following rules. In car accidents, if the victim (being a pedestrian or a cyclist) is under 14, only acts of the victim which are intentional or reckless, bordering on intentional, can be taken into account in the divison of damages. If the victim is 14 or over, unless the victim has acted intentionally or recklessly (bordering on the intention), a minimum of fifty per cent of the damages will always be imputed to the driver. Whether more than fifty per cent of the damages can be imputed to the driver, will be determined according to the general rule of Article 6:101 new Dutch Civil Code. An

---

3   Hoge Raad 1 juni 1990, *NJ* 1991, 720 (Ingrid Kolkman); Hoge Raad 31 mei 1991, *NJ* 1991, 721 (Marbeth van Uitregt); Hoge Raad 28 februari 1992, *NJ* 1993, 566 (IZA/Vrerink); Hoge Raad 15 januari 1993, *NJ* 1993, 568 (Puts/Ceha); Hoge Raad 24 december 1993, *RvdW* 1994, 11 (Anja Kellenaers).

insurer of the victim cannot profit from these equity-based rules and if an insurer takes action against the driver, the general rule of Article 6:101 will be applied.

c Another development worth mentioning is the publication by the Lord Chancellor of England, in May 1991, of a consultative paper on compensation for victims of road accidents. The official summary of this document is as follows:

— The scheme provides for compensation without proof of fault; people injured in road accidents would not have to show fault on the part of anyone in order to establish a claim.

— Claims would be limited to personal injuries arising out of road accidents involving one or more vehicles. The scheme would not extend to claims for vehicle damage.

— An upper limit on claims of £ 2,500 is proposed, with a lower limit of £ 250 below which claims would not be allowed.

— The scheme would be funded and operated by the insurance industry via motor vehicle premiums.

— The scheme would cover the United Kingdom as a whole.

— Most cases under the scheme would be settled without going to court.

— Existing tort law rights would be preserved.

— Cases involving larger sums would continue to be dealt with in court.

The Lord Chancellor's Department received a great many replies to the consultation document of May 1991 and is still considering how to proceed.

3 Another reason why the present contributor does not feel the need for a lengthy consideration of the present laws is that most of them, in Europe, are based on a philosophy of liability for fault and non-liability for no-fault, while a modern law should be based on a philosophy of compensation for accidental damage. This is a philosophy which has roots in ancient law, which was accepted by Roman law in some cases (damage caused by animals, things thrown from a building, tumble-down building), transmitted in these cases to the French and a number of other Civil Codes. It is now accepted in industrial injuries and partly in traffic accidents. It should be recognized in its autonomy[4] and should be the basis of a modern law of traffic accidents.

4 If the present laws of European countries do not seem to be a satisfactory basis for a uniform European law of traffic accident compensation, it is submitted that our source of inspiration should be the proposals advanced in 1968 by the *American Insurance Association* (AIA).[5] This is a large federation of insurance companies; in 1968, its share of the market of automobile insurance amounted to 38%.It came out in favour of no-fault compensation of all traffic victims through first-party insurance. Its efforts received limited success, due to some scepticism from other insurers, but mainly to the strong opposition of well organized sections

---

4   André Tunc, Responsabilité civile et droit des accidents, *Festschrift für Werner Lorenz*, 1991, p. 805 et s.

5   On the AIA proposals, see Tunc, *op.cit.* (n.1), s. 168-176.

of the lawyers associations. This experience will lead us to ask three questions: (a) Why a no-fault law? (b) What type of insurance? (c) What should be the scope of a chapter on traffic accident of a European Civil Code compensation and what is its feasibility?

5 Before trying to answer these questions, a preliminary remark should be made: we should concern ourselves only with personal injury and death, not with property damage, especially damage to vehicles.

Two reasons justify this exclusion. First, in many European countries, the problem of vehicle damage is settled in a relatively satisfactory fashion by arrangements made between insurance companies, and there is no need to interfere. Secondly, while compensation for a serious personal injury or for a death may be vital to a family, this is not the case for car damage; the owner of a car may take out such insurance as he wishes, and all economic research has demonstrated that, as regards property, insurance by the owner provides compensation much more cheaply and satisfactorily than civil liability.

I Why No-fault Compensation?

6 There are many reasons why all victims of traffic accidents should receive compensation without having to prove fault and without regard to their possible 'fault'.

Motor vehicle traffic creates a risk,[6] a risk which every day generates deaths and injuries. Materializations of the risk result from combinations, which are often difficult to analyze, of mechanical and human failures and sheer bad luck. Victims usually expect compensation. From a social point of view also, compensation is desirable.

This is the reason why most European countries admit a *prima facie* liability of the motorist toward the victim and require the motorist to take out a liability insurance. But most laws refuse compensation to a person injured by his or her own fault. There is a fallacy here, which should be denounced.

If 'fault' is defined, through various formulas, as the behaviour which would not have been the one of a *'bonus pater familias'* (the careful citizen, mindful of his duties toward himself and his fellow citizens), the conclusion is inescapable that one should not qualify as 'faults' the multiple errors, inadvertences, blunders, clumsiness which all of us may commit and that, as a matter of fact, we all more or less permanently do commit. *Errare humanum est.* Victims of such errors, be it their own, are victims of human nature exposed to traffic risk. At first blush, it may seem fair that such risk should be borne by those who create it. As said by Keeton and O'Connell, the 'automobile should pay its way through society'.

It is true that faults in the precise sense of the word are often committed and are the causes of too many accidents. Great attention is presently given, in France and probably in other countries, to dangerous behaviours, in particular excessive speed and driving while under the influence of alcohol. However, according to AIA

---

6   André Tunc, Accidents de la circulation: faute ou risque?, *Dalloz*, 1982. chr. 103.

findings, a true fault can be observed in only 5% of cases of collisions between motor vehicles and 10% of the cases of collisions against a fixed obstacle. If these proportions are not valid in Europe at the present time (which we ignore), it remains true that excessive speed and alcohol are much more often the authors of damage than of victims. And, when a dangerous driver is himself the victim of his behaviour, his punishment is often very tragically severe when compared to his fault.

7 Another reason to entirely disregard the victim's behaviour is that it is often difficult, in practical cases, to judge and to decide whether it was faultless, erroneous, or faulty. Most of the time, the circumstances of the accident are not known with a sufficient precision to permit the judgment.

Furthermore, it is easy to say, for instance, that everyone should stop at a 'Stop' signal. But a driver, in heavy rain at night, may approach in intersection very slowly and carefully and nevertheless fail to see the Stop signal. A physician or a surgeon, after a very heavy day, may have a lapse of concentration which only a jurist in his armchair will call a fault.

It is important to underline, as the AIA does, that this difficulty of judgment bears heavily upon the fate of all victims, even the ones who will be judged to be faultless. Even in countries where there is a *prima facie* liability of the motorist, the insurer will be prompt to invoke a 'fault' on the part of the victim and oblige the latter to engage in long discussions and often in an expensive litigation.

8 Finally, account must be taken of the automobile insurance. Automobile liability insurance everywhere is either compulsory or taken out by all responsible drivers. It is a terrible paradox that, on the road, one may kill or injure his neighbour in full civil immunity, while the injured party is liable for the slightest of his errors. If the consequences of an error or a fault committed by a driver author of a damage is legitimately spread on a collectivity of drivers, *a fortiori* should the same collectivity bear the cost of any damage occasioned by this driver, whatever the victim's behaviour. If causing a damage is an inescapable risk of traffic, suffering one should be considered in the same way.

One may regret, it is true, that insurance entirely disregards the behaviour of the author of the damage. Some behaviours should not be covered by insurance without a recourse against their authors. Unfortunately, such a recourse does not seem practicable. Accident prevention should be sought in regulation, enforcement and penal law. If it could have some value in civil law, it should be borne by the authors of accidents, not by the victims!

9 A further benefit of no-fault compensation is that it allows a system of first-party insurance.

II What type of insurance?

10 There is little doubt on the type of insurance which should be adopted once the idea is accepted of compensation to all victims on a no-fault basis.

Presently, in the case of a collision between motor vehicles, the driver and the passengers of vehicle A claim compensation from the insurer of vehicle B and *vice versa*. It would obviously be much simpler to replace this 'third-party insurance' by a 'first-party insurance', *i.e.* to permit the victims in each vehicle to obtain compensation directly from the vehicle's insurer. Furthermore, first-party insurance would provide compensation in cases where the law of civil liability does not: when the vehicle has hit a fixed obstacle. It is true that first-party insurance would not always be able to work: it should be accompanied by a third-party insurance for the benefit of pedestrians and cyclists hit by the vehicle.

The AIA is so keen on first-party insurance that it has suggested that, when a pedestrian or cyclist is hit by a motor vehicle, he should seek compensation, if he himself is a driver or a member of the family of a driver, from his own insurer. In our opinion, this is going too far and rather complicating the process of settlement without sufficient reason.

A model of the desirable law may be found in a draft prepared by an international colloquium which was held in the Sorbonne on May 8 and 9 1981.[7]

11 Why is the AIA so keen on first party insurance?

An obvious benefit is the simplification of the settlements. In theory at least, each insurer could ignore the other. No exchange of documents, no discussion would have to occur between them. In practice, the insurers might feel safer in sending a letter to their colleague, but experience might lead them to drop even this simple communication.

Again from a purely administrative point of view, first-party insurance would permit the insurer to take notice of the social status of his clients and thus facilitate the coordination of automobile insurance compensation and collateral benefits.

12 One may hope that first-party insurance would greatly change the relations between victims and insurers.

Presently, these relations are bad. Too often, victims try to obtain unreasonable and sometimes dishonest compensation from an insurer that they never expect to meet again. In their part, insurers usually try to reduce and delay the payment of justified compensation. One may hope that each side would feel the need to have better relations with the other party, to whom he would have to apply in others occasions. The insurer, for instance, would have a certain knowledge of his client and know to what extent he may rely on his statements. On the other hand, in order to increase his business, he would have to gain a good reputation, a reputation of reasonable and prompt settlements. Not only would the 'climate' be changed for the better, the perception of the insurance industry by the public would also be improved.

---

7   The various reports presented at the colloquium are reproduced in André Tunc (ed.), *Pour une loi sur les accidents de la circulation*, 1981. The draft is reproduced as Annex 2. Art. 7 was introduced as an option, but should not be considered as essential.

13 Finally, first-party insurance would facilitate the adjustment of the premiums to the record and specificities of each client, thus bringing more justice to each party.

III The Scope and Feasibility of a Chapter
on Traffic Accident Compensation of a European Civil Code

14 The preceding developments dealt with the need of a no-fault compensation system based on first-party insurance. This is a basic point in the matter of traffic victim compensation, but it is not the only one.

Another difficult problem is the determination of proper compensation. The matter is the subject of Resolution (75)7 of the Council of Europe. It has more recently been considered by an international colloquium held in Paris in November 1988.[8]

The conclusions emerging from the latter may be summarized and briefly commentated upon as follows:

a Distinction should be made between economic (pecuniary) losses and non-economic losses.

b Economic losses, should, as much as possible, receive full compensation, evaluated on the basis of the circumstances.

c Important economic losses should be compensated by periodic payments, capable of revision according to the evolution of the incapacity.

d Non-economic losses, if they are important, should be compensated by a lump sum, specified in schedules. This type of loss has no monetary value. While a periodic payment may compensate a salary , no amount of money will compensate an arm, or a leg, or a child or a wife. Payment of a certain amount of money is hardly more than recognition of a suffering. There is no reasonable room for discussion of the proper amount. To permit a discussion is to imply that the child or the wife had a value. The main concern of the legislature should be, on the contrary, to avoid such discussion. Experience shows that any discussion in those matters only generates further suffering and, whatever the amount finally paid, frustration.

e The amount of the compensation should be determined in consideration of the country where the victim normally lives.

These conclusions might be embodied in a European Civil Code.

15 The problem of the coordination of automobile insurance compensation and collateral compensation, is most important and difficult. However, the matter is closely related to the suitability of the national systems of social security to be unified of a European level.

It might be wise to state only the principle of non-cumulation of automobile insurance compensation and social compensation, and to provide that, during a certain period after a claim has been addressed by the victim to his insurer, the

---

8   See André Dessertine (sous la direction de), *L'évaluation du préjudice corporel dans les pays de la C.E.E.*, 1991.

persons or institutions having received from the victim a claim based on the same accident will notify the insurer, which will reduce the compensation accordingly.

16 The final question may be whether a chapter of the European Civil Code based on the foregoing principles would have any chance of being ratified.

All over the world, traffic accident compensation reform faces two possible adversaries: insurers and practising lawyers.

Insurers should find comfort in the fact that the foregoing project differs from the AIA project only by more timidity. Furthermore, French experience and British proposals have confirmed the fact that a significant reform can be made without any change of structures of the insurance industry. First-party insurance even entertains competition among the various insurers.

As to the practising lawyers, who have succeeded in distorting reforms in most of the States of the United States and in delaying reforms elsewhere, they now realize that in Europe, international business law is a field of activity largely more promising than divorces and traffic accidents.

A reform also faces the general feeling that liability for fault is a pillar of our civilization. While this feeling is respectable and largely justified, it has no authority in the field of accidents, which are statistically more or less unavoidable and should be dealt with on a principle of solidarity.[9]

17 Finally, it is a false assumption to believe that the cost of a non-fault system is prohibitive. The present writer may be excused if, in order not to remain in abstractions, he offers his own example. The owner of a Peugeot 405 and living in Paris, his annual 'reference' premium amounts to Frs 2 134, of which Frs Frs 1991 for civil liability. As a 'good driver' on the basis of his record, he enjoys a 50% discount and thus pays Frs Frs 995.50 to cover his liability. This amount covers: (a) liability for personal injury (on the basis of comparative negligence if the victim is a driver; on a quasi-absolute liability basis otherwise); (b) his liability for property damage (practically: on a comparative negligences basis as far as damage to cars is concerned; on a strict liability basis for other damage). Furthermore, he has subscribed for him and the members of his family to an additional full coverage (*i.e.* for the amount which would be awarded by a court) in case of personal injury or death by traffic accident, whatever the circumstances of the accident (and, therefore, even if the accident results from his fault or from a collision with a fixed obstacle). The cost of such additional protection amounts to Frs Frs 280 per year. Therefore, the cost of liability under a regime which is complicated, but close to a no-fault coverage of all personal injuries (plus a coverage of property damage) amounts to less than Frs Frs 1 280. If the driver is not considered as a 'good driver', the amount would still be Frs Frs 2 280. This figure gives a fair idea of the financial feasibility of a no-fault system of compensation of personal injuries when administrative costs are reduced.

---

9   See Tunc, *op.cit.* (n. 3).

CHAPTER 19

Environmental Liability

Gerrit Betlem*

One of the main topics of European Community environmental policy in the 1990s is non-contractual liability for damage to the environment. It can therefore be expected that if and when a European Civil Code were to be adopted in the more distant future, a uniform or at least harmonised environmental liability regime would already be in place in the European Community. This contribution will discuss the possible European Community activity regarding tortious liability for environmental damage in the light of insertability in a future European Civil Code. Furthermore, the need for coordination of unification at Community level with developments at global level will be dealt with.

1 Duty to Legislate

According to the fifth environmental action programme *Towards Sustainability*, 'an integrated Community approach to environmental liability will be established. (...) Liability will be an essential tool of last resort to punish despoilation of the environment. In addition — and in line with the objective of prevention at source — it will provide a very clear economic incentive for management and control of risk, pollution and waste'.[1] In the context of 'a broader mix of "instruments"',[2] it is intended to have a system of liability in place in the year 2000.[3] The Commission's first step towards this goal was taken on 17 March 1993 with the publication of the Green Paper on environmental liability.[4] One of the conclusions of this discussion paper is that: 'Civil liability is a useful legal instrument for recovering the costs of restoring environmental damage as well as for its prevention and enforcement functions'.[5] Given large enforcement deficits in the field of Community environmental protection policy, it is, in the words of the Court of Auditors, 'essential that [environmental directives] are backed up by other

---

*   The author would like to thank Aster Veldkamp for her incisive 'proof-reading'.
1   A European Community programme of Policy and Action in relation to the Environment and Sustainable Development, COM(92) 23 final - Vol. II, p. 68, see also p. 54 and 77; *O.J.* 1993 C 138/5; approved by the Council in its resolution of 1 February 1993, *O.J.* 1993 C 138/1.
2   Ibid, p. 64.
3   Ibid, p. 56.
4   Communication from the Commission to the Council and Parliament and the Economic and Social Committee: Green Paper on Remedying Environmental Damage, COM(93) 47. See also Communication from the Commission 'A Common Policy on Safe Seas', COM(93) 66 final, p. 23.
5   Ibid, p. 27.

incentives to reduce pollution ...'.[6] It can therefore be concluded that, for policy reasons, the European Community should develop uniform environmental liability rules. In other words, 'Without a uniform method to emphasize the importance of environmental laws, Western European governments are actually encouraging corporations to forum-shop and select the country with the most lenient environmental laws'.[7]

Moreover, the Community and all the member states are under an international law obligation to develop environmental liability law, for they have adopted Principle 13[8] concerning environmental (state) liability of the Rio Declaration.[9] Leaving aside state liability under public international law, Principle 13 obliges states to develop domestic law concerning liability for environmental damage. Although the Rio Declaration is an instrument of soft law, under public international law, this does not detract from the duty to legislate. As is apparent from the Conclusions of the Lisbon European Council and, in particular, from the Council's Resolution concerning the fifth environmental action programme, the European Community and its member states have committed themselves to implement the Rio Declaration.[10] Also, as will be examined further in the next paragraph, EC Directive 84/631 obliges the Council to legislate on civil liability for waste.

2 A Regulation on Environmental Liability

In my view, it is both desirable and feasible to lay down uniform rules on liability for environmental damage in a regulation within the meaning of Article 189 (2) EC Treaty.[11] This has the following advantages.[12] First, the well-known problems

---

6   Court of Auditors Special Report No. 3/92, concerning the environment, *O.J.* 1992 C 245/1, p. 19; see also the Common Policy on Safe Seas, *loc. cit.*, note 4, p. 16.
7   G. Nelson Smith, 'The Procedural Implementation Process and a Model Substantive Approach Towards the Storage, Treatment, and Disposal of Hazardous Waste in Western Europe,' (1992) 13 *University of Pennsylvania Journal of International Business Law*, 351, 406.
8   Principle 13 reads: 'States shall develop national law regarding liability and compensation for the victims of pollution and other environmental damage. States shall also cooperate in an expeditious and a more determined manner to develop further international law regarding liability and compensation for adverse effects of environmental damage caused by activities within their jurisdiction or control to areas beyond their jurisdiction.'
9   United Nations Conference on Environment and Development: Rio Declaration on Environment and Development, Rio de Janeiro, 14 June 1992, 31 *I.L.M.* 874 (1992); Stanley P. Johnson, *The Earth Summit: The United Nations Conference on Environment and Development (UNCED)* (London etc. 1993).
10   Lisbon European Council 26 and 27 June 1992, *Bull. EC* 6-1992, p. 13: the so-called eight-point plan, a follow-up measure to UNCED; Resolution of 1 February 1993, *O.J.* 1993 C 138/4.
11   Article 189 EC reads as follows: 'In order to carry out their task and in accordance with the provisions of this Treaty, the European Parliament acting jointly with the Council, the Council and the Commission shall, in accordance with the provisions of this Treaty, make regulations, issue directives, take decisions, make recommendations or deliver opinions.

regarding the non or incorrect transposition of a directive into national law do not arise. Secondly, the aim of uniform applicability is better served because harmonisation by directives 'only' results in an adaptation of national law; a complex system is created in which national law must be applied in conformity with the underlying directive.[13] A regulation is more 'truly' European than a directive, which must be regarded as a second-best approach.[14] Thirdly, an Environmental Liability Regulation could serve as a useful 'pilot study' for a possible European Civil Code, which should preferably — given the need for a systematic and coherent approach — be adopted in the form of a regulation.[15] Finally, if and when a European Civil Code would be adopted, it would simply be a matter of inserting the Environmental Liability Regulation as a separate Title into the Code without there being any need for an adaptation of national laws as in the case of a directive.

Support for this proposition may be found in the increasing use of regulations in the environment sector by the Community legislature. It goes without saying that the regulation is the appropriate legal instrument for establishing funds or institutions.[16] However, environmental regulations have also been created in order to lay down uniform substantive rules of law. This occurs, for example, in the Whale Products Regulation,[17] the regulation that implements CITES,[18] the Ozone

---

A regulation shall have general application. It shall be binding in its entirety and directly applicable in all Member States.

A directive shall be binding, as to the result to be achieved, upon each Member State to which it is addressed, but shall leave to the national authorities the choice of form and methods.

A decision shall be binding in its entirety upon those to whom it is addressed. Recommendations and opinions shall have no binding force.'

12   See also Müller-Graff, Chapter 2 of this book; cf. the Gazis Report of the European Parliament's Commission on Legal Affairs and the Rights of the Citizen on Harmonisation of Private Law, PE DOC A 2-157/89, p. 13.

13   See Case C-32/74 *Haaga* [1974] ECR 1201; Case C-111/75 *Mazzalai* v *Ferrovia del Renon* [1976] ECR 657; Case C-270/81 *Felicitas* v *Finanzamt für Verkehrsteuern* [1982] ECR 2771, in particular Opinion of A-G Slynn at 2792; and C.W.A. Timmermans, 'Directives: Their Effect within the National Legal Systems,' 16 *CMLRev.* (1979) 533, 536.

14   Müller-Graff, Chapter 2 of this book.

15   At least not by a directive: the Gazis Report, *op.cit.*, note 12, p. 7 and 13; F.J.A. van der Velden, 'Europa 1992 en het eenvormig privaatrecht,' in: D. Kokkini-Iatridou and F.W. Grosheide, eds., *Eenvormig en vergelijkend privaatrecht 1990* (Lelystad 1990), p. 25.

16   See for example Council Regulation 1210/90 on the establishment of the European Environment Agency and the European environment information and observation network, *O.J.* 1990 L 120/1 and Council Regulation 1973/92 establishing a financial instrument for the environment (LIFE), *O.J.* 1992 L 206/1.

17   Council Regulation 348/81 on common rules for imports of whales or other cetacean products, *O.J.* 1981 L 39/1.

18   Council Regulation 3626/82 on the implementation in the Community of the Convention in international trade in endangered species of wild fauna and flora, *O.J.* 1982 L 384/1; latest amendment: Commission Regulation 1970/92, *O.J.* 1992, L 201/1.

Layer Regulation,[19] the Eco-label Regulation[20] and the regulation on export and import of dangerous chemicals.[21] The most interesting regulation in this connection is Council Regulation 259/93 on the supervision and control of shipments of waste within, into and out of the European Community.[22] Not only does it replace a directive[23] concerning the same subject matter, it is also closely related to civil liability.

Why was the directive replaced by a regulation? According to the preamble and the Memorandum of Explanation,[24] the Community's signing of the UNEP Basel Convention[25] as well as other international law instruments, necessitated the adoption of a regulation; moreover, a uniform and simultaneous applicability in all the member states could only be ensured by a regulation. The experiences with the lack of simultaneous applicability of the directive proved to have resulted in a disorderly and unverifiable situation. Consequently, the above-mentioned more general problematic features of directives, as opposed to regulations, have led to the adoption of this instrument.

The Waste Control Regulation is related to liability issues in two or possibly three ways. First, according to Article 11 (3) of Directive 84/631,[26] the Council is under a duty to regulate the liability for damage caused by waste. Although this obligation has applied since 6 December 1984, legislative progress has so far only resulted in an Amended proposal for a Council Directive on civil liability for damage caused by waste.[27] Moreover, the status of the proposal was described as follows by a Commission official: 'It is sleeping.' Be that as it may, it can be expected, given the policy direction referred to in § 1, that the proposal will be 'overtaken' by more general rules of environmental liability.[28]

---

19 Council Regulation 594/91 on substances that deplete the ozone layer, *O.J.* 1991 L 67/1 as amended by Council Regulation 3952/92 [amending Regulation (EEC) No 594/91] in order to speed up the phasing-out of substances that deplete the ozone layer, *O.J.* 1992 L 405/41.

20 Council Regulation 880/92 on a Community eco-label award scheme, *O.J.* 1992 L 99/1.

21 Council Regulation 2455/92 concerning the export and import of certain dangerous chemicals, *O.J.* 1992 L 251/13 (replacing Regulation 1734/88, *O.J.* 1988 L 155/2).

22 *O.J.* 1993 L 30/1; applicable as of 6 May 1994.

23 Council Directive 84/631 on the supervision and control within the European Community of the transfrontier shipment of hazardous waste, *O.J.* 1984 L 326/31.

24 COM(90) 415 def.

25 Basel Convention on the Control of Transboundary Movements of Hazardous Wastes and their Disposal, Basel 22 March 1989, *Trb.* 1990, 12; 28 *I.L.M.* 649 (1989); (1989) 1 *JEL* 255; in force since 5 May 1992; see Katharina Kummer, 'The International Regulation of Transboundary Traffic in Hazardous Wastes: the 1989 Basel Convention,' (1992) 41 *I.C.L.Q.* 530.

26 It reads: 'The Council shall, acting in accordance with the procedure referred to in Article 100 of the Treaty, determine not later than 30 September 1988 the conditions for implementing the civil liability of the producer in the case of damage or that of any other person who may be accountable for the said damage and shall also determine a system of insurance.'

27 *O.J.* 1991 C 192/6; see for an extensive commentary: Peter v. Wilmowsky and Gerhard Roller, *Civil Liability for Waste* (Frankfurt am Main etc. 1992), Studies of the Environmental Law Network International, Vol. 2.

28 See also Patrick Thieffry, 'Les nouveaux instruments juridiques de la politique communautaire de l'environnement,' *RTD eur* 28 (4) 1992, p. 683.

Secondly, since the waste regulation concerns the implementation of the afore mentioned Basel Convention in the European Community, the possible future implementation of the Protocol to the Basel Convention on Liability and Compensation should also, for the e reasons, take place by way of regulation.

According to Article 12 of the Basel Convention,[29] the state parties are to discuss the adoption of a liability protocol. On the basis of elements which were put forward by an *ad hoc* working group of legal and technical experts, Draft Articles have been formulated.[30] It was decided at the First Meeting of the Conference of the Parties in Montevideo, 30 November — 4 December 1992, to consider and develop the Protocol further.

The third, possible, connection between the public law regime of the Waste Control Regulation and non-contractual liability concerns the responsibility for ensuring the removal of waste which has been disposed of due to illegal traffic. That is to say that the notifier (as defined by Article 2g) is then obliged to re-import the waste; the relevant state must ensure that the waste is taken back.[31] It may well be that, under Dutch law, these obligations are best enforced by the use of injunctions on pain of an *astreinte*. In particular in cases where a state wants to take legal action against waste generators based outside its territory, private law remedies are the only available option (the Dutch case of Benckiser[32] may be referred to as an example in point). Appropriate financial incentives seem to be called for in addition to the required financial guarantee of Article 27 Waste Control Regulation, because those engaged in illegal traffic are not likely to put down deposits with the competent authorities.[33]

In my view, in addition to the arguments put forward in connection with the Waste Control Regulation, the decisive factor for the choice of instrument harmonising environmental liability rules is its object and purpose. This issue is closely related to the next topic of discussion: what is the correct legal basis for an Environmental Liability Regulation?

---

29 Article 12 Basel Convention states: 'The Parties shall co-operate with a view to adopting, as soon as practicable, a protocol setting out appropriate rules and procedures in the field of liability and compensation for damage resulting from the transboundary movement and disposal of hazardous wastes and other wastes.'

30 UNEP/CHW.1/WG.1/1/5.

31 See Article 26 of the Regulation; similar duties apply under Articles 25 and 34.

32 HR 14 April 1989, *NJ* 1990, 712 CJHB and JCS; see for a comprehensive discussion of this case which is written in English: Gerrit Betlem, *Civil Liability for Transfrontier Pollution* (London etc. 1993), Ph.D. thesis, University of Utrecht, passim.

33 Cf. Kummer, *loc. cit.*, note 25, p. 554 on remedies to be provided by states; this could involve the use of private law.

3 Legal Basis

It is interesting to note that the Waste Control Regulation is based on Article 130S EEC Treaty.[34] Indeed the same applies to all the other regulations cited above.[35] Conversely, the Product Liability Directive[36] was based on Article 100 EEC:[37] the general harmonisation provision for the common market.[38] Similarly, the Commission based its proposal for the liability for waste directive on Article 100A EEC:[39] the general harmonisation provision for the internal market. Incidentally, one of the differences between Article 100A and Article 100 is that the latter is confined to directives, whereas the former speaks of 'measures'. A future Environmental Liability Regulation could thus be based on Article 100A EC. However, the Council has declared that the Commission must give precedence to directives in order to harmonise the domestic legislation.[40] Whatever the significance of this declaration, such a regulation should, in my view, be based on Article 130S EC rather than on Article 100A.[41]

The aims of an environmental liability instrument should be limited to environmental considerations instead of including internal market considerations.[42]

---

34 Article 130S EEC provides as follows: 'The Council, acting unanimously on a proposal from the Commission and after consulting the European Parliament and the Economic and Social Committee, shall decide what action is to be taken by the Community.
    The Council shall, under the conditions laid down in the preceding sub-paragraph, define those matters on which decisions are to be taken by a qualified majority.'

35 With the exception of those issued before the existence of Article 130S, of course; but they were based on Article 235 EEC (the residual competence provision) and not on the general harmonisation Article: Article 100 EEC.

36 Directive 85/374 on liability for defective products, *O.J.* 1985 L 210/29.

37 Article 100 EEC states: 'The Council shall, acting unanimously on a proposal from the Commission, issue directives for the approximation of such provisions laid down by law, regulation or administrative action in Member States as directly affect the establishment or functioning of the common market.
    The European Parliament and the Economic and Social Committee shall be consulted in the case of directives whose implementation would, in one or more Member States, involve the amendment of legislation.'

38 R.H. Lauwaars and J.M. Maarleveld, *Harmonisatie van wetgeving in Europese organisaties* (Deventer 1987), Europese Monografieën No. 33, p. 52.

39 Article 100A EEC (1) reads: 'By way of derogation from Article 100 and save where otherwise provided in this Treaty, the following provisions shall apply for the achievement of the objectives set out in Article 8a. The Council shall, acting by a qualified majority on a proposal from the Commission in co-operation with the European Parliament and after consulting the Economic and Social Committee, adopt the measures for the approximation of the provisions laid down by law, regulation or administrative action in Member States which have as their object the establishment and functioning of the internal market.'

40 P.J.G. Kapteyn and P. VerLoren van Themaat, Laurence W. Gormley, ed., *Introduction to the Law of the European Communities*, 2nd ed. (Deventer-Boston 1990), p. 473, 474.

41 See also House of Lords Select Committee on the European Communities Report, *Paying for Pollution. Civil Liability for Damage Caused by Waste* (HL Paper 84-I, London: HMSO 1990), No. 155, suggesting that the waste liability directive should be based on Art. 130S.

42 See also the criticisms of the Court of Auditors, *op. cit.*, note 6, No. 4.13.

This is particularly relevant to the interpretation of such a possible regulation in cases of doubt: *in dubio pro ambiente*. Moreover, a double aim — environmental protection and facilitation of the internal market — would probably mean that Article 100A EC would have to be used as a legal basis, with the ensuing risk of a predominance of internal market considerations. Consequently, it is not only desirable that Article 130S is used, it is necessary, in the light of the following judgment of the European Court in the case of *Re Titanium Dioxide*.[43]

In this case the Court upheld the Commission's complaint that a directive concerning the titanium dioxide industry should be based on Article 100A EEC rather than on Article 130S EEC. The main reason was that the directive pursued a double aim (prevention of distortions of competition and environmental protection). Given the fact that the procedural differences between the two provisions precluded joint application, the European Court annulled the directive because it should have been based on Article 100A EEC. Many commentators observed that the Court's judgment would significantly reduce the scope of Article 130S EC as a basis for future Community environmental law; the Court was considered to have given precedence to the objective of increasing the role of the European Parliament over environmental protection.[44]

However, in an interesting recent judgment the European Court made it clear that it had not sacrificed environmental protection on the altar of democracy: *Re Waste Directive*.[45] This time the Court rejected a similar claim of the Commission for the annulment of a directive in the waste sector on the ground of incorrect legal basis (Article 130S EEC). The judgment may be summarized as follows. The Court pointed out that, under consistent case law, the choice of legal basis of a Community measure must be based on objective factors susceptible to judicial control, in particular the aim(s) and contents of the measure. The Court concluded that the directive in issue pursued environmental protection alone. To the argument that the directive also concerned free movement of goods, *in casu* waste, the Court said the following.

Citing *Re Waste in Wallonia*,[46] it acknowledged that wastes are indeed goods within the meaning of the EEC Treaty; however, mandatory requirements of environmental protection justify exceptions to the free movement of goods. Finally, the Court held that the mere fact that a measure affects the internal market does not prompt application of Article 100A EEC and concluded that:

---

43 Case C-300/89 *Commission* v *Council* [1991] ECR I-2867; 29 *CMLRev.* (1992) 140 annotation by Somsen; (1992) 17 *E.L.Rev.* 127 annotation by Barnard; *NJ* 1993, 729.

44 See the annotations referred to in the previous note and Anneke Sewandono, 'Beginsel van democratie versus milieu?' *NJB* 1992, p. 63.

45 Case C-155/91 *Commission* v *Council* [1993] ECR nyr (judgment of 17 March 1993); *NJB*-katern 1993, p. 203, No. 19; 30 *CMLRev.* (1993) 1051 annotation by Wachsmann; (1993) 18 *E.L.Rev.* 418 annotation by Geradin; see also Case C-70/88 *Parliament* v *Council* [1991] ECR I-4529 (*Re Chernobyl*).

46 Case C-2/90 *Commission* v *Belgium* [1992] ECR nyr (judgment of 9 July 1992); 30 *CMLRev.* (1993) 351 note by Hancher and Sevenster; (1993) 18 *E.L.Rev.* 144 note by Geradin.

19 (...) Il résulte, en effet, de la jurisprudence de la Cour que le recours à l'article 100A n'est pas justifié lorsque l'acte à adopter n'a que accessoirement pour effet d'harmoniser les conditions du marché à l'interieur de la Communauté (arrêt du 4 octobre 1991, Parlement/Conseil, C-70/88, Rec. p. I-4529, point 17 [*Chernobyl*]).

It follows from this judgment that the case law of the European Court does not object to the adoption of environmental protection measures on the basis of Article 130S EC, in spite of their affecting the internal market. They must be based on Article 100A only when they have as their object and purpose (in contradistinction to their effect) the regulation of the conditions of competition on the internal market.[47] If it were otherwise, practically all the environmental legislation would have to be seen as internal market measures: there will always be repercussions on the conditions of competition.[48]

It is submitted that this judgment is in keeping with the amendments to the EEC Treaty laid down in the Maastricht Treaty on European Union.[49] Not only has the word 'Economic' disappeared — a 'European Community' is established — but also the new Article 2 of this EC Treaty[50] requires that economic growth shall be sustainable and respects the environment. Consequently, 'Maastricht' reinforces my view that Article 130S EC constitutes the proper legal basis for a single aim Environmental Liability Regulation.

Now that the Maastricht Treaty has entered into force (1 November 1993), a possible significant change to Community environmental law has come into effect.[51] Under current law, any environmental measure by the Community must be compatible with the objectives of the Community, i.e. sustainable development. Under previous law, all actions could be tested against Article 130R EEC.[52]

---

47 See also the Opinion of A-G Tesauro of 1 December 1992, Case C-155/91, nyr, Nos. 4, 7 and 10.
48 Ibid, No. 11.
49 The Maastricht Treaty on European Union, *Europe Documents* No. 1759/60, 7 February 1992; *O.J.* 1992 C 191, C 224; 31 *I.L.M.* 247 (1992); *Trb.* 1992, 74.
50 Article 2 EC reads: 'The Community shall have as its task, by establishing a common market and an economic and monetary union and by implementing the common policies or activities referred to in Articles 3 and 3a, to promote throughout the Community a harmonious and balanced development of economic activities, *sustainable* and non-inflationary growth *respecting the environment*, a high degree of convergence of economic performance, a high level of employment and of social protection, the raising of the standard of living and quality of life, and economic and social cohesion and solidarity among Member States [emphasis added].'
51 See Thieffry, *loc.cit.*, note 28, p. 670 and David Wilkinson, 'Maastricht and the Environment: the Implications for the EC's Environment Policy of the Treaty on European Union', (1992) 4 *JEL* 221; contra: H.G. Sevenster, *Milieubeleid en gemeenschapsrecht* (Deventer 1992), Ph.D. thesis, University of Leiden, Europese Monografieën No. 38, p. 418, 419.
52 As far as it is relevant here, Article 130R EEC reads: '1. Action by the Community relating to the environment shall have the following objectives: (i) to preserve, protect and improve the quality of the environment; (ii) to contribute towards protecting human health; (iii) to ensure a prudent and rational utilisation of natural resources. 2. Action by the Community relating to the environment shall be based on the principles that preventive action should be taken, that environmental damage should as a priority be rectified at source, and that the polluter should pay. Environmental protection requirements shall be a component of the Community's other policies.

Indeed, such a case is currently pending before the European Court.[53] It may be underlined that, accordingly, directives and regulations could be declared void for their lack of compatibility with, *inter alia*, the polluter pays principle.[54]

It should be added to this that a measure may similarly be tested against the subsidiarity principle, as laid down in the new Article 3b European Community Treaty.[55] It is a matter of some controversy whether subsidiarity is indeed justiciable.[56] However, a subsidiarity objection to EC action does not seem feasible, because it is of course a truism that pollution does not respect national borders. Most issues of environmental protection will therefore require, in compliance with the subsidiarity principle, a Community solution rather than a purely national approach.[57]

As a final observation on the legal basis issue, a comparison with product liability is required. Could it be argued that, since the product liability was based on Article 100 EEC, a similar measure concerning environmental liability should also be based on a provision regarding harmonisation? In my view, nothing compels the Community legislator to adopt this position. As is apparent from the preamble to the Product Liability Directive, it serves a double aim: protection of the consumer and facilitating the common market ('... approximation of the laws of the Member States (...) is necessary because the existing divergences may distort competition and affect the movement of goods within the common market ...').[58] One could thus argue, in keeping with *Re Titanium Dioxide*,[59] that a future Environmental Liability Regulation should be based on Article 100A EC, because the same internal market considerations apply in the environment sector. To this the following arguments may be advanced.

(...)'

53   See Case C-407/92 *An Taisce and WWF* v *Commission*, O.J. 1993 C 27/4.
54   See J.H. Jans, *Europees Milieurecht in Nederland* (Groningen 1991), p. 21.
55   Article 3b EC provides as follows: 'The Community shall act within the limits of the powers conferred upon it by this Treaty and of the objectives assigned to it therein. In areas which do not fall within its exclusive competence, the Community shall take action, in accordance with the principle of subsidiarity, only if and in so far as the objectives of the proposed action cannot be sufficiently achieved by the Member States and can therefore, by reason of the scale or effects of the proposed action, be better achieved by the Community.
      Any action by the Community shall not go beyond what is necessary to achieve the objectives of this Treaty.'
56   See Nicholas Emilou, 'Subsidiarity: An Effective Barrier Against "the Enterprise of Ambition"?' (1992) 17 *E.L.Rev.* 382, 402; A.J.C. de Moor-van Vugt, 'Een nieuw tijdperk in het bestuursrecht?' in: *Kroniek van het bestuursrecht 1987-1992* (Zwolle 1993), p. 109; the German Bundesverfassungsgericht's Maastricht judgment of 12 October 1993, *RIW* Beilage 5, 12/1993.
57   Cf. the European Parliament's 'Entschliessung' of 19 January 1993, as reported in *EuZW* 1993, p. 207; see also Trevor C. Hartley, 'Constitutional and Institutional Aspects of the Maastricht Agreement,' (1993) 42 *I.C.L.Q.*, 213, 217; L.J. Brinkhorst, *Subsidiariteit en Milieu in de Europese Gemeenschap* (Leiden 1993).
58   See also L. Dommering-van Rongen, *Produktenaansprakelijkheid* (Deventer 1991), Ph.D. thesis, University of Utrecht, Europese Monografieën No. 37, § 3.4 concerning the question whether the directive lays down minimum or maximum rules.
59   Above, note 43.

First, the mere statement that divergences between the laws of the member states *may* distort competition, is not entirely convincing.[60] Apart from the fact that a mere possibility is apparently regarded as sufficient, no mention is being made of any empirical research that substantiates the proposition.[61] Secondly, the free movement of goods is not sacrosanct. Indeed, it is exactly the object and purpose of recent Community environmental measures to reduce this movement (principle of proximity).[62] Thirdly, at the material time the product liability directive could not have been based on a specific consumer policy provision; there was no choice available in the comsumer law field, like a choice between the Articles 100A and 130S EEC in the field of environmental law. However, in the post-Maastricht era, there is such a provision: Article 129A EC.[63] A similar question as the above mentioned choice between legal bases of environment measures will arise as regards the choice between the Articles 100A and 129A EC.[64]

4 Coordination with Global Unification

As mentioned in § 2, the parties to the 1989 Basel Convention are currently developing a Protocol on Liability and Compensation for Damage Resulting from the Transboundary Movement of Hazardous Wastes and their Disposal.[65] Given the early stage of the drafting process and the scope of this article, it is sufficient to draw attention to the fact that unification at global level necessitates coordination with similar activities at Community level. However, the following interesting features of the Draft Articles may be noted.

---

60 Cf. Lauwaars/Maarleveld, *op.cit.*, note 38, p. 218.

61 See also the House of Lords Report, above note 41.

62 Opinion of A-G Tesauro of 1 December 1992, Case C-155/91 *Commission* v *Council* (Re Waste Directive), nyr, No. 9.

63 Article 129A EC provides as follows: '1. The Community shall contribute to the attainment of a high level of consumer protection through:
(a) measures adopted pursuant to Article 100a in the context of the completion of the internal market;
(b) specific action which supports and supplements the policy pursued by the Member States to protect the health, safety and economic interests of consumers and to provide adequate information to consumers. 2. The Council, acting in accordance with the procedure referred to in Article 189b and after consulting the Economic and Social Committee, shall adopt the specific action referred to in paragraph (b). 3. Action adopted pursuant to paragraph 2 shall not prevent any Member State from maintaining or introducing more stringent protective measures. Such measures must be compatible with this Treaty. The Commission shall be notified of them.'

64 See also H.A.G. Temmink, 'Het verdrag van Maastricht en Europees consumentenbeleid,' *TvC* 1992, p. 58, § 9.

65 A similar exercise is foreseen by Article 12 of the OAU Bamako Convention on the Ban of the Import into Africa and the Control of Transboundary Movement and Management of Hazardous Wastes within Africa, 29 January 1991, 30 *I.L.M.* 773 (1991). As far as waste generation within Africa is concerned, Article 4(3)(b) states: 'Each Party shall: Impose strict, unlimited liability as well as joint and several liability on hazardous waste generators'.

Similar to my arguments put forward in section 3, Draft Article 1 defines the purpose of the Protocol in terms of compensation and environmental protection aims.[66] This definition therefore confirms the view that a possible Environmental Liability Regulation should not be concerned with internal market issues but with environmental considerations alone. The proposed definition of damage not only expressly deals with pure economic loss (next to personal injury and damage to property), it also extensively covers ecological damage.[67] The Draft Articles envisage compulsory insurance for financially unlimited liability, the absence of time limits in the case of illegal traffic, and the establishment of an Emergency Fund, and, possibly, of a Compensation Fund. The provision regarding international jurisdiction foresees a scheme similar to Articles 2 and 5(3) of the EEC Brussels Convention,[68] as interpreted by the European Court in *Bier*.[69] Finally, a provision on recognition and enforcement of judgments, unlike Article 27(1) of the Brussels Convention, does not allow non-recognition on the ground of public policy.[70]

Furthermore, the globally or regionally unified liability regimes for oil pollution[71] and nuclear accidents are to remain untouched by unified Community law.[72] Coordination with these regimes had already been foreseen in the proposal for the directive on civil liability for waste;[73] Article 2(2) excludes application of the provisions of the directive insofar as the rules of the special regimes apply. Similarly, the Council of Europe's Convention on Civil Liability for Damage Resulting from activities Dangerous to the Environment is limited in the same way.[74]

---

66 Article 1 Draft Article states: The objective of this Protocol is to provide for adequate and prompt compensation, including reinstatement of the environment, for damage resulting from the transboundary movement of hazardous wastes and other wastes and their disposal. (UNEP/CHW.1/WG.1/1/5).

67 As far as relevant in the present context, Draft Article 2(2) refers to impairment of the environment and measures of reinstatement.

68 Brussels Convention of 27 September 1968 on Jurisdiction and the Enforcement of Judgments in Civil and Commercial Matters, consolidated version in: *O.J.* 1990 C 189/1.

69 Case C-21/76 *Handelskwekerij G.J. Bier B.V.* v *Mines de Potasse d'Alsace S.A. (MDPA)* [1976] ECR 1735; *NJ* 1977, 94 JCS.

70 Draft Article 12 reads: 'Any judgment of a court competent shall, if it is enforceable in the State of origin, be recognized in any Contracting State and shall be enforceable without review of the merits of the case.'

71 International Convention on Civil Liability for Oil Pollution Damage, Brussels 29 November 1969, *Trb.* 1970, 196; 9 *I.L.M.* 45 (1970).

72 Convention on Third Party Liability in the Field of Nuclear Energy, Paris 29 July 1960, *Trb.* 1964, 175; Convention Supplementary to the Paris Convention of 29 July 1960 and Annex, Brussels 31 January 1963, *Trb.* 1963, 176; as amended by the Additional Protocol, Paris 28 January 1964, *Trb.* 1964, 178.

73 Amended proposal for a Council Directive on civil liability for damage caused by waste, *O.J.* 1991 C 192/6.

74 Lugano, 21 June 1993, *European Treaty Series*/150.

5 Conclusions

The European Community is obliged to develop civil liability for environmental damage. This article proposes that, to this end, a Regulation should be adopted. The adoption of a regulation could function as a 'pilot study' for a more comprehensive codification of liability rules in the more distant future. Also, it would be easy to insert the provisions of this Regulation into a possible future European Civil Code. Moreover, the implementation of and coordination with a unification of liability rules in the context of the UNEP 1989 Basel Convention is facilitated.

In my view, the proper legal basis for an Environmental Liability Regulation is Article 130S EC. The main reason for this choice is that this regulation should be concerned with environmental aims alone, and not also with internal market considerations; this view is supported by recent case law of the European Court: *Re Waste Directive*. In doing so, the teleological interpretation of the instrument will better serve the ultimate aim: sustainable development.

C – Law of Property and Real Security

CHAPTER 20

Transfer of Property

Ulrich Drobnig

1 Introductory Remarks

In the context of the present book, the topic must be limited to contractrual transfers of property, thus excluding statutory transfers (such as succession). Both its economic importance and its legal complexity are obvious: the contractual transfer of property usually (although not always) signifies a change of attribution of an economic asset from one person or enterprise to another. Market economies are based upon such changes of attribution so as to facilitate the optimal use of assets by citizens and professional market participants.

It is the specific aspect of a market economy that such transfers are effectuated voluntarily by both parties to the transaction; legally speaking, they are based upon a contract. Contractual transfers of property, therefore, are located at the cross-roads of contract and property, and this feature creates, as we will see, one of the major difficulties for legal regulation.

At first glance, though, a lawyer familiar with only one legal system may regard the contractual transfer of property as a relatively simple, if not simplistic topic. Its central rules must be mastered by any first-year law student. A comparative survey, however, quickly reveals unanticipated difficulties: not only do the basic rules differ profoundly between the various European countries, but it also becomes apparent that a considerable number of subsidiary rules have to be taken into account in order to obtain a true and complete picture.

These legal complexities explain and excuse two further limitations of this study: it will be restricted to the transfer of property in corporeal movables, thus excluding transfers of immovables as well as transfers of intangibles, such as the assignment of monetary claims (or debts).

2 Diverging Principles

A brief comparative survey of the basic rules on transfer of property reveals a disquieting variety of diverging basic principles.

The weight and practical relevance of the different principles involved is best revealed if they are related to the three basic issues which are involved in the transfer of property.[1]

---

[1] A similar exposition of the issues is offered by Sacco, 'Le transfert de la propriété des choses mobilières determinées par acte entre vifs', in: *General Reports to the 10th International Congress of Comparative Law* (1981) 247 ff., 252, 258.

The first and most basic dichotomy exists between the principle of consent and the principle of delivery. Many authors regard this dichotomy as the only issue in the field.[2] These two principles purport to answer the question whether property passes from the transferor to the transferee by mere consent of the parties with respect to that transfer; or whether, in addition to such consent, delivery of the object of the transfer is required.

The second issue is whether the necessary consent resides in, or is to be derived from, the primary contractual relationship between the parties, for example a contract of sale. The alternative is an additional, or secondary, agreement between the parties only for the purpose of determining whether a delivery transfers title or merely possession (or any other minor right) to the transferee. Since this special agreement relates to proprietary aspects of the transaction, it may be called a 'real agreement.'[3] Whether such an additional agreement is required, depends upon the relationship between the primary general contract concluded by the parties and the secondary special agreement as to the transfer of property. The issue is whether the secondary agreement is more than one among many terms of the contract, or whether as a separate agreement it performs and ought to perform an independent function.

It would be treacherous and misleading, however, if comparison would be confined only to an exposition, juxtaposition and evaluation of these lofty principles. Rather, a sober analysis and appreciation of the basic two principles requires that for each of them a certain number of subsidiary and complementary rules be taken into account.

3 Consent or Delivery

3.1 The Principle of Consent

3.1.1 The Principle
According to the principle of consent property passes from the transferor to the transferee by virtue of any contract between those parties providing for such a transfer of property.

This solution was evolved in the French Civil Code of 1804 where it is consistently stated in the texts of various provisions, both in the law of property (cc Article 711: 'La propriété des biens s'acquiert et se transmet par ... et par l'effet des obligations') and in the law of contracts: for contracts to give in general (cc

---

2   Cf., e.g., Waelbroeck, *Le transfert de la propriété dans la vente d'objets mobiliers corporels en droit comparé* (Bruxelles 1961) 15; and also the recent Swiss thesis by Röthlisberger, 'Traditionsprinzip und Konsensprinzip bei der Mobiliarübereignung' (*Schweizer Studien zum internationalen Recht* 28) (Zürich 1982).

3   '*Dingliche Einigung*' in German.

Article 1138)[4] as well as for contracts of sale (cc Article 1583)[5] and an accepted promise of a gift (cc Article 938).[6] These last three provisions expressly mention that the passing of property occurs even if the asset has not been delivered.

Belgium and Luxembourg, having preserved the French Civil Code, have retained the French solution as well. Italy also follows the same approach. However, the relevant Italian general provision (Article 1376 cod.civ.) adds two important elements here. Firstly, the rule applies only to contracts for the transfer of a 'specific' good. Furthermore, the consent of the parties must have been 'legitimately manifested'.

Codified English sales law has taken the same course, although in a more differentiated way. The English Sale of Goods Act (SGA) of 1979 distinguishes between 'absolute' and 'conditional' contracts of sale (s. 2 (3)). An absolute contract is a 'sale' 'by which the seller transfers ... the property in goods to the buyer' (s. 2 (4) and (1)). A conditional contract is an agreement to sell by which the seller 'agrees to transfer the property in goods to the buyer' at a future time or subject to some condition.[7] It is remarkable to note how the time of the passing of the property exerts a strong influence upon the qualification of the contract of sale! The decisive criterion is the intention of the parties (s. 17 SGA 1979). Where the parties have not expressed their intentions, a number of presumptions has been established; the most important of these being the one contained in section 18 Rule 1 SGA (1979) under which, in an unconditional contract, the property passes at the time of the making of the contract.[8]

3.1.2 Refinements

The English and Italian provisions, which were enacted much later than the French Civil Code, contain three useful refinements to the basic principle which are worthy of note. These three refinements are also implicit in the original French rule. All of them have therefore been accepted in each of the other major countries, especially in France itself.

Both the English and the Italian provisions specify that the general rule applies only to the transfer of property in specific goods.[9] The English provision

---

4   'L'obligation de livrer la chose est parfaite par le seul consentement des parties contractantes...
     — Elle rend le créancier propriétaire et..., encore que la tradition n'en ait point été faite, à moins
     que ...'
5   'Elle est parfaite entre les parties, et la propriété est acquise de droit à l'acheteur à l'égard du
     vendeur, dès qu'on est convenu de la chose et du prix, quoique la chose n'ait pas encore été livrée
     ni le prix payé.'
6   'La donation dûment acceptée sera parfaite par le seul consentement des parties; et la propriété
     des objets données sera transférée au donataire, sans qu'il soit besoin d'autre tradition.'
7   SGA 1979 s. 2 (3), (5) and (1).
8   'Where there is an unconditional contract for the sale of specific goods, in a deliverable state, the
     property in the goods passes to the buyer when the contract is made, and it is immaterial whether
     the time of payment or the time of delivery, or both, be postponed.'
9   Encyclopédie Dalloz, Repertoire de Droit Civil VIII s.v. Vente (Généralités) (cited: *Dalloz-Civil,
     Vente en général*) no. 53-54.

emphasizes the primary importance of the intention of the parties with respect to the transfer of property.[10] One particularly important application of this rule is the contract of sale with a reservation of ownership where property does not pass to the buyer before he has paid the purchase price (or other debts). This topic, however, will not be pursued here since it reaches — in fact if not in law — into the broad field of security rights.

The Italian provision expressly demands the validity of the parties' consent.[11]

3.1.3 Qualifications

The transfer of property *solo consensu* is subject to a number of restrictions and qualifications. The true scope of the principle of consent cannot be assessed unless these qualifications are duly taken into account.

a Generic and Future Goods

As mentioned before, transfer of property by consent is effective only with respect to specific goods.[12] Property in generic goods passes to the transferee only after they have been appropriated to the contract.[13] Where in contracts of sale the goods are transported to the buyer by an independent carrier, appropriation usually takes place upon delivery to the carrier;[14] this is usually regarded as delivery of possession to the buyer.

Similar rules have been developed for the transfer of property in future goods.[15]

b Effects *inter partes*

The transfer of property by mere consent gives full legal effects primarily between the parties. This is expressly spelled out in French sales law[16] and results indirectly also from the text of the English SGA 1979.[17] The situation is quite different however with respect to third parties, as we now shall see.

c Effects vis-à-vis Third Persons

The provisions and rules which provide for a transfer of property by mere consent and without delivery as far as the relationship between transferor and transferee is concerned (supra b), obviously imply that such a transfer of property must not necessarily be fully effective vis-à-vis third persons. This is indeed the case, as will be demonstrated. We shall discuss seriatim dispositions made by the transferor in possession of transferred goods and by the non-possessing transferee as well as the

---

10 Dalloz, Vente en général no. 38-52; Ghestin/Desché, *Traité des Contrats. I: Vente* (Paris 1990) 621 ss.

11 This rule is implied and rarely expressed; cf. in England Benjamin (-Guest), *Benjamin's Sale of Goods* (ed. 3 London 1987) no. 476.

12 Supra 3.1.1 and 3.1.2.

13 Elaborate express provisions in s. 16 and 18 rule 5 SGA 1979. Italian cod.civ. Article 1378 first sentence. For France, Dalloz, Vente en général no. 61-64.

14 Expressly s. 18 rule 5 (2) SGA 1979 and Italian cod.civ. Article 1378 sent. 2. For France, see Ghestin/Desché no. 544.

15 Benjamin (-Guest) no. 353; Ghestin/Desché no. 550; cf. Italian cod.civ. Article 1472.

16 Cc Article 1583, cf. supra n. 5. Cf. Dalloz, Vente en général no. 36.

17 Sections 16-20 SGA are placed under the title 'Transfer of Property as between Seller and Buyer'.

effects of the transfer of property in the event of the transferor's or transferee's insolvency.

1 Dispositions by Transferor in Possession

Both English and French law regard dispositions by the transferor in possession to a second transferee under certain circumstances as effective even though the transferor is no longer the owner. The second transferee prevails if two conditions are met: firstly, the asset must have been delivered to him, and secondly, he must have been 'in good faith and without notice of the previous sale'.[18] The same rule prevails in Italy.[19]

2 Dispositions by a Non-possessing Transferee

The non-possessing transferee disposes as an owner and can therefore transfer property to his sub-transferee. However, he cannot transfer more rights than he himself holds. The sub-transferee, even if in good faith, cannot acquire more rights than his transferor — the first transferee — since the general rules for a *bona-fide* acquisition require possession by the first transferee which is missing here.

Consequently, the original transferor's rights vis-à-vis the first transferee remain effective also vis-à-vis the second transferee. He remains entitled to possession according to the terms of the contract.

In addition, both English and French law grant to an unpaid seller a right of retention — a lien — and a right of stoppage.[20] These rights are not affected by the first buyer's dispositions.[21] In England, the seller may in the exercise of his rights resell the goods; the second buyer then acquires 'a good title to them as against the original buyer.'[22]

3 Transferor's Insolvency

In English and French sales law, the non-possessing buyer, as the owner, may claim his purchased good in the event of the seller's insolvency.[23] However, if the seller is still unpaid at the time of insolvency, his right of retention prevails.[24]

4 Transferee's insolvency

English and French sales law again agree. Against a buyer's claim for delivery of goods, based upon his ownership, an unpaid seller in possession may invoke his

---

18 For sales s. 24 SGA 1979; the provision explains the result by a fictitious authorisation of the seller 'by the owner of the goods'. In France the general rule of cc Article 1141; cf. for its clarifying interpretation Ghestin/Schedé no. 540.

19 Italian cod.civ. Article 1155.

20 S. 39-44 SGA 1979. In France, the seller in possession has, until payment, a right to retain the goods sold, cc Article 1612.

21 S. 47 (1) SGA 1979.

22 England: s. 48 (2) SGA 1979; France: Dalloz, Repertoire de Droit Commercial III, s.v. Faillite — Redressement Judiciaire (Phase de traitement — les créanciers) no. 251-323. This rule is in keeping with the rule set out supra no. 1.

23 England: Atiyah, *The Sale of Goods* (ed. 7 London 1985) 219; Benjamin (-Guest) no. 269.

24 The holder of a lien is a 'secured creditor', see Insolvency Act 1986, s. 383 (2).

lien or right of retention and even resell the goods. The second buyer will acquire property in them, even against the first buyer.[25]

Overall, the transferee's position is inferior in case of dispositions by a possessing transferor, unless the second transferee is *mala fide*. In the event of the transferor's insolvency the transferee cannot claim the goods if he has not yet paid the transferor; the transferor may then effectively sell the unpaid asset to a second transferee. The same is true if the transferee disposes of his property to a sub-transferee. In the transferee's insolvency, the unpaid transferor may rely on his right of retention and effectively transfer the buyer's goods to a second transferee. The transferee's position is markedly improved only after delivery of the goods to him. Effective dispositions by the transferor are then precluded, whereas the transferee himself now is able to transfer full property.

In essence, under the principle of consent, the transfer of property takes place in two stages: by mere consent and without delivery, a right of property with limited effects vis-à-vis third parties is transferred. This diminished right of property becomes fully effective only upon delivery of the assets to the transferee. English and French authors have criticized this two-step system on practical grounds as being 'extremely complicated' and have contrasted this to the simpler Roman law system of consent and delivery.[26] It has been pointed out that the parties' consent is of relatively small importance.[27] Probably the most devastating criticism has been expressed by a leading Belgian author; De Page summarizes his critique in the recommendation: 'On renoncera à l'effet translatif des contrats, qui n'est qu'un non-sens, un nid à difficultés, et que la plupart des législations contemporaines eurent la sagesses de ne pas emprunter au Code civil français.'[28]

3.2 The Principle of Delivery

3.2.1 The Principle
The other main principle for transferring property is that of delivery or transfer of possession. This principle is, however, not a complete alternative but rather adds an additional requirement. The principle of delivery requires both the consent of the parties as to the transfer of property and delivery of the asset to the transferee.

---

25 England: S. 41 (1) (c) and 48 (2) SGA 1979; cf. Benjamin(-Guest) no. 269 and Atiyah 218. France: cf. Law no. 85-98 on reorganisation and judicial liquidation of enterprises of 25 Jan. 1985, artt. 116, 118-119.

26 Atiyah 221; Ghestin/Desché no. 542.

27 Ghestin/Desché no. 542.

28 De Page, *Traité élémentaire de droit civil belge VI* (1942) 86. References supporting the three main objections are omitted.

This principle originates from Roman law which demanded *titulus* and *modus*. Several European countries still follow this system, especially Germany,[29] Greece,[30] the Netherlands[31] and Scotland.[32] In the first three countries the codified provisions are drafted in very similar terms. They all mention first delivery (or transfer) to the transferee and only thereafter some of them deal with the consent of the parties as to the passing of property.

This sequence is not accidental. Delivery has indeed primary importance but delivery (or transfer of possession) in itself is ambiguous. Delivery may occur for different reasons; in particular, it may or may not coincide with an intention of the parties to transfer property. The intention of the parties therefore is necessary to specify the meaning of the delivery.

3.2.2 Refinements and Qualifications

The principle of delivery and consent is, like its antipode, subject to a certain number of exceptions and qualifications with respect to the requirement of delivery. Some of these are more in the nature of refinements, others are genuine qualifications.

a Brevi manu traditio

A refinement is involved where the asset to be delivered is already held by the transferee. Since in this case delivery is superfluous all codes agree that the parties' consent as to the passing of property suffices.[33]

b Asset Held by a Third Person

Somewhat more complicated rules have been developed for situations in which the asset to be transferred is in the custody of a third person, for example a warehouseman.

Strictly speaking, two different techniques are used, either an assignment of the transferor's claim for the return of the asset or an agreement between transferor and transferee.

German law and also parts of Greek law take recourse to assignment: the transferor must assign his claim against the third party possessor for the return of the asset.[34] However, the two countries differ as to the nature of the claim which is to be assigned: in Greece, the text of the relevant provision makes it clear that

---

29   § 929 sent. 1 German CC provides: The transfer of property in a movable thing requires that the owner transfers the thing to the transferee and that both agree that property is to pass.

30   Article 1034 Greek CC adopts almost literally the German provision quoted in the preceding note.

31   In the new Dutch Civil Code book 3 which entered into force on 1 Jan. 1992, Article 3:84 par. 1 defines the principle of delivery as follows: 'Transfer of property of an asset requires delivery pursuant to a valid title by the person who has the right to dispose of the asset.' The term 'asset' (*goed*) comprises both things and patrimonial rights (Article 3:1). Cf. also Article 3:90.

32   Walker, *Principles of Scottish Private Law* III (ed. 4 1989) 418 ff. Scots law basically still follows Roman law, except insofar as English statutes are applicable. This exception is true with respect to sales law since the English Sale of Goods Acts were extended to Scotland.

33   German CC § 929 sent. 2; Greek CC Article 976 sent. 2; Dutch CC Article 3:115 lett. b.

34   German CC § 931; Greek CC Article 1035.

the transferor's proprietary claim for the return (*rei vindicatio*) is assigned;[35] in Germany on the other hand, the claim to be assigned is the contractual claim for the return of the asset which arises from the contractual relationship between the transferor and, for example, his warehouseman.[36] The difference between these two solutions is due to the fact that assignment in Germany is the only method of constructive transfer of possession with respect to an asset held by a third person,[37] whereas Greek law disposes of a second way.

Dutch law and to a certain extent Greek law too, use a seemingly different approach. In these countries, the transferor and the transferee must agree that the holder of the asset shall henceforth hold it for the transferee and the holder must be notified accordingly[38] or, alternatively in the Netherlands, the holder must acknowledge the transfer.[39]

In essence, the two solutions coincide. An agreement between the transferor and the transferee that the third person shall henceforth hold the asset for the transferee would in Germany be regarded as an implied assignment.[40] Neither in Germany nor in Greece does the validity of an assignment depend upon notification to the debtor.[41] Notification is, however, advisable for the protection of the transferee since otherwise the holder may be discharged by returning the assets to the transferor.

c Transferor in Possession

Frequently, the transferor is to remain the holder of the assets although he has transferred property in them; this is especially so if a security transfer of property is involved.[42] Germany, Greece and the Netherlands essentially agree that a transfer of property in this situation is also possible and that physical delivery is not required. They further agree that delivery must be replaced by an agreement between transferor and transferee (*constitutum possessorium*). Only the contents of this agreement is in dispute. Germany and Greece require that the transferor's continued holding of the assets must be expressed by a specific legal relationship.[43] In practice, usually a gratuitous loan for use is concluded.[44] It must be admitted, however, that this requirement has degenerated into an empty formality. Therefore the Dutch solution of requiring a mere contractual clause

---

35 However, this applies only if the third person possesses the asset as his own, cf. Article 1035 in conjunction with Article 974.

36 In Germany it is held that the proprietary claim for return of an asset cannot be assigned as such since it is accessory to property, cf. Baur, *Lehrbuch des Sachenrechts* (ed. 14 1987) 459.

37 German law, contrary to Greek law, does not distinguish between possession and detention. It regards persons holding for the owner also as possessors.

38 Dutch New CC Article 3:115 litt. c, Greek CC Article 977 for the case where the third person holds the asset for another (detentor).

39 Dutch New CC Article 3:115 litt. c.

40 Baur 459.

41 German CC § 398, Greek CC Article 455.

42 The Dutch New CC Article 84 par. 3 now expressly declares such security transfers to be invalid. In the present context, the security aspects of such transfers will not be pursued.

43 German CC § 930, Greek CC Article 977.

44 Cf. Baur 570.

acknowledging that the transferor holds in future for the transferee[45] is a sensible improvement.

'Constructive' delivery by agreement between a transferor remaining in possession (or becoming a holder) and the transferee creates a situation which resembles that existing under the system of consent when the transferor remains in possession:[46] property and possession (or retention) of the assets are separated, the transferee being a 'naked' owner and the transferor still being a holder of the assets.

All three countries restrict the protection of the transferee's property. In the first place, a third person to whom the transferor transfers may acquire property, provided the third person in good faith regards his transferor as the owner.[47]

The Dutch New Civil Code adds two further situations where the non-possessory transferee is not protected. The first is a second disposition by the transferor to another transferee; that transfer does not become valid vis-à-vis the first transferee unless factual delivery has been made to the second transferee.[48] This corresponds to the rule laid down for the same situation by the countries following the principle of consent.[49] A similar rule applies to a double transfer of future assets.[50]

3.3 Evaluation

After having presented the two competing principles of transfer of property by mere agreement on the one hand, and by delivery plus agreement on the other, an evaluation of and choice between them remains to be made. This evaluation can be short since the merits and demerits of both principles have already become reasonably clear.

1   A first major disadvantage of the principle of consent is that it cannot be directly applied to the greater part of modern commercial transactions involving transfer of property. Subsidiary rules are needed to apply the principle to transfers of generic goods and of future goods.[51]

2   Its limited effects create a second major disadvantage. Primarily, the principle of consent governs the legal situation between transferor and transferee. *Inter*

---

45   New CC Article 3:115 litt. a.
46   See supra 3.1.3.
47   Under the general rules on good-faith-acquisition; for details cf. German CC § 932 ff., Greek CC artt. 1036 ff. and Dutch New CC Article 3:86.
48   New CC Article 3:90 par. 2.
49   Cf. supra 3.1.3, L, no. 1.
50   New CC Article 3:98 par. 2.
51   This objection is regarded as decisive by von Caemmerer, 'Rechtsvergleichung und Reform der Fahrnisübereignung' *Zeitschrift für ausländisches und internationales Privatrecht* 12 (1938/39) 675 ff. (689 - 693).

partes, however, the terms of their underlying contract and the supplementary general rules of contract law provide the relevant regulation.

By contrast, the relationship vis-à-vis third persons, be they acquirers from or creditors of one of the parties, is influenced by several rules which negate the effects of the transfer of property by virtue of the contract. In this respect, the principle of consent is a treacherous rule since it 'promises' more than it can fulfill.

3   From a dogmatic point of view, the distinction between a contract's proprietary effects between the parties and towards third persons is not only unfortunate and regrettable. It also conflicts with the basic principle of property law that real rights have effects *erga omnes.*

4   The scepticism against the principle of consent is confirmed by highly critical voices from countries which have adopted this system and have worked with it.

5   On all the foregoing three substantive aspects, the competing principle of delivery and consent furnishes solutions which can be derived directly from the principle, except where substitute forms of delivery are being used. The principle of delivery is therefore, on the whole, clearer and much less subject to exceptions. It maintains the unitary concept of property since it need not distinguish between the effects of a transfer of property *inter partes* and *erga omnes.*

6   For these practical as well as theoretical reasons, a European Civil Code should make the transfer of property subject to delivery of the asset to the transferee and to an accompanying agreement of the parties on the passing of property.[52]

7   If a uniform provision on the passing of property upon delivery and consent would be adopted, the countries currently following the principle of consent will have to examine whether adaptations of subsidiary rules which are based upon the consent principle may be necessary.[53]

4 The Agreement for the Transfer of Property

The other aspect of the transfer of property by virtue of, or according to, a contract is also controversial between the European countries. In some countries, the parties' consent to the transfer of the property is found in the underlying contractual relationship providing for a transfer of property to the transferee, such as a contract of sale, work, or gift. Other countries demand an additional term or even agreement providing specifically for the transfer of property, that is to say a 'real' agreement.

This issue seems to be closely related to the basic dichotomy between the principle of consent and the principle of delivery accompanied by consent, which

---

52   The same conclusion was reached earlier by Waelbroeck (supra n. 2) 166 - 172.
53   Some considerations in Waelbroeck 172 - 181.

have already been discussed (supra III). This correspondence provides a convenient starting point for the following survey. It may, however, turn out that the similarities are more apparent than real.

4.1 The 'Real' Agreement

a Countries Requiring Delivery
Germany and the Netherlands, the two most prominent representatives of the principle of delivery plus consent, clearly separate the contractual agreement providing for the transfer of property from the 'real' agreement which is necessary (in addition to delivery) for the transfer to be effectual. Nevertheless, there are important differences between the two countries, as will appear.

In German law, the 'real' agreement of the parties is required for any disposition of proprietary rights and is therefore regulated by the provisions in Book 3 of the Civil Code governing property.[54] The required contents of the 'real' agreement for the transfer of property in movables is expressly defined in CC § 929 in the first sentence: the transferor as owner must agree with the transferee 'that property is to pass'. This agreement is defined as an appendix to the necessary delivery. In fact, the 'real' agreement must exist at the time of delivery.[55]

Notionally, the 'real' agreement is separate from the underlying contract of the parties providing for transfer of property, although in fact it may be contained in one of the terms of that contract. The contract as such (merely) creates the obligations of the parties; insofar as the transferor obliges himself to transfer property to the transferee, this promise must be executed by delivering the promised asset with the intention of transferring property to the transferee and the latter must accept this intention.

There are three elements of the 'real' agreement which clearly indicate that it is distinct from the parties' underlying contractual agreement. Firstly, the Civil Code uses a special term for the 'real' agreement (*Einigung*) which differs from the term contract (*Vertrag*). Secondly, the 'real' agreement is regulated by Book 3 on property. Thirdly, the 'real' agreement is revocable by each party until delivery has taken place.[56] An illustration: the courts have held, and most legal commentators agree, that a seller who has contracted to sell and transfer property unconditionally may upon delivery reserve his property, that is to say that the transfer of property to the buyer is made under the condition precedent of being paid by the latter.[57]

---

54   Cf. CC § 873, 877 in general, § 925 for transfer of property in immovables, § 929 for that in movables.
55   Baur 445.
56   Baur 445.
57   Federal Supreme Court 9 July 1975, BGHZ 64, 395, 397 with references; cf. also F.S.Ct. 14 Nov. 1977, NJW 1978, 696. The courts demand, however, an unambiguous declaration at the time of delivery at the latest; in these two cases the requirements were not met.

Dutch law is much less explicit than the German Civil Code. The Dutch New Civil Code merely requires delivery (Article 3:84 par. 1). For immovables, delivery takes place by a notarial deed of the parties intended for delivery, which must be registered.[58] Also in the cases where constructive possession is transferred by agreement, a 'real' agreement is involved.[59] Apart from these special cases and in spite of the silence of the code, many writers generally insist upon the requirement of a 'real' agreement.[60] However, there are also strong opponents to this idea.[61]

So far, certain differences between the two countries, although not major ones, have become apparent. There is, however, one decisive difference between the Dutch and the German 'real' agreement, and that concerns its relationship to the underlying contract between the parties. In the Netherlands, the validity of the transfer and therefore also of the 'real' agreement effectuating it, depends upon the validity of the underlying contract. This is clearly spelled out by the relevant provision which demands 'delivery pursuant to a valid title'.[62] This so-called 'causal' nature of the 'real' agreement is also unanimously accepted in Dutch literature.

In contrast, the German 'real' agreement is, in principle, independent of the underlying contract. Its existence and validity, and therefore also the validity of the transfer to the transferee, does not depend upon the prior or continuing existence of an underlying contract or its validity. That is not expressly spelt out by the Civil Code but is implied and is the unanimous view of both courts and writers.[63]

Thus, although the two legal systems require delivery, they differ profoundly on the role of the 'real' agreement. In the Netherlands, the 'real' agreement has merely a descriptive function. It designates that term of the contract which fixes the proprietary effects agreed upon, for example whether a transfer of property should be unconditional or subject to a specific condition. The 'real' agreement is completely integrated into the contractual context since its existence and validity is on a par with all other contractual clauses. It only differs as to its effects, since these are proprietary and not contractual. The Dutch controversy about the 'real'

---

58   New CC Article 3:89 par. 1.
59   Cf. New CC Article 3:115 and supra 3.2.2; cf. Pitlo (-Brahn), *Het Nederlands Burgerlijk Wetboek. II. Het Zakenrecht* (ed. 9 1987) 169.
60   See, inter alia, Asser (-Beekhuis), *Handleiding tot de Beoefening van het Nederlands Burgerlijk Recht* vol. 3 part I: Zakenrecht Algemeen Deel (ed. 11 1980) 162 ff.; Schoordijk, *Vermogensrecht in het algemeen naar Boek 3 van het nieuwe B.W.* ... (1986) 254 ff., with extensive discussion of other views; Mijnssen/Schut, *Bezit, levering en overdracht* (ed. 3 1991) 55-68; Hartkamp, *Compendium van het vermogensrecht volgens het nieuwe Burgerlijk Wetboek* (ed. 3 1988) no. 91 who reasons that the necessity of separate delivery implies that of a 'real' agreement.
61   See especially Vriesendorp, *Het eigendomsvoorbehoud* (1985) 9-31; Den Dulk, *De zakelijke overeenkomst* (1979) for movables; Pitlo (-Brahn) 168-170.
62   'levering krachtens geldige titel', New CC Article 3:84 par. 1.
63   Baur 41-45 with many references.

agreement therefore is purely conceptual and without practical relevance,[64] except where the Civil Code expressly provides for it.[65]

Interestingly enough, Greek law takes a middle position between Germany and the Netherlands. The transfer of property in immovables is, as in the Netherlands, causal.[66] This rule has been introduced to protect the transferors of immovables.[67] By contrast, the parties' agreement to transfer property in movables does not require a valid title;[68] it is abstract in order to protect transferees.[69] In both cases, a 'real' agreement is required. But it may be assumed that its role in the two situations differs as much as does its role in the Netherlands on the one hand and in Germany on the other.

b Countries Requiring Only Consent

In England and France, the idea of a special 'real' agreement is almost unknown.[70] The absence of a 'real' agreement is easily explicable. Both countries proceed from the principle that property is transferred by mere consent.[71] That consent is to be found in the terms of the underlying contract.

Continuing the preceding analysis of the discussion in the Netherlands[72] one could, of course, designate those clauses in a contract that determine the time and conditions of the transfer of property as the 'real' agreement. However, it has been shown above that this is a purely conceptual exercise. Those clauses, while dealing with the intended proprietary effects, are otherwise completely integrated into the contractual framework. They have no constitutive function apart from other contractual terms, as does a 'real' agreement in Germany.

4.2 The Necessity of an Abstract 'Real' Agreement

Since the 'real' agreement was 'invented' in Germany and this country is its major proponent, the following inquiry as to its necessity must concentrate on German law.

---

64   Vriesendorp 23 has clearly recognized that in a 'causal' system of transfer of proprietary rights a 'real' agreement is not a constitutive element of such transfers.
65   See text supra.
66   According to Greek CC Article 1033, the parties' agreement on transfer of property in immovables must be based upon 'a legitimate cause'. Cf. also Symeonides in Keramäus/Kozyris (ed.), *Introduction to Greek Law* (1988) 61.
67   Oral information by Professor Keramäus, Athens.
68   Greek CC Article 1034; cf. Symeonides 61-62.
69   See supra n. 67.
70   Atiyah 34 remarks on a sale, invoking SGA 1979 s. 2 (1), that the contract suffices to transfer the property in the goods, i.e. it may 'operate both as a conveyance and a contract.' But this observation is not pursued further.
71   Cf. supra 3.1.
72   Cf. supra a.

The principle of abstraction may well be regarded as a general feature of German law since it permeates several fields of law. Apart from property law, the rules concerning representation also clearly separate an agent's power of authority vis-à-vis third persons from the contract of agency which determines his relationship towards the principal. The general idea which inspires all the rules distinguishing between the two related legal relationships and insulating one from the other is the desire to protect third persons from the impact of possible defects existing in that other relationship.

We briefly turn first to the historical background and then to the contemporary effects of the 'real' agreement.

a Historical Background

The German *jus commune* followed the old Roman law principle of *'Nemo dat quod non habet.'* In order to mitigate the negative effects of this rule on legal transactions involving the transfer of goods, Von Savigny developed, in the middle of the 19th century, the theory of the 'real' agreement.

Its function was to insulate the transfer of a proprietary right to the transferee from possible defects of the underlying transaction (such as illegality, avoidance for mistake or non-observance of a formal requirement). True, as between the parties the transferee would be obliged to retransfer the asset received since he was unjustly enriched. But with respect to third persons, especially sub-transferees and creditors, the first transferee would retain the property until re-transfer to the original transferor. Consequently, he would be able to pass good title to a sub-transferee and his creditors could satisfy themselves from these assets.

In some fields, similar effects could be achieved by a different route, namely the protection of the good-faith sub-transferee from the transferee. This new practice was indeed introduced on a broad scale into the German Civil Code of 1900.[73] Nevertheless, the abstract 'real' agreement was retained for purely dogmatic reasons without reflecting on its relationship to the new rules on good-faith acquisition.[74]

b The Effects of the Abstract 'Real' Agreement

Today, scepticism towards the abstract 'real' agreement is gradually increasing in Germany. If one compares its effects with the basic ideas of good-faith acquisition, it appears that the latter achieves more reasonable results than the former. The decisive defect in the abstract 'real' agreement is that its protective effects go too far.

First, as regards sub-transfers by the transferee, the abstract 'real' agreement protects a sub-transferee blindly without asking whether this person had or should have had knowledge as to the position of the transferee at the time of the transfer. In other words, the abstract 'real' agreement protects sub-transferees even in the absence of good faith. Secondly, the abstract 'real' contract protects in effect the

---

73 Cf. CC § 932-935.
74 Details in Zweigert/Kötz, *An Introduction to Comparative Law* (1977) vol. I 181.

transferee's (and the sub-transferee's) creditors - an advantage not available under the general rules.[75]

Courts and writers have developed several means of avoiding the undesirable effects of the abstract 'real' agreement. One is an express agreement of the parties derogating from the abstract rule by making the validity of the transfer depend upon the validity of the underlying contract. Second, in the absence of an express term the courts may interpret the contract as containing such a term. Third, recourse may also be made to the provision on the partial nullity of a contract; CC § 139 establishes in this case a rebuttable presumption that, if one part of a legal transaction is void, the whole transaction is void.

Some prominent German writers also conclude that the abstract 'real' agreement should be abandoned as a general principle of property law.[76] Of course, nothing prevents the parties from insulating, by an express term, a transfer from the underlying contract.

4.3 Conclusion

A future European Civil Code should avoid making a transfer of property depend upon an abstract 'real' agreement of the parties. Most European countries do not know this intricate practice and even in Germany there are important sceptical voices.

If that recommendation is adopted, it will be necessary to carefully review the two legal systems that hitherto follow the principle of the abstract 'real' agreement. Both the German and the Greek legislatures will have to examine all fields of civil law to determine whether adaptations to the new system are necessary.

In particular, the equivalence of the proprietary claim for return of a thing (*reivindicatio*) with a claim of restitution based on unjust enrichment must be examined carefully. Under the present German law, both the conditions and the effects of these two claims differ in certain respects. If it is desired to retain, in effect, the present solutions, certain adaptations will be necessary.[77]

---

75   See especially Kegel, 'Verpflichtung und Verfügung — Sollen Verfügungen abstrakt oder kausal sein?' In: *Festschrift F.A. Mann* (1977) 57-86; cf. also Ferrari, 'Vom Abstraktionsprinzip und Konsensualprinzip zum Traditionsprinzip,' *Zeitschrift für Europäisches Privatrecht* 1993, 52 ff, 65 f.

76   Kegel 85-86; Larenz, *Lehrbuch des Schuldrechts* II 1 (1986) 20-21. For similar considerations of the Dutch legislator cf. *Parlementaire Geschiedenis van het Nieuwe Burgerlijk Wetboek. Boek 3: Vermogensrecht in het algemeen* (1981) 317.

77   Cf. van Caemmerer (supra n. 51) 704 and also Waelbroeck (supra n. 53).

5 Conclusion

For the contractual transfer of property in corporeal movables, a future European Civil Code should be guided by the following two rules:

1   The transfer of property should be subject to delivery to the transferee and an agreement of the parties to pass property to him.
2   The agreement of the parties as to the transfer of property should depend upon an existing and valid contract providing for such a transfer.[78]

These two rules would modify the existing legal situation in the countries of the consent principle on the one hand and in the countries of the abstract 'real' agreement on the other. Both groups of countries will have to investigate any undesired indirect effects which may result from a new uniform rule on the transfer of property.

It is also indispensable that such indirect effects are taken into account when drafting other parts of a future European Civil Code. A civil code is a highly complex and integrated whole; especially the rules on obligations and property are interdependent to such a degree that an isolated unification of rules of such central importance is not advisable.

---

78   The same solution was recently proposed by Ferrari (supra n. 75) 77 f.

CHAPTER 21

Security in Movable and Intangible Property. Finance Sales, Future Interests and Trusts

Jan H. Dalhuisen

1 Modern Security Devices

There are many types of secured interests, sometimes also called charges or liens (the latter especially in the US). They all aim at giving creditors some proprietary or, in civil law terms, *in rem* protection for their advances which otherwise would result in no more than a competing personal claim in the bankruptcy of the debtor. Security of this type normally means the setting aside of certain of the debtor's assets to guarantee his debts and implies a power of sale for the creditor in these assets upon default with a right to set-off the original debt against any sales proceeds. The result is a priority, whilst only any excess value is returned to the debtor or his (bankrupt) estate. It follows, at least in civil law countries, that the assets so set aside must be sufficiently identifiable and that the claims secured thereon must have a minimum of specificity. This satisfies at the same time the quest for clarity in the creation of proprietary rights and in their coverage and also avoids tying down too many random assets for unspecific claims, leading inexorably to excess security, unproductive encumbrances of future assets, and (further) prejudice to unsecured creditors.

There is generally less of a problem in this context if the security is registered, like the old mortgage for real estate, or is possessory, meaning that the secured asset enters the possession of the creditor, like under the old pledge in respect of movables, even though for the latter there may still be problems in the precise description of the loan or other advances the pledge is meant to ensure, as beyond the surrender of possession itself the pledge may be quite informal. Surrender of possession is now rarely convenient, however, except for negociable instruments, documents of title and capital market instruments like shares and bonds, as the movable assets concerned normally need to function in the current business of the debtor. Hence the increasing emphasis on non-possessory charges in movables and intangibles, like receivables, the latter being non-possessory *per se*. These modern non-possessory charges increasingly aspire to covering generalities of goods including replacement and future assets and are now often meant not only to secure present but also past and future debt. This poses more urgently the problem of their legal limitations in terms of identification and specificity. For the secured creditor, they further present the danger of the secured assets being lost or moving out of sight or reach. For third parties they are likely to create an erroneous appearance of credit worthiness of the debtor. It raises the question of their publication as an alternative form of protection for creditors, which was for movable assets traditionally limited to assets like ships and aircraft for which there was an established register. These then resulted in so-called chattle mortgages. Modern security registers are likely to be very differently organised in view of their different purpose.

The modern non-possessory security devises basically come in two forms:

a   to cover present and future equipment, inventory and receivables as security to acquire working capital in a business, mainly to finance these assets themselves, and
b   to better protect payment of goods sold, mainly through reservation of title, possibly extending to the goods in which they are subsequently incorporated.

Ad a
At least the first type of these modern non-possessory securities in movables often results in some kind of floating charge (a term not used in the US), as distinguished from a fixed charge, which, like in the case of the traditional mortgage, chattel mortgage or pledge, normally relates to specific assets. The principal feature of a floating charge is that it covers varying assets, like inventory, but normally allows such assets to be sold by the debtor free and clear of any charge in his ordinary course of business, whilst new inventory is automatically added. It may not only entail the creation of a security interest in present or future tangible assets of the business, but might even include an automatic assignment to the creditor of (future) receivables resulting from any sale of inventory with a licence for the latter to collect the proceeds rather than go through execution (foreclosure). This shift to proceeds suggests at the same time an enhancement in the value of the security since the sales price is likely to be higher than the original cost price. The charge may also cover any other income from assets, like that on shares, a facility not implied in fixed charges (except if on claims themselves, like on receivables or bonds, allowing the secured creditor to collect without foreclosure), although there is still a type of security in France which gives the creditor a claim to income (only) from real estate, automatically reducing the debt thereby, the so-called *antichrèse* of Art. 2085 Cc, earlier called the *vifgage* or *vivum vadium*. In common law countries, particularly in the UK, the floating charges may sometimes cover whole businesses, including real estate, which is uncommon elsewhere.

These floating charges are often intended not only to insure present advances but also past and (ever changing) future indebtedness. As suggested above, their true scope in terms of the future assets and past or future debt covered remains in the meantime a matter of debate in many countries against the background of the prevailing requirements of identification and specificity, which are nevertheless put under increasing pressure. Can next years harvest e.g. be given in security in this manner or any future crop resulting from next year's seeds? This may remain vague even in modern codes, like in the new Civil Code in the Netherlands, and will then depend on case law for further elaboration. Inclusion of past debt may in any event be deemed to create a voidable preference under the applicable laws against fraudulent conveyances or preferences (*actio Pauliana* or *actio revocatoria*). As mentioned above, the other issue is likely to be the need for registration or other forms of publication to protect the non-possessory creditor and warn the unweary (especially in the US and the UK) or only to establish time and (implicitly) rank (now in The Netherlands). It needs not to amount to the creation of mere chattle mortgages as the nature of this type of publication or registration is likely to be very different and may allow for the floating elements and even advance filing of the charge (like in the US). In France, there was traditionally particular concern with deceptive outward signs of credit worthiness generally, therefore with all hidden charges, although since 1980 French law has started to relax, an easier attitude long obtaining in Germany and The Netherlands.

Ad b
The second modern security device, more specifically geared to protecting payment of deliveries, is most likely to take the form of a reservation (or retention) of title. It may replace or reinforce statutory purchase money security and statutory or contractual rescission or reclaiming rights upon default. Even this reservation of title may acquire some floating elements when it is agreed e.g. that it may shift to replacement goods upon conversion or into a security in receivables upon resale, normally allowing collection of proceeds by the creditor. It may also require accounting of proceeds of any subsale by the buyer. It is less likely to cover any other unrelated pre-existing or later claims of the same creditor against the debtor, so that in this aspect there may not be an identification or specificity problem. This is made explicitly clear in the new Dutch Civil Code (Art. 3.92(2)). Publication or other forms of registration is also likely to be a lesser issue here as it may be considered too burdensome for habitual sellers, often of small items.

Security in the above sense is normally considered to give rise to a proprietary or (in civil law terminology) *in rem* right for the creditor in the assets thus set aside for his protection. It means foremost that the secured creditor retains his rights in the assets regardless of any transfer of ownership by the debtor (*droit de suite*), although subject to any protection of *bona fide* purchasers for value of movables or free and clear sales in the ordinary course of business, and may collect and execute the asset regardless of the bankruptcy of the debtor . To that extent, at least a first mortgagee or other first security holder may ignore executions by others, although particularly in modern reorganisation procedures the own separate execution rights of secured creditors may be curtailed as it is likely to effectively render continuation of a business impossible during the reconstruction period, cf. See. 362 Bankruptcy Code 1979 and Art. 33 and 47 French Bankruptcy Act 1985. As mentioned before, the process of execution or foreclosure of securities (or collection under secured receivables) further implies a set-off, creating a priority (*droit de préférence*) for the secured creditor but also some guarantees for the debtor in terms of obtaining market value for the secured assets and the return of any excess proceeds or collections. Another aspect of security is that it is normally ancillary to the debt, that is to say that if the claim is transferred to another party, the security remains attached to it, but is, on the other hand, automatically terminated once the debt is paid, at the same time giving rise to a resumption of full title by the debtor, except where provisions can be made to the contrary, like in the German *Grundschuld* (or *Schuldbrief* in Switzerland), which facility survives repayment and is transferable separately from the debt. It is on the other hand also possible to embody claim and security in one negociable instrument, common in so-called asset-backed securities. There is another form of this in Belgium where mortgage instruments may be to bearer allowing a transfer without need to amend the property register, in that country otherwise required notwithstanding the ancillary nature of the security.

2 Indirect Security Rights and their Contractual Enhancements

Retention Right

Meanwhile, particularly banks may wish to claim for themselves extensive retention rights, preferably covering all they retain or may receive on behalf of a client in order to protect any credit lines or other types of client indebtedness, present or future. The traditional statutory retention right is, at least in civil law countries of the French type, of a much more limited nature and normally restricted to a right to hold, but not to sell or appropriate specific assets until expenses incurred in connection therewith, notably in respect of repairs, are reimbursed. It may now sometimes be combined with a priority in the proceeds upon an ordinary attachment followed by execution, cf. e.g. Art. 3.292 new Dutch Civil Code, but is still meant mainly to protect basic expenditure relating to the asset itself. In common law countries, the retention right (for which the term 'lien' is sometimes reserved, especially in the UK) may well be more general and figure as purchase money security with a separate execution right (power of sale), a situation in civil law normally only achieved through a contractual enhancement of the retention right, by bankers often attempted through their general terms of business. This contractual enhancement of retention rights may then result in some form of possessory floating charge (even though there may be no signed document), allowing the debtor nevertheless to make ordinary payments out of his accounts and buy and sell securities in the custody of his bank (at least as long as the bank allows it). There are, however, likely to be the usual problems of identification and specificity in both the secured assets and the debts they are meant to insure, creating particular doubts as to the coverage of future debt. There may also be problems in terms of registration or publication and of voidable preferences. The protection may in any event lack the nature of a charge proper in the assets them-selves and may thus remain limited to a preference in the execution proceeds only.

Right of Sett-off

Another important indirect but also traditional security may be found in the right of set-off, which is ultimately at the heart of direct securities as well. Its impact will vary according to the existence of off-settable due counter-claims (and may further be limited to claims expressed in the same currency). It commonly derives from the mere operation of the law, might be automatic or require some declaration (as in Germany, Sec. 388 BGB, and now also in The Netherlands, Art. 6.127 CC). It is normally available even if the claims are unrelated, although in the latter case, in common law countries, there may still be a need for legal proceedings, which, however, are implicit in executions and bankruptcies. The right of set-off might also be contractually enhanced through the introduction of contractual accelleration and valuation clauses for the event of (cross) default or insolvency so as to result in all debts of the non-bankrupt party payable to the estate immediately falling due in this context (monetary claims against the bankrupt automatically mature upon insolvency) and, if non-monetary, being valued according to an agreed formula, thereby becoming off-settable. In the context of the set-off, the object is thus to settle as many mutual claims of whatever nature as possible and to that effect immediately reduce through accelleration all outstanding executory matters to money claims, a much widened set-off attempt therefore.

This contractual accelleration of maturity to gain a better set-off may, however, not always be (fully) effective, particularly not in France and Belgium, if not triggered before insolvency as, from that moment, all is considered frozen in these countries, cf. Art. 33 and 47 French Bankruptcy Act. In the US there is the already mentioned general stay of individual creditors' action, Sec. 362. Moreover, accelleration is generally curtailed in bankruptcy (Sec. 365(e) Bankruptcy Code), also to prevent an early disintegration of the business. An exception is now created for securities contracts, futures, repurchase agreements and swaps (Secs. 555, 556, 559 and 560). In the UK, Sec. 175(2) Insolvency Act 1986 covering the repudiation facility of the trustee of burdensome contracts is not believed to bar contractual rescission and valuation clauses either. Settlement payments, at least in commodity contracts, forward transactions, securities contracts and repos, may always be immediately set-off in the US(Sec. 362(b)(6) and (7).[1] A similar system would appear to result in the UK under Sec 159 Companies Act 1989, but only if exchanges or clearing house rules support it.

Netting

The result of this much widened contractual set-off, wherever allowed, is often called netting and the scope of this facility is of particular importance in the financial world, notably in the area of contracts for differences and in repurchase agreements (repos). The former are two sided contracts, like swaps, in which e.g. a floating rate income stream is exchanged for a fixed rate income stream giving

---

1   Cf. *Matter of Bevill, Bresler and Schulman Asset Management*, 896 F2d 54 (1990)).

rise to regular off-setting interest payments during the term of the agreement, depending on the movement in the (floating) exchange interest rate. The essence for netting purposes is to view such a swap as one transaction rather than as two closely related parallel borrowings amongst which a bankruptcy trustee might chose to continue the (for him) profitable side whilst repudiating the other, often referred to as the 'cherry picking' option. Rather than relying on the principle of set-off, there may in this manner result a wider form of netting within the damage calculation following termination. Through a master agreement, all swap contracts between the same parties might even be deemed to be part of one contract terminated in the case of bankruptcy of either party, leading to a still broader netting, although as mentioned above it depends on applicable execution or bankruptcy law to what extent this will be effective. A not dissimilar netting arrangement is usually foreseen in master agreements concerning repos, the additional aspect being the valuation of the assets (shares or bonds) involved. It may (and is intended to) further impede the trustee's option rights and may therefore not be acceptable everywhere either. The netting principle has proved particularly relevant for banks who must otherwise allocate more regulatory capital to their swap and repo business as, without it, their risk exposure will be deemed to be accordingly increased. It may thus be seen that the status and effect of contractual enhancements of direct and particularly indirect security rights, notably retention rights and set-offs, have become issues of the greatest importance.

Rescission Rights

There may finally also be a statutory rescission right for creditors (*lex commissoria tacita*) upon default of a debtor, creating a further possibility of an indirect security right. In more modern codifications, this statutory rescission right may result in a right to reclaim title and possession without (default) proceedings upon mere notice (cf. Art. 6.267 Dutch CC). In the new Dutch Civil Code, this statutory rescission right may no longer be used to reclaim property from a bankrupt estate pursuant to a failed sales agreement, however (Art. 2.269) and only a contractual clause can now achieve this result (*lex commissoria expressa*, Art. 3.84(4)). In Germany, both rescission rights remain available, but with respect to the reclaiming of title thereunder only to the extent the relevant assets have not yet reached the bankrupt. In France and countries following its tradition, these rescission rights also exist but, like the accelleration, are frustrated by the bankruptcy principle that conditions may no longer be fulfilled after the opening of the proceedings and the rescission right must therefore, in order to be effective, as a minimum have been invoked before. In the US (under Sec 365(e) Bankruptcy Code), the effect of these rescission clauses, like accelleration (with the above mentioned exceptions), is more generally curtailed in order not to trigger an early demise. The choice of continuation remains then with the bankruptcy trustee, at least in executory contracts, which are contracts not yet fully performed by either party.

This common bankruptcy facility is in fact the origin of his so-called 'cherry picking' option and it may be seen that accelleration and rescission with subsequent netting are meant to curtail this option, particularly in swaps and repos, to avoid the trustee electing to maintain the profitable side and repudiating the other. Should the trustee wish to discontinue, he might face a claim for (non-secured) damages; if he wishes to continue he may, on the other hand, have to give adequate security for his own continuing performance.

3 The Finance Sale

Modern financial transactions are often cloaked in terms of conditional sales under which certain assets or rights therein are transferred subject to return upon payment of the debt or fulfillment of other conditions rather than that these assets are given as security. Especially when no clear interest structure is foreseen, many of these transactions cannot easily be qualified as secured lending. Inherent in this approach is the possibility of appropriation or forfeiture upon fullfillment or non-fullfillment of the condition, as the case may be. It deprives the counterparty at the same time of the protection of an execution sale and an objective evaluation with a set-off under which excess value will be returned. In common law, there is here particularly the concept of the equity of redemption under which a defaulting debtor may reclaim the forfeited asset, at least for some time after appropriation, which is supervised by the courts under the rules of foreclosure.[2] This concept is thus unavoidably under pressure in the more modern financial techniques based on finance sales, although a mere reservation of title does not normally require any execution sale either, not even under the new Dutch Civil Code (Art. 3.92 CC), but in the US specifically required under the Uniform Commercial Code (pursuant to Sec. 9-102 (2)). Floating charges often take the form of sales of assets as well and may or may not then require a further execution sale upon default. It would appear that the nature of the transaction itself provides the guide as to any necessity of foreclosure. When the protections inherent in foreclosure procedures are missing, they might, however, be replaced by notions of unjust enrichment.

These so-called finance sales are increasing in frequency, value and types all the time and are substantially eclipsing secured transactions, partly because they are more flexible and subject to less formality (e.g. in terms of publication or registration), particularly attractive in international financings with assets moving between countries, as the sales and ownership concepts are more universal than the concept of security, whilst (cumbersome) local formalities concerning secured transactions may have no significance or may not give any particular protection in other countries where the secured assets may eventually emerge. They are then better avoided. Also identification and specificity problems might be lessened in this manner. More importantly, these finance sales may not serve as substitutes for secured lending at all, but may rather have a logic of their own, which is becoming

---

2   Cf. Cheshire and Burns, *Modern Law of Real Property*, 638 (1988).

the more likely scenario. They are then often based on ownership rights being transferred or split up in different parts whilst options or temporary/future interests are granted therein to achieve particular forms of financings or particular cash flews and more speculative objectives. The result is often referred to as the unbundling of the ownership right, which may lead to temporary or conditional transfers of the assets concerned, in a manner principally determined by the parties, as part of what is now often called financial engineering. Reservation of title and hire purchases are probably the more traditional, and repurchase agreements (repos), finance leases and factoring the more modern examples of this new approach, the former more security related, the latter more like transactions in their own right. The question is in how far these finance sales result in split proprietary rights proper, as such in principle enforcable against all the world.

A simple example may demonstrate the point. A person requiring cash may solicit an advance from a bank and offer his car as a pledge, therefore as a possessory security. But a non-possessory arrangement may be preferred and the car owner may therefore seek to split-off and grant the bank an option to acquire the car upon default. This would not, however, normally provide the bank with a proprietary right in a bankruptcy of the debtor and may therefore be of little value. In civil law terms, there would only be a personal right of the bank to the asset upon default. However, the debtor could also sell the car and transfer the ownership to the bank whilst retaining possession, and cash the proceeds upon the condition that the whole transaction is automatically reversed upon repayment of a certain sum at a certain time. In this latter construction, the bank might have an ownership right on which it may continue to rely in the case the erstwhile car owner does not fulfil the repayment condition and goes bankrupt. On the other hand, the former car owner might have a conditional property right (or *in rem* option in civil law terms), which he may be able to maintain even in a bankruptcy of the bank upon his lender of timely payment. Registration where required for non-possessory security would not appear necessary, at least not if the device was not meant as a clear substitute for a secured transaction. Although in this example this may still appear to be the case, it need not be so when e.g. a flow of temporarily surplus assets passes between a customer and his bank (or any other entity) in exchange for cash (or other commodities) until such time that there may be no further need or the customer requires the assets. In the meantime, the bank might make an own use of the asset and create an own income therefrom as its reward. The result is more like a swap. In most forms of repos, in financial leases or in factoring, no security substitution is normally the objective, as these financing techniques operate differently and have an own market value and price not directly related to the prevailing interest rates. There is therefore no credit agreement proper.

These finance sale techniques are understandably giving rise to much debate and the greater formality attached to secured transactions, especially if non-possessory, in some countries e.g. in terms of publication or registration, requires in any event a clear criterion to distinguish them from finance sales under applicable law. There is also the question of safeguards e.g. in terms of specificity and enforcement. It has, however, proved difficult to find a clear distinctive element, even though it is becoming clearer all the time that not all proprietary rights exchanged or emerging in a financing are automatically indicative of a secured loan. The new Dutch Civil Code, which has attempted to narrow the concept of security and now requires a form of registration for non-possessory charges, has at the same time tried (in Art. 3.84 (3)) to eliminate any substitutes by introducing a substantive criterion requiring that all proprietary transactions beyond registered or possessory security must have as their purpose and intent the passing of the asset concerned into the patrimony of the other party. This criterion is unclear, however, as it does not explain what 'passing into the patrimony' in this context really means and to what extent this is deemed necessary.

The idea is more generally to avoid any kind of ownership rights devised by the parties including any double ownership through a combination of present and future interests, but only in the next subsection (Art. 3.84 (4)), the new Dutch Code is forced to allow in a closed system of ownership rights the conditional transfer, of which the reservation of title and the hire purchase are themselves explicit further examples, cf. resp. Art. 3.92 CC and Art. 1576h CC (old). It unavoidably leads to defeasible and prospective ownership rights operating side by side in the same asset, which under the new Code would appear to lack proprietary effect only to the extent a clear attempt at creating a substitute security right is made. It is likely that much uncertainty will persist in this area in The Netherlands for some time, particularly affecting the status of repos, finance leases and factoring. Art. 3.84 (3) is probably unrealistic in its aspirations and likely to have been a legislative mistake, even though motivated by an altogether understandable systemic concern caused by the proliferation of proprietary rights and, although apparently to some lesser extent, its effect in terms of the resulting priorities affecting the *pari passu* treatment of common creditors.

As to the distinction between secured transactions and finance sales elsewhere, especially with a view to the need to register corporate charges, English law might be more readily inclined towards the more formal criterion of interest having been agreed.[3] Consequently, English law might confirm that only if there is a clear interest rate structure, the transaction is likely to be considered a loan and any proprietary rights transferred or emerging therein may then be considered securities, subject to registration as the case may be, although registration as a charge may in any event not always be necessary in the UK, either under the Bills of Sale Act or Companies Act, under the latter at least not as long as no floating charge is created or other debt is covered. In case law in the US, there are also indications of this approach at least for repos (cf. Bevill, Bresler and Schulman Asset Management Corp., 896 F 2d 54 (1990)). As far as finance leases are concerned, the new Article

---

3   Cf. Oditah, 'Financing Trade Credit', *Journal of Business Law*, 541 (1992).

2A of the UCC on Equipment leasing together with the amended Sec. 1-201(37) UCC suggest that there is still substantial uncertainty in the matter and no clear distinctive criterion has so far been formulated in the US where the facts of the case decide the issue. It is obvious therefore that these more modern financing techniques still suffer from a lack of legal definition in many countries. A particular problem also remains the ancillary or alternatively independent nature of the property rights so created. This is particularly relevant as to the automatic nature of any retransfer upon fulfilment of the conditions at the end of the agreed term, which may be more problematic if there is independence.[4]

As a general background, it is well known that under common law parties are freer in arranging their proprietary affairs. This affects the modern developments in financial techniques worldwide, as they are mainly inspired by the Anglo-American practice, and is the main cause of the need to rethink civil law approaches in this area. This greater choice notably applies to the manner, time and place of transfer of title to property. In common law, it may occur at the time of the contract or upon delivery and be made subject to all kinds of conditions parties elect. This provides flexibility and security rights consequently have often been more readily cast in terms of a conditional sale/transfer, notably also the traditional mortgage. They may also operate through use of the trust concept, although the courts even then have been concerned about proper foreclosure, the equity of redemption or other ways of returning excess value. Nevertheless, particularly in the UK, there remains on the whole considerable flexibility and freedom in the creation of new proprietary devices. The US approach limits the traditional common law flexibility in this area with respect to movables as it requires all movable security interests to be embedded in the system of Chapter 9 UCC, but, as shown above, it does not attempt to outlaw the finance sale as such, particularly not in the case of repos, and finance leases, is therefore different in its attitude from the new Dutch Civil Code.

German law, which does not require publication or registration of security in movables, has always accepted hidden charges and appears as a consequence less concerned in the matter of finance sales as the distinction, in the absence of registration requirements and other formalities, is less important, although still relevant e.g. in terms of forfeiture and execution sales, (automatic) return of title, and in the disposition rights and rights to income and capital gains in the meantime. In fact, modern analysis of all secured transactions in terms of conditional or temporary ownership rights or of expectations with proprietary effect is not unknown in Germany since Raiser suggested it already in 1961 (*Dingliche Anwartschaften*). In France, the statutory system of passing of title upon the signing

---

4   Comparative studies remain rare in this area of proprietary rights, even of securities themselves, although as to the latter the compilation of contributions edited by Sauveplanne in 1973 in Security over Corporeal Moveables remains relevant and also Drobnig's contribution in the *Uncitral Yearbook* 171 (1977), see further, Dalhuisen *International Bankruptcy and Insolvency*, 3-343 ff and 3-381 ff (1986).

of the contract itself (even without subsequent delivery, cf. Art. 1138 Cc) also clearly allows for conditional *sales*, cf. also Art. 1584 Cc, although this can have unexpected results as upon bankruptcy conditions can no longer be fulfilled. It could leave the wrong party with full ownership and render the device entirely ineffective e.g. in bankruptcy of a buyer in possession under a reservation of title if the asset was not surrendered by him beforehand. The alternative theory of a delayed *tranfer* until payment would leave the seller with the risk of loss of the goods (if not transferred by contract).[5] and in his bankruptcy create problems with regard to the instalments paid as title can no longer be transferred to the buyer upon the latter's full performance.

French (and Belgian) law opted as a consequence for a number of specific non-possessory chattle mortgages instead, the so-called *nantissements*, including one on equipment, leases and good-will (as defined) of a company: the *nantissement de fonds de commerce*. However, in France, a law of 1980 lifted the above mentioned bankruptcy law restrictions in respect of the reservation of title (cf. Art. 115 and 121 French Bankruptcy Act 1985) and laws of 1981 (*Loi Dailly*) and 1984 introduced the legal basis for the assignment of receivables for security purposes by lifting the prior notification requirement of Art. 1689/Art.1690 Cc, confirmed in Art. 107(4) of the French Bankruptcy Act of 1985, whilst recent French proposals concerning the introduction of the *fiducia* (Art. 2062 ff. Cc) will generally allow a conditional transfer of tangible assets (including real estate), thereby also creating a floating charge facility which may be combined with the assignment of receivables, both to be effective in bankruptcy. In the meantime, finance leases are covered in France by a special Act of 1966 on the *credit-bail* (finance lease) and *cession-bail* (sale and lease back).

Another aspect of finance sales may be to what extent they are covered by the 1980 Vienna Convention on the international sale of goods in those countries that are parties to it (which notably still excludes the UK). The Convention is clearly not written for this type of sales but may nevertheless well be considered to be applicable, e.g. in terms of responsibility for the goods and risk, except if the goods sold are shares, bonds or other negotiable instruments or investment securities (Art. 2(d)). In any event, the Vienna Convention does not apply to the proprietary consequences of a sale.

---

5   See for a discussion of the French law in this area, Von Breitenstein, 'La clause de reserve de propriété et le risque d'une perte fortuite de la chose vendue', Decision French Cour de Cassation, Nov. 20 1979, 33 *Rev. Trim. de Droit Commercial*, 43 (1980).

4 The Repo, Financial Lease and Factoring

Repo

Repos, financial leases and factoring are the most important modern structures supporting international financings and examples of finance sales as distinguished from secured transactions. The repo or repurchase agreement is based on two mirror transactions of sale: in order to finance a short term bond portfolio investment, the owner may sell and deliver his securities and collect the agreed price, whilst arranging at the same time a repurchase date and repayment price. The initiative may, however, also emanate from the lender in what is then called a reverse repo. The price difference between the two contracts is called the repo rate and is related to the market price for this type of activity in which standard interest rates for the type of money market advance the original owner may so receive may play a role but are not necessarily the determining factor. The key is that the repo rate may be lower. This type of financing may thus be cheaper than available alternatives. Repos may on the other hand not be meant as a financing instrument at all but be used in lieu of so-called bond lending against a fee to allow the bond borrower to cover his short positions, the fee being replaced by the benefit of cheap money in the repo structure. In practice, bond financing and bond lending are hard to distinguish as most major security houses have made a separate business out of the repo activity altogether. Formalities are minimal as the normal sales and settlement techniques of the bond markets are used instead of a specialised credit agreement with security provisions or a bond lending contract, as the case may be, which cause delay and add to the costs. The repo now competes with these more conventional approaches.

Financial Lease

In the finance lease, the lessor, as the legal owner, puts the assets at the disposition of the lessee who will pay him for the use, usually in regular instalments, until the end of the term when the lessee will normally become the owner of the leased asset against payment of a pre-set residual (nominal) price, or at least receive an option to acquire ownership. Particularly in real estate transactions, they may be tantamount to a mortgage, but avoid mortgage charges, allow 100% financing and produce an off-balance sheet item. Although the regular and final payments relate to the capital cost of the asset, funded by the lessor/financier, and will assume an element of interest and risk reward, they cannot be equated to capital repayment and interest either. The whole point of the arrangement for financiers is the higher rewards they may so obtain; for users it is often the convenience of off-balance sheet assets which need not be financed. The consequence is that this type of lease also has an own market value and justification, separate from the interest rate structure, there being specific value in providing this kind of facility. A particular form is a sale-lease back, under which an owner of an asset temporarily surrenders title in exchange for a lease (often to obtain off-balance sheet financing), subject to similar regular payments during the useful life of the asset, after which full title reverts to the former owner.

Factoring

The factoring technique, long known domestically, but now also used increasingly in international financings, aims at the collection of receivables by an organisation which professionally handles debt administration, provides credit in the interim and (often) guarantees the payments. In that context, it may abandon any recourse (at a price), resulting in so-called non-recourse factoring. Factoring may then result in an outright sale of existing receivables (at a discount) or in respect of future receivables up and until accruing to an agreed amount beyond which any excess may be returned and any transfer rescinded. The plurality of receivables distinguishes factoring from forfeiting which is normally related to a one-off collection, often of a large amount, effectuated through a transfer of the receivable together with any personal security in terms of letters of credit or other guarantees or the (extra) discounting of a bill of exchange drawn on and accepted by the original buyer.

Bankruptcy

As far as these more common types of modern finance sales are concerned, on the analogy of a secured transaction, the repo could be considered to result in a possessory security interest comparable to an enhanced short term retention right or pledge in respect of securities for which a financier is extending credit. The finance lease could be considered to result in a non-possessory interest of the financier, a situation for the creditor comparable to a reservation of title, which might, however, not apply to a sale-lease back as the reservation of title is often limited to the protection of purchase money only. The modern factoring might then be comparable to a floating charge on receivables. The key feature in all these new techniques is, however, to understand that not only do these techniques not adopt the form of a security but they do not necessarily mean to reach a similar result either. They elaborate on the conditional or temporary transfer of title for other reasons, resulting in split ownership rights under which *both* parties may have proprietary interests. Not recognising this, unavoidably gives either the one or the other party the upper hand with either an excess or too little protection and may reduce in this way the finance lease e.g. to no more than a personal right of the lessee which may terminate upon a bankruptcy of the lessor (under the 'cherry picking' option of the latter's trustee), and factoring to no more than a licence to collect, terminating upon the bankruptcy of the assignor.

These modern financing techniques unavoidably give rise to considerable problems if their proprietary status as split ownership rights are not recognised. For the repo, the problem is then particularly in the status of the second contract in the case of intervening bankruptcy of either party, particularly relevant if the price of the underlying assets has changed. Has the original seller or his trustee a proprietary right to the assets earlier sold whilst offering payment, or can the trustee of buyer opt to retain the asset subject to a competing personal claim for damages by the other party only? May the second party alternatively, upon default of the first one, retain ownership in the assets and/or, if the assets decreased in value, force a set-off relying on the accrued income in the meantime, even if he is not strictly speaking entitled to the income accrued on the assets under the repo itself. Or has the buyer in the bankruptcy of the original seller a security right (pledge) in the assets and, if so, a power of sale and a priority in the proceeds including accrued interest? May other debt be covered? May on the other hand both agreements contractually be tied together in such a way that an automatic form of netting results in the event of default under either and 'cherry picking' by the bankruptcy trustee of either is avoided? On the other hand, in the case of repos of investment securities, notably bonds and shares, the fungible character of these assets may defeat any proprietary claims of the original seller,[6] but not necessarily any set-off or any proprietary right of the original seller in the coupons or dividends.

For the finance lease with an automatic purchase by the lessee, the question may be whether this right may still exist after a bankruptcy of the lessor, even if not all instalments are due and paid. The trustee's option to demand continuation may be more valuable here, especially in the case of a bankruptcy of the lessor as the asset might not have much value outside the existing relationship. In the case of reorganisation proceedings against the lessee, the continuation of the lease will normally also have a high priority. In factoring, discontinuation of the arrangement by the trustee of the assignor may expose a lender/guarantor unduly. The latter may want to exercise any option to continue to collect and even obtain more receivables in order to amortise his advance, although he is unavoidably exposed, as the flow of receivables is likely to come to an end. These problems can only be resolved by revisiting the ownership concepts themselves. In this context it is also necessary, however, to consider related problems like those concerning the disposition rights of either party to a split ownership right, the protection of *bona fide* third parties, the rights to income and capital gains, the risk of damage to or loss of the property, the position of attachors or trustees in bankruptcy, any unjust enrichment as the consequence of collecting over-value and the manner of retrieval of the assets upon fulfillment of the conditions or at the end of the agreed term, either through revindication of ownership or as a personal claim only.

5 Legal Status and Relative Priorities. Privileges

Although the essence of all the above techniques, resulting in direct or indirect securities or conditional or temporary proprietary rights, is now known in most modern countries and has in one form or another found (some) expression or recognition in most domestic legal systems, including their execution or bankruptcy laws, there may still be substantial differences in approach, especially in the legal form required and in the type of proprietary right created; the aspects of identification and specificity under floating charges; formalities, particularly in

---

6   Cf. in the US, *Matter of Bevill, Bresler and Schulman Asset Management*, 896 F2d 54 (1990).

terms of publication or registration; disposition rights, especially in the possibility for the debtor to sell inventory to third parties free and clear of any charges or for the latter, if *bona fide*, to acquire full title; separate execution rights of the creditor with or without a power to sell (subject to foreclosure proceedings with their own guarantees) or appropriate the assets concerned in reliance on his proprietary right; acceptance of enhanced retention rights (with power of sale) and of rescission or accelleration clauses with the possibilities of a subsequent return of assets or an enhanced set-off or netting facility. In finance sales, there are the particular problems associated with dual ownership, as there are the disposition rights, the protection of *bona fide* third parties, the entitlement to income and capital gains, the risk of damage or loss, the position in attachments and bankruptcy of either party, the question of any retrieval of over-value through an unjust enrichment action and the automatic return of assets upon fulfillment of the conditions at the end of the agreed term.

There may be considerable differences in views in all these aspects in different countries, as we saw probably foremost in the validity, coverage and treatment of the most modern non-possessory security devices, themselves often of a hybrid nature, in the status of the conditional or temporary ownership (or leaseholds) under finance sales, and in netting. The relative status, rank or priority of all these direct or indirect charges, conditional or temporary ownership rights in a liquidation need further be considered. This is not only important whenever their validity and precise coverage remains uncertain in terms of entitlement to possessions and enjoyment or future rights thereto, but also where they are competing, as most commonly a floating charge on inventory, protecting bank lending, and a reservation of title (or any other purchase money security) in the same assets, protecting the suppliers.

Also other property interests of third parties, like usufructs, commercial leases or life interests (and equitable interests in common law countries) may compete with these charges or conditional (financial) ownership or leasehold rights. The basic rule remains here that, in matters of proprietary rights of whatever nature, the older charge or property right prevails over the younger (according to the rule: *prior tempore, potior iure*), except that the grantor is always postponed or subordinated, although likely to be (automatically) reinstated in full at the end of the term of the granted limited proprietary right or, if conditional, when it becomes clear that the conditions will not be fulfilled. In civil law terms, this (automatic) reversion is sometimes referred to as the elasticity of the concept of ownership, whilst the ranking results from the *in rem* effect of all these proprietary rights, which, in this system, may be maintained against all the world, except against the owner of any prior proprietary right unless he is the grantor. Any attendant priority in an execution subsequently derives from the implicit set-off right.

There may be exceptions to this traditional seniority rule. Purchase money security e.g. might in particular be protected, even if created later in order to safeguard the

375

ordinary flow of goods. A reservation of title thus often prevails over a floating charge, another reason being that it is likely to be the more specific. It may even prevail over other possessory charges, although possession itself may sometimes give better rights. Then there is the purchaser in the ordinary course of business or the *bona fide* purchaser for value who is likely to be protected as succeeding owner under general legal principles concerning ownership of movables on the European Continent or by specific case law or statutory exception under common law. Lack of proper formalities, like registration, may void the security or proprietary right altogether, at least vis a vis third parties, although it is also possible that actual knowledge of the charge or ownership right may still uphold it in respect of the person with this knowledge.

Most importantly, there are sometimes also statutory preferences, notably in favour of tax and social security authorities, often given super rank, even though not necessarily expressed in terms of a (statutory) charge, lien or security interest. On the European Continent, particularly in countries of the French legal tradition, it is not uncommon in this connection to see so-called *privilèges*, which create a statutory priority right, not normally to any asset, but rather to execution proceeds upon an ordinary attachment or in a bankruptcy. As a consequence, they do not result in own separate execution rights or in a possibility of separate recovery through a power of sale in favour of the beneficiary. They are ancillary to the debt but lost if title in the assets is transfered. They may be general, covering the whole estate, or specific, covering the proceeds of a special asset in respect of which it arose, normally because of repairs, maintenance or upkeep charges. A special instance may be the privilege of the unpaid seller. Debts made by the bankruptcy trustee in the winding up or reorganisation of the estate may be of a similar (generally) privileged nature, that is to say that they are given priority in any bankruptcy distributions without being proprietary charges proper.

Normally the rank of privileges is lower than those of security interests (amongst each other, the specific ones usually rank higher than the general ones) and these privileges have in any event a weaker status than securities as they have no proprietary status whilst their benefit is lost altogether when the goods pass on to third parties, a situation approximated in the modern non-possessory floating charges in goods that are meant to trade. However, especially the status of (general) governmental privileges, which have now also been introduced in the UK and the US[7] may be higher than proprietary security rights within the own jurisdiction, even though not commonly recognised in executions or bankruptcies elsewhere. The underlying claims might, however, still be presented in other countries as common debt.[8]

---

7   Cf. Sec. 89 UK Bankruptcy Act 1985 and Sec. 507(a)(7) cq. Sec. 1129(a)(9) US Bankruptcy Code.

8   Cf. e.g. Art. 8 of the Belgian-Austrian Bankruptcy Treaty.

6 The Status of Modern Security Interests. Property and other *in Rem* Rights. Future Interest and Trusts

Whatever legal doctrine or statutory law may dictate, there can be little doubt that most modern securities can be and are increasingly cast in terms of conditional or temporary ownership. The floating charge probably started in that manner in both Germany and The Netherlands. Even though this construction now appears eliminated in the new Dutch Civil Code, it is still explicitly recognised to apply to reservation of title in that country and to hire purchases. More generally, even in The Netherlands the concept of conditional ownership enjoying *in rem* effect was unavoidably maintained, Art. 3.84 (4), cf. also Art. 3.38 for the contractual aspect, although the transfer for a specific time might surprisingly be construed as a usufruct (Art. 3.85). Thus modern financial transactions using the conditional sale or transfer techniques might in The Netherlands still operate but not, it seems, if patently meant as a security device. Ownership thus clearly may be conditional and divisible in time everywhere, at least in some circumstances. The problem is that this is not the traditional civil law approach to proprietary rights, which theoretically only allows the unbundling of the ownership right in a pre-ordained and restricted manner, therefore only in terms of certain clearly defined rights, like the usufruct, some forms of leasing and specific secured interests. By using conditional and temporary rights and more so in combining them, flexibility results in the kind of proprietary (*in rem*) rights created, depending on their terms and conditions. It is this flexibility that is used and sought out in modern financings. As mentioned before, it is the normal common law approach towards future interests, compatible with the traditional common law system of creating securities like the mortgage as an estate in land. These future interests existed originally only in land in fee simple determinable, in fee simple subject to a condition subsequent and in fee simple subject to executory interests, but are now also accepted in movables and intangibles allowing great flexibility in the nature of the conditions. They all have, in civil law terminology, a measure of *in rem* or proprietary effect. It is to be noted in this respect that common law does not maintain the notion of ownership as absolute right (*dominium*) but sees it rather as a better or longer right in terms of possession, use or enjoyment and always in relation to the rights of others.[9]

Trust

In setting aside assets for a specific purpose and by dividing and adjusting the ownership rights accordingly, the trust construction unavoidably surfaces. Under common law, this construction, which through the terms of the trust deed provides the ultimate in flexibility, has long been used to create floating charges or indenture trusts, which allow particular assets or cash flows to back up certain indebtedness,

---

9   Cf. for this basic difference in view, notably Lawson, *Introduction to the Law of Property*, 87 (1958).

as in asset backed securities. Much more traditionally, the trust replaces mortgages in many States of the US. Note that in a system of conditional ownership rights, with two interested parties sharing proprietary rights, the interposition of a (kind of) trustee is easily imaginable. This person would take over legal title to the assets, allow possession by either party as agreed and use his power e.g. in the case of purchase money security either to transfer the full interest to the debtor upon full payment or otherwise to claim possession and sell the asset to provide satisfaction for the creditor out of the proceeds with overvalue to be returned to the buyer.

Separation of assets and differences in ranking, in any event, emerge all the time, also in civil law. The separation of assets for specific purposes through new legal entities, all kinds of joint property and partnerships, or through the technique of ring-fencing, is well known to create different levels of rights between creditors of the separated assets and those of the others. The lifting of the corporate veil on the other hand may amalgamate assets and liabilities, although there may still be some ranking between creditors of the former separate entity and those of the participants becoming (more) fully liable. In the US, there may be equitable subordination in bankruptcy (Sec. 510 B.A.), particularly in situations in which insiders, like related companies, might otherwise obtain *pari passu* treatment for their claims. There may also be contractually agreed subordination, very common in bond-issues and other forms of corporate financings.

The treatment of client moneys, the handling of decedent estates or of the assets of minors or incapacitated persons everywhere creates mixtures of proprietary rights, with the need for ever stronger protection of beneficiaries or economic owners through the increasing recognition of fiduciary duties in a common law sense, which, in order to deal with conflicts of interests, are much more specific and stronger than the general civil law notions of equity and reasonableness (*Treu und Glauben*), particularly whilst giving rise in appropriate instances to proprietary claims of the beneficiaries. A related development is that, even in the civil law, the tracing concept increasingly surfaces where moneys have been improperly handled or misappropriated by asset managers, brokers and the like, or where proprietary interests are allowed to shift to replacement goods, receivables and proceeds. It shows a need which in the law of obligations earlier lead everywhere to increased possibilities of specific performance.

Civil law remains, nevertheless, uncomfortable with any conditional or temporary rights and their *in rem* effect, therefore their property status. If, however, the Hague Convention (1985) on the recognition of foreign trusts were ratified in civil law countries (as it is in Italy and proposed in France and The Netherlands), at least foreign trusts would be recognised (and might even cover assets in the recognising country itself), notwithstanding the civil law idea of a closed system of clearly defined proprietary rights. Common law is not similarly concerned, although the proliferation of indirect security rights and the uncertainties they may create in the priority ladder is noted and limited under the UCC in the US. As common law is not given to clear concepts of ownership and property, however, the unbundling of rights with proprietary effect generally remains much less structured and geared to dividing user rights and expectations therein with third party effect being determined from case to case. It notably does not use the sharp civil law distinction between *in rem* and *in personam* rights in this context either; this terminology is only basic to the common law of jurisdiction.

Split ownership rights, future interests and trust concepts were earlier also known on the European Continent, notably in the *German Treuhand* (creating *Sondervermoegen* or *Treugut*) and in the Roman *fiducia cum amico and cum creditore*. The concept is alive in Germany and Switserland eventhough it cannot be used in the latter country to create non-possessory security in movables (Art. 717 ZGB). As noted above, France is now reintroducing the *fiducia* through statutory amendment. Although the new Dutch Code has tried to reverse the tide in eliminating any *in rem* effect from the *fiducia cum creditore* (in Art. 3.84(3)), it shows its confusion by allowing the conditional transfers with *in rem* effect in only the next sub-paragraph (Art.3.84(4)) and in the reservation of title and hire purchase. It would seem inconceivable to construe a modern legal system without it. Even the Dutch are now comtemplating the general recognition of foreign trusts. The question is not therefore whether this trend of informalising proprietary rights should be accepted in civil law - it is unavoidable - but rather how its contours should be defined, which is no less a continuing process under common law.

7 The Organisation of the Floating Charge

A type of non-possessory floating charge on movables and intangibles resulted in Germany and even in The Netherlands (before the new Code) originally from a conditional transfer of movable property by the borrower to the lender. This technique was possible as, in these countries, title only passes upon delivery. It allowed a sale with a conditional transfer of ownership, a technique further aided by the possibility to transfer property whilst leaving it in the possession of the former owner (the so-called delivery *constituto possessorium*). Therefore, there could be a delivery without an actual change in possession, whilst the fulfilment of the condition (payment) would allow in The Netherlands, although not necessarily in Germany, an automatic retransfer to the original owner without any further physical act.

In Germany and The Netherlands, this technique of creating a non-possessory security right became prevalent in the early part of the 20th century and was subsequently expanded to include receivables through a conditional assignment to a creditor, normally accompanied by the (implied) right to collect proceeds. In these countries, this was easy as this assignment for its validity did not require notice to the debtor (an approach now abandonned in The Netherlands except if the assignment is meant to create a security right and is then subject to the applicable formalities), which also allowed an assignment of future claims. From the perspective of the lender, the aim thus became the inclusion in one secured transaction of as many present and future assets of the debtor as possible to achieve the widest possible floating charge. From his perspective, such a security would preferably serve to protect also other past, present and future advances or claims against the same debtor with the same rank (rather than creating subsequent and therefore lower ranking security rights in the same assets whenever new claims arose). Future claims were thus intended to benefit from the original high rank.

There were largely two methods of achieving this type of floating charge on movables and intangibles. The first method was an automatic shift of the charge or lien to related assets, like replacement goods upon conversion or to a co-mingled quantity of goods, and to any receivables upon sale with a licence to cash any related proceeds. It is an approximation of the concept of tracing, better known in common law. The second method meant to include more generally also unrelated (future) assets. As mentioned before, especially in the latter case, the problem arose how far out one could go: the harvest of next year, other goods that might eventually be acquired by the debtor, receivables from clients who were not yet known in respect of unspecified sales or deliveries? It would appear largely to depend on the required measure of specificity and identification. The new Dutch Civil Code suggests a fairly restrictive approach (in the details still largely based on previous case law) in that tangible assets must be determinable (Art. 3.84(2)). The precise meaning of this requirement remains unclear but it may imply that the tangible asset must either exist in principle or be in the process of accruing and, in any case, either belong to the debtor or be contracted to be acquired by him. For a valid assignment of receivables or claims, the relationship out of which they arise for the debtor must in principle exist at the time the security interest is created (Art. 3.239).

As for the contractually enhanced retention right for banks, the inclusion of any future balances in the current account or future financial instruments in the custody accounts may give rise to further problems as their assignment or transfer could be considered preferential and therefore voidable under statutes against preferences or fraudulent conveyances (*actio recovatoria* or *Pauliana*) because of their coincidental nature in the absence of a specific assignment or pledge of respectively the underlying receivables (with the possible limitation to those that arise from an existing legal relationship with the debtor) or of the tangible assets (in as far as they are determinable and accrue to the debtor). In any event, any floating security may perfect only when the asset emerges in the ownership of the grantor of the security interest and it might take its rank only as of that time (except in cases of advance filing in the US), whilst the whole arrangement obtains a fixed (instead of floating) aspect merely upon default when the creditor starts to exercise his rights (crystallisation in the UK). It is thus conceivable that separate status and priority are determined only as of that moment. The accumulation of security in future assets under floating charges is in any event likely to stop at the opening of the bankruptcy (except for the pending harvest under new Dutch law) and any after-acquired or maturing assets would be for the benefit of the general body of creditors, at least in countries where after-acquired property is normally considered part of the bankrupt estate, which is not the case in Germany and the US. Individual attachments do not normally have this interrupting effect, but where, like in Germany and the US, they result in a priority, they may prevail over or have the same rank as the security.

Another aspect of the modern floating charge, especially in respect of a whole business, is the practical problem of conveying to the creditor a generality of goods. In many countries, such a conveyance is deemed impossible which would suggest individual conveyance per asset. Where there is a security document indicating and describing the contents, some bulk transfer might, nevertheless, be deemed to result as long as no physical changes in the assets is required, e.g. where they remain either with the debtor or under third parties (like in the case of a floating charge on a whole business or a charge on a portfolio of shares or bonds in the hands of a custodian). Any unspecified assets or excess stock remain in this approach at the disposition of the general body of creditors. In Germany, the floating charge (*Sicherungsübereignung*) may include some specific constructions to cover in a limited manner some generality of goods, for tangible assets through the *Raumsicherungsvertrag* in respect of assets in a separate depot or place, and for receivables in the *Globalzession* in respect of classes of credits that can be clearly identified in the account of the debtor. In the Netherlands, the traditional method was implementation by presenting regular assignment lists, now more properly called pledge lists, where receivables were given as security. As individual registration appears now to be necessary, this has created substantial practical problems.[10]

8 Floating Charges in Western Europe and the USA

In The Netherlands, in the meantime, the new Code creates a special registered (but not published) security right in this area, Art.3.237. It expressly abolishes the use of the earlier conditional transfer of ownership in this connection (Art. 3.84(3)), although beyond this much of the original case law would appear to remain pertinent. Upon payment, the security is automatically lifted. In Germany, the sales approach remains the normal technique under the so-called *Sicherungsübereignung*. It means in the absence of a full elaboration of the conditional sales approach, that the assets after payment may not automatically retransfer to the erstwhile debtor, who, without further arrangements, only has a personal claim to them. The creditor, on the other hand, does not have a separate recovery right (power of sale) under this type of floating charge (except if especially provided), but merely a priority to

---

10   See on these complications, Heyman, *WPNR* 6070 (1992).

the execution proceeds, much like under a privilege in France. This is thought to be so because of the disposition rights of the debtor, if operating in the normal course of his business. In Germany, this type of security remains in the meantime fully covered by case law. Public policy (concepts of *gutte Sitten*) is used to curb excess in individual cases. The identification and specificity requirements may limit its scope further.

As suggested above, other countries, most notably those with a common law approach, may be more relaxed regarding the creation of floating security rights, the principles of identification and specificity and the technique of bulk transfers and the manner of their publication. On the other hand, whereas Dutch and German law still allows the resulting liens to be secret, even though in The Netherlands registration is now required if the charge is non-possessory (not to achieve publicity, however, but only certainty as to the effective date of the security, which in turn determines its relative rank), others, notably common law countries, may require greater formality on this point and even publication.

This may, as in the US, simultaneously widen the possibilities of creating floating charges in future goods through the technique of advance filing. This fixes the date of the security (perfection) upon the emergence of the asset in the possession of the debtor as of the date of the original filing and publication, bringing forward its rank and eliminating the need for repeated filings. Future assets, except next year's crop under Article 9 of the Uniform Commercial Code (UCC), may therefore easily be included and virtually all may thus be given as security in this manner. Naturally, it does not mean that financiers will accept the ensuing collateral as satisfactory security, but it achieves simplicity and contrasts with the Dutch approach of (in principle) individual registration in all non-possessory cases, which is costly and burdensome. In the UK, there is the concept of crystallisation in this respect, meaning that the floating charge becomes fixed as of the moment of the appointment of a receiver under it. The status and priority of the charge whilst still floating is not entirely clear, one reason why the floating charge is often seen as a weak security right in the UK.

As to floating charges in the UK (although differently organised in England and Scotland), UK banks appear to have considerable flexibility and will normally create so-called debentures (by themselves no more than documented debt instruments) secured by a transfer of whole businesses, including real estate, to a trust-like structure with own liquidation rules and trustees or receivers in the case of default. These structures may also be used by suppliers, although this is less common. In the case of default, they result in a separate liquidation under the charge regardless of any bankruptcy and may be initiated or continued in bankruptcy proceedings. They are in fact sometimes created for no other reason than to protect the separate execution of fixed charges on specific business assets from any interference by bankruptcy trustees in reorganisation proceedings, although this separate status does not necessarily give floating charges the highest protection. Governmental charges may prevail over them under the 1986 UK Bankruptcy Act. If operating in the commercial field, these debentures must be published in the companies register and are then for corporates exempt from the Bills of Sales Act (1878/1882), which otherwise requires special publication whenever charges are created without change of possession. These so-called bills of sales have long had a bad reputation, operating, unlike debentures, mainly in the small money lenders world.

Meanwhile, French, Italian and Belgian law remained particularly restrictive in the area of floating charges, partly because the conditional transfer is much more difficult to place in their legal systems under which the ownership in movable propertly is conveyed by law as from the moment of the contract of sale (cf. Art. 1138 Cc.) and assignments of receivables require prior notice to the debtor of the receivable for their effectiveness (cf. Art. 1689/1690 Cc.), restrictions and limitations increasingly lifted in France since 1980, a country now also contemplating the introduction of the fiducia, as more extensively discussed above.

9 The Organisation of Other Security Interests

Reservation of Title
Of the other modern security interests, the reservation of title is probably the most important. It already found expression in the German Civil Code of 1900 (Sec. 455) and subsequently in the German Code of Civil Procedure (Sec. 771). In The Netherlands, it was developed by case law, but is now covered by Art.3.92 of the new Dutch Civil Code. In England, it was introduced in 1976, also through case law,[11] which first recognised a Dutch reservation of title in respect of assets subsequently shipped to the UK. It has now become a most important security device in England, although it had always been technically possible under Sec. 19(1) Sales of Goods Act 1974 and under Sec 17(1) of its predecessor of 1893. Until the Romalpa decision, the hire purchase, with the purchaser's option to acquire ownership upon payment of the instalments, was the more common non-possessory security device in sold but unpaid goods in the UK.

In Germany and The Netherlands, the reservation of title remains a secret lien. Registration is also not felt necessary in the UK if neither a floating charge is intended nor the coverage of prior (unrelated) debt. In the US, under the UCC, this type of reserved ownership is now automatically converted into an ordinary security interest, normally requiring an execution sale and publication, except to the extent it figures as purchase money security. In most other countries (also under the new Dutch Civil Code), the reservation of title still allows appropriation of the property by the original seller upon default, which may produce for him a capital gain if the

---

11   *Romalpa case*, (1976) 2 All E Rep 552.

asset has appreciated in value in the meantime. On the other hand, any capital loss reducing the asset value to less than the claim, might still lead to further enforcement action.

Particularly in Germany, the scope of the reservation of title has been broadened and now allows special provisions to include converted property (*Verarbeitungsklausel*) and a resale possibility implying the simultaneous assignment of the receivable (*Vorausabtretungsklausel*), which together create a so-called *verlängerter Eigentumsvorbehalt*. The new Dutch Code covers the former (Art. 5:16) and may imply the latter if the sale is in the ordinary course of business. In Germany, it is even possible to agree a general reservation of title in all goods passing between the same parties until payment of all outstanding debt between them (*Saldoklausel*), probably not possible in The Netherlands (Art. 3:92(2)). Reservation of title with a *Verarbeitungsklausel* or a *Saldoklausel* eliminates in Germany the possibility of repossession upon default, and only leads to recovery by priority out of the proceeds upon an execution sale, therefore to a type of privilege much like in the case of the *Sicherungsübereignung*.

As mentioned before, in France, the reservation of title suffered from similar limitations as the floating charge in that a conditional transfer of ownership is difficult to construe, whilst an immediate transfer to the buyer conditional upon later non-payment would not result in any protection for the creditor in a France bankruptcy of the buyer at all. Only a delayed transfer to the buyer until payment was likely to help, but would create the improper impression of credit worthiness in someone who has possession, long particularly offensive to French law, and would in any event have created problems if the good was not returned before a bankruptcy of the buyer. Only through an amendment of the Bankruptcy Act in 1980, reservation of title was fully accepted in France, provided the property is reclaimed within 3 months after bankruptcy, cf. Art. 121 io. Art. 115 French Bankruptcy Act 1985. It is not likely to shift to converted or co-mingled property or to proceeds (in the latter case, the receivable may, however, now be separately assigned). According to Art. 122 BA, the original seller may also lay claim to any resale receivables (until payment). In Belgium, there remains the traditional French approach requiring that the reserved property must be reclaimed before the start of the bankruptcy. It is a severe limitation on the effectiveness of the reservation of title in that country even though it may still have some use outside a bankrupcy situation.

10 Aspects of Conditional or Temporary Property Rights

Where modern financing techniques increasingly depend on finance sales, it is also necessary to look closer at some of the details of these sales to determine their effect. In practice, it is probably the most efficient to look at the subject of split ownership rights from a number of perspectives: disposition rights, the effect of attachments or bankruptcy, the risk in terms of reduction in value and harm that the asset may cause to third parties, and the entitlement to income out of the assets, always assuming a certain flexibility for participants to arrange their own affairs, including in principle their own protection arrangements as may be seen in the ever evolving modern financing techniques.

Disposition Rights
As far as disposition rights are concerned, the financier until (re) payment will normally appear as the legal owner of the relevant assets in all modern financial instruments, like a conditional sale, a reservation of title, a bank's enhanced retention right in respect of all it holds or receives for its client, the repo, the finance lease or the factoring arrangement. However, the financier may not normally dispose of the asset, except where it is in its nature, for him mainly relevant in the collection of receivables to amortise his advance or loan, of which financial factoring, a banker's enhanced retention right and a collection arrangement for proceeds under a retention of title or under a floating charge are the most explicit examples. In any event, in many countries the financier would need possession to deliver assets, which will only be the case in the bank's enhanced retention right and in the repo, although in the former case, the bank's customers might still be able to make the normal changes in their investment portfolio and continue payments from their current account. In the case of the repo, the fungible nature of securities will itself allow trading, which may, as mentioned above, at the same time weaken any proprietary claims of the other party.

The debtor in this scenario is equally barred from disposing of the assets since he is not the full owner either, even if he has possession, like in the conditional sales leading to floating charges, the reservation of title and in the finance lease. There is an exception in this respect for assets traded in the ordinary course of business, like mostly inventory, particularly relevant for the floating charge and reservation of title, but less likely in the finance lease which normally concerns capital goods. As, however, the debtor will normally have it in his sole power to fulfill the condition and thereby make himself full owner, his position might be thought to be the stronger also in respect of disposition rights.

Beyond the situation in which the nature of the goods or intangibles itself suggest otherwise, both parties in a split ownership may only be able to legally dispose free and clear together. Each one alone can only dispose of his proprietary right subject to that of the other. It is in fact not much different from a situation where there is a usufruct operating besides the residual ownership or reversion. Unsuspecting third parties will then depend for their protection on their *bona fides*, their acquisition for value, and (probably) actual or constructive possession. This protection is of a general nature in civil law countries in respect of movables (except sometimes for stolen goods and probably also mostly for intangibles), but in common law only obtains in respect of sales by an unauthorised trustee or on markets overt and is otherwise dependent on statutory intervention, like in the UK under Sec. 9 of the

385

Factors Act and Sec. 25(2) of the Sales of Goods Act. In the US there are several such provisions in the UCC. Note that in Germany, custom in the particular branch also has a bearing on the subject and *bona fides* is more narrowly construed upon reservation of title than upon *Sicherungsübereignung*, both charges being secret liens in principle. It means that the third party purchaser in the case of a floating charge is more likely to be protected whilst the financier has a stronger position under the reservation of title. The result of all this is nevertheless that non-possessory liens on movables are much less likely to follow the asset, in Germany in any event unlikely in the case of a *Sicherungsübereignung* and a reservation of title with a *Verarbeitungsklausel*.

Attachment

In the matter of individual attachments, Sec. 771 of the German CCP has a special rule for reservation of title and allows the buyer's creditors to attach the latter's rights, although the seller may object in order to protect his title against a judicial sale or subsequently allege unjust attachment. Under German case law, the buyer may similarly object to an attachment of the asset by seller's creditors. In a seller's bankruptcy, the trustee prevails over the buyer under a reservation of title if the latter does not perform (Sec.17 German Bankruptcy Act); in a buyer's bankruptcy the seller retakes the asset.

Where an attachment does not itself result in a charge, which is the situation in most West European countries, including the UK (but not in Germany and the US), the measure is a mere order to preserve or execute the asset. Although sometimes characterised as affecting the disposition rights of the attachee, this would not seem relevant when, like here in the case of dual ownership, he has no disposition right proper. Such an attachment actually levied would, in any event, remain subject to existing liens and charges and would not affect underlying ownership or security rights. It means that as long as the debtor has not repaid his advance or paid the purchase price (so that the full title remains in limbo), an attachment order on either party is not likely to have much effect. It would not likely lead to an execution sale of any meaning. This sale could at most achieve a transfer without delivery, subject to all existing proprietary rights in the assets. In bankruptcy, the trustee of the financier would have to wait until the maturity date before he could take action against the property. In a bankruptcy of the debtor, the debt matures and the financier might be able to exercise his full ownership right immediately if there is no payment by the trustee. Alternatively, the bankruptcy trustee could make use of any right to dispose of the asset free and clear, as possible under the US Bankruptcy Code, whilst settling all other rights in the property out of the proceeds according to their rank, a facility an attachor does notably not have and neither might bankruptcy trustees in other countries.

Risk of Loss and Right to Income

As to the risk of holding the goods in terms of third party's liability or appreciation/depreciation of the asset, maintenance costs and the right to any income, in principle these risks and rights accrue to the debtor/borrower, except if there is an agreement to the contrary. Liability for any harm done to third parties is as determined by modern product liability statutes and the contractual arrangement cannot affect it.

11 Conclusions

The reality of modern securities, certainly in international financial transactions, is that they are all increasingly expressed in terms of conditional or split ownership rights by way of finance sales, probably because there is generally greater familiarity with the notion of ownership than of security, which more obviously breaks down in local variants, whilst the former avoids registration requirements and other formalities that may be particular to secured transactions but because of their purely local status not meaningful when assets are intended to move across border or, as in the case of intangibles, their location is difficult to determine. Also it is a traditional common law approach. Finance sales may in any event go well beyond mere secured transactions and may have their own logic of which the absence of a clear interest rate structure is likely to be a strong indication. Their status remains nevertheless uncertain under most domestic laws.

If one takes the perspective of the international practice, accepts the current flexibility developed therein and greater freedom for the parties with regard to the use or unbundling of the ownership concept, this might entail or facilitate some harmonisation, in that extreme variations in local security devices of the various sort may be avoided. The further elaboration of any internationalised and partly contractualised ownership concept in the above manner may produce a measure of common ground between common and civil law, facilitating at the same time the process of characterisation, recognition, adjustment and accommodation of the proprietary status when the assets concerned surface or play a role in (proceedings in) other countries. From an international perspective, local codifications are not likely to be helpful in this regard as is proven by the Dutch ambivalence on the subject of finance sales and in the narrowing attitude of the UCC in the US, which, even if realistic at home, are likely to be confusing elsewhere. Much more important is the acceptance of a measure of openness of the proprietary system. In the process of recognition of security in assets after moving trans-border, the relativity of the proprietary structures becomes in any event only too obvious and the undeniable own autonomy of the courts assuming jurisdiction in recognition matters will at the same time lead to the acceptance of (some) foreign proprietary devises and notions, if only in the interest of continuing trade.

Another most important aspect of modern financial transactions is the (contractual) enhancement of direct or indirect security rights, particularly through accelleration or rescission clauses leading to a broadening of the set-off facilities and the concept of netting. The true issues are here the limitation of the 'cherry picking' option of bankruptcy trustees particularly in swaps and repos, the possibility to also reduce to money any non-monetary obligations of the non-bankrupt, and the ability to liquidate and involve in the set-off all similar contracts existing between the same parties (like all swaps or repos). This widened set-off and its status in enforcement proceedings remain in the meantime also contentious, further complicated because it can often not be predicted where enforcement might take place. This has in turn an adverse effect on the capital requirements for banks again particularly in their swap and repo exposures, which is now receiving the attention of banking regulators (the Basle Commitee on Banking Supervision of the G10).

The best development in these areas may remain through practice and doctrine, which has in fact been the conduit for the development of most modern security rights and their enhancements and for finance sale concepts wherever obtaining. Nationally, case law is sometimes able to reflect the modern trends and market practices,[12] whilst, as to determining the extra-territorial effect, a measure of discretion of the courts in proprietary matters, indirect securities and privileges may be helpful rather than destructive and is in any event unavoidable.

In a wider multi-state context, uniform treaty law in this area presents considerable dangers of rigidity, thus also curtailing development. Within the area of such uniform law, the result would in any event be uncertain because of lack of harmonisation in other aspects of the law, notably in the proprietary concepts generally, the ranking and other enforcement questions, like the extent of separate execution rights. It is of interest that the attempt made by Unidroit in the field of International Financial Leasing in 1988 did not manage to present a coherent view of the proprietary aspects of the finance lease.

In the conflicts area, the Hague Conference made an attempt in 1958 to formulate some rules on the subject in its Convention on the Law Governing Transfer of title in the International Sales of Goods, which never became effective. It is likely to be more successful in its Convention on the Law Applicable to Trusts and on their Recognition of 1985. Acceptance of the Trust Convention, since 1992 effective between the UK, Canada, Australia and Italy, and now considered for ratification in France and the Netherlands, introduces foreign trusts in domestic law even in respect of assets located in the recognising country except if contrary to its policy. The introducing statute (Art. 4) and accompanying government memorandum in the Netherlands seek to limit policy considerations in this connection and invite thereby a more serious discussion on the openness of the Dutch system of proprietary rights. Such a discussion would appear unavoidable in all civil law countries introducing the (foreign) trust concept in this manner and more so if also introducing it domestically, like in France, especially in view of the flexibility of the trust which can be put to many uses. In civil law terms, the introduction of the

---

12   Cf. e.g. Tribunal de Commerce de Paris, Third Chamber, Oct 28 1992 (with respect to swaps).

trust concept in the law of ownership is likely to have a similar opening-up effect as the introduction of the notions of fairness and reasonableness (*Treu* and *Glauben*) had in contract law.

All efforts in this area would seem to require as a minimum a clear insight into the nature of finance sales as distinguished from or replacing secured transactions, would need a clear view on the scope and status of contractual enhancements of the (indirect) security rights and notably on the concept of netting, on the respective relationships of all these devises as well as of privileges and similar protections, on the status of third party successors and rights of creditors of all these parties, and ultimately on the reach and impact of their extra-territorial effect. It may well be that the result will be largely dependent on one's views on the desirable level of protection of the small local creditors, therefore on the *par conditio creditorum* in respect of unsuspecting local parties. Rather than frustrating the further development of the proprietary notions to this effect amongst professionals internationally, it may be better to focuss on giving these weaker parties a special status as a group locally (although difficult to define), further to be protected through the creation of domestic subpools in international enforcements. It is a different problem that in any event cannot be solved by the continuing fractioning of the ownership concept along national lines.

CHAPTER 22
Real Security Regarding Immovable Objects

Reflections on a Euro-Mortgage

Hans G. Wehrens[*]

1 Introduction

In a future European Civil Code statutory provisions on *real securities regarding immoveable property* will be indispensable, irrespective of whether corresponding regulations or directives of the European Union (EU) will already exist at the time of codification or not. In both cases the preparatory work in this sector which has been carried out under the provisional title *'Euro-mortgage'*, (*'Eurohypothek'*, *'Eurohypothèque'*) can serve as a basis.

What does 'Euro-mortgage' mean and where does this new legal term come from?[1]

---

[*]   The author would like to thank Dirk Voß for his translation of this chapter.
[1]   Up to now, the term 'Euro-mortgage' has mainly been used in the following publications (in chronological order):
— CACE/UINL: *La Cédule hypothécaire suisse et la dette foncière allemande-Etude comparative, base d'une future Euro-hypothèque.* Published by Stichting tot bevordering der notariële wetenschap (French/German), Amsterdam 1988.
— Wehrens: 'Der schweizer Schuldbrief und die deutsche Briefgrundschuld- Ein Rechtsvergleich als Basis für eine zukünftige Eurohypothek', *Österreichische Notariats-Zeitung* 1988, p. 181.
— Hamou: 'L'hypothèque marocaine sur soi-même et l'eurohypothèque', *La Semaine Juridique* 1989, p. 241.
— Van Velten: 'Hypotheek en Europese Gemeenschap', *WPNR* 6001, 1991, p. 241.
— Stöcker: *Die 'Eurohypothek'— Zur Bedeutung eines einheitlichen nicht-akzessorischen Grundpfandrechts für den Aufbau eines 'Europäischen Binnenmarktes für den Hypothekarkredit'*, doctoral thesis of the Universität Würzburg, Verlag Duncker & Humblot, Berlin 1992.
— Uwe H. Schneider: 'Europäische und internationale Harmonisierung des Bankvertragsrechts-Zugleich ein Beitrag zur Angleichung des Privatrechts in der Europäischen Gemeinschaft', *Neue Juristische Wochenschrift* 1991, p. 1985.
— Hofmeister: 'Das Liegenschaftsrecht im Zeichen der Annäherung Österreichs an die Europäische Gemeinschaft', *Österreichische Notariats-Zeitung* 1991, p. 282.
— Stürner: 'Das Grundpfandrecht zwischen Akzessorietät und Abstaktheit und die europäische Zukunft', *Festschrift für Rudolf Serick*, Heidelberg 1992.
— CACE/UINL: *L'Eurohypothèque; Rapport de la 'Commission des Affaires de la Communauté Européenne' au sein de l'Union Internationale du Notariat Latin (CACE/UINL).* Published by Stichting tot bevordering der notariële wetenschap (French/German), Amsterdam 1992.

The twelve Member States of the European Union have already grown so closely together in the economic sector that cross-border mortgage credits are becoming increasingly frequent. For this reason the occupational groups mainly dealing with this topic- the mortgage banks and the notaries- have for a couple of years especially raised the following questions:[2]

—   Is it possible to simplify and unify the very different statutory provisions in existing legislation on mortgage within the particular EU Member States by means of *contractual agreements*?
—   Will it be of any use, if the objective cannot be reached in this way, to introduce a new uniform right in rem within the EU, i.e. the *Euro-mortgage*?
—   To what extent should this new European regulation include *uniform provisions* for all EU Member States and in how far should existing domestic peculiarities be preserved?

The clarification of these questions lies in the interest of the persons who have to apply the law or in that of the 'consumers' who will no longer have to accept avoidable disadvantages in the future. A uniform regulation would also increase the importance and the volume of *cross-border mortgage credits*, since immoveable property is, due to its stability, the most common security for loans and will retain this position within the European internal market.

The endeavours to reach a simplification of cross-border operation of mortgage credits up until now can be summarized as follows:

a The *'Segré Report'* of 1966[3] considered it to be of primary importance to approximate and harmonize the different types of land charges within the EC; at the same time the authors pleaded for the introduction of a uniform type of land charge as a contribution to the integration of the capital markets.

— Vegter: 'Over het rechtskarakter van de Eurohypotheek', *WPNR* 6077, 1993, p. 55.

— Wehrens: 'Das Projekt einer Eurohypothek — Rückblick und Ausblick', *WPNR* 6126, 1994, p. 170.

2   Cf. the CACE/UINL reports mentioned in footnote 1 and in addition:

EC Mortgage Federation: *L'Hypothèque sur soi-même*, Brussels 1972.

EC Mortgage Federation: *Examen de droit comparé des procédures de saisie. Crédit transfrontalier au logement — Les incompatibilités*, Brussels 1983.

EC Mortgage Federation: *Ordre des privilèges et hypothèques*, Brussels 1984.

EC Mortgage Federation: *Les conditions minimales des hypothèques conventionnelles*, Brussels 1985.

EC Mortgage Federation: *Hypothèques libellées en monnaie étrangère*, Brussels 1985.

EC Mortgage Federation: *Variability of interest rates on mortgage loans in the EC*, Brussels 1989 (also available in other languages).

EC Mortgage Federation: *Mortgage credit in the European Community*, 2nd ed. 1990, Domus-Verlag Bonn (also available in French and German).

3   Report of an expert committee set up by the EC-Commission on the topic: 'The building of a European Capital Market', Brussels November 1966; due to its chairman Prof. Claudio Segré it is generally called the 'Segré- Report'.

b Since its foundation the *European Community Mortgage Federation* in Brussels has tried to show the obstacles existing on the national level to a Europeanization of the mortgage credit and to create the conditions necessary for them to be surmounted.[4]

c In 1987, a commission composed of civil law notaries and solicitors of the EC states was established on the European level within the *International Union of the Latin Notariat*, dealing with legal questions within the framework of community law (Commission des Affaires de la Communauté Européenne — CACE/UINL). It bears a French name since French was agreed on as the main working language. In 1983 this commission set up a special committee dealing with the legal possibilities for a uniform European mortgage.[5]

d The *EC Commission* has recently[6] reaffirmed the necessity for the short-term creation of a specific regulation on the operation of mortgage credits. In this context the Commission referred to the amended proposal for a Council directive on the freedom of establishment and the free supply of services in the field of mortgage credit. This proposal acknowledges the differences in the conditions for the operation of mortgage credits in the various Member States. Nevertheless it does not provide for a complete harmonization of these conditions which would be a very laborious and lengthy task, but for a mutual recognition of the financing techniques.

The EC Commission and the EU Member States have not yet finished the discussion on whether the amended proposal for a directive on mortgage credit[7] should be taken up again or whether the liberalization of mortgage credits could be reached by other means; moreover they want to wait and see what effects the two banking directives have on the markets for mortgage credits of the Member States.[8]

2 Survey of the Existing Laws of Mortgage within the EU

Whereas the greatest obstacles for activities abroad of business banks have been removed since the First and Second Banking Directive of the EC came into force,[9] the operation of mortgage credits across the border of a EU Member

---

4 Cf. the works of the European Mortgage Federation mentioned in footnote 2.

5 The works of the CACE/UINL on the Euro-mortgage are listed in footnote 1.

6 O.J. C 47/8.

7 The proposal amended several times for this EC-Directive on the free supply of services in the field of mortgage credit provides in Art. 3 that credit institutions may grant mortgage credit secured by mortgages on real property situated in another Member State. The original proposal of 18 February 1985 can be found in O.J. C 42 and the amended proposal in O.J. C 161.

8 This can be gathered from the address of Martin Bangemann held on the annual meeting of the European Mortgage Federation in Brussels on 22 June 1990.

9 1st Directive of 17 December 1988 — O.J. L 322/30 — and 2nd Directive of 15 December 1989 — O.J. L 386/1 —.

State still faces considerable — legal and practical — difficulties, since the Member States of the EU have very different systems regarding the law of mortgage as well as the law of land registration. These systems can only be presented briefly at this place.[10]

In all states the mortgage entitles the creditor to enforce his claim, if necessary, by realising the charged real property with priority to other creditors and he can do so no matter whether the initial debtor is still the owner of this property or not.

In most states, the legal regulations up to now only provide for a *mortgage strictly accessory to the underlying debt* meaning that its coming into being; its size and discharge depend on the existence and respective actual size of the debt. The advantages of a land charge independent from the underlying debt like the Swiss *Schuldbrief / cédule hypothécaire* or the German *Grundschuld* are still quite unknown in most of the Member States. The same is true for the advantages of a *Hypothekenbrief* (an officially issued transferable mortgage certificate) or of an owner's charge or owner's mortgage.

The principle of *accessoriness* of mortgage and debt as derived from older codifications influenced by Napoleonic legislation has nevertheless been abandoned in practice by several auxiliary arrangements. There are already more or less far reaching exceptions mainly in the Netherlands and in Denmark. Thus, the mortgage can exist at least for a certain period without an exactly determined underlying debt; moreover, it can serve as security for a debt, the size of which varies permanently, e.g. as security for an overdraft.

Considerable differences can be observed in regard to the time at which the mortgage starts to exist. In France, Belgium, and Luxembourg, the mortgage already comes into existence at the moment of the recording by the notary, whereas the subsequent entry into the *Hypothec Register* (Mortgage Register) gives the mortgage legal effect in regard to third parties and determines the specific rank of the mortgage in relation to other charges. On the other hand, the mortgage does not exist before registration in Germany, Austria, Switzerland, the Netherlands, Italy, Greece or Spain.

In most countries it is sufficient if only the owner of the charged property who is at the same time the personal debtor signs the mortgage deed since there exist no particular formal requirements regarding the consent of the mortgage creditor according to substantive law. However, in France, the Netherlands and Belgium the creditor has to participate in the creation of the mortgage.

---

10   More details can be found in the brochure *Mortgage credit in the European Community*, edited by the European Mortgage Federation in Brussels (footnote 2). Cf. moreover the series 'Recht der Kreditsicherheiten in europäischem Ländern', vol. I — VII, edited by the 'Institut für internationales Recht des Spar-, Giro- and Kreditwesens' at the University of Mainz, Verlag Duncker & Humbolt, Berlin 1976 until 1988. Moreover Jackson: 'Die Grund-pfandrechte in den Rechtsordnungen Dänemarks, Irlands sowie des Vereinigten Köningreichs von Großbritannien und Nordirland'; expertise of 1976 for the EC Commission — Directorate General Internal Market — and the corresponding expertise of the Max-Planck-Institute in Hamburg: 'Die Grundpfandrechte in Recht der Mitgliedstaaten der EG', Hamburg 1971.

There are basically two different procedures for the *entry of the mortgage* into the Land Register or into the Hypothec Register respectively[11]

a   According to the *Grundbuchsystem* (a system of comprehensive land registration providing for a complete recording of the particulars of all real property e.g. ownership and charges in rem on it, established in Germany, Switzerland, Austria, in a modified form also Spain, Alsace-Lorraine and South Tyrol,[12] the applicant or the notary has to file an original or an authenticated copy of the mortgage deed to the Land Registry together with the application for registration of the mortgage according to its intended specific rank. Before registration is effected, application and enclosures are examined in regard to formal and substantive requirements by a legally trained official of the Land Registry (a judicial officer or Land Registry judge). The official of the Land Registry formulates the intended text of the registration on his own as an abridged version of the filed mortgage deed. The registration itself is effected — handwritten, typed or computer aided — by 'writing in'. Afterwards, creditor debtor and notary each receive a copy of the effected registration; on request they can also receive a complete excerpt from the Land Register revealing all entries effected up to now including the specific rank of the mortgage in relation to other charges.

b   According to the *Publication System (Publikationssystem:* France, Belgium, Luxembourg, the Netherlands,[13] Italy etc.) not only does the applicant have to file the mortgage deed to the Hypothec Registry but he must also file two signed certificates of entry. One of them is handed back to the applicant bearing a confirmation of the performance of the entry; it serves as proof of the right. The examination of the application is limited to the fulfillment of the formal requirements; in France, the examining officer does not even belong to the judiciary but to the fiscal administration. The registration itself is in some countries not performed by a 'writing in' but the submitted documents and the second certificate of entry are merely filed away.

---

11   Fundamental: v. Hoffmann, *Das Recht Des Grundstückkaufs*, Tübingen 1982, p. 27 ff. Cf. also Burseau, 'L'organisation de la publicité foncière et l'hypothèque conventionelle dans divers pays de l'Europe occidentale', *Juris-Classeur Périodique* 1968 No. 2174-Doctrine.

12   In their comparative study 'Das moderne Grundbuch', the Austrian writers Herbert Hofmeister and Helmut Auer call this system the 'mitteleuropäisches Grundbuchsystem' (central European system of land registration), No. 58 of the Schriftenreihe des Bundesministeriums für Justiz, Wien 1992.

13   In the Netherlands, the former system based on two certificates of entry has been replaced by a new registration system on the basis of two authenticated copies of the contracts since the entering into force of the new Civil Code (1 january 1992).

Finally, divergent regulations can be found regarding the question of whether the amount of mortgage debt and interest rates may only be stated in the national currency or in a foreign currency as well. At present, only the national currency is permitted in Germany, Spain and France, whereas for example in Belgium, Italy, Greece, the Netherlands and Denmark a foreign currency can also be chosen. Further peculiarities have to be observed in regard to the language used in the mortgage deed. Only the national language may be used in France, Italy, Greece, Spain, whereas in Belgium all three national languages and in Luxembourg French and German are permitted. On the other hand, in Germany, UK, Ireland and the Netherlands foreign languages can be used as well on the condition of a corresponding knowledge of the respective language; an authenticated translation into the national language has nevertheless to be added for the Land or Hypothec Registry.

3 A Uniform Mortgage for Cross-border Credits

For the above-mentioned reasons the following considerations have been made by the CACE:

Instead of a harmonization of the mortgage laws of all EU Member States, which is neither practicable nor desirable, this field of law should — at least as it concerns cross-border operation of credits — be simplified in such a way that it will be possible to provide mortgage credits across the borders according to uniform legal provisions.

For banks and borrowers, a uniform Euro-mortgage should be *optionally* available *besides* the different types of mortgage already existing in the several Member States. When required it should also be possible to use it for domestic credits.

This uniform Euro-mortgage could largely be shaped according to the model of the Swiss *Schuldbrief*[14] since this Swiss type of land charge is even more suitable for this purpose than the German *Grundschuld*.[15] Moreover, it could partially be based on the trilingual legal regulation of the *Schuldbrief* in the Swiss Civil Code.[16]

In this way a negotiable and versatile type of mortgage would be offered to banks and borrowers as an *alternative* to the types of mortgage already existing within the various Member States. Doing this could avoid difficulties and

---

14 By the *Schuldbrief* or *cédule hypothécaire* the debtor agrees to pay a certain amount of money including interest rates for which he accepts personal liability. This personal claim is secured at the same time by a land charge (the *Schuldbrief*; Art, 842 of the Swiss Zivilgesetzbuch).

15 The Grundschuld is a land charge according to which a certain amount of money including interest rates and other additional performances have to be paid to the creditor, the charged real property being liable for this obligation while this liability is in principle independent from the existence of an underlying debt (§ 1191 Bürgerliches Gesetzbuch).

16 For more details see Wehrens, Der schweizer Schulbrief und die deutsche Briefgrundschuld (footnote 1).

complications arising from the observance of the different mortgage laws in the various Member States.

In this way, the legal, economic and practical disadvantages of the conventional hypothec depending strictly on the underlying debt could be avoided as well; at the moment land charges not depending on the underlying debt do not exist in the EU Member States except for Germany and Switzerland, but only types of mortgage which are — apart from the very few legal makeshifts developed in practice (e.g. adaptation of the interest rate in the case of inflation or other amendments of the credit conditions) — closely linked to the personal claim.

For the operation of mortgage credits across the borders of two adjoining states like e.g. France and Germany the Euro-mortgage would not strictly be worth the troubles of lengthy preparatory work. But since the method suggested for the mortgage credit could be operated in a uniform way in twelve or more states, the efforts towards achieving a Euro-mortgage are worthwhile.

Difficulties can mainly arise from the fact that states with a 'Napoleonic' hypothec law can only slowly be convinced of the advantages of a mortgage independent from an underlying claim and will have difficulties in accepting the 'security contract' as a substitute for the close connection to the claim. If the Anglo-Saxon states should insist on preserving their existing system this would not cause complications due to the optional character of the Euro-mortgage.

Shaping the Euro-mortgage largely according to the Swiss model would be relatively simple; in contrast, the uniform shaping of the execution of the real estate will be very difficult. Therefore a way should be found in which the execution can be carried out according to existing domestic law while approximating only terms and costs.

The members of the working group of the CACE all agreed that the *term* 'Euro-mortgage' is preferable to the other expressions suggested until now like 'Hypothèque sur soi-même', 'Engagement foncier', 'Hypothèque indépendante du crédit' or 'Dette foncière'.

Searching for an appropriate expression the working group of the CACE started out by observing that the term indicating the new mortgage, uniformly valid within the entire EU, must not give rise to confusion with types of mortgage already existing. The name should be generally understandable in all Member States; this requires that it is short but significant, impressive and easy to translate. But it must also fit within the abbreviations already used within the EU. For these reasons the working group of the CACE decided in favour of the term 'Euro-mortgage' (*'Eurohypothek'*, *'Eurohypothèque'*) which is meanwhile commonly used.

The following objections have mainly been put forward to the other expressions used in the initial stages:

The term 'Hypothèque sur soi-même' means 'owner's mortgage', 'mortgage for the property owner's own benefit' or 'mortgage on the own real property', but the Euro-mortgage comprises much more than the function of an *Eigentümerhypothek* or an *Eigentümergrundschuld* (land charges for the owner's

397

own benefit in German law). Moreover, in German law this expression could lead to confusions with the corresponding subject of §§ 1163 and 1177 BGB. The final objection was that, from 1795 there existed a 'hypothèque sur soi-même' in French law which was not satisfactory in practice and was therefore abolished soon afterwards.

The suggestion 'Engagement foncier' was not convincing either. The occasionally used term 'dette foncière' is not suitable because in the German translation it can be confused with the *Grundschuld* and in the other EU-member states this expression is not meaningful enough.

4 Shaping the Euro-Mortgage as a right *in rem*

The suggested *Euro-mortgage* will not exclude the different types of mortgage already existing in the various Member States but be added to the existing regulations as an *additional possibility*. In this the Euro-mortgage is primarily meant to be used for securing cross-border credits; however, if required and as far as it is wanted, it can, after a transitional period, also be used for domestic credits besides the conventional types of mortgage.

The *introduction* of the Euro-mortgage by a future European Civil Code requires that if one voluntarily chooses the Euro-mortgage instead of one's usual national type of mortgage one has to observe provisions regarding the particulars of the Euro-mortgage and its existence from its creation until its discharge which have to be codified at the same time; therefore a short but sufficient minimum regulation should be incorporated into the new Civil Code uniformly for the entire EU. It could be comparable, for example, to the clear regulation of the Swiss *Schuldbrief*. The success of this new type of mortgage will depend not so much on coping with the legal and technical problems as on its economic advantages. The development in Switzerland and in Germany can be presented as an example for the success of a mortgage separated from the underlying personal claim. During the last 30 years, legal practice in both states switched for economic considerations from the *Hypothek* which is strictly con-nected to the underlying credit, to the more flexible *Schuldbrief* (Switzerland) and to the more economic *Grundschuld* (Germany).

The Euro-mortgage can be *defined* as a land charge which is independent from the existence of a concrete personal claim; and as the creation of the Euro-mortgage also includes an abstract acknowledgment of indebtedness it allows access to the charged real property (real liability) as well as to the personal property of the debitor (personal liability).

According to its purpose, the *creation* of the Euro-mortgage will depend on the composition of the respective national system of land registration. In states having a *Grundbuchsystem*, the Euromortgage will be created by notarial recording of the mortgage contract, entry of the mortgage into the land charge register and handing over of the mortgage certificate connected with a notarial declaration of executionability. In states having either only a *Grund-*

stücksregister (a system of real estate registration) or only a system of *Hypothec Registration* the creation of the Euro-mortgage deed connected with the notarial declaration of executionability. If a *Hypothekenbrief* for the Euro-mortgage should be provided for, it would moreover be necessary to legally regulate whether the notary or the registry is in charge of issuing this certificate.

Finally, in those EC countries not having the institution of the Latin notariat, it has to be legally determined that the Euro-mortgage comes into existence with the minimum content prescribed as soon as it is created according to the conventional procedures of those states and the mortgage deed has been handed over; as until now, the advantages of the notarial declaration of executionability could not be enjoyed in these states.

In order to simplify the description, the peculiarities of the three EU Member States having common law systems will be left out of consideration in the following remarks.[17]

The Euro-mortgage can already be created *before the granting of the credit* or to a higher amount than that of the actual debt. Accordingly, the interest rates could, for the purpose of registration, be fixed at a higher level than that of the real interest rates usual at the time of creation.

It could be registered *in reserve* in order to be immediately available on a later occasion if required.

It could be created as security for an *overdraft* or for a credit ceiling.

It could serve as security in cases where the credit is not granted to the property owner but *to a third party* but where nevertheless the property owner is prepared to give his land as real security. The owner's liability is then limited to the land and this does not affect his residual property, whereas the borrower is liable towards the creditor with his entire assets. The same applies if it shall serve as security for the liabilities of several debtors.

The Euro-mortgage is an appropriate means to *secure* a cross-border credit operation against *currency fluctuations* if the total amount entered into the Land Registry is fixed at a high enough level. This is important in cases where the mortgage can only be registered in the currency of the state in which the charged land is situated but the credit secured shall be paid out in another currency.

After the total redemption of a credit, it can be used for the *securing of a new credit* granted by the same creditor, even if many years have passed in between, since an automatic discharge of the Euro-mortgage as a result of time expiry does not exist according to the system suggested.

If in the case just mentioned *another creditor* grants the new credit, the old creditor has to assign the Euro-mortgage to the new creditor. This assignment is to be performed by a corresponding declaration of the old creditor, for reasons of security preferably recorded by a notary, and the handing over of the

---

17   Reference can be made to the publication of the European Community Mortgage Federation
       on the mortgage credit within the EC (Footnote 2), p. 423 ff.

Hypothekenbrief (*cédule hypothécaire*) at the same time. The assignment should be entered into the Land Registry (deviating from the Swiss model).

Even in the case of an alienation of the property charged with the Euro-mortgage this mortgage can continue to exist, if the new creditor agrees, and subsequently be used by the property owner being the new debtor.

It is also possible to create and register the Euro-mortgage initially *for the property owner's own benefit* thus enabling him, if required, to assign the Euro-mortgage which is already entered into the Land Register to a creditor of his choice by handing over the transferable mortgage deed (Hypothekenbrief).

The *Hypothekenbrief* (officially issued transferable mortgage certificate) shows some features of a negotiable instrument (marketability and easy transferability). As far as this is not desired one has to deviate from the Swiss model.

For the practice of credit operation, the Euro-mortgage delivers a reliable and at the same time comfortable form of security. It is safe in its creation (independent from the initial debt), secured in its continued existence (in case of an alteration of the initial debt), and finally secured in its transferability and thus easy to re-finance.

The Euro-mortgage is an ideal legal institute for the borrower (consumer) as well, especially if permanently changing interest rates have to be secured or if after the redemption of the first credit a second one shall be secured by the same Euro-mortgage or if the creditor changes. The considerable additional costs for annulment and deletion of the old mortgage and the creation of a new one could be avoided. The same is true for the other financing techniques to which some banks have resorted, e.g. absolute guarantees, pledging of moveables, assignments of financial claims or claims against insurances. These securities which can in some individual cases perhaps be comfortable for the borrower hold considerable risks for the consumer and his guarantor. These disadvantages could largely be avoided by the creation of the Euro-mortgage. When shaped in the right way it satisfies the interests of the creditor as well as the interests of the borrower, especially since the consumer is in the first place interested in a security which is both economical and contains the minimum of risk to his property.

5 The Obligatory Contract[18] Creating the Security

The legal relationship between the creditor on the one side and the borrower as well as the owner of the real property on the other side consists of three elements:

The basic legal relationship is the *loan contract* between creditor and borrower, thus without participation of the owner of the real property if he is

---

18 In this context the term 'obligatory' shall mean the right *in personam* (contract *in personam*).

not identical to the borrower. To the essentials of this loan contract belong provisions concerning the volume of the credit, interest rates and redemption as well as a description of the securities which the borrower has to provide.

The second element is the *Euro-mortgage* created for the creditor allowing access to the charged real property (real liability) *and*, by the abstract acknowledgment of indebtedness connected to it, to the personal property of the respective debtor (personal liability).

Of special importance is the obligatory *security contract* concluded between creditor and borrower; the property owner should advisably participate in this conclusion if he is not identical to the borrower.

While the loan contract needs no further explanation in this context and the content of the Euro-mortgage has already been outlined, the importance and main content of the 'security contract' will be described right now.

The *'security contract' (Sicherungsvertrag)*[19] contains the obligatory relations between creditor and borrower as far as they are covered neither by the loan contract nor by the Euro-mortgage or the abstract acknowledgment of indebtedness connected to it; these are especially the obligation of the borrower to create the Euro-mortgage and the obligation of the creditor to use this security only under the conditions agreed to in the contract. In this way the *accessoriness* between the Euro-mortgage on the one hand and the debt in its real size on the other is restored on the obligatory level, since for the reasons mentioned above it would have been a hindrance to realize it on the level of a right in rem (as content of the Euro-mortgage). The security contract contains the *causa* of the Euro-mortgage; therefore one could also call it a 'pactum de hypothecando'. The security contract makes it possible that the creditor enjoys the unlimited position of a Euro-mortgage in his *external relations* whereas he is bound by the particular of this legal shaping the Euro-mortgage should as far as possible be limited to the securing of credits granted by institutional creditors (banks, savings banks, building societies, insurances and state creditors).

Normally, the content of the security contract will contain provisions regarding the creation of the Euro-mortgage, the determination of its purpose, the possibilities of a refinancing or an assignment of the Euro-mortgage as well as the obligation of the creditor to reassign the Euro-mortgage to the property owner or to agree to the cancellation of its entry (waiver). Moreover, it can be provided that the Euro-mortgage shall secure only one particular personal debt and therefore must not be assigned, or that the rights arising out of the Euro-mortgage may not be enforced before the maturity (or the paying out) of the credit. Finally, special provisions are required if the borrower and the property owner are not the same person.

Because of the far-reaching importance of the security contract it seems to be advisable that the minimum content or the basic conditions of a typical security contract should be determined by law; this would create a softened

---

19   For details see Stöcker (footnote 1), p. 218 f. and 222.

accessoriness which supplies the property owner with sufficient protection against the initial creditor as well as against later assignees.[20] Under no circumstances may the shaping of the security contract be left totally to the discretion of the persons involved or to national legislation.[21] In the continental European states entrusting the certification of the Euro-mortgage to the impartial notary it could be legally prescribed at the same time that either the security contract has to be recorded as well or that it has at least to be presented on the occasion of the recording of the Euro-mortgage in order to facilitate the control of its compliance with the minimum content determined by law. Furthermore, one could ensure in this way the necessary instruction of the parties about the legal consequences of Euro-mortgage and security contract.

6 Important Questions Regarding Details

Parallel to a legal regulation of a future Euro-mortgage, important questions regarding details have to be solved. These details include the question of which way the valid *creation* of the Euro-mortgage, its *specific rank* and its later *assignment* can be made *known to the public* in states without a system of land registration. But it comprises also the difficult decision of which peripheral legal fields have to be regulated in a uniform way and which particulars can still be treated according to provisions of national law.

Because of the differing systems of land and land charge registration it will be advisable in the interest of legal certainty to introduce an official confirmation of the proper registration of the Euro-mortgage and of its specific rank in relation to other charges on the respective land (lettre de confirmation uniforme). The uniform text of this *certificate of registration and specific rank* should be formulated so broadly that it fits within the legal relations in all EU Member States. The certificate could include declarations on the valid creation according to the *lex loci actus*, on the validity of the declaration of executionability connected to the mortgage certificate, on the valid registration of the Euro-mortgage according to the *lex loci actus* and on the resulting specific rank of the Euro-mortgage in relation to other land charges. Moreover, it could contain peculiarities of the individual case, e.g. references to the creation of a transferable mortgage document and to the person to whom it has been handed over. Such a certificate could indicate which assignments have taken place or which amendments to the original content of the Euro-mortgage have been effected.

Such certificates will advisably be issued by those persons, authorities or institutions which are generally in charge of the certification of the Euro-mortgage according to the respective domestic law. *Publizitätswirkung* (in how

---

20   Cf. the succinct formulation of Stürner (footnote 1), p. 388.
21   Stürner, *loc. cit.* (footnote 19).

far can it be treated as *notice to the whole world?*) and *öffentlicher Glaube* (public reliance) of this certificate should be regulated by law as well; the same applies to the legal consequences of a divergence between the contents of the certificate and actual legal position.

In practice, it will also be of considerable importance, whether the Euro-mortgage — as an alternative to the conventional kinds of land charge in the respective states — may *only* be created for or assigned to *institutional creditors* in the widest sense and not for or to private persons. A further problem is caused by the much-discussed question of whether it should be permitted to create the Euro-mortgage initially as an *owner's mortgage* in order to facilitate an assignment to the final creditor on a later occasion. The practising lawyers seem to agree that each *assignment* should be subject to the same formal requirements as the creation of the Euro-mortgage itself. It will be incompatible with the future Euro-mortgage to subject this land charge to a time limitation set by law as applied at present to inter alia mortgages according to French law.

7 Results and Prospect

The problems the practice of credit operation is faced with in regard to the cross-border securing of credits by immoveable property cannot be solved by contemporary Private International Law.

The principle of mutual recognition does not bring about a breakthrough to the European International Market in the field of land charges; mainly in France and Spain numerous difficulties arise from the cumbersome nature of the *accessoriness* of the mortgage to the underlying debt.[22]

For these reasons, all possible efforts should be made to introduce — besides the national kinds of land charge which continue in existence — a Euro-mortgage being uniformly in force within the EU. Not only economic considerations but also the principles of a well-understood consumer protection count in favour thereof. The Euro-mortgage could be shaped according to the Swiss *Schuldbrief*, embody a personal as well as a real title, be independent of an underlying debt and transferable; moreover, the specific rank of the Euro-mortgage revealed by the Land Register should not be substantially interfered with by legal privileges and prerogatives not being registered.[23]

On the basis of the experiences of the practice of credit operation in Europe it can be recommended to introduce the Euro-mortgage *in addition* to the national kinds of mortgage continuing in force. In this way it can prove its value in free competition with the traditional kinds of land charge of domestic law.

The Euro-mortgage will experience this test at first in regard to the cross-border operation of credits secured by immoveable property which soon will be

---

22 This has been made clear by the Thesis of Stöcker (footnote 1).
23 Discussed in detail by Stöcker (footnote 1), p. 84 ff. and *Der Hypothekarkredit in der EG* (footnote 2) p. 222 ff.

very common in the European Internal Market. The disadvantages of the mortgage accessory to the debt which have already been demonstrated in relation to domestic mortgage credits will be multiplied in relation to cross-border financing, not least as a result of the different laws applicable according to Private International Law.

The time remaining should be used to discuss and to develop the suggestions at hand and perhaps also to add further alternatives. Those competent to do this are in the first place the European law institutes of the universities. Cooperation with the European Community Mortgage Federation in Brussels and with the CACE/UINL would be advisable.

Principles of European Contract Law*

PART 1
Performance and Non-performance of Contracts

CHAPTER 1: GENERAL PROVISIONS

Article 1.101 *Application of the principles*
(1) These Principles are intended to be applied as general rules of contract law in the European Communities.
(2) These Principles will apply when the parties have agreed that their contract is to be governed by them.
(3) These Principles may be applied
    (a) when the parties have agreed that their contract is to be governed by 'general principles of law', the 'lex mercatoria' or the like; or
    (b) when the parties have not chosen any system or rules of law to govern their contract.
(4) These Principles may provide a solution to the issue raised where the system or rules of law applicable do not do so.

Article 1.102 *Exclusion or Modification of the Principles*
The parties may exclude the application of any of these Principles or derogate from or vary their effects except as otherwise provided in the Principles.

Article 1.103 *Usages and Practices*
(1) The parties are bound by any usage to which they have agreed and by any practice they have established between themselves.
(2) The parties are bound by a usage which would be considered generally applicable by persons in the same situation as the parties, except where the application of such usage would be unreasonable.

Article 1.104 *Interpretation and Supplementation*
(1) These Principles should be interpreted and developed in accordance with their purposes. In particular, regard should be had to the need to promote good faith and fair dealing, certainty in contractual relationships and uniformity of application.
(2) Issues within the scope of these Principles but not expressly settled by them are so far as possible to be settled in accordance with the ideas underlying the Principles. Failing this, the legal system applicable by virtue of the rules of private international law is to be applied.

Article 1.105 *Meaning of Terms*
In these Principles, except where the context otherwise requires:
(1) 'act' includes omission;

---

*   This document is the most recent draft of the PECL. The final text and comments will be published by Martinus Nijhoff Publishers.

(2) 'court' includes arbitral tribunal;

(3) an 'intentional' act includes an act done recklessly;

(4) 'non-performance' denotes any failure to perform an obligation under the contract and includes delayed performance, defective performance and failure to co-operate in order to give full effect to the contract.

Article 1.106 *Good Faith and Fair Dealing*
(1) In exercising his rights and performing his duties each party must act in accordance with good faith and fair dealing.

(2) The parties may not exclude or limit this duty.

Article 1.107 *Duty to Cooperate*
Each party owes to the other a duty to cooperate in order to give full effect to the contract.

Article 1.108 *Reasonableness*
Under these Principles reasonableness is to be judged by what persons acting in good faith and in the same situation as the parties would consider to be reasonable. In particular, in assessing what is reasonable the nature and purpose of the contract, the circumstances of the case, and the usages and practices of the trades or professions involved should be taken into account.

Article 1.109 *Imputed Knowledge and Intention*
(1) A party is to be treated as having known or foreseen a fact, or as being in a position where he should have known or foreseen it, if any person for whom he was responsible knew or foresaw the fact, or should have known or foreseen it, unless that person was not involved in the making or performance of the contract.

(2) A party is to be treated as having acted intentionally or with gross negligence or not in accordance with good faith and fair dealing if a person to whom he entrusted performance or who performed with his assent so acted.

Article 1.110 *Notice*
(1) Notice given pursuant to these Principles has effect if given by any means, whether in writing or otherwise, appropriate to the circumstances.

(2) If pursuant to these Principles one party gives notice to the other because of the other's non-performance or because such non-performance is reasonably anticipated by the first party and the notice is properly dispatched or given, a delay or error in the transmission of the notice or its failure to arrive does not prevent it from having effect. The notice shall have effect from the time at which it would have arrived under normal circumstances.

(3) In any other case, notice does not have effect unless and until it reaches the person to whom it is given.

(4) For the purpose of this Article, 'notice' includes a declaration, demand, request or any other form of communication.

CHAPTER 2: TERMS AND PERFORMANCE OF THE CONTRACT

Article 2.101 *Determination of Price or Other Contractual Terms*
Where the contract does not fix the price or the method of determining it, the parties are to be treated as having agreed on a reasonable price. The same rule applies to any other contractual term.

Article 2.102 *Unilateral Determination by a Party*
Where the price or any other contractual term is to be determined by one party whose determination is grossly unreasonable, then notwithstanding any provision to the contrary, a reasonable price or other term shall be substituted.

Article 2.103 *Determination by a Third Person*
(1) Where the price or any other contractual term is to be determined by a third person, and he cannot or will not do so, the parties are presumed to have empowered the court to appoint another person to determine it.
(2) If a price or other term fixed by a third person is grossly unreasonable, a reasonable price or term shall be substituted.

Article 2.104 *Reference to a Non Existent Factor*
Where the price or any contractual term is to be determined by reference to a factor which does not exist or has ceased to exist or to be accessible, the nearest equivalent factor shall be substituted.

Article 2.105 *Quality of Performance*
If the contract does not specify the quality, a party must tender performance of at least average quality.

Article 2.106 *Place of Performance*
(1) If the place of performance of a contractual obligation is not fixed by or determinable from the contract it shall be:
    (a) in the case of an obligation to pay money, the creditor's place of business at the time of the conclusion of the contract;
    (b) in the case of an obligation other than to pay money, the obligor's place of business at the time of conclusion of the contract.
(2) If a party has more than one place of business, the place of business for the purpose of the preceding paragraph is that which has the closest relationship to the contract, having regard to the circumstances known to or contemplated by the parties at the time of conclusion of the contract.
(3) If a party does not have a place of business his habitual residence is to be treated as his place of business.

Article 2.107 *Time of Performance*
A party has to effect his performance:
(1) if a time is fixed by or determinable from the contract, at that time;
(2) if a period of time is fixed by or determinable from the contract, at any time within that period unless the circumstances of the case indicate that the other party is to choose the time;

(3) in any other case, within a reasonable time after the conclusion of the contract.

Article 2.108 *Early Performance*
(1) A party may decline a tender of performance made before it is due except where acceptance of the tender would not unreasonably prejudice his interests.
(2) A party's acceptance of early performance does not affect the time fixed for the performance of his own obligation.

Article 2.109 *Contract for an indefinite Period*
A contract for an indefinite period may be ended by either party by giving notice of reasonable length.

Article 2.110 *Form of Payment*
(1) Payment of money due may be made in any form used in the ordinary course of business.
(2) A creditor who, pursuant to the contract or voluntarily, accepts a cheque or other order to pay or a promise to pay is presumed to do so only on condition that it will be honoured. The creditor may not enforce the original obligation to pay unless the order or promise is not honoured.

Article 2.111 *Currency of Payment*
(1) The parties may agree that payment shall be made only in a specified currency.
(2) In the absence of such agreement, a sum of money expressed in a currency other than that of the place where payment is due may be paid in the currency of that place according to the rate of exchange prevailing there at the time when payment is due.
(3) If, in a case falling within the preceding paragraph, the debtor has not paid at the time when payment is due, the creditor may require payment in the currency of the place where payment is due according to the rate of exchange prevailing there either at the time when payment is due or at the time of actual payment.

Article 2.112 *Appropriation of Performance*
(1) Where a party has to perform several obligations of the same nature and the performance tendered does not suffice to discharge all of the obligations, then subject to paragraph 4 the party may at the time of his performance declare to which obligation the performance is to be appropriated.
(2) If the performing party does not make such a declaration, the other party may within a reasonable time appropriate the performance to such obligation as he chooses. He shall inform the performing party of the choice. However, any such appropriation to an obligation which:
    (a) is not yet due, or
    (b) is illegal, or
    (c) is disputed,
is invalid.
(3) In the absence of an appropriation by either party, and subject to paragraph 4, the performance is appropriated to that obligation which satisfies one of the following criteria in the sequence indicated:
    (a) the obligation which is due or is the first to fall due;
    (b) the obligation for which the obligee has the least security;

(c) the obligation which is the most burdensome for the obligor,

(d) the obligation which has arisen first.

If none of the preceding criteria applies, the performance is appropriated proportionately to all obligations.

(4) In the case of a monetary obligation, a payment by the debtor is to be appropriated, first, to expenses, secondly, to interests, and thirdly, to principal, unless the creditor makes a different appropriation.

Article 2.113 *Property Not Accepted*

(1) A party who is left in possession of tangible property other than money because of the other party's failure to accept or retake the property must take reasonable steps to protect and preserve the property.

(2) The party left in possession may discharge his duty to deliver or return:

(a) by depositing the property on reasonable terms with a third person to be held to the order of the other party, and notifying the other party of this; or

(b) by selling the property on reasonable terms after notice to the other party, and paying the net proceeds to that party.

(3) Where, however, the property is liable to rapid deterioration or its preservation is unreasonably expensive, the party must take reasonable steps to dispose of it. He may discharge his duty to deliver or return by paying the net proceeds to the other party.

(4) The party left in possession is entitled to be reimbursed or to retain out of the proceeds of sale any expenses reasonably incurred.

Article 2.114 *Money Not Accepted*

Where a party fails to accept money properly tendered by the other party, that party may after notice to the first party discharge his obligation to pay by depositing the money to the order of the first party in accordance with the law of the place where payment is due.

Article 2.115 *Stipulation in Favour of a Third Party*

(1) A third party may require performance of a contractual obligation when his right to do so has been expressly agreed upon between the promisor and the promisee, or when such agreement is to be inferred from the purpose of the contract or the circumstances of the case. The third party need not be identified at the time the agreement is concluded.

(2) If the third party renounces the right to performance the right is treated as never having accrued to him.

(3) The promisee may by notice to the promisor deprive the third party of the right to performance unless:

(a) the third party has received notice from the promisee that the right has been made irrevocable, or

(b) the promisor or the promisee has received notice from the third party that the latter accepts the right.

Article 2.116 *Performance by a Third Person*

(1) Except where the contract requires personal performance the obligee cannot refuse performance by a third person if:

(a) the third person acts with the assent of the obligor; or

(b) the third person has a legitimate interest in performance and the obligor has failed to perform or it is clear that he will not perform at the time performance is due.

(2) Performance by the third person in accordance with paragraph (1) discharges the obligor.

Article 2.117 *Change of Circumstances*
(1) A party is bound to fulfil his obligations even if performance has become more onerous, whether because the cost of performance has increased or because the value of the performance he receives has diminished.
(2) If, however, performance of the contract becomes excessively onerous because of a change of circumstances, the parties are bound to enter into negotiations with a view to adapting the contract or terminating it, provided that:

> (a) the change of circumstances occured after the time of conclusion of the contract, or had already occured at that time but was not and could not reasonably have been known to the parties, and
> (b) the possibility of a change of circumstances was not one which could reasonably have been taken into account at the time of conclusion of the contract, and
> (c) the risk of the change of circumstances is not one which, according to the contract, the party affected should be required to bear.

(3) If the parties fail to reach agreement within a reasonable period, the court may:

> (a) terminate the contract at a date and on terms to be determined by the court; or
> (b) adapt the contract in order to distribute between the parties in a just and equitable manner the losses and gains resulting from the change of circumstances; and
> (c) in either case, award damages for the loss suffered through the other party refusing to negotiate or breaking off negotiations in bad faith.

CHAPTER 3: NON-PERFORMANCE AND REMEDIES IN GENERAL

Article 3.101 *Remedies Available*
(1) Whenever a party fails to perform an obligation under the contract and the failure is not excused under Article 3.108, the aggrieved party may resort to any of the remedies set out in Chapter 4.
(2) Where a party's failure to perform is excused under Article 3.108, the aggrieved party may resort to any of the remedies set out in Chapter 4 except claiming performance and damages.
(3) A party may not resort to any of the remedies set out in Chapter 4 to the extent that his own act caused the other party's non-performance.

Article 3.102 *Cumulation of Remedies*
Remedies which are not incompatible may be cumulated. In particular, a party is not deprived of his right to damages by exercising his right to any other remedy.

Article 3.103 *Fundamental Non-Performance*
A non-performance of an obligation is fundamental to the contract if:

> (a) strict compliance with the obligation is of the essence of the contract; or
> (b) the non-performance substantially deprives the aggrieved party of what he was entitled to expect under the contract, unless the other party did not foresee and could not reasonably have foreseen that result; or
> (c) the non-performance is intentional and gives the aggrieved party reason to believe that he cannot rely on the other party's future performance.

Article 3.104 *Cure by Non-Performing Party*
A party whose tender of performance is not accepted by the other party because it does not conform to the contract may make a new and conforming tender where the time for performance has not yet arrived or the delay would not be such as to constitute a fundamental non-performance.

Article 3.105 *Assurance of Performance*
(1) A party who reasonably believes that there will be a fundamental non-performance by the other party may demand adequate assurance of due performance and meanwhile may withhold performance of his own obligations so long as such reasonable belief continues.
(2) Where this assurance is not provided within a reasonable time, the party demanding it may terminate the contract if he still reasonably believes that there will be a fundamental non-performance by the other party and gives notice of termination without delay.

Article 3.106 *Notice Fixing Additional Period for Performance*
(1) In any case of non-performance the aggrieved party may by notice to the other party allow an additional period of time for performance.
(2) During the additional period the aggrieved party may withhold performance of his own reciprocal obligations and may claim damages, but he may not resort to any other remedy. If he receives notice from the other party that the latter will not perform within that period, or if upon expiry of that period due performance has not been made, the aggrieved party may resort to any of the remedies that may be available under chapter 4.
(3) If in a case of delay in performance which is not fundamental the aggrieved party has given a notice fixing an additional period of time of reasonable length, he may terminate the contract at the end of the period of notice. The aggrieved party may in his notice provide that if the other party does not perform within the period fixed by the notice the contract shall terminate automatically. If the period stated is too short, the aggrieved party may terminate, or, as the case may be, the contract shall terminate automatically, only after a reasonable period from the time of the notice.

Article 3.107 *Performance Entrusted to Another*
A party who entrusts performance of the contract to another person remains responsible for performance.

Article 3.108 *Excuse Due to an Impediment*
(1) A party's non-performance is excused if he proves that it is due to an impediment beyond his control and that he could not reasonably have been expected to take the impediment into account at the time of the conclusion of the contract, or to have avoided or overcome the impediment or its consequences.
(2) Where the impediment is only temporary the excuse provided by this article has effect for the period during which the impediment exists. However, if the delay amounts to a fundamental non-performance, the obligee may treat it as such.
(3) The non-performing party must ensure that notice of the impediment and of its effect on his ability to perform is received by the other party within an reasonable time after the non-performing party knew or ought to have known of these circumstances. The other party is entitled to damages for any loss resulting from the non-receipt of such notice.

Article 3.109 *Clause Limiting or Excluding Liability*
The parties may agree in advance to limit or to exclude their liability for non-performance except where the non-performance is intentional or the limitation or exclusion is unreasonable.

CHAPTER 4: PARTICULAR REMEDIES FOR NON-PERFORMANCE

SECTION 1: RIGHT TO PERFORMANCE

Article 4.101 *Monetary Obligations*
(1) The creditor is entitled to recover money which is due.
(2) Where the creditor has not yet performed his obligation and it is clear that the debtor will be unwilling to receive performance, the creditor may nonetheless proceed with his performance and may recover any sum due under the contract unless:
    (a) he could have made a reasonable cover transaction without significant effort or expense; or
    (b) performance would be unreasonable in the circumstances.

Article 4.102 *Non-monetary Obligations*
(1) The aggrieved party is entitled to specific performance of an obligation other than one to pay money, including the remedying of a defective performance.
(2) Specific performance cannot, however, be obtained where:
    (a) performance would be unlawful or impossible; or
    (b) performance would cause the obligor unreasonable effort or expense; or
    (c) the performance consists in the provision of services or work of a personal character or depends upon a personal relationship, or
    (d) the aggrieved party may reasonably obtain performance from another source.
(3) The aggrieved party will lose the right to specific performance if he fails to seek it within a reasonable time after he has or ought to have become aware of the non-performance.

Article 4.103 *Damages Not Precluded*
The fact that a right to performance is excluded under this Section does not preclude a claim for damages.

SECTION 2: RIGHT TO WITHHOLD PERFORMANCE

Article 4.201 *Right to Withhold Performance*
(1) A party who is to perform simultaneously with or after the other party may withhold performance until the other has tendered performance or has performed. The first party may withhold the whole of his performance or a part of it as may be reasonable in the circumstances.
(2) A party may similarly withhold performance for as long as it is clear that there will be a non-performance by the other party when the other party's performance becomes due.

SECTION 3: TERMINATION OF THE CONTRACT

Article 4.301 *Right to Terminate the Contract*
(1) A party may terminate the contract if the other party's non-performance is fundamental.
(2) In the case of delay the aggrieved party may also terminate the contract under Article 3.106 (3).

Article 4.302 *Contract to be Performed in Parts*
If the contract is to be performed in separate parts and in relation to a part to which the counter performance can be apportioned, there is a fundamental non-performance, the aggrieved party may exercise his right to terminate under this Section in relation to the part concerned. He may terminate the contract as a whole only if the non-performance is fundamental to the contract as whole.

Article 4.303 *Notice of Termination*
(1) A party's right to terminate the contract is to be exercised by notice to the other party.
(2) The aggrieved party loses his right to terminate the contract unless he gives notice within a reasonable time after he has or ought to have become aware of the non-performance.
(3) (a) When performance has not been tendered by the time it was due, the aggrieved party need not give notice of termination before a tender has been made. If a tender is later made he loses his right to terminate if he does not give such notice within a reasonable time after he has or ought to have become aware of the tender.
(b) If, however, the aggrieved party knows or has reason to know that the other party still intends to tender within a reasonable time, and the aggrieved party unreasonably fails to notify the other party that he will not accept performance, he loses his right to terminate if the other party in fact tenders within a reasonable time.
(4) If a party is excused under Article 3.108 through an impediment which is total and permanent, the contract is terminated automatically and without notice at the time the impediment arises.

Article 4.304 *Anticipatory Non-Performance*
Where prior to the time for performance by a party it is clear that there will be a fundamental non-performance by him the other party may terminate the contract.

Article 4.305 *Effects of Termination in General*
(1) Termination of the contract releases both parties from their obligation to effect and to receive future performance, but, subject to Articles 4.306, 4.307 and 4.308, does not affect the rights and liabilities accrued up to the time of termination.
(2) Termination does not affect any provision of the contract for the settlement of disputes or any other provision which is to operate even after termination.

Article 4.306 *Property Reduced in Value*
A party who terminates the contract may reject property previously received from the other party if its value to the first party has been fundamentally reduced as a result of the other party's non-performance.

Article 4.307 *Recovery of Money Paid*
On termination of the contract a party may recover money paid for a performance which he did not receive or which he properly rejected.

Article 4.308 *Recovery of Property*
On termination of the contract a party who has supplied properly which can be returned and for which he has not received payment or other counterperformance may recover the property.

Article 4.309 *Recovery for Performance that Cannot be Returned*
On termination of the contract a party who has rendered a performance which cannot be returned and for which he has not received payment or other counterperformance may recover a reasonable amount for the value of the performance to the other party.

SECTION 4: PRICE REDUCTION

Article 4.401 *Right to Reduce Price*
(1) A party who accepts a tender of performance not conforming to the contract may reduce the price. This reduction shall be proportionate to the decrease in the value of the performance at the time this was tendered compared to the value which a conforming tender would have had at that time.
(2) A party who is entitled to reduce the price under the preceding paragraph and who has already paid a sum exceeding the reduced price may recover the excess from the other party.
(3) A party who reduces the price cannot also recover damages for reduction in the value of the performance but remains entitled to damages for any further loss he has suffered so far as these are recoverable under Section 5 of this Chapter.

SECTION 5: DAMAGES AND INTEREST

Article 4.501 *Right to Damages*
(1) The aggrieved party is entitled to damages for loss caused by the other party's non-performance which is not excused under Article 3.108.
(2) The loss for which damages are recoverable includes:
　　(a) non-pecuniary loss; and
　　(b) future loss which is reasonably likely to occur.

Article 4.502 *General Measure of Damages*
The general measure of damages is such sum as will put the aggrieved party as nearly as possible into the position in which he would have been if the contract had been duly performed. Such damages cover the loss which the aggrieved party has suffered and the gain of which he has been deprived.

Article 4.503 *Foreseeability*
The non-performing party is liable only for loss which he foresaw or could reasonably have foreseen at the time of conclusion of the contract as a likely result of his non-performance, unless the non-performance was intentional or grossly negligent.

Article 4.504 *Loss Attributable to Aggrieved Party*
(1) The non-performing party is not liable for loss suffered by the aggrieved party to the extent that:
  (a) the aggrieved party contributed to the non-performance or its effects, or
  (b) his loss could have been reduced by his taking reasonable steps.
(2) The aggrieved party is entitled to recover any expenses reasonably incurred in attempting to reduce the loss.

Article 4.505 *Cover Transaction*
Where the aggrieved party has terminated the contract and has made a cover transaction within a reasonable time and in a reasonable manner, he may recover the difference between the contract price and the price of the cover transaction as well as damages for any further loss so far as these are recoverable under this Section.

Article 4.506 *Current Price*
Where the aggrieved party has terminated the contract and has not made a cover transaction but there is a current price for the performance contracted for, he may recover the difference between the contract price and the price current at the time the contract is terminated as well as damages for any further loss so far as these are recoverable under this Section.

Article 4.507 *Delay in Payment of Money*
(1) If payment of a sum of money is delayed, the aggrieved party is entitled to interest on that sum from the time when payment is due to the time of payment at the average commercial bank short-term lending rate to prime borrowers prevailing for the contractual currency of payment at the place where payment is due.
(2) The aggrieved party may in addition recover damages for any further loss, so far as these are recoverable under this Section.

Article 4.508 *Agreed Payment for Non-performance*
(1) Where the contract provides that a party who fails to perform is to pay a specified sum to the aggrieved party for such non-performance, the aggrieved party shall be awarded that sum irrespective of his actual loss.
(2) However, despite any agreement to the contrary the specified sum may be reduced to a reasonable amount where it is grossly excessive in relation to the loss resulting from the non-performance and the other circumstances.

Article 4.509 *Currency by which Damages to be Measured*
Damages are to be measured by the currency which most appropriately reflects the aggrieved party's loss.

UNIDROIT Principles for International Commercial Contracts *

PREAMBLE (ex Arts. 1.1 and 1.2)
(*Purpose of the Principles*)

These Principles set forth general rules for international commercial contracts.
They shall be applied when the parties have agreed that their contract be governed by them.
They may also be applied when the parties have agreed that their contract be governed by
'general principles of law', the 'lex mercatoria' or the like. They may [among others]
provide a solution to an issue raised when it proves impossible to establish the relevant rule
of the applicable law.
They may be used to interpret or supplement international uniform law.
They may in addition serve as a model for national and international legislators.

Chapter 1
GENERAL PROVISIONS

Article 1.1 *Freedom of contract*
The parties are free to enter into a contract and to determine its content.

Article 1.2 *No form required*
Nothing in these Principles requires a contract to be concluded in or evidenced by writing.
It may be proved by any means, including witnesses.

Article 1.3 *Binding character of the contract*
A contract validly entered into is binding upon the parties. It can only be modified or
terminated in accordance with its terms or by agreement or as otherwise provided under
these Principles.

Article 1.4 *Mandatory rules*
Nothing in these Principles shall restrict the application of mandatory rules, whether of
national, international, or supranational origin, which are applicable in accordance with the
relevant rules of private international law.

Article 1.5 *Exclusion or modification by the parties*
The parties may exclude the application of these Principles or derogate from or vary the
effect of any of its provisions, except as otherwise provided in the Principles.

Article 1.6 *Interpretation and supplementation of the Principles*
(1) In the interpretation of these Principles, regard is to be had to their international
character and to their purposes including the need to promote uniformity in their application.

---

* This document does not represent the final views of UNIDROIT. It is the text as modified by
the Editorial Committee and the Governing Council of Unidroit (November 1993).

(2) Issues within the scope of these Principles but not expressly settled by them are so far as possible to be settled in accordance with their underlying general principles.

Article 1.7 *Good faith and fair dealing*
(1) Each party must act in accordance with good faith and fair dealing in international trade.
(2) The parties may not exclude or limit this duty.

Article 1.8 *Usages and practices*
(1) The parties are bound by any usage to which they have agreed and by any practices which they have established between themselves.
(2) The parties are bound by a usage that is widely known to and regularly observed in international trade by parties in the particular trade concerned except where the application of such a usage would be unreasonable.

Article 1.9 *Notice*
(1) Where notice is required it may be given by any means appropriate to the circumstances.
(2) A notice is effective when it reaches the person to whom it is given.
(3) For the purpose of paragraph (2) a notice 'reaches' a person when given to the person orally or delivered to that person's place of business or mailing address.
(4) For the purpose of this article 'notice' includes a declaration, demand, request or any other communication of intention.

Article 1.10 *Definitions*
In these Principles
    — 'court' includes arbitration tribunal;
    — where a party has more than one place of business the relevant 'place of business' is that which has the closest relationship to the contract and its performance, having regard to the circumstances known to or contemplated by the parties at any time before or at the conclusion of the contract.
    — 'obligor' refers to the party who is to perform an obligation and 'obligee' refers to the party who is entitled to performance of that obligation.

Chapter 2
FORMATION

Article 2.1 *Definition of offer*
A proposal for concluding a contract constitutes an offer if it is sufficiently definite and indicates the intention of the offeror to be bound in case of acceptance.

Article 2.2 *Withdrawal of offer*
(1) An offer becomes effective when it reaches the offeree.
(2) An offer, even if it is irrevocable, may be withdrawn if the withdrawal reaches the offeree before of at the same time as the offer.

Article 2.3 *Revocation of offer*
(1) Until a contract is concluded an offer may be revoked if the revocation reaches the offeree before he has dispatched an acceptance.

418

(2) However, an offer cannot be revoked:
  (a) if it indicates, whether by stating a fixed time for acceptance or otherwise, that it is irrevocable; or
  (b) if it was reasonable for the offeree to rely on the offer as being irrevocable and the offeree has acted in reliance on the offer.

Article 2.4 *Rejection of offer*
An offer is terminated when a rejection reaches the offeror.

Article 2.5 *Mode of acceptance*
(1) A statement made by or other conduct of the offeree indicating assent to an offer is an acceptance. Silence or inactivity does not in itself amount to acceptance.
(2) An acceptance of an offer becomes effective at the moment the indication of assent reaches the offeror.
(3) However, if, by virtue of the offer or as a result of practices which the parties have established between themselves or of usage, the offeree may indicate assent by performing an act without notice to the offeror, the acceptance is effective at the moment the act is performed.

Article 2.6 *Time of acceptance*
An offer must be accepted within the time the offeror has fixed or, if no time is fixed, within a reasonable time, due account being taken of the circumstances of the transaction, including the rapidity of the means of communication employed by the offeror. An oral offer must be accepted immediately unless the circumstances indicate otherwise.

Article 2.7 *Acceptance within a fixed period of time*
(1) A period of time for acceptance fixed by the offeror in a telegram or a letter begins to run from the moment the telegram is handed in for dispatch or from the date shown on the letter or, if no such date is shown, from the date shown on the envelope. A period of time for acceptance fixed by the offeror by means of instantaneous communication begins to run from the moment that the offer reaches the offeree.
(2) Official holidays or non-business days occurring during the period for acceptance are included in calculating the period. However, if a notice of acceptance cannot be delivered at the address of the offeror on the last day of the period because that day falls on an official holiday or a non-business day at the place of business of the offeror, the period is extended until the first business day which follows.

Article 2.8 *Late acceptance. Delay in transmission*
(1) A late acceptance is nevertheless effective as an acceptance if without delay the offeror so informs the offeree or gives a notice to that effect.
(2) If a letter or other writing containing a late acceptance shows that it has been sent in such circumstances that if its transmission had been normal it would have reached the offeror in due time, the late acceptance is effective as an acceptance unless, without delay, the offeror informs the offeree that it considers the offer as having lapsed.

Article 2.9 *Withdrawal of acceptance*
An acceptance may be withdrawn if the withdrawal reaches the offeror before or at the same time as the acceptance would have become effective.

Article 2.10 *Modified acceptance*

(1) A reply to an offer which purports to be an acceptance but contains additions, limitations or other modifications is a rejection of the offer and constitues a counter-offer.

(2) However, a reply to an offer which purports to be an acceptance but contains additional or different terms which do not materially alter the terms of the offer constitutes an acceptance, unless the offeror, without undue delay, objects to the discrepancy or gives a notice to that effect. If he does not so object, the terms of the contract are the terms of the offer with the modifications contained in the acceptance.

Article 2.11 *Writings in confirmation*

If a writing which is sent within a reasonable time after the conclusion of the contract and which purports to be a confirmation of the contract contains additional or different terms, such terms will become part of the contract, unless they materially alter the contract or the recipient, without undue delay, objects to the discrepancy or gives notice to that effect.

Article 2.12 *Conclusion of contract dependent on agreement on specific matters or in a specific form*

Where one of the parties in the course of negotiations insists that a contract not be concluded until there is agreement on specific matters or in an specific form, the contract is not concluded before there is agreement on these matters or in that form.

Article 2.13 *Contract with terms deliberately left open*

(1) If the parties intended to conclude a contract, the fact that they have intentionally left a term to be agreed upon in further negotiations or to be determined by a third person does not prevent a contract from coming into existence.

(2) The existence of the contract is not affected by the fact that subsequently

    (a) the parties reach no agreement on the term, or

    (b) the third person does not determine the term, provided that there is an alternative means of rendering the term definite that is reasonable in all of the circumstances, including any intention of the parties.

Article 2.14 *Negotiations in bad faith*

(1) A party is free to negotiate and is not liable for failure to reach an agreement.

(2) However, a party who has negotiated or broken off negotiations in bad faith is liable for the losses caused to the other party.

(3) It is bad faith, in particular, for a party to enter into or continue negotiations intending not to make an agreement with the other party.

Article 2.15 *Duty of confidentiality*

If information is given as confidential by one party in the course of negotiations, the other party is under a duty not to disclose that information or use it improperly for his own purposes whether or not a contract is subsequently concluded. Where appropriate, the remedy for breach of that duty may include compensation based on the benefit received by the other party.

Article 2.16 *Merger clauses*
A contract in writing which contains a clause indicating that the writing completely embodies the terms on which the parties have agreed cannot be contradicted or supplemented by evidence of prior statements or agreements. However, such statements or agreements may be used to interpret the writing.

Article 2.17 *Written modification clauses*
A contract in writing which contains a clause requiring any modification or termination by agreement to be in writing may not be otherwise modified or terminated by agreement. However, a party may be precluded by this conduct from asserting such a clause to the extent that the other party has relied on that conduct.

Article 2.18 *Contracting under standard terms*
(1) Where one party or both parties use standard terms in concluding a contract, the general rules on formation apply, subject to Articles 2.17 - 2.19.
(2) Standard terms are provisions which are prepared in advance for general and repeated use by one party and which are actually used without negotiation with the other party.

Article 2.19 *Surprising terms*
No term contained in standard terms which by virtue of its content, language or presentation is of such a character that the other party could not reasonably have expected it, shall be effective, unless is has been expressly accepted by that party.

Article 2.20 *Conflict between standard terms and non-standard terms*
If there is a conflict between a standard term and a term which is not a standard term the latter prevails.

Article 2.21 *Battle of forms*
If both parties use standard terms and they reach an agreement except on those terms, a contract is concluded on the basis of the agreed terms and any standard terms which are common in substance unless one party clearly indicates in advance or later, without undue delay, informs the other that he does not intend to be bound by such a contract.

Chapter 3
VALIDITY

Article 3.1 *Matters not covered*
These Principles do not deal with invalidity arising from
(a) lack of capacity;
(b) lack of authority;
(c) immorality or illegality.

Article 3.2 *Validity of mere agreement*
A contract is concluded, modified or terminated by the mere agreement of the parties, without any further requirement.

Article 3.3 *Initial impossibility*
(1) The mere fact that at the time of the conclusion of the contract the performance of the assumed obligation was impossible shall not effect the validity of the contract.
(2) The mere fact that at the time of the conclusion of the contract a party was not entitled to dispose of the assets to which the contract relates, shall not effect the validity of the contract.

Article 3.4 *Definition of mistake*
Mistake is an erroneous assumption relating to facts or to law existing when the contract was concluded.

Article 3.5 *Relevant Mistake*
(1) A party may only avoid a contract for mistake if when the contract was concluded the mistake was of such importance that a reasonable person in the same situation as the party in error would have contracted only on materially different terms or would not have contracted at all if the true state of affairs had been known, and
> (a) the other party made the same mistake, or caused the mistake, or knew or ought to have known of the mistake and it was contrary to reasonable commercial standards of fair dealing to leave the mistaken party in error, or
> (b) the other party has not at the time of avoidance acted in reliance on the contract.
(2) However, a party may not avoid the contract, if
> (a) it committed the mistake with gross negligence, or
> (b) the mistake relates to a matter in regard to which the risk of mistake was assumed or, taking into account all the relevant circumstances, should be borne by the mistaken party.

Article 3.6 *Error in expression or transmission*
An error occurring in the expression or transmission of a declaration is considered to be a mistake of the person from whom the declaration emanated.

Article 3.7 *Remedies for non-performance*
A party shall not be entitled to avoid the contract on the ground of mistake if the circumstances on which he relies afford, or could have afforded, him a remedy for non-performance.

Article 3.8 *Fraud*
A party may avoid the contract when he has been led to conclude it by the other party's fraudulent representation, including language or practices, or fraudulent non-disclosure of circumstances which according to reasonable commercial standards of fair dealing he should have disclosed.

Article 3.9 *Threat*
A party may avoid the contract when he has been led to conclude it by the other party's unjustified threat which, having due regard to the circumstances, is so imminent and serious as to leave him no reasonable alternative. In particular, a threat is unjustified if the act or omission with which a party has been threatened is wrongful in itself, or it is wrongful to use it as a means to obtain the conclusion of the contract.

422

Article 3.10 *Gross disparity*

(1) A party may avoid a contract or an individual term if at the time of the making of the contract the contract or term unjustifiably gives the other party an excessive advantage. Regard is to be had to, among other things,

    (a) the fact that the other party has taken unfair advantage of the avoiding party's dependence, economic distress or urgent needs, or of his improvidence, ignorance, inexperience or lack of bargaining skill, and

    (b) the nature and purpose of the contract.

(2) Upon the request of the party entitled to avoidance, a court may adapt the contract or term in order to bring it in accordance with reasonable commercial standards of fair dealing.

(3) A court may also adapt the contract or term upon the request of the party receiving notice of avoidance, provided that that party informs the other party of its request promptly after receiving such notice and before the other party has relied on it. The provisions of Article 3.13(2) apply accordingly.

Article 3.11 *Third persons*

(1) Where a fraud, a threat, a gross disparity or a party's mistake is imputable to, or is known or ought to be known by, a third person for whose acts the other party is responsible, the contract may be avoided under the same conditions as if the behaviour or knowledge had been that of the party itself.

(2) Where a fraud, a threat or a gross disparity is imputable to a third person for whose acts the other party is not responsible, the contract may be avoided if the other contracting party knew or ought to have known of the fraud, the threat or the disparity, or has not at the time of avoidance acted in reliance on the contract.

Article 3.12 *Confirmation*

If the party who is entitled to avoid the contract expressly or impliedly confirms the contract after the period of time for giving notice of avoidance has begun to run, avoidance of the contract is excluded.

Article 3.13 *Adaptation of contract*

(1) If a party is entitled to avoid the contract for mistake but the other party declares himself willing to perform or performs the contract as it was understood by the party entitled to avoid, the contract shall be considered to have been concluded as the latter understood it. The other party must make such a declaration or render such performance promptly after having been informed of the manner in which the party entitled to avoid had understood the contract and before that party has acted in reliance on a notice of avoidance.

(2) After such a declaration or performance the right to avoid is lost and any earlier notice of avoidance is ineffective.

Article 3.14 *Notice of avoidance*

The right of a party to avoid the contract is exercised by notice to the other party.

Article 3.15 *Time limits*

(1) Notice of avoidance must be given within a reasonable time, having due regard to the circumstances, after the avoiding party knew or could not have been unaware of the relevant facts and became capable of acting freely.

(2) Where an individual term of a contract may be avoided by a party under Article 3.10, the period of time for giving notice of avoidance begins to run when that term is asserted by the other party.

Article 3.16 *Partial avoidance*
If a ground of avoidance affects only individual terms of a contract, the effect of an avoidance is limited to those terms unless, having regard to the circumstances of the case, it is unreasonable to uphold the remaining contract.

Article 3.17 *Retroactive effect of avoidance*
(1) Avoidance shall take effect retroactively.
(2) On avoidance either party may claim restitution of whatever it has supplied under the contract or the part of it avoided, provided that it concurrently makes restitution of whatever it has received under the contract or the part of it avoided, or, if it cannot make restitution in kind, it must make an allowance for what it has received.

Article 3.18 *Damages*
Irrespective of whether or not the contract has been avoided, the party who knew or ought to have known of the ground for avoidance is liable for damages so as to put the other party into the same position it would have been in if it had not concluded the contract.

Article 3.19 *Mandatory character of the provisions*
The provisions of this chapter are mandatory, except insofar as they relate.

Article 3.20 *Unilateral declarations*
The provisions of this Chapter apply with appropriate adaptations to any communication or intention addressed by one party to the other.

Chapter 4
INTERPRETATION

Article 4.1 *Intention of parties*
(1) A contract shall be interpreted according to the parties' common intention if such an intention can be established.
(2) If such an intention cannot be established, the contract shall be interpreted according to the meaning which reasonable persons of the same kind as the parties would give to it in the same circumstances.

Article 4.2 *Interpretation of statements and other conduct*
(1) A party's statements and other conduct shall be interpreted according to that party's intention, if the other party knew or could not have been unaware of that intention.
(2) If the preceding paragraph is not applicable, such statements and other conduct shall be interpreted according to the meaning that a reasonable person of the same kind as the other party would give to it in the same circumstances.

Article 4.3 *Relevant circumstances*
(1) In applying Articles 4.1 and 4.2, regard shall be had to all the circumstances, including:

(a) any preliminary negotiations between the parties;
(b) any practices which the parties have established between themselves;
(c) any conduct of the parties subsequent to the conclusion of the contract;
(d) the nature and purpose of the contract;
(e) any meaning commonly given to terms and expressions in a trade concerned; and
(f) any usages.

Article 4.4 *Reference to contract or statement as a whole*
Terms and expressions shall be interpreted in the light of the whole contract or statement in which they appear.

Article 4.5 *All terms to be given effect*
Contract terms shall be interpreted so as to give effect to all the terms rather than to deprive some of them of effect.

Article 4.6 *Contra proferentem rule*
If contract terms supplied by one party are unclear, an interpretation against that party is preferred.

Article 4.7 *Linguistic discrepancies*
If a contract is drawn up in two or more language versions being equally authoritative, in case of discrepancy between the versions there is a preference for the interpretation according to the version in which it was originally drawn up.

Article 4.8 *Supplying an omitted term*
(1) Where the parties to a contract have not agreed with respect to a term which is important for a determination of their rights and duties, a term which is appropriate in the circumstances is supplied.
(2) In determining what is an appropriate term regard shall be had, among other factors, to
    (a) the intention of the parties;
    (b) the nature and purpose of the contract;
    (c) good faith;
    (d) reasonableness.

Chapter 5
CONTENT

Article 5.1 *Express and implied obligations*
The contractual obligations of the parties may be express or implied.

Article 5.2 *Implied obligations*
Implied obligations stem from
    (a) the nature and purpose of the contract;
    (b) practices established between the parties and fair dealing;
    (c) reasonableness.

Article 5.3 *Cooperation between the parties*
Each party shall cooperate with the other party, when such cooperation may reasonably be expected for the performance of that party's obligations.

Article 5.4 *Duty to achieve a specific result, duty of best efforts*
(1) To the extent that an obligation of a party involves a duty to achieve a specific result, that party is bound to achieve that result.
(2) To the extent that an obligation of a party involves a duty of best efforts that would be made by a reasonable person of the same kind in the same circumstances.

Article 5.5 *Determination of kind of duty involved*
In determining the extent to which an obligation of a party involves a duty of best efforts in the performance of an activity or a duty to achieve a specific result, regard shall be had to the following circumstances, among others:
    (a) the way in which the obligation is expressed in the contract;
    (b) the contractual price and other terms of the contract;
    (c) the degree of risk normally involved in achieving the expected result;
    (d) the other party's ability to influence the performance of the obligation.

Article 5.6 *Determination of quality of performance*
If the quality of performance is not fixed by nor determinable from the contract, a party is bound to render a performance of a quality that is reasonable and not less than average in the circumstances.

Article 5.7 *Price determination*
(1) If a contract does not fix or make provision for determining the price, the parties are considered, in the absence of any indication to the contrary, to have made reference to the price generally charged at the time of the conclusion of the contract for such performances under comparable circumstances in the trade concerned, or if no such price is available, to a reasonable price.
(2) Where the price is to be determined by one party and that determination is manifestly unreasonable, a reasonable price shall be substituted, notwithstanding any contract term to the contrary.
(3) Where the price is to be fixed by a third person, and he cannot or will not do so, the price shall be a reasonable price.
(4) Where the price is to be fixed by reference to factors which do not exist or have ceased to exist or to be accessible, the nearest equivalent factor shall be treated as a substitute.

Article 5.8 *Contract for an indefinite period*
A contract for an indefinite period may be ended by either party by giving notice a reasonable time in advance.

Chapter 6
PERFORMANCE

SECTION 1: PERFORMANCE IN GENERAL

Article 6.1.1 *Time of performance*
A party must perform its obligations:
  (a) if a time is fixed by or determinable from the contract, at that time;
  (b) if a period of time is fixed by or determinable from the contract, at any time within that period unless circumstances indicate that the other party is to choose a time; or
  (c) in any other case, within a reasonable time after the conclusion of the contract.

Article 6.1.2 *Performance at one time or in instalments*
In cases under Article 6.1.1(b) or (c), a party must perform its obligations at one time, if that performance can be rendered at one time and the circumstances do not indicate otherwise.

Article 6.1.3 *Partial performance*
(1) The obligee may reject an offer to perform at the time performance is due, whether or not coupled with an assurance as to the balance of the performance, unless he has no legitimate interest in doing so.
(2) Additional expenses caused to the obligee by partial performance are to be borne by the obligator without prejudice to any other remedy.

Article 6.1.4 *Order of performance*
(1) To the extent that the parties' performances can be rendered simultaneously, the parties are bound to render them simultaneously unless the circumstances indicate otherwise.
(2) To the extent that the performance of only one party requires a period of time, that party is bound to render its performance first, unless the circumstances indicate otherwise.

Article 6.1.5 *Earlier performance*
(1) The obligee may reject an earlier performance unless he has no legitimate interest in doing so.
(2) A party's acceptance of an earlier performance does not affect the time for the performance of his own obligation if it has been fixed irrespective of the performance of the other party's obligations.
(3) Additional expenses caused to the other party by earlier performance are to be borne by the performing party, without prejudice to any other remedy.

Article 6.1.6 *Place of performance*
(1) If the place of performance is not fixed by nor determinable form the contract, a party is to perform:
  (a) a monetary obligation, at the creditor's place of business;
  (b) any other obligation, at its own place of business.
(2) A party must bear any increase in the expenses incidental to performance which is caused by a change in his place of business subsequent to the conclusion of the contract.

Article 6.1.7 *Payment by check or other instruments*
(1) Payment can be made in any form used in the ordinary course of business at the place of payment.
(2) However, an obligee who accepts, either by virtue of paragraph (1) or voluntarily, a check, an other order to pay or a promise to pay, is presumed to do so only on condition that it will be honored.

Article 6.1.8 *Payment by funds transfer*
(1) Unless the obligee has indicated a particular account, payment can be made by a transfer to any of the financial institutions in which the creditor has made it known he has an account.
(2) In case of payment by a transfer the obligation of the obligor is discharged when the transfer to the obligee's financial institution becomes effective.

Article 6.1.9 *Currency of payment*
(1) If a monetary obligation is expressed in a currency other than that of the place of payment, it may be paid by the obligor in the currency of the place of payment unless
    (a) that currency is not freely convertible; or
    (b) the parties have agreed that payment should be made only in the currency in which the monetary obligation is expressed.
(2) If it is impossible for the obligor to make payment in the currency in which the monetary obligation is expressed, the obligee may require payment in the currency of the place of payment, even in the case envisaged by paragraph (1)(b).
(3) Payment in the currency of the place of payment is to be made according to the applicable rate of exchange prevailing there when payment is due.
(4) However, if the obligor has not paid at the time when payment is due, the obligee may require payment according to the applicable rate of exchange prevailing either when payment is due or at the time of actual payment.

Article 6.1.10 *Currency not expressed*
If a monetary obligation is not expressed in a particular currency, payment must be made in the currency of the place where payment is to be made.

Article 6.1.11 *Costs of performance*
Each party shall bear the costs of performance of its obligations.

Article 6.1.12 *Imputation of payments*
(1) A obligor owning several monetary obligations to the same obligee may specify at the time of payment the debt to which he intends the payment to be applied. However, the payment discharges first any expenses, then interests due and finally the principal.
(2) If the obligor does not make such a specification, the obligee may, within reasonable time after payment, declare to the debtor the obligation to which he imputes the payment, provided that obligation is due and undisputed.
(3) In the absence of imputation under paragraphs (1) or (2), payment is imputed to that obligation which satisfies one of the following criteria in the sequence indicated:
    (a) an obligation which is due or which is the first to fall due;
    (b) an obligation for which the obligee has least security;
    (c) the obligation which is the most burdensome for the obligor;
    (d) the obligation which has arisen first.
If none of the preceding criteria applies, payment is imputed to all the obligations proportionally.

Article 6.1.13 *Imputation of non-monetary obligations*
Article 6.1.11 applies with appropriate adaptions to the imputation of performances of non-monetary obligations.

Article 6.1.14 *Application for public permission*
Where the law of a State requires a public permission affecting the validity of the contract or its performance and that law or the circumstances do not indicate otherwise
(a) if only one party has his place of business in that State, that party shall take the measures necessary to obtain the permission; and
(b) in any other case the party whose performances requires permission shall take the necessary measures.

Article 6.1.15 *Procedure in applying for permission*
(1) The party required to take the measures necessary to obtain the permission shall do so without undue delay. He shall bear any expenses incurred.
(2) That party shall whenever appropriate give the other party notice of the grant or refusal of such permission without undue delay.

Article 6.1.16 *Permission neither granted nor refused*
(1) If, notwithstanding the fact that the party responsible took all measures required, permission was neither granted nor refused within an agreed period, or where no period has been agreed, within a reasonable time from the conclusion of the contract, either party is entitled to terminate the contract.
(2) Where the permission affects only some terms, paragraph (1) does not apply, if, having regard to the circumstances of the case, it is reasonable to uphold the remaining contract even if the permission is refused.

Article 6.1.17 *Permission refused*
(1) The refusal of a permission affecting the validity of the contract renders the contract void. If the refusal affects the validity of only some terms, only such terms are void if, having regard to the circumstances of the case, it is reasonable to uphold the remaining contract.
(2) Where the refusal of a permission renders the performance of the contract impossible in whole or in part, the rules on non-performance apply.

SECTION 2: HARDSHIP

Article 6.2.1 *Contract to be observed*
If the performance of a contract becomes more onerous for one of the parties, he is nevertheless bound to perform his obligations subject to the following provisions on hardship.

Article 6.2.2 *Definition of hardship*
There is of hardship where the occurrence of events fundamentally alters the equilibrium of the contract whether because the cost of a party's performance has increased or because the value of the performance a party receives has diminished, and
(a) the events occur or become known to the disadvantaged party after the conclusion of the contract;
(b) the events could not reasonably have been taken into account by the disadvantaged party at the time of the conclusion of the contract;
(c) the events are beyond the control of the disadvantaged party; and

(d) the risk of the events was not assumed by the disadvantaged party.

Article 6.2.3 *Effects of hardship*
(1) In a case of hardship the disadvantaged party is entitled to request renegotiations. The request shall be made without undue delay and shall indicate the grounds on which it is based.
(2) The request for renegotiation does not in itself entitle the disadvantaged party to withhold performance.
(3) Upon failure to reach agreement within a reasonable time either party may resort to the court.
(4) If a court finds hardship it may, if reasonable,
      (a) terminate the contract at a date and on terms to be fixed, or
      (b) adapt the contract with a view to restoring its equilibrium.

Chapter 7
NON-PERFORMANCE

SECTION 1: GENERAL PROVISIONS

Article 7.1.1 *Non-performance defined*
Non-performance is failure by a party to perform any of its obligations under the contract, including defective performance or late performance.

Article 7.1.2 *Other party's interference*
A party may not rely on the other party's non-performance to the extent that such non-performance was caused by the first party's act or omission or by another event as to which the first party bears the risk.

Article 7.1.3 *Withholding performance*
(1) Where the parties are to perform simultaneously, either party may withhold performance until the other party tenders its performance.
(2) Where the parties are to perform consecutively, the party that is to perform later may withhold its performance until the first party has performed.

Article 7.1.4 *Cure by non-performing party*
(1) Subject to the right of the aggrieved party to terminate, the non-performing party may, at its own expense, cure any non-performance, including by repair or replacement, provided that cure is appropriate to the circumstances, is effected promptly on reasonable notice by the non-performing party, and the aggrieved party has no legitimate interest in refusing cure.
(2) In case of cure the aggrieved party retains the right to claim damages for delay as well as for harm caused or not prevented by the cure.
(3) The aggrieved party may withhold performance pending cure, but rights inconsistent with the non-performing party's performance are suspended by a proper notice of cure until the time for cure has expired.

Article 7.1.5 *Additional period for performance*

(1) In any case of non-performance the aggrieved party may by notice to the other party allow an additional period of time for performance.

(2) During the additional period the aggrieved party may withhold performance of his own reciprocal obligations and may claim damages but he may not resort to any other remedy. If he receives notice from the other party that the latter will not perform within that period, or if upon expiry of that period due performance has not been made, the aggrieved party may resort to any of the remedies that may be available under this chapter.

(3) If in a case of delay in performance which is not fundamental the aggrieved party has given notice allowing an additional period of time of reasonable length, he may terminate the contract at the end of that period. If the additional period allowed is not of reasonable length it shall be extended to a reasonable length. The aggrieved party may in his notice provide that if the other party fails to perform within the period allowed by the notice the contract shall automatically terminate.

(4) Paragraph (3) does not apply when the obligation which has not been performed is only a minor part of the non-performing party.

Article 7.1.6 *Exemption clauses*

A term which limits or excludes one party's liability for non-performance or which permits one party to render performance substantially different from what the other party reasonably expects may not be invoked if it would be grossly unfair to do so, having regard to the purpose of the contract.

Article 7.1.7 *Force majeure*

(1) A party's non-performance is excused if that party proves that the non-performance was due to an impediment beyond its control and that it could not reasonably be expected to have taken the impediment into account at the time of the conclusion of the contract or to have avoided or overcome it or its consequences.

(2) When the impediment is only temporary, the excuse shall have effect for such period as is reasonable taking into account the effect of the impediment on performance of the contract.

(3) The party who fails to perform must give notice to the other party of the impediment and its effect on its ability to perform. If the notice is not received by the other party within a reasonable time after the party who fails to perform knew or ought to have known of the impediment, it is liable for damages resulting from such non-receipt;

(4) Nothing in this article prevents a party from exercising a right to terminate the contract or withhold performance or request interest on money due.

SECTION 2: RIGHT TO PERFORMANCE

Article 7.2.1 *Performance of monetary obligation*

If a party who is obliged to pay money does not do so, the other party may require payment.

Article 7.2.2 *Performance of non-monetary obligation*

If a party who owes an obligation other than one to pay money does not perform, the other party may require per-formance, unless

    (a) performance is impossible in law or in fact;

(b) performance or, when relevant, enforcement is unreasonably burdensome or expensive;

(c) the party entitled to performance may reasonably obtain performance from another source;

(d) performance is of an exclusively personal character; or

(e) the party entitled to performance does not require performance within a reasonable time after he has, or ought to have, become aware of the non-performance.

Article 7.2.3 *Repair and replacement of defective performance*
The right to performance includes in appropriate cases the right to require repair, replacement or other cure of a defective performance. The provisions of Articles 7.2.1 and 7.2.2 apply accordingly.

Article 7.2.4 *Judicial penalty*
(1) Where the court orders a party to perform, it may also direct that this party pay a penalty if he does not comply with the order.
(2) The penalty shall be paid to the aggrieved party unless mandatory provisions of the law of the forum provide otherwise. Payment of the penalty to the aggrieved party does not exclude any claim for damages.

Article 7.2.5 *Change of remedy*
(1) An aggrieved party who has required performance of a non-monetary obligation and who has not received performance within a period fixed or otherwise within a reasonable period of time may invoke any other remedy.
(2) If the decision of a court for performance of a non-monetary obligation cannot be enforced, the aggrieved party may invoke any other remedy.

SECTION 3: TERMINATION

Article 7.3.1 *The right to terminate the contract*
(1) A party may terminate the contract if the failure of the other party to perform an obligation under the contract amounts to a fundamental non-performance.
(2) In determining whether a failure to perform an obligation amounts to a fundamental non-performance regard shall be had, in particular, to whether
  (a) the non-performance substantially deprives the aggrieved party of what he was entitled to expect under the contract unless the other party did not foresee and could not reasonably have foreseen such result;
  (b) strict compliance with the obligation which has not been performed is of essence under the contract;
  (c) the non-performance is intentional or reckless;
  (d) the non-performance gives the aggrieved party reason to believe that he cannot rely on the other party's future performance;
  (e) the defaulting party will suffer disproportionate loss as a result of the preparation or performance if the contract is terminated.
(3) In the case of delay the aggrieved party may also terminate the contract if the other party fails to perform before the time allowed him under Article 6.1.5 has expired.

Article 7.3.2 *Notice of termination*
(1) A party's right to terminate the contract is to be exercised by notice to the other party.
(2) If performance has been offered late or otherwise does not conform to the contract the aggrieved party will lose his right to terminate the contract unless he gives notice to the other party within a reasonable time after he has or ought to have become aware of the offer or of the non-conforming performance.

Article 7.3.3 *Anticipatory non-performance*
Where prior to the date for performance by one of the parties it is clear that there will be a fundamental non-performance by him, the other party may terminate the contract.

Article 7.3.4 *Adequate assurance of due performance*
A party who reasonably believes that there will be a fundamental non-performance by the other party may demand adequate assurance of due performance and may meanwhile withhold his own performance. Where this assurance is not provided within a reasonable time the party demanding it may terminate the contract.

Article 7.3.5 *Effects of termination in general*
(1) Termination of the contract releases both parties from their obligation to effect and to receive future per-formance.
(2) Termination does not preclude a claim for damages for non-performance.
(3) The termination does not affect any provision in the contract for the settlement of disputes or any other term of the contract which is to operate even after termination.

Article 7.3.6 *Restitution*
(1) On termination of the contract either party may claim restitution of whatever he has supplied, provided that he concurrently makes restitution of whatever he has received. If restitution in kind is not possible or appropriate allowance should be made in money whenever reasonable.
(2) However, if performance of the contract has extended over a period of time and the contract is divisible, such restitution can only be claimed for the period after termination has taken effect.

SECTION 4: DAMAGES AND EXEMPTION CLAUSES

Article 7.4.1 *Right to damages*
Any non-performance gives the aggrieved party a right to damages either exclusively or in conjunction with any other remedies except where the non-performance is excused under these Principles.

Article 7.4.2 *Full compensation*
(1) The aggrieved party is entitled to full compensation for harm as a result of the non-performance. This harm includes both any loss which he suffered and any gain of which he was deprived, taking into account any gain to the aggrieved party resulting from his avoidance of cost or harm.
(2) Such harm may be non-pecuniary and includes, for instance, physical suffering or emotional distress.

433

Article 7.4.3 *Certainty of harm*
(1) Compensation is due only for harm, including future harm, that is established with a reasonable degree of certainty.
(2) Compensation may be due for the loss of a chance in proportion to the probability of its occurrence.
(3) Where the amount of damages cannot be established with a sufficient degree of certainty, the assessment will be at the discretion of the court.

Article 7.4.4 *Foreseeability of harm*
The non-performing party is liable only for harm which he foresaw or could reasonably have foreseen at the time of the conclusion of the contract would be likely to result from his non-performance.

Article 7.4.5 *Proof of harm in case of replacement transaction*
Where the aggrieved party has terminated the contract and has made a replacement transaction within a reasonable time and in a reasonable manner it may recover the difference between the contract price and the price of the replacement transaction as well as damages for any further harm.

Article 7.4.6 *Proof of harm by current price*
(1) Where the aggrieved party has terminated the contract and has not made a replacement transaction but there is a current price for the performance contracted for, it may recover the difference between the contract price and the price current at the time the contract is terminated as well as damages for any further harm.
(2) Current price is the price generally charged for goods or services delivered or rendered in comparable circumstances at the place where the contract should have been performed or, if there is no current price at that place, the current price at such other place that appears reasonable to take as a reference.

Article 7.4.7 *Harm due in part to the aggrieved party*
When the harm is due in part to the aggrieved party's act or omission or to another event as to which that party bears the risk, the amount of damages shall be reduced to the extent these factors have contributed to the harm, having regard to the conduct of each of the parties.

Article 7.4.8 *Mitigation of harm*
(1) The non-performing party is not liable for harm suffered by the aggrieved party to the extent that the harm could have been reduced by its taking reasonable steps.
(2) The aggrieved party is entitled to recover any expenses reasonably incurred in attempting to reduce that harm.

Article 7.4.9 *Interest for failure to pay money*
(1) If a party does not pay a sum of money when it falls due the aggrieved party is entitled to interest upon that sum from the time when payment is due to the time of payment.
(2) The rate of interest shall be the average bank short-term lending rate to prime borrowers prevailing for the currency of payment at the place for payment, or where no such rate exists at that place, then the same rate in the State of the currency of payment. In the absence of

such a rate at either place the rate of interest shall be the appropriate rate fixed by the law of the State of the currency of payment.

(3) The aggrieved party is entitled to additional damages if the non-payment caused it a greater harm.

Article 7.4.10 *Interest on damages*

Unless otherwise agreed, interest on damages for non-performance of non-monetary obligations accrues as from the time of non-performance.

Article 7.4.11 *Manner of monetary redress*

(1) Damages are to be paid in lump sum. However, they may be payable in instalments when the nature of the harm makes this appropriate.

(2) Damages to be paid in instalments may be indexed.

Article 7.4.12 *Currency in which to assess damages*

Damages are to be assessed either in the currency in which the monetary obligation was expressed or in the currency in which the harm was suffered whichever is more appropriate.

Article 7.4.13 *Agreed payment for non-performance*

(1) Where the contract provides that a party who does not perform is to pay a specified sum to the aggrieved party for such non-performance, the aggrieved party is entitled to that sum irrespective of its actual harm.

(2) However, despite any agreement to the contrary the specified sum may be reduced to a reasonable amount where it is grossly excessive in relation to the harm resulting from the non-performance and the other circumstances.

Table of Cases

440

Table of Statutes and other Legislation

445

448

Index

About the Authors

Gerrit Betlem
Researcher at the Centre for Enforcement of European Law/NISER (Netherlands Institute for Social and Economic Law Research), University of Utrecht. FIELD OF SPECIALISATION: Tort law, European Community Private Law. CORRESPONDENCE ADDRESS: NISER, Boothstraat 6, NL-3512 BW Utrecht, The Netherlands

Ted M. de Boer
Professor of Law, Deputy Judge District Court Alkmaar. FIELD OF SPECIALISATION: Private International Law and Comparative Law. CORRESPONDENCE ADDRESS: Faculty of Law, University of Amsterdam, P.O. Box 1030, NL-1000 BA Amsterdam, The Netherlands

Carlos Bollen
Researcher, Substitute Judge's Clerk. FIELD OF SPECIALISATION: Copyright and Neighbouring Rights, Comparative Law. CORRESPONDENCE ADDRESS: Hoogbrugstraat 56, NL-6221 CS Maastricht, The Netherlands

Jan H. Dalhuisen
Executive Director, IBJ International, London; Professor of International Commercial Law at the University of Utrecht. FIELD OF SPECIALISATION: Commercial and Banking Law, Comparative Law, Transnational Law, Private International Law. CORRESPONDENCE ADDRESS: Molengraaff Institute, Nobelstraat 2A, NL-3512 EN Utrecht, The Netherlands

Ulrich Drobnig
Director at the Max-Planck-Institute for Foreign Private and Private International Law, Hamburg and Professor at the Faculty of Law, University of Hamburg. FIELD OF SPECIALISATION: Comparative Law, Private International Law. CORRESPONDENCE ADDRESS: Max-Planck-Institute, Mittelweg 187, D-20148 Hamburg, Germany

Sjef van Erp
Associate Professor of Private Law and of English and American Law, Tilburg University, The Netherlands; Deputy Judge in the District Court of Amsterdam. FIELD OF SPECIALISATION: Dutch and European Private Law, Private International Law, Comparative Law, English and American Law. CORRESPONDENCE ADDRESS: Tilburg University, Faculty of Law, P.O.B. 90153, NL-5000 LE Tilburg, The Netherlands, E-mail: J.H.M. vErp@KUB.NL

Dennis Faber
Member of the staff of the Business and Law Research Centre of the Faculty of Law and Lecturer in Civil Law, Catholic University Nijmegen. FIELD OF SPECIALISATION: Dutch Civil Law. CORRESPONDENCE ADDRESS: Faculteit der Rechtsgeleerdheid, Katholieke Universiteit Nijmegen, P.O. Box 9049, 6500 KK Nijmegen, The Netherlands

Gerard-René de Groot
Professor of Comparative Law and Private International Law at the University of Limburg. FIELD OF SPECIALISATION: Comparative Law, Private International Law, Nationality Law. CORRESPONDENCE ADDRESS: Ambyerstraat Zuid 79, NL-6225 AD Maastricht, The Netherlands

Arthur Hartkamp
Advocate-General at the Supreme Court; Professor of Private Law, University of Utrecht. FIELD OF SPECIALISATION: Dutch Private Law and Comparative Law. CORRESPONDENCE ADDRESS: De Hoge Raad der Nederlanden, P.O. Box 20303, NL-2500 EH The Hague, The Netherlands

Ewoud Hondius
Professor of Law, University of Utrecht; President, Netherlands Association of Comparative Law. FIELD OF SPECIALISATION: Consumer Protection and Contract Law. CORRESPONDENCE ADDRESS: Molengraaff Instituut voor Privaatrecht, Nobelstraat 2A, NL-3512 EN Utrecht, The Netherlands

Geraint Howells
Senior Lecturer in Law, University of Sheffield. FIELD OF SPECIALISATION: Consumer Law. CORRESPONDENCE ADDRESS: Faculty of Law, University of Sheffield, P O Box 598, Sheffield S10 1FL, United Kingdom

Bas Kortmann
Professor of Civil Law at the Catholic University of Nijmegen. FIELD OF SPECIALISATION: Dutch Civil Law, Comparative Law. CORRESPONDENCE ADDRESS: Faculteit der Rechtsgeleerdheid, Katholieke Universiteit Nijmegen, P.O. Box 9049, NL-6500 KK Nijmegen, The Netherlands

Ole Lando
Professor emeritus at the Copenhagen Business School. FIELD OF SPECIALISATION: Comparative Law and Conflicts of Law. CORRESPONDENCE ADDRESS: Legal Department, Copenhagen Business School, Nansensgade 19, DK-1366 Copenhagen, Denmark

Gerrit van Maanen
Professor of Private Law at the University of Limburg (Maastricht). FIELD OF SPECIALISATION: Dutch Private Law (Torts, Law of Property). CORRESPONDENCE ADDRESS: Faculty of Law, P.O. Box 616, NL-6200 MD Maastricht, The Netherlands

Basil Markesinis
Denning Professor of Comparative Law at the University of London; Professor of Anglo-American Private Law, University of Leiden; Corresponding Member of the Royal Belgian Academy; Bencher of Gray's Inn. FIELD OF SPECIALISATION: Law obligations, Comparative Law. CORRESPONDENCE ADDRESS: 27 Barrow Road, Cambridge CB2 2AP, United Kingdom

Peter-Christian Müller-Graff
University Professor of Private Law, Commercial and Economic Law, Law of the European Communities and Comparative Law at the University of Trier.
FIELD OF SPECIALISATION: Private Law, Commercial and Economic Law, Law of the European Communities and Comparative Law. CORRESPONDENCE ADDRESS: Universität Trier, FB Rechtswissenschaft, Postfach 3825, D-54296 Trier, Germany

Madeleine van Rossum
Senior Lecturer at the University of Limburg. FIELD OF SPECIALISATION: Dutch Private Law, Comparative Law. CORRESPONDENCE ADDRESS: University of Limburg/Maastricht, Postbus 616, NL-6200 MD Maastricht, The Netherlands

Marcel Storme
Professor at the University of Gent (Belgium). FIELD OF SPECIALISATION: Procedural Law, European Law. CORRESPONDENCE ADDRESS: Coupure 3, B-9000 Gent, Belgium

Matthias E. Storme
Professor at the Katholieke Universiteit Leuven and the Universiteit Antwerpen (Belgium). FIELD OF SPECIALISATION: Law of Property and Obligations, Comparative Law, Procedural Law. CORRESPONDENCE ADDRESS: Zuidbroek 49, B-9030 Gent, Belgium

William John Swadling
Lecturer in Law, Faculty of Laws, Queen Mary & Westfield College, University of London. FIELD OF SPECIALISATION: English Law of Property and English Law of Restitution. CORRESPONDENCE ADDRESS: Faculty of Laws, Queen Mary & Westfield College, Mile End Road, London E1 4NS, United Kingdom

463

Denis Tallon
Professor at the University Panthéon-Assas (Paris II). FIELD OF SPECIALISATION: French Civil Law, Comparative Law. CORRESPONDENCE ADDRESS: Université Panthéon-Assas (Paris II), 12 Place du Panthéon, F-75231 Paris Cedex 05, France

André Tunc
Professor emeritus, University of Paris. FIELD OF SPECIALISATION: Comparative Law, mainly for Tort Law and Company Law. CORRESPONDENCE ADDRESS: Université de Paris I, 112 Rue de Vaugirard, F-75006 Paris, France

Hans G. Wehrens
Vice-President of the Commission for European Community affairs — International Union of Latin Notariat. FIELD OF SPECIALISATION: European Civil Law, German Private Law. CORRESPONDENCE ADDRESS: Postfach 1126, D-55477 Kirchberg, Germany

Reinhard Zimmermann
Chair of Private Law, Roman Law and Comparative Legal History, University of Regensburg. FIELD OF SPECIALISATION: German Private Law, Roman Law, Roman-Dutch Law and History of European Private Law. CORRESPONDENCE ADDRESS: Faculty of Law, University of Regensburg, Universitätsstrasse 31, D-93053 Regensburg, Germany

Dit boek is aangeleverd op floppy, opgemaakt bij Uitgeverij Ars Aequi Libri te Nijmegen, gedrukt door Boekdrukkerij F.E. MacDonald te Nijmegen en gebonden door Boekbinderij Van den Burg te Weurt (gebrocheerde uitgave) en door Boekbinderij Callenbach te Nijkerk (gebonden uitgave).